Corrections in the 21st Century

FIRST EDITION

Norman A. Carlson

Kären M. Hess

Christine M. H. Orthmann

Corrections
in the 21st Century

A PRACTICAL APPROACH

West/Wadsworth
I(T)P® An International Thomson Publishing Company

Belmont, CA   Albany, NY   Boston   Cincinnati   Johannesburg   London   Madrid   Melbourne
Mexico City   New York   Pacific Grove, CA   Scottsdale, AZ   Singapore   Tokyo   Toronto

Criminal Justice Editor: Sabra Horne
Development Editor: Dan Alpert
Project Development Editor: Claire Masson
Editorial Assistant: Cherie Hackelberg
Marketing Manager: Mike Dew
Project Manager: Debby Kramer
Print Buyer: Karen Hunt
Permissions Editor: Yanna Walters
Production: Cindy Hass/Shepherd, Inc.
Designer: Leigh McClellan
Copy Editor: Joan Lyon
Cover Design: Polly Christensen
Compositor: Shepherd, Inc.
Printer: R.R. Donnelley & Sons Company
Cover Printer: Phoenix Color Corp.

Printed in the United States of America 1 2 3 4 5 6 7 8 9 10

For more information, contact Wadsworth Publishing Company, 10 Davis Drive, Belmont, CA 94002, or electronically at http://www.wadsworth.com

International Thomson Publishing Europe
Berkshire House
168–173 High Holborn
London, WC1V 7AA, United Kingdom

Nelson ITP, Australia
102 Dodds Street
South Melbourne
Victoria 3205 Australia

Nelson Canada
1120 Birchmount Road
Scarborough, Ontarlo
Canada M1K 5G4

International Thomson Editores
Seneca, 53
Colonia Polanco
11560 México D.F. México

International Thomson Publishing Asia
60 Albert Street
#15-01 Albert Complex
Singapore 189969

International Thomson Publishing Japan
Hirakawa-cho Kyowa Building, 3F
2-2-1 Hirakawa-cho, Chiyoda-kμ
Tokyo 102, Japan

International Thomson Publishing Southern Africa
Building 18, Constantia Square
138 Sixteenth Road, P.O. Box 2459
Halfway House, 1685 South Africa

Library of Congress Cataloging-in-Publication Data

Carlson, Norman A.
    Corrections in the 21st century : a practical approach / Norman A.
    Carlson, Kären M. Hess, Christine M.H. Orthmann.—1st ed.
        p.   cm.
    Includes bibliographical references and index.
    ISBN 0–534–53496–1 (alk. paper)
    1. Corrections—United States.   2. Punishment—United States.
  3. Criminals—Rehabilitation—United States.   4. Prisons—United
  States.   I. Hess, Kären M.   II. Orthmann, Christine M.
H.   III. Title.
HV9469.C37   1998
364.6' 0973– –dc21   98–4016

✼ This book is printed on acid-free recycled paper.

Contents

SECTION I Theoretical and Historical Context

1 An Overview of Corrections and the Criminal Justice System

2 The Origins of Corrections—Penology

3 The Evolution of Corrections in the United States

SECTION II Sentencing Alternatives

4 Perspectives on Sentencing

5 Alternatives to Incarceration: Probation and Other Intermediate Sanctions

6 Jail: Detention and Short-Term Incarceration

7 Prisons

SECTION III The Human Factor—Behind the Bricks and Mortar

8 Correctional Clients: Adult Offenders

9 Correctional Clients: Juvenile Offenders

10 Special Needs Offenders

11 Correctional Management

12 Other Correctional Personnel

SECTION IV Corrections at Work

13 Special Challenges for Corrections

14 Prisoners' Rights and Other Legal Issues

15 A Look Toward the Future: Corrections in the Twenty-First Century

Preface

Corrections is a complex, challenging component of our criminal justice system. Its charge is to carry out the sentences imposed by the courts and to do so while protecting society, vindicating victims, protecting the rights of those placed into their custody and, in most cases, rehabilitating offenders so they can return to society as productive citizens.

This text explores the delicate balance corrections seeks to maintain between the rights of society and the rights of individuals convicted of infringing upon society's rights. The tension between societal and individual rights and between concern for crime control and due process will become apparent as you proceed through the text.

Section I describes the theoretical and historical context from which our present correctional system has evolved. It explores how society has viewed crime throughout the ages and how punishments for crime have varied.

Section II presents the numerous sentencing alternatives within the system, ranging from probation to the most severe penalty—the death penalty. Between these two extremes are intermediate sanctions and incarceration. Intermediate sanctions discussed include fines, forfeitures, restitution, community service, intensive supervision programs, house arrest, electronic monitoring, day reporting centers and residential community facilities. Incarceration may be in jails or prisons. Boot camps are also discussed.

Section III explores the human factor in corrections, going beyond the bricks and mortar to describe the correctional clients within the system, their culture and their unique challenges, as well as the correctional personnel who manage them.

Section IV describes corrections at work, including special challenges such as gangs, riots, drugs and overcrowding; prisoners' rights and other legal issues; and a look toward the future of corrections.

How to Use This Text

This text is structured to enhance your understanding and remembering of the main concepts presented. To get the most from the text, first look through the table of contents to give yourself a framework for the subject. Think about the specific areas included in the topic of corrections as a whole. Then read the section openers for a closer look at the four broad divisions of the text. Finally, complete the following steps for each chapter:

1. Read the "Do You Know" questions at the beginning of the chapter. These questions present the chapter objectives in a way that should get you thinking about your current level of knowledge. For example, "Do you know the primary purposes of corrections?"

2. Scan the list of terms and consider your current level of understanding of each term.

3. Read the chapter, highlighting, underlining or taking notes. Watch for answers to the "Do You Know" questions, which are highlighted in the text like this:

> The primary purposes of corrections are retribution, deterrence, incapacitation and rehabilitation.

   Also watch for words in **bold** type. These are the key terms for the chapter. The definitions should be clear from the text. You may also want to read the definitions given in the glossary.

4. Read the chapter summary. You will find that you have now read the key concepts three times. This triple-strength approach should take the information from your short-term memory into your long-term memory.

5. To solidify the information, return to the "Do You Know" questions at the beginning of each chapter and answer each question. Write down any questions you have about the information in the chapter. Look at the list of key terms and make certain you understand and can define each term.

6. Read the discussion questions at the end of the chapter and think about what you can contribute to a class discussion of each.

7. Periodically (for example, each Friday) review your highlighting, the text highlighting and the summary for each chapter.

If you follow these seven steps, you should master the content of this text. Additional learning aids may also be available if your professor has included them with this text.

Crime Scenes: An Interactive Criminal Justice CD ROM The first introductory criminal justice CD ROM available. This interactive CD ROM places the student in various roles as she explores all aspects of the CJ system: Policing/Investigations, Courts, Sentencing and Corrections.

InfoTrac Gives students access to full-length articles from over 600 scholarly and popular periodicals. Students can print complete articles or use the cut/paste and email techniques. Includes readings from U.S. News and World Report, Corrections Today, Prison Journal, American Criminal Law Review and much more.

Internet Investigator, II Includes new Criminal Justice related web sites categorized by course for ease of use: policing, investigations, courts, corrections, research, juvenile delinquency and much, much more! Save students money by bundling with the book.

Acknowledgments

We would like to thank the following individuals for their careful review of the manuscript for this text and their helpful suggestions for improving it:

Thomas McAninch
Scott Community College

Charles Conner
Lakeland College

Lawrence Travis III
University of Cincinnati

Mark Hansel
Moorhead State University

Tom Durkin
University of Florida

Susan McGuire
San Jacinto College North

Avon Burns
Mott Community College

Steve Atchley
Delaware Technical & Community College

Harry Spiller
John A. Logan College

Additional thanks go to the Florida Department of Corrections and the staff and inmates at the Columbia Correctional Institution (Florida); Dr. Delores Craig, Wichita State University; and Dale L. Carlton, for their contributions to the content of the text. Thank you also to those contributors who wished to remain anonymous.

Finally, thank you to our team at Wadsworth Publishing: Criminal Justice Editor, Sabra Horne; Project Editor, Debby Kramer; and Project Development Editor, Claire Masson; to our photo researcher, Roberta Spieckerman; and to the senior project editor at Shepherd, Inc., Cindy Hass.

Any errors in content or expression are the sole responsibility of the authors.

About the Authors

Coauthor Norman A. Carlson has received his B.A. degree in sociology and his M.A. in criminology. He has worked as a correctional officer at the Iowa State Penitentiary; as a case manager at the Federal Correctional Institution in Ashland, Kentucky; as a parole officer at the U.S. Penitentiary in Leavenworth, Kansas; as assistant supervisor of the Division of Institutional Programs in Washington, DC; and as a project director for the developing Community Treatment Center (halfway house program). Mr. Carlson was appointed the fourth director of the Federal Bureau of Prisons in 1970 and served for 17 years before retiring in 1987. He also served as president of the American Correctional Association from 1978 to 1980 and is a fellow in the National Academy of Public Administration. Mr. Carlson also served as a special master for the U.S. District Court in Maryland.

Since his retirement from the FBOP, Mr. Carlson has participated in management studies of the United States Immigration and Naturalization Service

and the Bureau of Indian Affairs as well as the Departments of Correction in Hawaii, Utah and Michigan. He is currently an adjunct professor in the department of sociology at the University of Minnesota and is a member of the advisory board of the National Institute of Corrections.

Coauthor Kären M. Hess has a master's degree in educational psychology, a Ph.D. in English and instructional design and a Ph.D. in criminal justice. Dr. Hess has written extensively in the field of law enforcement and criminal justice and is an instructor at

Normandale Community College. She is a member of the National Criminal Justice Association and the American Correctional Association. Among the publications she has coauthored for West/Wadsworth Publishing Company are *Introduction to Law Enforcement and Criminal Justice*, 5th ed.; *Criminal Investigation*, 5th ed.; *Juvenile Justice*, 2nd ed.; *Management and Supervision in Law Enforcement*, 2nd ed.; *The Police in the Community: Strategies for the 21st Century*, 2nd ed.; *Seeking Employment in Criminal Justice and Related Fields*, 2nd ed.; *Police Operations*, 2nd ed.; *Criminal Procedure;* and *Constitutional Law for Criminal Justice Professionals*.

 Coauthor Christine M. H. Orthmann has her bachelor's and master's degrees and is currently senior researcher for Innovative Programming Systems, Inc. She was the key researcher for this text, conducting an extensive review of the literature as well as developing and conducting surveys whose results appear in the text. Ms. Orthmann also developed several of the graphics for this text, including the time lines. In addition, she was responsible for developing the instructor's guide and test bank.

Corrections in the 21st Century

SECTION I

Theoretical and Historical Context

Corrections is an exceedingly complex area which can be approached from several perspectives. Any attempt to isolate specific subjects within corrections is artificial, but necessary for the student to come to an understanding of the field. Although specific subjects are discussed, always keep in mind that, in reality, the subjects are integrally related.

Section I begins with a discussion of what corrections is, how our criminal justice system was established, the purposes corrections has served within this system, the ideologies underlying these purposes, the models that have prevailed at various times, a sociological view of punishment and an exploration of a new paradigm being recommended for corrections (Chapter 1). This is followed by a description of the origins and evolution of the criminal justice system with an emphasis on the correctional component of that system (Chapter 2). The section concludes with a look at the evolution of the criminal justice system in the United States (Chapter 3).

History is important because it illustrates cycles as well as what seems to work and what does not. It helps practitioners learn from the mistakes of others. And it shows how in any given area the pendulum of change swings from one extreme to a middle position and then to the opposite extreme. This pendulum effect is readily observed in the history of the criminal justice system and corrections (see Figure 1–4).

The chapters in this section provide a framework for the remainder of the text. Corrections as it exists today and may exist in the future can most readily be understood with an understanding of this background.

1

An Overview of Corrections and the Criminal Justice System

Do You Know

➤ What corrections is?

➤ What two basic principles underlie our representative democracy?

➤ What three branches of government are established by our Constitution? In which branch corrections falls?

➤ What the primary purposes of corrections are?

➤ What two views influence the direction corrections takes?

➤ What four ideologies underlie corrections?

➤ What models of dealing with offenders have been in vogue?

➤ What two most basic rationales have been used to justify punishment throughout the ages?

➤ Which view of punishment was held by the Greek philosopher Plato?

➤ What a sociological view of punishment means?

➤ How punishment has been viewed?

➤ How the Durkheimian perspective sees punishment? The Marxist perspective?

➤ What a paradigm is? A shift in paradigms?

➤ What shift in paradigms has been suggested for corrections?

Today in our nation we hear the deafening drum beat of build, build, build as more facilities go up. We see people put in chains. We hear that 10-year-olds are being imprisoned and that kids are being sent to adult facilities. . . . America now faces the challenge of what to do to stem violence, crime and destruction—a complex set of problems with no easy, quick-fix solutions.

—James A. Gondles, Jr.
Executive Director, American Correctional Association

Can You Define

anomie

classical view

deterrence

discretion

distributive justice

federalism

funnel effect

general deterrence

ideologies

incapacitation

just deserts

justice model

lex talions

medical model

panopticism

paradigm

paradigm shift

penology

positivist view

recidivism

rehabilitation

restorative justice

retribution

sociological view
    of punishment

specific deterrence

Introduction

As the twenty-first century approaches, our entire criminal justice system is at a crossroads. Violence, an increase in the gang and drug problem, overcrowded jails and prisons and recidivism rates all suggest that our criminal justice system is not functioning as intended. It is neither preventing crime nor ensuring peaceful communities.

A Gallup poll reported on the public's confidence level with 15 selected institutions, including Congress, big and small business, organized labor, the U.S. Supreme Court, organized religion, banks, newspapers, public schools, the police and the criminal justice system (Newport, 1997). Only 19 percent of those polled said they had "a great deal" or "quite a lot" of confidence in the criminal justice system, the lowest confidence rating of the 15 institutions. Interestingly, 50 percent expressed confidence in the U.S. Supreme Court, and 59 percent expressed confidence in the police, the third highest ranking. This would indicate that perhaps the public does not understand what constitutes the criminal justice system or how one component influences the other. (Figure 1–1 illustrates the public's confidence levels concerning the courts, the police and the criminal justice system.) Furthermore, corrections is the only one of the three criminal justice components not specifically inquired about in the Gallup poll. Might it be that the low confidence rating for the criminal justice system as a whole is really a reflection of the public's loss of faith in corrections?

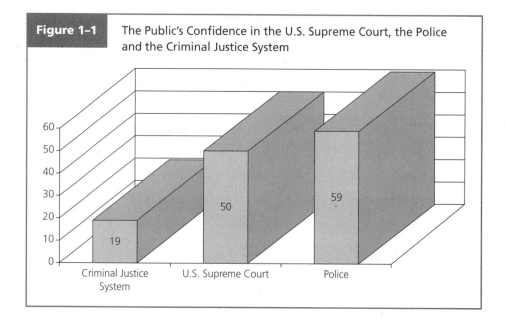

Figure 1–1 The Public's Confidence in the U.S. Supreme Court, the Police and the Criminal Justice System

As noted by Innes (1993, p. 220): "The public appears to have an abstract commitment to justice, wants the criminal justice system to work properly, and is frustrated that it does not appear to do so." And, as suggested by several criminal justice researchers, the system may not be *capable* of doing so. Many researchers feel that the system has become isolated from the community it is intended to protect and that it has strayed from the ancient legacy of people joining together into societies for mutual self-help and protection.

This chapter begins with a discussion of what corrections is and its major components. It then presents an explanation of how our present criminal justice system was established, where corrections fits within this system and what the primary purposes of corrections are. This is followed by a discussion of three basic ideologies underlying approaches to dealing with those who do not conform to the law. Next comes the presentation of several competing models developed in the evolution of corrections and a theoretical discussion of punishment and how it has been viewed throughout history. The chapter concludes with a discussion of a new paradigm that some criminal justice researchers are calling for.

Corrections Defined

To the general public, the term *corrections* is almost synonymous with punishment. But in the United States the term is relatively new. Prior to the 1950s, the terms *penal system* and *penology* were used, terms that emphasized the
➤ punishment focus placed on those convicted of crimes. Although **penology** is defined as "the study of the reformation and rehabilitation of criminals and of the management of prisons," the term is based on the root word *penal*, which is derived from the Latin word *poenalis* meaning "punishment" and a similar Greek word *poine* meaning "penalty" or "fine." It was not until 1954 that the American Prison Association changed its name to the American Correctional Association, thus reflecting a fundamental shift in the philosophy of handling those who break the law. Not only was punishment a valid objective; so too was the rehabilitation, or correction, of persons found guilty of crime.

Corrections is that portion of the criminal justice system charged with carrying out the sentences of our courts. It is one of the three key components of the criminal justice system and, itself, consists of several components. The other two components are law enforcement and the courts, to be described shortly.

Corrections refers to the programs, services, agencies and institutions responsible for supervising persons charged with or convicted of crimes.

Components of Modern Corrections

Corrections is not simply a one-size-fits-all service for those who violate the law. It is a conglomeration of programs and facilities designed to handle a wide variety of individuals and their unique needs.

As stated, the purpose of corrections is to carry out the sentence of the court, with various correctional components handling specific types of sentences. Some components are devoted to providing pretrial services for those entering the criminal justice system. Other components, such as jails, handle individuals of both pre- and postconviction status. The majority of correctional components, however, deal with persons who have appeared before the court and have been found guilty of one or more crimes. These components include probation services, community services, day reporting centers, electronic monitoring programs, intensive supervision programs, jails, prisons, boot camps, parole services and halfway houses. Furthermore, specific elements of corrections are designed to handle juvenile offenders only. Each of these components is discussed in greater detail later in the text.

Establishment of Our Democracy

The United States Constitution, signed in 1787, established the foundation of our democracy and became the supreme law of the land. Determined to depart from the unified systems so common throughout European countries, our founding fathers adopted principles to guarantee that powers in this

The signing of the U.S. Constitution in Philadelphia in 1787.

new country would be dispersed. Those principles—separation of powers and federalism—have produced an *intentionally* fragmented criminal justice system.

> The Constitution established a representative democracy based on two basic principles, separation of powers and federalism, which resulted in an intentionally fragmented system.

Separation of Powers

Separation of powers was established in the first three articles of the Constitution, which created the branches of government. Article I created the *legislative branch*, the Congress of the United States, giving it the power to make laws to govern the country: "All legislative powers herein granted shall be vested in a Congress of the United States, which shall consist of a Senate and House of Representatives." This is the branch of government that passes our laws, including those establishing what constitutes a crime and what the punishment for each crime is to be.

Article II created the *executive branch*, giving a portion of power to the president and vice-president of the United States: "The executive power shall be vested in a President of the United States of America. He shall hold his office during the term of four years, and together with the Vice-President, chosen for the same term, be elected as follows . . . ." The executive branch's responsibility is to enforce the laws passed by Congress. Law enforcement and corrections are under the authority of this branch of government and receive their power from this article.

Article III created the *judicial branch*, including the Supreme Court: "The judicial power of the United States shall be vested in one Supreme Court, and in such inferior courts as the Congress may from time to time ordain and establish." The court component of the criminal justice system is charged with determining when laws have been broken and imposing sentence on those found to be guilty. In some states, parts of corrections, for example, probation, are also part of the judicial branch.

> The three branches of our government—legislative, executive and judicial—serve as checks and balances on each other, ensuring, as the founding fathers intended, that one will not become all-powerful. Corrections is primarily part of the executive branch. In some states, parts of corrections are also part of the judicial branch.

Federalism

➤ The Constitution also established **federalism,** a form of government where several states join together, yet retain certain powers at the state level. The granting of power to the states is made clear in the Tenth Amendment which states that any powers not specifically granted to the federal government shall be retained by the states. The states, in turn, can allow local jurisdictions to retain certain powers not specified in the state's constitution.

The principle of federalism results in varying levels of courts and corrections as well as the establishment of federal and state laws.

Establishment of the Criminal Justice System

The criminal justice system reflects the basic principles of separation of powers and federalism and consists of numerous agencies at the federal, state and local levels. In this country, we have 1 federal system, 50 state systems, over 3,000 county systems and thousands of city and local municipality systems, each having responsibility for criminal justice within its own jurisdiction. Decisions made in one part of the criminal justice system influence decisions made in other parts. Corrections, particularly, is influenced by the law enforcement and judicial components in the system. Agents within the law enforcement component have considerable discretion. How many people are arrested and for what types of crimes certainly affects the number of individuals in community corrections, jail and prison and whether these populations are overloaded.

Further, the kinds of sentences imposed also directly affect the correctional system. In most jurisdictions, judges have considerable discretion as to what sentences they impose. Decision making in one component does not require the approval of the other two components. Since corrections is the endpoint in the system, it is directly affected by decisions made by other criminal justice entities, regardless of the rationality of those decisions.

This problem was noted over 20 years ago by our Department of Justice's National Advisory Commission on Criminal Justice Standards and Goals (1973, p. 5):

> A substantial obstacle to development of effective corrections lies in its relationship to police and courts, the other subsystems of the criminal justice system. Corrections inherits any inefficiency, inequity, and improper discrimination that may have occurred in any earlier step of the criminal justice process. Its clients come to it from the other subsystems; it is the consistent heir to their defects.

In fact, the goals of the agencies at opposite ends of the criminal justice system appear to be at odds with each other. Law enforcement seeks to maintain law and order by arresting people who commit crimes—getting them off the street. The more individuals arrested, the more crowded the court dockets

(*Left*)A goal of law enforcement is to remove offenders from the streets. This Manhattan police officer is arresting a robbery suspect. (*Right*) A common goal of corrections, in contrast, is to rehabilitate offenders so that they may one day return to society. This cycle has been criticized as revolving-door justice.

| Figure 1–2 | Criminal Justice System Overview |

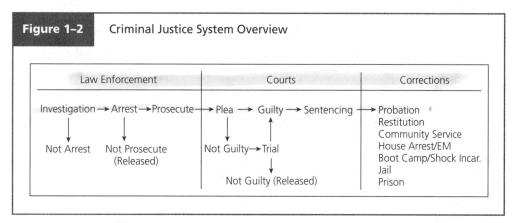

Note: This is an oversimplification to illustrate the key events in a person's "journey" through the criminal justice system and into the corrections component of the system.

become and, ultimately, the more crowded correctional facilities become. In addition, law enforcement officers frequently have to deal with the pain and suffering of victims of crime and, consequently, may be more punishment-oriented toward offenders than judges or correctional officers and administrators.

While law enforcement removes lawbreakers from the community, corrections often seeks to treat or rehabilitate offenders so they may be reintegrated into society. When inmates are released, law enforcement officers may see these offenders as a threat to the law and order of their comunity and as adding to their already heavy workload.

The various components of the criminal justice system are illustrated in Figure 1–2.

Theoretically, the criminal justice system is designed to control crime and to ensure a safe, orderly society. In doing so, however, each component of the system has a great deal of discretion.

Discretion within the System

► **Discretion** refers to freedom to make judgments. Legislators may decide what laws to pass, what actions to label as crimes and what punishments to attach to these crimes. For example, prohibition laws led to severe prison overcrowding in the 1920s, much like the drug laws are doing today.

Law enforcement officers also exercise great discretion. A 13-year-old caught writing graffiti on a bridge may be warned, taken home and turned over to the parents or turned over to juvenile court. Prosecutors decide whether to file charges and what types of crimes they will pursue most forcefully. For example, most prosecutors would hesitate to prosecute an 80-year-old senile woman who shoplifts a bottle of aspirin.

Judges decide whether to issue warrants, what evidence to admit into court and what sentences to pass. Correctional officials may decide to reward or punish inmate behavior, to allow or deny privileges, to stress punishment or rehabilitation. Parole officers may recommend that parole be rescinded. The wide array of discretionary decisions operating in our criminal justice system is summarized in Table 1–1. The existence of so much discretion within the system results in what is often referred to as the funnel effect.

The Funnel Effect

► The **funnel effect,** as originally described by the President's Commission in 1967, refers to the fact that the number of those committing crimes and the

Table 1–1	Who Exercises Discretion?
Officials	**Discretionary Power**
Legislators	Primary power brokers who define policy; enact laws and determine type of sentence; authorize funding.
Police	Enforce specific laws; investigate specific crimes; search people, vicinities, buildings; arrest or detain people.
Prosecutors	File charges or petitions for adjudication; seek indictments; drop cases; reduce charges or plea bargain.
Judges or magistrates	Set bail or conditions for release; accept pleas; dismiss charges; impose sentence; revoke probation.
Correctional officials	Assign to type of correctional facility; award privileges; punish for disciplinary infractions.
Paroling authority	Determine date and conditions of parole; revoke parole.

Source: Bureau of Justice Statistics. *Report to the Nation on Crime and Justice,* 2nd ed. Washington, DC: United States Department of Justice, March 1988, pp. 2–3.

number being processed by the criminal justice system becomes fewer at each stage of the process, as illustrated in Figure 1–3.

At the top of the funnel are all crimes committed in a given period. Of these crimes, only a portion become known to the police. The large portion of crimes not reported, referred to as *the dark figure of criminality,* has been estimated to be as high as 50 percent. (The National Crime Victimization Survey [NCVS] has methods for estimating the total number of crimes committed, reported and nonreported.) Of offenses known to law enforcement, investigation solves only a portion. Even in some cases that are solved, an arrest may not be made because of problems with the investigation or for numerous other reasons.

The *Sourcebook of Criminal Justice Statistics* (1995, p. 425) reports that only 21.4 percent of offenses known to police were cleared by arrest in 1994. Those who are arrested may not be prosecuted because of a weak case, lack of

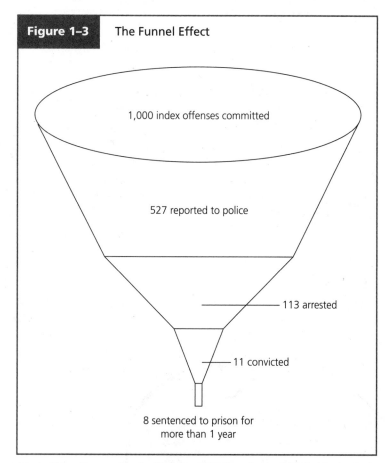

| Figure 1–3 | The Funnel Effect |

1,000 index offenses committed

527 reported to police

113 arrested

11 convicted

8 sentenced to prison for more than 1 year

Adapted from: Bureau of Justice Statistics. *1995 Sourcebook of Criminal Justice Statistics.* Washington, DC: U.S. Department of Justice, 1995.

evidence or witnesses or because it is of low priority for a particular jurisdiction (for example, prostitution). As noted by the 1995 *Sourcebook* (p. 427), from 1982 to 1993 the percent of suspects declined for prosecution by U.S. attorneys ranged from 26.9 percent (1982) to 30.9 percent (1993).

Those who are prosecuted may avoid a trial by plea bargaining (80 to 90 percent of cases go this route) and perhaps receive only a fine or probation, avoiding incarceration. Those who go to trial may be found not guilty. Even those who are found guilty may receive only a fine and probation, avoiding incarceration. A very small percent of all criminals end up incarcerated.

The funnel effect has also been called the *screening* or *sieve effect*. Those interested in the crime and violence problem in the United States should recognize that correctional clientele are negatively selected—most individuals involved in crime do not end up in corrections. With the funnel effect in mind, how can crime be effectively reduced by treatment, deterrence or incapacitation? This important issue faces not only corrections but the entire criminal justice system—when law enforcement can't catch them and the courts won't sentence them, how can corrections "correct" them?

This leads to another consideration in the study of corrections: what purpose or purposes can or should corrections accomplish?

The Purposes of Corrections

As will be demonstrated in the historical overview of corrections and the criminal justice system, society has dealt with lawbreakers in a multitude of ways and has emphasized different goals and different methods to accomplish those goals. The pendulum has swung from pure revenge or vengeance to a medical model where the criminal is viewed as being ill and in need of treatment. It has swung from very public punishment to very private punishment. And as the pendulum swings, the primary purpose of corrections also shifts.

Recall Figure 1–2, which illustrated a person's journey through the criminal justice system and how corrections follows the courts and sentencing, and it becomes apparent that the purpose of corrections is to carry out whatever sentence the court imposes on various individuals. The variety of correctional alternatives available to the court also indicates the different objectives and purposes sought by the court in the imposition of such sentences. No matter where the emphasis is placed, however, it is generally conceded that corrections can serve four basic, often overlapping, purposes.

The primary purposes of corrections are

- Retribution.
- Deterrence.
- Incapacitation.
- Rehabilitation.

This simple statement belies the complexity of the issues. What purpose(s) corrections should serve has been and continues to be the subject of heated debate.

Retribution

➤ **Retribution** is punishment for the sake of punishment and was most prevalent in ancient societies, existing in such approaches as just deserts and *lex talions*.
➤ **Just deserts** means individuals "get what's coming to them." They
➤ deserve what they get. *Lex talions* is a closely related concept based on the notion of "an eye for an eye." Retribution is probably the oldest of the four purposes, a principle dating back at least to biblical times, as found in the Old Testament of the Christian Bible: "Life shall go for life, eye for eye, tooth for tooth, hand for hand, foot for foot" (Deut. 19:21).

Retribution is focused on the offense committed and on the past. It assumes that offenders are responsible for their own actions, that they chose to break the law and deserve to be punished. It is a way for society to "get even" with those who would violate its laws, to pay them back for their unsocial behavior.

Criminals must repay society for breaking the law. The just deserts approach to corrections was influenced by Andrew von Hirsch's *Doing Justice*, published in 1976. In this work, von Hirsch contends that criminals should be punished for actions they have already committed, not for what they might do in the future or what others might do without the example of what happens to those who break the law. Retribution focuses almost exclusively on the crime itself rather than on the offender's needs or the needs of the community. It is almost entirely reactive.

More recently retribution has come to include restitution, whereby an offender reimburses the victim, most often with money though occasionally with services. Retribution is discussed in greater detail in Chapter 5.

Deterrence

➤ **Deterrence** as a correctional objective views punishment as a means to prevent future criminal actions. In this sense it is more functional and proactive. It is intended to show offenders and would-be offenders that the price for committing crimes is too steep. The pain is greater than the gain.
➤ Deterrence aimed at offenders, called **specific deterrence,** attempts to make the consequences of committing crime so severe that when the offenders are returned to society, they will not commit further crimes. Deterrence in-
➤ tended to serve as an example to others is called **general deterrence.**

One corrections issue that tests the effectiveness of deterrence is capital punishment. Does the threat of losing one's own life deter a potential murderer? And even if it does, is it justice to take the life of a murderer simply to serve as an example, or, as some argue, to take a life to save a life? This sensitive and highly controversial issue is discussed in Chapter 4.

Incapacitation

➤ **Incapacitation** refers to making it impossible for the offender to commit further offenses. One important goal of our entire criminal justice system is to protect law-abiding citizens from crime, especially crimes of violence.

Incapacitation can take many forms. One of the earliest forms was banishment, also referred to as social death. Some people feel this is the ultimate punishment, more devastating then being executed. In preliterate societies, offenders were often cast out from the village. More recently England banished its outlaws and undesirables to Australia and the United States.

Other forms of incapacitation make it physically impossible for a criminal act to be repeated. A thief whose hands are cut off will not easily steal again. A castrated male will be unable to rape again. An incarcerated child molester will not be able to abuse children while in prison. And, obviously, a murderer who is executed will kill no more.

Like retribution, incapacitation is reactive, and yet, like deterrence, it attempts to predict and influence future behavior. Offenders are confined not only for what they have done, but for what it is feared they may do in the future.

Rehabilitation

➤ **Rehabilitation** sees the purpose of corrections to be clearly stated in its name—to correct deviant behavior. Rehabilitation is a more humane purpose, one that has been in and out of popular practice throughout the development of the criminal justice system. This purpose is reflected in the medical model, or treatment model, which assumes that criminal behavior is a form of pathology that can be treated and cured. It is similar to a doctor who diagnoses and treats a medical problem over which the patient has limited control. Voltaire expressed belief in the rehabilitation of offenders when he said: "The punishment of criminals should be of use—when a man is hanged he is good for nothing."

Another proponent of this function of corrections was Warren E. Burger, former chief justice of the United States Supreme Court, who stated (1983): "When society places a person behind walls and bars it has an obligation to change that person before he or she goes back into the stream of society."

This purpose is clearly proactive and focused on the needs of offenders as well as the needs of the community to which the offenders may return. The issue
➤ of **recidivism,** or repeat offenders, raises questions about whether corrections can effectively rehabilitate offenders. Closely related to this purpose is the goal of reintegrating offenders into society as productive, law-abiding citizens.

The purposes that are most appropriate for corrections are directly affected by the environment in which corrections operates and another theoretical consideration: how crime and criminals are viewed by society, that is, the prevailing view underlying how society treats those who violate its laws.

Rehabilitating offenders frequently involves helping them develop marketable skills so they may find jobs following their release. These inmates at a private prison in Texas are receiving computer training.

Two Competing Views

For centuries, fervent debate has centered on who or what is responsible for crime. Two distinct and opposing views exist.

> ➤ The **classical view** holds that humans have free will and are responsible for their
> ➤ own actions. The **positivist view** holds that humans are shaped by their society and
> are the product of environmental and cultural influences. The classical view focuses
> on crime; the positivist view on the criminal.

Although these two views exist at opposite ends of the continuum of correctional thought, both have made significant contributions to the field. The classical view, in focusing on crime, encouraged due process of law and endorsed restrictions on the arbitrary use of judicial authority. The positivist view, by focusing on the criminal, helped advance experimental methods of research in the field of criminology.

Most people do not believe completely in one view or the other but see some combination of free will and determinism governing human behavior. The majority, however, also tend to place greater credence in one view over the other, and this directly influences how they view crime and criminals as well as what they consider to be the primary purpose of corrections.

This difference in view has resulted in two distinct models within not only corrections, but the entire criminal justice system: the *medical model* and the
➤ *justice model*, summarized in Table 1–2. The **medical model** assumes offenders are victims of society and their environment who need to be cured. The
➤ **justice model** assumes offenders are self-directed, acting on free will and responsible for their crimes. Although this table includes only portions of the

Table 1–2	Comparison of the Medical versus the Justice Model	
Issue	**Medical Model 1930–74**	**Justice Model 1974–Present**
Cause of Crime	Disease of society or of the individual.	Form of rational adaptation to societal conditions.
Image of Offender	Sick, product of socio-economic or psychological forces beyond control.	Capable of exercising free will; of surviving without resorting to crime.
Object of Correction	To cure offender and society; to return both to health; rehabilitation.	Humanely control offender under terms of sentence; offer voluntary treatment.
Agency/Institution Responsibility	Change offender, reintegrate back into society.	Legally & humanely control offender; adequate care & custody; voluntary treatment; protect society.
Role of Treatment & Punishment	Voluntary or involuntary treatment as means to change offender; treatment is mandatory, punishment used to coerce treatment, punishment & treatment is viewed as same thing.	Voluntary treatment, only; punishment & treatment not the same thing. Punishment is for society's good, treatment is for offender's good.
Object of Legal Sanctions (Sentence)	Determine conditions which are most conducive to rehabilitation of offender.	Determine conditions which are just re: wrong done, best protect society and deter offender from future crime.
Type of Sentence	Indeterminant, flexible; adjust to offender changes.	Fixed sentence (less good time).
Who determines release time?	"Experts" (parole board for adults, institutional staff for juveniles).	Conditions of sentence as interpreted by Presumptive Release Date (PRD) formula.

Source: D. F. Pace. *Community Relations Concepts.* Copyright © 1991, p. 145. Copperhouse Publishing Company. Incline Village, NV. Reprinted by permission.

twentieth century, you will find societies throughout the ages vacillating from one model to the other, with intermediate models in between.

Correctional Ideologies and Models

The complexity of corrections is evident in the interrelatedness of purpose, basic views and correctional ideologies. Closely related to the purposes of corrections and the fundamental views just discussed are the basic ideologies underlying society's response to criminal behavior.

➤   Correctional **ideologies** are complex bodies of ideas, adopted because they provide answers to an entire range of questions, such as the causes of crime, moral significance of crime, the proper response to crime and so on. Understanding these ideologies is important to understanding the current state of corrections and the problems and issues facing it, for these ideas are historically conditioned and change, in part, due to matters unrelated to criminal justice policy or practice (for example, the 1960s youth culture and the civil rights movement). Considering these complex sets of ideas, a variety of purposes or philosophies of punishment become more or less attractive to society. Thus, the rhetorical strategies of one era differ from those of another—"penitentiaries" give way to "reformatories," and "big houses" or "prisons" give way to "correctional institutions."

Most of the ideologies applied to correctional actions over the years fall into one of four categories: *punishment, control, treatment* or *prevention.* These categories may overlap; for example, some forms of punishment might also be perceived as methods of control.

> Four correctional ideologies are punishment, control, treatment and prevention.

Punishment and the Justice Model

In a *punishment ideology,* punitive actions of various forms can serve several purposes previously discussed. The most common purpose is retribution or vengeance.

> Punishment is associated with the justice model.

The idea of "getting even" or "an eye for an eye" goes far back in history. The fundamental principle underlying the justice model is that society has a duty to punish those who break its laws and that this threat of punishment is vital in implementing the law. Punishment is discussed in greater depth at the end of this chapter.

    Another common reason for using punishment is for deterrence. As behavior modification experts stress, to be effective the negative consequences for a negative act must be immediate, certain and personal. These conditions are readily observable as one trains a pet or raises a child. Unfortunately, our criminal justice system has numerous loopholes (lack of certainty) and usually moves slowly (lack of immediacy), greatly reducing the effectiveness of the punishment. These conditions may partially account for the reasoning of a police or corrections officer who "dispenses his or her own justice" rather than relying on the system.

    A third purpose of punishment is incapacitation, previously discussed. Banishing or incarcerating offenders makes them incapable of doing further harm to society.

Control and the Custodial Model

The *control ideology* and its resulting custodial model is the least complex and often most prevalent. The focus is on the present and on the immediate need to restrain the behavior of those accused or convicted of crimes.

> Control is associated with the custodial model.

    Correctional officials often have all they can do simply to maintain control over their institutions. Punishing those who fail to comply may be one extremely important means of doing so and may be counterproductive to the other, more humanitarian purposes often set forth for corrections. Many critics of our prisons contend that they are nothing more than human warehouses, violent places of confinement.

Treatment and the Medical Model

The *treatment ideology* views offenders as capable of rehabilitation or of being corrected. Although many people criticize this ideology as being "soft" on criminals, it has room for punishment, unlike the punishment ideology which leaves little room for treatment.

> Treatment is associated with the medical model.

    Emphasis on the treatment ideology occurred during three distinct periods in our history. The first was the Quaker reform movement of the late eighteenth century. It was believed that offenders were sinners and needed to be put back in touch with God. The treatment was isolation, reading the Bible and doing penance.

The second period was the late nineteenth century and the reformatory movement. Offenders were seen as disadvantaged, and the treatment was education and training with an emphasis on vocational skills.

The third period was from 1930 to 1974 with the development of the medical model and the emphasis on individualized treatment for inmates. This model parallels the steps taken by a physician dealing with an ill patient: examine, diagnose, prescribe, treat and follow up.

The Prevention Ideology and the Reintegration Model

The *prevention ideology* considers both the offender and the offender's environment. A goal of both the punishment and treatment models is to *prevent* further offenses.

> Prevention is associated with the reintegration model.

In the late 1960s the reintegration model was popular. During this period it was believed that the community was somehow responsible for offenders' behavior. Societal factors were at the core of the crime problem; therefore, treatment consisted of finding ways to use community resources to help offenders become productive citizens.

The Pendulum Swings

The next two chapters describe how each of these ideologies arose and when each was most prevalent. As with the opposing basic views of crime and criminals, the ideologies can be placed on a continuum with punishment and prevention on the opposite extremes (Figure 1–4).

Currently the high crime rates and media coverage of violent crimes across the nation have resulted in a mood that is most supportive of the punishment ideology. This mood is reflected in the comments made by President Clinton in his January 25, 1994, State of the Union address: "Those who commit crimes should be punished, and those who commit repeated violent crimes should be told when you commit a third violent crime, you will be put away and put away for good—three strikes and you are out." Clinton is not alone. According to an article in the National Criminal Justice Association's *Justice Bulletin* ("Governors Seek Greater Sanctions," 1994, p. 1):

> Governors across the nation in January outlined new get-tough strategies for keeping violent criminals behind bars, dealing more effectively with dangerous juvenile offenders, and taking firearms out of the hands of felons and teenagers. . . .

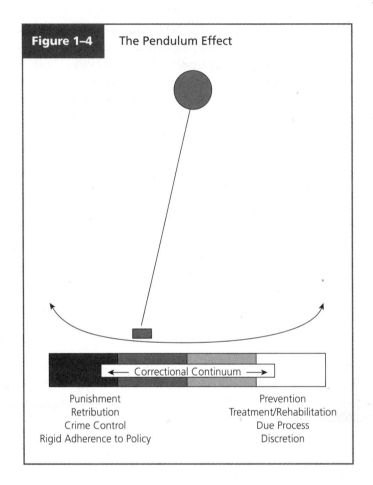

Figure 1–4   The Pendulum Effect

Correctional Continuum

Punishment	Prevention
Retribution	Treatment/Rehabilitation
Crime Control	Due Process
Rigid Adherence to Policy	Discretion

Although most states are experiencing slight decreases in serious crime rates, many governors have moved crime control to the top of their political agendas. . . .

In their annual status reports, governors voiced a strong desire to halt the "revolving door" of justice for violent criminals and repeat offenders—both adult and juvenile—with stricter sentencing laws, more police, and new prison facilities. The chorus of calls for a crackdown on violent crime represents a shift of focus from the governors' preoccupation with the drug war in recent years.

Not all those who study criminal justice believe the punishment ideology is the answer. According to Allen and Simonsen (1992, p. 91): "The correctional 'nonsystem' will stagger through the 1990s in a continuing state of indecision as to what to embrace as its core ideology. . . . Despite the increased reliance on punishment and the conservative backlash that has so negatively impacted corrections in the late 1980s and early 1990s, there remains strong support for both treatment and prevention among legislators as well as the general public."

Although every era and civilization has incorporated some form of punishment into their dealings with criminals, the philosophies behind the use of punishment have varied greatly throughout history.

Competing Perspectives on Punishment and Corrections

Traditionally, punishment has been seen as a way to control crime, as a means to the obvious end of reducing crime rates and restraining individual criminals. In civilized societies, the punishment has been administered by the government rather than the victim. The concept that crimes are offenses against *all* members of a society is central to our modern criminal justice system and its approach to punishment.

What Justifies Punishment

Punishment has historically served a multitude of purposes and has been administered in a variety of ingeniously barbaric ways.

> The two basic justifications for use of punishment through the ages have been retribution and utilitarian.

Retribution, as discussed previously, was most prevalent in ancient societies. Because retribution focuses on the offense committed and on the past, it is backward-looking. A utilitarian justification, in contrast, has punishment serving a useful purpose such as incapacitation, deterrence or rehabilitation. Since utilitarian approaches are about social engineering, they are forward-looking or proactive.

> The earliest known advocate of punishment as utilitarian was the Greek philosopher Plato.

In one of his best known dialogues, Plato (427–347 B.C.) set forth the following argument:

> If you will think, Socrates, of the nature of punishment, you will see at once that in the opinion of mankind, virtue can be acquired; no one punishes the evil-doer under the notion, or for the reason, that he has done wrong—only the unreasonable fury of a beast acts in that manner. But he who desires to inflict rational punishment does not retaliate for a past wrong which cannot be undone; he has regard to the future, and is desirous that the man who is

punished, and he who sees him punished, may be deterred from doing wrong again. He punishes for the sake of prevention, thereby clearly implying that virtue is capable of being taught (Jowett, 1952, p. 45).

Debate between these two justifications has existed for thousands of years and continues today. Another approach to understanding punishment, which is so often equated with corrections, is to take a sociological view of punishment.

A Sociological View of Punishment

According to Garland (1991, p. 161): "[P]unishment should be considered in the same kind of way and in the same kind of depth as other social institutions."

> A **sociological view of punishment** takes a broad view, perceiving punishment as a social institution.

Garland cautions that the sociology of punishment is not a single, unified framework but rather a set of competing philosophies, a "noisy clash of perspectives" and varying points of view (p. 121). Four such perspectives are described by Garland.

> Punishment may be viewed as a moralizing mechanism for social solidarity, a component of class rule, an exercise of power and a reflection of our cultural sensibilities.

Punishment and Social Solidarity—The Durkheimian Perspective

Emile Durkheim (1858–1917), a pioneer in modern sociology, contended that social solidarity was impossible if society was deviant and immoral. However, he also regarded crime as a normal, in fact, necessary, element of society, providing a form of individual expression that society allowed to exist in much the same way it permitted a "genius to carry out his work" (Durkheim, 1938 [1895], p. 71). Durkheim (1951 [1897], p. 252) also developed a concept known as
> **anomie,** the breakdown of societal norms as a result of society's failure to distinguish between right and wrong, often in response to rapid change: "[W]hen society is disturbed by some painful crisis or by beneficent but abrupt transition, it is momentarily incapable of exercising [control over the individual]."

Durkheim argued that punishment is a moral process to preserve the shared values of a society, that is, its collective conscience. When individuals deviate from this collective conscience, society is outraged and seeks revenge and to restore the moral order.

> The Durkheimian perspective sees punishment as revenge and as a way to restore and solidify the social order.

One key element of Durkheim's perspective is that the general population is involved in the act of punishing, giving it legitimacy. A second key element is its deeply emotional, passionate reactions in response to crime. Garland (p. 123) suggests:

> In Durkheim's view, the rituals of punishment are directed less at the individual offender than at the audience of impassioned onlookers whose cherished values and security had been momentarily undermined by the offender's actions. Punishment's significance is best conceived as social and moral rather than purely penological.
>
> Punishment is thus an occasion for the practical realization of the moral values that make up the conscience collective. It responds to the criminal's attack on morality and solidarity by reaffirming the strength of that moral order, restating its terms, and reasserting its authority. . . . Punishment thus transforms a threat to social order into a triumph of social solidarity.

Durkheim emphasized condemnatory rituals. Ritual produces or reinforces social solidarity by evoking certain emotions and by affirming the importance of certain ideas or relationships. Some ideas and relationships are more important than others. The most important have a religious-like quality (even in secular society). Crime, according to Durkheim, is any act that people consider a violation or threat to those core ideas.

In essence, Durkheim saw punishment as "sentiment-based, morality-affirming, solidarity-producing" (Garland, p. 123) rather than as a means of crime control. When society punishes those who break its rules, it demonstrates that it is in control. This perspective on punishment helps explain many forms of corporal punishment used in earlier times. Today, arrest and public trial are justice system components that illustrate the Durkheimian perspective, for example, the emotional jubilation felt across the country at the Timothy McVeigh verdict and sentencing decision. Similarly, the acquittals of other high-profile defendants have elicited vigorous public response, reflecting society's sense that moral injustice had not been righted.

The question arises, however, especially in modern times, as to whether we have a collective conscience. This issue is addressed in the Marxist perspective.

Punishment and Class Conflict—The Marxist Perspective

Rather than viewing punishment as a means of providing social solidarity, Karl Marx (1818–1883) saw punishment as a way to enhance the power of the upper class and an inevitable result of capitalism. In the *Manifesto of the Communist Party* (1848), Marx and Engels wrote: "The history of all hitherto existing society is the history of class struggles. Freeman and slave, patrician and plebeian, lord and serf, guild-master and journeyman, in a word, oppressor and oppressed stood in constant opposition to one another, carried on an uninterrupted, now hidden, now open fight, a fight that each time ended in either a revolutionary reconstruction of society at large, or in the common ruin of the contending classes."

Marx referred to the lower class as a "slum proletariat" made up of vagrants, prostitutes and criminals. "In effect, penal policy is taken to be one element within a wider strategy of controlling the poor; punishment should be understood not as a social response to the criminality of individuals but as a mechanism operating in the struggle between social classes" (Garland, p. 128).

> The Marxist perspective sees punishment as a way to control the lower class and preserve the power of the upper class.

This perspective is supported by the way in which punishment has frequently taken the form of hard physical labor ranging from shackled prisoners rowing huge vessels across the ocean to chain gangs. This physical labor was also intended to instill in the prisoners the discipline needed to become productive workers in society.

The Marxist view is not necessarily in conflict with the Durkheimian view. While supporters of the Marxist perspective are not likely to talk about the collective conscience, neither will they emphasize the way public condemnation of criminals reinforces shared moral beliefs in a community. The Marxist is interested in how laws are made deliberately and perhaps conspiratorially to protect privilege and how they are enforced selectively. There is great concern for social justice questions ("the rich get richer and the poor get prison") and little for the way punishment reinforces the moral sentiments of the social elite.

This rationale was doubtless operating throughout the Middle Ages, Renaissance, Reformation and into the nineteenth century. Society was divided into a small ruling class, a somewhat larger class of artisans and a vastly larger class of peasants. Intimidation through a brutal criminal law was an important form of social control. Organized police forces and prisons did not exist. Punishment was severe, either capital or corporal or both, and convicted criminals were dealt with swiftly.

In the twentieth century, hard labor was often avoided by those who could afford to pay a fine which, according to Garland (p. 130), "in the twentieth century has come to be the most frequently deployed penal measure and the epitome of rationalized capitalist penal law." This perspective does have its hazards, however, for if offenders see their punishment as an unjust imposition of the establishment's power and authority, and if that belief is reinforced by other offenders, punishment may simply encourage them to commit further criminal acts.

The Power and Knowledge Perspective

Some research has focused on the evolution of forms of punishment and on penal control—how power is exercised and people are controlled. The change can be traced from the scaffold to the prison and reflects a change in the character of justice itself. The body becomes "an instrument for transforming the soul rather than as a surface on which to inflict pain" (Garland, p. 135).

This perspective focuses on correction rather than on punishment—a distinctive kind of disciplinary power that masters the human body, making it both obedient and useful. Correction, in turn, relies on understanding the individual violators and knowing what actions can be taken to transform them into conforming members of society. Experts in various fields contribute to this understanding and knowledge.

➤ Control is maintained through constant, uninterrupted surveillance, inspections and discipline. This perspective formed the basis for **panopticism,** applying the technology of control through systematically observing and gathering information. In addition, as noted by Garland (p. 138):

> Key principles of modern penology—the investigation of "the criminal" behind the crime, the concern with correction and adjustment, the involvement of experts whose task is to observe, to assess, and to cure—are all hallmarks of this disciplinary process, as are the standard penitentiary techniques of isolation, work, individualized treatment, and the adjustment of sentence to reflect behavioral improvement.

Punishment and Sensibilities

Another view of punishment looks at what is culturally and emotionally acceptable. Punishments such as torture, maiming, stoning, whipping and drawing and quartering are no longer acceptable in most societies. Painful, violent or disturbing events are removed from public view:

> Sex, violence, bodily functions, illness, suffering, and death gradually become a source of embarrassment and distaste and are more and more removed to various private domains such as the domesticated nuclear family, private lavatories and bedrooms, prison cells, and hospital wards. Lying behind this process is the tendency to suppress the more animalistic aspects of human conduct as being signs of the crude and the uncultivated (Garland, p. 145).

The civilizing process is very evident in the evolution of punishment. In early times, barbaric forms of punishment were conducted in public. Hangings brought out crowds of onlookers. Entire communities participated in stoning offenders to death. By the seventeenth and eighteenth century, such displays of suffering were regarded as distasteful, and punishment was removed from public view, most often to prisons.

The civilizing distaste for violence can also be seen in the search for an acceptable form of capital punishment. The movement from a personal executioner such as the hangman or the firing squad to mechanical means such as the gas chamber or the electric chair parallels this civilizing process. More recently, the use of lethal injection "encapsulates many of the important characteristics of modern punishment—its privatization, its sanitization, and the careful denial of its own violence . . ." (Garland, p. 151).

A more recent example comes from the headlines in U.S. papers on March 4, 1994: "Singapore to Flog U.S. Teen Who Vandalized Cars." The sentence of being flogged six times with a rattan cane and put in prison for four months caused public outrage. As noted in the *Los Angeles Times:*

> The punishment is far more severe than the word "caning" might imply. A half-inch-thick rattan cane that has been soaked in water is used, and it is wielded by an official trained in martial arts. Prisoners often go into shock during caning, and the punishment leaves permanent scars on their buttocks. . . .
>
> The government has long been a believer in Draconian sentencing in criminal cases as a deterrent. Possession of even minute amounts of marijuana, for example, can lead to the death penalty.

Multiple Interpretations

To understand our current forms of punishment and their role in the broader criminal justice system, punishment must be viewed in its historical, social and cultural context as a social institution that has evolved over the centuries. As noted by Garland (p. 159):

> Like all complex institutions, the prison simultaneously pursues a number of objectives and is kept in place by a range of forces. Crime control—in the sense of reforming offenders and reducing crime rates—is certainly one of these objectives but by no means the only one. As we have seen, the prison also serves as an effective means of incapacitation, securely excluding offenders from society, sometimes for very long periods, and containing those individuals who prove too troublesome for other institutions or communities. . . . Most important, the prison provides a way of punishing people—of subjecting them to hard treatment, inflicting pain, doing them harm—that is largely compatible with modern sensibilities and conventional restraints on open, physical violence.

This last objective, punishing people, can be traced from the use of public stocks and branding in our early history to the private use of solitary confinement and even electrocution or lethal injection.

Punishment vs. Corrections: Call for a New Paradigm

➤ A **paradigm** is a model or a way of viewing an aspect of life such as education, politics, medicine or the criminal justice system.

➤ A **paradigm shift** is a new way of thinking about a given subject.

Such a paradigm shift is seen in police departments that have adopted community policing.

In an address to the American Correctional Association Winter Conference in January 1992, Portland Police Bureau Assistant Chief Wayne R. Inman (1992, p. 192) stated:

> No longer can we sit idly by and blame other components of the criminal justice system or society in general. We are a part of rather than apart from that system and society.
>
> Crime is a symptom; it is not a cause. Crime has its roots in such dysfunctional institutions as the family, where physical and mental abuse occur and where children are not taught values and life skills, have no role models and suffer from low self-esteem.
>
> Crime has its roots in the schools, where gangs often flourish as surrogate parents, where classrooms are too crowded, where the quality of instruction is sometimes lacking, and where children are not given the opportunity and encouragement to feel valued and worthy of a significant place in society.
>
> Crime has its roots in the workplace, where unemployment and underemployment breed contempt for the work ethic and frustration and despair abound. Crime has its roots in racism, where factors such as skin color and national origin discriminate and segregate and people are judged by standards unrelated to their objective contributions to society. . . .
>
> The basic premise of community policing is that resolving crime and disorder is the responsibility of all people and all organizations in society.

Inman concluded his address with a challenge to corrections to begin thinking along similar lines.

Rees (1990, p. 104) also calls for a new way of looking at our justice system: "Sadly, we have not progressed to any significant degree in more than 200 years. The solutions are to be found by moving forward and embracing novel, never-tried possibilities. The solutions do not lie in the past, where models and philosophies have failed dismally and brought us to where we are today."

Crier (1993, p. 142) reminded the attendees at the opening session of the ACA's 123rd Congress of Corrections that: "Albert Einstein said we cannot cure the problems today with traditional thinking because, after all, that's the kind of thinking that got us here in the first place. It's time to shake up the status quo. It's time to dream outrageous dreams and make them come to pass."

A Princeton University Study Group funded by the Bureau of Justice Statistics (BJS) has explored how this paradigm shift might be accomplished: examining how the criminal justice system is viewed and how this view might need changing. Their first discussion paper (DiIulio, 1992, p. 6) described the multiple, vague, contradictory purposes served by the criminal justice system in our country:

> The history of the American criminal justice system is a history of swings in public mood. Americans have long been ambivalent about the purposes of criminal justice. Among other things, they have wanted a criminal justice system that apprehends and visits harm upon the guilty (*punishment*); makes offenders more virtuous or at least more law-abiding (*rehabilitation*); dissuades would-be offenders from criminal pursuits (*deterrence*); protects innocent citizens from being victimized by convicted criminals (*incapacitation*); and enables most criminals to return as productive citizens to the bosom of the free community (*reintegration*). They have wanted the system to achieve these contradictory goals without violating the public conscience (*humane treatment*), jeopardizing the public law (*constitutional rights*), emptying the public purse (*cost containment*), or weakening the tradition of State and local public administration (*federalism*).

During different periods of our history the criminal justice system has emphasized specific purposes, for example in the 1960s and 1970s the focus was on fighting poverty and rehabilitating criminals. Constitutional rights and humane treatment were prized. Since the 1980s the focus has been on getting harder on criminals, building more prisons and imposing longer sentences. But crime and violence continue to escalate. As noted by Rees (p. 104): "We know through history that warehousing inmates with a variety of structures, models, treatments, and goals is not the solution."

The BJS Princeton Project suggested (DiIulio, p. 8): "A modern, democratic vision of the justice system's public purposes and limitations is both necessary and desirable. Such a vision emerges from the realization that all citizens have the right and responsibility to participate in the system. Citizens are co-producers of justice." Such a paradigm shift would hold a neighborhood accountable for the quality of life in that neighborhood. The shift also encompasses four civic ideals (DiIulio, p. 10):

- Doing justice.
- Promoting secure communities.
- Restoring crime victims.
- Promoting noncriminal options.

Doing justice. The study group defined justice as "the quality of treating individuals according to their civic rights and in ways that they deserve to be treated by virtue of relevant conduct." To "do justice" implies that offenders are held fully accountable for their behavior, that their constitutional and legal rights are protected, that like offenses are treated alike, and that both the offense and the offender are considered.

Promoting secure communities. This goes beyond neighborhood watches and citizen patrols. It entails a geographic community becoming a community sociologically as well. According to Klockars (1991, pp. 247–48): "Sociologically, the concept of community implies a group of people with a common history, common beliefs and understandings, a sense of themselves as 'us' and outsiders as 'them,' and often, but not always, a shared territory." In communities lacking this commonality, crime and violence may flourish. Goldstein (1990, p. 25) suggests: "Areas of cities requiring the most police attention are usually those with few shared values and little sense of community."

Restoring crime victims. Van Ness (1990, p. 62), the originator of restorative justice, notes: "The Western view of crime and justice has become skewed. Rather than admitting that crimes injure victims, our laws define them as only offenses against government. . . . Contemporary criminal justice is preoccupied with maintaining public order and punishing offenders. Victims are often ignored."

Traditionally justice in the United States has focused on the offender and the state punishing that offender. The victim and the community have been overlooked.

> **Restorative justice** seeks to use a balanced approach involving offenders, victims, local communities and government in alleviating crime and violence and obtaining peaceful communities.

Van Ness (p. 64) sees restorative justice as involving three basic principles:

- Crimes result in injuries to victims, communities and offenders; therefore, the criminal justice process must repair those injuries.
- Not only government, but victims, offenders and communities should be actively involved throughout the entire criminal justice process.
- In promoting justice, the government should preserve order, and peace should be maintained by the community.

According to Umbreit (1996, p. 1): "Unlike conventional criminal justice approaches which center mainly on the offender, restorative justice offers a triple focus: individual victims, victimized communities, and offenders. Crime is understood to consist of acts against people within communities, as opposed to the traditional notion that crime is an offense against the state. . . . Restoration of material and emotional loss is seen as far more important than imposing ever-increasing levels of costly punishment on offenders. In turn, offenders are encouraged to work to restore their victims' and community's sense of peace."

While it may seem appealing in theory, some criticism has fallen on restorative justice and its functionality in practice. Many advocates of restorative justice miss how fundamentally our basic approach to law and the criminal justice system must be changed in order to achieve restorative justice. Critics claim restorative justice is an absurdity in today's anonymous society, being little more than intellectualized nostalgia for the lost intimacy of traditional communities. These critics also state the implications of restorative justice are unsettling, given the wide range of offenses that constitute crimes in our society—everything from vandalism and other relatively benign property crimes to rape and murder. Can restorative justice really be applied in cases involving such crimes against persons?

Promoting noncriminal options. Numerous alternatives to incarceration exist. And even within prison, the punishment of confinement need not totally interfere with an offender's opportunity to take part in meaningful, constructive activities. Table 1–3 summarizes some of the basic changes involved in the suggested paradigm shift.

Paradigm shifts are hard to comprehend because they change the way we see and understand everything around us. It may be that even this shift is lacking in fully understanding justice. One way to better understand justice is to consider what it is *not*.

Most would agree that it is unjust to send accused criminals who are poor to jail while those who have the financial means are able to hire high-powered lawyers, post bail and pay fines.

Another form of injustice may exist in failing to have the punishment fit the crime done to society. Our criminal law has harsh penalties for doing drugs, prostitution and other so-called victimless crimes. In contrast, minor penalties—usually financial—are imposed for corporations engaging in white-collar crimes, environmental crimes or hazardous working conditions for employees.

➤   Yet another form of injustice identified by sociologists relates to **distributive justice** or social justice—the fairness of how property, money and prestige are divided within a society. Too frequently distributive and retributive justice are not differentiated and critics claim that retributive justice has failed when, in effect, it has no power over the failure. The criminal justice system is often blamed for injustice over which it has little or no control.

That distributive injustice exists was acknowledged by President Clinton in his January 25, 1994, State of the Union address:

> I urge you to consider this: As you demand tougher penalties for those who choose violence, let us also remember how we came to this sad point. In our toughest neighborhoods, on our meanest streets, in our poorest rural areas, we have seen a stunning simultaneous breakdown of community, family, and work, the heart and soul of civilized society. This has created a vast vacuum which has been filled by violence and drugs and gangs. So I ask you to remember that even as we say no to crime, we must give people, especially our young people, something to say yes to.

Table 1–3	Paradigms of Justice—Old and New

Old Paradigm Retributive Justice	New Paradigm Restorative Justice
1. Crime defined as violation of the state	1. Crime defined as violation of one person by another
2. Focus on establishing blame, on guilt, on past (did he/she do it?)	2. Focus on problem-solving, on liabilities and obligations, on future (what should be done?)
3. Adversarial relationships and process normative	3. Dialogue and negotiation normative
4. Imposition of pain to punish and deter/prevent	4. Restitution as a means of restoring both parties; reconciliation/restoration as goal
5. Justice defined by intent and by process: right rules	5. Justice defined as right relationships; judged by the outcome
6. Interpersonal, conflictual nature of crime obscured, repressed; conflict seen as individual vs. state	6. Crime recognized as interpersonal conflict; value of conflict recognized
7. One social injury replaced by another	7. Focus on repair of social injury
8. Community on sideline, represented abstractly by state	8. Community as facilitator in restorative process
9. Encouragement of competitive, individualistic values	9. Encouragement of mutuality
10. Action directed from state to offender: • victim ignored • offender passive	10. Victim and offender's roles recognized in both problem and solution: • victim rights/needs recognized • offender encouraged to take responsibility
11. Offender accountability defined as taking punishment	11. Offender accountability defined as understanding impact of action and helping decide how to make things right
12. Offense defined in purely legal terms, devoid of moral, social, economic, political dimensions	12. Offense understood in whole context—moral, social, economic, political
13. "Debt" owed to state and society in the abstract	13. Debt/liability to victim recognized
14. Response focused on offender's past behavior	14. Response focused on harmful consequences of offender's behavior
15. Stigma of crime unremovable	15. Stigma of crime removable through restorative action
16. No encouragement for repentance and forgiveness	16. Possibilities for repentance and forgiveness
17. Dependence upon proxy professionals	17. Direct involvement by participants

Source: Howard Zehr. "Restorative Justice." *IARCA Journal,* March 1991, p. 7. Reprinted by permission.

The following chapters trace the origins of the theories and concepts discussed in this chapter and help explain the complexity of corrections as it exists today.

Summary

Corrections refers to the programs, services, agencies and institutions responsible for supervising persons charged with or convicted of crimes.

The Constitution established a representative democracy based on two basic principles, separation of powers and federalism, resulting in an intentionally fragmented system. The Constitution also established three branches of our government—legislative, executive and judicial—to serve as checks and balances on each other, ensuring, as the founding fathers intended, that one will not become all-powerful. Corrections is primarily part of the executive branch. In some states, parts of corrections are also part of the judicial branch.

The primary purposes of corrections are retribution, deterrence, incapacitation and rehabilitation. Which purpose is emphasized is influenced by a person's view of crime and criminals. The classical view holds that humans have free will and are responsible for their own actions. The positivist view, in contrast, holds that humans are shaped by their society and are the product of environmental and cultural influences. The classical view focuses on crime; the positivist view on the criminal.

Adding to the complexity of corrections are four correctional ideologies that influence and are influenced by views of crime and criminals and the purposes emphasized: punishment, control, treatment and prevention. Punishment is associated with the justice model, control is associated with the custodial model, treatment is associated with the medical model, and prevention is associated with the reintegration model.

The two basic justifications for use of punishment through the ages have been retribution or utilitarian. The earliest known advocate of punishment as utilitarian was the Greek philosopher Plato. The sociological view of punishment takes a broad view, perceiving punishment as a social institution. Punishment may be viewed as a moralizing mechanism for social solidarity, a component of class rule, an exercise of power and a reflection of our cultural sensibilities. The Durkheimian perspective sees punishment as revenge and as a way to restore and solidify the social order. In contrast, the Marxist perspective sees punishment as a way to control the lower class and preserve the power of the upper class.

A paradigm is a model or a way of viewing an aspect of life such as education, politics, medicine or the criminal justice system. A paradigm shift is a new way of thinking about a given subject. Paradigm shifts recently suggested for corrections include doing justice, promoting secure communities, restoring crime victims and promoting noncriminal options. Restorative justice seeks to use a balanced approach involving offenders, victims, local communities and government in alleviating crime and violence and obtaining peaceful communities.

Discussion Questions

1. In today's society, is the separation of powers good or bad? What are the advantages and disadvantages of such an arrangement?

2. Do police officers, judges and correctional officers have too much discretion (power)?

3. Have you ever been involved in an act of discretion (for example, pulled over for speeding and let go with a warning)? Was your experience positive or negative?

4. Can you think of examples of the funnel effect in other areas of life (for example, the employment process)?

5. Which of the four purposes of corrections do you feel is most important and why?

6. Which view is most believable to you—the classical or positivist view? Why?

7. What if a 22-year-old inmate kept robbing other inmates, getting caught and then being released before the paperwork was completed? After repeated incidents, is it understandable that a correctional officer might punish the offender rather than taking him or her before the warden? Is it legal?

8. Although the national crime rate has been decreasing for the past few years, public perception continues to be that things are getting worse. What might be some reasons for this?

9. Why do you think the police and the courts receive such high marks of public confidence while the criminal justice system as a whole falls to the bottom of the confidence list? How might the public's confidence in the criminal justice system be raised?

10. What impacts will the new "get tough" and "three strikes" laws have on corrections?

References

Allen, Harry E. and Simonsen, Clifford E. *Corrections in America: An Introduction*, 6th ed. New York: Macmillan Publishing Company, 1992.

Bureau of Justice Statistics. *1995 Sourcebook of Criminal Justice Statistics*. Washington, DC: U.S. Department of Justice, 1995.

Burger, Warren E. Commencement address at Pace University, June 11, 1983.

Crier, Catherine. "It's Time to Take Responsibility for Fixing Our Nation's Problems." *Corrections Today,* December 1993, pp. 142–143.

DiIulio, John J., Jr. "Rethinking the Criminal Justice System: Toward a New Paradigm." Washington, DC: Bureau of Justice Statistics, December 1992.

Durkheim, Emile. *The Rules of Sociological Method* (1895), edited by G.E.G. Catlin. Glencoe, IL: The Free Press, 1938.

Durkheim, Emile. *Suicide* (1897). Glencoe, IL: The Free Press, 1951.

Garland, David. "Sociological Perspectives on Punishment." *Crime and Justice: A Review of Research,* Vol. 14, pp. 115–165, edited by Michael Tonry. Chicago: The University of Chicago Press, 1991.

Goldstein, Herman. *Problem-Oriented Policing.* New York: McGraw-Hill Publishing Company, 1990.

"Governors Seek Greater Sanctions Against Violent Offenders." *NCJA Justice Bulletin,* Vol. 14, No. 1, January 1994, pp. 1–2, 8–11.

Inman, Wayne R. "Portland Law Enforcement Officer Poses Challenge to ACA Members." *Corrections Today,* August 1992, pp. 188–193, 230.

Innes, Christopher A. "Recent Public Opinion in the United States Toward Punishment and Corrections." *The Prison Journal,* Vol. 73, No. 2, June 1993, pp. 220–236.

Jowett, Benjamin (translator). "Protagoras." *The Dialogues of Plato* (Great Books of the Western World Series). Chicago: Encyclopedia Britannica, Inc., 1952.

Klockars, Carl B. "The Rhetoric of Community Policing." In *Community Policing: Rhetoric or Reality,* edited by Jack R. Greene and Stephen D. Mastrofski, pp. 239–258. New York: Praeger Publishing, 1991.

Marx, Karl and Engels, Friedrich. *Manifesto of the Communist Party* (1848). Chicago, IL: Encyclopedia Britannica, Inc., p. 419.

National Advisory Commission on Criminal Justice Standards and Goals. *Corrections.* Washington, DC: U.S. Department of Justice, 1973.

Newport, Frank. "Small Business and Military Generate Most Confidence in Americans." Public releases from Gallup poll results on the Internet (www.Gallup.com), July 25–27, 1997.

President's Commission on Law Enforcement and Administration of Justice. *The Challenge of Crime in a Free Society.* Washington, DC: U.S. Government Printing Office, 1967.

Rees, Chuck. "Will We Learn from Our Mistakes or Continue to Build on Them?" *Corrections Today,* February 1990, pp. 102–104.

"Singapore to Flog U.S. Teen Who Vandalized Cars." *Los Angeles Times,* quoted in Minneapolis/St. Paul *Star Tribune,* March 4, 1994, p. A1.

Umbreit, Mark S. "Restorative Justice Through Mediation." *Overcrowded Times,* June 1996, pp. 1, 9–11.

Van Ness, Daniel W. "Restoring the Balance: Tipping the Scales of Justice." *Corrections Today,* February 1990, pp. 62–66.

2

The Origins of Corrections—Penology

The farther backward you can look, the farther forward you are likely to see.
—Winston Churchill (1871–1947)

Can You Define

Bridewell
corporal punishment
determinism
free will

gaols
hulks
indeterminate sentence

Inquisition
mark system
social contract

Introduction

T his chapter describes the origins of our criminal justice system, going back to preliterate societies. Figure 2–1 provides a time line to guide you on this historical overview and to illustrate the overlap of influences at different times in history.

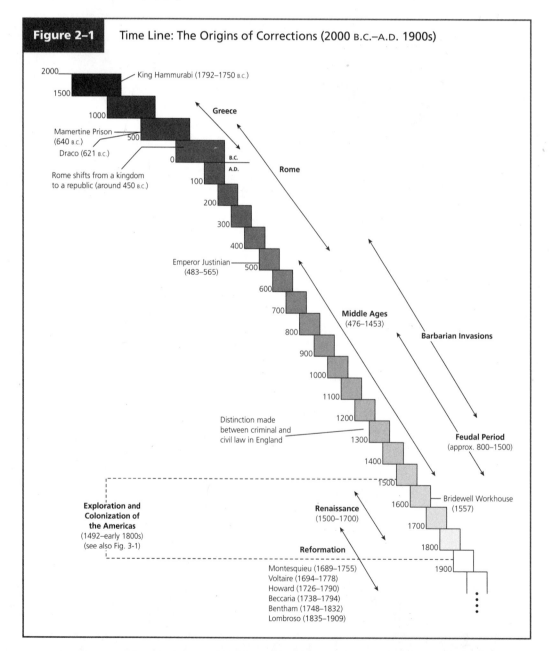

| **Figure 2–1** | Time Line: The Origins of Corrections (2000 B.C.–A.D. 1900s) |

As civilizations developed, their methods for maintaining social control also evolved and provided the historical beginnings of our criminal justice system, including the component we now call corrections. The swinging of the pendulum from harsh punishment to a call for reform and back to harshness is readily apparent in the following pages.

Social Control in Preliterate Societies

Anthropologists conclude that from the earliest times, individuals who broke society's laws were punished. Even the most primitive tribe exercised some form of social control over its members' behavior. In preliterate societies, *retaliation* was the accepted way to deal with tribe members who broke the rules. Personal revenge was sometimes broadened so that the victim's entire family or tribe retaliated against the offender's family or tribe, resulting in blood feuds. Blood feuds were avoided by establishing a system whereby the wrongdoer could pay the victim money or give the victim property.

> Preliterate societies stressed the importance of the victim and the need for personal revenge or retaliation.

As tribal leaders emerged, they began to help victims by imposing fines and punishments on wrongdoers. If the wrongdoer refused to pay the fine or accept the punishment, that person was declared an *outlaw*, that is, outside the law of the tribe and therefore banished, probably to be eaten by wild animals or killed by the elements. Banishment was one of the earliest forms of social vengeance. This is also the forerunner of our criminal law, taking *public* action against those who do not obey the rules of the society.

> Eventually, tribal leaders and rulers took over the task of punishing those who broke the law.

As societies developed language and writing skills, they began to record their laws. One of the earliest known codes was that of Hammurabi, the King of Babylonia (the region now called Iraq). King Hammurabi (1792–1750 B.C.), acting as sole legislator and supreme judge for his kingdom, set forth rules establishing offenses and punishments, a code whose influence was felt throughout the Middle East.

Historians view the *Code of Hammurabi* as the first comprehensive description of a system society used to regulate behavior and at the same time take vengeance on those who disobeyed its rules. The code contained 282 clauses concerning such behaviors as false accusations, witchcraft, military service, family laws, tariffs, loans and debts.

> The underlying principle of the *Code of Hammurabi* was that of *lex talions*—an eye for an eye.

This principle can be seen in the portion of the code dealing with buildings:

> If a builder builds a house for a man and does not make its construction firm and the house collapses and causes the death of the owner of the house—that builder shall be put to death. If it causes the death of a son of the owner—they shall put to death a son of the builder.

Punishments were severe and public, including forced labor, branding, whipping, mutilating, burning at the stake, crucifying, hanging and drowning.

Ancient Greece and Rome

Greek life was centered in a city-state governed by aristocrats who considered themselves superior beings. The aristocrats and commoners clashed frequently. Finally the commoners demanded and got a written code of laws, which dealt mainly with homicide, contracts and rules for appointing officials. As noted by Bowra (1965, p. 13): "From the first Greek lawgivers stems the whole majestic succession of the West's legal system. The Romans, great lawmakers in their own right, learned from the Greeks. In turn, the comprehensive codes of Gaius and Justinian gave rise to most modern legal systems."

Later Greek society was organized into city-states, with criminals handled by kings and elders. Victims or their families presented their case to the king in public. The onlookers could cheer or jeer depending on if they believed or disbelieved the defendants.

> The Greeks' public participation in meting out justice is the forerunner of our jury system.

For those found guilty, a brutal death penalty was often prescribed such as being strapped to a board and left to die of exposure or starvation or being hurled off a cliff.

In addition to the death penalty, ancient Greece and Rome also used imprisonment as a punishment for lesser offenses. In 640 B.C. Mamertine Prison was built. This prison consisted of a vast series of dungeons under Rome's main sewer. Ancient Greece and Rome also used strong cages and

rock quarries as prisons. These prisons held not only criminals but also political dissidents and social misfits.

The need for workers to perform hard physical labor on numerous public
works encouraged the use of penal servitude, reserved for the lower classes. A
sentence to penal servitude usually meant a life in chains working in the galleys of ships, toiling in the mines or building immense structures decreed by
the ruler. It also meant giving up citizenship (civil death) and all possessions,
including property, to the state.

➤ In Greece, the harsh, cruel Code of Draco, ruler in 621 B.C., called for **corporal punishment**—inflicting bodily pain—so extensively it was rumored to
be written in blood. The word *Draconian* became synonymous with extreme
cruelty. Among the punishments set forth were flogging, branding, drawing
and quartering, stretching on the rack and mutilating. Thieves had their
hands cut off. Liars had their tongues cut out. Rapists' genitals were removed,
and adulterers had an "A" branded on their forehead. The minor offense of
stealing cabbages was punishable by death. The less advanced the society, the
greater the likelihood of corporal punishment being used.

Around 450 B.C. Rome shifted from a kingdom to a republic, and the common people demanded more fairness in the administration of justice. The
Twelve Tables put custom into writing and became the foundation of law in
Rome. The laws set forth in the Twelve Tables were in effect for a thousand
years. During this time many thousand volumes of laws and legal opinions
were generated, resulting in a Roman law that was disjointed and, for the
most part, ignored.

Up to the Middle Ages, many criminals were handled privately under *lex
talions*, the law of retribution or retaliation.

The Middle Ages (A.D. 476–1453)

In the sixth century A.D., Emperor Justinian (483–565), wanting to restore
Rome to its former glory, called together 12 experts to review the laws of
Rome and to organize them into a document called the *Corpus Juris Civilis*. A
key part of the *Corpus* was the *Justinian Code*. The work took three years to
complete, and its lasting influence can be seen by reviewing some of the code's
provisions (Hadas, 1965, p. 166):

- No one suffers a penalty for what he thinks.
- Anything not permitted the defendant ought not be allowed the plaintiff.
- The burden of proof is upon the party affirming, not on the party denying.
- A father is not a competent witness for a son, nor a son for a father.
- In inflicting penalties, the age and inexperience of the guilty party must
  be taken into account.

The provisions of the Justinian Code were the law throughout most of Europe until modern times, and they greatly influenced our law as well.

Art of this period shows the first rendering of the scales of justice, illustrating that punishments were to be balanced by the crimes committed. Banishment was frequent and was, in effect, capital punishment because offenders were sent away and forbidden food or shelter for hundreds of miles. An extensive system of fines was also established. The Justinian Code fell when the Roman Empire crumbled, but it provided the base from which most of the Western world's laws evolved.

After the fall of the Roman Empire, general disorder prevailed. Kings were in complete authority, making laws and enforcing them as best they could. Kings sought to suppress threats to their rule by executing those who opposed them. Every castle had a dungeon, and, as noted by Fremantle (1965, p. 20):

Punishments were primitive, coarse and cruel. Men were beaten, branded, mutilated, their eyes gouged out or their hands cut off. Torture was habitual; it only grew more refined as time went on.

Additional attempts to maintain order and control involved cities building walls with strong gates, bridge abutments and fortresses to protect themselves against roving bands of thieves. When gunpowder was invented, the effectiveness

Capital punishment was public and quite brutal during the late 1500s.

of these fortresses was lost, and many were converted into prisons for political dissidents, the poor, social misfits and criminals. These prisons were the forerunners of contemporary corrections, especially in England and Scotland. Debtors' prisons were established for those who could not pay their debts but also confined criminals and social misfits, typically under miserable, custodial conditions. No treatment or rehabilitation was even considered. The sole purpose was punishment. Individuals were put in prison to receive punishment, not as a punishment in itself. Many died there.

The Feudal Period (Ninth to Fifteenth Century)

In the English tradition, crimes committed prior to the thirteenth century were considered harms against all individuals, and a common punishment for those breaking the law of the feudal lord was forfeiting land and property. During the thirteenth century, however, the distinction was made in England between criminal and civil law. The importance of this differentiation is (1) it was politically grounded and (2) it was the structural reason that led some to think of restorative justice as a good idea. (Recall how restorative justice seeks to use the combined effort of offenders, victims, communities and government to reduce crime and achieve peace, a concept predicated on the distinction between civil and criminal law.) A violation of the criminal law was viewed as a harm against the state, with the state seizing victim status for a specific set of offenses which were relabeled *crimes*. What was left over was covered by civil law. A violation of the civil law was seen as a wrong against an individual. Civil law's goal was victim restitution as in ancient times.

Religion and Criminal Justice

Religion has affected laws and punishments since ancient times. Religion was especially influential during the Middle Ages. The church's form of trial was "the ordeal," some sort of dangerous or painful test to determine innocence, for example, being thrown into water. Those who sank (and often drowned) were believed to be innocent. The "guilty" would float and, thus, be dragged from the water and put to death. This seemingly lose-lose "ordeal by water" displayed the reliance of some religions on pagan philosophy and illustrated a millennium-old connection to Greek civilization. The reasoning behind the drowning of innocents was rooted in the Greeks' four pure elements: earth, air, fire and water. A pure (innocent) person was like the water and mixed with it (sank); a guilty one was like wood and floated. Another ordeal forced a person accused of heresy (an opinion at odds with established beliefs) to grasp a red-hot iron bar. If no festering occurred within three days, the person was declared innocent.

In addition, most monasteries and abbeys had sanctuaries where those who violated religious law were placed in solitary confinement for long periods. This approach to reforming individuals through isolation and prayer influenced later attempts at reforming criminal offenders and is the origin of the term *penitentiary*.

➤   Another important church contribution to corrections was the idea of **free will**—people choose to act as they do and are responsible for those actions. This concept is at the ethical core of our criminal law and is the heart of the classical approach to criminology (introduced in Chapter 1 and to be discussed in greater detail shortly). Free will is also central to the contemporary return to retribution.

> Religion played a role in law and punishment by placing violators in solitary confinement, thereby attempting to reform individuals through isolation and prayer. Religion also affected corrections by contributing the idea of free will—people choose to act as they do and are responsible for those actions.

➤   The **Inquisition,** begun in the thirteenth century, was one powerful means of holding people responsible for their actions. The Roman Catholic Church held tribunals (trials) to suppress heresy. Although acting in the name of the church, the Inquisition also functioned as an arm of the state. The Spanish Inquisition religious tribunal sentenced Joan of Arc in 1431 to be burned at the stake for alleged witchcraft. Religious nonconformists were confined in dungeons. Alleged heretics were viciously tortured to extract confessions. Thousands died during the Inquisition. This illustrates what can occur when religious intolerance becomes politically dominant. Modern manifestations of this include the Iranian Revolution and the moral crusade in the United States against drugs (a sort of culture war). Certain criminal actions, such as hate crimes against homosexuals, may have religious roots.

The Renaissance

The Middle Ages are generally thought to have ended with the discovery of America in 1492. The next two centuries in Europe are often referred to as the Renaissance and marked the transition from medieval to modern times. The Renaissance was characterized by an emphasis on art and the humanities as well as a more humanistic approach to criminal justice.

In sixteenth century England, Sir Thomas More refused to subscribe to the Act of Supremacy, which required accepting the king as the head of the church. More wrote scathing social satire, including *Utopia* (Ogden, 1949, p. 7):

Simple theft is not so great a crime that it ought to cost a man his life, and no punishment however severe is sufficient to restrain a man from robbery who can find no other livelihood. In this not only you in England but a great part of the world seem to imitate bad masters, who are readier to punish their pupils than to teach them. Severe and horrible punishments are enacted against theft, when it would be much better to enable every man to earn his livelihood, instead of being driven to the fatal necessity of stealing and then dying for it.

In More's Utopia, laws are few, simple and known to all (p. 61): "They think it highly unjust to bind men by laws that are too numerous to be read and too obscure to be readily understood. As for lawyers, a kind of men who handle matters craftily and interpret laws subtly, they have none at all. . . .There might as well be no laws at all as to have laws which only men of great ability and long training can interpret."

> Sir Thomas More wrote that punishment would not prevent crime and that it would be better to look at conditions that caused crime.

More was imprisoned and ultimately beheaded on a charge of treason. Although now four centuries old, his rather basic idea of focusing on conditions that lead to crime is still considered today. The answers, however, are not easy to come by.

Up until the middle of the sixteenth century, prisons were used primarily to incarcerate those awaiting some other form of punishment such as banishment or execution. The earliest people to be incarcerated for other reasons were the poor, the insane and those convicted of petty crimes. Poor laws enacted during this century required that paupers, vagrants and vagabonds be put to work on public or private projects or as galley ship rowers, perpetuating a Marxist philosophy of trying to exert social and economic control over the so-called dregs of society.

> The Bridewell Workhouse was established in 1557 in London to house and employ the "dregs" of the city.

➤ **Bridewell** was not intended as a prison, but rather as a way to take care of and train the poor and to instill in them the Judeo-Christian work ethic that hard manual labor benefits a person's soul as well as society. In effect, the workhouse's purpose was rehabilitative. Although intended as a humanitarian institution, it was actually private profiteering. Over time, the workhouse and prisons became indistinguishable.

The Bridewell was so popular that in 1576 Parliament required every county in England to construct a Bridewell-style house. Most bridewells did not separate men and women, young and old, sick and healthy. Prisoners had to pay for their food, have family or friends bring them food or starve. Sanitary conditions were deplorable, and typhus (called "jail fever") flourished in these wretched conditions, often spreading to surrounding cities.

Nonetheless, bridewells became highly profitable enterprises. These sixteenth century "houses of correction" were in essence slave labor camps to exploit prisoners and produce saleable goods inexpensively. They were also part of the social control of the poor. When a surplus of labor existed, the punishment for crimes was often execution.

> Penology in the sixteenth and seventeenth centuries stressed punishment for the purposes of deterrence and retribution.

During the sixteenth century, efforts were made to control the increasingly costly burden of caring for poor people. In fact, much of the criminal law was directed against idleness. For example, the Elizabethan Vagabonds Act of 1597 listed several classes of undesirables including idle people, rogues, sturdy beggars and vagabonds. Such people could avoid spending time in a debtors' prison or receiving corporal punishment by enlisting in the military.

Also during the sixteenth century, naval vessels used galley slaves as rowers. Prisoners sentenced to death might be reprieved from execution and sent to the galleys instead. As many as 200 rowers, chained four to a bench, were needed for a single naval vessel.

John Howard visiting a debtors' prison in England. Many inmates were imprisoned for the "crime" of poverty, putting them in debt to greedy landlords.

From 1600 to 1776 England also sent over half of its unwanted social, political and religious misfits and criminals to America or Australia as indentured servants. This form of punishment was called *penal banishment*. Much like the bridewells, the conditions aboard the ships transporting the prisoners were deplorable.

Up to the eighteenth century, public corporal punishment of some form was the most common method of "correction." Imprisonment as a form of punishment did not begin until the eighteenth century in Europe and the nineteenth century in the United States, but the origin of locking people up as punishment can be found in the Middle Ages in the form of workhouses and
➤ jails, called **gaols** in Europe.

The Reform Movement (Seventeenth to Nineteenth Century)

By the eighteenth century, conditions in workhouses, gaols and houses of correction throughout Europe had deteriorated to the extent that they could be described as human cesspools. Caldwell (1965, p. 494) described a typical English gaol like this:

> Devoid of privacy and restrictions, its contaminated air heavy with the stench of unwashed bodies, human excrement, and the discharge of loathsome sores, the gaol bred the basest thoughts and the foulest deeds. The inmates made their own rules, and the weak and the innocent were exposed to the tyranny of the strong and the vicious.

In addition, the jailers often added to the misery of the prisoners. Wilson (1934, p. 186) notes that the jailers were often "low bred, mercenary and oppressive, barbarous fellows, who think of nothing but enriching themselves by the most cruel extortion, and have less regard for the life of a poor prisoner than for the life of a brute." But, because places of confinement were physically located away from the general population, the public was unaware of the deplorable conditions. "Out of sight, out of mind" describes this period of corrections.

Also, as noted by Vass (1990, p. 5): "The condition of impressment[1] as a regular statutory penal sanction for the enlistment of people sentenced to death, transportation, or imprisonment was particularly relevant in the eighteenth century following the gradual curtailment and eventual abolition of transportation to the colonies and plantations." The urgent need for recruits to expand the military and contribute to the war effort made this an attractive option. In addition, such enlistments into the military could reduce somewhat the severe overcrowding in the jails.

---

[1]The practice of placing individuals into public service, such as serving in the military.

Another problem existed in the laws themselves and how they were administered. The variety of laws which had accumulated throughout the previous centuries were often duplicative and contradictory. Class-based political conditions allowed criminal justice officials to abuse their authority through corruption and brutality, with court-imposed sentences based on the power, wealth and status of the convicted. The complete lack of accountability of criminal justice officials resulted in frequent abuses of justice, where torture was commonly used to gain confessions, secret trials ended with harsh prison sentences, and severe physical punishment was allowed for relatively minor offenses. Conditions were ripe for reformers to come forth demanding change.

Enlightenment and Social Reforms

Historians have labeled the eighteenth century as the beginning of the Age of Enlightenment. During the eighteenth and nineteenth centuries French, English and Italian philosophers and reformers openly criticized the deplorable conditions in places of confinement as well as use of corporal punishment. Among the reformers was a French historian and philosopher, Charles-Louis de Secondat, Baron de La Brède et de Montesquieu (1689–1755), a founder of political science.

➤   Montesquieu's philosophy centered around the **social contract** whereby free, independent individuals agree to form a community and to give up a portion of their individual freedom to benefit the security of the group. He also criticized inhumane punishment and argued that the punishment should fit the crime. He believed that harsh punishment undermined morality and that a better way to prevent crime was to appeal to an individual's sense of decency and what was morally and socially right.

Another French philosopher, François-Marie Arouet Voltaire (1694–1778), was the leading figure of eighteenth century Enlightenment. Two imprisonments in the Bastille (1717 and 1726) and a visit to England (1726–1729) fostered a hatred of arbitrary absolutism and admiration for English liberalism. Voltaire was also horrified at the injustices of the French penal system. Believing that fear of shame could deter crime, Voltaire fought against torture. Voltaire's work was immense, and not all serious, as shown by his observation: "In general, the art of government consists in taking as much money as possible from one class of citizens to give it to the other."

The writings of Montesquieu and Voltaire greatly influenced the key penology reformers of the Enlightenment.

Among the key penology figures of the Enlightenment were philosophers Beccaria and Lombroso and reformers Howard and Bentham.

Beccaria

An Italian economist, Milanese aristocrat, jurist and criminologist, the marchese di Cesare Bonesana Beccaria (1738–1794) was the most influential writer of the period. Influenced by Montesquieu and Voltaire, he brought about local economic reforms and stimulated penal reform throughout Europe. At the core of Beccaria's philosophy was the social contract set forth earlier by Montesquieu, part of which stated that people must obey society's laws, and offenders must be punished (Beccaria, 1963 [1764]).

> Beccaria was the founder of the classical school of criminology stressing the social contract, the prevention of crime and the need to make any punishment fit the crime committed.

A basic assumption of Beccaria was that people are rational and responsible for their acts. He also contended that laws should be structured to permit the greatest amount of happiness to the largest number of people. In 1764 he wrote his best known work, an essay entitled *On Crimes and Punishments*, outlining his philosophy. This short treatise became a classic in criminological literature. Nonetheless, many opposed his philosophy, including the Vatican. Among the principles he advocated are the following (Barnes and Teeters, 1959, p. 322):

- All social action should be based on the utilitarian concept of the greatest good for the greatest number.
- Crime is an injury to society, the only rational measure of which is the extent of the injury.
- Preventing crime is more important than punishing those who commit crime. To do so the public must be educated about what the laws are, their support for the law enlisted, and virtue rewarded.
- Secret accusations and torture should be abolished. Those accused of crimes should have speedy trials and be treated humanely before, during, and after the trial.
- The purpose of punishment should be to deter crime, not to obtain revenge for an offended society. It is not the severity of the punishment, but the certainty and swiftness that will result in deterring crime. Penalties must fit the crime, with crimes against property being punished by fines or imprisonment for those who cannot pay the fine. Capital punishment should be abolished as life imprisonment is a more effective deterrent.
- Imprisonment should be more widely used but improved by having better physical facilities and separating prisoners by age, sex, and degree of criminality.

Beccaria also stressed that the law serves the needs of society rather than enforcing moral virtues. Therefore, law should be limited to the most serious offenses. Beccaria had an immense impact on French criminal law. The four individual rights advocated by Beccaria for those accused of crimes were included in the French Code of Criminal Procedure in 1808 and the French Penal Code of 1810:

- Individuals should be regarded as innocent until proven guilty.
- Individuals should have the right to employ legal counsel and to cross-examine the state's witnesses.
- Individuals should not have to testify against themselves.
- Individuals should have the right to a prompt, public trial, usually by a jury.

These rights should sound familiar because they influenced the framers of the U.S. Constitution. In addition, many of our current criminal laws reflect Beccaria's philosophy, which was a strong influence on the transition from punishment to rehabilitation.

Lombroso

Toward the end of the eighteenth century, opposition to the classical view increased and continued into the next century. Among the leading opponents was Cesare Lombroso (1835–1909).

Lombroso, considered the father of the positivist school of criminology, maintained that criminals were born with a predisposition to crime and needed exceptionally favorable conditions in life to avoid criminal behavior.

Lombroso was serving as a physician in mental institutions when he developed an interest in studying criminals. During a visit to an Italian prison, Lombroso had the opportunity to meet one of the most notorious highway robbers of the time. When the imprisoned robber died, Lombroso received permission to conduct an autopsy on the body. His examination of the robber's brain was quite surprising: the region of the brain normally well developed in "higher" animals, such as primates and humans, was rather undeveloped, whereas another region typically well developed in lower mammals and birds was unusually overdeveloped in the robber (Shoham and Hoffmann, 1991, p. 20). This discovery led Lombroso to postulate that criminality resulted from a biological reversion to an earlier evolutionary stage, that criminals were developmental throwbacks to more primitive creatures (Lombroso, 1968).

Although Lombroso's study was widely criticized, he had started people thinking about other causes for criminal behavior than free will. Building on Lombroso's idea that environmental factors influenced criminal behavior, ➤ some scholars developed the positivist view based on the concept of **determinism.** Determinism views human behavior as the result of various environmental and cultural influences; crime is viewed as a consequence of many factors such as population density, economic status and legal definitions of crime. This positivist multiple-factor causation theory directly conflicts with the free-will concept.

Howard

An important penal reformer, John Howard (1726–1790), was appointed sheriff of Bedfordshire in 1773. In this position he became painfully aware of the ➤ inhuman conditions in the **hulks** (unseaworthy ships) and gaols being used to house prisoners. The hulks were originally meant as a temporary solution to the inability to transport prisoners to America because of the revolution. Howard undertook a study of these "human cesspools" and also traveled to other countries to study their prisons.

Howard looked at institutions in other countries and was especially impressed by the Hospice (hospital) of San Michele in Rome. Built in 1704 by Pope Clement XI, the Hospice of San Michele was one of the first institutions designed exclusively for youthful offenders. Incorrigible youth under age 20 ate and worked in silence in a large central hall, but slept in separate cells. The emphasis was on reading the Bible and hard work. An inscription placed over the door by the Pope is still there: "It is insufficient to restrain the wicked by punishment unless you render them virtuous by corrective discipline." This sentiment is strikingly similar to a favorite motto of Howard: "It is doing little to restrain the bad by punishment unless you render them good by discipline."

Howard devoted his life and his money to prison reform. Greatly concerned with penal discipline, he advocated rigorous religious teaching, highly routine daily schedules and productive hard labor. He also advocated sanitary prison conditions, separating women from men and young offenders from older offenders, paying jailers a salary rather than relying on payments from prisoners for food and using isolation for reflection and penance. His work influenced Parliament to abolish many abuses and to pass the Penitentiary Act in 1779.

> Howard is often thought of as the father of prison reform. To this day the John Howard Society continues to carry forth his ideas.

Bentham

Another influential reformer of English criminal law was philosopher and lawyer, Jeremy Bentham (1748–1832). Bentham read Howard and was influenced by him. Bentham was a firm believer in "the greatest good for the greatest number"—a practical, utilitarian approach to crime inspired by Beccaria and referred to by Bentham as "the greatest happiness principle." Punishment was society's means of balancing individuals' uncurbed pursuit of happiness with the needs of an orderly society.

Like Beccaria, Bentham believed punishment could deter crime, but only if it negated whatever positive results the criminal obtained from the crime. According to Bentham, two fundamental drives control individual actions: "Nature has placed man under the governance of two sovereign masters, pain and pleasure. It is for them alone to point out what we ought to do, as well as to determine what we shall do" (1948 [1789], p. 125). Bentham's *An Introduction to the Principles of Morals and Jurisprudence* (privately printed in 1780; published in 1789) set forth a plan to make punishments much more severe than any gains criminals might receive from their deeds.

> Bentham wrote that if punishments were known to be swift, severe and certain, and if the pain exceeded the gain, criminals would be deterred.

He also advocated a system of graduated penalties to make the punishment more closely fit the crime.

Bentham is also credited with designing the panopticon (from two Greek words meaning "everything" and "place of sight") as a national penitentiary to house felons who were temporarily incarcerated in horrid conditions in hulks in rivers and harbors. Parliament passed a bill in 1779 to build a national penitentiary, but never funded the project. Bentham and King George III argued over the panopticon for 23 years.

Using his own money, Bentham designed a huge prison with a glass roof and central control area allowing supervision of each cell. The underlying idea was that staff would be an omnipresent surveillant of the inmate's behavior, that is, the inmates would be continuously watched, 24 hours a day. The cells were arranged like spokes on a wheel. This radiating spoke design for prisons was used in many of the massive institutions built in the nineteenth century. The design was used for the prison in Statesville, Illinois, in 1919. This prison was considered a model here and abroad for many years.

According to Vass (p. 7):

By the middle of the nineteenth century the prison was firmly established as the bastion of the criminal justice system by changing its characters from a mere depot for recruits, people awaiting trial or sentence and transportation, to an

(Left) A view inside the panopticon-styled cellhouse at the Statesville (Illinois) Prison. *(Right)* The panopticon design was also used at this state prison in Philadelphia (now vacant).

authoritative and organized penal institution for the containment and discipline of criminals; and which symbolized a new epoch of the philosophy of authority and the exercise of class power in general. . . . [T]he prison was presented as a unique opportunity to reform, contain and deter its inmate populations as well as acting as a form of general deterrence to outsiders.

This emphasis on prisons as a means to control crime would have a profound influence on the development of corrections in the United States. Another influence was the development of the mark system and the indeterminate sentence in Australia.

The Mark System and Indeterminate Sentence

An estimated 130,000 to 160,000 undesirables and criminals were banished from England to Australia from 1787 to 1857. Many died during the 10-month voyage. Once in Australia they were assigned to a settlement managed by military and naval officers.

Those who committed further crimes were labeled "doubly convicted" and sent to one of four penal settlements, the most infamous being that on Norfolk Island some 930 miles off the continent of Australia. According to Barry (1957, p. 5): "Conditions were so bad at Norfolk that men reprieved from the death penalty wept, and those who were to die thanked God." It was to this hellhole that an Englishman, Captain Alexander Maconochie, was assigned, with the task of supervising the Norfolk Island prison colony. In 1840 this prison colony housed some 2,000 of England's doubly convicted criminals.

One of the first actions taken by Maconochie was to eliminate the flat sentence and replace it with a **mark system.** In this system prisoners could earn points (marks) for good behavior, thereby shortening their sentence, or lose marks for bad behavior, lengthening their sentence. This is the forerunner of modern "good time."

> Maconochie's system rewarded positive behavior and punished negative behavior using marks the prisoners could earn or lose. This created, in essence, an **indeterminate sentence.**

The mark system had five key elements:

- Sentences were for a specified quantity of labor, not a specific time period.
- The quantity of labor was stated as a specific number of marks to be earned by improving conduct, living frugally and working diligently. For example, 800 marks was the quantity specified to free an offender from a life sentence.
- Prisoners had to earn all they received, paid for with their marks.
- Prisoners who were well disciplined could work in groups of six or seven, with the group responsible for the actions of each member.
- As prisoners neared obtaining the needed number of marks for release, they still earned their daily tally of marks, but had less rigorous discipline to prepare themselves for their return to society.

Maconochie's administration at Norfolk was based on two underlying principles: (1) cruel and brutal treatment demeans not only the persons subjected to them, but also undermines the society that deliberately uses or allows them for social control and (2) treatment of offenders while imprisoned should be intended to make them fit for release into society. Maconochie's philosophy and innovative ideas would later influence reformers in Europe as well as in the United States.

One person so influenced was an Irishman, Sir Walter Crofton, who used Maconochie's success with the indeterminate sentence to develop the Irish system. This system consisted of several stages beginning with solitary confinement and monotonous work. The next stage was laboring on public works, with each level within this stage shortening the length of time to be served. The final stage was confinement in an intermediate prison where the prisoners worked without supervision and were free to move about in the community. Those prisoners who obeyed all the laws and social customs of the community and who were able to find a job were given a "ticket of leave," what is referred to as parole in modern corrections.

> Good behavior could result in a ticket of leave, the forerunner of our parole system.

The ticket of leave could be revoked at any time during the period of the original fixed sentence for any infractions of the rules established.

Summary

Preliterate societies stressed the importance of the victim and the need for personal revenge or retaliation. Eventually, tribal leaders and rulers took over the task of punishing those who broke the law. The emphasis on revenge or retaliation was incorporated into the *Code of Hammurabi*, whose underlying principle was that of *lex talions*, an eye for an eye. This same emphasis could be seen in ancient Greece and Rome. The Greeks' public participation in meting out justice is the forerunner of our jury system. The provisions of the Justinian Code were the law throughout most of Europe until modern times, and they greatly influenced our law as well.

Religion, especially influential during the Middle Ages, played a role in law and punishment by placing violators in solitary confinement, thereby attempting to reform individuals through isolation and prayer. Religion also affected corrections by contributing the idea of free will—people choose to act as they do and are responsible for those actions.

Centuries later, in England, Sir Thomas More wrote that punishment would not prevent crime and that it would be better to look at conditions that caused crime. Among the conditions thought to cause crime were idleness and poverty. In response to this, the Bridewell Workhouse was established in 1557 in London to house and employ the dregs of the city, a rehabilitative purpose. For the most part, however, sixteenth and seventeenth century penology stressed punishment for the purposes of deterrence and retribution.

Two French philosophers who wrote extensively about crime and punishment and greatly influenced the key reformers of the Enlightenment were Montesquieu and Voltaire. Among the key penology figures of the Enlightenment were philosophers Beccaria and Lombroso and reformers Howard and Bentham. Beccaria was the founder of the classical school of criminology stressing the social contract, the prevention of crime and the need to make any punishment fit the crime committed. Lombroso, considered the father of the positivist school of criminology, maintained that criminals were born with a predisposition to crime and needed exceptionally favorable conditions in life to avoid criminal behavior. Howard is often thought of as the father of prison reform. To this day the John Howard Society continues to carry forth his ideas. Bentham wrote that if punishments were known to be swift, severe and certain, and if the pain exceeded the gain, criminals would be deterred.

Reform also occurred in the way sentences were carried out and the length of time prisoners spent behind bars. Maconochie's system rewarded positive behavior and punished negative behavior using marks the prisoners could earn or lose. This created, in essence, an indeterminate sentence. Good behavior could result in a ticket of leave, the forerunner of our parole system.

Discussion Questions

1. Some cultures (for example, Eskimos) continue to use banishment as punishment for crimes. Is this likely to be effective in modern times? Discuss the problems with this sanction.

2. Do you support *lex talions?* In what circumstances?

3. Do you believe our jury system today is as effective as it should be?

4. What is your view on corporal punishment? While other countries embrace the practice (for example, Singapore), why does the United States still denounce such punishment? Do you think public opinion is shifting regarding the use of corporal punishment?

5. What are some modern day examples of the thirteenth century Inquisition?

6. Four centuries have passed since More's *Utopia* satirized legal practices. Can you think of examples today where the crime and corresponding punishment are greatly mismatched? Consider violent offenses committed by juveniles.

7. Which do you feel has the greatest credibility—the classical or positivist view of criminality? Why?

8. Discuss your thinking toward Howard's favorite motto: "It is doing little to restrain the bad by punishment unless you render them good by discipline."

9. Do you believe today's criminal justice system is effective in producing "swift, severe and certain" punishment?

10. Can you identify current instances in which a type of mark system is used?

References

Barnes, Harry E. and Teeters, Negley K. *New Horizons in Criminology,* 3rd ed. Englewood Cliffs, NJ: Prentice Hall, 1959.

Barry, John V. "Captain Alexander Maconochie." *Victorian Historical Magazine,* 27, June 1957, p. 5.

Beccaria, Cesare. *On Crimes and Punishments* (1764). New York: Bobbs-Merrill, 1963.

Bentham, Jeremy. *An Introduction to the Principles of Morals and Jurisprudence* (1789). Oxford: Blackwell, 1948.

Bowra, C.M. *Classical Greece*. New York: Time Incorporated, 1965.

Caldwell, Robert G. *Criminology*. New York: Roland Press, 1965.

Fremantle, Anne. *Age of Faith*. New York: Time Incorporated, 1965.

Hadas, Moses. *Imperial Rome*. New York: Time Incorporated, 1965.

Lombroso, Cesare. *Crime: Its Causes and Remedies*. Montclair, NJ: Patterson Smith, 1968.

Ogden, H.V.S., ed. Thomas More's *Utopia*. New York: Appleton-Century-Crofts, 1949.

Shoham, A. Giora and Hoffmann, John P. *A Primer in the Sociology of Crime*. New York: Harrow and Hesston Publishers, 1991.

Vass, Antony A. *Alternative to Prison: Punishment, Custody and the Community*. Newbury Park, CA: Sage Publications, 1990.

Wilson, Margaret. *The Crime of Punishment*. London: Jonathan Cape, 1934.

3

The Evolution of Corrections in the United States

Do You Know

➤ Where our modern correctional system originated?

➤ What significance the Walnut Street Jail has for corrections?

➤ How the Auburn and the Pennsylvania systems for prisons differed? Which system eventually prevailed?

➤ Who is known as the father of probation?

➤ What event marked the beginning of the National Prison Association?

➤ What the Three Prisons Act did?

➤ What characterized the Progressive Era?

➤ When the Federal Bureau of Prisons was established and what function it was to serve?

➤ What "environments" have influenced corrections?

Crime is a dangerous and cancerous condition which, if not curbed and beaten down, will soon eat at the very vitals of the country.
                                                                    —*J. Edgar Hoover*

Can You Define

Auburn system   congregate system   Pennsylvania system

Introduction

Because so many colonists were from England, our system of criminal justice has its roots in the English system. Yet many colonists greatly resented the harsh European criminal codes, especially those who had been banished to America as criminals. They supported changing the system of punishing criminals. The conflicting views on crime and criminals existing in Europe were also evident in the American colonies as our criminal justice system evolved from its European roots.

This chapter covers the evolution of corrections in the United States. Figure 3–1 provides a time line, which overlaps the end of the time line provided in Figure 2–1, to identify the significant events and individuals that shaped our nation's correctional system.

The Colonial Period

The most common penalty in the early colonial days was whipping and a stiff fine. Initially, public humiliation was also common using stocks, pillories, ducking stools, branks, flogging and branding. Those sentenced to the stocks were made to sit on a wooden bench with their hands and feet thrust through

Elder Anderson in the pillory, as a sign on his chest tells for what crime he is being punished.

ELDER ANDERSON IN THE PILLORY.

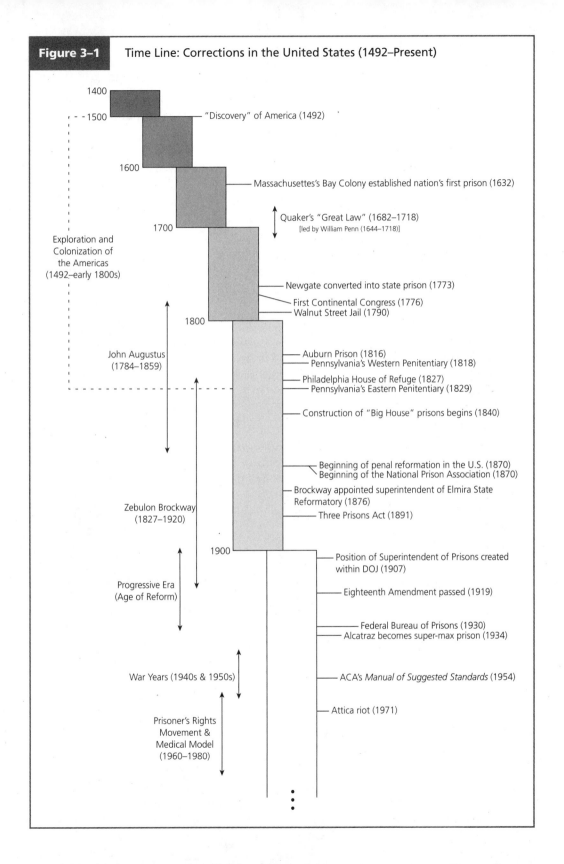

Figure 3–1 Time Line: Corrections in the United States (1492–Present)

1400

1500

"Discovery" of America (1492)

1600

Massachusettes's Bay Colony established nation's first prison (1632)

Quaker's "Great Law" (1682–1718)
[led by William Penn (1644–1718)]

1700

Exploration and Colonization of the Americas (1492–early 1800s)

Newgate converted into state prison (1773)
First Continental Congress (1776)
Walnut Street Jail (1790)

1800

John Augustus (1784–1859)

Auburn Prison (1816)
Pennsylvania's Western Penitentiary (1818)
Philadelphia House of Refuge (1827)
Pennsylvania's Eastern Penitentiary (1829)

Construction of "Big House" prisons begins (1840)

Beginning of penal reformation in the U.S. (1870)
Beginning of the National Prison Association (1870)
Brockway appointed superintendent of Elmira State Reformatory (1876)
Three Prisons Act (1891)

Zebulon Brockway (1827–1920)

1900

Position of Superintendent of Prisons created within DOJ (1907)

Progressive Era (Age of Reform)

Eighteenth Amendment passed (1919)

Federal Bureau of Prisons (1930)
Alcatraz becomes super-max prison (1934)

War Years (1940s & 1950s)

ACA's *Manual of Suggested Standards* (1954)

Attica riot (1971)

Prisoner's Rights Movement & Medical Model (1960–1980)

holes in a securely locked wooden frame. Those sentenced to the pillory were made to *stand* with their heads and hands through a wooden frame. The townspeople would pass by those confined in the stock or pillory and spit on them, taunt them and throw garbage and rocks at them.

If a ducking stool was the punishment ordered, the person was tied to a chair or platform at the end of a long lever which was then lowered into a river or lake. If a person was found guilty of lying, the punishment was often the brank. The brank was a cage containing a plate of iron with sharp spikes placed over a liar's head so that the spikes went into the person's mouth. Any movement of the tongue resulted in being stabbed. Such public corporal punishment was very effective because in these small communities everyone knew everyone else, and the physical pain and psychological humiliation the offenders underwent were seen by all the citizens as well. Deterrence was a clear goal of such punishment.

In 1632 the Massachusetts Bay Colony established the nation's first jail, a small wooden building in Boston. Later other local jails were built throughout the country. Jails became more and more necessary as the population migrated to urban areas and the church, family and community began to lose some of their social control.

More humane treatment of offenders was advocated by William Penn (1644–1718), founder of Pennsylvania and leader of the Quakers. The Quakers were a religious group who emphasized silence in their practices and had derived their name through the admonition to quake at the word of the Lord. The Quakers' "Great Law," in effect from 1682 to 1718, eliminated capital punishment and established a house of corrections where offenders performed hard labor. Each county was to build such a house of corrections, similar to our jails of today.

> Many historians note that our modern correctional system originated in Pennsylvania under the leadership of Penn and the Quakers' Great Law.

This code was in effect until Penn died in 1718 when it was repealed and replaced with the English Anglican code which advocated harsh punishment, including corporal and capital punishment.

The Rise of Prisons

During the late 1700s and early 1800s states began constructing prisons. In 1773 Connecticut converted an abandoned shaft in a copper mine in Simsbury into a state jail. For some 50 years this mine provided both housing and work for the inmates. Although the conditions in the jail were miserable, it was considered an improvement over corporal or capital punishment. The first institutional rebellions occurred in this mineshaft prison. It eventually was closed as a jail, however, because the mineshaft could not be made habitable and the public did not support the project.

In 1776 the Continental Congress decreed that state and county jails could be used to confine prisoners charged with federal crimes. As noted by Keve (1991, p. 5): "At that point, the only facility of any size, other than Simsbury, was the new Walnut Street Jail in Philadelphia. . . . Soon after the Walnut Street Jail opened, it was commandeered by the Continental Congress for federal use, an action that would seem to qualify this institution as the first federal prison in the United States."

In September 1787, the Constitutional Convention in Philadelphia completed its work and presented its proposed Constitution to the states. A year later the necessary nine states had ratified it. As noted in Chapter 1, the Constitution established the three branches of government: legislative, executive and judicial.

One of the first actions taken by the first Congress was authorizing a federal court system. The Judiciary Act of 1789 established the Supreme Court and also divided the country into districts, each with a district court. At the time, only 13 states had been admitted to the Union, yet the act provided for each new state admitted to become part of a district and to be served by a district court. The act also created the positions of U.S. attorney and U.S. marshal for each district. No provision was made for federal prisons. Instead, U.S. marshals were to scout for prison cells available for the most reasonable fee. So for more than the first hundred years, federal corrections depended on the states.

As the nation developed following the revolution, Pennsylvania again turned to Penn's code, this time under the leadership of Dr. Benjamin Rush (1745–1813). Rush formed the Philadelphia Society for Alleviating the Miseries of Public Prisons, a reform group seeking to make prisons more orderly and humane. In 1790, under pressure from the Quakers, the Pennsylvania legislature called for renovating the prison system. The result was construction of a separate wing of Philadelphia's Walnut Street Jail to confine convicted felons, making it a prison. A law passed in 1794 directed that everyone convicted of a crime (except murder) would be sent to the Walnut Street Jail, thus establishing the first prison.

> The Walnut Street Jail is considered the United States' first state prison.

Keve (p. 10) notes: "The Walnut Street jail, when expanded after the Revolution, was the first of the penitentiary type of prisons—implementing the new effort to use fewer harsh corporal penalties and resort instead to solitary confinement with labor." Prisoners were locked in separate cells, isolated from one another for their entire sentence. Each cell contained a Bible, which prisoners were expected to read in the hope that they would become penitent—the origin of the term *penitentiary*, as noted previously. As the wing, called the *penitentiary house*, became more crowded, inmates were placed two in a cell. Another change was to give the inmates piecework to occupy their time. The Walnut Street Jail was modeled after the European prisons of Ghent and Gloucester and would later serve as a model for the Pennsylvania system of prisons.

By 1797 the jail was using a four-level classification of prisoners based on how socially dangerous the inmate was perceived to be. The most dangerous were placed into solitary confinement for their entire sentence. Between 1797 and 1817, 10 other prisons were built, as summarized in Table 3–1.

In 1827 Pennsylvania again provided leadership in establishing the Philadelphia House of Refuge, an institution designed to separate juvenile delinquents and poor children from adult criminals.

In the early decades of the nineteenth century, partly as a result of the social upheaval caused by the Industrial Revolution, prisons, mental hospitals (asylums) and almshouses (for debtors) proliferated. A major factor behind the increase in such institutions was the perceived threat to aristocratic class values posed by the lower and working classes, in particular immigrant groups. As with the poor laws enacted in sixteenth century England, these activities in the United States were seen by some critics as a reflection of the Marxist perspective of punishment and class conflict and an attempt to preserve the power of the upper class. In addition, public punishments were becoming less popular. The crowds witnessing such punishments often became unruly and sometimes even sided with the prisoner. When a prisoner was to be hanged, the procession to the gallows often turned into a mob, resulting in moving the executions to just outside the prison gates and eventually inside to be conducted privately.

Table 3–1	American Prisons Built between 1790 and 1817	
Pennsylvania	Walnut Street Jail, Philadelphia	1790
New York	Newgate Prison, New York City	1797
New Jersey	State Penitentiary, Lamberton	1798
Kentucky	State Penitentiary, Frankfort	1800
Virginia	State Penitentiary, Richmond	1800
Massachusetts	State Prison, Charlestown	1805
Vermont	State Prison, Windsor	1809
Maryland	State Penitentiary, Baltimore	1812
New Hampshire	State Prison, Concord	1812
Ohio	State Penitentiary, Columbus	1816
Georgia	State Penitentiary, Milledgeville	1817

Early in the century, New York and Pennsylvania were having difficulty dealing with their burgeoning prison populations. Each developed a system to deal with the problem.

The Auburn System

New York built a new prison at Auburn in 1816. This prison well represented American pragmatism and efficiency and became the model for maximum security prisons throughout the country. The design was based on that of the Walnut Street Jail. In this prison the cells were built vertically on five floors of the structure, so it is sometimes referred to as the *tier system*. (See Figure 3–2.)

Individuals were confined in poorly lit, unsanitary cells for sleeping, but not for eating or working. Rigid regimentation prevailed. Criminals were perceived as defective in morals and mind.

> ➤   The **Auburn system** emphasized crime prevention through strict silence and fear of brutal punishment. Because the prisoners worked and ate as a group, the system is
> ➤   sometimes referred to as the **congregate system**.

It was at Auburn that the lockstep prison shuffle was developed. Prisoners lined up in close formation with their hands under the arms or on the shoulders of the prisoner in front. The entire line shuffled forward rapidly in unison, the prisoners' feet never leaving the ground, faces turned toward the watching guards, eyes to the ground. Strict silence was enforced. It was also at Auburn that the practice of having prisoners eat seated at long tables face-to-back was instituted, greatly reducing the opportunity for any form of communication between prisoners.

The warden at Auburn was a strict disciplinarian who believed in brutal punishments and degrading practices to break the convicts' spirits so they could then be reformed. This included wearing degrading, bizarre prison uniforms whose color indicated whether the prisoner was a first-time offender or a repeater and being known by a number rather than a name. Prisoners could receive no visitors or mail, and the only reading allowed was the Bible.

Discipline was so severe and obedience so complete that when Auburn became full and the warden selected 100 inmates to build a new prison at Sing Sing in 1825, over the three years only two prisoners tried to escape even though quartered in an open field with minimal supervision.

The classification system used at Auburn divided inmates into three groups based on age and prior crimes. The older, hardened criminals were placed in solitary confinement for the entire sentence. Those younger and less hardened were initially placed in solitary confinement until they showed repentance, at which time they were freed to join the other inmates to eat and work. The very young and those convicted of petty crimes were placed into the system immediately.

Figure 3–2 The Auburn System

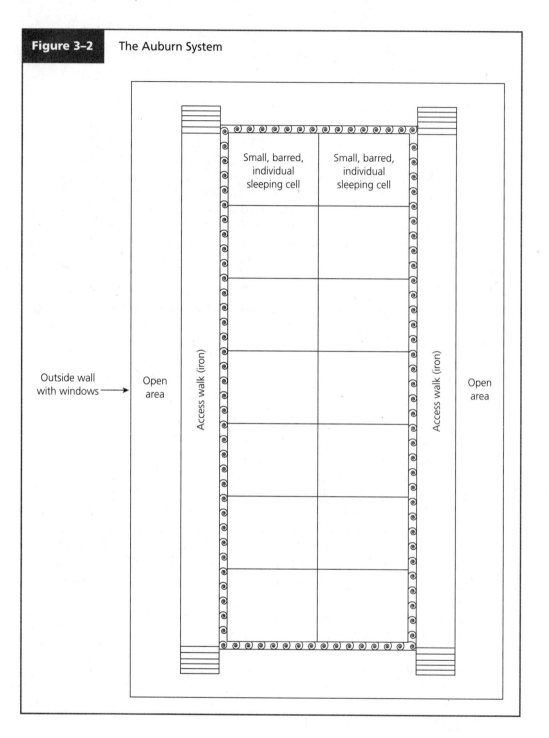

Outside wall with windows →

Open area

Access walk (iron)

Small, barred, individual sleeping cell

Small, barred, individual sleeping cell

Access walk (iron)

Open area

The dining room at the St. Cloud State Prison, circa 1900. Inmates at
this Auburn-style prison were made to eat silently, no one face-to-face.
Source: Time-Life Books. *This Fabulous Century, Prelude: 1870–1900,* p. 53.

The Pennsylvania System

In 1818, Pennsylvania built a new state prison in Pittsburgh. Called the Western
Penitentiary, this prison was modeled after the cellular isolation wing of the Walnut Street Jail. Each inmate was confined in a single cell with a solitary exercise
yard. Prisoners were never to encounter one another. The prison was built in the
traditional outside-cell design. (See Figure 3–3.)

It provided only solitary confinement, no labor. In 1829 a second such
prison was built on Cherry Hill in Philadelphia, called the Eastern Penitentiary. This massive structure, built by architect John Haviland, was the largest
structure in America at the time and resembled a medieval castle. It was
world famous, with foreign travelers often requesting its inclusion on their
itineraries. This penitentiary well represented the coherence between architecture and penal ideas. In addition, every cell contained a Bible with the ex-
pectation that the prisoner would turn to it and become penitent.

> The **Pennsylvania system** is sometimes referred to as the *separate system* because
> the prisoners were so totally isolated. The Pennsylvania system's philosophy empha-
> sized religion and penitence, hence the name *penitentiary.*

The Debate

Fierce debates occurred between advocates of the Pennsylvania system and the
Auburn system, forerunners of prison reform in the United States. Both systems
stressed the importance of isolating criminals from society and subjecting them

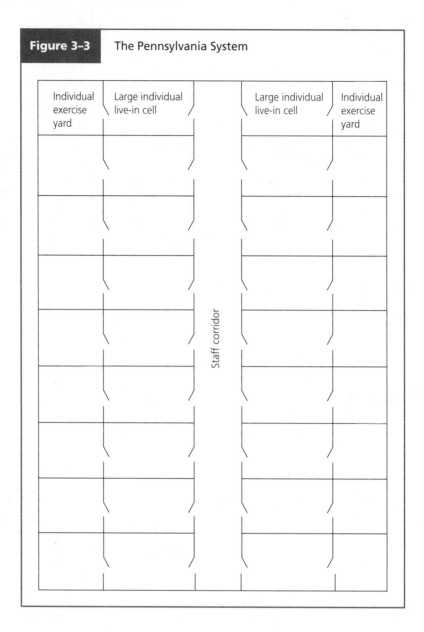

Figure 3–3   The Pennsylvania System

| Individual exercise yard | Large individual live-in cell | | Large individual live-in cell | Individual exercise yard |

to a strict routine of discipline and physical labor. But they differed radically in how this was to be accomplished, as reflected in their physical design.

In the Auburn or congregate system, prisoners worked together using the factory model of mass production. In contrast, the Pennsylvania or separate system used individual, craft-based labor performed in their cells.

Proponents of the Auburn system argued that the system was more flexible, that it was more efficient since convicts could share machinery as they worked and that it was more humane. Many suggested that the total isolation of the Pennsylvania system led to insanity. In addition, the Auburn system could house more inmates in less physical space since separate exercise yards and larger cells to accommodate working were not needed.

Proponents of the Pennsylvania system, on the other hand, contended that total isolation was more likely to cause repentance. Further, the Auburn system required more guards and more rules. Because these rules were likely to be broken, harsh discipline was the frequent consequence. The Auburn and Pennsylvania systems are compared and contrasted in Table 3–2.

The debate between advocates of the Auburn system and the Pennsylvania system was long and bitter. In the end, according to most scholars, it was the pragmatic cost advantage of Auburn that led to the wide emulation of this design. Furthermore, Auburn was efficient, helping it become the model for other U.S. prisons. The Pennsylvania system represented a religious idea and ideals that were whole-heartedly attempted, yet were unsuccessful.

As other states built their prisons, most followed the Auburn system.

Table 3–2	Auburn and Pennsylvania Systems Compared	
Component/Characteristic	**Auburn System**	**Pennsylvania System**
Also referred to as . . .	Congregate system	Separate system
Cell design and purpose	Smaller, single occupancy, for sleeping only	Larger, single occupancy, for sleeping, eating and working
Contact with other prisoners	Eating, working	None
Correctional emphasis	Rigid regimentation, strict silence, fear of brutal punishment	Religion and penitence
Advantages/arguments of proponents	More flexible, more efficient by allowing prisoners to share machinery, more humane, could house more inmates in less physical space, more cost-effective	Total isolation more likely to cause repentance
Disadvantages/arguments of opponents	Required more guards and more rules	Total isolation led to insanity

From 1825 to 1869 over 30 state prisons adopted the Auburn system. Among the best known were Sing Sing, built in New York in 1825, and San Quentin, built in California in 1852.

John Augustus and Probation

One reformer especially important to corrections was John Augustus (1784–1859). Augustus was a prosperous Boston shoemaker with several employees in his shop. One August morning in 1841 he was in court when a wretched looking man was brought into court and charged with being a drunkard. Knowing the man would most likely be sentenced to prison, Augustus felt a better alternative existed. Augustus spoke briefly with the man and then provided the man's bail on the provision he sign a pledge to never drink spirits again and to return to court at a set time as a reformed man.

For the next 18 years, Augustus attended court and provided bail for drunkards and prostitutes. Initially he and his wife took them into their home. Later they established a House of Refuge. Augustus's actions are viewed as the origin of probation and community-based corrections.

> John Augustus is known as the father of probation and an originator of community corrections.

From 1841 to 1851 Augustus provided bail for more than a thousand men and women, some as young as eight years old.

The Civil War and Its Aftermath

The penitentiary system was firmly established by the time of the Civil War. During the Civil War (1861–1865), prisons became major producers of boots, shoes, clothing and furniture. Following the war, prisoner labor was extremely important in the southern states where so much of the country had to be rebuilt. The war destroyed most southern prisons, so many prisoners were contracted out to work for private firms. Many southern states built flimsy barracks as temporary housing for prisoners until they could be leased to private contractors. The prisoners were chained together and wore horizontal black-and-white striped, loose-fitting, heavy cotton uniforms. This post–Civil War prison labor occurred in the context of a very weak national labor movement, and for a short period, police were known to shoot strikers and their families on occasion.

Convicts working on a Florida prison farm, circa 1910.

Following the war, the Thirteenth Amendment abolished slavery and involuntary servitude except as punishment for a crime:

> Neither slavery nor involuntary servitude, except as a punishment for crime whereof the party shall have been duly convicted, shall exist within the United States or any place subject to their jurisdiction.

This amendment, in effect, officially authorized involuntary servitude as a punishment in the United States. In addition, the country needed to rebuild its industries and transportation system which had been damaged during the war. Prisoners were one important source of labor. Among the prison industry systems used were the following:

- The account system, with the state running the industry, including marketing, financing and either profiting or losing money.
- The closed-market system, which limited sale of prison-produced goods to governmental and nonprofit agencies.
- The contract system, whereby the state sold their prisoners' labor to individuals or private businesses for a set fee per day for each inmate.
- The lease system, where the state actually gave up physical control of the inmates and received a fixed annual fee for the work the prisoners did for others.
- The piece-price system, a modified form of the contract system, where a contractor supplied the raw materials and paid the state a set price for each unit produced by prison labor.

By 1870, however, trade unions voiced opposition to this competition, resulting in some restriction on interstate commerce in prison-produced goods.

The Reform and Reformatory Movement

The year 1870 marked the beginning of the reformation of penology in the United States, a process that is still occurring today. In June of 1870, President Ulysses S. Grant signed the act creating the Department of Justice. Still there was no provision for federal prisons. The confinement in state or local institutions of prisoners who had violated federal law was unquestioned. Also in 1870, a group of distinguished citizens formed the National Congress of Penitentiary and Reformatory Discipline, which held an "exhilarating" conference in Cincinnati, providing an opportunity for corrections experts from around the country and foreign prison workers to meet and discuss needed reforms.

> The conference held by the National Congress of Penitentiary and Reformatory Discipline in 1870 (the Cincinnati Conference) marked the beginning of the National Prison Association, which later became the American Correctional Association (ACA).

Rutherford B. Hayes (U.S. president 1877–1881) was elected the first president of the association, which changed its name a few years later to the American Prison Association and more recently, in 1983, to the American Correctional Association, paralleling a change in emphasis in the correctional system. At the conference, correctional leaders of the old school were advised strongly to reject their former practices of corporal punishment and accept the principle that rehabilitation of offenders was now their goal. Reformers persuaded those in attendance to sign off on a radically new *Declaration of Principles* to guide the reformation of the nation's prisons. Of the 37 principles set forth in the declaration, the following are most relevant to the history of criminal justice and corrections:

- Reformation, not punishment, should be the purpose of penal treatment of prisoners.
- Classification should be based on a mark system.
- Good conduct should be rewarded.
- The political appointment of prison officials and unstable management are obstacles to prison reform.
- Prison management should be centralized at the state level.
- Prison officials should be trained for their positions.
- Indeterminate, rather than fixed, sentences should be used and inequities in sentences eliminated.
- Prisoners later found to be innocent should be indemnified.
- The pardon should be used more judiciously.

- Religion and education are the most important agencies of reform.
- Prison discipline should gain the support of prisoners and preserve their self-respect.
- Vocational training should be provided.
- Prison contract labor should be abolished.
- Laws regarding treatment of insane criminals should be revised.
- Prisons should be small with separate institutions for different types of offenders.
- Prison architecture should provide for air and sunlight.
- Uniform penal statistics should be established.
- Society must realize its responsibility for crime conditions.

Many of these ideas came from abroad and were slow to be adopted in the United States. The *Declaration of Principles* of the National Prison Association officially recognized the importance of programs and activities to assist offenders, stressing that appropriate treatment could bring about moral regeneration of criminals.

Among the participants at the national conference in Cincinnati was Zebulon Brockway (1827–1920), then warden of the Detroit House of Correction. His paper "The Ideal Prison System for a State" was proclaimed the outstanding contribution of the convention and influenced the *Declaration of Principles* significantly. In his paper, Brockway urged the administrators of prisons to adopt a new view, replacing vengeance with treatment. Included within his proposed system were primary schools for educating children from the almshouses, reform schools for juveniles, district reformatories for adult misdemeanants, a graduated series of reformatory institutions for adults and separate reformatories for women.

In 1876 Brockway was given the chance to put several of these principles into practice when he was appointed superintendent of the Elmira State Reformatory in New York and structured his administration around a rehabilitation or reform model. Organized along military lines, prisoners wore military uniforms and practiced close order drills. Elmira incorporated individualized treatment using a mark system, education, indeterminate sentences and vocational training. Brockway also possessed the institutional means to accomplish more fully what Maconochie had envisioned several decades earlier with his mark system. With a parole system tied to the use of marks, Brockway had all the elements of discretionary parole in place. He may not have had career parole and probation officers, but he did provide community supervision. Furthermore, Elmira would provide an impetus for establishing a separate juvenile court system.

Another development during the reformatory movement was a massive type of prison called the "Big House." Construction began in 1840 and continued for

An example of a typical "Big House" prison, New York City, circa 1948.

over a century. These institutions had immense stone cellblocks and were surrounded by high brick walls with armed guard towers overlooking the yard.

Throughout the 1870s and 1880s calls for a federal prison system became more frequent. Among the most vocal was the National Prison Association, a constant critic of the federal government's boarding-out practices. The association was instrumental in passage of legislation creating the first federal prisons.

The Three Prisons Act (1891) established the first federal prisons in Leavenworth, Kansas; McNeil Island, Washington; and Atlanta, Georgia.

This marked the second phase of the development of the federal prison system, the first phase having been the use of state and local facilities to board out prisoners. Keve (p. 35) notes: "The three-prison act was a profoundly significant new development. For the first time, the federal government was committed to the idea of having its own prisons to house its own prisoners."

The first federal penitentiary was a former military prison at Leavenworth, Kansas, acquired by the Department of Justice. Keve (pp. 39–40) describes the rules for guards and prisoners at this first federal prison:

Rules recorded in 1898 specified that "guards shall refrain from whistling, scuffling, immodest laughter, profanity, boisterous conversation, exciting

> discussion on politics, or other subjects calculated to disturb the harmony and good order of the penitentiary. . . ."
>
> Rules for prisoners were as repressive here as in all prisons of the time. A gray uniform was issued to each new prisoner, and later, subject to good behavior, it was exchanged for one of blue. The common black and white striped uniform was not worn, except by prisoners in the "third class": recaptured escapees and others under punishment.

By 1910 Leavenworth had more than 1,000 inmates and within 10 years it had double that. The facility had insufficient staff and hordes of visitors.

The second federal prison to be constructed was the United States Penitentiary at Atlanta, Georgia. Keve (p. 59) notes that this new federal prison also faced many problems:

> In Atlanta Warden Moyer had many of the same problems that McClaughry faced in Leavenworth. Moyer struggled with both population pressures and protracted construction. He contended with a guard force that was insufficient for the job and increasingly restive about the low pay and long hours.
>
> In Atlanta, too, the problem of visitors reached dimensions that seem incredible today. Moyer once told an audience of other prison officials that when he arrived at Atlanta, "every day was visiting day and . . . indiscriminate visitors, sometimes to the number of three thousand, were admitted and shown through the prison in one day during business hours."

The third penitentiary was located on McNeil Island in Washington. It had originally been a territorial jail.

The State of American Corrections at Century's End

The nineteenth century saw a great emphasis on incarceration. By the end of the century, prison conditions had deteriorated considerably and two trends in American corrections had become apparent: the continued decline of penal institutions and a broad acceptance of capital punishment. Solitary confinement in small, dark cells with starvation-portion meals was common. Corporal punishment was rampant; whippings, beatings, hanging by the thumbs and starvation were common. It was becoming clear to many that the prisons were not rehabilitating the inmates. The need for reform was apparent in the United States just as it had been in England previously.

Capital punishment was still commonly practiced in the western states, with invitations sent to guests as illustrated in Figure 3–4.

Toward the end of the century the reformers also tried to abolish capital punishment, but were thwarted by hard-liners including the police commissioner of New York City from 1895 to 1897, Theodore Roosevelt, who stated: "You don't want any mushy sentimentality when you are dealing with criminals. One of the things that many of our good reformers should learn is that fellow-feeling for the criminal is out of place" (Bowen, 1970, p. 52).

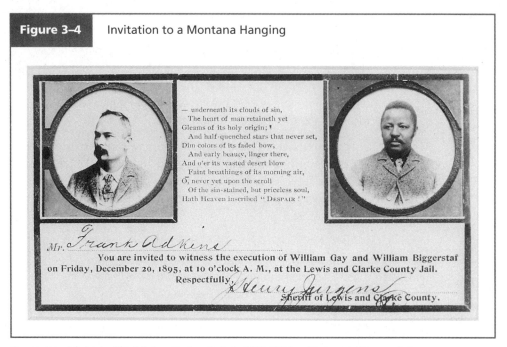

| Figure 3–4 | Invitation to a Montana Hanging |

— underneath its clouds of sin,
  The heart of man retaineth yet
Gleams of its holy origin; •
  And half-quenched stars that never set,
Dim colors of its faded bow,
  And early beauty, linger there,
And o'er its wasted desert blow
  Faint breathings of its morning air,
O, never yet upon the scroll
  Of the sin-stained, but priceless soul,
Hath Heaven inscribed " DESPAIR ! "

Mr. *Frank Adkins*

You are invited to witness the execution of **William Gay and William Biggerstaf** on Friday, December 20, 1895, at 10 o'clock A. M., at the Lewis and Clarke County Jail.
Respectfully, *Henry Jurgens*
Sheriff of Lewis and Clarke County.

Source: Time-Life Books. *This Fabulous Century, Prelude: 1870-1900,* p. 52. Reprinted by permission.

In summary, the highlights of the reformatory movement include the National Prison Association's *Declaration of Principles,* Brockway's innovations in correctional administration, the flourishing of the Big House prison design and the establishment of the first federal prisons.

The Twentieth Century

During the twentieth century, 27 Big House prisons were built. These immense physical institutions restricted architectural and programming innovations. In addition, emphasis continued to be placed on reforms affecting prison conditions, but not prison administration. Of the noteworthy developments in the twentieth century were the establishment of the Federal Bureau of Prisons in 1930, the prisoners' rights movement between 1960 and 1980, the outbreak of riots causing national concern and a shift from a punishment model to a treatment model.

The Progressive Era

The first quarter of the twentieth century is often referred to as the Progressive Era or the Age of Reform, a time of intellectual and institutional revolution in corrections and criminology. The reformers were optimistic people who believed that individualized treatment based on the inmate's history was critical. They also advocated indeterminate sentences, probation, parole and a system of prisoner classification. The classification system was based on the need for security, separating inmates into three categories—those needing minimum, medium and maximum security.

Ideologically during this time, the principle of offender rehabilitation presented at the Cincinnati Conference of 1870 was more widely adopted and given institutional expression. Furthermore, the juvenile court movement exploded during this period, with juvenile probation and parole expanding across most of the nation in 20 years. Although adult probation and parole expansion occurred more slowly than that for juveniles, these correctional practices also spread throughout the states during this time.

The Progressive Era also saw a fundamental shift in the ideology of criminology, away from the classical approach of free will emphasized by the church toward a more secular, positivist approach. The focus turned more toward the criminal instead of the crime committed and the moral consequences of such crime. Ideologically, however, there was little agreement about the causes of crime, and what agreement did exist was negative—criminal behavior is not simply an individual choice; choices are shaped by one's social environment, economic conditions, genetics, exposure to alcohol and drugs, negative peer influences and so on. Additionally, reform at this time focused on social control of the poor, particularly the immigrant.

> The Progressive Era called for *normalization,* converting the oppressive, brutal prison environment to a more humane, community-like environment. Education and vocational training were stressed. Probation and parole are the most notable institutional additions of this era. The positivist ideology of crime gained support and momentum.

In 1907 corrections took a further step toward becoming a bureaucracy when the attorney general created the position of superintendent of prisons within the Department of Justice.

Women's Prisons. During this time the need for separate facilities for women and youth was stressed by some reformers. One such reformer, Ellen Foster, found deplorable conditions for the female prisoners and urged that the department build a separate cell house at Leavenworth and that they be employed making convict clothing. The attorney general approved construction, but when Foster died, the project was given up.

Another advocate for women and youth was Mabel Walker Willebrandt, who became assistant attorney general with responsibility for prisons in 1923. Willebrandt established three major goals for prisons (Keve, p. 80):

- Employment for federal prisoners.
- A reformatory for young men.
- An industrial farm prison for female prisoners.

Willebrandt was joined in her crusade for female prisoners by such organizations as the Daughters of the American Revolution, the National Council of Jewish Women and the politically powerful Women's Christian Temperance Union. Her efforts were further aided when the small town of Alderson, West Virginia, determined to have the institution in their community, offered the government 202 acres of land. In March 1925, the first construction money was authorized. Willebrandt appointed Dr. Mary Belle Harris superintendent of the new prison. In 1927 the first three women were admitted to this open, campus-like women's federal prison at Alderson.

Decline of the Progressive Movement. Despite these goals, the Progressive Movement declined, partially because it focused on the individual criminal and largely ignored the penal institutions and their administration. Prisons were still primarily custodial, punitive institutions. In addition, because a basic tenet of the Progressive Era was that imprisonment was positive and would lead to a change in criminal behavior, more inmates came under the states' control, the result being severe overcrowding.

This overcrowding was an impetus to the growth of the reformatory. Although the reformatory had been pioneered by Brockway at Elmira State Reformatory in New York from 1876 to 1900, it was not widely supported until prison reform itself became an issue. The reformatory was seen as not only a new model to rehabilitate young adults but also as a means to segregate them from hardened criminals and simultaneously lessen the problems of overcrowding. The Elmira Reformatory became the model for the nation.

Another change occurring at this time concerned criminology and the perception of criminals. Beginning in the mid-1920s, some no longer viewed criminals as sinners who needed to atone for their sins, but rather as people suffering from an affliction that caused them to commit crime. This view later became known as the medical model. The emphasis shifted to the cause of deviancy as being rooted in the failure of the family, the community and religion to instill moral values. Because the deviancy was no longer seen as originating in the individual (the Calvinist view) but in the environment, emphasis shifted to the internal regimen of the penitentiary environment and efforts to retrain and rehabilitate inmates. Labor, however, was still used extensively.

Prison Labor. Following the Depression, in an effort to control competition from prison labor, the Hawes-Cooper Act stipulated that prison products would be subject to the laws of the state to which they were shipped. Furthermore, during the 1930s, the labor movement became very strong and was able to leverage its influence to protect itself from certain sources of competition, including prison labor. Within a few years most states had passed laws in some way restricting prison products.

The Federal Bureau of Prisons (FBOP)

During the first three decades of the twentieth century, federal prisons were built, often on military reservations scattered around the country. Little coordination existed, although the prisons shared many common problems, including overcrowding as the result of federal legislation: the Harrison Act of 1914 (narcotics), the Volstead Act of 1919 (prohibition) and the Automobile Theft (Dyer) Act. In addition to severe overcrowding, federal prisons also had problems of inconsistent administration and the political spoils system, whereby wardens were appointed on the basis of patronage. In response to these problems and the lack of coordination, Congress established the Federal Bureau of Prisons. The FBOP is also abbreviated as BOP.

> In 1930 Congress established the Federal Bureau of Prisons (FBOP). The goal of federal corrections was to protect society's right to be free from fear while at the same time developing a more unified system.

At this time some 12,000 offenders were confined in seven autonomous federal prisons. The FBOP's charge was to create a federal *system*, including classification and ways to rehabilitate inmates through vocational and educational training. President Hoover appointed Sanford Bates as the first director of the Bureau of Prisons. Mr. Bates had a long and illustrious career as director of prisons in Massachusetts. According to Keve (p. 94): " [Bates] took federal prisons out of politics. . . . He was a political realist, but again, because he did not ask for his job or engage in any political bargaining to obtain it, he was free to put sound management practices ahead of most political accommodations."

The Federal Bureau of Prisons became one of the leading agencies in American corrections, with many of its innovations being adopted by state prisons. A major innovation was using professionals such as psychiatrists and psychologists to help in inmate rehabilitation. Bates was a strong advocate of individualized treatment of prisoners. He also instituted staff training intended to replace control by force with control by intelligence and leadership using knowledge from the behavioral sciences. Keve (p. 112) suggests: "Perhaps Bates is best remembered for introducing a newly human attitude toward prisoners as people."

One important contribution of the Federal Bureau of Prisons was its classification system. Under this system institutions began to specialize in custody and treatment based on the risk level and needs of its inmates. Federal facilities were classified as penitentiaries, reformatories, prison camps, medical hospitals and treatment facilities for drug addicts. Each type of facility further classified inmates by age, sex and offense.

(Left to right) Sanford Bates, James V. Bennett, Myrl E. Alexander and Norman A. Carlson, on the occasion of Carlson's swearing in as director of the Bureau of Prisons. (Bureau of Prisons)

At the same time the Bureau of Prisons was created, Congress also authorized an extensive expansion of institutional facilities, including a new penitentiary in Lewisburg, Pennsylvania, regional jails and several camps. The camps were barrack-type dormitories intended to house the multitude of inmates serving short sentences for making moonshine during Prohibition.

Other Influences on Corrections

A number of influential individuals and organizations called for harsher treatment of criminals, including the director of the FBI, J. Edgar Hoover (appointed in 1924 at age 29). Hoover used statistics to show the severity of the crime problem and verbalized public criticisms of those who would be soft on criminals (Bowen, 1969, p. 112):

> Hoover intensified his fire in a new broadside of speeches aimed not only at crooks, but at anyone who, he felt, sympathized with them. This included "shyster lawyers and other legal vermin," "sob-sister judges," political liberals and other "sentimental moo-cows" who believed in lightening the sentences of "criminal jackals."

With the passage of the Eighteenth Amendment in 1919 and the coming of Prohibition, new ruthless gangsters, some with tremendous wealth, surfaced, including Al Capone. Other predatory criminals were also making

Alcatraz—it was hoped prisoners couldn't get here from there.

headlines: John Dillinger, George "Machine Gun" Kelly and the kidnapper of the Lindbergh child. The need for a new maximum security prison for racketeers, kidnappers and other predators became apparent.

Hoover's efforts helped turn Alcatraz into a federal prison. Alcatraz, built on a 12-acre site in the San Francisco Bay, was originally a U.S. military fort designed to protect the San Francisco Harbor. In 1859 it was converted into a military prison and remained as such until 1934, when Hoover's personal backing helped develop Alcatraz into a super-maximum prison. It was considered by many to be escape-proof and, consequently, housed America's most dangerous criminals. Well-known inmates included Dillinger, Al Capone, George "Machine Gun" Kelly and Baby Face Nelson. According to Keve (p. 186): "[T]his prison was not intended for reformatory purposes; according to Bates, it was intended only to exercise unique control over the dangerous few who would otherwise disrupt the system." (The Bureau closed Alcatraz in 1963. It has subsequently been converted to a tourist attraction by the National Park Service as a classic representation of a Big House prison.)

In 1937, Bates resigned to become president of the Boys Club of America. He was replaced by James V. Bennett, who had been one of his assistant directors. One of the first steps Bennett took was to construct medium and minimum security facilities. He also believed that prisoners needed to work, an unpopular idea during the Great Depression when millions were unemployed. Congress had passed legislation severely curtailing prison industries, but Bennett got around this obstacle by establishing a government corporation to manufacture products for use by the federal government. The Federal Prison Industries established by Bennett was profitable immediately. Bennett was also faced with a new problem prisoner—the drug addict.

1940 to 1960

The 1940s and 1950s were the war years. Prisoners helped in the war effort by manufacturing rope cargo nets, stripping salvaged electrical cable and producing huge quantities of food for military use. The war had another effect. It created an influx of very nontraditional inmates who challenged prison conditions and practices, including conscientious objectors who found themselves in federal prisons. Hunger strikes among these dissidents were common.

The middle of the twentieth century saw the rapid rise of social welfare programs. The crime rate was relatively stable, around 100,000 adults indicted on specific offenses each year, and the American people believed that their criminal justice system was working to control crime.

The major prison emphasis was again on rehabilitation: less harsh discipline, educational programs and more privileges. During the 1950s and 1960s the main goal of prisons was considered to be rehabilitation, with emphasis on the individual. Despite such efforts at reform, the 1950s saw violence increase in the prisons once again, with numerous major rebellions throughout the country. An investigation by the American Correctional Association of the more than 100 riots or major disturbances occurring in American prisons between 1950 and 1966 revealed the following main causes:

- Inequitable sentencing and parole practices.
- Inadequate financial support.
- Inferior personnel.
- Idleness.
- Lack of professionalism.
- Official and public indifference.
- Excessive overcrowding.
- Politically motivated management.

In 1954 the American Correctional Association published *A Manual of Suggested Standards*. Cautiously presenting basic minimum conditions that should exist in prisons throughout the country, this was the forerunner of the current accreditation system.

1960 to 1980

Correctional experts often refer to efforts during the 1960s and 1970s as a *medical model* seeking to rehabilitate inmates. The 1970s also placed much emphasis on ways to reintegrate offenders into society. Numerous alternatives to incarceration were investigated, as discussed in Chapter 5.

The 1960s were turbulent times with

- President Lyndon Johnson's Great Society programs designed to eradicate poverty.
- The unpopular Vietnam War and its accompanying protests and demonstrations.
- Greater social awareness.
- Increased activism by numerous groups.
- The civil rights movement.
- The extensive reinterpretations of criminal law.
- Public exposure of abuses in prisons.
- The assassinations of President John F. Kennedy and Reverend Dr. Martin Luther King, Jr.
- The rise of a drug-using counterculture.

These tensions and pressures were also felt inside prisons as racial mixtures began to change. Prior to the 1960s, prison populations in the northern states were predominantly White, with Black and Hispanic inmates comprising a relatively small, docile minority. In many correctional facilities, interracial violence destroyed the "live-and-let-live" attitude among prisoners.

These conditions resulted in frequent violent riots which helped to raise public awareness of prison conditions. Reforms included the classification system, medical care, work programs, and education and vocational programs. The emphasis in corrections was on rehabilitation.

A Change in Court Attitude

During the 1960s courts changed their approach from a hands-off policy to more attention to prisoners' civil rights. Before this time, most complaints had been about conditions within the prisons, but not about the violation of inmates' civil rights. Courts began hearing cases challenging how prisons were run. One such case, *Cooper v. Pate* (1964), established that prisoners have the right of access to the courts. The 1970 ruling in *Holt v. Sarver* effectively threw out the hands-off policy, allowing the courts a role in setting standards of correctional care. (Prisoners' rights are discussed in detail in Chapter 14.)

This emphasis was dampened, however, as crime rates soared. Many attributed the increase in crime and violence to "softness" of the system and called for a return to getting tough on crime. Adding to the problem was the prison riot in New York State Penitentiary at Attica in 1971. During this riot 11 guards and 32 prisoners were killed. A commission appointed by the governor of New York determined that the main causes of the riot were conditions of confinement as well as racial discrimination.

By the mid-1970s, sentences were longer, and many became disillusioned about the potential of the system to rehabilitate. The pendulum swung back toward an emphasis on punishment and a get-tough-with-criminals stance. Today, this attitude appears stronger than ever.

Environmental Influences

Williamson (1990, pp. 29–41) suggests that corrections since the 1960s has been greatly influenced by several "environments," illustrated in Figure 3–5.

Corrections is influenced by the social, political, bureaucratic, legal, institutional, system and community environments in which it functions.

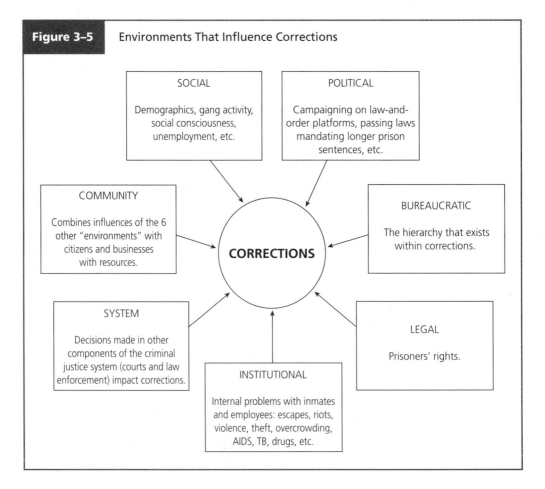

Figure 3–5   Environments That Influence Corrections

SOCIAL

Demographics, gang activity, social consciousness, unemployment, etc.

POLITICAL

Campaigning on law-and-order platforms, passing laws mandating longer prison sentences, etc.

COMMUNITY

Combines influences of the 6 other "environments" with citizens and businesses with resources.

CORRECTIONS

BUREAUCRATIC

The hierarchy that exists within corrections.

SYSTEM

Decisions made in other components of the criminal justice system (courts and law enforcement) impact corrections.

INSTITUTIONAL

Internal problems with inmates and employees: escapes, riots, violence, theft, overcrowding, AIDS, TB, drugs, etc.

LEGAL

Prisoners' rights.

The *social environment* was changing dramatically. According to Williamson (p. 31):

> Corrections prior to the 1960s, operating without significant influence from outside forces, was clearly a closed system. The influence of social change, however—including the major effects of demography, social consciousness, gang activity, unemployment, and many other factors—forced corrections to become an open system.

Today's information technologies continue the trend begun in the 1960s to open up the correctional system. Via on-line services, citizens have access to state and federal prison data, prisoners can get information to the media and numerous other methods of data flow can occur. This impacts correctional management dramatically, as bureaucratic supervisors, politicians, the media and the public are made aware of institutional happenings almost immediately.

The *political environment* also changed. Politicians who had previously ignored the criminal justice system, and corrections in particular, began campaigning on law-and-order platforms. They passed laws making longer prison sentences mandatory. Despite this public show of concern for law and order, however, often dollars to accomplish the desired results were not allocated.

The *bureaucratic environment* involves the hierarchy existing within corrections. Bureaucracies, by their nature, tend to be rigid, rule-producing and impersonal, and tend to stifle innovation. But they are necessary. Professionals who must function within a bureaucracy often find themselves hindered by rules and protocols, tied to how things have been done in the past, unappreciated and finally burned out.

The *legal environment* has changed dramatically from the anonymous, immune warden operating in virtual secrecy to wardens being sued for violating prisoners' rights. It is important to understand that the legal environment is a strong influence on correctional programs. In many states, entire correctional systems have been ruled unconstitutional and are under court order to change, but no funds have been allocated to make the mandated changes.

The *institutional environment* greatly affects the direction corrections can take. As noted by Williamson (pp. 35–36):

> Prisons have always had internal problems with inmates and employees. Escapes, riots, inmate violence, theft, and other problems are endemic to any population such as that housed in prisons. However, prior to the 1960s, prisons were surprisingly predictable places. Highly regimented and controlled behavior kept the institutional environment relatively safe, predictable, and unambiguous.
>
> The changes occurring since the 1960s have caused prison environments to change quite dramatically. Overcrowding, health problems (such as the Acquired Immune Deficiency Syndrome or AIDS), drugs, violence among inmates, and the implementation of various treatment programs have served to decrease the stability and predictability of inmate populations.

The *system environment* was previously discussed in Chapter 1. Corrections is not an isolated entity but part of the criminal justice system. Decisions made and actions taken in the other two components of the system greatly affect corrections.

Finally, the *community environment,* which consists of all the preceding environments with the addition of citizens and businesses with resources, can either assist or hamper corrections. In many areas an emphasis has been placed on finding alternatives to prison within the community, as discussed in depth in Chapter 5.

And the Pendulum Swings

Since the colonial times, reform and reaction have alternated. Each reform has led to periods of public apathy, indifference and worsening of conditions until again, public indignation or the emergence of new ideas causes the pendulum to swing toward reform. Throughout our history the pendulum has swung between optimism and disillusionment with the correctional system and its ability to achieve the desired purpose—which also changes as the pendulum swings.

Summary

Many historians note that our modern correctional system originated in Pennsylvania under the leadership of Penn and the Quakers' Great Law. The Walnut Street Jail is important in the development of corrections because it is considered the United States' first state prison.

In the 1800s two distinct prison systems developed, the Auburn system and the Pennsylvania system. The Auburn system emphasized crime prevention through strict silence and fear of brutal punishment. Because the prisoners worked and ate as a group, the system is sometimes referred to as the congregate system. The Pennsylvania system, in contrast, is sometimes referred to as the separate system because the prisoners were totally isolated. The Pennsylvania system's philosophy emphasized religion and penitence, hence the name *penitentiary.* In the Auburn or congregate system, prisoners worked together using the factory model of mass production. In contrast, the Pennsylvania or separate system used individual, craft-based labor performed in their cells. As other states built their prisons, most followed the Auburn system.

John Augustus is known as the father of probation and an originator of community corrections. He built a House of Refuge for those on probation, and his actions are viewed as the origin of community-based corrections.

The conference held by the National Congress of Penitentiary and Reformatory Discipline in 1870 (the Cincinnati Conference) marked the beginning of the National Prison Association, which later became the American Correctional

Association (ACA). At the end of the nineteenth century the Three Prisons Act established the first federal prisons in Leavenworth, Kansas; McNeil Island, Washington; and Atlanta, Georgia.

The Progressive Era called for normalization, converting the oppressive, brutal prison environment to a more humane, community-like environment. Education and vocational training were stressed. Probation and parole are the most notable institutional additions of this era. The positivist ideology of crime gained support and momentum.

In 1930 Congress established the Federal Bureau of Prisons (FBOP). The goal of federal corrections was to protect society's right to be free from fear while at the same time developing a more unified system.

Today corrections is influenced by the social, political, bureaucratic, legal, institutional, system and community environments in which it functions.

Discussion Questions

1. Recall how, in the early nineteenth century, correctional institutions proliferated, partly as the result of the perceived threat to aristocratic class values posed by the lower and working classes, in particular immigrant groups. Does today's upper class feel the same way toward the lower and working classes, particularly immigrants? What about the middle class? Is there any class that does *not* feel threatened by the others?

2. Discuss the following item listed in the National Prison Association's *Declaration of Principles:* "Society at large should be made to realize its responsibility for crime conditions." Do you believe this has been achieved? What still needs to be done?

3. Why is it necessary to have separate state and federal prisons?

4. Although one of the principles set forth in the declaration stated that prisons should be small, Big House prisons continued to be built for more than a century. Why?

5. Do you think the medical model removed too much responsibility from the criminal for his or her own actions?

6. Overcrowding seems to be a recurring theme in the history of our prisons. Could something have been done earlier to prevent the continued overcrowding situation that exists to this day? What might be done now?

7. Separating prisoners according to race constitutes discrimination, yet interracial violence remains a problem for correctional facilities and a frequent source of riots and rebellions. What might be done to overcome this challenge?

8. Which environment do you think has the greatest impact on corrections today: social, political, bureaucratic, legal, community, institutional or system? The least?

9. How has economics guided the progress of corrections? Does the bottom line too often undermine the effectiveness of corrections and the value placed on public safety?

10. Are we closer to or farther from the correctional philosophy that prevailed when this country began? Which way are we moving?

References

Bowen, Ezra, ed. *This Fabulous Century, Prelude: 1870–1900*. New York: Time-Life Books, 1970.

Bowen, Ezra, ed. *This Fabulous Century: 1930–1940*. New York: Time-Life Books, 1969.

Keve, Paul. *Prisons and the American Conscience: A History of U.S. Federal Corrections*. Carbondale: Southern Illinois University Press, 1991.

Williamson, Harold E. *The Corrections Profession*. Newbury Park, CA: Sage Publications, 1990.

Cases

Cooper v. Pate, 378 U.S. 546 (1964).

Holt v. Sarver, 309 F.Supp. 362, E.D. Ark. (1970).

SECTION II

Sentencing Alternatives

The sentencing phase of the criminal justice process has a great impact on the field of corrections, for it is corrections personnel who must carry out such sentencing decisions. Section II begins with a look at past and present views on sentencing; the goals served by various sentences; types of sentences; current issues in sentencing, including overcrowding, parole reform and capital punishment; sentencing innovations; and corrections' role and interest in sentencing (Chapter 4).

This is followed by a discussion of alternatives to incarceration, including the sentencing options of probation and a variety of intermediate sanctions (Chapter 5). Intermediate sanctions exist along a continuum of increasing restriction and supervision and include day fines, forfeitures, restitution, community service, intensive supervision programs (ISPs), house arrest, electronic monitoring, day reporting centers and residential community corrections.

The sentencing alternative of jail is presented next (Chapter 6), with a look back at the roots of today's jail and an examination of jail populations and jail facilities. Ways to get out of jail are then followed by a discussion of critical issues facing jails today. The section concludes with a chapter on prisons (Chapter 7) and a discussion of their history in this country, prison populations, the prison facility, getting out of prison and an in-depth look at parole. Chapter 7 concludes with a presentation of some critical issues facing prisons today.

4

Perspectives on Sentencing

➤ What goals sentences may serve?

➤ What a PSI report is, what information it contains, who prepares it and what functions it serves?

➤ What plea bargaining is and how it is used?

➤ What types of sentencing exist and the characteristics of each?

➤ What two sentencing reform models appeared in the 1970s and what each was based on?

➤ What impact mitigating and aggravating circumstances have on sentence length?

➤ What two factors are considered in presumptive sentencing grids like the one used in Minnesota?

➤ What the purpose of the federal Sentencing Reform Act was and how it affected sentence disparity?

➤ What the Greenwood scale attempts to measure and what its intended use is?

➤ How selective and collective incapacitation differ?

➤ What the Supreme Court's position on capital punishment has been?

➤ If capital punishment has been proven to be an effective deterrent for crime?

➤ What Supreme Court cases uphold the constitutionality of executions of juveniles and those mentally ill or retarded?

Punishment, that is justice for the unjust.
—Saint Augustine (A.D. 345–430)

Can You Define

aggravating circumstances

collective incapacitation

determinate sentences

discretionary sentences

good time

Greenwood scale

incarceration sentences

indeterminate sentences

justice model

limited discretionary sentences

mandatory sentences

mitigating circumstances

nondiscretionary sentences

nonincarceration sentences

plea bargaining

presumptive sentences

retributivist model

selective incapacitation

selective release

sentencing commission

Sentencing Reform Act

Introduction

Sentencing is that stage in the criminal justice process where a judge formally determines how the convicted offender will "pay for" the crime(s) committed. It is also the stage that has the greatest impact on corrections, for it is corrections personnel who must carry out such sentencing decisions.

Sentencing is where policy and practice either collide or complement. First, different philosophies of punishment have different implications for sentencing structures. Different approaches suggest different minimum "meaningful" sentences and different maximum sentences (what is "cruel and unusual"). Second, economic and other environmental differences affect the movement from one sentencing structure to another. Finally, the sociology of punishment can be connected to the sentencing material. Some sentencing structures emphasize the condemnatory (Durkheim); mandatory sentencing structures are arguably class control structures (Marx), for example, federal sentences for crack and powder cocaine. The evolution of capital punishment reflects shifting sensibilities in this country. The pragmatic mentality is reflected in periodic proposals to predicate sentences on "dangerousness" (selective incapacitation, the Greenwood scale, early parole guidelines and the earlier Minnesota state sentencing guidelines that included a prediction scale). Watch for these interconnections as you read this chapter.

A variety of sentencing options are available to judges. Jail and prison sentences are but two of the options. Other sentencing alternatives include fines, forfeitures, probation, intensive supervision, electronic monitoring and community corrections. These specific sentencing options will be discussed in greater detail in the following chapters; this chapter will focus on the general issues related to the arrival at and imposition of criminal sentences.

Goals of Sentencing

The sentencing options available to judges are usually selected based on the particular goal sought.

Sentences may serve to

- Protect society.
- Punish the convicted criminal.
- Obtain restitution for the victim's loss.
- Treat and rehabilitate offenders so they may be reintegrated into society as functional citizens—sentences can correct the underlying causes that led them to commit crime.

The nineteenth century prison reform movement was based on the presumption that the prison's function was to reform the offender. Singer notes: "Criminologists long accepted the view that an offender's criminal misbehavior could be analogized to a disease, which could be cured if properly treated in a proper institution. Cure became a major goal of both sentencing and incarceration." Singer goes on to state: "This rehabilitative outlook shaped even the vocabulary of criminal punishment. Prisons were often called 'correctional' institutions; those for young adults were often called 'reformatories.'" In fact, the field of corrections came by its name as a result of these early goals of sentencing.

Rehabilitation remained the dominant goal of sentencing and the correctional system for nearly a century, until reform in the 1970s led to a fundamental shift. Although rehabilitation still remained a correctional goal, other primary goals surfaced, such as incapacitation and retribution. With this shift in correctional goals came changes in the types of sentences being handed down. When the primary goal of corrections is retribution, the courts are likely to emphasize lengthy incarceration. However, when the focus is on rehabilitation and reintegration of the offender into society, the courts tend to downplay incarceration and focus on probation and community-based programs.

Most citizens are familiar with California's three-strikes law and the increasing public demand to get tough on crime. The prevailing public attitude toward crime and those who commit it has led judges nationwide to "come down hard" on convicted criminals. The result: our country's prisons are now bursting at the seams. This situation has forced another sentencing goal upon our judges—avoiding dangerous prison overcrowding by selecting alternative sentences to incarceration. This in/out decision is made daily as judges consider such alternatives to incarceration as probation, home detention and community service. In some cases, however, the in/out decision has been taken from judges through the creation of mandatory sentences enacted by state and federal legislatures for certain offenses, such as crimes committed with a firearm.

> An additional goal of sentencing may be to reduce prison populations by using alternatives to incarceration.

The sentence imposed on a convicted criminal results from a judicial evaluation of which goals that sentence should seek to achieve. One tool used by judges in determining the appropriate sentence is the presentence investigation report.

The Presentence Investigation (PSI) Report

The presentence investigation, or PSI, report is a valuable instrument to a judge when determining which sentence to impose on an offender. Typically prepared by a probation officer, the PSI report provides information about the offender, as well as professional recommendations concerning the appropriate disposition of the case.

No standard format exists for PSI report preparation, although many PSIs are patterned after those used by the Administrative office of the U.S. Courts (1984). The first formal PSI was drafted by that office in 1943 and has since undergone several revisions. Included in the PSI report is

- Personal information, such as the offender's name, address, birth date and location, educational history, employment history, marital status and family history, financial condition, physical description, mental stability and any known addictions or medical conditions.
- Offense information, such as the current offense and date of offense, the offender's version of the conviction offense, the prosecution's version of the conviction offense, possibly a victim impact statement, witness statements, statutory penalties for the conviction offense and any prior record of juvenile or adult offenses.
- An evaluation of the offender by the probation officer and recommendations concerning sentencing of the offender.

A relatively new development under the rules of disclosure is that offenders and their lawyers can read the PSI to check its accuracy.

> A PSI report is prepared by a probation officer and contains personal information about the offender, offense, relevant criminal information about the offender and recommendations to the judge concerning sentencing of the offender.

The recommendations given in these PSI reports have been shown to factor heavily in judges' sentencing decisions. In some instances, the acceptance rate is between 80 and 90 percent. It should be noted, however, that where sentencing guidelines exist, the PSI has less impact on sentencing because judges' discretion is limited.

Not only are PSI reports useful to judges at the sentencing stage, they also assist probation officers' supervisory efforts during probation and parole and aid correctional agencies in the classification, institutional programming and release planning of inmates. In a majority of jurisdictions, the contents of the PSI are presented to the court immediately before a sentencing hearing. These reports are prepared with the eventual phase of sentencing in mind and are one method used to influence sentencing outcomes. Another method used to influence sentencing is plea bargaining.

Plea Bargaining

> **Plea bargaining** is a preconviction agreement where a defendant pleads guilty in exchange for some concession from the prosecution. Such agreements are generally made with the expectation that the defendant will receive a more favorable sentence as a result of pleading guilty.

Those who favor plea bargaining claim the process eases the burden on the already overcrowded court dockets and spares the defendant significant legal fees. Those who oppose plea bargaining state it denies defendants their constitutional rights by allowing alleged offenders to be considered guilty before having their case tried in court. Furthermore, judges may tend to give more severe sentences to defendants who refuse to "cop a plea." Regardless of which side one favors, plea bargaining is highly used, involving more than 90 percent of all criminal convictions. Only 10 percent go to trial.

> Plea bargaining is a preconviction agreement where a defendant enters a guilty plea in exchange for some concession from the prosecution. Plea bargaining accounts for more than 90 percent of all criminal convictions.

Offenders plead guilty for a variety of reasons:

- They feel guilty and want to confess.
- They hope to get a better deal from the judge.
- They believe the evidence against them is too overwhelming.

With nine out of ten criminal convictions arising as a result of this process, plea bargaining obviously plays a large role in sentencing our nation's convicts. Without plea bargaining, the courts would be gridlocked. The criminal justice system is based on pleas. Contrary to public opinion, trials are rare.

Nonetheless, plea bargaining is not accepted by many citizens, as noted by Thrash (1996, p. 54): "Many citizens question whether the law is actually working for them or for the criminals." Justice negotiated through plea bargaining is especially troublesome to victims of crime and to law enforcement officers. Says Thrash (p. 55):

> Obviously, a crime victim usually wants as much if not more punishment as is available for a criminal brought to answer for their offenses. Any reduction of charges or sentencing can bring hostile resentment toward a system that outwardly appears to operate without concern for the victim or for justice.

Police officers can also become embittered by a system of perceived revolving door justice. Officers who have worked hard to build cases and arrest hardened criminals can become jaded when crooks get off easy with a plea bargain.

However, plea bargaining remains a necessity (Thrash, p. 55): "Conservative estimates indicate that we would have to double our staff and double the amount of courts [judges and staff] to not bargain anything."

Types of Sentences

Twenty to thirty years ago, sentences were either prison or probation. Now judges have a host of intermediate choices available, as shown in Figure 4-1. These options are frequently categorized according to whether the offender is incarcerated.

➤   **Nonincarceration sentences** include fines, restitution or victim compensation, probation, home confinement or house arrest, electronic monitoring and community service. Table 4–1 illustrates how different populations of felons (male, female, White, Black) tend to receive differing sentences.

Table 4–1 seems to indicate that a greater percentage of female felons receive probation than do male felons and that White felons receive probation more often than do Black felons. Conversely, judges *appear* to hand more incarceration sentences to male and Black or Hispanic felons than to female and White felons. However, a number of factors are involved, including the offender's prior record.

➤   **Incarceration sentences** include shock incarceration, placing offenders in confinement for a set period and then releasing them to serve probation, confinement in jail and confinement in prison. Incarceration sentences are of four basic types:

➤   • **Indeterminate sentences,** also called **discretionary sentences,** in which judges and parole authorities have a great deal of latitude in determining the length of the sentence. The maximum sentence is determined by the legislature. Judges can't exceed this but can give a lesser sentence.

➤   • **Determinate sentences,** one of the two types of **limited discretionary sentences,** in which a degree of judicial discretion is removed but a range of sentence lengths is still allowed.

➤   • **Presumptive sentences,** the other type of limited discretionary sentence, again removing a degree of judicial discretion but still allowing a range of sentence lengths.

➤   • **Mandatory sentences,** also known as **nondiscretionary sentences,** in which the sentence is fixed by law and must be given upon conviction, eliminating any judicial discretion to suspend the sentence or grant probation.

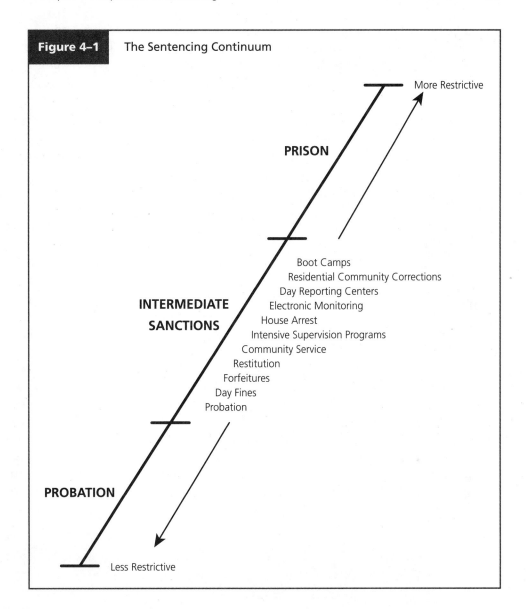

Figure 4–1   The Sentencing Continuum

More Restrictive

PRISON

Boot Camps
Residential Community Corrections
Day Reporting Centers
Electronic Monitoring
House Arrest
Intensive Supervision Programs
Community Service
Restitution
Forfeitures
Day Fines
Probation

INTERMEDIATE
SANCTIONS

PROBATION

Less Restrictive

These different sentencing systems—indeterminate, determinate, presumptive and mandatory—result in great variation among the states in sentences imposed for the same crime.

Indeterminate Sentencing

Indeterminate sentencing, as the name implies, is open-ended as to sentence length, with no fixed minimum (that is, the sentence can be from zero years to life). Recall that prison reform in the 1800s sought to rehabilitate, or cure,

| Table 4–1 | The Relative Percentage of Adults on Probation, in Jail, in Prison or on Parole, by Sex and Race, 1995 |

		Sex		Race		
	Total	Male	Female	White	Black	Other*
Total	5,400,000					
Probation	3,100,000	54%	78%	65%	48%	38%
Jail	499,300	10%	6%	6%	10%	45%
Prison	1,100,000	22%	8%	17%	26%	13%
Parole	700,000	14%	8%	12%	16%	4%
U.S. adult resident population	192,857,000					
Percent under correctional supervision	2.8%					

*Most often = Hispanic
Source: Adapted from Bureau of Justice Statistics. *Correctional Populations in the United States, 1995.* Executive summary, June 1997 (NCJ-163917).

offenders. Reformers argued that since the sentencing judge would have no way of knowing how long the rehabilitation process would take for a particular individual, the determination of when to release an offender into society was best left to correctional administrators. The legislature determined maximum sentence length. These maximum-length sentences were given with the understanding that, should an offender reform and be ready to face life in the "real world" before completing the entire sentence, parole officials would have the authority to terminate the incarceration and release.

> Indeterminate sentencing is a discretionary, open-ended sentencing scheme with no fixed minimum or maximum sentence length. It involves decisions by parole boards to determine release dates of inmates.

Following the adoption of the 1870 *Declaration of Principles* by the National Prison Association, indeterminate sentencing became the standard to which states were advised to adhere. Eventually most did. Prison administrators approved of this system, as it encouraged inmates to behave to expedite their release.

Indeterminate sentencing remained the primary form of sentencing in state and federal courts for nearly a century, well into the 1960s. The pendulum began to swing the other way, however, late in the decade. By the 1970s, sentencing practices in the United States were undergoing another reform. Critics of indeterminate sentences objected to the uncertainty and general unfairness of the sentences. The disparity in sentence lengths for similar crimes became obvious. Two offenders committing the same crime and with similar backgrounds could get completely different sentences because of judicial discretion. Inmate discontent led to an increase in prison riots across the country; 43 people were killed in the 1971 riot at Attica, New York. Furthermore, the public started to perceive that dangerous criminals were being released into the community at the whim of lenient parole boards and, indeed, studies of postrelease activities indicated high rates of recidivism.

Critics alluded to the extensive discussion of sentencing disparity in the late 1960s and early 1970s. Their goal was to limit judicial (or parole board) discretion and eliminate or at least minimize sentencing disparity. However, they did not consider the role of the prosecutor and the fact that any sentencing scheme is a tool prosecutors may use to secure guilty pleas. As long as the prosecutor's virtually unreviewable power, *nollo pros,* exists, the connection between criminal conduct and sentence is uncontrollable. Sentencing merely controls the connection between charge and sentence. The American Bar Association (ABA) standards for the prosecutor support this broad discretionary power at the prosecutorial level.

The Transition from Indeterminate to Determinate Sentencing—Two New Models

By the early 1970s, indeterminate sentencing had come to be considered unjust, ineffective and soft on crime. Reform efforts sought to limit discretion by judges and parole boards, reduce discrimination and restore justice by eliminating sentence disparity and ensuring more fairness in sentencing. Several new models were proposed to solve the problems that plagued the sentencing system—problems created by indeterminate sentencing and rehabilitative ideals that had fallen short of their mark.

➤   One approach to sentencing, introduced in 1975 and known as the **justice model,** first proposed a fundamental shift in sentencing philosophy, such as replacing indeterminate sentences with determinate (flat-time) sentences, creating mandatory sentences for particularly serious offenses, establishing sentencing commissions and providing stricter guidelines for parole release decisions. This model also recognized the hypocrisy within the sentencing and corrections systems and called for a change in the procedures that treated inmates unfairly. Ironically, the very system charged with correcting and releasing prisoners was being criticized for the potentially unlawful use of power and blatant disparity in sentencing.

➤   Another model, the **retributivist model,** appeared in 1976. This model also rejected indeterminate sentencing schemes and the idea that rehabilitating criminals was the solution to the country's crime problems. The retributivist model took the stance that criminal sentences should be based solely on the seriousness of the crime committed and provide a "just deserts" level of punishment. As with the justice model, this model took the focus away from rehabilitation of the offender and looked to other approaches for achieving justice.

> Both the justice and retributivist models rejected the principles of indeterminate sentencing and called for nationwide sentencing reforms.

Also, in 1976, a Task Force on Criminal Sentencing advanced the notion that the disparity resulting from indeterminate sentencing practices promoted an unfairness that would inevitably breed disrespect for the law. Criminal justice scholars argued that the indeterminate sentencing system was aggravating the crime problem by treating those it sentenced unfairly and unjustly. This widespread criticism of indeterminate sentencing prompted many states to reverse themselves and adopt determinate sentencing systems.

Determinate Sentencing

Determinate sentencing systems are limited discretionary schemes which fix definite terms for the various crimes contained in the penal code, the length of the term reflecting the seriousness of the offense. A basic difference between determinate and indeterminate sentences is that determinate sentences are not subject to early termination by parole boards. The only way a determinate sentence may be shortened is through the accumulation of "good time" credits. Such discretion may make determinate sentencing closely resemble indeterminate sentencing.

> Determinate sentencing is a limited discretionary scheme which fixes definite terms for crimes, involves no parole boards and allows the use of good time to hasten the release from a correctional institution.

➤   Originally used in the mark system by Maconochie, **good time** is credit earned by an inmate which reduces the duration of the incarceration. It is determined by prison staff at the administrator's discretion. Good time may be earned simply by demonstrating good behavior, or it may result from participating in institutional programs.

Different correctional facilities use different methods of apportioning good time to inmates. Some facilities treat good time as a reward and allow inmates to earn it through model behavior. This earned good time is "banked" for the inmates and is not subject to revocation. Negative behavior prevents the accumulation of good time, but whatever time is already in the bank is protected from loss. Other facilities, however, allow the accumulation of good time but retain the authority to revoke any and all earned good time following an infraction of the rules. Presently, the use of good time is being reduced and is undergoing considerable scrutiny.

Whichever method is used, good time systems allow correctional staff some authority with sentencing functions by allowing considerable control over the length of sentences served by inmates. According to some correctional administrators, good time programs have also been cited as one way to maintain control over an inmate population. Inmates are motivated to behave when they know such behavior may significantly reduce the time they spend behind bars. For example, many states allow sentences to be cut in half by giving one day's credit for one good day served. Texas allows two days' credit for every good day served, potentially shortening an original sentence by two-thirds.

Several states have implemented determinate sentencing reform (Alaska, Arizona, California, Connecticut, Colorado, Illinois, Indiana, Maine, Minnesota, North Carolina, Pennsylvania and Washington), and many others are considering such reform. When asked what effects the determinate sentencing law had on corrections in his state, Washington's secretary of the Department of Corrections, Chase Riveland, responded (Bartollas and Conrad, 1992, p. 152):

> Actually, it has met a couple of objectives. One, its original objective was intended to put violent offenders in for a longer period of time and to divert nonviolent offenders from the system. For the most part, that has occurred. . . .
>
> Second, the new law has served the purpose of improving at least the parity and equity issues of sentences across the state, in ethnicity, gender, as well as geographic analysis. . . . Also, from a practitioner's perspective, it is very attractive that its finiteness allows us to do very accurate population projections. I think for planning purposes and for keeping a corrections system stable and matching the resources to the need, that's very important.

Determinate sentences are categorized as limited discretionary sentences, but many argue discretion is not limited enough, and efforts at determinate sentencing reform have often fallen short of reducing discretion. For example, at the front end of the system, a form of plea bargaining called *charge bargaining* may still occur, where a defendant may plead guilty to a lesser included charge or to fewer than all of the charges against him or her. At the back end of the system, the length of the sentence actually served remains open to great discretion and disparity due to variations in the granting of good time credit by prison officials.

In other words, determinate sentences, while supposedly protected from substantial judicial or prosecutorial discretion, do little to actually limit this discretion and may actually achieve the same end results as indeterminate sentencing. In addition, determinate sentencing has a potential impact on prison population growth, prison security, correctional officers' morale, prisoner suicide, mental illness and prison rebellions. Another limited discretionary sentencing system is presumptive sentencing.

Presumptive Sentencing

Presumptive sentencing is based on a predetermined range of minimum, average and maximum terms set by a **sentencing commission.** Sentencing commissions are not parole boards, but instead consist of ex officio members and members appointed by the governor or mandated by the legislature (for example, the director of corrections and the attorney general). Most states also require a certain number of judges and prosecutors to be members of the state sentencing commission. Their purpose is to develop and monitor presumptive sentences. Sentencing guideline commissions in Minnesota and in the federal system are administrative committees with permanent staffs. The legislature in Minnesota approves any changes, but they do not vote on the details. They accept or reject the entire sentencing guideline.

Such commissions not only develop the sentencing guidelines but also monitor judicial decisions, requiring a written explanation in instances where the judge has ruled outside the designated sentencing range. Under presumptive sentencing guidelines, average sentence lengths are provided by law and allow the judge to impose shorter or longer sentences, within limits, depending on mitigating or aggravating circumstances. The legislature gives maximum sentencing guidelines and develops a presumptive range of sentences.

> Presumptive sentencing is a limited discretionary scheme that uses sentencing commissions to predetermine minimum, average and maximum terms for specific crimes and allows for the consideration of mitigating and aggravating circumstances.

➤   **Mitigating circumstances** weigh in favor of the defendant and serve to shorten the imposed sentence length. (For example, the defendant was only a fringe participant in the criminal act or had a personality disorder, thus being
➤ more easily led into committing a crime.) **Aggravating circumstances,** on the other hand, serve to increase sentence length. Aggravating circumstances include having a prior record of incarceration, causing severe bodily harm to the victim and preying on particularly vulnerable victims such as the elderly or the mentally or physically handicapped. For example, Minnesota has a presumptive sentencing structure that provides three options to the sentencing judge, as seen here for the crime of burglary:

1. Aggravating circumstances—7 years.
2. Presumptive (average) sentence—5 years.
3. Mitigating circumstances—3 years.

> Mitigating circumstances serve to shorten the imposed sentence length whereas aggravating circumstances serve to increase sentence length.

Mitigating and aggravating circumstances are also subject to judicial and prosecutorial discretion. For example, having severe emotional problems or being mentally retarded may be considered mitigating circumstances by some courts, and the defendant may receive a lighter sentence as a result.

To arrive at the appropriate sentence range, the judge uses a formula that factors in an offender's prior record or criminal history, mitigating and/or aggravating circumstances, the length of previous incarcerations and other considerations.

A number of states have adopted presumptive sentencing structures to guide their courts. For example, the Minnesota Sentencing Guidelines Commission has devised a table to direct judges in their sentencing decisions (Table 4-2). The table takes into account the offender's criminal history, listed along the horizontal axis, and the severity of the conviction offense, listed along the vertical axis.

> Presumptive sentencing grids factor together the offender's criminal history and the severity of the conviction offense to arrive at an appropriate sentence.

Note the bold zigzag line across the grid. This is the in/out line, separating those sentences that require a prison term (below the line) from those sentences requiring alternatives to prison (above the line), such as a jail term or probation. Pennsylvania's sentencing guidelines grid shows in greater detail how various sentences may be imposed and how aggravating and mitigating circumstances may affect sentence length (Table 4–3). Commenting on the revision of the Pennsylvania guidelines, Kempinen (1997, p. 1) states: "[T]he changes expand the range of offenders for whom intermediate punishments are authorized, and accompany a substantial increase in state funding for community-based penalties."

Some states' sentencing guidelines, such as those of Minnesota, legally require the sentencing commission to adjust the application of the guidelines to avoid overcrowding. Such systems thereby attempt a built-in mechanism for achieving the sentencing goal of preventing prison overcrowding. Minnesota Commissioner Orville Pung voiced concern about the increasing penalties called for in some state sentencing guidelines (Bartollas and Conrad, p. 158):

> In the old indeterminate sentence, the parole board would review a case and say, "That happened 15 years ago. Look what he's done for the first 15 or 10 years." It might have been a little easier to say we're not going to give him another 15 years because the victim's family may have moved, or the judge may have died. I think I'm seeing that longer and longer sentences are being handed down. That's going to continue and I don't know where that's going to lead us because we have sex offenders in prison now who have a longer sentence than if they'd killed the victim and got first-degree murder. You play an elevation game and continue to increase the thing proportionately.

Another type of sentencing system that uses legislatively determined sentences is mandatory sentencing.

Table 4–2	Minnesota Sentencing Guidelines Grid

Presumptive Prison Sentence Lengths in Months

Less Serious ◄─────────────────────────────► More Serious

Severity of Offense (Illustrative Offenses)	Criminal History Score						
	0	1	2	3	4	5	6 or more
Sale of Simulated Controlled Substance	12	12	12	13	15	17	19 *18–20*
Theft Related Crimes ($2,500 or less) Check Forgery ($200–$2,500)	12*	12*	13	15	17	19	21 *20–22*
Theft Crimes ($2,500 or less)	12	13	15	17	19 *18–20*	22 *21–23*	25 *24–26*
Nonresidential Burglary Theft Crimes (over $2,500)	12	15	18	21	25 *24–26*	32 *30–34*	41 *37–45*
Residential Burglary Simple Robbery	18	23	27	30 *29–31*	38 *36–40*	46 *43–49*	54 *50–58*
Criminal Sexual Conduct, 2nd Degree	21	26	30	34 *33–35*	44 *42–46*	54 *50–58*	65 *60–70*
Aggravated Robbery	48 *44–52*	58 *54–62*	68 *64–72*	78 *74–82*	88 *84–92*	98 *94–102*	108 *104–112*
Criminal Sexual Conduct, 1st Degree Assault, 1st Degree	86 *81–91*	98 *93–103*	110 *105–115*	122 *117–127*	134 *129–139*	146 *141–151*	158 *153–163*
Murder, 3rd Degree Murder, 2nd Degree (felony murder)	150 *144–156*	165 *159–171*	180 *174–186*	195 *189–201*	210 *204–216*	225 *219–231*	240 *234–246*
Murder, 2nd Degree (with intent)	306 *299–313*	326 *319–333*	346 *339–353*	366 *359–373*	386 *379–393*	406 *399–413*	426 *419–433*

▨ At the discretion of the judge, up to a year in jail and/or other non-jail sanctions can be imposed instead of prison sentences as conditions of probation for most of these offenses. If prison is imposed, the presumptive sentence is the number of months shown.

☐ Presumptive commitment to state prison for all offenses.

Notes: 1. Criminal history score is based on offender's prior record and seriousness of prior offenses. 2. Numbers in italics represent the range of months within which a judge may sentence without the sentence being deemed a departure from the guidelines. 3. First degree murder is excluded from the guidelines by law and carries a mandatory life sentence.

*One year and one day

Source: Minnesota Sentencing Guidelines Commission. Effective August 1, 1994. William M. DiMascio. *Seeking Justice: Crime and Punishment in America,* 1995, p. 24. Reprinted by permission.

Table 4–3   Pennsylvania Sentencing Guidelines Grid

		Prior Record Score								
	OSG	0	1	2	3	4	5	RFEL	REVOC	AGG/MIT
LEVEL 5 State Incar	14	72–240	84–240	96–240	120–240	168–240	192–240	204–240	240	+/−12
	13	60–78	66–84	72–90	78–96	84–102	96–114	108–126	240	+/−12
	12	48–66	54–72	60–78	66–84	72–90	84–102	96–114	120	+/−12
	11	36–54 BC	42–60	48–66	54–72	60–78	72–90	84–102	120	+/−12
	10	22–36 BC	30–42 BC	36–48	42–54	48–60	60–72	72–84	120	+/−12
	9	12–24 BC	18–30 BC	24–36 BC	30–42 BC	`36–48 BC	48–60	60–72	120	+/−12
LEVEL 4 State Incar/ RIP trade	8 [F1]	9–16 BC	12–18 BC	15–21 BC	18–24 BC	21–27 BC	27–33 BC	40–52	NA	+/−9
LEVEL 3 State/ Cnty Incar RIP trade	7 [F2]	6–14 BC	9–16 BC	12–18 BC	15–21 BC	18–24 BC	24–30 BC	35–45 BC	NA	+/−6
	6	3–12 BC	6–14 BC	9–16 BC	12–18 BC	15–21 BC	21–27 BC	27–40 BC	NA	+/−6
LEVEL 2 Cnty Incar RIP RS	5 [F3]	RS–9	1–12 BC	3–14 BC	6–16 BC	9–16 BC	12–18 BC	24–36 BC	NA	+/−3
	4	RS–3	RS–9	RS–<12	3–14 BC	6–16 BC	9–16 BC	21–30 BC	NA	+/−3
	3 [M1]	RS–1	RS–6	RS–9	RS–<12	3–14 BC	6–16 BC	12–18 BC	NA	+/−3
LEVEL 1 RS	2 [M2]	RS	RS–2	RS–3	RS–4	RS–6	1–9	6–<12	NA	+/−3
	1 [M3]	RS	RS–1	RS–2	RS–3	RS–4	RS–6	3–6	NA	+/−3

Key:
AGG = aggravated sentence addition
BC = boot camp
CNTY = county
F = felony
INCAR = incarceration
M = misdemeanor

MIT = mitigated sentence subtraction
OGS = offense gravity scale
RFEL = repeat felony 1 and felony 2 offender category
REVOC = Repeat violent offender category
RIP = restrictive intermediate punishments
RS = restorative sanctions
<;> = less than; greater than

1. Shaded and cross-hatched areas of the matrix indicate restrictive intermediate punishments may be imposed as a substitute for incarceration.
2. When restrictive intermediate punishments are appropriate, the duration of the restrictive intermediate punishment program shall not exceed the guideline ranges.
3. When the range is RS through a number of months (e.g., RS–6), RIP may be appropriate.

Source: Pennsylvania Commission on Sentencing, 1997. Cynthia Kempinen. "Pennsylvania Revises Sentencing Guideline." *Overcrowded Times,* August 1997, p. 17. Reprinted by permission.

Mandatory Sentencing

Mandatory sentencing requires a judge to impose a specific incarcerative sentence for a particular crime. Sentence length is set by law, and judicial discretion concerning sentence suspension, probation and immediate parole is eliminated. However, as with determinate sentences, some jurisdictions allow earning good time to reduce sentence length.

> Mandatory sentencing is a nondiscretionary sentencing scheme that requires offenders convicted of particular crimes to receive statutorily determined incarcerative sentences. Offenders may be allowed to earn good time to achieve early release in some jurisdictions.

All 50 states have some mandatory sentencing statutes which apply to a range of offenses, including, for example, violent crimes, drug-related crimes and crimes committed with guns. These statutes effectively eliminate the court's discretion in such cases. Alabama has a two-year minimum sentence for those convicted of selling drugs. The sentence is increased by five years if the sale occurs within three miles of a school or housing project and by ten years if it happens within three miles of both (*Seeking Justice*, 1995, p. 19).

California's "use a gun—go to prison" statute requires adding a two-year penalty to the sentence of any person in possession of a firearm when involved in a felony or an attempted felony. Several other states, including Michigan and Hawaii, have similar laws setting mandatory incarceration sentences for offenders who use a lethal weapon while committing a felony. Although these laws are designed to discourage offenders from using weapons during criminal acts, thereby resulting in less harm to victims, limited evidence supports a significant reduction in the involvement of weapons in states that have such mandatory sentences. One study in Massachusetts, where one year was automatically added on for using a gun in committing a crime, showed some reduction in the use of weapons.

Criticisms of mandatory sentencing abound. Mandatory sentences targeting drug offenders have recently begun to fall under attack as prisons across the nation are filling up with "minor-league druggies," leaving less space for murderers, rapists and robbers. According to one article ("Drug Sentences," 1993, p. A22): "Drug offenders now make up 60 percent of the federal inmate population—up from 22 percent in 1980. As Attorney General Janet Reno has noted, that increase is prompting some prisons to release violent offenders in order to fulfill Congress' demand for mandatory sentences for drug offenders." Dickey (1993, p. 3) notes: "In New York, which makes extensive use of mandatory minimums for drug offenses, the percentage of violent offenders in prison declined from 63 percent in 1982 to 34 percent in 1992. The state of Florida has been forced to release thousands of offenders, many of them convicted of assaultive offenses, in order to create prison space for drug offenders serving mandatory sentences."

The famed California three-strikes law falls into the category of mandatory sentencing and attempts to address the issue of the habitual offender. Table 4–4 shows the mandatory penalties in the 50 states regarding habitual offender laws and laws concerning drugs and guns. According to Proband

Table 4–4	State Mandatory Penalties								
State	Habitual Offender Laws		Specific Crimes		State	Habitual Offender Laws		Specific Crimes	
	2/3 Strikes	Other	Drugs	Guns		2/3 Strikes	Other	Drugs	Guns
Alabama	✔		✔	✔	Montana	✔		✔	✔
Alaska	✔		✔	✔	Nebraska	✔		✔	
Arizona	✔	✔	✔	✔	Nevada	✔		✔	✔
Arkansas	✔		✔	✔	New Hampshire	✔	✔	✔	✔
California	✔	✔	✔	✔	New Jersey	✔		✔	✔
Colorado	✔	✔	✔	✔	New Mexico	✔	✔		
Connecticut			✔	✔	New York	✔	✔	✔	✔
Delaware	✔	✔	✔	✔	North Carolina	✔		✔	✔
Florida			✔	✔	North Dakota				✔
Georgia	✔	✔	✔	✔	Ohio			✔	✔
Hawaii	✔	✔	✔	✔	Oklahoma	✔		✔	✔
Idaho	✔		✔	✔	Oregon	✔	✔		✔
Illinois	✔	✔	✔	✔	Pennsylvania	✔		✔	✔
Indiana	✔	✔	✔	✔	Rhode Island	✔	✔	✔	✔
Iowa	✔		✔	✔	South Carolina	✔		✔	✔
Kansas	✔	✔	✔	✔	South Dakota			✔	✔
Kentucky	✔	✔	✔	✔	Tennessee				
Louisiana	✔		✔	✔	Texas	✔		✔	✔
Maine				✔	Utah				✔
Maryland	✔	✔	✔	✔	Vermont				
Massachusetts			✔	✔	Virginia		✔	✔	✔
Michigan		✔	✔	✔	Washington		*		
Minnesota		✔	✔	✔	West Virginia	✔	✔	✔	✔
Mississippi	✔		✔	✔	Wisconsin			✔	
Missouri		✔		✔	Wyoming	✔			

*Washington passed a "4 Strikes and You're Out" law requiring life without parole in 1993.
Note: "2/3 Strikes" Laws call for enhanced penalties for offenders with one or two prior felony convictions. Most require a term of years in addition to the penalty for the current offense. "Other" habitual offender laws relate to specific prior crimes such as violent or sex offenses.
Source: Bureau of Justice Statistics. *State Justice Sourcebook of Statistics and Research,* 1992. Stan C. Proband. "Habitual Offender Law Ubiquitous." *Overcrowded Times,* February 1997, p. 7. Reprinted by permission.

(1994, p. 7): "[H]abitual offender laws went out of vogue from the 1960s until recently. Like mandatory minimums, they were often applied to low-level, not frightening, offenders, and were widely circumvented by plea bargaining. Also like mandatory minimums, they have not been shown to be effective deterrents but to cause offenders to be retained in prison long after they cease to pose meaningful threats to public safety."

One very real concern about three-strikes laws is that they frequently do not distinguish between violent criminal acts and crimes such as nonviolent property offenses. They also do not distinguish between people who use real weapons and offenders who merely pretend to have a weapon. According to Clark (1994, p. 1): "Larry Lee Fisher, who has been in and out of jails since he was a teen-ager, has become a poster boy of sorts for those who oppose 'three strikes' laws." Fisher, now in his mid-30s, was arrested on his third strike in January 1994, after robbing a restaurant of $150 by pretending his concealed finger was a gun. His first strike occurred in 1986, when he knocked his grandfather down and stole $390 from him. The second strike came in 1988, when he used his finger as a gun to rob a restaurant of $100. The new three-strikes law means if Fisher is convicted of this third offense, he faces life imprisonment without parole, instead of a 22-month prison sentence.

Another concern of the three-strikes laws focuses on the fact that most of these offenders are relatively young, with many years of life ahead of them. The cost to keep these offenders imprisoned into their 60s, 70s and beyond, and the increased medical care that frequently accompanies the aging process pose significant financial burdens to those states opting to impose such sanctions. Mauer (1994, p. 15) states: "Criminology studies have documented that young males commit a disproportionate amount of all violent crime. . . . Offenders over the age of 60 commit just 1 percent of all serious crime. Thus, incarcerating offenders beyond the age of 50, 60, or 70 is likely to have a very minimal impact on crime." Mauer also asserts: "The '3 Strikes' proposals, politically popular in a time of concern about crime, represent a corrections time bomb likely to have an enormous fiscal impact with virtually no gains in crime control."

An NCJA Justice Bulletin ("More Judges Opposing," 1994, p. 3) reports more and more federal and state judges are taking a stand against mandatory-minimum sentences by refusing to impose them. This raises an important issue: what good are mandatory sentences if they aren't mandatory? Seemingly, prosecutors are invoking some discretion by allowing defendants to plead guilty to lesser charges, thereby avoiding mandatory-minimum charges. Dickey (p. 3) states: "Studies in several jurisdictions have revealed that prosecutors sometimes refuse to file mandatory-bearing charges or use creative plea bargaining to avoid these statutes."

Another shortcut around mandatory minimums is contained in the federal crime bill safety valve. The federal crime bill, which was signed into law by President Clinton in September 1994, contains a clause allowing federal judges to reduce mandatory-minimum sentences for offenders meeting a certain set of requirements ("More Judges Opposing," p. 15).

Mandatory sentences have their share of problems. In jurisdictions where prison overcrowding is of critical concern, mandatory sentences only compound the problem. Furthermore, no evidence supports the effectiveness of mandatory terms to deter crime. Mandatory sentences were designed to eliminate sentencing disparity in cases of a particularly serious nature, but such sentencing tactics have come up short in this area as well.

Issues in Sentencing

Disparity in sentencing is of great concern in our criminal justice system and is but one of the critical issues facing sentencing practices in the United States. Other issues include sentencing guidelines, prison overcrowding and the question of whether to incarcerate, abolition of parole and the controversial topic of capital punishment.

Disparity in Sentencing

Sentencing disparity is an inevitable consequence where judges are allowed any degree of discretion. Although they are expected to act fairly and impartially as they dispense justice, in an imperfect world judges are necessarily less than unbiased. This is a situation similar to one everyone has probably experienced in high school or college regarding grades. What one instructor considers A-level work, another may consider merely average, or C-level. The same holds true for judges—what one throws the book at and hands down a 15-year prison sentence, another may treat with a probation term or community service.

Johnson (1993, p. 54) notes: "Studies have consistently found that people receive very different punishments for similar crimes as judges apply their subjective opinions." Furthermore, other studies seem to indicate that the race of the victim plays a large part in the determination of the offender's sentence, with crimes against Whites receiving stiffer penalties than crimes against others. To complicate matters even further, "many criminal codes have irrational punishments built in." For example, as mentioned by Commissioner Pung, some sentencing structures have sex offenders serving longer sentences than those convicted of first-degree murder, and a certain Michigan law provides a greater penalty for writing a bad check than for engaging in child abuse.

Sentencing structures such as presumptive and mandatory sentencing were designed to eliminate a degree of this disparity, yet, even these methods are not without fault. In fact, as reported by McDonald and Carlson (1994, p. 1), the passage of the Sentencing Reform Act (SRA) of 1984 by Congress had an unpredictable effect:

> [R]acial and ethnic differences in imprisonment sentence grew wider *after* implementation of guidelines. Sentences imposed on blacks grew increasingly more severe, on average, relative to whites and Hispanics. . . . . The black/white

differences result mostly from sentencing for cocaine trafficking. Most (two-thirds) of the difference results from a congressional decision to impose much harsher penalties for crack cocaine offenses than for powder cocaine offenses . . . [and] we discovered a significant difference in the frequency with which whites and blacks were convicted of trafficking in crack as opposed to powdered cocaine, which accounts for much of the apparent racial differences in sentencing.

Consequently, even intentional efforts to create more uniformity, or to eliminate disparity, in sentencing have backfired because of variances in the populations that commit certain types of offenses.

Sentencing Guidelines

Efforts to standardize sentencing and eliminate disparity led to the creation of sentencing guidelines. A number of states have adopted their own guidelines, and many states are presently overhauling their entire sentencing systems. Tables 4–2 and 4–3, showing Minnesota's and Pennsylvania's presumptive sentencing grids, are but two of many state-implemented sentencing guidelines.

Federal guidelines also exist. In 1984 Congress passed the Comprehensive Crime Control Act which abolished parole (effective November 1987). Furthermore, the **Sentencing Reform Act** of 1984 created the United States Sentencing Commission, whose first function was to draft a new set of guidelines to establish flat terms for all federal prisoners. The purpose of the Sentencing Reform Act was to achieve:

1. *Honesty*—assuring that sentences were served (known as "truth in sentencing").

2. *Uniformity*—imposing similar terms for similar crimes to eliminate racial or gender disparity.

3. *Proportionality*—considering the severity of offenses and imposing appropriate levels of punishment.

> The Sentencing Reform Act sought to achieve honesty, uniformity and proportionality in sentencing, although many argue the act actually contributed to increases in sentencing disparity.

The federal presumptive sentencing guidelines implemented in 1987 and amended in 1992 are shown in Table 4–5. Like the Minnesota and Pennsylvania grids, this table places offense categories along the vertical axis in order of increasing severity and the criminal history of the offender along the horizontal axis, giving judges a range of appropriate sentence lengths (in months).

Table 4–5	U.S. Sentencing Commission Sentencing Table (in Months of Imprisonment)

	Criminal History Category (Criminal History Points)					
Offense Level	**I** (0 or 1)	**II** (2 or 3)	**III** (4, 5, 6)	**IV** (7, 8, 9)	**V** (10, 11, 12)	**VI** (13 or more)
1	0–6	0–6	0–6	0–6	0–6	0–6
2	0–6	0–6	0–6	0–6	0–6	1–7
3	0–6	0–6	0–6	0–6	2–8	3–9
4	0–6	0–6	0–6	2–8	4–10	6–12
5	0–6	0–6	1–7	4–10	6–12	9–15
6	0–6	1–7	2–8	6–12	9–15	12–18
7	1–7	2–8	4–10	8–14	12–18	15–21
8	2–8	4–10	6–12	10–16	15–21	18–24
9	4–10	6–12	8–14	12–18	18–24	21–27
10	6–12	8–14	10–16	15–21	21–27	24–30
11	8–14	10–16	12–18	18–24	24–30	27–33
12	10–16	12–18	15–21	21–27	27–33	30–37
13	12–18	15–21	18–24	24–30	30–37	33–41
14	15–21	18–24	21–27	27–33	33–41	37–46
15	18–24	21–27	24–30	30–37	37–46	41–51
16	21–27	24–30	27–33	33–41	41–51	46–57
17	24–30	27–33	30–37	37–46	46–57	51–63
18	27–33	30–37	33–41	41–51	51–63	57–71
19	30–37	33–41	37–46	46–57	57–71	63–78
20	33–41	37–46	41–51	51–63	63–78	70–87
21	37–46	41–51	46–57	57–71	70–87	77–96
22	41–51	46–57	51–63	63–78	77–96	84–105
23	46–57	51–63	57–71	70–87	84–105	92–115
24	51–63	57–71	63–78	77–96	92–115	100–125
25	57–71	63–78	70–87	84–105	100–125	110–137
26	63–78	70–87	78–97	92–115	110–137	120–150
27	70–87	78–97	87–108	100–125	120–150	130–162
28	78–97	87–108	97–121	110–137	130–162	140–175
29	87–108	97–121	108–135	121–151	140–175	151–188
30	97–121	108–135	121–151	135–168	151–188	168–210
31	108–135	121–151	135–168	151–188	168–210	188–235
32	121–151	135–168	151–188	168–210	188–235	210–262
33	135–168	151–188	168–210	188–235	210–262	235–293
34	151–188	168–210	188–235	210–262	235–293	262–327
35	168–210	188–235	210–262	235–293	262–327	292–365
36	188–235	210–262	235–293	262–327	292–365	324–405
37	210–262	235–293	262–327	292–365	324–405	360–life
38	235–293	262–327	292–365	324–405	360–life	360–life
39	262–327	292–365	324–405	360–life	360–life	360–life
40	292–365	324–405	360–life	360–life	360–life	360–life
41	324–405	360–life	360–life	360–life	360–life	360–life
42	360–life	360–life	360–life	360–life	360–life	360–life
43	life	life	life	life	life	life

Source: U.S. Sentencing Commission. *Sentencing Guidelines Manual,* 1992. David Yellen. "Little Progress in Federal Sentencing after Ten Years of Guidelines." *Overcrowded Times,* June 1997, p. 5. Reprinted by permission.

Yellen (1997, p. 1) notes: "The guidelines are ambitious and complex. A sentencing judge's task begins with selecting the appropriate offense guideline, usually but not always based on the statutes of conviction. . . . There are then upward, and occasionally downward, adjustments based on 'specific offense characteristics.' " Once an adjusted offense score is reached, it is plotted against the offender's criminal history score and a sentencing range is given. According to Yellen (p.4): "Only at the lowest levels, where the range is 0–6 months, may the judge freely impose probation. There is a small portion of the table where the court may combine probation with some confinement. On most of the table, however, a prison sentence is required."

The constitutionality of these guidelines was challenged on the grounds they violated the separation of power between the legislature and the judiciary. However, the 1989 U.S. Supreme Court ruling in *Mistretta v. United States* stated there was no compromise in the independence of the judiciary, upholding the constitutionality of such guidelines.

Voluntary guidelines have been tried in some states, such as Michigan, but are often rather ineffective. Advantages to these guidelines are that no legislative action is required, no sentencing commissions are involved, implementation is inexpensive and judges retain a high degree of discretionary power because they can ignore the guidelines altogether. However, many argue "What's the point?" when the end result is the same as having an indeterminate sentencing scheme.

Prison Overcrowding—To Incarcerate or Not to Incarcerate?

One of the biggest issues facing sentencing and the entire criminal justice system is prison overcrowding. Indeed, as Michael Tonry asserted in a debate over sentencing policy ("Tonry, Fein Debate," 1993, p. 56): "[P]rison populations have tripled since 1980 and jail populations are up by about the same amount." Singer (p. 3) reveals: "[A] criticism of sentencing reform is that it has contributed to recent increases in prison crowding, first by causing the sentencing to prison of many offenders who previously would have received probation, and second by removing the 'safety valve' of early release on parole in the event of overcrowding." Many point to the mandatory sentencing of drug offenders as a major reason for prison overcrowding, and few signs indicate this incarceration policy has had any positive impact of the level of drug abuse throughout the country. The Campaign for an Effective Crime Policy has suggested that perhaps these mandatory-minimum sentences need to be repealed if they don't begin to show evidence of aiding crime control (Dickey, p. 2).

Prison populations have risen in nearly every state, with overcrowding a severe problem for many. These states have had to seek ways to alleviate the pressure of prison crowding by modifying sentencing policies, thereby affecting both the number of individuals sentenced and the length of time each individual stays incarcerated. Some states, such as Minnesota, have built-in measures to avoid overcrowding, but it is little consolation knowing convicted criminals who *should* receive a prison sentence are being funneled into other programs or that those already incarcerated are being released early to make room for newly sentenced offenders.

Such circumstances pose potentially serious threats to the public safety. For example, California's sentencing practices during the early 1980s had judges sentencing more than 70 percent of the state's felons to probation in an effort to alleviate the prison overcrowding crisis. Studies conducted on this group of felony probationers revealed many were poor candidates for probation. During a 40-month period, 65 percent of these probationers were arrested, 51 percent were convicted of a new crime and one-third ended up behind bars (Petersilia et al., 1985). Furthermore, 75 percent of the offenses committed by this group of probationers fell into the categories of robbery, theft, burglary and other violent crimes which directly threatened public safety.

As noted, mandatory sentences have removed some of the in/out decisions judges need to make, but where judges do have sentencing discretion, they are faced with the often difficult task of predicting the future behavior of those who come before the court for sentencing. Such judicial predictions are often the basis for whether the offender receives probation or is sentenced to time behind
➤ bars. The **Greenwood scale,** devised by Peter Greenwood (1982) of the Rand Corporation, presumably provides a relatively accurate prediction of which offenders are most likely to commit future crimes. One test of this scale conducted with data about more than 10,000 inmates from the 1979 *U.S. Survey of Inmates of State Correctional Facilities* found that inmates with higher Greenwood scale scores averaged a higher number of prior convictions than those with lower scores, although predictions in individual cases were highly inaccurate. This study determined that generalizations about a group of offenders were not necessarily applicable to any particular individual, as is often the case when looking at such data. It was argued that total reliance on predictors such as Greenwood scale scores was not recommended, for it could likely lead a judge to impose an inappropriate sentence. Researchers have found the best predictor of chronicity is if the offender spent time in prison as a juvenile.

> The Greenwood scale attempts to predict offender dangerousness and public risk, although it is not accurate for individuals.

Peter Greenwood intended his scale to be a useful tool for judges when making that in/out decision. He proposed a means of controlling the increas-
➤ ing crime rates through a method of selective incapacitation. **Selective incapacitation,** as the name implies, seeks to keep those selected offenders predicted of future dangerousness (those with high Greenwood scale scores) locked behind bars while releasing nondangerous offenders (those with low

Greenwood scale scores) on probation. Numerous factors are considered, including offenders' prior criminal records and, in particular, whether an offender had been incarcerated as a juvenile. Unfortunately, as studies have seemed to indicate, the Greenwood scale leaves much to be desired in predicting the actual dangerousness of a particular individual.

Some researchers have challenged the application of prediction scale results, claiming such scales may be more effective in identifying who should be
➤ released—a concept known as **selective release**—than who should remain locked up. According to Hayes and Geerken (1997, p. 368): "A modified version of Greenwood's predictive scale performed best in predicting low-rate offenders, especially when property, violent, and index offenses were considered. The scale performed much less well in predicting high-rate offenders across all offense categories examined." One benefit of selective release may be a reduction in the need for jail and prison space. Another benefit might be that shorter incarcerations for low-rate offenders may spare them the criminogenic effects of a lengthy prison term, a concept discussed in the next chapter.

Another issue with the selective incapacitation method is the potential for false positives, or inaccurate predictions of future dangerousness. An offender identified as a public safety risk is labeled "positive." When this offender truly is a risk, it is a "true positive," and when the offender is mistakenly diagnosed as dangerous, it is a "false positive." Persons may be wrongly detained in incarcerative facilities because of inaccuracies of the prediction process, resulting in a clear transgression of justice. The converse scenario of "false negatives" may also exist, when offenders who truly do pose a significant threat to society are predicted, for whatever reasons, as being nondangerous and are released into society.

David Stanley (1976, p. 56) echoes the earlier criticism of using prediction to determine sentences: "The trouble with prediction is simply that it will not work—that is, it will not work for individuals, only for groups. A parole board may know that of 100 offenders with a certain set of characteristics, 80 will probably succeed and 20 will fail on parole. But the board members do not know whether the man who is before them belongs with the 80 or the 20."

➤ An alternative to selective incapacitation is the concept of **collective incapacitation,** which seeks to impose lengthy terms of incarceration for all convicted offenders regardless of whether they are deemed a "poor risk" or a future danger to society. Such an across-the-board attitude toward keeping offenders behind bars is, however, unlikely to succeed for several reasons.

First, given the already critical overpopulation of many correctional facilities and the trend toward faster turnover of inmates, such a policy of keeping everyone locked up for a long time is not feasible. Second, the cost to construct the necessary facilities to hold these numbers of inmates is more than many communities can, or want to, handle.

Third, numerous studies reveal that lengthy terms, such as those proposed by collective incapacitation policies, are *not* effective means for controlling or reducing the level of crime. Although the crime rate is currently down and some credit the decrease to increased incarceration rates, this may or may not actually be true. For example, as reported by Austin and McVey (1989, p. 6): "In both the United States and Canada, the rates of crime do not go down with increased imprisonment. Instead, the rates of crime go up when the proportion of offenders per 100,000 who are sentenced to prison is raised." Furthermore, as noted in *Seeking Justice* (p. 3): "In recent years, the U.S. criminal justice system has responded to the public's fear of crime by locking up more offenders for longer periods of time. This practice has not been correlated with a significant reduction in crime rates. In fact, states that incarcerate the most offenders continue to have the highest crime rates." Some researchers, however, disagree with this correlation.

Some studies indicate that a substantial proportion of crime is caused not by repeat or career criminals but by first-time offenders, especially young offenders. These people have no prior record and, obviously, would not have been kept from committing their crimes because of a decision to lengthen their period of incarceration—they were never behind bars to begin with. Therefore, many scholars argue collective incapacitation efforts are futile in their attempts to significantly reduce crime.

> Selective incapacitation seeks to keep those selected offenders predicted of future dangerousness locked behind bars while releasing nondangerous offenders on probation. Collective incapacitation seeks to impose lengthy terms of incarceration for all convicted offenders "across the board," regardless of whether they are deemed a poor risk or a future danger to society.

Incarceration remains a mixed bag for sentencing judges, appealing from the get-tough perspective so many citizens and communities are now calling for, yet unattractive due to prison overcrowding and pressures from state legislatures to reduce the number of inmates. Probation, however, is not always the best solution either. Many questions remain about how effective either incarceration or probation are in rehabilitating or correcting those sentenced to them.

Parole Reform

Parole boards were created as part of the indeterminate sentencing structure, to determine when an inmate had been sufficiently rehabilitated and was ready for release. These boards have fallen under criticism, however, for their contributions to sentencing disparity. Recent reform efforts in sentencing have also included attempts at reform in parole practices or total abolition of parole.

Total abolition of parole boards does not always result in reducing sentencing disparity, as was the experience in Maine. Oregon enacted parole guidelines in an effort to reduce differences in sentence lengths, which has had a positive effect on such disparities. Oregon's parole reform also addressed the uncertainty caused by indeterminate sentences and provided for a decision to be made relatively early in the sentence concerning the inmate's release date. This release date may be extended only by a maximum of 90 days and only for serious misconduct.

The disposition of parole is discussed in detail in Chapter 7.

Capital Punishment

"More than 3,200 people are on death row nationwide, and 13 of the 38 states with capital punishment laws have carried out executions this year [1997]" (Associated Press, 1997, p. A4). During 1995, 26 state prison systems and the federal prison system received 310 prisoners under sentence of death, although only 56 of the prisoners already on death row were executed (Snell, 1996, p. 1). Death sentences are being handed down more frequently than they are being carried out, and our country's death rows are filling up, although the national execution rate in 1997 was the highest it has been since 1957 (Associated Press, p. A4). Figure 4–2 shows the number of persons under

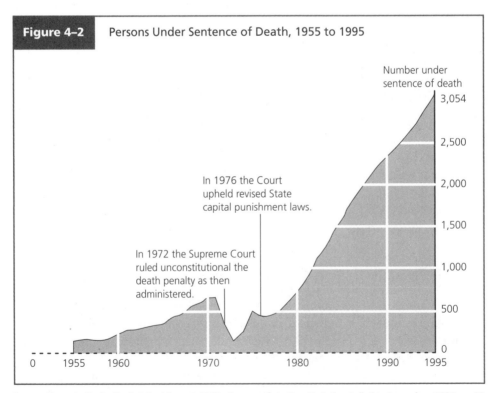

Figure 4–2   Persons Under Sentence of Death, 1955 to 1995

Number under
sentence of death

In 1976 the Court
upheld revised State
capital punishment laws.

In 1972 the Supreme Court
ruled unconstitutional the
death penalty as then
administered.

Source: Tracy L. Snell, *Capital Punishment 1995.* Bureau of Justice Statistics Bulletin, December 1996, p. 12 (NCJ-162043).

sentence of death from 1955 to 1995; Figure 4–3 shows the number of persons executed from 1930 to 1995. Table 4–6 provides a list of states having performed executions in 1995 and how many each state conducted.

Capital punishment as a sentencing option is highly controversial. Many articles have been written, both for and against the death penalty. Indeed, entire books have been devoted to the subject. The practice of sentencing criminals to death has existed for thousands of years, but it has not always gone unchallenged.

More than two centuries ago, Cesare Beccaria criticized capital punishment's usefulness on the grounds that it set a barbaric example for the crime of homicide. He found it ridiculous to punish an act of killing with an act of killing, and many today argue the very same.

In 1972, the U.S. Supreme Court found that the way capital punishment was being applied was unconstitutional and placed a moratorium on the death penalty (*Furman v. Georgia,* 1972). In this case, it was contended that the death penalty was discriminatorily applied mainly to Black offenders, while White offenders convicted of the same crime usually avoided sentences of death. The

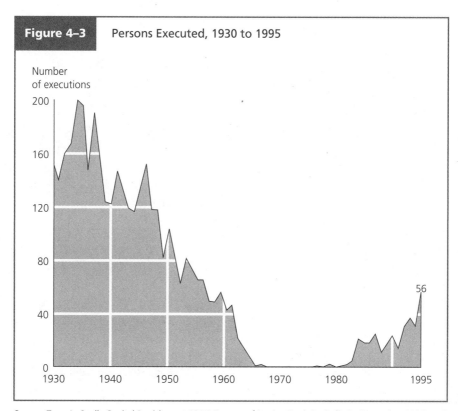

Figure 4–3   Persons Executed, 1930 to 1995

Number of executions

Source: Tracy L. Snell, *Capital Punishment 1995.* Bureau of Justice Statistics Bulletin, December 1996, p. 2 (NCJ-162043).

Table 4–6	Executions during 1995	
	Texas	19
	Missouri	6
	Illinois	5
	Virginia	5
	Florida	3
	Oklahoma	3
	Alabama	2
	Arkansas	2
	Georgia	2
	North Carolina	2
	Pennsylvania	2
	Arizona	1
	Delaware	1
	Louisiana	1
	Montana	1
	South Carolina	1
	Total	56

Source: Tracy L. Snell. *Capital Punishment 1995.* Bureau of Justice Statistics Bulletin, December 1996, p. 1 (NCJ-162043).

arbitrary and capricious manner in which capital punishment was applied was declared unconstitutional. The Court concluded in a five-to-four decision that capital punishment *as practiced* was, in fact, cruel and unusual punishment, a violation of the Eighth Amendment and therefore unconstitutional (that is, capital punishment in itself was not unconstitutional; the manner in which it was *administered* was unconstitutional).

Four years later, however, in *Gregg v. Georgia* (1976), the Court, by a seven-to-two margin, ruled on how the death penalty could be imposed without violating the Eighth Amendment, stating:

> A punishment is unconstitutionally cruel and unusual only if it violates the evolving levels of decency that define a civilized society. The death penalty today in the United States does not do that—as is proved by public opinion substantially favoring executions, by legislatures enacting death penalty statutes or refusing to repeal them, and by courts willing to sentence hundreds of murderers to death every year (Ecenbarger, 1994, p. A12).

Furman v. Georgia (1972) was the landmark case in which the Supreme Court called for a moratorium on the death penalty as practiced, ruling it as "cruel and unusual punishment." *Gregg v. Georgia* (1976) was the Supreme Court decision that ended the moratorium on the death penalty by describing how capital punishment should be imposed.

Although the *Gregg* decision declared capital punishment constitutional in crimes of murder, other cases have challenged the constitutional applicability of the death penalty where the crime was not that of murder. For example, in *Coker v. Georgia* (1977), the Supreme Court ruled that capital punishment for rape in which a life was not taken was excessive and therefore a violation of the Eighth Amendment. Also, in *Woodson v. North Carolina* (1976), although the crime for which capital punishment was sentenced was murder, it was, by statute, a mandatory sentence unaffected by either aggravating or mitigating circumstances, and for that reason, the Supreme Court ruled it unconstitutional.

McClesky v. Kemp (1987) challenged the constitutionality of the death penalty based on statistical studies that suggested Blacks convicted of murder were far more likely than Whites convicted of the same crime to receive capital punishment. The Supreme Court, however, ruled five to four that the death penalty was still a constitutional act.

Although the death penalty is a matter of great seriousness, there have been cases that can only be described as absurd. Consider, for example, the case of Mitchell Rupe, who was convicted of killing two bank tellers during a 1981 robbery in Washington state. He was given his choice of death: lethal injection or hanging. Rupe chose hanging and then went on an eating binge, ballooning to more than 400 pounds. At that point, he challenged his death sentence, claiming he'd be decapitated if he were hanged. Surprisingly, the judge agreed, stating that such an execution would indeed be cruel and unusual punishment.

Despite the Supreme Court ruling that capital punishment is constitutional, it is still opposed by many. Today's arguments denouncing the death penalty are founded not only on moral or logistic ground; they also have statistical evidence to support them.

James Q. Wilson, a criminal justice scholar and professor of political science, believes support for the death penalty fluctuates with the crime rate (Dionne, 1990, p. 181). As illustrated in Figure 4–3, the number of executions reached a high point during the mid-1930s, when crime was prevalent in communities across America. Support for capital punishment began to decline during the early 1960s, reaching an all-time low in 1966, when a Gallup poll revealed only 42 percent of Americans favored the death penalty. However, a Gallup poll conducted in August 1997 showed a shift in attitude, with 61 percent of Americans polled favoring capital punishment as the penalty for murder. Several criminal justice scholars believe this rising support of the death penalty is due to the public's *perception* that violent crime is increasing (even if data indicates a decline in the overall crime index), their disgust with the entire legal system and their belief that criminals don't serve long enough sentences (Dionne, p. 182). Capital punishment is a get-tough answer to the problems of the "soft on crime" criminal justice system.

Interestingly, the ABA recently voted for a moratorium on capital punishment, stating such penalties are administered through "a haphazard maze of unfair practices" and calling for "greater fairness and due process [for] criminal defendants" ("ABA Votes," 1997, p. A1). Similar to the central issue facing the Supreme Court in *Furman v. Georgia,* the ABA's conflict with the death penalty "should not be taken as outright opposition to capital punishment. Instead, they said they oppose the current process under which it is administered." Proponents of the moratorium claim many death penalty defendants are represented by incompetent counsel or that their defense is otherwise compromised by inadequately paid lawyers. Furthermore, according to supporters of the capital punishment moratorium ("ABA Votes," p. A9): "Hundreds of the more than 3,000 men and women on death row have no legal counsel in post-conviction appeals, which focus on possible violations of a defendants' constitutional rights. . . ."

The debate between those who support and those who oppose capital punishment centers on these basic issues: deterrence; retribution; life imprisonment, the loopholes and cost-effectiveness; disparity; the nature of the punishment as cruel and unusual; and the potential for error. Other side issues concern the age and mental fitness of those sentenced to die.

Deterrence. Proponents of capital punishment have long argued that it provides a strong deterrent to potential murderers. These supporters justify state-sanctioned killings by stating homicides are prevented when the state makes it clear that the punishment for such crimes is death. However, some critics feel this deterrent value is greatly overestimated, and that capital punishment as a crime-fighting tool is relatively useless.

> Capital punishment has not been proven to be an effective deterrent for criminal activity.

Murphy (1995, p. 11A) reports the findings of a poll of police chiefs and sheriffs throughout the country, in which most stated their belief that capital punishment was a hollow deterrent and an ineffective law enforcement tool. The same poll revealed most police chiefs and sheriffs (82 percent) believed killers did *not* weigh the possible penalties before committing the crime. Other studies back up this belief by documenting the small percentage of murderers who actually receive a capital punishment sentence. Zimring and Laurence (p. 2) note: "The actual probability that a murderer will receive a death sentence is quite low and the risk of being executed even smaller, about 1 per 1,000 killings in 1984." Cook and Slawson (1994, p. 23) report: "Recent history suggests that approximately 10 percent of the death-sentenced defendants [in North Carolina] will be executed," and Wunder (1994, p. 9) articulates: "A prisoner sentenced to death who leaves death row has only an 11 percent likelihood of leaving death row for the death chamber." The remaining 89 percent either have their sentences commuted to life imprisonment, are taken off death row for a new trial and resentencing, die prior to the execution or have their charges dropped altogether.

Several compelling arguments have been put forth which suggest execution may actually arouse the urge to kill and promote homicide through a sort of brutalization effect. Some argue that such state-sanctioned killings cheapen the value of human life and dull our society to issues concerning intentional death. Others fear the death penalty may be interpreted by some as a green light to extinguish those they feel have wronged them, a phenomenon identified as "villain identification" or "lethal vengeance."

During a debate on the crime bill in April 1994, a prominent representative told the story of the assassination attempt made on President Franklin D. Roosevelt on a 1933 trip to Miami (Schmickle and Christensen, 1994, p. A19). The assassin missed his mark, instead killing Chicago Mayor Anton Cermak. Thirty-five days later, the assassin was executed by electrocution. The representative applauded the swift response, saying: "The people in America who had seen the horror of Mayor Cermak being killed could remember, 35 days later, why the man was being executed." Today, the delay between sentencing and execution has grown so long that the public often has forgotten the horror of the crime for which the death penalty was imposed, severely hindering any deterrent effect the capital punishment might have. Snell (p. 1) states: "The persons executed in 1995 were under sentence of death an average of 11 years and 2 months."

Some argue that the person who is finally executed, five or ten years after the fact, is not always the "same" person who committed the crime. These opponents argue that people *do* mature and change, that they can still make positive contributions to society if given the chance—a chance due to life imprisonment without parole as opposed to execution. (Consider, for example, Karla Faye Tucker, executed February 3, 1998, for a double-murder she committed fifteen years earlier. Tucker's claim to have "found God" and her marriage to a prison chaplain convinced many that she had truly repented, no longer presenting a threat to society and perhaps deserving to have her death penalty commuted.) But as quickly as this oppositional argument is heard, supporters of the death penalty respond with, "What chance did the victim have? Why should the killer be allowed to live?" Faced with data that the death penalty does not deter acts of killing, supporters of capital punishment have turned to retribution to justify the execution of convicted murderers.

Retribution. Those who assign a retributionist justification to the death penalty are basically stating that murderers *deserve* to be killed. Such an argument is impossible to confirm or deny based on empirical evidence. No studies are available to support whether those who kill should or should not be killed—it is a matter of religious or philosophical principle. Murphy (p. 11A) notes: "While a majority of the police chiefs surveyed support the death penalty philosophically . . . they are also keenly aware that government spending is being cut and budgets are tight. Support must be given to programs that work."

Studies show that 87 percent of the executions performed in the United States since 1930 have been for the crime of murder, and nearly 12 percent have been for convictions of rape. These two crimes have accounted for almost 99 percent of the capital punishment sentences carried out in the last 50 years. Supporters of capital punishment point to the heinousness of these crimes as justification for the death penalty. Opponents, however, argue that the state's act of sentencing and putting to death those convicted of such crimes is actually "more calculated and cold-blooded than that of many murderers" (Zimring and Laurence, p. 3).

Life Imprisonment, the Loopholes and Cost-Effectiveness. Many opponents to capital punishment suggest life imprisonment with no chance of parole as a suitable alternative to execution. These people bolster this argument by citing the potential good the inmate might do if allowed to live, including providing restitution to the victim's family and participating in the rehabilitation of other inmates (on and off death row). Wunder (p. 10) tells the story of Wilbert Rideau, an inmate at the Louisiana State Penitentiary at Angola:

> In 1961, Rideau was sentenced to death by the electric chair. Rideau spent eleven years on death row before his sentence was commuted to life when the Supreme Court struck down Louisiana's death penalty statute. During those eleven years Rideau taught himself to write and developed a voracious appetite for books. Today, Rideau—still serving his life sentence—is the highly-respected editor of the highly-acclaimed prison magazine, the Angolite.

Supporters of the death penalty argue, however, that a sentence of life imprisonment does not always guarantee a life behind bars, and that many prisoners serving time for murder are eligible for parole after only a dozen or so years. Only when the guarantee of no parole is given do many people side with the life imprisonment alternative.

Given the relatively young age at which many murderers commit their crimes, and the likelihood these prisoners will spend many years behind bars if given a life sentence without parole, concern over the cost to warehouse these criminals has become another issue of the debate. Murphy (p. 11A) reports: "The death penalty was rated as the least cost-effective method for controlling crime. Police chiefs would rather spend their limited crime-fighting dollars on such proven measures as community policing, more police training, neighborhood watch programs and longer prison sentences."

Conflicting data exists concerning which is more expensive: housing an inmate for 50 or more years under a life sentence or covering the expenses that accompany the death penalty, such as longer investigations, additional expert testimony and postconviction appeals. Cook and Slawson (p. 23) have found: "[I]n North Carolina, it costs taxpayers $329,000 more to convict and execute a murderer than it does to convict the same person and give him or her a 20-year prison term." Consider, however, that many life sentences will extend well beyond 20 years. Schmickle and Christensen (pp. A19, A22) report: "California spends $600,000 on each prisoner it executes, much more than those it locks up for life." Capital punishment proponents estimate that at $10,000 to $20,000 a year, a 20-year-old who lives 60 years in prison would cost society more than $1 million. However, dollar estimates for executions that include the full cost of appeals are also often in the millions.

Disparity. As with sentencing in general, imposition of the death penalty has been criticized as being applied arbitrarily and unfairly. Some statistics support the claim that death sentences are not handed down equitably. These statistics focus on the race of the offender, the race of the victim, the socioeconomic status of the offender, where the crime was committed and the sex of the offender.

The financial status of the offender and the setting of the offense may play a role in whether that individual receives a death sentence. Some studies have concluded offenders able to afford private attorneys are less likely to be sentenced to death than those offenders having court-appointed representation. Another variable in determining who receives a death sentence is the location of the crime. Studies indicate that courts in large cities impose capital punishment less often than courts in rural and suburban regions.

Perhaps one of the most obvious disparities concerning the death penalty centers on the gender of the offender. Women are conspicuously absent on death row. Of the more than 3,000 prisoners under sentence of death, fewer than 2 percent are women (Snell, p. 1), even though roughly 15 percent of persons arrested for murder are women. Table 4–7 shows the number of women under sentence of death at year-end 1995 and the states where they were imprisoned. Juries in the past have appeared reluctant to sentence women to death, and the number of women on death row continues to climb slowly.

Another concern regarding disparity and the death penalty concerns not the characteristics of the defendant but rather the jury. Jury selection has become a field in itself, complete with consultants and techniques designed to choose jurors who will vote in favor of one side or the other. Such a screening process may not elicit a well-rounded jury of one's peers but rather a group of people preselected to think one way or another. As noted by Blankenship et al. (1997, p. 326): "In *Witherspoon v. Illinois* (1968), the U.S. Supreme Court allowed trial courts to exclude jurors who stated that they could not vote to impose the death penalty because they opposed its use. A plethora of research

Table 4–7	Number of Women under Sentence of Death, Year-End 1995		
State	**Total**	**White**	**Black**
Total	48	32	16
California	8	6	2
Florida	6	4	2
Texas	6	4	2
Oklahoma	5	4	1
Illinois	5	2	3
Alabama	4	3	1
Pennsylvania	4	1	3
Missouri	2	2	0
North Carolina	2	2	0
Mississippi	2	1	1
Arizona	1	1	0
Idaho	1	1	0
Tennessee	1	1	0
Nevada	1	0	1

Source: Tracy L. Snell. *Capital Punishment 1995.* Bureau of Justice Statistics Bulletin, December 1996, p. 7 (NCJ-162043).

followed that demonstrated 'death-qualified' juries are more likely than other juries to find the accused guilty and to impose a death sentence."

Furthermore, sentencing instructions are not always written clearly and concisely, leading some juries to misinterpret the law. Blankenship et al. examined jurors' ability to comprehend sentencing instructions used in death penalty cases in Tennessee (p. 326): "Several studies suggest . . . that jurors have difficulty in comprehending sentencing instructions. . . . When sentencing instructions are ambiguous or confusing, jurors may resort to 'event schemas'—that is, what they think they know about the law—during sentencing deliberations." Such misinterpretation may have dire consequences for death penalty defendants. As these authors state: "[I]n actual cases in Tennessee, death sentences may have been imposed unconstitutionally. . . . [P]oorly worded or vague or ambiguous sentencing instructions may invite precisely the arbitrary and capricious application of the death penalty that the U.S. Supreme Court sought to avoid in *Furman*."

Cruel and Unusual Punishment. History shows many brutal methods have been used to accomplish the death of a criminal, including being buried alive, flayed alive, thrown to wild animals, drawn and quartered, boiled in oil, burned,

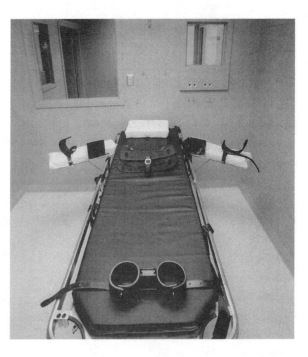

The execution chamber at Oregon State Penitentiary in Salem where Harry Charles Moore was willingly put to death by lethal injection in April 1997. Moore was the last "volunteer" for the death penalty, and opponents of capital punishment hope Oregonians will begin to oppose such executions as other inmates are led unwillingly to their deaths.

stoned, drowned, impaled, crucified, pressed to death, smothered, stretched on a rack, disemboweled and beheaded. Although today's practices seem more civilized, accounts of witnesses to executions leave one wondering if any progress has been made.

Executions in America "evolved" as states searched for more humane ways of killing its condemned—from hangings in the early years of our nation, to the first electrocution in 1890, the invention of the gas chamber in 1923, the use of a firing squad and finally the adoption of lethal injections in 1977. Table 4–8 shows the various methods of execution used by states having a death penalty.

Although lethal injection is the predominant method of execution in the United States and is often heralded as the most humane method, five of the eleven botched executions between 1979 and 1990 involved the lethal injection technique (Pittman, 1990). Such foul-ups during an execution may cause tremendous agony for the executionee and have been a major source of concern of opponents to capital punishment. Opponents are also quick to point out that very few other advanced democracies participate in the killing of their criminals. Table 4–9 illustrates the company the United States is keeping in practicing capital punishment. Ecenbarger (p. A12) claims the United States is the only country to use a variety of methods in its executions, further noting: "Indeed, the three most common American ways of death—electrocution, asphyxiation and lethal injection—are used nowhere else in the world."

Potential for Error. Debate has also erupted over the possibility of innocent people being executed. Some studies have reported instances where an

| Table 4–8 | Method of Execution, by State, 1995 | | | |

Lethal Injection		Electrocution	Lethal Gas	Hanging	Firing Squad
Arizona[a,b]	New Hampshire[a]	Alabama	Arizona[a,b]	Delaware[a,c]	Idaho[a]
Arkansas[a,d]	New Jersey	Arkansas[a,d]	California[a,e]	Montana[a]	Oklahoma[f]
California[a,e]	New Mexico	Florida	Maryland[g]	New Hampshire[a,h]	Utah[a]
Colorado	New York	Georgia	Mississippi[a,j]	Washington[a]	
Connecticut	North Carolina[a]	Kentucky	Missouri[a]		
Delaware[a,c]	Ohio[a]	Nebraska	North Carolina[a]		
Idaho[a]	Oklahoma	Ohio[a]	Wyoming[a,j]		
Illinois	Oregon	Oklahoma[f]			
Indiana	Pennsylvania	South Carolina[a]			
Kansas	South Carolina[a]	Tennessee			
Louisiana	South Dakota	Virginia			
Maryland[g]	Texas				
Mississippi[a,j]	Utah[a]				
Missouri[a]	Virginia[a]				
Montana	Washington[a]				
Nevada	Wyoming[a]				

Note: The method of execution of Federal prisoners is lethal injection, pursuant to 28 CFR, Part 26. For offenses under the Violent Crime Control and Law Enforcement Act of 1994, the method is that of the State in which the conviction took place, pursuant to 18 USC 3596.

[a]Authorizes 2 methods of execution.

[b]Arizona authorizes lethal injection for persons sentenced after 11/15/92; those sentenced before that date may select lethal injection or lethal gas.

[c]Delaware authorizes lethal injection for those whose capital offense occurred after 6/13/86; those who committed the offense before that date may select lethal injection or hanging.

[d]Arkansas authorizes lethal injection for persons committing a capital offense after 7/4/83; those who committed the offense before that date may select lethal injection or electrocution.

[e]Use of lethal gas is currently prohibited in California pending a legal challenge in Federal court.

[f]Oklahoma authorizes electrocution if lethal injection is ever held to be unconstitutional and firing squad if both lethal injection and electrocution are held unconstitutional.

[g]Maryland authorizes lethal injection for all inmates, as of 3/25/94. One inmate, convicted prior to that date, has selected lethal gas for method of execution.

[h]New Hampshire authorizes hanging only if lethal injection cannot be given.

[i]Mississippi authorizes lethal injection for those convicted after 7/1/84 and lethal gas for those convicted earlier.

[j]Wyoming authorizes lethal gas (if lethal injection is ever held to be unconstitutional.

Source: Tracy L. Snell. *Capital Punishment 1995.* Bureau of Justice Statistics Bulletin, December 1996, p. 5 (NCJ-162043).

Table 4–9	Abolitionist Countries and Countries with the Death Penalty[1]

Abolitionist Countries

The following countries have abolished capital punishment. Those marked with an asterisk (*) have abolished the death penalty for all but the most exceptional crimes (e.g., wartime crimes). Those marked with a double asterisk (**) are de facto abolitionists; they legally retain the death penalty but have had no executions in the past ten years or more.

Andorra	Djibouti**	Madagascar**	Romania
Angola	Dominican Republic	Maldives**	Rwanda**
Argentina*	Ecuador	Malta*	Samoa (Western)**
Australia	El Salvador*	Marshall Islands	San Marino
Austria	Federal Republic of Germany	Mexico*	Sao Tome & Principe
Bahrain**	Fiji*	Micronesia	Senegal**
Belgium**	Finland	Monaco	Seychelles*
Bermuda**	France	Mozambique	Slovak Republic
Bhutan**	Gambia	Namibia	Slovenia
Bolivia**	Greece	Nauru**	Solomon Islands
Brazil*	Guinea-Bissau	Nepal*	Spain*
Brunei Darussalam**	Haiti	Netherlands	Sri Lanka**
Cambodia	Honduras	New Zealand	Sweden
Canada*	Hong Kong	Nicaragua	Switzerland
Cape Verde	Hungary	Niger**	Togo**
Colombia	Iceland	Norway	Tonga**
Comoros**	Ireland	Panama	Tuvalu
Costa Rica	Israel*	Papua New Guinea**	United Kingdom*
Cote D'Ivoire**	Italy*	Paraguay*	Uruguay
Croatia	Kiribati	Peru*	Vanuato
Cyprus*	Liechtenstein	Philippines**	Vatican City State
Czech Republic	Luxembourg	Portugal	Venezuela
Denmark	Macedonia		

Total: 90 Countries & Territories

Countries with the Death Penalty

The following countries legally retain and currently practice capital punishment.

Afghanistan	Equatorial Guinea	Lebanon	Somalia
Albania	Eritrea	Lesotho	South Africa
Algeria	Estonia	Liberia	Sudan
Antigua & Barbuda	Ethiopia	Libya	Suriname
Armenia	Gabon	Lithuania	Swaziland
Azerbaydzhan	Georgia	Malawi	Syria
Bahamas	Ghana	Malaysia	Tadzhikistan
Bangladesh	Grenada	Mali	Taiwan
Barbados	Guatemala	Mauritania	Tanzania
Belarus	Guinea	Mauritius	Thailand
Belize	Guyana	Moldova	Trinidad & Tobago
Benin	India	Mongolia	Tunisia
Bosnia-Herzegovina	Indonesia	Morocco	Turkey
Botswana	Iran	Myanmar	Turkmenistan
Bulgaria	Iraq	Nigeria	Uganda
Burkina Faso	Jamaica	Oman	Ukraine
Burundi	Japan	Pakistan	United Arab Emirates
Cameroon	Jordan	Poland	United States of America
Central African Republic	Kazakhstan	Qatar	Uzbekistan
Chad	Kenya	Russia	Vietnam
Chile	Korea (North)	St. Christopher & Nevis	Yemen
China	Korea (South)	St. Lucia	Yugoslavia
Congo	Kuwait	St. Vincent & the Grenadines	Zaire
Cuba	Kyrgyzstan	Saudi Arabia	Zambia
Dominica	Laos	Sierra Leone	Zimbabwe
Egypt	Latvia	Singapore	

Total: 103 Countries & Territories

[1]As of December 1993.

Source: Amanda Wunder. "Capital Punishment, 1994." *Corrections Compendium,* November 1994, p. 16. Reprinted by permission.

innocent person was mistakenly convicted of murder. Error, however unfortunate, is inevitable in any decision, including conviction for a capital offense. Many argue that the potential for even one mistake should be reason enough to abolish capital punishment.

Addressing this potential for error, New York State Senator Dale Volker (Verhovek, 1995, p. A2) asserts: "You would hope that would never happen, but the mere fact that you might fail does not argue that you shouldn't do it." This opinion is echoed by many supporters of the death penalty, who contend the scrutiny given to each case adequately protects against errors. Some argue that to abolish the death penalty out of fear of error is to second-guess the integrity of the system or to undermine the very credibility of our criminal justice system.

Sentencing Juveniles, the Mentally Handicapped and the Mentally Ill to Death. The execution of youth and the mentally handicapped is a hotly contested issue. Many believe a lack of maturity and the inability to comprehend the nature of the capital punishment are mitigating circumstances which should disqualify an individual from receiving the death penalty. Table 4–10 shows the minimum age the various states use in determining eligibility for death sentences.

The constitutionality of juvenile executions was upheld by the Supreme Court in two 1989 decisions. *Stanford v. Kentucky* involved the sentencing of a 17-year-old for murder, and *Wilkins v. Missouri* involved a young man who, at the age of 16, killed a convenience store clerk. Both young men were minors when the crimes were committed and when they were sentenced. The Supreme Court ruled the minimum age for executions prescribed by common law was 14 and therefore, imposition of the death penalty did not constitute cruel and unusual punishment. At year-end 1995, the youngest inmate on death row was 18 (Snell, p. 1).

Several states, including Arizona and Colorado, have included statutory provisions making mentally ill or mentally retarded persons ineligible to receive death sentences. Other states, such as Texas, have no such provision and are criticized by many for engaging in such executions. The Supreme Court has also upheld the constitutionality of these executions in the ruling on the 1989 case of *Penry v. Lynaugh*. Penry, convicted of rape and murder, was evaluated as having an IQ of 54 and a mental age of six, yet the Court determined that such mental deficiencies did not preclude the sentence of death.

Stanford v. Kentucky (1989) and *Wilkins v. Missouri* (1989) are two landmark cases in which the Supreme Court upheld the constitutionality of juvenile executions. In *Penry v. Lynaugh* (1989) the Supreme Court ruled it was not unconstitutional to execute a mentally retarded convict.

A diagnosis of mental illness often eliminates the death penalty as a sentencing option for the offender. According to Wunder (p. 10): "[It is] unlawful to execute someone who is legally insane and incapable of appreciating the

Table 4–10		Minimum Age Authorized for Capital Punishment, 1995		
Age 16 or Less	**Age 17**	**Age 18**	**Age 19**	**None Specified**
Alabama (16)	Georgia	California	New York	Arizona
Arkansas (14)[a]	New Hampshire	Colorado		Idaho
Delaware (16)	North Carolina[b]	Connecticut[c]		Louisiana
Florida (16)	Texas	Federal system		Montana
Indiana (16)		Illinois		Pennsylvania
Kentucky (16)		Kansas		South Carolina
Mississippi (16)[d]		Maryland		South Dakota[e]
Missouri (16)		Nebraska		Utah
Nevada (16)		New Jersey		
Oklahoma (16)		New Mexico		
Virginia (14)[f]		Ohio		
Wyoming (16)		Oregon		
		Tennessee		
		Washington		

Note: Reporting by States reflects interpretations by State attorney general offices and may differ from previously reported ages.

[a]See Arkansas Code Ann.9-27-318(b)(1)(Repl. 1991).

[b]The age required is 17 unless the murderer was incarcerated for murder when a subsequent murder occurred; then the age may be 14.

[c]See Conn. Gen. Stat. 53a-46a(g)(1).

[d]The minimum age defined by statute is 13, but the effective age is 16 based on interpretation of a U.S. Supreme Court decision by the State attorney general's office.

[e]Juveniles may be transferred to adult court. Age can be a mitigating factor.

[f]The minimum age for transfer to adult court is 14 by statute, but the effective age for a capital sentence is 16 based on interpretation of a U.S. Supreme Court decision by the State attorney general's office.

Source: Tracy L. Snell. *Capital Punishment 1995.* Bureau of Justice Statistics Bulletin, December 1996, p. 5 (NCJ-162043).

severity of the punishment of death." A person can be under a death sentence and become insane, at which time the death sentence is commuted until the prisoner regains sanity and is able to be executed.

Whatever legal authorities exist for the perpetuation of capital punishment, the issue remains one of the most volatile in criminal justice today. Other topics gaining notice of a more positive nature are several innovations in sentencing practice throughout the country.

Sentencing Innovations

Sentencing in America has been evolving for over a century, and the reform continues today. Some states have made more progress than others, yet, as Reitz and Reitz (1994, pp. 5–6) note:

Most jurisdictions continue to operate under traditional regimes of indeterminate sentencing. Most states do not have permanently-chartered sentencing commissions or a culture of active appellate review of sentences. No state has developed an adequate plan for structuring the use of intermediate punishments. Most states allow criminal justice policy to lurch forward without systemic oversight, and without coordination of available resources.

Hopefully the most recent edition of the Criminal Justice Standards for Sentencing Law and Procedure, published by the ABA in 1994, will help guide the states still using "outmoded practices of indeterminate sentencing," as well as those in the very early stages of sentencing reform or those that have not even begun their sentencing reform. These ABA standards outline four goals each state should seek to achieve concerning sentencing reform:

1. A permanent sentencing commission or equivalent entity should be created to determine state sentencing policies.

2. The sentencing commission should draft determinate sentencing provisions, including presumptive sentences, for judges to follow unless "substantial" reasons for departure exist.

3. Presumptive sentences should be extended to apply to the entire scope of criminal sanctions, including restitution, community service, probation, home detention and incarceration.

4. All sentencing provisions should be drafted such that their execution does not exceed the available resources.

As Reitz and Reitz point out: "[The ABA standards] suggest a framework for sentencing decisions that is simpler and less mechanical than the federal guidelines and preserves greater discretion for sentencing judges." An awareness exists that the current sentencing structures still need significant improvement, while it is also clear that such innovations must be carried out under strict budgetary constraints. Several states have taken the initiative and are trying some innovative sentencing practices.

In Dakota County, Minnesota, a pilot sentencing project was implemented in October 1993, allowing three county judges to delegate some of their sentencing discretion to probation officers (Adams, 1993, p. A1). The unique approach involved only nonviolent offenders, the judges determined the length of the sanction and the probation officer decided which type of sanction was most appropriate.

Legislation in Florida during 1994 requires courts to place liens on current and future assets of convicted felons. This approach, the first of its kind in the nation, was taken in an attempt to force criminals to make restitution to their victims and to reimburse local and state governments for the costs of incarceration. It was also implemented to prevent criminals from cashing in on their crimes by selling book, television or movie rights to their criminal experience. According to the new law (Kleindienst, 1994, p.12A): "A life felony—such as sexual battery on a child under 12—will cost $15,000. If the crime caused someone's death, another $25,000 will be added. On top of that, criminals will be liable for repaying the state up to $250,000 for their imprisonment." Some are quick to point out that many criminals turn to crime because they have little or no assets, and future earnings after release from prison may be minimal. Nonetheless, the concept remains highly praised and some funds will be collected as a result of this new law.

Whenever sentencing reform efforts are undertaken and achieved, the field of corrections has a role and an interest.

Corrections' Role and Interest in Sentencing

U.S. sentencing reform has been a major contributor to the prison population explosion over the past two decades. Clearly, sentencing policy has a substantial impact on the field of corrections and affects what corrections personnel must deal with daily. The American Correctional Association's (ACA) draft policy statement concerning sentencing reads: "It is important for correctional professionals and their association to take an active role in voicing concerns and providing input into the establishment of sound sentencing policies." Perry Johnson, past ACA president, advocates having corrections professionals become more involved in sentencing reform. Those who work in corrections have unique, valuable knowledge concerning the success of various sentences and should offer their experiences as part of the effort, locally and nationally, to make sentencing more effective.

Summary

Sentencing is that stage in the criminal justice process where a judge formally determines how the convicted offender will "pay for" the crime(s) committed. It is also the stage that has the greatest impact on the field of corrections, for it is corrections personnel who must carry out the sentencing decisions.

Sentences may serve to protect society, punish the convicted criminal, obtain restitution for the victim's loss, or treat and rehabilitate offenders so they may be reintegrated into society as functional citizens. An additional goal of sentencing may be to reduce prison populations by imposing alternatives to incarceration.

A PSI, or presentence investigation, report is prepared by a probation officer and contains personal information about the offender, offense, relevant criminal information about the offender and recommendations to the judge concerning sentencing of the offender.

Plea bargaining is a preconviction agreement where a defendant enters a guilty plea in exchange for some concession from the prosecution. Plea bargaining accounts for more than 90 percent of all criminal convictions.

A variety of sentencing alternatives are available to today's judges. These options are categorized according to whether the offender is incarcerated. Intermediate (nonincarceration) sentences include fines, restitution or victim compensation, probation, home confinement or house arrest, electronic monitoring and community service. Incarceration sentences include shock incarceration, placing offenders in confinement for a set period and then releasing them to serve probation, confinement in jail and confinement in prison. Incarceration sentences are further classified as indeterminate (discretionary), determinate (limited discretionary), presumptive (limited discretionary) and mandatory (nondiscretionary) sentences.

Indeterminate sentencing is a discretionary, open-ended sentencing scheme that involves decisions by parole boards to determine release dates of inmates. Both the justice and retributivist models rejected the principles of indeterminate sentencing and called for nationwide sentencing reforms. Determinate sentencing is a limited discretionary scheme that fixes definite terms for crimes, involves no parole boards and allows the use of good time to hasten the release from a correctional institution.

Presumptive sentencing is a limited discretionary scheme that uses sentencing commissions to predetermine minimum, average and maximum terms for specific crimes and allows for the consideration of mitigating and aggravating circumstances. Mitigating circumstances weigh in favor of the defendant and serve to shorten the imposed sentence length. Aggravating circumstances, on the other hand, serve to increase the length of sentence.

Presumptive sentencing grids factor together the offender's criminal history and the severity of the conviction offense to arrive at an appropriate sentence. Mandatory sentencing is a nondiscretionary sentencing scheme that requires offenders convicted of particular crimes to receive statutorily determined incarcerative sentences. Offenders may be allowed to earn good time to achieve early release in some jurisdictions.

Issues in sentencing include disparity in sentencing, sentencing guidelines, prison overcrowding and the question of whether to incarcerate, parole reform and the controversial topic of capital punishment. The Sentencing Reform Act sought to achieve honesty, uniformity and proportionality in sentencing, although many argue the act actually contributed to increases in sentencing disparity.

The Greenwood scale attempts to predict offender dangerousness and public risk and is intended to be used as a method of selective incapacitation. Selective incapacitation seeks to keep those selected offenders predicted of future dangerousness locked behind bars while releasing nondangerous offenders on probation. Collective incapacitation seeks to impose lengthy terms of incarceration for all convicted offenders across the board, regardless of whether they are deemed a poor risk or a future danger to society.

Capital punishment as a sentencing option is a highly controversial issue that has not been proven to be an effective deterrent for criminal activity. A number of Supreme Court cases have focused on the constitutionality of capital punishment. *Furman v. Georgia* (1972) was the landmark case in which the Supreme Court called for a moratorium on the death penalty as practiced, ruling such practice as "cruel and unusual punishment." *Gregg v. Georgia* (1976) was the Supreme Court decision that ended the moratorium on the death penalty by describing how capital punishment should be imposed. *Stanford v. Kentucky* (1989) and *Wilkins v. Missouri* (1989) are two landmark cases in which the Supreme Court upheld the constitutionality of juvenile executions. In *Penry v. Lynaugh* (1989) the Supreme Court ruled it was not unconstitutional to execute a mentally retarded convict.

Discussion Questions

1. Given the history of corrections and how punishment has worked (or not worked) in the past, should today's sentencing efforts be focused on rehabilitation or retribution?

2. As a whole, is plea bargaining positive or negative? Do you think criminals assume they'll be able to "plea down" their charges, should they get caught?

3. Do you think offenders deserve to earn good time credits toward early release, after having chosen to act illegally in the free society? Why or why not?

4. How successful has the Sentencing Reform Act been in achieving its stated purposes?

5. In considering the Greenwood scale and attempts to predict an offender's future dangerousness, which is worse: a false positive or a false negative?

6. Do you believe some mandatory sentences, such as the federal laws on crack vs. powder cocaine, serve as class control structures?

7. Do you think any modifications should be made to current capital punishment practices? Do they "violate the evolving levels of decency that define a civilized society"?

8. Should age be a mitigating factor in any case?

9. What do you think about the United States practicing forms of execution used nowhere else in the world?

10. How can corrections professionals make a positive impact on today's sentencing practices?

References

"ABA Votes for Death Penalty Moratorium." (Minneapolis/St. Paul) *Star Tribune*, February 4, 1997, pp. A1, A9.

Adams, Jim. "Dakota County to Try Unique Sentencing Plan for Nonviolent Criminals." (Minneapolis/St. Paul) *Star Tribune*, October 18, 1993, pp. A1, A8.

Associated Press. "Pace of U.S. Executions Reaches a 40-Year High." (Minneapolis/St. Paul) *Star Tribune*, October 3, 1997, p. A4.

Austin, James and McVey, David. *The 1989 NCCD Prison Population Forecast: The Impact of the War on Drugs*. San Francisco: National Council on Crime and Delinquency, 1989, p. 6.

Bartollas, Clemens and Conrad, John P. *Introduction to Corrections*, 2nd ed. New York: Harper Collins Publishers, 1992.

Blankenship, Michael B.; Luginbuhl, James; Cullen, Francis T.; and Redick, William. "Jurors' Comprehension of Sentencing Instructions: A Test of the Death Penalty Process in Tennessee." *Justice Quarterly*, Vol. 14, No. 2, June 1997, pp. 325–351.

Clark, Jacob R. " 'Three-Strikes and You're Out' May Be Popular, but Some Say It's No Grand Slam." *Law Enforcement News*, February 14, 1994, p. 1.

Cook, Philip J. and Slawson, Donna B. "Death Penalty Cost Study Now Available." *Corrections Compendium*, August 1994, p. 23.

Correctional Populations in the United States, 1995. Bureau of Justice Statistics, Executive Summary, June 1997 (NCJ-163917).

Dickey, Walter J. "Evaluating Mandatory Minimums." *Overcrowded Times*, December 1993, pp. 2–3.

Dionne, E.J., Jr. "Capital Punishment Gaining Favor as Public Seeks Retribution." *Corrections Today*, August 1990, pp. 178, 180–182.

"Drug Sentences: A Chance to Reverse Mandatory Madness." (Minneapolis/St. Paul) *Star Tribune*, November 3, 1993, p. A22.

Ecenbarger, William. "A Good Kill Is Gruesomely Hard to Find." (Minneapolis/St. Paul) *Star Tribune*, July 15, 1994, p. A12.

Hayes, Hennessey D. and Geerken, Michael R. "The Idea of Selective Release." *Justice Quarterly*, Vol. 14, No. 2, June 1997, pp. 353–370.

Johnson, Perry M. "Corrections Should Take the Lead in Changing Sentencing Practices." *Corrections Today*, April 1993, pp. 52, 54–55, 130–131.

Kempinen, Cynthia. "Pennsylvania Revises Sentencing Guidelines." *Overcrowded Times*, August 1997, pp. 1, 14–18.

Kleindienst, Linda. "New Florida Law Will Impose Liens on Felons' Assets." (Ft. Lauderdale) *Sun-Sentinel*, July 1, 1994, p. 12A.

Mauer, Marc. "3 Strikes and You're Out." *Corrections Compendium*, July 1994, pp. 15–16.

McDonald, Douglas C. and Carlson, Kenneth E. "Drug Policies Causing Racial and Ethnic Differences in Federal Sentencing." *Overcrowded Times*, December 1994, pp. 1, 8–10.

"More Judges Opposing Mandatory-Minimum Sentencing." *NCJA Justice Bulletin*, September 1994, pp. 3–4, 14–15.

Murphy, Patrick V. "Death Penalty Useless: Poll of Police Chiefs Finds That Most Say Capital Punishment Is a Hollow Deterrent; They'd Choose Other Methods to Reduce Crime." *USA Today*, February 23, 1995, p. 11A.

Petersilia, Joan et al. *Granting Felons Probation*. Santa Monica, CA: Rand Corporation, 1985.

Pittman, Robert. "Electric Chair Marks a Century of Use—And It Still Seems Cruel and Unusual." (Minneapolis/St. Paul) *Star Tribune*, August 15, 1990.

Proband, Stan C. "Habitual Offender Laws Ubiquitous." *Overcrowded Times*, February 1994, p. 7.

Reitz, Kevin R. and Reitz, Curtis R. "American Bar Association to Publish New Sentencing Standards." *Overcrowded Times*, June 1994, pp. 5–6.

Schmickle, Sharon and Christensen, Jean. "Death Row: A House Divided." (Minneapolis/St. Paul) *Star Tribune*, April 17, 1994, pp. A19, A22.

Seeking Justice: Crime and Punishment in America. New York: The Edna McConnell Clark Foundation, 1995.

Singer, Richard. "Sentencing." *Crime File Study Guide*, National Institute of Justice, n.d. (NCJ-97233).

Snell, Tracy L. *Capital Punishment 1995*. Bureau of Justice Statistics Bulletin, December 1996 (NCJ-162043).

Stanley, David. 1976, p. 56. In Richard Hawkins and Geoffrey P. Alpert. *American Prison Systems: Punishment and Justice*. Englewood Cliffs, NJ: Prentice Hall, 1989, p. 123.

Thrash, Paul D. "Plea Bargaining and Justice." *Law Enforcement Technology*, September 1996, pp. 54–57.

"Tonry, Fein Debate Sentencing Policy." *Corrections Today*, October 1993, pp. 56, 58, 60, 62–63.

Verhovek, Sam Howe. "Is Death Penalty Worth the Risk?" (Minneapolis/St. Paul) *Star Tribune*, January 8, 1995, p. A2.

Wunder, Amanda. "Living on Death Row." *Corrections Compendium*, December 1994, pp. 9–21.

Yellen, David. "Little Progress in Federal Sentencing After Ten Years of Guidelines." *Overcrowded Times*, June 1997, pp. 1, 4–7.

Zimring, Franklin E. and Laurence, Michael. "Death Penalty." *Crime File Study Guide*, National Institute of Justice, n.d. (NCJ-97219).

Cases

Coker v. Georgia, 433 U.S. 584, 97 S.Ct. 2861, 53 L.Ed.2d 982 (1977).

Furman v. Georgia, 408 U.S. 238 (1972).

Gregg v. Georgia, 428 U.S. 153 (1976).

McClesky v. Kemp, 481 U.S. 279, 107 S.Ct. 1756, 95 L.Ed.2d 262 (1987).

Mistretta v. United States, 109 S.Ct. 647 (1989).

Penry v. Lynaugh, 109 S.Ct. 2934 (1989).

Stanford v. Kentucky, 109 S.Ct. 2969 (1989).

Wilkins v. Missouri, 109 S.Ct. 2969 (1989).

Witherspoon v. Illinois (1968).

Woodson v. North Carolina (1976).

5

Alternatives to Incarceration: Probation and Other Intermediate Sanctions

Do You Know

➤ What alternatives to incarceration exist?

➤ What intermediate sanctions are?

➤ What standard probation is?

➤ What day fines are and what they are based on?

➤ What forfeiture is?

➤ What restitution is?

➤ What community service is?

➤ What intensive supervision programs involve?

➤ What house arrest entails?

➤ What electronic monitoring is?

➤ What day reporting centers are?

➤ What residential community corrections includes?

➤ If any of the intermediate sanctions are perceived by offenders as being more punitive than prison sentences?

The fundamental value in the corrections continuum is that the least restrictive method should be used to manage offender behavior consistent with public safety. This principle is important regardless of whether the corrections system expands or contracts, and should guide us in how we do our jobs.

—Frank A. Hall, Director
Oregon Department of Corrections

Can You Define

alternatives to incarceration

community service

criminogenic

day fines

day reporting center

electronic monitoring

forfeiture

house arrest

intensive supervision programs

intermediate punishments

intermediate sanctions

net widening

residential community corrections

restitution

standard probation

Introduction

A wide variety of correctional options exist for those who decide what to do with our country's offenders. As stated in the chapter opening quote, the decision of which correctional method to use centers on selecting an option that balances public safety with the need to control the offender in the "least restrictive" manner. Although time behind bars is a viable and often necessary alternative, particularly for violent and predatory offenders, with a majority of states under federal court order to reduce prison and jail overcrowding, the consideration of numerous alternatives to incarceration has become a correctional necessity. As expressed by Petersilia and Deschenes (1994, p. 307), these alternatives provide "a range of sanctions that reflects the range of criminality."

➤ **Alternatives to incarceration** in jail or prison include probation, straight fines and day fines, forfeitures, restitution, community service, intensive supervision, house arrest and electronic monitoring, day reporting centers and residential community corrections. Boot camps are another alternative, discussed in Chapter 7. Parole is an option for those who have already served time in an institution, and is often administered by the same personnel who oversee probation. It is important to recognize the distinction between probation and parole. Probation avoids incarceration altogether; parole is supervision *after* a period of incarceration. Parole as a correctional option is discussed later in the text.

> Alternatives to incarceration include probation, straight fines and day fines, forfeitures, restitution, community service, intensive supervision, house arrest and electronic monitoring, day reporting centers and residential community corrections.

These alternatives are also referred to as *community-based corrections,* since the offender serves the sentence not behind bars but within the community at large. Such community-based correctional sanctions have been gaining popularity throughout the United States for the past two decades, as more and more states have sought ways to ease the burden on their overcrowded jail and prison facilities. Shilton (1992, p. 4) notes: "Since Minnesota adopted the first community corrections act ("CCA") in 1973, at least 17 other states have passed legislation."

The American Bar Association has drafted a Model Adult Community Corrections Act providing an overview of community corrections, descriptions of the sanctions within the realm of community corrections and brief discussions of program criteria and sentencing determinations. According to McCarthy and McCarthy (1997, p. 26):

This Model Act varies from earlier community corrections proposals in that it emphasizes community safety and offender accountability as well as reintegration, cost effectiveness, and the desirability of employing the least restrictive criminal sanction.

This willingness to acknowledge multiple goals is becoming a hallmark of contemporary community corrections.

Probation is usually considered the least restrictive of the alternatives to incarceration. The remaining correctional alternatives (fines, forfeitures, restitution, community service, intensive supervision, house arrest and electronic monitoring, day reporting centers and residential community corrections) constitute a continuum of increasing supervision and restriction between standard probation and incarceration and are grouped into a category known as **intermediate sanctions** or **intermediate punishments.**

> Intermediate sanctions, or intermediate punishments, refer to the continuum of increasingly restrictive correctional alternatives between standard probation and incarceration.

As noted by McCarthy and McCarthy (p. 174): "Years ago, before the term 'community corrections' came into vogue, 'alternatives to confinement' meant either *probation* or *parole*. . . ." Today, however, the community has assumed a more prominent role in the criminal justice system, evidenced by community policing programs as well as community corrections efforts. According to McCarthy and McCarthy (pp. 174–175):

> The current era of community corrections is defined by *intermediate sanctions.* The importance of intermediate sanctions is not a result of their widespread use. Although most states report that a variety of intermediate sanctions are in use in their jurisdictions, the vast majority of offenders continue to be placed on probation or parole rather than assigned to the "newer" intermediate punishments. . . . Yet recognition of the values underlying intermediate sanctions is essential to an understanding of contemporary community corrections. Those values are best understood by an examination of the objectives of intermediate sanctions . . . : to protect the community, to create a continuum of correctional punishments that provide a better fit between the offender and his or her sanction than can be achieved by probation or prison, and to reduce correctional costs.

According to O'Leary and Raleigh (1994, p. 3), criminal sanctions must be determined by considering both punishment dimensions and risk dimensions. From Figure 5–1 it is seen how intermediate sanctions fill a broad niche in the correctional continuum, ranging from moderate punishment objectives for those posing a low risk to the community to high punishment objectives for those posing a high risk to community safety.

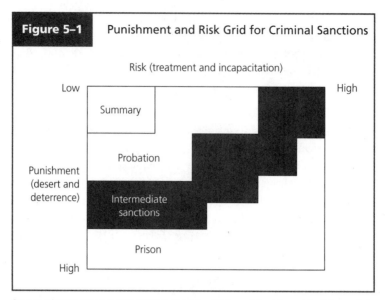

Figure 5–1 Punishment and Risk Grid for Criminal Sanctions

Source: Vincent O'Leary and William Raleigh. "Risk and Punishment in Intermediate Sanctions." *Community Corrections Report,* 1 (7), September/October 1994, p. 3. Belinda J. McCarthy and Bernard J. McCarthy. Community-Based Corrections, 3rd ed., p. 31. Copyright © 1997 by Wadsworth Publishing Company. Reprinted by permission.

This chapter begins with a discussion of probation as the least restrictive correctional alternative to incarceration. It then moves up the continuum, presenting intermediate sanctions of increasing restrictions and supervision: day fines, forfeitures, restitution, community service, intensive supervision programs (ISPs), house arrest, electronic monitoring, day reporting centers and residential community corrections.

Probation

The use of probation as an alternative to incarceration is an American innovation. It is more widely used here than anywhere else in the world. The father of probation, Boston's John Augustus, was concerned about drunks being put in jail to dry out. He felt they needed help, so he took them into his home as an act of compassion. Since Augustus's successful supervision and reformation of the nation's first probationer in 1841, probation has become the most commonly used alternative in the country, with nearly four times as many offenders serving probation as are sentenced to our nation's prisons.

The first state to pass a probation statute, authorizing the hiring of probation officers and the organization of a formal probation program, was Massachusetts in 1878. The National Probation Act, passed in 1925, allowed federal district courts outside the nation's capital to hire probation officers. By 1927, juvenile probation services were available in every state, but it was not until 1957 that every state had adopted similar programs for adult offenders.

Standard probation is the least restrictive and most common of the correctional alternatives. At year-end 1995, nearly 3.1 million adults were on probation in the United States (*Correctional Populations,* 1997, p. 1). The American Correctional Association defines probation as:

> [A] judicial disposition (sentencing alternative) that establishes the defendant's legal status under which his freedom in the community is continued subject to the supervision by a probation organization and subject to conditions imposed by the court.

➤ **Standard probation** is the least restrictive and most common of the correctional alternatives, allowing the offender to remain in the community under the limited supervision of a probation agency and subject to conditions set by the court.

Who Gets Probation?

Consideration of the presentence investigation (PSI) report and state statutes help guide the court in determining whether an offender is a suitable candidate for probation. Some statutes involving mandatory sentences, discussed in Chapter 4, preclude the option of probation for certain offenders, though exceptions do exist. For example, probation is generally not granted to those convicted of murder, sex crimes or other serious assaults and is frequently denied to those with a serious prior record. Probation is most commonly granted to first-time offenders, property offenders, low-risk offenders and nonviolent offenders and involves minimal levels of supervision and restriction. People who receive standard probation are those for whom jail sentences were most likely never a serious option.

One indication of the low level of supervision associated with standard probation is that it may or may not involve personal contacts between the probation officer and the offender. In many jurisdictions, standard probation involves no supervision of any kind or very minimal telephone or mail contacts with clients.

Many probation officers' caseloads are so massive it is virtually impossible for them to maintain regular face-to-face contact with all their clients. Probation officers in Los Angeles are expected to handle as many as 1,000 offenders at a time (Labaton, 1990). A recent survey (Wunder, 1995, pp. 9–15) indicates probation officers in 24 states handle an average monthly caseload in excess of 100 cases. Using statistics from several sources, Petersilia (1997, p. 3) states: "Given an estimated 50,000 probation employees in 1994, and given that 23 percent of them (11,500 officers) were supervising about 2.9 million adult probationers, the average caseload that year was 258 adult offenders per line officer. This contrasts with what many believe to be the ideal caseload of 30 adult probationers per line officer."

Clearly such caseloads prevent much active supervision on the part of probation officers and, indeed, this is anticipated by the courts when sentencing individuals to such limited supervision. Often, the probationer is simply instructed on the conditions of the probation and advised that any violations of such conditions will result in the revocation of probation and the imposition of a more serious sanction by the court. If the offender maintains a law-abiding lifestyle, adheres to the conditions of the probation and avoids any future contacts with the police, it is possible the probation officer and probationer will not meet again until the conclusion of the probation period.

Most probation officers classify their caseload into high-, medium- and low-risk offenders. They concentrate on the high-risk offenders rather than those at low risk of violating probation.

Conditions of Probation

The conditions of probation may vary depending on the nature of the offense and the goals sought by the court. Although the overall purpose of probation is to help offenders maintain law-abiding behavior, some courts are more treatment-oriented in assigning conditions while other courts are more punitive.

One universal condition for all probationers is to obey the law. Other conditions suggested by the American Bar Association (1981, p. 45) as appropriate for certain offenders under particular circumstances are

- Cooperating with a program of supervision.
- Meeting family responsibilities.
- Maintaining steady employment or engaging or refraining from engaging in a specific employment or occupation.
- Pursuing prescribed educational or vocational training.
- Undergoing available medical or psychiatric treatment.
- Maintaining residence in a prescribed area or in a special facility established for or available to persons on probation.
- Refraining from consorting with certain types of people or frequenting certain types of places.
- Making restitution of the fruits of crime or reparation for loss or damage caused thereby.

A frequent condition of probation is that clients undergo periodic or random testing for use of drugs and/or alcohol. Such clients may be required to also sign a document stating that they will refrain from eating any foods containing poppy seeds because poppy seeds can cause a person to test positive for drugs.

Certain activities may require the probation officer's permission, such as traveling outside the county or state. Furthermore, many probation sentences carry the condition of regular maintenance fee payments to offset administrative costs or drug and alcohol screening costs. Late payment of these fees may lead to increased contact between the probation officer and probationer, or worse, to probation revocation. These conditions constitute a set of rules the probationer must follow. Failure to adhere to any of the conditions of probation results in a *technical violation,* which may lead to the judge revoking probation. Breaking the law is also grounds for probation revocation.

Two important U.S. Supreme Court decisions have involved the due process rights of offenders during probation revocation procedures. In *Mempa v. Rhay* (1968), the Court ruled that the Sixth Amendment right to counsel may be extended to probationers during revocation hearings. In a later case, *Gagnon v. Scarpelli* (1973), the Court ruled that the right to counsel in revocation hearings should be decided case by case and not automatically extended in all cases. Many have criticized the court's decision, claiming the case-by-case determination of the right to counsel is unjustly arbitrary.

Having probation revoked is a serious matter for the offender, as it will most likely mean serving time behind bars. Probation revocation is also a serious matter for the correctional system, as it means a failed attempt at an alternative to incarceration.

Functions of Probation

When John Augustus assumed responsibility for the first probationer, his focus was not on public safety or the punishment and deterrence of unlawful behavior. His mission was to rehabilitate the convicted offender. Today, although rehabilitation remains a hoped-for result of probation and every other correctional option, other goals are being sought from probation, including punishment, deterrence, community reintegration and crime control.

Granted, the punishment value of standard probation is not particularly harsh. Many probationers are allowed to live in their own homes, drive their cars, go to work and exist in the community as normal citizens. If the probationer adheres to all the conditions of the probation and avoids the criminal activity that led to probation in the first place, life is basically the same as it is for the citizens in the community who are not on probation. However, this freedom is not absolute for probationers. The ever-present possibility exists of having that freedom revoked. Activities such as traveling out of state on a whim or not showing up for work could result in a period of incarceration for the probationer.

The deterrent value of probation is frequently debated by criminal justice experts. Recidivism rates are the most commonly used measure in determining whether a correctional program is effective, yet experts often disagree on what rate constitutes an acceptable level or demonstrates the success of a program. Some studies have shown that standard probation correlates to higher rates of recidivism than other, more intensively supervised programs. Others show probation to be a far more successful correctional alternative than incarceration in jails or prisons.

A third goal sought from probation is community reintegration. Some criminal justice scholars argue that jail and prison environments are highly
➤ **criminogenic,** meaning they contribute to the criminal attitude and outlook of those confined within their walls. Keeping first-time and nonviolent offenders out of these institutions through probation may prevent their becoming more hardened criminals. Furthermore, potential hardships endured by the offender's family are avoided by allowing the offender to remain at home, employed and able to continue supporting the family. Some programs place a great deal of emphasis on the connection between probation and the community. According to Lurigio and Martin (1997, p. 104):

> . . . the Chicago-based Cook County Adult Probation Department (CCAPD) has worked to create a partnership between probation, nonprofit service providers and community organizations. The goals of these efforts are to strengthen probation's links with the community; to provide a full-service model of probation; to protect the community; to hold offenders accountable for their crimes; and to help probationers reintegrate into the community as productive, law-abiding citizens.

The goal of crime control is an obvious objective of any correctional option. How well probation achieves this goal remains uncertain, especially when considering the heavy caseload of most probation officers and their limited ability to closely monitor those on standard probation.

Probation Officers and Approaches to Supervision

The role of the probation officer, or PO, has changed. Probationers used to come in to see the probation officer as a therapist or counselor. Today the emphasis is on supervision and surveillance (for example, drug testing). The various functions of probation illustrate the dichotomy of the job performed daily by probation officers across the nation: to control offenders and to provide social services. The style chosen by the probation officer depends on how the job is perceived. Some probation professionals see themselves as enforcers and stress control over probationers' activities and maintaining public safety. Other probation officers regard themselves more as social workers, seeking ways to counsel and rehabilitate probationers. Furthermore, as noted by McCarthy and McCarthy (p. 103): "The administrative structure of U.S. probation services reflects the decentralized and fragmented character of contemporary corrections. As with other forms of corrections, there does not appear to be a single model or standard for organizing or operating a probation agency."

In many jurisdictions the task of supervising both probationers and parolees falls upon one agency. As noted by Camp and Camp (1997, p. 180):

"Of the total 2,931 probation and parole offices operated by agencies, 812, or 27.7%, were probation offices, 486, or 16.6%, were parole offices, and 1,633, or 55.7% were probation and parole offices." Supporters of the combined system state limited resources are better conserved when probation and parole are handled within the same agency. Opponents, however, argue that probationers, particularly first-time offenders, need to be kept separate from parolees.

Some states allow private agencies to become involved in administering probation services. Florida, for example, has the Salvation Army Misdemeanant Program (SAMP), begun in 1974, which handles 90 percent of the state's probation caseload. Other states are allowing private investigators to prepare PSI reports for the court, thereby easing some of the workload on the overburdened probation agencies.

Probation as Part of an Intermediate Sanction

Probation is presently the fastest growing form of penal sanction, the number of probation sentences having doubled during the last decade (Reeves, 1992, p. 76). In fact, many criminal justice professionals agree with Barajas (1993, p. 30) that: "The most severe and potentially dangerous correctional crowding is not in prisons or jails but in probation." Unfortunately, although use of probation as a correctional sanction has doubled, funding has not kept pace. The result has been that probation officers, saddled with unmanageable caseloads, have had to limit the amount of supervision and services provided to probationers. According to Reeves (p. 76): "This has fostered a demand for the development of effective, truly diversionary community-based programs," known as intermediate sanctions. Often, standard probation is combined with forms of intermediate punishment to increase the level of punishment and restriction imposed on the offender.

Intermediate Sanctions

The Center for Effective Public Policy has produced *The Intermediate Sanctions Handbook*, describing intermediate sanctions as a combination of programs and policies and defining intermediate sanctions as (1993, p. 18):

A. A range of sanctioning options that permit the crafting of sentences to respond to:
- the particular circumstances of the offender and the offense; and
- the outcomes desired in the case.

B. A coherent policy to guide their use that:
- specifies goals and outcomes;

- specifies the place and purpose of every sanction within the total range; and
- ensures that the sanctions are used for the offenders for whom they were created.

Petersilia and Deschenes (p. 307) explain intermediate punishments as:

> . . . sanctions that are tougher than traditional probation but less stringent—and expensive—than imprisonment. Intermediate sanctions offer an alternative to the "either/or" sentencing policy found in many states, that is, either prison or probation. They are predicated on the assumption that the two extremes of punishment—prison and probation—are both used excessively, with a near vacuum of useful punishments in between.

Use of the term *intermediate sanctions* has been criticized as contributing to negative public perceptions about how the criminal justice system is handling convicted criminals. A common interpretation of the word *intermediate* is "halfway" or "partial," and the public often takes such intermediate *sanctions* to mean that criminals are getting off easy by receiving only partial punishment. In this decade of the get-tough philosophy toward crime and criminals, people want society's lawbreakers locked away behind bars. The public often thinks anything but prison is soft on crime. However, most taxpayers are unaware of the substantial costs required to lock up these offenders. An examination of the average annual cost of intermediate sanction and treatment options in California (Petersilia, 1995, p. 6) revealed the following:

- One year in a state prison $21,800
- One year in a county jail $19,700
- Boot camp (1/3 prison time; 2/3 ISP) $11,700
- House arrest with electronic monitoring $3,500–$8,500
- Routine supervision probation/parole $200–$2,000
- Outpatient substance abuse treatment $2,900

Considering the staggering number of adults serving correctional sentences in the communities of America—over three million (Taxman, 1995, p. 46)—the cost to house all of them in prisons or jails is prohibitively high. Furthermore, most criminal justice scholars believe incarceration is not always the best or most appropriate correctional alternative, particularly for first-time and nonviolent offenders.

Castle (1991, p. 2) notes: "When the Edna McConnell Clark Foundation asked hundreds of Alabama residents how they would sentence 20 convicted offenders, virtually all thought prison appropriate. After some explanation of costs and alternatives, the same people 'resentenced' most of these cases to intermediate sanctions. This demonstrates that an educated public will support alternative sanctions."

It must be understood that these alternatives to incarceration are intended to divert nonviolent, prison-bound offenders from serving their sentence behind bars, thereby freeing up critically scarce prison space for those truly violent individuals who *should* be locked up as a matter of public safety. Unfortunately, judges have been known to divert non–prison-bound offenders, those for whom simple, standard probation is appropriate, into intermediate sanctions programs. This displacement of offenders from regular probation into more restrictive and supervised alternatives contributes to the phenomenon known as *net widening*.

➤   **Net widening** is a negative consequence of diversion attempts, typically describing what happens when "more diversion 'to' other programs or agencies has occurred than true diversion 'away' from the system" (Drowns and Hess, 1995, p. 58). Net widening results in misallocation of resources. With offenders in programs who don't need that much supervision, the result is that the programs are watered down for those who do need them. Unfortunately, all intermediate sanctions are vulnerable to net widening. Some judges cannot deny the "benefit" of program XYZ to certain individuals or a class of persons (for example, kids from single parent households), even if it is not the most appropriate alternative, thus widening the net.

A further complication of intermediate sanctions is noted by Harland (1993, p. 35): "Increasing the range of choices expands the prospect of improving sanctioning practices, but it also makes the task of deciding on the 'right' response to criminal conduct an even more complex and challenging proposition than in the past." Table 5–1 shows which states' probation and parole agencies provide each of the various intermediate sanctions to offenders.

Day fines, forfeitures and restitution exist at the low end of control and restriction on the intermediate sanctions continuum and, when combined with probation, have been shown to provide an effective level of punishment for many offenders. Community service, intensive supervision, house arrest and electronic monitoring are sanctions further up the correctional continuum. Day reporting centers and residential community corrections programs exist at the most restrictive end of the correctional continuum, one step away from incarceration.

Day Fines

➤   **Day fines,** so named because they are based on the offender's daily income, differ from traditional, straight fines in that the judge determines the amount of the fine based not only on the nature of the crime but also on the offender's ability to pay. Day fines have been common sentences in northern European countries for many years. Their use in the United States, however, has only recently received attention. Traditionally, fine sentences in this country have been based on the nature of the crime alone, imposing severe financial penalties on low-income offenders but presenting little or no financial punishment for wealthy offenders.

Table 5–1 Programs Administered by Probation & Parole Agencies on January 1, 1997

State	Type of Agency	Programs						
		Resti-tution	Cmty. Service	Intensive Supv.	Supv. Home Rel.	Group Homes	Halfway Houses	Shock Prob.
Alabama	Prob. & Parole	□		□	□			
Alaska	Probation	□	□				□	
	Parole	□	□	□			□	NA
Arizona	Probation	□	□	□			□	□
	Parole		□		□			NA
Arkansas	Probation	□	□	□	□			□
	Parole		□	□	□			NA
California	Probation	□	□	□	□			□
	Parole	□	□	□			□	NA
Colorado	Probation	□	□	□				
	Parole	□		□	□			NA
Connecticut	Probation	□	□	□				
	Parole		□	□			□	NA
Delaware	Prob. & Parole		□	□	□		□	
Dist. of Col.	Probation	□	□	□	□			
	Parole			□				NA
Florida	Prob. & Parole	□	□	□	□			
Georgia	Probation	□	□	□	□		□	□
	Parole	□						NA
Hawaii	Probation			□				
	Parole			□		□	□	NA
Idaho	Prob. & Parole	□	□	□	□		□	□
Illinois	Probation	□	□	□	□			
	Parole			□	□			NA
Indiana	Probation	□			□			
	Parole			□				NA
Iowa	Prob. & Parole	□	□	□			□	□
Kansas	Probation	□	□	□	□			
	Parole	□	□				□	NA
Kentucky	Prob. & Parole	□	□	□	□		□	□
Louisiana	Probation	□			□		□	
	Parole	□		□	□		□	NA
Maine	Prob. & Parole	□						
Maryland	Probation	□	□	□				
	Parole	□		□	□			NA
Massachusetts	Probation	□	□	□	□			
	Parole			□				NA
Michigan	Parole	□	□	□	□		□	NA
Minnesota	Probation	□	□	□	□			
	Parole			□	□			NA
Mississippi	Probation	□	□		□			□
	Parole	□	□		□			NA

Table 5–1   Continued

State	Type of Agency	Resti-tution	Cmty. Service	Intensive Supv.	Supv. Home Rel.	Group Homes	Halfway Houses	Shock Prob.
Missouri	Prob. & Parole	✓	✓	✓	✓		✓	✓
Montana	Prob. & Parole			✓	✓			✓
Nebraska	Probation		✓	✓	✓			
	Parole		✓	✓	✓			NA
Nevada	Prob. & Parole	✓	✓	✓	✓			
New Hampshire	Prob. & Parole	✓	✓	✓	✓			✓
New Jersey	Probation	✓	✓	✓	✓			
	Parole	✓		✓				NA
New Mexico	Prob. & Parole	✓	✓	✓			✓	
New York	Parole		✓	✓				NA
North Carolina	Prob. & Parole			✓	✓			✓
North Dakota	Prob. & Parole	✓	✓	✓	✓			
Ohio	Prob. & Parole							✓
Oklahoma	Prob. & Parole	✓	✓	✓				
Oregon	Prob. & Parole	✓	✓	✓	✓		✓	
Pennsylvania[1]	Parole		✓	✓	✓		✓	NA
Rhode Island	Probation		✓	✓				
	Parole				✓			NA
South Carolina	Prob. & Parole	✓	✓	✓	✓			
South Dakota	Parole	✓	✓	✓				NA
Tennessee	Probation		✓	✓	✓		✓	✓
	Parole			✓				NA
Texas	Probation	✓	✓	✓	✓	✓	✓	✓
	Parole	✓	✓	✓	✓		✓	NA
Utah	Probation	✓	✓	✓			✓	
	Parole	✓		✓			✓	NA
Vermont	Prob. & Parole				✓			
Virginia[2]	Probation	✓	✓	✓	✓		✓	✓
	Parole		✓	✓	✓		✓	NA
Washington	Probation	✓	✓		✓			
	Parole	✓	✓		✓			NA
West Virginia	Probation	✓	✓	✓	✓			
	Parole				✓			NA
Wisconsin	Prob. & Parole	✓	✓	✓	✓		✓	
Wyoming	Prob. & Parole	✓		✓	✓			✓
Federal[3]	Probation	✓	✓	✓	✓			
	Parole		✓	✓	✓			NA

✓ = yes
[1] Halfway houses are offered in connection with the DOC.   [2] Halfway houses are offered but contracted out.   [3] As of 1/1/96.
Source: Adapted from George M. Camp and Camille Graham Camp, *The Corrections Yearbook, 1997*. South Salem, NY: The Criminal Justice Institute; 1997, pp.166–167.

> Day fines involve financial penalties based not only on the nature of the crime but also on the offender's ability to pay.

Until recently, the use of fines has suffered as an American correctional alternative due to widespread skepticism concerning the courts' ability to make fixed fine amounts work for a wide range of offenders. Fines set too high would go unpaid by poor offenders; fines set too low served no punishment or deterrent value for wealthy offenders. According to Winterfield and Hillsman (1993, p. 2):

> [T]he day fine approach consists of a simple, two-step process. First, the court uses a "unit scale" or "benchmark" to sentence the offender to a certain number of day-fine units . . . according to the gravity of the offense and without regard to income. . . . The value of each unit is then set at a percentage of the offender's daily income, and the total fine amount is determined by simple multiplication.

A pilot study on day fines conducted in Staten Island, New York, revealed the following consequences of the day fine approach (Winterfield and Hillsman, pp. 3, 5):

- After introduction of the day fine, average fines imposed for penal law offenses rose 25 percent.
- The total amount of the fines imposed by the court in penal law cases increased by 14 percent during the pilot year (from $82,060 to $93,856).
- Despite the substantial increase in average fine amounts, introduction of the day-fine system did not undermine the court's high collection rates.
- While the introduction of day fines did not diminish the court's success in collecting fines, day fines did take longer to collect than fixed fines prior to the experiment.
- The day-fine program significantly reduced the number of arrest warrants issued for failure to appear at postsentence hearings.

Hillsman (1990, p. 4) notes several other appealing aspects of using fines as correctional options:

> Fines are unmistakably punitive; they can deprive offenders of ill-gotten gain; they are relatively inexpensive to administer; and they provide revenue to cover such things as the cost of collection or compensation to victims. Furthermore, recent research has tended to support their deterrent impact: fines are associated with lower rates of recidivism than either probation or jail for offenders with equivalent criminal records and current offenses.

The use of day fines as an intermediate sanction, while not particularly severe, does appear to provide effective punishment and deterrence. Day fines also allow the offender to remain in the community, able to tend to family needs.

Forfeitures

Forfeitures, like day fines, impose a financial penalty on the offender. Unlike fines, however, which are currency-based penalties, forfeitures involve the loss of property. They are usually an add-on punishment, not a sole alternative. In most cases, forfeiture is part of another sentence or used in conjunction with another sentence. According to Green (1994, p. 14): "Civil forfeiture is a legal concept by which property that is illegally used or acquired is seized for forfeiture to the government upon an initial showing of probable cause—without the necessity of a criminal conviction for the underlying crime."

> **Forfeiture** is a financial penalty involving the seizure of the offender's illegally used or acquired property or assets.

Civil forfeiture has been particularly useful in drug trafficking cases due to the abundance of assets needed to run a successful trafficking organization, including vehicles, aircraft, stash houses and cash. Often, these seized assets are auctioned off, the proceeds going to the law enforcement agency that handled the case, to charitable organizations or to victims of crime.

According to Green (p. 14): "[T]he concept of forfeiture dates back to Biblical times . . . [h]owever, the application of forfeiture to separate criminals from

As displayed prominently on its side, this vehicle was taken from a convicted drug dealer and is being used to help fight the war on drugs. Such seizures send a message to dealers and would-be dealers that, when caught, they'll lose not only their freedom but also the property used in committing their crimes.

the profits of their crimes is fairly recent." In fact, the rise in use of asset forfeiture programs around the country seems to coincide with the heating up of the war on drugs initiated during the Reagan administration (Martin, 1993, p. 46).

The constitutionality of forfeitures has been at issue in several Supreme Court cases, particularly where the proportionality of the forfeiture is in question. The Eighth Amendment prohibits the imposition of "excessive fines," and the courts must be certain that the value of the assets to be forfeited does not exceed the severity of the crime (Kime, 1993, p. 12). To facilitate this endeavor, the Department of Justice, in collaboration with the DEA, FBI and other law enforcement agencies, has drafted a "National Code of Professional Conduct for Asset Forfeiture," detailing the standards of conduct for agencies involved in asset seizure (Green, p. 15). Although asset forfeiture remains under attack by the media and members of the judiciary as an infringement upon the constitutional rights of U.S. citizens, it remains a successful method for "attacking the economics of criminal profits" (Green, p. 14).

Restitution

➤ **Restitution** is traditionally reimbursement of the victim by the offender, most often with money though occasionally with services. Since the 1970s, restitution has become an increasingly common criminal sanction, often imposed as a condition of probation, although it appears to be used more frequently with juvenile offenders than with adult offenders.

> Restitution is an increasingly common sanction whereby the offender reimburses the victim, most often with money.

Often cited as the first of such efforts, Minnesota's Restitution Program, begun in 1972, gave convicted property offenders the chance to shorten or avoid a prison sentence by working to pay restitution to their victim. Courts in other states began following Minnesota's lead and devising their own restitution programs. Restitution as a sentencing option is now being used in nearly every state.

The goal of such financial penalties is not only to reform or rehabilitate the offender but to punish and deter future illegal conduct and to provide compensation, or retribution, to the victim. Restitution also appears to be a popular sentencing alternative among criminal justice professionals, victims and offenders alike, although for different reasons. Many criminal justice professionals consider restitution an effective sentencing alternative, believing it to be more severe and punitive than either fines or standard probation. Restitution is a popular sentencing option from the victims' point of view for the obvious reason that it provides compensation for their loss. It is also hoped that effective restitution programs may increase the number of crimes reported, as victims see the direct benefits of getting involved. Offenders also benefit from restitution, as they avoid cell time and are allowed to remain in the community to serve their sentences while maintaining their jobs and supporting their families.

Although the case for restitution is strong in theory, Weitekamp (1992, p. 6) notes several shortcomings in actually implementing restitution programs. He argues restitution is

- Applied unsystematically in many jurisdictions.
- Used only for property offenders and first-time offenders.
- Rarely used purely as an *alternative* to incarceration, instead being used as an add-on to probation or parole.
- Applied to favor White and middle-class offenders.
- Frequently used only for juvenile offenders and not adults.

In addition, restitution amounts are usually a fraction of the actual loss. Furthermore, Weitekamp argues, little research has been done to evaluate the effects of restitution on recidivism rates.

Another problem associated with restitution is its enforcement. According to McCarthy and McCarthy (p. 170): "Because restitution is frequently a condition of probation or parole, the enforcement of restitution conditions through revocation proceedings is a common problem. Imprisonment for debt is a violation of the U.S. Constitution." This situation effectively ties many probation officers' hands when it comes to offenders who choose not to adhere to the restitution schedule.

Despite the apparent shortcomings in its application, restitution continues to grow in its use as an intermediate sanction. Closely related to the concept of victim restitution is the idea of community service, where the offender makes reparations not to a specific victim but to the community at large.

Community Service

Like restitution, community service is often imposed not as a sole penalty but rather as a condition of probation, enhancing the level of punishment and restriction of the sentence. **Community service** generally involves public service for nonprofit organizations. It usually involves the performance of *unpaid* labor by the offender in an attempt to pay a debt to society, with assignments ranging from cleaning litter from roadsides and performing lawn maintenance on government facilities, to janitorial work in churches or schools, to building parks and playgrounds, repairing public housing and serving as a volunteer in a hospital or rehab center. Occasionally, the community service duties are related to the offense, for example, drug offenders performing volunteer services in a drug treatment facility.

These five offenders are part of a court-ordered cleanup crew performing community service in Hollywood, California.

Community service involves unpaid labor by the offender in an attempt to pay a debt to society.

Also like restitution, community service as a sentencing option has been gaining popularity over the past two decades. Community service as a formal sentencing option originated in 1966 in California, when judges sought ways to punish indigent women who violated traffic and parking laws (McDonald, 1990). Fines were an unreasonable alternative, since these women were too poor to pay them, but a jail sentence imposed too great a hardship on their families. The sentencing option of community service gradually expanded to include other types of offenders, including males, juveniles and those convicted of more serious crimes.

In 1978, the Vera Institute of Justice in New York City implemented a community service sentencing project in the Bronx Criminal Court to study the effectiveness of unpaid labor as punishment. The project focused on chronic property offenders and sought to punish, not to rehabilitate. According to McDonald (p. 8): "Within a few years, the project had spread to all the city's major misdemeanor courts. In 1989, community service orders (CSOs) became a fully-institutionalized feature of the city's criminal justice system." Evaluation of the project showed mixed results. The communities undoubtedly benefited from the thousands of hours of free labor, and the city government saved money by not having to jail some offenders. It was also found that "[t]hose given a CSO were rearrested at exactly the same rate as similar persons sent to jail for short terms and then released" (McDonald, p. 8). This result was not of major concern, however, considering the goal of the project was not to rehabilitate offenders.

Other community service programs have sprung up around the country and have met with varying levels of success. The sentencing to service (STS) program in Minnesota has been growing since 1986, with most of the state counties now participating (Adams, 1992, p. B7). Offenders perform a variety of services, including cleaning up illegally dumped tires, mowing lawns and painting park buildings. One supervisor of a cleanup crew believes offenders sentenced to the STS program benefit more from their sentence than do offenders left sitting in jail, and the offenders apparently agree. Offenders with families appreciate being able to stay home; offenders released from jail to work receive lesser sentences; and other offenders actually come out of the program feeling good about the work they have performed.

Today, community service remains an underused sentencing option, with only a small fraction of the courts imposing it with any regularity. Although community service programs may ease the burden on jail and prison crowding, such programs require a significant amount of planning and staffing. Additional difficulty is encountered in locating agencies willing to accept felons as volunteers (Hudson and Galaway, 1990, p. 73). Nonetheless, community service is increasing in acceptance.

Intensive Supervision Programs (ISPs)

Intensive supervision programs, also called intensive supervised probation or ISP, have been called the "heart of the intermediate sanction program" (Lemov, 1992, p. 139). As the name implies, this correctional alternative uses a greater degree of supervision and restriction than does standard probation and places "an overriding emphasis on offender control and surveillance rather than treatment" (Fulton and Stone, 1992, p. 80). Petersilia and Turner (1993a, p. 2) note the distinction between two types of ISPs:

1. *Diversion* ISPs function as a "front door" mechanism to limit the number of offenders entering prison. Lower risk offenders are diverted into an ISP as a substitute for a prison term.

2. *Enhancement* ISPs select offenders already sentenced to probation (or parole) who have either shown evidence of failure under standard probation or parole programs or who have committed more serious offenses than those typically supervised under standard probation.

ISPs attempt to reduce prison crowding by diverting low-risk offenders and expanding the range of correctional options to ensure more serious offenders do not slip through the cracks of standard probation. One objective of ISPs is to enhance efforts to protect the public via closer monitoring of offenders released to serve their sentences in the community (Petersilia and Turner, 1991, p. 20).

Various reports place typical officer caseloads between 10 and 50 for ISPs, compared to the hundreds of clients handled by officers under standard probation practices. Fewer cases obviously correlate to a greater amount of time and supervision allowed for each individual probationer. Although no one specific model exists for ISPs, common elements found in the various programs across the country include

- Frequent personal contact between the offender and probation officer, allowed for by smaller caseloads (for example, several times a week at the offender's home or work).
- Strict enforcement of conditions such as curfews through frequent home visits.
- Random, unannounced drug and alcohol testing.
- Payment of victim restitution and performance of community service.
- Requirement to hold a job and provide proof (weekly paycheck stubs).
- Possible use of house arrest and electronic monitoring.
- Participation in treatment programs, education classes and so on.
- Routine checks of local and state arrest records.

➤ **Intensive supervision programs** (ISPs) emphasize offender control and surveillance by using frequent contacts between the probation officer and the offender, strict enforcement of conditions, random drug and alcohol testing, fulfillment of restitution and community service obligations, mandatory employment, house arrest and electronic monitoring, programs to help offenders "better" themselves (treatment programs, education classes) and regular checks of local and state arrest records.

ISPs have been gaining popularity as an intermediate sanction since the late 1970s. By 1990, jurisdictions in every state had implemented some form of ISP. Georgia's ISP, often cited as being one of the most stringent and best known programs in the country, includes the following requirements:

- Five face-to-face contacts each week.
- 132 hours of mandatory community service.
- Mandatory curfew.
- Mandatory employment.
- Weekly checks of local arrest records.
- Automatic notification of arrest elsewhere via the State Crime Information Network Listing.
- Routine, unannounced alcohol and drug testing.

Clearly, such programs provide a greater degree of offender supervision than standard probation, which often involves little or no personal contacts between the probation officer and the probationer.

ISPs have reportedly been successful in achieving some of their goals, such as enhanced levels of offender surveillance and the provision of effective intermediate sanctions (Petersilia and Turner, 1993a, p. 5). However, ISPs have fallen short of several other goals. Many jurisdictions adopted ISPs believing they would reduce recidivism rates by rehabilitating offenders and would reduce overall costs to the correctional system. Yet several studies have shown these intensive supervision programs have not always met such expectations. A Rand study reveals it is often difficult for agencies to establish and maintain effective ISPs (Bennett, 1995, p. 86). The study also concludes: "[T]here is some indication that ISP makes offenders likelier to participate in treatment and that treatment participation is associated with lower recidivism. The evaluation also shows, however, that ISP by itself seldom achieves other things—reduced recidivism, reduced prison populations, lower costs—that it is widely believed to achieve" (Petersilia and Turner, 1993b, p. 6). Additionally, "generating community support for funding of offender treatment programs is a major hurdle" ("Intermediate Sanctions," 1993, p. 3).

A report issued by the National Institute of Justice ("Intensive Supervision," 1993, p. 7) states: "Intensive supervision probation/parole (ISP) programs may not reduce offender recidivism rates more than regular probation or prison and in fact could increase prison populations in the long run," leading to higher overall costs to the correctional system. Furthermore, "because of the intense supervision, ISP was found to be costlier than routine probation and roughly comparable in cost to prison" ("Intermediate Sanctions," p. 4). Interestingly, it is theorized that the very intensive supervision which defines ISPs "may be so stringent as to increase the probability that crimes (and technical violations) will be detected and an arrest made" (Petersilia and Turner, 1993a, p. 5).

Another complication for ISPs has proven to be offender selection (Fulton and Stone, p. 82). Faulty selection of offenders for ISP—for example, sentencing a high-risk offender who should be incarcerated to intensive supervision in an attempt to reduce prison admissions—increases the likelihood that the ISP method of correction will fail.

Despite the mixed results, ISPs, like other intermediate sanctions, continue to grow in their use across the nation as a correctional alternative. However, Petersilia and Turner (1993a, p. 9) caution: "If jurisdictions are primarily interested in reducing recidivism, prison crowding, and system costs, ISP programs as currently structured may not meet all their expectations. . . . If jurisdictions target objectives based more on intermediate sanctions principles, ISP's hold promise."

House Arrest

House arrest, also known as home confinement or home detention, is an intermediate sanction "one step up from intensive supervision in terms of the severity of the punishment" (Whitehead, 1992, p. 156). However, the distinction between intensive supervision programs and house arrest is often blurred, as both sanctions involve many of the same conditions. Used with those juveniles and adults whose crimes are more serious and for whom the court and probation officer have determined enhanced supervision and restriction are necessary, **house arrest** requires the offender to remain within the confines of the home during specified times and to adhere to a strict curfew. Additional conditions, such as restrictions on visitors and the prohibition of drug or alcohol use, vary by program (Baumer and Maxfield, 1991, p. 4). The offender is normally allowed to leave only for work and reasons such as grocery shopping, community service assignments and doctor appointments.

> House arrest requires offenders to stay home during specified times and to adhere to a strict curfew. Restrictions may be placed on visitors and the use of drugs and alcohol.

House arrest as a criminal penalty has existed for thousands of years and has been used to confine a variety of transgressors, including such well-known people as St. Paul the Apostle, Galileo and Lenin. As a sanction in the United States, house arrest was first used in 1971 by the city of St. Louis to confine juvenile offenders. Home detention programs began spreading around the country as a means to relieve prison crowding and as a way of handling certain "special needs" offenders, such as pregnant women until the birth of the baby. It wasn't until 1983, however, when Florida passed the Correctional Reform Act, that house arrest was implemented as an intermediate sanction anywhere statewide. At the time, the cost of home confinement in Florida was about 10 percent of the cost of imprisonment.

According to Bennett (p. 88): "At least two jurisdictions, Alabama and Florida, have had large numbers of offenders in such a program. Although the research has not been rigorous, the general findings about house arrest have been positive." Joan Petersilia, a researcher for the Rand Corporation, evaluated house arrest as an intermediate sanction and compiled a list of advantages and disadvantages (1985, pp. 2–4).

Advantages of house arrest include the potential cost-effectiveness of such programs; the social benefits of allowing the offender to keep a job, avoid the breakup of family networks and escape the stigma associated with going to prison; the responsiveness and flexibility of the program to meet local and offender needs; and the ease with which such programs can be implemented.

Disadvantages and criticisms of house arrest include the potential for such programs to widen the net of social control by allowing judges to sentence those for whom routine probation with minimal supervision is appropriate to more intense supervision under house arrest; the potential to narrow the net of social control by allowing those who should be sentenced to prison to serve their time at home under house arrest; the possibility that attempts to rehabilitate the offender will dwindle as the focus shifts primarily to offender surveillance; the fact that house arrest is intrusive and possibly illegal, with numerous court cases having already been decided regarding the constitutionality of such sanctions; the potential for race and class bias to enter into participant selection, as house arrest requires that the offender has a place to live, and if electronic monitoring is to be used, the offender must have a telephone; and the possibility that house arrest compromises public safety, as several instances have occurred in which house arrestees have broken their curfew and committed violent crimes.

While allowing cost savings on the one hand, by keeping the offender at home, house arrest programs can also be very labor intensive (Baer and Klein-Saffran, 1990, p. 30), resulting in less savings than initially appears. Maximum caseloads may be similar to those found in intensive supervision programs because of the constant need of the probation officer to check up on the offender. However, the success of house arrest programs has been bolstered by the use of electronic monitoring devices, which not only enhance the level of supervision directed toward each offender but also allow probation officers to handle slightly larger caseloads.

Electronic Monitoring

➤ **Electronic monitoring** (EM) uses telemetry devices to supervise an offender's whereabouts. First used in the United States in the early 1960s to monitor

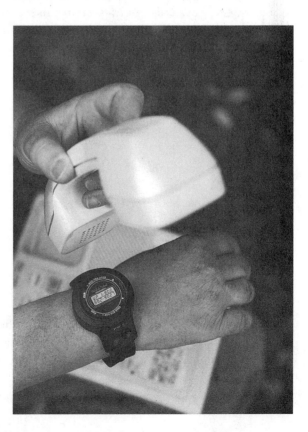

An electronic monitoring bracelet worn on an offender's wrist. Signals from the wristband are transmitted over the phone lines to ensure offenders are where they are supposed to be.

mental patients and certain parolees, electronic monitoring has been paired with house arrest to create an intermediate sanction which is now used in every state in the nation. According to Lilly (1995, p. 112), it is estimated more than 70,000 offenders nationwide are supervised via electronic monitoring. Whitehead (p. 156) notes: "Rather than a sanction, [electronic monitoring] is a means of enforcing the curfew component of intensive supervision or the more stringent restrictions of house arrest." Goss (1990, p. 80) states succinctly: "[EM] is not a program itself—it is a tool that makes the home incarceration program work." House arrest can be labor intensive, requiring the frequent monitoring of offenders through a combination of telephone contacts and field visits. The application of electronic monitoring equipment to house arrest programs automates much of the monitoring that would otherwise be conducted manually by probation officers.

> Electronic monitoring uses telemetry devices to keep track of an offender's whereabouts and is commonly used in conjunction with house arrest.

Two basic types of electronic monitoring systems are currently used: (1) passive, or programmed contact, systems and (2) active, or radio frequency, systems. Both systems use a transmitter bracelet securely placed around the offender's ankle or wrist and a piece of equipment connected to the offender's phone line. Passive monitoring systems call the offender's home at random times and direct the offender to insert the transmitter into the verifier connected to the phone. Additionally, a recording of the offender's voice may be taken during the setup phase of the monitoring system to create a "voice print," which can then be compared to the voice of the person responding to the random call. This is another way to verify the presence of the offender at home.

Active monitoring, also called radio frequency monitoring, uses a continuous signal from the transmitter bracelet to an attachment on the telephone. Most active monitoring systems have a range around 150 feet, effectively tethering the offender to the immediate confines of the house. If the offender moves beyond the range of the equipment during a curfew period, the continuous signal is broken and an alarm is sent to the monitoring agency.

The technology of monitoring equipment continues to advance, simplifying the entire process for both the probation officer and the offender. Papy (1994, p. 132) notes: "New units combine cellular technology, pager technology, drive-by options and video technology. . . . Cellular technology allows offenders without phone service to participate in electronic monitoring programs, and . . . [a] new mobile unit allows supervising officers to check on offenders and hold a two-way conversation with them without ever having to leave their vehicles."

Papy (p. 132) goes on to explain how the rapid expansion of such technology has led at least one state to devise certification rules for monitoring systems: "In June 1991, Ohio began codifying its law governing electronically monitored house arrest, certification of monitoring devices and establishment of a device fund. Many other jurisdictions have followed Ohio's lead."

If the offender attempts to remove or tamper with the transmitter bracelet, a signal is sent to the monitoring agency. Penalties vary for tampering with the transmitter and breaking the conditions of confinement, although revocation of probation and incarceration in jail or prison remain a likely consequence.

Despite the apparent benefits of this technology, there are a number of criticisms of electronic monitoring. Perhaps most important is that offenders can figure out how to beat the system. Defective equipment and signal interference compromise offender supervision and may place the community at significant risk. McCarthy and McCarthy (p. 215) state: "Incompatible phone lines provide perhaps the most widespread challenge. Unreliable power supplies and the sensitivity of tamper alarms are continuing issues." Furthermore, locations close to radio stations, faulty telephone lines, call-waiting features, power surges and computer downtime can all interfere with electronic monitoring. As noted by Christianson (1995, p. 3): "Two recently decided civil cases involved offenders under supervision in the community who somehow 'beat' their monitoring system and subsequently committed murder." Such instances have caused EM to lose popularity as an alternative.

Some critics argue that the price tag on monitoring systems is too high to be considered a cost-effective alternative to incarceration, yet many EM programs now have the offenders paying monthly fees to cover their own supervision. However, this practice raises other criticisms concerning legal issues and constitutional guarantees. A monograph published by the Bureau of Justice Assistance (BJA) (*Electronic Monitoring*, 1989, p. 5) states: "A principal legal concern of any electronic monitoring application, irrespective of design, is that the technology allows the state to intrude into an offender's home, an action severely restricted by law." Consequently, opponents of electronic monitoring have attempted to raise challenges regarding violations of the Fourth Amendment's right to privacy and protection from unreasonable searches and seizures, the Fifth Amendment's right against self-incrimination, the Eighth Amendment's protection against cruel and unusual punishment and the Fourteenth Amendment's Equal Protection Clause. So far, the courts have upheld the constitutionality of electronic monitoring but caution that conditions imposed on offenders must be

- Related to the protection of society and/or the rehabilitation of the offender (*Port v. Templar*).

- Clear (*Panko v. McCauley*).
- Reasonable (*State v. Smith*).
- Constitutional (*Sobell v. Reed*) (*Electronic Monitoring*, p. 5).

In spite of the potential technical difficulties and legal challenges, electronic monitoring continues to be used. Although typically used for nonviolent first offenders such as those convicted of drunk driving or petty theft, Papy (p. 134) notes: "Some agencies recently have added drug and sex offenders to electronic monitoring programs, and judges are beginning to impose electronic monitoring in domestic violence cases."

As one judge found, when he voluntarily submitted to a week of house arrest with electronic monitoring, the home can be an unpleasant place when you're required to stay there for any length of time (Abrahamson, 1991, p. 76). A correctional alternative that also uses increased levels of surveillance but gets the offenders out of the home is the day reporting center.

Day Reporting Centers

➤ **Day reporting centers,** or DRCs, are nonresidential locations at which offenders must appear daily. They were first used in the United States during the 1970s for juvenile offenders and deinstitutionalized mentally ill persons (McCarthy and McCarthy, p. 221). The first adult day reporting center in the United States started in 1986 in Massachusetts and was originally used as an early release option for incarcerated offenders (Larivee, 1990, p. 84). Today's day reporting centers serve as an alternative to sending both juvenile and adult offenders to jail or prison.

Until the early 1990s, the growth and acceptance of day reporting centers as a sentencing alternative was slow. However, by 1995, more than 100 DRCs were operating in 22 states (Parent et al., 1995, p. 3). McCarthy and McCarthy (p. 221) note:

> The rapid growth of DRCs in the 1990s seems to be a result of the search for different organizational strategies for the provision of community sanctions as well as an effort to provide innovative programs. DRCs are facilities that offer surveillance, treatment programs, and other services to offenders on community release. . . .
>
> The programs are designed to protect the community, while saving money and providing a punishment more onerous than traditional probation but less severe than incarceration.

The emphasis at day reporting centers is on helping offenders get jobs, but a variety of counseling and treatment programs are often also available (Table 5–2). Offenders not only participate in programs at these centers but also work out a schedule with a staff member, detailing the remainder of their day outside the center. Gowdy (1993, p. 5) states:

Table 5–2	Types and Locations of Services Offered by Day Reporting Centers			
			Location of Service	
Type of Service	**Percent of DRCs That Provide Services**	**At DRC**	**Elsewhere**	**Both**
Job-seeking skills (N = 53)	98%	79%	13%	8%
Drug abuse education (N = 52)	96	69	17	14
Group counseling (N = 51)	96	80	12	8
Job placement services (N = 50)	93	62	34	4
Education (N = 49)	93	55	31	14
Drug treatment (N = 48)	92	31	54	15
Life skills training (N = 49)	91	92	6	2
Individual counseling (N = 47)	89	72	17	11
Transitional housing (N = 32)	63	13	81	6
Recreation and leisure (N = 31)	60	74	16	10

Source: Dale Parent, Jim Byrne, Vered Tsarfaty, Laura Valade and Julie Esselman. *Day Reporting Centers.* Washington, DC: National Institute of Justice, 1995, p. 13.

Reports from 13 centers in the United States and 1 in Canada indicate that generally in these programs offenders must not only physically report to their centers daily but also provide a schedule of planned activities and participate in designated activities. In addition, offenders must call the centers by phone throughout the day; they can also expect random phone checks by center staff both during the day and at home following curfew. In some programs, offenders must contact their respective centers an average of 60 times weekly and, in all but one, take random drug tests.

Larivee (pp. 84–86) tells how a day reporting center in Massachusetts works:

An offender placed in the center lives at home while remaining under the jurisdiction of a correctional administrator. He or she reports to the center daily—usually in the late afternoon or early evening—and completes a 24-hour itinerary.

The itineraries, prepared with case managers, list when and where the offenders will be the following day and how they will get from place to place. Offenders must call the center at least twice a day, and they receive two calls a day from the center verifying their whereabouts. They are randomly tested for drug and alcohol use at least twice each week.

While in the program, inmates either work or go to school, and they regularly participate in treatment programming, usually in the evening. Each offender gives at least four hours a week to a community service assignment and adheres to a curfew.

> Day reporting centers are nonresidential locations at which offenders must appear daily to participate in programmed activities and to work out a schedule detailing their activities outside the center. Offenders are also required to maintain frequent phone communications with center staff and to submit to random drug testing.

In addition to the standard educational and drug abuse treatment programming, the Cook County (Illinois) sheriff's department's day reporting center provides AIDS prevention, stress management and nutritional education programs (Turnbaugh, 1995).

A National Institute of Justice survey compiled the following composite of common characteristics among the nation's DRCs (Parent et al., p. 40):

- Accepts primarily male offenders who are on probation or have violated conditions, who abuse alcohol and other drugs, and who pose a low risk to the community.
- Is open five days a week with a program duration of about five months.
- Handles less than 100 offenders at any given time.
- Maintains a strict level of surveillance and requires more contacts with offenders than other forms of community supervision.
- Directs successful offenders through three, sometimes four, phases, with increasingly less stringent requirements as progress is made.
- Requires five weekly on-site contacts during the most intensive phase, and monitors offenders off-site through telephone and field contacts and electronic surveillance nearly 70 hours per week.
- Tests offenders for drug use at least five times each month during the most intensive phase.
- Provides numerous services on-site to address clients' employment, education, and counseling needs; refers offenders off-site for drug-abuse treatment.
- Requires offenders to perform community service.
- Has one line staff for every seven offenders, and has a relatively low staff turnover.
- Costs about $20 per day, per offender.

Parent et al. (p. 40) also note: "Private programs differ from this composite in that they provide more services, have fewer staff and higher staff turnover, are slightly larger and more expensive, and recruit more offenders released early from jail or prison."

Clearly, being sentenced to report to a day reporting center is a restrictive, highly controlled sentencing option. For those offenders for whom live-in sanctions are more appropriate, residential community corrections are available—an alternative just a step away from incarceration.

Residential Community Corrections

Residential community corrections take many forms, including halfway houses, prerelease centers, transition centers, work furlough and community work centers, community treatment centers and restitution centers. Residents may live either part-time or full-time at such centers, depending on other conditions set forth by the court. These residential programs provide a semisecure correctional environment within the community while addressing the dual objectives of community protection and offender reintegration.

➤ **Residential community corrections** fall just short of actual incarceration and may take many forms. Residents may live either part-time or full-time at the center, depending on conditions set forth by the court.

According to McCarthy and McCarthy (p. 238): "The precise origin of halfway houses is unknown. Some writers suggest that they grew out of early acts of Christian charity." These authors also suggest the halfway house may have evolved from Sir Walter Crofton's Irish system stating (p. 238):

> This system of penal servitude provided for incarceration in a maximum security prison followed by work in the free community and residence in an intermediate institution. This intermediate institution, with its emphasis on work in the community and preparing the offender for release, seems to be the most direct forerunner of the contemporary halfway house.

McCarthy (1992, p. 174) notes: "Diversity is the essence of community residential centers. . . . Unlike other forms of intermediate punishments, no uniform model exists regarding how these programs should be organized or run. The programs vary in degree of supervision and services provided but they may impose considerable restrictions on the liberty of the offenders residing in them." McCarthy goes on to state (p. 175):

> In recent years the halfway house concept has been expanded to include a full range of services to the entire criminal justice system. They accommodate pretrial offenders unable to make bail, persons on probation who require close supervision, inmates assigned to work release, prereleasees and parolees, and more recently, as an intermediate sanction for offenders who violate the terms of their probation and parole.

McCarthy and McCarthy (p. 235) elaborate on this diversity:

The type of population served varies from community to community and from halfway house to halfway house, depending upon the characteristics of the specific program and the services the halfway house provides. Some halfway houses are administered by correctional agencies and accept only offenders as residents. Others, especially those that provide special treatment programs for alcoholics, drug abusers, or persons with mental health problems, accept individuals referred from social service agencies and self-referrals as well as offenders. Still others focus the majority of their efforts on nonoffenders and accept criminal justice clients only occasionally. Programs that accept both offenders and nonoffenders are often administered by public health or welfare agencies or by private organizations.

Of the more than 900 residential community corrections centers operating in the United States, over 90 percent are privately administered (Camp and Camp, 1995, p. 64). The average capacity of residential community corrections centers is 25 residents, although some facilities house only 6 residents while others can take up to 140 residents.

As noted, these types of centers may be used as an alternative to sending an offender to jail or prison or may be a transitional stop for offenders just released from incarceration, to determine if they are ready to return to society. Although the details may vary greatly between different community residential facilities, one common philosophy shared by all goes back to the chapter opening quote and the concept of the least restrictive alternative. It is presumed that many "offenders can be punished justly and effectively in a community setting"

After years of watching the same offenders come and go through New York City's jails, prison chaplain Roberto Rodriguez decided to create a halfway house by refurbishing a run-down, three-story building over his basement church in Bedford-Stuyvesant, one of Brooklyn's poorest neighborhoods. Reverend Rodriguez helps former inmates and addicts dry out, train for jobs and renew themselves spiritually. Here, residents at the Good News Regeneration House say grace before dinner.

(McCarthy, p. 176), and community residential centers provide such a place for nondangerous offenders and those requiring more supervision than occurs under house arrest.

As McCarthy (p. 177) points out, the goals of community residential centers include the following:

- To assist in the reintegration of offenders.
- To reduce or ease overcrowding in jails or prisons.
- To reduce correctional costs by providing a cost-effective intermediate sanction.
- To provide an appropriate setting for the treatment of substance abuse problems.

In the context of this chapter, community residential centers serve as a last stop before incarceration and are the most restrictive intermediate sanction available. This sanction may also be combined with other intermediate sanctions, such as restitution, community service and day reporting centers to further expand the level of supervision and enhance the structure and discipline afforded to each offender. Other types of community residential corrections programs will be discussed in future chapters, as they relate to release from jail and prison.

As with many intermediate sanctions, residential community corrections have not yet achieved their full potential as a correctional alternative. McCarthy (p. 190) states: "Community residential centers represent a promising, yet underutilized, resource in the search for effective and cost-efficient intermediate punishments." One reason it is difficult to establish residential correctional programs is cost. Per capita costs are very high, almost as high as incarceration.

Another factor is community opposition—the *"Not In My Back Yard"* (NIMBY) syndrome. McCarthy and McCarthy (p. 253) note: "[A]lthough no research has indicated that the establishment of a halfway house in any way reduces neighborhood security or leads to higher crime rates, the public's fear of such occurrences is real and pervasive. It appears that most citizens are extremely reluctant to have a halfway house established in their own residential area."

Some programs, however, have successfully overcome this strong opposition by the community. One such program is the Griffin Diversion Center in Griffin, Georgia. Established in the early 1970s, the center has "earned high praise from the community, in part because the director and staff aggressively built relationships with judges and the local business community" (*Seeking Justice*, 1995, p. 40). James Fletcher, former director of the center, states: "Work, education and the community are the foundation of this program," as shown by the following description:

> Residents work eight hours a day, take care of all the Center's maintenance, perform community service on weekends, attend classes or counseling sessions in the evening and submit to regular drug testing. They also participate in sports tournaments and organize food and clothing drives. Residents are

considered valuable workers by area businesses, and the program has faced virtually no resistance from its neighbors.

Rand Study

Intermediate sanctions have often come under attack by those who claim offenders are being let off easy due to prison overcrowding and judges' reluctance to incarcerate all but the most dangerous criminals. A study by the Rand Corporation reveals, however, that many offenders do not perceive such intermediate sanctions as cakewalk sentences. The study examined how both inmates and correctional personnel ranked the severity of several criminal sanctions. The results support what many proponents of intermediate sanctions have said all along: "It is no longer necessary to equate criminal punishment solely with prison" (Petersilia and Deschenes, p. 306).

Figures 5–2 and 5–3 illustrate some of the Rand study findings regarding the perception of sanction severity and the ranking of equivalent punishments, respectively.

It is interesting to note that inmate and corrections staff responses were very similar, often running parallel in Figure 5–2. Inmates, as a group, ranked five

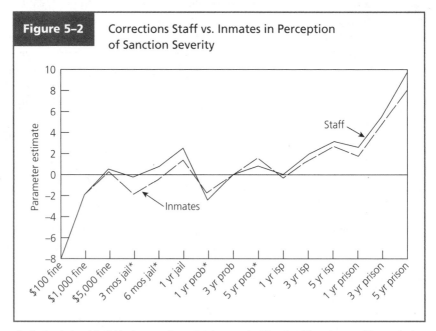

Figure 5–2   Corrections Staff vs. Inmates in Perception of Sanction Severity

*Indicates tests of individual parameter estimates are significantly different, $p > .05$, comparing inmates and staff. Model chi-square difference = 40.4, $df = 15$.

Source: Joan Petersilia and Elizabeth Piper Deschenes. "Perceptions of Punishment: Inmates and Staff Rank the Severity of Prison Versus Intermediate Sanctions." *The Prison Journal,* Vol. 74, No. 3, September 1994, p. 321. Copyright © 1994, Pennsylvania Prison Society. Reprinted by permission of Sage Publications, Inc.

years of intensive supervision probation as more severe than a year in prison, with three years of intensive supervision probation about equal to a year in prison. In fact, an earlier study (Petersilia and Deschenes, p. 310) revealed the following:

> Oregon implemented an intensive supervision probation (ISP) program in 1989, and selected nonviolent offenders were given the choice of either serving a prison term or returning to the community to participate in ISP, which incorporated drug testing, mandatory employment, and frequent home visits by the probation officer. During the first year, about a third of the offenders given the option of participating in ISP chose prison instead.

Gowdy (p. 5) echoes: "Evidence also suggests that the offenders themselves viewed ISP's as more punitive and restrictive of freedom than prison." A separate survey of 128 convicted felons also revealed that 75 percent of the offenders thought a stiff fine or serious probation sanction was more punitive than three months of incarceration (Spelman, 1995).

Several studies reveal that inmates often consider intermediate sanctions such as ISPs to be more punitive than prison sentences.

Figure 5–3	Inmate and Staff Ranking of Equivalent Punishments	

	Inmates	Staff
Least serious		
Group #1	$100 fine	$100 fine
Group #2	$1,000 fine 3 months jail* 1 yr probation	$1,000 fine 1 yr probation
Group #3	6 months jail 3 yr probation 1 yr intensive probation $5,000 fine	3 months jail* 6 months jail 3 yr probation 1 yr intensive probation $5,000 fine
Group #4	3 yr intensive probation 1 yr jail 5 yr probation* 1 yr prison	3 yr intensive probation 1 yr jail 5 yr intensive probation* 1 yr prison
Most serious		
Group #5	5 yr intensive probation	
Group #6	3 yr prison	3 yr prison
Group #7	5 yr prison	5 yr prison

Note: Each group statistically significant from another group. *Indicates differences in sanctions are included in the groups.
Source: Joan Petersilia and Elizabeth Piper Deschenes. "Perceptions of Punishment: Inmates and Staff Rank the Severity of Prison Versus Intermediate Sanctions." *The Prison Journal,* Vol. 74, No. 3, September 1994, p. 321. Copyright © 1994, Pennsylvania Prison Society. Reprinted by permission of Sage Publications, Inc.

Table 5–3	Comparison of Perceived Relative Severity of Criminal Sanctions, in Increasing Order of Severity (Citizens vs. Inmates/Staff)

Penalty	Citizen Perception of Severity[a]	Inmates/Staff Perception of Severity[b]
$1,000 fine	1	1
$5,000 fine	2	6
1 year of probation	3	2
3 years of probation	4	4
1 year of ISP	5	5
6 months of incarceration	6	3
3 years of ISP	7	7
1 year of incarceration	8	8
3 years of incarceration	9	9
5 years of incarceration	10	10

Source: [a]Adapted from Joan Petersilia and Elizabeth Piper Deschenes. "Perceptions of Punishment: Inmates and Staff Rank the Severity of Prison Versus Intermediate Sanctions." *The Prison Journal,* Vol. 74, No. 3, September 1994, p. 321. [b]Adapted from Robert Harlow, John Darley and Paul Robinson. "The Severity of Intermediate Penal Sanctions: A Psychophysical Scaling Approach for Obtaining Community Perceptions." *Journal of Quantitative Criminology,* Vol. 11, No. 1, 1995, p. 85.

Harlow et al. (1995, p. 85) surveyed citizens in New Jersey on the perceived severity of criminal sanctions, the results of which are compared to the Rand study results of inmate and correctional staff perceptions (see Table 5–3). The various sanctions are ranked according to increasing perceived severity. Note that citizens' perceptions coincide with those of inmates and staff at both extremes. A $1,000 fine is viewed as the least punitive. Three years of intensive supervision probation is seen as quite severe, followed by one year in prison and three years in prison, with five years in prison perceived as the most punitive sanction, relative to the other sanctions provided. In the middle of the relative severity continuum, however, citizen perception less closely matches that of inmates and correctional staff, providing perhaps some insight as to why the public may often think of intermediate sanctions as letting offenders off easy. For instance, inmates and correctional staff consider six months of incarceration *less* severe than three years of probation or one year of ISP, whereas citizens perceive six months of incarceration as *more* severe than either of the two nonincarcerative alternatives.

The Rand study indicates that intermediate sanctions *do* fulfill a punitive function and some are considered by inmates and correctional staff as more

Table 5–4	Proposed Ratios of Prison to Intermediate Sanctions			
Type of Sanction	**Minnesota**	**Louisiana**	**Pennsylvania**	**United States Sentencing Commission**
Jail	1:1	1:1	1:1	1:1
Intensive supervision probation	1:3	1:5.3	1:1	1:3
Home confinement	NA	1:5.3	1:1	1:2
Standard probation	1:5	NA	not permitted	not permitted
Community service	NA	1:320 hrs	not permitted	not permitted
Inpatient treatment	NA	1:5.3	1:1	1:1

Note: Ratios represent months in prison to months in intermediate sanction.
Source: Joan Petersilia and Elizabeth Piper Deschenes. "Perceptions of Punishment: Inmates and Staff Rank the Severity of Prison Versus Intermediate Sanctions." *The Prison Journal,* Vol. 74, No. 3, September 1994, p. 325.Copyright © 1994, Pennsylvania Prison Society. Reprinted by permission of Sage Publications, Inc.

punitive than prison. Some states, as well as the U.S. Sentencing Commission, have developed proposed ratios of prison to certain intermediate sanctions, shown in Table 5–4.

Note that Pennsylvania's proposed system allows one year of prison to be substituted with one year of ISP or a year of home confinement, whereas the U.S. Sentencing Commission has proposed three years of ISP for every year of prison and two years of home confinement for every year of prison. Obviously, debate remains concerning how much of an intermediate sanction equals a specific period of incarceration, but many states are now recognizing that sentences other than prison terms do have punitive value.

Special Needs Offenders and Intermediate Sanctions

Certain populations have special needs and require special consideration when it comes to intermediate sanctions. According to Knapp (1994, p. 4):

> Women are more likely than men to commit property or drug offenses and less likely to commit violent offenses. They are less likely to have prior felony records. They are more likely to suffer from substance abuse, to be involved in dysfunctional dependent relationships with criminally-involved spouses, to obtain support from public assistance, and to be a custodial parent. They are less likely to respond positively to confrontational correctional programs and more likely to respond positively to nurturing programs.

Unfortunately, as Knapp points out, such programs are quite rare, although several jurisdictions around the country are now involved in policy planning for female offenders. Female offenders are discussed at length in Chapter 8.

Another population that requires special consideration are chemically dependent offenders. Note that the last sanction listed in Table 5–4 is inpatient treatment. As the link between drugs and crime became more apparent, many advocated treatment programs for persons convicted of street crimes when it was demonstrated that the offender was drug-dependent. Thus was created the Treatment Alternative to Street Crime, or TASC. The approach was to force an addict to submit to treatment and apply criminal sanctions only if the offender failed to comply with the conditions of the treatment.

The first TASC program opened in 1972 in Wilmington, Delaware, providing "pretrial diversion for opiate addicts with nonviolent criminal charges who were identified in jail by urine tests and interviews" (*Treatment Alternatives*, 1992, p. 5). Other TASC programs were implemented in more than 50 cities across the nation during the 1970s, and although federal funding for such programs was withdrawn in 1982, system participants have maintained fiscal support for these projects. Addicted offenders are included as a special needs group in Chapter 10.

Summary

Alternatives to incarceration include probation, straight fines and day fines, forfeitures, restitution, community service, intensive supervision, house arrest and electronic monitoring, day reporting centers and residential community corrections. Intermediate sanctions, or intermediate punishments, refer to the continuum of increasingly restrictive correctional alternatives between standard probation and incarceration.

Standard probation is the least restrictive and most common of the correctional alternatives, allowing the offender to remain in the community under the limited supervision of a probation agency and subject to conditions set by the court. Day fines involve financial penalties based not only on the nature of the crime but also on the offender's ability to pay. Forfeiture is a financial penalty involving the seizure of the offender's illegally used or acquired property or assets. Restitution is an increasingly common sanction whereby the offender reimburses the victim, most often with money.

Community service involves unpaid labor by the offender in an attempt to pay a debt to society. Intensive supervision programs (ISPs) emphasize offender control and surveillance by using frequent contacts between the probation officer and the offender, strict enforcement of conditions, random drug and alcohol testing, fulfillment of restitution and community service obligations, mandatory employment, house arrest and electronic monitoring, programs to help offenders "better" themselves (treatment programs, education classes) and regular checks of local and state arrest records. House arrest requires offenders to stay home during specified times and to adhere to a strict curfew. Restrictions may be placed on visitors and the use of drugs and alcohol. Electronic monitoring uses telemetry devices to keep track of an offender's whereabouts and is commonly used in conjunction with house arrest.

Day reporting centers are nonresidential locations at which offenders must appear daily to participate in programmed activities and to work out a schedule detailing their activities outside the center. Offenders are also required to maintain frequent phone communications with center staff and to submit to random drug testing. Residential community corrections fall just short of actual incarceration and may take many forms. Residents may live either part-time or full-time at the center, depending on conditions set forth by the court.

Several studies reveal that inmates often consider intermediate sanctions such as ISPs to be more punitive than prison sentences.

Discussion Questions

1. Is it acceptable that many of those given the alternative of standard probation receive little or no supervision by a probation officer? Does this diminish the validity of such "sentences"?

2. Have you known anyone who has spent time behind bars? If so, did they generally agree or disagree that the jail/prison environment was highly criminogenic?

3. If you were a probation officer, which style would you more likely adopt: enforcer or counselor?

4. In your opinion, in the case of forfeitures, how common is it that law enforcement officers become "cash-crazed" as critics contend, focusing more on acquiring money and property than on apprehending those who break the law?

5. Does your local law enforcement agency make much use of asset forfeiture laws? If so, how do they use the revenue collected?

6. Do you think it is possible to have an effective house arrest program without some type of electronic monitoring?

7. Does the use of electronic monitoring discriminate against poorer people who don't have phone service? What about homeless persons convicted of crimes?

8. What does it say about the harshness of prison sentences when a significant number of offenders would rather be sentenced to prison than to ISPs, where they had to work, submit to random drug tests and receive frequent visits by a probation officer?

9. Discuss the net widening effects often occurring with the use of sentencing alternatives.

10. In most cases, do you think intermediate sanctions effectively provide "the least restrictive method . . . to manage offender behavior consistent with public safety," or do many fall short? Which ones are adequate? Which ones need restructuring?

References

Abrahamson, Alan. "Home Unpleasant During House Arrest, Judge Learns." *Corrections Today,* July 1991, p. 76.

Adams, Jim. "It's Better Than Being Behind Bars: Offenders Willingly Exchange Labor for Jail Time." (Minneapolis/St. Paul) *Star Tribune,* October 8, 1992, p. B7.

American Bar Association. *Standards Relating to Probation.* Chicago: American Bar Association, 1981.

American Correctional Association. *Manual of Correctional Standards.* College Park, MD, 1975.

Baer, Benjamin F. and Klein-Saffran, Jody. "Home Confinement Program: Keeping Parole Under Lock and Key." *Corrections Today,* February 1990, pp. 17–18, 30.

Barajas, Eduardo, Jr. "Defining the Role of Community Corrections." *Corrections Today,* April 1993, pp. 28–32.

Baumer, Terry L. and Maxfield, Michael G. "Electronically Monitored Home Detention." *Overcrowded Times,* September 1991, pp. 4, 16.

Bennett, Lawrence A. "Current Findings on Intermediate Sanctions and Community Corrections." *Corrections Today,* February 1995, pp. 86–89.

Camp, David and Camp, Camille. *The Corrections Yearbook, 1995.* South Salem, NY: The Criminal Justice Institute, 1995.

Camp, George M. and Camp, Camille Graham. *The Corrections Yearbook, 1997.* South Salem, NY: The Criminal Justice Institute, 1997.

Castle, Michael N. "Alternative Sentencing: Selling It to the Public." *Research in Action.* National Institute of Justice, September 1991 (NCJ-129875).

Center for Effective Public Policy. *The Intermediate Sanctions Handbook: Experiences and Tools for Policymakers,* edited by Peggy McGarry and Madeline M. Carter. Washington, DC: National Institute of Corrections, 1993.

Christianson, Scott. *Community Corrections Report.* Civic Research Institute, Inc., July/August 1995.

Correctional Populations in the United States, 1995: Executive Summary. Bureau of Justice Statistics, June 1997 (NCJ-163917).

Crime and Corrections in Oregon: Tough Issues, Hard Facts. Oregon Department of Corrections, September 1994.

Drowns, Robert W. and Hess, Kären M. *Juvenile Justice,* 2nd ed. St. Paul, MN: West Publishing, 1995. Reprinted by permission.

Electronic Monitoring in Intensive Probation and Parole Programs. Monograph. Bureau of Justice Assistance, U.S. Department of Justice, February 1989 (NCJ-116319).

Fulton, Betsy and Stone, Susan. "Evaluating the Effectiveness of Intensive Supervision." *Corrections Today,* December 1992, pp. 80–87.

Goss, Mike. "Serving Time Behind the Front Door: Electronic Monitoring Programs Provide Prison Alternative." *Corrections Today,* July 1990, pp. 80–84.

Gowdy, Voncile B. *Intermediate Sanctions.* National Institute of Justice, 1993 (NCJ-140540).

Green, Stephen H. "Changing Trends in Asset Forfeiture." *The Police Chief,* January 1994, pp. 14–22.

Harland, Alan T. "Defining a Continuum of Sanctions: Some Research and Policy Development Implications." In Center for Effective Public Policy. *The Intermediate Sanctions Handbook: Experiences and Tools for Policymakers.* Washington, DC: National Institute of Corrections, 1993, pp. 35–42.

Harlow, Robert; Darley, John; and Robinson, Paul. "The Severity of Intermediate Penal Sanctions: A Psychophysical Scaling Approach for Obtaining Community Perceptions." *Journal of Quantitative Criminology,* Vol. 11, No.1, 1995, pp. 71–95.

Hillsman, Sally T. "Day Fines: An Overview." *Overcrowded Times,* September 1990, p. 4.

Hudson, Joe and Galaway, Burt. "Community Service: Toward Program Definition." *Federal Probation,* June 1990.

"Intensive Supervision Merits Questionable, Says NIJ Report." *NCJA Justice Bulletin,* July 1993, pp. 7–9.

"Intermediate Sanctions Producing Mixed Results, Says NIJ." *NCJA Justice Research,* July/August 1993, pp. 3–5.

Kime, Roy Caldwell. "The Future of Asset Forfeiture." *The Police Chief,* August 1993, pp. 10–12.

Knapp, Kay. "Planning Intermediate Sanctions for Female Offenders." *Overcrowded Times,* February 1994, pp. 4, 14.

Labaton, Stephen. "Glutted Probation System Puts Communities in Peril." *New York Times,* June 19, 1990, pp. A-1, A-10.

Larivee, John. "Day Reporting Centers: Making Their Way from the U.K. to the U.S." *Corrections Today,* October 1990, pp. 84–89.

Lemov, Penelope. "The Next Best Thing to Prison." *Corrections Today,* April 1992, pp. 134-141.

Lilly, J. Robert. "Electronic Monitoring in the U.S." In *Intermediate Sanctions in Overcrowded Times,* edited by Michael Tonry and Kate Hamilton. Boston: Northeastern University Press, 1995, pp. 112–116.

Lurigio, Arthur J. and Martin, Nancy. "Making 'Community' the Operative Word in Community Corrections." *Corrections Today,* July 1997, pp. 104–107.

Martin, Deirdre. "Assets Seizure: Poetic Justice or Taking Justice Into One's Own Hands?" *Law Enforcement Technology,* October 1993, pp. 46–50.

McCarthy, Belinda Rodgers and McCarthy, Bernard J., Jr. *Community-Based Corrections,* 3rd ed. Belmont, CA: Wadsworth Publishing Company, 1997. Reprinted by permission.

McCarthy, Bernard J. "Community Residential Centers: An Intermediate Sanction for the 1990s." In *Corrections: Dilemmas and Directions,* edited by Peter J. Benekos and Alida V. Merlo. Cincinnati, OH: Anderson Publishing Co., 1992, pp. 173–192.

McDonald, Douglas C. "Community Service Sentences." *Overcrowded Times,* March 1990, p. 8.

O'Leary, Vincent and Raleigh, William. "Risk and Punishment in Intermediate Sanctions." *Community Corrections Report,* Vol.1, No.7, September/October 1994, pp. 3–5, 14, 15.

Papy, Joseph E. "Electronic Monitoring Poses Myriad Challenges for Correctional Agencies." *Corrections Today,* July 1994, pp. 132–135.

Parent, Dale; Byrne, Jim; Tsarfaty, Vered; Valade, Laura; and Esselman, Julie. *Day Reporting Centers.* Washington, DC: National Institute of Justice, 1995.

Petersilia, Joan. "How California Could Divert Nonviolent Prisoners to Intermediate Sanctions." *Overcrowded Times,* Vol.6, No.3, 1995, p. 6.

Petersilia, Joan. "Probation in the United States: Practices and Challenges." *National Institute of Justice Journal,* September 1997, pp. 2–8.

Petersilia, Joan et al. *Granting Felons Probation.* Santa Monica, CA: Rand Corporation, 1985.

Petersilia, Joan and Deschenes, Elizabeth Piper. "Perceptions of Punishment: Inmates and Staff Rank the Severity of Prison Versus Intermediate Sanctions." *The Prison Journal,* Vol. 74, No.3, September 1994, pp. 306–328.

Petersilia, Joan and Turner, Susan. "Objectively Evaluating ISPs." *Corrections Today,* June 1991, pp. 20-28.

Petersilia, Joan and Turner, Susan. "Evaluating Intensive Supervision Probation/Parole: Results of a Nationwide Experiment." *Research in Brief,* National Institute of Justice, May 1993a.

Petersilia, Joan and Turner, Susan. "Evaluating Intensive Supervision Probation and Parole." *Overcrowded Times,* October 1993b, pp. 6, 8–10, 16.

Reeves, Rhonda. "Finding Solutions to the Most Pressing Issues Facing the Corrections Community." *Corrections Today,* December 1992, pp. 74–79.

Seeking Justice: Crime and Punishment in America. New York: The Edna McConnell Clark Foundation, 1995.

Shilton, Mary K. "Community Corrections Acts." *Overcrowded Times*, April 1992, pp. 4, 14.

Spelman, William. "The Severity of Intermediate Sanctions." *Journal of Research in Crime and Delinquency*, Vol.32, No.2, May 1995, pp. 107–135.

Taxman, Faye S. "Intermediate Sanctions: Dealing with Technical Violators." *Corrections Today*, February 1995, pp. 46–57.

Treatment Alternatives to Street Crime: TASC Programs, 2nd ed. Program Brief. Bureau of Justice Assistance, U.S. Department of Justice, April 1992, (NCJ-129759).

Turnbaugh, Kristi. "Cook County Sheriff's Day Reporting Center." *The Compiler*, Winter/Spring, 1995.

Weitekamp, Elmar. "Restitution: An Overview." *Overcrowded Times*, June 1992, p. 6.

Whitehead, John T. "Control and the Use of Technology in Community Supervision." In *Corrections: Dilemmas and Directions*, edited by Peter J. Benekos and Alida V. Merlo. Cincinnati, OH: Anderson Publishing Co., 1992, pp. 155–172.

Winterfield, Laura A. and Hillsman, Sally T. "The Staten Island Day-Fine Project." *Research in Brief*, National Institute of Justice, January 1993 (NCJ-138538).

Wunder, Amanda. "Parole and Probation Officer Profile." *Corrections Compendium*, February 1995, pp. 8–19.

Cases

Gagnon v. Scarpelli, 441 U.S. 778 (1973).

Mempa v. Rhay, 339 U.S. 128 Cir. 3023 (1968).

6

Jail: Detention and Short-Term Incarceration

Do You Know

➤ When and where jails originated and what their purpose was?

➤ What a jail is and what dual functions it serves?

➤ Who the majority of jail inmates are by one-day counts?

➤ How many jails currently operate in the United States? If most are large or small? New or old?

➤ What the three basic architectural designs of jails are and how they differ?

➤ What impact the Americans with Disabilities Act (ADA) has had on jails?

➤ Who controls the jail in most jurisdictions?

➤ How jail duty used to be perceived and what efforts are currently underway to improve the quality of jail personnel?

➤ What five basic operational responsibilities concerning inmates jails have?

➤ What services jails are responsible for providing to inmates?

➤ What optional services and programs jails might provide and what factors prevent the availability of such services and programs?

➤ How the Bail Reform Act of 1984 differed from the Bail Reform Act of 1966?

➤ When pretrial release programs began in this country and what types of pretrial release alternatives are available to judges?

➤ What types of posttrial release options are available?

➤ What are some of the critical issues facing jails today?

The goals and missions of local jails have changed drastically in the past 20 years. Outside influences, coupled with our changing criminal justice system and the diversity of inmate populations, have forced local jails to adapt. Jail staff must be versatile in order to accept changes and prepare for the challenges they create.
                                                                        — Marvin J. Wilson

Can You Define

bail

classification

conditional release

direct supervision

field citations

first generation jails

fully secured bail

jail

lockup

new generation jails

percentage bail

pretrial detention

pretrial release

privately secured bail

release on own
      recognizance (ROR)

second generation jails

station house citations

summons

supervised release

third generation jails

third-party release

unsecured bail

weekend jail

work release

Introduction

J ails are an important element in our nation's correctional system, serving as the most commonly used type of confinement in the United States. In fact, "some communities are beginning to use jails as the most punitive component in a continuum of coordinated intermediate sanctions" (Wells and Brennan, 1995, p. 58).

Jails in America have had a long and sometimes sordid history. O'Toole (1993, p. 8) states:

> Although jails date back many centuries, they were not generally included under the broader umbrella of corrections until the 1960s. Once this happened, jails were quickly identified as the least developed correctional component.
>
> Indeed, when the National Institute of Corrections was authorized nearly 20 years ago, one of its advisory board's first acts was to focus attention on improving conditions in the nation's jails. The creation of the NIC Jail Center in 1977 marked the first time federal funding was targeted specifically to solving the many problems in the nearly 3,400 jails throughout the country.

As expressed by Goldfarb (1976) two decades ago: "Generations of neglect have earned American jails the label of the 'ultimate ghetto of the criminal justice system.' " The squalor existing in our nation's jails was practically legendary. While these negative perceptions may have been true in the 1960s and 1970s, things have changed. Recent efforts have attempted to reverse these perceptions and improve the function and image of jails in the United States. Improvement has occurred, much of it court mandated.

Jails have also suffered in the shadow of the plight of prisons. While much media attention and political rhetoric have been devoted to issues concerning American prisons, jails have frequently been overlooked in correctional reform efforts. This chapter examines the pivotal role of jails in the criminal justice system, beginning with how jails came to this country. This is followed by the definition and function of jails and a look at today's jail populations. Next, the jail facility is examined, with a discussion and comparison of first, second and third generation jails. Ways of getting out of jail are presented next, and the chapter concludes with the critical issues facing jails today.

The Roots of Today's Jail

Today's jails have their roots in medieval Europe. In 1166, King Henry II of England ordered every sheriff to establish a gaol, pronounced "jail," in his shire for the purpose of securing offenders until they could be brought before the king's court. Eventually, the same gaols were also used to contain prison-ers after trial as a means of punishment. The sheriff was responsible for ad-ministering to the needs of those jailed, although by many accounts, the prisoners were often badly neglected (recall from Chapter 2 how gaols were described as human cesspools).

> Jails can be traced back to 1166, when King Henry II of England ordered every sheriff to establish and administer a gaol to secure offenders until they could be brought be-fore the court.

Furthermore, jailers were often unsalaried, earning a living by collecting fees from those they kept incarcerated. Prisoners were charged such fees to cover the costs of food, clothing and shelter. The amount of the fee typically depended on the socioeconomic class of the prisoner, with wealthier persons paying higher fees, an approach strikingly similar to that used today with the day fines. This system fell easy prey to corruption, however, as jailers discov-ered that more prisoners translated into more revenue. Unscrupulous jailers frequently pocketed this money, allowing the jail cells to fill up and overflow with hungry inmates. Workhouses, or bridewells, also evolved during this time, providing additional profit to greedy jailers who "hired out" their prison-ers to local merchants.

As jail conditions worsened and the number of citizens incarcerated rose, the call for reform intensified. Finally, during the seventeenth century, legislation was drafted granting prisoners some fundamental rights (Goldfarb, pp. 36–37):

1. The 1628 Petition of Rights assured the right to freedom before trial.

2. The 1679 Habeas Corpus Act provided a remedy for improper incarceration.

3. The 1689 English Bill of Rights outlawed the imposition of excessive bail.

These rights set the precedent for some of what later became the U.S. Constitution and the Bill of Rights.

Reform efforts were also undertaken by John Howard, the father of prison reform. His efforts affected jails, as he helped persuade Parliament in 1774 to allow salaries for jailers, thereby eradicating the corrupt fee system.

When the first colonists arrived in America, they brought with them the concept of the English gaol, including the local administration by the county sheriff and the imposition of fees. Early American jails were built not with in-dividual cells but with several small dormitories, each holding over two dozen inmates. An example of one of these colonial jails is shown in Figure 6–1.

Although the first colonial jail was built in Virginia, the Pennsylvania jails actually became the model used by other states. Philadelphia's Walnut Street Jail was considered quite progressive because it (1) separated prisoners based

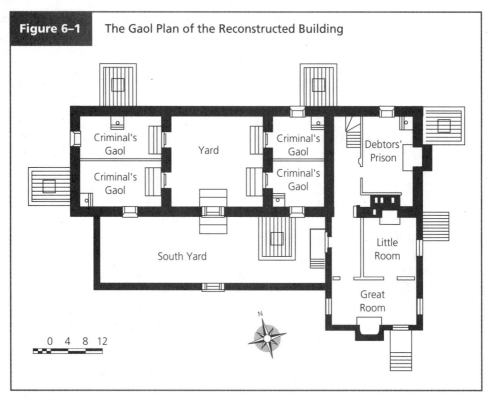

| Figure 6–1 | The Gaol Plan of the Reconstructed Building |

Source: Clemens Bartollas and John P. Conrad, *Introduction to Corrections,* 2nd ed. New York: Harper Collins Publishers, 1992, p. 289. Reprinted by permission of Colonial Williamsburg Foundation.

on the seriousness of their offenses, (2) separated serious offenders from the rest of the prisoner population through the use of solitary confinement and (3) separated female and male prisoners. However, this jail was soon converted into a state penitentiary, starting a movement of prison development which spread across the nation, leading reformers to shift their focus from jails to prisons.

Progress that did occur during the nineteenth century included removing juveniles and the mentally ill from jails for placement into more appropriate facilities and reducing the number of debtors held in jail. These actions, however, did little to improve the conditions within the jail, nor did they enhance the public image of the jail.

The U.S. Census Bureau, in an effort to better understand the population confined within the nation's jails, began collecting data in 1880, but most of the attention and research on incarceration was focused on the nation's prisons. Information concerning American jails was quite sparse, until the 1970s. A census of the nation's jails is now conducted every five years.

A holding cell at the Los Angeles County Jail.

What Is a Jail?—Definition and Function

Jails go by a variety of names, including houses of detention and houses of corrections, but their definitions are the same. A **jail** is a place of confinement, typically administered by the county, with the sheriff in charge. Occasionally jails are run by a regional or state law enforcement agency. Jails serve the multiple functions of (1) detaining individuals waiting to appear before the court, either for trial (preconviction) or for sentencing (postconviction), (2) holding offenders who have been sentenced and are awaiting transfer to prison and (3) holding those sentenced to a year or less of incarceration.

> A jail is a place of confinement, typically administered by the county, with the sheriff in charge, and used to detain individuals prior to adjudication, sentenced offenders awaiting transfer to prison and those sentenced to a year or less of incarceration.

A jail differs from a **lockup** in that lockups, commonly located in city halls or police stations, are temporary holding facilities, authorized to hold individuals for a maximum of 48 hours. A city or county jail differs from a prison in that (1) prisons are state- or federally administered and (2) prisons hold only those convicted of a crime and sentenced, not those awaiting trial, sentencing or transfer to prison.

Jail Populations

A variety of individuals, adult and juvenile, male and female, may be found in our nation's jails, including the mentally ill, the drunk and chemically dependent, the homeless, prostitutes and other members of society's underclass. Such people have been called society's rabble. According to Irwin (1985, p. xiii), the purpose of jails is to manage society's rabble, and because these people are often ignored and disregarded by society at large, the facilities that deal with such people (jails) are neglected as well. This philosophy of the jail's purpose leans heavily toward the Marxist perspective discussed in Chapter 1.

Jails also hold

- Those who have violated the conditions of their probation or parole.
- Juvenile offenders under preventive detention.
- Individuals being held for military authorities.
- Witnesses needing protective custody.
- Those found in contempt of the court.
- Prison inmates for whom no space is available in the overcrowded prison.
- Individuals wanted by other jurisdictions for whom a detainer warrant exists.

Given this conglomerate of individuals, jails are often frightening places for those kept inside. According to some criminal justice scholars, this situation commonly forces jailees into a plea bargaining arrangement. Upon arrest, some offenders cannot afford private legal counsel or bail. They therefore sit in jail until their public defender and jail conditions encourage them to plea bargain. This is how the system works for them. Enhanced sentencing, excessive bail and overcrowded, dangerous conditions in jails may force defendants to plead guilty to get out of jail—even if it means serving time in prison.

One-Day Counts

A one-day count taken on June 28, 1996, revealed local jails in the United States held a total of 518,492 persons (Gilliard and Beck, 1997 p. 1), a 102.1 percent increase from the number in jail in 1985. These researchers state (p. 6): "Since 1985 the Nation's jail population has nearly doubled on a per capita basis." This count also revealed an estimated 8,100 juveniles (under age 18) being held in local jails, an increase of 17.6 percent from June 30, 1995. Of the inmates incarcerated on June 28, 1996:

- 89 percent were male (approximately 1 out of every 207 adult men in the U.S.).

- 11 percent were female (approximately 1 out of every 1,828 adult women in the U.S.).
- 41.6 percent were White non-Hispanic.
- 41.1 percent were Black non-Hispanic.
- 15.6 percent were Hispanic.
- 1.7 percent were categorized as "other" for race.

A substantial proportion of those in jail have not yet been convicted of a crime. On June 28, 1996, only 48.8 percent of all adult inmates had conviction status, meaning a majority (51.2 percent) of adults in jail on that day had not been convicted of a crime (Gilliard and Beck, p. 7).

According to one-day counts conducted on June 28, 1996, the majority of jail inmates in America were adult, male, White and of preconviction status.

In addition to the 518,492 offenders housed in local jails on June 28, 1996, jail authorities supervised an additional 72,977 offenders in alternative programs outside the jail facilities. Gilliard and Beck (p. 5) state: "For the first time in 1995 the Annual Survey of Jails obtained counts of the number of offenders under community supervision." The distribution of these offenders is shown in Table 6–1.

On this particular day, June 28, 1996, the overall jail occupancy was 92 percent of the rated capacity, down from previous years' counts of 93 percent (1995), 96 percent (1994) and a record high 108 percent (1989) (Gilliard and Beck, p. 7). Overcrowding of jails, like other areas of corrections, is an important issue, and many facilities are currently under court order to reduce inmate population, as will be discussed later in the chapter.

Table 6–2 shows the 25 largest jurisdictions in 1996 and how many inmates each jurisdiction held from 1994 to 1996. Keep in mind that most jails across the country are smaller in size and number of personnel, housing far fewer inmates than those shown in this table.

The turnover rate in these facilities is very high and jail populations constantly fluctuate, with numerous admissions and releases occurring every day. Many of those booked into jail are chronic offenders whose repeated admissions and releases skew the population figures. Nonetheless, millions go through our jails annually.

The Jail Facility

Uncertainty exists as to how many jails are operating in the United States, partially because the definition of "jail" is inexact. Some counts include only locally operated facilities designated specifically as jails, whereas other counts include

Table 6–1	Persons under Jail Supervision, by Confinement Status and Type of Program, Midyear 1995 to 1996		
		Number of Persons under Jail Supervision	
Type of Supervision		**1996**	**1995**
Total		591,469	541,913
Held in jail		518,492	507,044
Supervised outside of a jail facility[a]		72,977	34,869
Electronic monitoring		7,480	6,788
Home detention[b]		907	1,376
Day reporting		3,298	1,283
Community service		17,410	10,253
Weekender program		16,336	1,909
Other pretrial supervision		2,135	3,229
Other work programs[c]		14,469	9,144
Treatment programs[d]		10,425	—
Other		517	887

—Not available.

[a]Excludes persons supervised by a probation or parole agency.

[b]Includes only those without electronic monitoring.

[c]Includes persons in work release programs, work gangs/crews, and other work alternative programs administered by the jail jurisdiction.

[d]Includes persons under drug, alcohol, mental health, and other medical treatment.

Source: Darrell K. Gilliard and Allen J. Beck. *Prison and Jail Inmates at Midyear 1996.* Bureau of Justice Statistics Bulletin, January 1997, p. 5 (NCJ-162843).

state-operated facilities, lockups, work release centers, farms for low-risk inmates and other similar facilities. One estimate places the number of jails currently operating in the United States at over 3,700 (Stojkovic and Lovell, 1992, p. 80), while others figure there to be approximately 3,400 (O'Toole, p. 8). A survey by the American Jail Association (1994) revealed a total of 3,272 county jails.

> An estimated three to four thousand jails currently operate in the United States. Most jails are small, hold fewer than 50 inmates and are more than a quarter-century old.

Most jails hold fewer than 50 inmates, and many facilities were constructed long before the courts or the profession considered correctional standards. Most of the jails operating in the United States today were built before 1970; many are more than a half-century old. Often, such facilities are no longer architecturally sound, and the old construction designs hinder effective inmate monitoring. However, in many jurisdictions, jails have been modernized and updated if not completely rebuilt.

| Table 6–2 | The 25 Largest Local Jail Jurisdictions: Number of Inmates Held, Average Daily Population and Rated Capacity, Midyear 1994 to 1996 |

Jurisdiction	Number of Inmates Held[a]			Average Daily Population[b]			Rated Capacity[c]			Percent of Capacity Occupied at Midyear[d]		
	1994	1995	1996	1994	1995	1996	1994	1995	1996	1994	1995	1996
New York City, NY	18,171	18,143	19,890	18,091	18,200	18,382	18,696	19,033	20,862	97%	95%	95%
Los Angeles County, CA	20,113	18,236	18,627	19,725	19,896	18,167	13,340	20,049	20,099	151	91	93
Cook County, IL[e]	7,320	8,626	8,713	8,950	10,837	9,169	8,032	9,317	9,617	91	93	91
Harris County, TX	10,716	8,825	7,703	10,282	8,962	7,140	8,698	8,698	8,698	123	101	89
Dade County, FL	6,338	6,653	6,357	6,656	6,728	6,499	6,752	6,604	6,387	94	101	100
Dallas County, TX	9,715	5,721	6,380	9,321	7,151	5,862	6,676	8,629	8,374	146%	66%	76%
Maricopa County, AZ	5,170	5,717	5,679	4,862	5,503	5,542	4,910	4,910	6,252	105	116	91
San Diego County, CA[e]	5,302	6,006	5,549	5,651	5,820	5,522	5,670	5,670	4,653	61	106	119
Orleans Parish, LA	5,351	5,558	5,368	5,231	5,549	5,433	7,174	7,174	7,174	75	77	75
Philadelphia City, PA	4,696	5,076	5,695	4,799	4,968	5,341	5,349	3,750	5,600	88	135	102
Shelby County, TN	5,124	5,247	5,264	4,891	5,091	5,153	6,344	5,512	6,364	81%	95%	83%
Orange County, CA	4,987	5,157	5,326	4,836	5,074	5,143	3,821	3,821	3,821	131	135	139
Santa Clara County, CA	4,303	4,174	4,213	4,103	4,161	4,314	4,088	3,774	3,774	105	111	112
San Bernardino County, CA	3,136	4,025	3,958	3,188	4,100	4,119	3,744	4,930	4,957	84	82	80
Alameda County, CA[e]	3,295	3,838	3,994	3,098	3,903	3,954	3,552	4,063	4,264	93	94	94
Broward County, FL	3,367	3,573	3,528	3,165	3,546	3,470	3,654	3,656	3,656	92%	98%	96%
Orange County, FL[e]	3,355	3,405	3,120	3,162	3,441	3,332	3,329	3,329	3,329	101	102	94
Baltimore City, MD	3,350	3,777	3,309	3,160	3,380	3,300	2,833	2,933	2,933	118	129	113
Sacramento County, CA	2,954	3,125	3,093	2,852	3,094	3,217	2,749	2,749	2,749	107	114	113
Tarrant County, TX	5,317	3,865	2,881	5,167	4,468	2,876	4,996	4,369	4,193	106	88	69
Bexar County, TX	4,301	3,099	3,058	3,882	3,569	2,821	3,640	3,640	3,640	118%	85%	84%
Wayne County, MI	2,499	2,598	2,711	2,400	2,600	2,800	2,545	2,628	2,658	98	99	102
Milwaukee County, WI	2,247	2,491	2,653	2,165	2,501	2,695	1,854	2,274	2,274	121	110	117
Hillsborough County, FL	1,992	2,536	2,661	2,108	2,384	2,679	2,445	2,649	2,757	81	96	97
Duval County, FL[e]	2,744	2,606	2,384	2,383	2,688	2,473	3,300	3,300	3,300	83	79	72

Notes: Jurisdictions are ordered by their average daily population in 1996.
[a]Number of inmates held in jail facilities.
[b]Based on the average daily population for the year ending June 30.
The average daily population is the sum of the number of inmates in jail each day for a year, divided by the number of days in the year.
[c]Rated capacity is the number of beds or inmates assigned by a rating official to facilities within each jurisdiction.
[d]The number of inmates divided by the rated capacity multiplied by 100.
[e]Previously published numbers for 1994 and 1995 have been revised to include only inmates held in jail facilities.
Source: Darrell K. Gilliard and Allen J. Beck. *Prison and Jail Inmates at Midyear 1996.* Bureau of Justice Statistics Bulletin, January 1997, p. 8 (NCJ-162843).

Considerable attention has been given to recent architectural designs for jails, however, to improve the conditions for both the inmates being housed in these facilities and the corrections professionals who work there.

Architecture, Construction and Design

Much consideration goes into the making of a jail. Sheridan (1993, p. 110) states: "The design process follows a logical sequence—planning, programming, designing, constructing and then activating a facility." A great deal can be learned about a jail's functionality, its strengths and weaknesses, by evaluating its design both before and after the actual construction.

Milwaukee County used an innovative technique to help identify potential design flaws before their new jail was actually built (Zens, 1992, p. 112). The full-scale mock-up program involved building a "dummy model" of the various jail components and allowing staff to test them out. The goal was to achieve a dress rehearsal of how the facility would operate in an effort to pinpoint problem spots before they were "cast in concrete." An evaluation of the award-winning mock-up program revealed savings in excess of $1 million when considering the cost to fix the problems postconstruction.

Another method used to achieve optimum jail design is with postoccupancy evaluations (POEs). This technique analyzes a facility after it has been occupied. It allows those designing new facilities to learn from others' mistakes. Wener et al. (1993, p. 98) state: "Although relatively few correctional facility POEs are conducted annually, several design firms use them to enhance their service—to make their organization a little smarter after each job or to give direction to a new project. . . . Ideally, POEs should be a regular part of the design and construction process."

A variety of structures have been used as jails. In some remote areas, World War II Quonset huts have housed offenders on a short-term basis. New York City has "converted obsolete ferry boats and barracks barges into correctional facilities" (Cottrell and Shanahan, 1992, p. 132). And according to Welch (1991, p. 150): "An abandoned gas station in Denton, Texas, was converted into a makeshift jail." Although such unique instances of jails exist, three basic jail designs, or "generations," are generally recognized.

> Three basic architectural designs of jails are (1) first generation or linear/intermittent surveillance, (2) second generation or podular/remote surveillance and (3) third generation or podular/direct supervision.

First Generation Jails. The earliest and oldest jails are typically categorized as **first generation jails,** illustrated in Figure 6–2. These jails were commonly designed with cells lined up in rows that radiated out from a central guard station like spokes on a wheel. Bars separated the inmates in the cells from the jail staff on patrol. This design allowed only intermittent surveillance of the inmates by correctional officers and fostered a reactive style of supervision. Correctional staff became involved with inmates only when trouble occurred, as a *reaction.* The philosophy behind this design was based on minimizing the interaction between jail inmates and staff, a design which evolved naturally from the first colonial jails. Recall the floorplan of the colonial jail shown in Figure 6–1 and how the inmates' cells were completely separated from the jailer's quarters. Since jails were considered holding tanks where communication

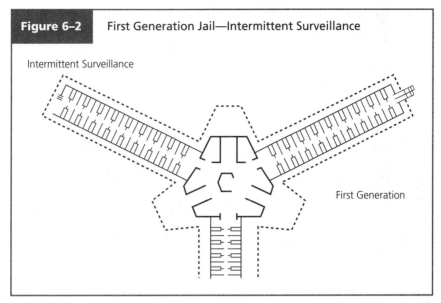

Figure 6–2 First Generation Jail—Intermittent Surveillance

Intermittent Surveillance

First Generation

Source: W. Raymond Nelson. *Cost Savings in New Generation Jails: The Direct Supervision Approach.* Washington, DC: National Institute of Justice, July 1988, pp. 2–3.

between inmates and jailers was not expected, the first generation design was well suited to the prevailing management philosophy.

> First generation jails allowed only intermittent surveillance of inmates by correctional staff, minimized the interaction between inmates and staff and fostered a reactive management philosophy.

A common complaint of officers working in first generation facilities was the prevalence of blind spots and the inability to observe all the inmates all the time. This concern led to a fundamental change in the design of these institutions and the birth of second generation jails.

➤ **Second Generation Jails. Second generation jails** placed cells in a podular configuration, as shown in Figure 6–3, with bars replaced by security glass, allowing for continuous visual supervision of the inmates. However, the correctional staff remained physically separated from the inmates in a safe, remote central observation station. This design also fostered a reactive style of supervision, in which the staff interacted with the inmates only after a disruption had occurred.

> Second generation jails used a podular configuration to remove blind spots and allow continuous visual supervision of inmates, but continued to keep inmates and staff physically separated and fostered a reactive management philosophy.

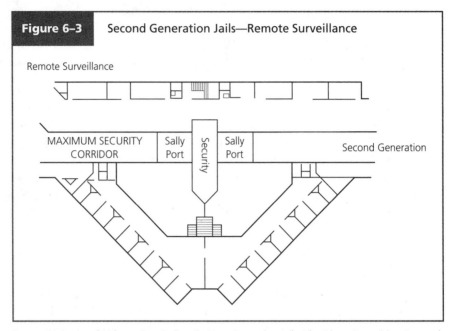

| Figure 6–3 | Second Generation Jails—Remote Surveillance |

Remote Surveillance

MAXIMUM SECURITY CORRIDOR | Sally Port | Security | Sally Port | Second Generation

Source: W. Raymond Nelson. *Cost Savings in New Generation Jails: The Direct Supervision Approach.* Washington, DC: National Institute of Justice, July 1988. pp. 2–3.

Second generation jails, while improving the level of supervision given to inmates, did little to enhance relationships between the jailers and jailees or improve the behavior of inmates. Violence continued to be a problem, as did vandalism of jail property and the marring of walls with graffiti. The problems in second generation jails built in the early 1980s led to development of the new generation jail, designed to maximize interaction between the staff and inmates.

➤ **Third Generation Jails.** These **new generation jails,** also called **third generation jails,** "began having a significant impact on jail design and inmate management practices after being successfully adopted in 1981 by Contra Costa County, Calif.," the first county to adopt the third generation jail design (O'Toole, p. 8). A major reason for the success of these new generation jails was they allowed for direct supervision of inmates. A significant advantage of third generation jails is more efficient surveillance. This concept dates back to Bentham's panopticon; the goals are the same. The idea has been around for a long time, but only recently has corrections married the ideas to bricks and mortar on a significant scale.

➤ **Direct supervision** was achieved by removing structural barriers, such as the remote security center prevalent in second generation jails (Figure 6–3), and placing correctional officers in the same living area with the inmates. Spears and Taylor (1990, p. 20) explain:

Third (new) generation jails are designed to make the most of staff interaction with the inmate population by placing them inside the inmate housing unit. This direct

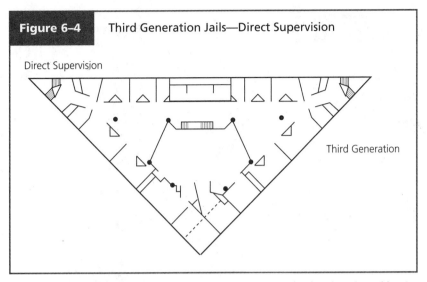

Figure 6–4   Third Generation Jails—Direct Supervision

Direct Supervision

Third Generation

Source: W. Raymond Nelson. *Cost Savings in New Generation Jails: The Direct Supervision Approach.* Washington, DC: National Institute of Justice, July 1988. pp. 2–3.

surveillance allows staff to change from being an inmate behavior monitor to being an inmate behavior manager. By supervising the inmates' activities directly, staff can help to actively change their behavior patterns, rather than just reacting to them.

The floorplan of a typical third generation jail is illustrated in Figure 6–4.

The housing unit, commonly referred to as a module or pod, consists of around 50 cells, sometimes more and sometimes less, and can be managed by a single officer. Figure 6–5 shows the configuration of a typical pod at the Niagara County Jail. Four pods comprise each housing floor. A case study performed at the Niagara County Jail reveals many benefits to this type of design (Krasnow, 1995, p. 4). For example:

> With respect to direct supervision, the basic triangular pod is the optimal configuration for sight lines, travel distances, and the orientation of cells and day space to the pod officer's desk. No location within the pod is more than 90 feet from the desk—the maximum distance at which facial features and expression can be discerned by the naked eye.
>
> The height of the platform relative to both levels of cells gives the pod officer a full view of all cell fronts, as well as an excellent vantage point from which to survey day space activities. Showers are located at the center of the hypotenuse on both levels and are visible from virtually every point within the day space.

In addition to enhanced visibility, the list of benefits offered by a new generation design is quite extensive. The podular design permits one officer to supervise as many as 50 or more inmates, a ratio that improves staffing efficiency. Another benefit is the ability to shut down a pod if inmate populations decline, thereby lowering operational costs of the facility. Many of these modular jails, such as the

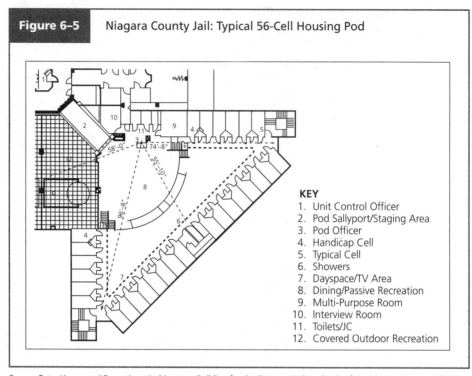

| Figure 6–5 | Niagara County Jail: Typical 56-Cell Housing Pod |

KEY
1. Unit Control Officer
2. Pod Sallyport/Staging Area
3. Pod Officer
4. Handicap Cell
5. Typical Cell
6. Showers
7. Dayspace/TV Area
8. Dining/Passive Recreation
9. Multi-Purpose Room
10. Interview Room
11. Toilets/JC
12. Covered Outdoor Recreation

Source: Peter Krasnow. "Corrections Architecture: Building for the Future—A Case Study of the Niagara County Jail." *Corrections Compendium,* May 1995, Volume XX, No. 5, p. 3. Copyright © 1995 by CEGA Publishing. Reprinted by permission.

one in Pinellas County, Florida, are built from precast concrete, allowing rapid construction at a substantially reduced cost to taxpayers.

Another advantage of these new generation jails is the opportunity for jail personnel to interact with inmates in an effort to avoid significant problems. Staff-inmate interaction is facilitated by literally placing them together. Staff must therefore be sensitive to inmate concerns. Stojkovic and Lovell (p. 92) note: "[T]his model attempts to be proactive in its management philosophy, relying on the skills and training of the officer to control and supervise the inmate population." Consequently, "the podular/direct supervision model is only as good as the staff that is supporting and implementing the fundamental principles associated with it. In short, the correctional officers are at the core of this type of jail design and management."

> Third generation, or new generation, jails also used a podular configuration but removed physical barriers between staff and inmates to allow for direct supervision and foster a proactive management philosophy.

Numerous studies have revealed positive responses by inmates to the environment of new generation jails. Inmates are allowed more personal space in third generation jails than in either first or second generation styles of jails,

Suffolk County Sheriff's Department officers inside the Suffolk
County Jail in Boston. The jail cost $54 million and has 453 cells, with
a decentralized design for enhanced security.

and they enjoy more freedom to interact with other prisoners (Clear and Cole,
1990, p. 226). These positive reactions, combined with or as a result of the
proactive management style, have led to a decrease in the number of assaults
and a reduction in the overall levels of violence and vandalism. The Reuben
Long Detention Center in South Carolina is a direct supervision facility built
in the late 1980s. After two years of operation, the facility was reportedly as
"quiet, clean and safe, and as sparkling . . . as it was when it opened" ("*Times*
Article," 1992, p. 5). Furthermore, the jail's director reported only three assaults during the first two years of operation, compared to the former jail's average of 250 assaults per year.

The decrease in the level of violence and vandalism has, in turn, had a
positive effect on correctional officers' attitudes, with correctional officers in
new generation jails reporting more job satisfaction and more positive attitudes about the work climate than officers in traditional jails. In addition, the
working conditions in new generation jails showed an overall improvement.
The new generation jail puts staff in charge rather than inmates. In traditional facilities, the toughest guy in the cellblock is the "boss"—he runs
things. The guards merely supervise. In contrast, third generation jails put
the power in the correctional officers' hands, improving morale and work
conditions.

Other Design Considerations. Recent studies have revealed that the physical
design of a correctional facility has a significant impact on the emotional reaction of those within the facility, both inmates and staff. Smith (1993, p. 88)
has identified eight architectural elements that "tend to reinforce inmates'

positive behavior and make officers' jobs easier, safer and less stressful." These essential characteristics are

1. Visibility.
2. Comfortable furniture.
3. Acoustical control.
4. Ample lighting.
5. Views of the outdoors.
6. Outside contact.
7. Outdoor recreation.
8. Dayroom as a classroom.

Smith (p. 88) states: "You will note that many of these characteristics apply to direct supervision facilities; the principles of manageability and livability have most relevance under direct supervision, a concept that is incorporated into almost all newly constructed prisons and jails."

Another interesting design consideration concerns color. According to Reeves (1992, p. 128): "Color has a noticeable effect on inmates' behavior." For instance, blue "has a calming effect and has been shown to lower blood pressure. Blue is ideal for spaces such as inmate day rooms, where a restful, peaceful environment is desired" (Reeves, p. 129). Red, on the other hand, "increases brain wave activity and stimulates the adrenal gland to release adrenaline into the blood stream." Consequently, red is suitable for social contact areas, such as dining rooms and visiting areas.

Although no laws or regulations require jails to incorporate the eight essential architectural elements identified by Smith or to paint rooms a certain color, a new law is having quite an impact on the design of all jails, old and new—the Americans with Disabilities Act (ADA).

ADA Requirements. Thompson and Ridlon (1995, p. 122) state: "The Americans with Disabilities Act (ADA) has been called the most sweeping civil rights legislation since the Civil Rights Act of 1964." Pulitzer and Bliek (1995, p. 90) elaborate: "Title II of the Americans with Disabilities Act (ADA) applies to all public institutions, including state and local governments and the agencies that operate under their auspices—prisons, jails and detention centers. This section of the law prohibits discrimination on the basis of disability and covers all programs, services and activities provided by these agencies."

Title I of the ADA requires accessibility for disabled correctional staff, as individuals with disabilities can no longer be denied jobs in the corrections profession because of their disabilities. Disabled offenders will be discussed in greater detail in Chapter 10, and the ADA will be covered more extensively in Chapter 13.

> The Americans with Disabilities Act (ADA) applies to all public buildings, including jails, and requires modification or new construction of such facilities to accommodate disabled inmates, visitors and staff.

No matter what changes are made, how well the jail functions is largely attributable to its administration, management and staffing.

Administration, Management and Staffing

Like their ancestors in medieval England, modern jails are usually under local control by the sheriff's office. In most jurisdictions, the sheriff is an elected official who may or may not have law enforcement or corrections experience. Many are former police officers or sheriff's deputies.

> In most jurisdictions, jails are under the local control of the sheriff, an elected official who may or may not have any law enforcement or corrections experience.

Some have criticized this practice of local control by an elected official, claiming it to be a key problem of many inadequate jails. The accountability of the sheriff to the county's voters necessarily makes the jail a very political institution. The possibility also exists for new administration to be voted in each election, resulting in discontinuity in management styles and policies. This discontinuity makes it difficult for the correctional staff to perform their jobs effectively. Potential alternatives to locally controlled jails include state-run facilities, cooperative (regional) arrangements, state subsidy programs and private jails.

The people with whom the sheriff and other jail administrators staff the facility may vary significantly in qualifications and skills. In fact, the reasons such people are selected to work within the jails may vary considerably as well. Clark (1991, p. 1) notes: "Because jails are usually managed by the police chief or sheriff, jail personnel must meet employment qualifications of the local agency rather than of a statewide personnel system. State and even national standards for this field may be generally consistent, but they are certainly not identical." The low status of jail correctional officers is reflected in the practice of some sheriffs who assign regular deputies to jailer duty as punishment for violating a department rule. This is unfortunate because competent staff are a critical feature in the success of today's jails. Clark's findings (p. 4) are encouraging, however: "Most departments have stopped using the jail as a punishment detail for those officers who could not perform well in patrol capacities."

Efforts to improve officer quality involve hiring more women, ethnic minorities and persons with college degrees. However, officers with more education may experience greater job dissatisfaction due to too much routine and limited challenge.

> Competent staff are a critical feature in the success of today's jails, and most departments no longer use the assignment of jail duty as a punishment. Attempts to improve the quality of jail personnel include raising educational requirements and hiring more women and minorities.

As the management philosophies of more jails assume the proactive approach of third generation jails, perhaps correctional officers will find more purpose, challenge and satisfaction in their positions. Corrections careers are discussed later in the text.

Operations

Although jails may vary considerably in their management and operational philosophies, the basic functions remain a common element between different facilities. Jail personnel are responsible for conducting the following specific operations:

- Intake of arrestees.
- Classification of inmates.
- Orientation of new residents.
- Transport of inmates for court appearances.
- Release of inmates.

> Jail personnel are responsible for the intake, classification, orientation, transportation to court and release of inmates.

During intake, the arrestee is transferred from the custody of law enforcement to the custody of the jail. Booking, fingerprinting, photographing, and logging and storing personal property are also part of intake. Once the jail has assumed custody of the individual, classification occurs.

➤ **Classification** separates and organizes inmates once they enter the jail facility. The purpose of classification, according to Wells and Brennan (p. 58) is "to assess inmate risk and make housing decisions. In many facilities, the offender's classification determines his or her access to various programs and privileges." Factors generally considered during classification are the offender's

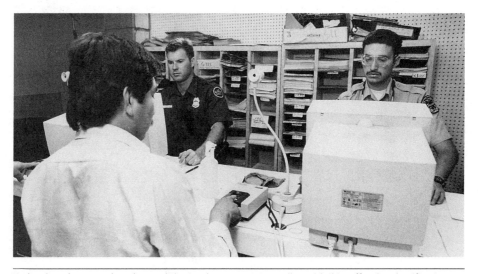

Technology has greatly enhanced the intake process, as well as aided in offender classification. Here an inmate is electronically fingerprinted.

age and gender, the category of offense charge, prior criminal history, special needs (medical, emotional) and available space within the facility. Turturici and Sheehy (1993, p. 104) note: "At San Joaquin, as in most direct supervision jails, inmate classification is based on predictable behavior rather than on specific crimes."

Wells and Brennan (p. 58) suggest: "An effective classification system also facilitates eligibility screening for programming—such as pre-trial release, day release or early release—and can provide a linkage with courts for monitoring, coordinating work release and fast-tracking." Jail personnel must often make classification decisions based on very limited information, and the accuracy with which jail personnel make these determinations will greatly influence how smoothly the remainder of the jail operations run. Clearly, classification of inmates is an important aspect of jail operations.

Following intake and classification, the inmate is oriented to the jail's rules and procedures. This orientation occurs regardless of how many times the individual has been to jail.

Jails are also responsible for arranging to transport inmates to and from the courthouse. The inmate first appears before the court usually within 48 hours of the arrest, unless a holiday or other special circumstance lengthens that time. If the inmate is denied bail or is ordered to remain behind bars, the jail may need to transport the inmate to and from the courthouse several times.

The final duty of the jail is to release the inmate. The nature of the release may vary from bail to dismissal of charges, transfer to another facility, completion of the sentence or for medical reasons. During this operational phase, positive identification of the releasee is crucial. Personal property is also returned at release.

Services and Programs

In addition to the five basic operational duties, jails are responsible for providing a wide variety of services to inmates, including

- Meal service.
- Clothing and laundry service.
- Sanitation service.
- Mail service.
- Visitation/interviewing facilities.
- Facility maintenance.
- Storage of personal property.
- Security of inmates, staff and the public by controlling contraband and preventing fires, which are often intentionally set by inmates.

> Jails are responsible for providing services to inmates such as meals, clothing, sanitation, mail, visiting opportunities, facility maintenance, storage of personal property and security in the form of controlling contraband and preventing fires.

Jails, particularly larger ones, may also provide services and programs to special needs inmates, such as medical service, mental health counseling or treatment for chemical dependency. However, shortages of personnel and lack of funding frequently prevent many jails from providing such services. Beck et al. (1993, p. 8) state: "Alcohol and drug treatment programs were offered in more than half of the large jail jurisdictions. . . . [and p]sychological or psychiatric counseling programs were provided in 212 of the large jurisdictions." While law enforcement officers are responsible for diverting arrestees to appropriate facilities if they notice the need (for example, detox centers or hospitals), many times these special needs go undetected and individuals find themselves in jail without access to proper treatment. Unquestionably, providing special services is a problem for many jails.

Some jails also provide innovative programs to help inmates overcome fundamental deficits, such as poor language skills or lack of job skills. These efforts should better equip inmates to pursue law-abiding lifestyles after release.

> Jails may provide medical service, mental health counseling, treatment for chemical dependency and language and job skills programs. However, shortages of personnel and lack of funding often prevent providing such optional services and programs.

According to Beck et al. (p. 8): "Educational programs (including literacy, basic education, and GED programs) were offered in more than two-thirds of the large jurisdictions." Henn (1996, p. 71) states: "As the analysis of inmate needs increased, program offerings expanded to incorporate subjects such as anger management, family relations, job interview skills, vocational training, gender issues, and a variety of imaginative programs, such as aerobics." Smith (p. 90) notes: "Inmate programs pioneered in Contra Costa County, Calif., and Orange County, Fla., are outstanding examples of a broad range of successful programs geared to these inmates' needs. For many inmates, these programs provide the opportunity to begin changing lifelong patterns of criminal behavior."

The Orange County, Florida, program allows inmates "the opportunity to make positive changes and acquire the tools necessary to become responsible citizens" (Allison, 1993, p. 93). Under this program, inmates are given a choice to determine their own fates: (1) accept responsibility for their lives and make some difficult and demonstrable changes by participating in rigorous volunteer and vocational training programs *or* (2) spend the duration of their sentence locked in their cells. As Allison (p. 93) explains:

> This [program] is . . . based on the notion that offenders should be held accountable to change or be warehoused with no rewards. In the continuum of care, individuals define and attain their needs by acting responsibly. If inmates choose not to accept responsibility for changing their lives, they are determining how the system should hold them accountable and what type of confinement is required. These inmates should be incarcerated in legal but spartan settings, for as long as the law provides.

A number of jails, particularly larger ones, conduct drug testing on inmates. According to Beck et al. (p. 7): "The 1992 Annual Survey of Jails asked the largest jurisdictions if and on whom they conducted urinalysis tests for drugs. Of all large jurisdictions, 308 said that they did." Most jurisdictions tested only upon suspicion; however, some performed random tests on the entire inmate population and others tested inmates upon their return from the community.

Some jails are able to provide special programs for inmates, such as work release, community service and weekend jail programs. An innovative program at the Hennepin County (Minnesota) Adult Correctional Facility is called the Productive Day: "Inmates are now required to mimic a day on the job and if they don't work, they have to be in class and, if they aren't in class, they have to stay locked alone in their 4- by 8-foot cells during the 3 1/2-hour morning and afternoon blocks" (Hodges, 1995, p. 1A). The program has several in-house jobs but also places inmates in positions outside the jail. According to one correctional staff member: "We are trying to develop contracts with businesses. We have a valuable resource of sober, available employees here" (Hodges, p. 16B).

Two factors usually determine if a jail provides programs for residents: the size of the facility and the average length of stay of inmates. Most jails are

small, and many inmates spend only a few hours behind bars before being released. Given the transient nature of the jail population and the high rate of
turnover, it is difficult to run programs for people who are there for only a short
time. Therefore, it is understandable that many jails are unable to offer special
programming to inmates. Those that do offer such programming or alternative-
to-incarceration programs tend to be the larger facilities which use these programs to relieve overcrowding. Such programs are one way to get out of jail.

Getting Out of Jail

There are many ways to be released from jail or to avoid jail altogether, once
an arrest has occurred. Some are pretrial measures; others occur posttrial.
Some arrestees, upon appearing before the court for the initial hearing (arraignment), are determined by the judge to be a flight risk or a potential danger to self or society, in which case the offender must remain in jail until the
➤ trial, a situation known as **pretrial detention.** However, often the judge will
➤ grant one of a variety of **pretrial release** sanctions as an alternative to holding the offender in jail until trial.

Pretrial Release

Like the history of the jail itself, the practice of pretrial release has its origins
in medieval England. Jailers, eager to make a profit, would allow offenders to
be released to a third party, usually a friend or family member, in exchange for
either money or their word that the accused would appear in court as
➤ arranged. This practice marked the beginning of the use of **bail,** which is
thought to be derived from the French word *bailer,* meaning "to hand over or
deliver." Releasing inmates on bail not only freed up space for more prisoners
but raised the possibility that the accused would fail to appear before the
magistrate, in which case the third party could be jailed or forced to pay a fine
to the sheriff. Either way, jailers profited from pretrial releases.

As with other aspects of the jail, the use of pretrial release and bail soon
succumbed to corruption, as jailers raised bail amounts to exorbitant heights.
These immoral practices prompted those who drafted the U.S. Constitution to
include protection from such corruption through the Eighth Amendment's
prohibition against "excessive bail."

Pretrial release programs have been gaining popularity and momentum in the
United States since the 1960s, when Louis Schweitzer founded the Vera Foundation (now known as the Vera Institute of Justice) to help judges gather information
needed to determine which offenders could appropriately be released on their own
recognizance (McCarthy and McCarthy, 1997, p. 72). Today, many jurisdictions
have adopted pretrial release programs as a way to manage offenders in the least
restrictive manner possible. According to several corrections professionals from

Dade County, Florida: "Pretrial release has been very successful for us. Nearly 98 percent of the people in the program show up for court when they are supposed to. It has earned several awards and has served as a model to agencies throughout the country" (Spears and Taylor, p. 22).

Numerous pretrial alternatives to jail, both financial and nonfinancial, exist along a continuum of increasing control, much like intermediate sanctions. These pretrial options are granted based on the perceived risk of the arrestee. Alternatives selected early in the judicial process—for instance, at the point of initial police contact—not only cost the system less by saving time and money but also have a more direct impact on jail populations. However, such decisions to release or divert may also have negative effects concerning the rights of the suspects or the safety of the community. Figure 6–6 shows several pretrial alternatives to detention and how the release mode and releasing authority relate to the length of time the arrestee is detained.

Prebooking Releases

Arrestees may be released prior to booking via summons, field citation or
➤ station house citation. McCarthy and McCarthy (p. 79) explain: "**Summons** are similar to arrest warrants, but they do not require the defendant to be taken into custody. A summons is a request that an individual appear at a

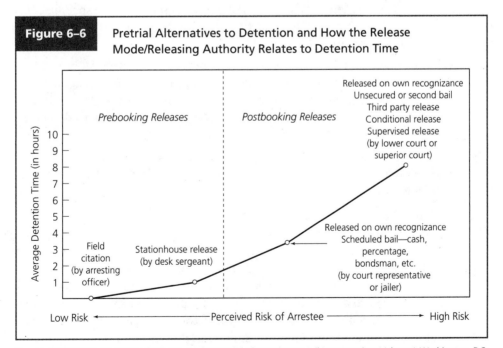

| **Figure 6–6** | Pretrial Alternatives to Detention and How the Release Mode/Releasing Authority Relates to Detention Time |

➤ future court proceeding." **Field citations** may be used by arresting officers to release misdemeanants "on the spot" if they do not demand to appear before a judge. In these cases, the initial hearing must generally take place
➤ within five days of the arrest. **Station house citations** occur once the misdemeanant is taken to the police station for verification of information. If the arresting officer or desk sergeant is satisfied that the information checks out, the arrestee may be released, again to appear before the judge within five days for arraignment.

Postbooking Releases

If neither a summons, field citation nor station house citation is issued, the arrestee is taken into custody and booked. Following booking, a number of release alternatives are available, including a variety of financial bonds and other alternative release options. Nonfinancial release options include

➤ 1. Monitored and unmonitored **release on own recognizance (ROR),** where the defendant basically exchanges his or her word, promising to appear in court, for pretrial freedom. This is the most commonly used pretrial release alternative.

➤ 2. **Third-party release,** where an individual other than the defendant offers his or her word, guaranteeing the defendant's appearance in court, in exchange for the defendant's pretrial freedom.

➤ 3. **Conditional release,** where the defendant agrees to meet specific court-ordered conditions, such as participating in drug counseling, in exchange for pretrial freedom.

➤ 4. **Supervised release,** where the defendant is monitored by a pretrial officer via frequent phone calls and regular visits to the officer's office. This alternative may also incorporate house arrest, electronic monitoring and drug testing as conditions of the release and is used with defendants who pose more of a flight risk or threat to society.

➤ 5. **Unsecured bail,** where no money is actually deposited with the court but the defendant is responsible for the full amount in the event he or she fails to appear in court.

Bail refers to the monetary guarantee, deposited with the court, that a defendant will appear in court if released before trial. The federal Bail Reform Act of 1966 required only that the judge consider whether the defendant was likely to appear in court if released. It did not provide for the detention of those who were a real threat to society. The federal Bail Reform Act of 1984 amended the 1966 act, requiring the judge to also consider public safety. This additional requirement led to an increase in the number of defendants denied bail and, consequently, an increase in pretrial detainees.

> The federal Bail Reform Act of 1966 required only that the judge consider whether the defendant was likely to appear in court if released. The amended federal Bail Reform Act of 1984 required the judge to also consider public safety, a requirement which increased the number of pretrial detainees in our nation's jails.

The various other types of bail or financial release options include:

➤ 1. **Percentage bail,** where the defendant deposits part of the full bail amount, generally 10 percent, but again is responsible for the remainder following failure to appear in court.

➤ 2. **Privately secured bail,** where a bondsman charges the defendant a fee (generally 10 percent of the bail amount) and agrees to cover the full bail amount should the defendant fail to appear in court.

➤ 3. **Fully secured bail,** where the defendant deposits the full bail amount with the court.

> Pretrial release programs have been gaining momentum in the United States since the 1960s and include the prebooking release options of (1) summons, (2) field citations and (3) station house citations, as well as the postbooking release options of (4) release on own recognizance, (5) third-party release, (6) conditional release, (7) supervised release, (8) unsecured bail, (9) percentage bail, (10) privately secured bail and (11) fully secured bail.

Posttrial Release

Several possible release options may be granted to offenders after going to
➤ trial and receiving a conviction. **Work release** allows inmates to maintain or obtain employment in the community while still serving their jail sentence. Inmates are allowed to leave jail only for work and must return to the jail
➤ every evening. **Weekend jail** programs are similar to work release programs except that offenders need report to the jail only on weekends, working *and living* in the community during the week.

> Posttrial release options include work release and weekend jail programs, both of which allow the inmate to work in the community and return to the jail to serve the sentence.

These posttrial release programs not only reduce the idleness and boredom suffered by inmates serving jail sentences—factors which lead to restlessness and, potentially, violence—but they also serve as population control, providing a degree of relief for the often overcrowded jail, one of many critical issues facing jails today.

Critical Issues Facing Jails Today

With jails receiving perhaps more attention today than ever before, the number of critical issues concerning jails is quite extensive, ranging from overcrowding to high suicide rates to accreditation and privatization of jail facilities.

Overcrowding

According to the Bureau of Justice Statistics (1990), overcrowding is the most critical concern for today's jail administrators. In addition to increases in their own populations, jails are expected to shoulder the overflow from crowded prisons. As O'Toole (p. 8) states: "Jail crowding was exacerbated in several states when legislation to ease state prison burdens resulted in increased population pressures at the local level. In a few of the harder hit states, some noted that prisons were becoming more like jails and vice versa."

According to Mumola and Beck (1997, p. 7): "At the end of 1996, 27 States reported a total of 31,508 State prisoners held in local jails or other facilities because of crowding in State facilities. . . . Overall, 2.9% of all State prisoners were confined in local jails due to State prison crowding, up slightly from 2.7% in 1995." Wilson (1996, p. 8) notes: "Juvenile crime compounds the problem of crowding, because the rising number of juveniles being adjudicated as adults and placed in our jails has forced jail operations to change their philosophies in order to be able to care for juveniles and meet their special needs." Juvenile offenders are the topic of Chapter 9.

Staffing

Staffing shortages are also a critical issue facing jail administrators. High turnover frequently leaves jail administrators scrambling to fill positions, and the quality of applicants has often left much to be desired.

Because jails are typically a low priority for funding, staff positions within jails have not always attracted highly qualified applicants. Additionally, the high levels of burnout and stress experienced in corrections lead to high turnover and a lack of seasoned professionals working within the country's jails. Statistics from Florida reveal turnover rates exceeding 95 percent in some agencies (Spears and Taylor, p. 26). A survey of jails with capacities of 200 prisoners or more revealed an average turnover rate of 16.2 percent for jail staff in 1996.

According to Camp and Camp (1997, p. 247): "The highest turnover rate for jailers was in Baltimore City, Maryland, where jailer turnover was 70%. Okaloosa County, Florida, reported 0.01 percent jailer turnover, the lowest." The loss of an experienced staff member can be financially damaging for any jail facility. As Spears and Taylor (p. 26) acknowledge: "Any experienced employee that is lost is a wasted resource. . . . What can an agency do but start all over and recruit, select and train new employees—a great expense for any department?"

Another issue concerning staffing is identified by Clark (pp. 1–2):

> One of the greatest controversies in the jail field is whether to establish a separate jail-related classification and career path for correctional workers or to use the jail position as a flexible, general assignment within the department's overall law enforcement staffing pattern. This issue adds to the identity problem for many local jurisdictions and for the profession at large, as job titles of correctional workers in jails may be a mix of positions, each with different requirements.

Accreditation

During the 1980s, the ACA, the National Sheriffs Association (NSA) and the American Jail Association (AJA) established an accreditation program whereby jails and other custodial facilities can obtain certification as having met certain minimum standards. According to Henn (p. 70): "Standards provide the direction to commit to policy, procedures and practice that protect [a jail] in litigation. Standards prevent [a jail] from making excuses and therefore developing higher levels of professionalism within [these] agencies." Nationwide, approximately 85 jails are accredited (Pinson, 1996, p. 73).

Accreditation has many benefits, including

- The protection of life, safety and health of both the jail staff and inmates.
- Assistance with and stronger defenses against lawsuits involving negligence or conditions of incarceration.
- The evaluation of operations, procedures and policies and the identification of the facility's strengths and weaknesses in an effort to maximize resources and make any necessary changes.
- Enhancement of the jail's credibility with courts.
- An increase in community support.
- Formal recognition of the facility's professionalism.
- Higher levels of both staff and inmate morale.

Despite the apparent benefits, many jail administrators fail to apply for accreditation because of limited funds and/or the belief that accreditation is unnecessary for proper jail administration.

Funding

Practically every jail in every jurisdiction faces some sort of funding problem. When jails are locally controlled, they also receive funding at the local level, meaning they must compete with the many referendums seeking money for local schools, community centers and other local concerns. Funding for jail operations is not usually a high priority in the community.

The jail in Macomb County, Michigan, uses an innovative program to ease funding problems. Amboyer (1993, p. 88) states: "[I]n 1985 . . . the Jail Reimbursement Program [was initiated] under provisions of the 1984 Inmate Reimbursement to the County Act. The law allows counties to collect fees of up to $30 a day from inmates for their incarceration." According to the program, inmates are not billed until they are released from the jail. Additionally, all expenses accrued by the inmate (room and board, medication and medical/dental treatment) are billed on a sliding scale, similar to day fines: "[O]ffenders with substantial assets or high paying jobs are assessed a higher daily fee than those with limited savings or minimum wage jobs" (Amboyer, p. 90).

Suicides

> Dan was a terrific human being. He was smart and earned a scholarship to the state university because of his grades. Dan was talented, the varsity center for his high school football team for three years and president of the school's debate society.
>
> In college he was very popular; he dated and socialized quite a bit. In fact, that's all he was doing last weekend. He'd been to an off-campus party with a few friends and had been drinking most of the night. At around two in the morning he was stopped and arrested for driving while drunk.
>
> The magistrate put a $100 bond on Dan. He didn't have enough cash to get out, so they locked him in a holding cell until he sobered up. Now he's dead. Gone. What a waste! Just because he thought his family and friends would abandon him because of a DWI charge. He was ashamed, so he killed himself (Gondles, 1991, p. 77).

In this story, Dan is a fictitious character but is based on real-life situations that happen all too frequently. The problem of suicides is one of the most serious issues facing jails today. Many criminal justice scholars believe the shock and shame felt by some who land in jail is enough to trigger suicidal behavior. Others suggest the jail population itself consists of suicide-prone, high-risk inmates.

In 1996, jails with capacities of 200 or more prisoners reported 76 suicides (Camp and Camp, p. 207). Hayes (1994, p. 182) reports: "Though an inmate can commit suicide at any time during incarceration, research shows that more than 50 percent of all suicides take place within the first 24 hours of incarceration, with almost a third occurring within the first three hours." Hayes also states: "The key to any prevention program is properly trained correctional staff, who are the backbone of any jail facility. . . . Simply stated, correctional officers are the only staff available in the jail 24 hours a day; thus, they form the front line of defense in suicide prevention." Hayes identifies the essential components in a suicide prevention program as

- Staff training—explanation of why jail environments are conducive to suicidal behavior, potential predisposing factors to suicide, high-risk suicide periods, warning signs and symptoms, self-awareness training regarding officers' own attitudes and biases toward suicidal inmates and a comprehensive review of the facility's overall prevention program.

- Intake screening—identification of a number of characteristics strongly related to suicide, including intoxication, emotional state, family history of suicide, recent significant loss, no prior incarceration, lack of a social support system and previous history of suicidal behavior.

- Communication—three levels of communication exist in preventing jail suicides: (1) between the arresting/transporting officer and jail staff; (2) between and among jail staff (including mental health and medical personnel); and (3) between jail staff and the suicidal inmate. Pay attention to statements like, "I feel so empty," or "I just want everything to be over."

- Housing—suicidal inmates should be housed within the general population, not isolated. Belts and shoelaces should be removed. Physical restraints (handcuffs, straightjackets) should be used only as a last resort.

- Supervision—two levels are recommended for suicidal inmates: (1) close supervision (observed at staggered intervals not to exceed 15 minutes) for inmates who are not actively suicidal but who have expressed suicidal thoughts or have a prior history of suicidal behavior and (2) constant supervision (observed continuously) for inmates who are actively suicidal, threatening or engaging in self-destructive behavior.

- Intervention—training in standard first aid and CPR, how to call for emergency assistance, never assuming inmate is dead but continuing first aid and life-saving measures until medical personnel arrive.

- Reporting—notifying jail officials through the chain of command, notifying family, submitting statements regarding full knowledge of the inmate and incident.

- Follow-up/review—may include critical incident stress debriefings (CISD), administrative review and any recommendations for changes in policy, training, operations, services and facility design.

The intake screening component is particularly crucial in preventing jail suicides. According to Hayes (p. 182): "Most jail suicides—80 percent—are committed by individuals who have made at least one prior attempt during their lifetime." Furthermore, ". . . more than 89 percent of all county jail victims had not been screened for potentially suicidal behavior prior to their death, while 97 percent of victims in police department lockups had not been screened." These statistics imply that proper screening and identification of suicidal inmates by correctional staff may go a long way toward reducing the number of jailees who take their own life.

Privatization of Jails

Another controversial issue involving jails is the privatization of jail management. Privatization began to enter the field of adult corrections during the 1980s and today, with limited funds, shrinking budgets and rising inmate populations, many argue the private sector is better equipped financially to take on the challenges of jail management. Jails already contract with private companies for such services as medical care, mental health care, food services, community-based programs, work programs, architectural services and facility construction. Some believe this public-private partnership is adequate and is more beneficial than the strict privatization of jail management (Cox and Osterhoff, 1991, p. 228).

Critics of privatization pose a variety of political and administrative questions: How will privatization affect the degree of control the government has over criminals? How will public policy concerning inmate punishment and treatment fit with private management? Will the quality of inmate care be compromised by privatization?

Unless state legislation specifically prohibits jail operation by private enterprise, little can legally prevent it. According to Thomas (1994, p. 6): "[A]lthough only Illinois expressly prohibits contracting [with private companies], roughly one-half of American jurisdictions have no statutory authority to contract." Jurisdictions in Arizona, California, Colorado, Florida, Louisiana, Mississippi, North Carolina, Texas and Virginia currently have private companies operating adult correctional facilities, although the data does not distinguish if these facilities are jails, prisons or both. Privatization disappearing from jail and prison management seems unlikely: "The best available evidence now suggests that the appeal of privatization is accelerating" (Thomas, p. 19). Privatization is discussed in Chapter 15 as one trend facing corrections in the twenty-first century.

Inmate Rights

The basic concept of "innocent until proven guilty" poses a variety of challenges for jails and is another area of much concern. Many individuals confined in our nation's jails have not yet been convicted of any crime. They are simply waiting to have their case heard by a judge. While society's tolerance of criminal misconduct is reaching new lows, and the belief that criminals should be stripped of many, if not all, of their rights seems to be gaining momentum, the fact remains that incarcerated individuals, convicted or not, do retain numerous basic constitutional rights, as discussed in detail in Chapter 14.

A variety of critical issues face jails today, including overcrowding, staffing, accreditation, funding, suicides, privatization and inmate rights.

Summary

Jails can be traced back to 1166, when King Henry II of England ordered every sheriff to establish and administer a gaol for the purpose of securing offenders until they could be brought before the court. A jail is a place of confinement, typically administered by the county, with the sheriff in charge, and used to detain individuals prior to adjudication, sentenced offenders awaiting transfer to prison and those sentenced to a year or less of incarceration. According to one-day counts conducted on June 28, 1996, the majority of jail inmates in America were adult, male, White and of preconviction status.

An estimated three to four thousand jails currently operate in the United States. Most jails are small, hold fewer than 50 inmates and are more than a quarter-century old. Three basic architectural designs of jails are (1) first generation or linear/intermittent surveillance, (2) second generation or podular/remote surveillance and (3) third generation or podular/direct supervision. First generation jails allowed only intermittent surveillance of inmates by correctional staff, minimized the interaction between inmates and staff and fostered a reactive management philosophy. Second generation jails used a podular configuration to remove blind spots and allow continuous visual supervision of inmates, but continued to keep inmates and staff physically separated and fostered a reactive management philosophy. Third generation, or new generation, jails also used a podular configuration but removed physical barriers between staff and inmates to allow for direct supervision and foster a proactive management philosophy.

The Americans with Disabilities Act (ADA) applies to all public buildings, including jails, and requires the modification or new construction of such facilities to accommodate disabled inmates, visitors and staff.

In most jurisdictions, jails are under the local control of the sheriff, an elected official who may or may not have any law enforcement or corrections experience. Competent staff are a critical feature in the success of today's jails, and most departments no longer use the assignment of jail duty as a punishment. Attempts to improve the quality of jail personnel include raising educational requirements and hiring more women and minorities. Jail personnel are responsible for the intake, classification, orientation, transportation to court and release of inmates. Jails are responsible for providing services to inmates such as meals, clothing, sanitation, mail, visiting opportunities, facility maintenance, storage of personal property and security in the form of controlling contraband and preventing fires. Jails may provide medical service, mental health counseling, treatment for chemical dependency and language and job skills programs for inmates. However, shortages of personnel and lack of funding often prevent the provision of such optional services and programs.

The federal Bail Reform Act of 1966 required only that the judge consider whether the defendant was likely to appear in court if released. The amended federal Bail Reform Act of 1984, however, required the judge to also consider public safety, a requirement which increased the number of pretrial detainees in our nation's jails. Pretrial release programs have been gaining momentum in the United States since the 1960s and include the prebooking release options of (1) summons, (2) field citations and (3) station house citations, as well as the postbooking release options of (4) release on own recognizance, (5) third-party release, (6) conditional release, (7) supervised release, (8) unsecured bail, (9) percentage bail, (10) privately secured bail and (11) fully secured bail. Posttrial release options include work release and weekend jail programs, both of which allow the inmate to work in the community and then return to the jail to serve the sentence.

A variety of issues face today's jails, including overcrowding, staffing, accreditation, funding, suicides, privatization and inmate rights.

Discussion Questions

1. Do you believe sheriffs and others who run jails should be required to have law enforcement or corrections experience?

2. Should the position of sheriff continue as an elected one, or would it be better as an appointed position?

3. Is the jail in your local community large or small? What is the capacity? Who runs it? How old is it? Is the construction first, second or third generation? What kinds of programs and services does it offer its inmates?

4. Should overcrowded prisons be allowed to send their "overages" to local jails? What might be a better solution?

5. Why do you think most direct supervision jails classify inmates according to predictable behavior rather than basing classification on specific crimes committed?

6. Do you think a separate jail-related career path is beneficial to corrections, or should "the jail position as a flexible, general assignment within the department's overall law enforcement staffing pattern" be used?

7. Considering there are between 3,000 and 4,000 jails in the United States and, as of 1996, only about 85 were accredited (according to a cited source), what might be done to encourage more jails to seek accreditation?

8. What are your own attitudes and biases toward suicidal inmates?

9. Is privatization of correctional facilities such as jails a good or bad idea? Why?

10. Considering most jail inmates are of preconviction status, do you believe it is true that these people are treated as "innocent until proven guilty" by correctional staff?

References

Allison, Tom L. "A New Vision: Making Offenders More Accountable and Offering Opportunity for Change." *Corrections Today,* October 1993, pp. 92–95.

Amboyer, Donald J. "Making Offenders Pay: Michigan County Requires Inmates to Defray Cost of Incarceration." *Corrections Today,* October 1993, pp. 88–90.

American Jail Association. *Who's Who in Jail Management.* Hagerstown, MD: American Jail Association, 1994.

Beck, Allen J.; Bonczar, Thomas P.; and Gilliard, Darrell K. *Jail Inmates 1992.* Bureau of Justice Statistics Bulletin, August 1993. (NCJ-143284).

Bureau of Justice Statistics. *Jail Inmates, 1989.* Washington, DC: U.S. Department of Justice, 1990.

Camp, George M. and Camp, Camille Graham. *The Corrections Yearbook, 1997.* South Salem, NY: The Criminal Justice Institute, 1997.

Clark, Frances. "Working in Jail: It Takes More Than a Badge and a Uniform." *Correctional Issues: Jails.* American Correctional Association, 1991, pp. 1–4.

Clear, Todd R. and Cole, George F. *American Corrections,* 2nd ed. Pacific Grove, CA: Brooks/Cole, 1990.

Cottrell, James H. and Shanahan, John H., Jr. "A Jail That Floats." *Corrections Today,* April 1992, pp. 132–133.

Cox, Norman R., Jr. and Osterhoff, William E. "Managing the Crisis in Local Corrections: A Public-Private Partnership Approach." In *American Jails,* Joel A. Thompson and G. Larry Mays, editors. Chicago: Nelson-Hall Publishers, 1991.

Gilliard, Darrell K. and Beck, Allen J. *Prison and Jail Inmates at Midyear 1996.* Bureau of Justice Statistics Bulletin, January 1997 (NCJ-162843).

Goldfarb, Ronald. *Jails.* Garden City, NJ: Anchor Books, 1976.

Gondles, James A., Jr. "Jail Suicides: Working to Prevent Tragedy." *Correctional Issues: Jails.* American Correctional Association, 1991, pp. 77–81.

Hayes, Lindsay M. "Developing a Written Program for Jail Suicide Prevention." *Corrections Today,* April 1994, pp. 182–187.

Henn, Frank. "Change: Whether You Want It or Not." *Corrections Today,* December 1996, pp. 70–71, 99.

Hodges, Parker. "Prisoner's Day Becomes 'Productive.'" (Bloomington, Minnesota) *Sun-Current Central Lifestyle,* April 19, 1995, pp. 1A, 16B.

Irwin, J. *The Jail: Managing the Underclass in American Society.* Berkeley, CA: University of California Press, 1985.

Krasnow, Peter. "Corrections Architecture: Building for the Future—A Case Study of the Niagara County Jail." *Corrections Compendium,* May 1995, Volume XX, No.5.

McCarthy, Belinda Rodgers and McCarthy, Bernard J., Jr. *Community-Based Corrections,* 3rd ed. Belmont, CA: Wadsworth Publishing Company, 1997. Reprinted by permission.

Mumola, Christopher J. and Beck, Allen J. *Prisoners in 1996.* Bureau of Justice Statistics Bulletin, June 1997 (NCJ-164619).

O'Toole, Michael. "The Changing Role of Local Jails." *Corrections Today,* October 1993, p. 8.

Pinson, Michael. "Accreditation Is Worth the Effort." *Corrections Today,* December 1996, pp. 72–75.

Pulitzer, Curtiss and Bliek, Jacob. "In Pennsylvania: Making the Transition to Meet ADA Requirements Systemwide." *Corrections Today,* April 1995, pp. 90–95.

Reeves, I.S.K., V. "Soothing Shades: Color and Its Effect on Inmate Behavior." *Corrections Today,* April 1992, pp. 128–130.

Sheridan, Francis J. "Taking Charge: Technology Selection Is Your Responsibility." *Corrections Today,* April 1993, pp. 108–110.

Smith, Wantland J. "Eight Essential Keys to Designing Manageable, Livable Housing Units." *Corrections Today,* April 1993, pp. 88–90.

Spears, Lois and Taylor, Don. "Coping with Our Jam-Packed Jails." *Corrections Today,* June 1990, pp. 20–26.

Stojkovic, Stan and Lovell, Rick. *Corrections: An Introduction.* Cincinnati, OH: Anderson Publishing Co., 1992.

Thomas, Charles W. "Growth in Privatization Continues to Accelerate." *Corrections Compendium,* April 1994, pp. 5–6, 19.

Thompson, Arthur P. and Ridlon, Wesley. "How ADA Requirements Affect Small Jail Design." *Corrections Today,* April 1995, pp. 122–126.

"Times Article Gives Boost to Direct Supervision Jails." *On The Line,* Vol. 15, No. 2, March 1992, p. 5.

Turturici, Jack and Sheehy, Gregory. "One County's Lesson: How Direct Supervision Jail Design Affects Inmate Behavior Management." *Corrections Today,* April 1993, pp. 102–106.

Welch, Michael. "The Expansion of Jail Capacity: Makeshift Jails and Public Policy." In *American Jails,* Joel A. Thompson and G. Larry Mays, editors. Chicago: Nelson-Hall Publishers, 1991.

Wells, David and Brennan, Tim. "Jail Classification: Improving Link to Intermediate Sanctions." *Corrections Today,* February 1995, pp. 58–63.

Wener, Richard; Farbstein, Jay; and Knapel, Carol. "Post-Occupancy Evaluations: Improving Correctional Facility Design." *Corrections Today,* October 1993, pp. 96–102.

Wilson, Marvin J. "The Ever-Changing Local Jail: The Challenges of Tomorrow." *Corrections Today,* December 1996, p. 8.

Zens, Jeffrey S. "Dress Rehearsal: Mockups Pinpoint Jail Design Flaws Before It's Too Late to Fix Them." *Corrections Today,* April 1992, pp. 112–118.

7

Prisons

Do You Know

➤ How prisons differ from jails?

➤ Which prison system set the precedent for today's minimum-, medium- and maximum-security prisons?

➤ How the national incarceration rate has changed since 1980?

➤ What race and gender the majority of prison inmates today are?

➤ Which category of offense has shown the greatest increase in incarceration rates over the past decade?

➤ What purpose prisoner classification serves?

➤ What features distinguish minimum-security prisons from maximum-security prisons?

➤ What the Federal Bureau of Prisons is and how federal facilities are classified?

➤ Which architectural designs are most commonly used for maximum-security prisons? For minimum-security prisons?

➤ How prison industries have been regarded throughout this century and how they are regarded today?

➤ How release from prison is categorized and which form is most common? Least common?

➤ What parole is?

➤ Which offenders are typically found in boot camp and what is emphasized in many boot camps?

➤ Whether most boot camps have succeeded in their goals to reduce recidivism, prison crowding and costs?

To put people behind walls and bars and do little or nothing to change them is to win a battle but lose a war. It is wrong. It is expensive. It is stupid.

—*Former Chief Justice Warren E. Burger*

Can You Define

amnesty
boot camp
classification
commutation
conditional release
discretionary release
educational release
executive clemency
furlough
halfway house
institutional
  classification

mandatory release
maximum-security
  prisons
medium-security prisons
minimum-security
  prisons
pardon
parole
parole board
parole hearing
prisonization

privatization
reclassification
release eligibility date
reprieve
shock incarceration
systemwide
  classification
total institution
unconditional release
work release

Introduction

Prisons are what come to mind when most Americans think of corrections, and they are the focus of numerous discussions concerning crime and punishment in today's society. A caution: our society assumes the legitimacy of its institutions and the given rationales for them. Hence, it does not make them problematic and does not ask hard questions about their intended or unintended effects. We do not look at the historical accidents that give us one practice or another. And we easily slide over routine practices. Keep this in mind.

Prison institutions are significantly different from the jail facilities discussed in the previous chapter.

> Prisons differ from most jails in that they hold convicted offenders sentenced to more than a year of incarceration. Prisons are also funded either by the state or federal government, as opposed to the local funding of most jails.

Prisons are like miniature cities, providing all the programs and services necessary for the long-term inmate population housed within. Social scientist, Erving Goffman, developed the concept of **total institution** to describe the environmental reality of prisons and their absolute dominance over prisoners' lives.

Much attention has been devoted to our state and federal prisons in recent years as the result of increasing incarceration rates. In fact, as one startling statistic reveals (Schoen, 1992, p. 217): "At the increasing rate the U.S. is locking up offenders, over one-half of all Americans will be in prison by 2052." Clearly, the pressure on our state and federal prisons is intensifying.

Corrections professionals in these institutions face many challenges, for they bear the burden of supervising an increasing influx of inmates, often without a corresponding increase in funds, facilities or other resources. As Bartollas and Conrad (1992, p. 146) state: "A correctional system has no control over the number of offenders it receives and the number it can release. It is like a hotel that must find room for all who come but that can evict no one."

This chapter looks at what are perhaps the most scrutinized and criticized institutions in America's correctional system—prisons. A brief recap of the history of American prisons is followed by a discussion of today's prison populations and the prison facility itself. Administration, management and staffing of prisons is covered briefly, followed by prison operations, prison industries and ways to get out of prison, including an in-depth look at parole. The chapter concludes with a discussion of some of the critical issues facing prisons today. Because the topic of prisons is so large, many aspects of this correctional alternative will also be discussed in other chapters. In addition, the chapter focuses on the "bricks and mortar" aspect of prisons. The human factors involved, including the prison culture and the role of correctional officers and administrators, are the focus of Section III.

A Brief Recap of the History of Prisons

Like jails, the concept of prisons was brought to this country by the colonists. John Howard, the English prison reformer, advocated prisons be places where inmates achieve penance for their crimes through hard and productive labor. However, Howard's philosophy of corrections underwent a significant, fundamental shift after being brought to the United States, focusing less on reform and rehabilitation and more on punishment.

American prisons have evolved into places unlike any other correctional institutions in the world. Our reliance upon and use of them is also unique, as "[w]e now imprison at a higher rate than any nation in the world, having recently surpassed South Africa" (Irwin and Austin, 1997, p. 1).

Arguably, the first state prison in the United States was established in Simsbury, Connecticut, in 1773. Inmates at this prison received strict punishment for their misdeeds, being shackled at the ankles and forced to work grueling hours for even relatively minor crimes. The Walnut Street Jail was built in Pennsylvania in 1790, and a small part of the jail was set aside as a prison, marking the beginnings of the Pennsylvania system of prisons. Over a period of 20 to 30 years, the Walnut Street Jail developed a regimen that was built into Eastern State Penitentiary, putting the Pennsylvania system into bricks and mortar.

A second type of prison, the Auburn system, developed in New York during the second decade of the 1800s. This system allowed some inmate interaction, as prisoners were permitted to eat and work together during the day, then locked in solitary cells at night. This system also classified and divided prisoners based on the seriousness of their crimes. Cell assignments were based on the inmates' classification, with various floors and areas of the prison designated for certain groups of prisoners. Different uniforms were also used to distinguish between the categories of criminals. By classifying offenders based on the nature of their offenses, and then housing them in distinct areas of the prison based on this classification, the Auburn system set the precedent for present-day minimum-, medium- and maximum-security penitentiaries.

Unlike the Pennsylvania system, the Auburn system allowed inmates to eat and work together during the day. It also divided prisoners based on the nature of their offenses, setting the precedent for today's minimum-, medium- and maximum-security prisons.

Many state prisons were built throughout the 1800s, including the Elmira State Reformatory at Elmira, New York, in 1876. This institution was considered innovative in its use of "good time" credits to increase inmate compliance and productivity, thereby decreasing the length of time served in prison. It was also during the late 1800s that the federal prison system began taking shape.

State and federal prison construction continued throughout the end of the nineteenth century and into the twentieth century, undergoing gradual and continual changes and reform in prison design and the philosophy of inmate management. Some of the old state and federal prisons constructed over a century ago are still in use, although increasing numbers of prisoners in the last half of this century have prompted a flurry of new prison construction. Recent data indicates there are currently 817 state prisons and 78 federal prisons (*Directory of Juvenile*, 1997).

The recent bustle of new prison construction is the combined result of rising incarceration rates and changes in sentencing philosophy, leading to a greater number of inmates spending longer periods of time behind bars. But who are the people who make up our prison population?

Prison Populations

As with other forms of correctional supervision (probation, jail), the number of people in our nation's prisons has been climbing steadily over the past several decades. According to Mumola and Beck (1997, p. 2), the total number of inmates held in state and federal prisons at year-end 1996 was 1,182,169.

National Incarceration Rates

The national rate of incarceration has been steadily increasing. Mumola and Beck (p. 1) state: "Overall, the Nation's prison population grew by 5%. . . . The 1996 increase was the equivalent of 1,075 more inmates per week." They also note (p. 2): "In absolute numbers the total prison population increase of 55,876 prison inmates was the second lowest of the 1990's, after the 1991 increase of 51,640. In contrast the prison population grew by 71,591 inmates during 1995." Since 1985 the number of inmates sentenced to prison per 100,000 U.S. residents has risen from 200 to 427. Figure 7–1 illustrates how the number of inmates in custody has increased.

The national incarceration rate has increased steadily over the past decade, with more than twice the number of sentenced inmates today than in 1985.

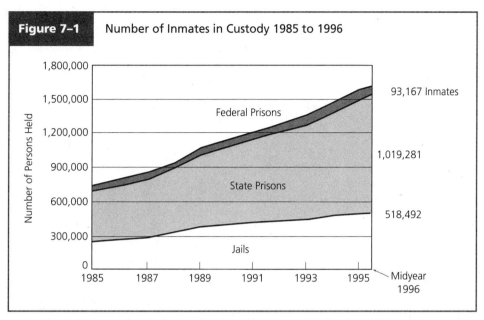

Figure 7–1 Number of Inmates in Custody 1985 to 1996

Source: Christopher J. Mumola and Allen J. Beck. *Prisoners in 1996.* Bureau of Justice Statistics Bulletin. June 1997, p. 2 (NCJ-164619).

Regional Differences in Prison Population

Mumola and Beck (p. 4) note that U.S. prison populations grew fastest in the West (9.6 percent). Midwest prison populations rose by 5.8 percent, followed by the South and the North, each reporting an increase of 2.8 percent. Furthermore (p. 2): "The sentenced State prison population experienced slower growth during the year than the Federal prison population (4.8% compared to 6.2%)." Table 7–1 shows the prison situation among several states at the end of 1996.

Gender and Race Differences in Prison Population

Besides regional differences in incarceration rates and prison populations, gender and race differences are also noted. Table 7–2 shows how prison populations increased from 1985 to 1995, with respect to sex and race.

Mumola and Beck (p. 5) state the growth rate of the female prison population was nearly twice that of males: "During 1996 the number of women under the jurisdiction of State and Federal prison authorities increased from 68,494 to 74,730, an increase of 9.1% . . . [t]he number of men grew from 1,057,799 to 1,107,439, an increase of 4.7%." At year-end 1996, 51 out of every 100,000 female U.S. residents was serving a sentence of more than one year. And while more women are being sentenced to time behind bars, the numbers are still only a fraction of the number of men in prison: "By 1996 women accounted for 6.3% of all prisoners nationwide." (Mumola and Beck, p. 5).

Table 7-1   The Prison Situation on December 31, 1996

Prison Population	Number of Prisoners	Incarceration Rates, 12/31/96	Sentenced Prisoners per 100,000 State Residents*	Percent Changes in the Prison Population			
				1-Year Growth, 1995–96	Percent Change	5-Year Growth, 1991–96	Percent Change
10 highest:							
California	147,712	Texas	686	North Dakota	18.8%	Texas	156.2%
Texas	132,383	Louisiana	615	New Mexico	15.8	Wisconsin	63.7
Federal	105,544	Oklahoma	591	Idaho	15.2	North Carolina	62.4
New York	69,709	South Carolina	532	Missouri	15.0	Mississippi	60.5
Florida	63,763	Nevada	502	Wisconsin	14.8	Iowa	53.0
Ohio	46,174	Mississippi	498	Utah	14.1	New Mexico	51.5
Michigan	42,349	Alabama	492	Rhode Island	12.7	South Dakota	50.2
Illinois	38,852	Arizona	481	Mississippi	12.7	Utah	50.1
Georgia	35,139	Georgia	462	Hawaii	12.7	Hawaii	48.6
Pennsylvania	34,537	California	451	Colorado	12.4	Minnesota	48.6
10 lowest:							
North Dakota	722	North Dakota	101	Vermont	-12.0%	District of Col.	-10.3%
Vermont	1,125	Minnesota	110	District of Col.	-4.3	Maine	-6.5
Maine	1,476	Maine	112	Florida	-.2	South Carolina	11.9
Wyoming	1,483	Vermont	137	Arkansas	0	Maryland	14.3
South Dakota	2,064	West Virginia	150	Massachusetts	.9	Michigan	16.3
New Hampshire	2,071	New Hampshire	177	Virginia	.9	New Jersey	17.1
Montana	2,073	Nebraska	194	Connecticut	1.4	Rhode Island	18.0
West Virginia	2,754	Utah	194	New Jersey	1.6	New York	20.5
Rhode Island	3,271	Rhode Island	205	New York	1.8	Arkansas	21.1
Nebraska	3,275	Iowa	222	Georgia	2.5	Oregon	28.7

*Prisoners with a sentence of more than a year. The Federal Bureau of Prisons and the District of Columbia are excluded.
Source: Christopher J. Mumola and Allen J. Beck. *Prisoners in 1996.* Bureau of Justice Statistics Bulletin, June 1997, p. 5 (NCJ-164619).

| Table 7–2 | Number of Sentenced Prisoners under State or Federal Jurisdiction, by Sex and Race, 1985 to 1995 |

Year	Total	Male			Female		
		All[a]	White[b]	Black[b]	All[a]	White[b]	Black[b]
1985	480,568	459,223	242,700	210,500	21,345	10,800	10,200
1986	522,084	497,540	258,900	232,000	24,544	12,400	11,800
1987	560,812	533,990	277,200	249,700	26,822	13,700	12,600
1988	603,732	573,587	292,200	274,300	30,145	15,500	14,200
1989	680,907	643,643	322,100	313,700	37,264	18,400	18,300
1990	739,980	699,416	346,700	344,330	40,564	20,000	20,100
1991	789,610	745,808	363,600	372,200	43,802	20,900	22,200
1992	846,277	799,776	388,000	401,700	46,501	22,100	23,800
1993	932,074	878,037	418,900	445,400	54,037	25,200	27,900
1994[c]	1,016,691	956,566	452,700	489,200	60,125	28,300	30,700
1995	1,085,363	1,021,463	493,700	510,900	63,900	31,700	31,000
Percent change, 1985–1995	126%	122%	103%	143%	199%	194%	204%

Note: Sentenced prisoners are those with a sentence of more than 1 year.

[a]Includes Asians, Pacific Islanders, American Indians, Alaska Natives, and other racial groups.

[b]The numbers for sex and race were estimated and rounded to the nearest 100. For men and women, the total number of sentenced prisoners was multiplied by the proportion of Black or White of the total population in each group. The reported racial distribution was used to estimate unreported data. For 1995, Hispanics were identified among unknown sentenced prisoners; then, race was estimated for those Hispanics based on the Survey of Inmates in State Correctional Facilities. Finally, estimation of sex and race was done, following the procedure used for previous years.

[c]The numbers of sentenced prisoners on December 31, 1994, have been updated and will differ from numbers reported in prior years.

Source: Christopher J. Mumola and Allen J. Beck. *Prisoners in 1996.* Bureau of Justice Statistics Bulletin, June 1997, p. 9 (NCJ-164619).

Note from Table 7–2 that in 1985 more White males were sentenced to prison than Black males, and more White females were sentenced than Black females. Not until 1991 did the number of Black males exceed the number of White males. Similarly, in 1990 the number of imprisoned Black females surpassed the number of White females. Mumola and Beck (p. 9) state: "In 1985 black males were about 6.3 times more likely than white males to be in prison; by 1995 they were 7.0 times more likely than white males to be in prison." Additionally, Mumola and Beck note: "Hispanics, who may be of any race, represent the fastest growing minority group being imprisoned, increasing from 10.9% of all State and Federal inmates in 1985 to 15.5% in 1995."

The majority of prison inmates today are Black males, although it was not until 1991 that the number of Black males exceeded the number of White males in prison.

Age Differences in Prison Population

It has long been held that crime is a young person's activity, and available data supports this concept. Figure 7–2 shows the age of offenders entering prison for the first time. This curve is similar to that illustrating the number of inmates already present in state and federal prisons (Snell, 1995, p. 50). There is concern that shifts in sentencing philosophy and efforts to make prisoners serve at least 85 percent of their sentences will cause the curve seen in Figure 7–2 to drop off less in the upper age ranges, a phenomenon referred to as the "graying" of the prison population. Currently, however, the majority of prisoners are in the 25 to 34 age bracket.

Educational Differences in Prison Population

Data reveals quite a diversity of educational levels attained by the nation's state and federal prisoners. As reported by Snell (p. 51), of the 846,277 sentenced prisoners under state or federal jurisdiction in 1992, 337,700 (40 percent) had not

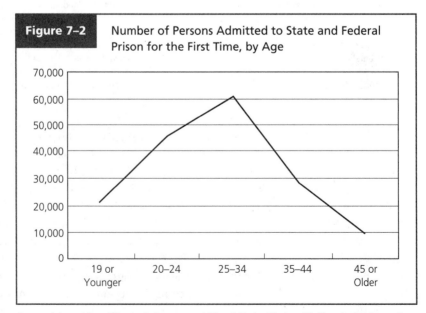

Figure 7–2 Number of Persons Admitted to State and Federal Prison for the First Time, by Age

Source: Adapted from Thomas P. Bonczar and Allen J. Beck. *Lifetime Likelihood of Going to State or Federal Prison.* Bureau of Justice Special Report, March 1997, p. 5 (NCJ-160092).

completed high school, 393,600 (46 percent) had graduated from high school and 114,900 (14 percent) had taken some college-level courses. Table 7–3 shows the levels of education attained by different age brackets of prisoners. Notice when the numbers are normalized for population (number of sentenced prisoners per 100,000 adult residents), the greatest proportion of every age bracket falls into the "less than high school" category.

Differences in Types of Crime Committed

Over the past decade and a half, the composition of prisoners has changed substantially based on type of offense. The recent stiffening of penalties for drug-related offenses and the growing intolerance by judges and juries for those convicted of such offenses has resulted in an unprecedented rise in the number of prisoners serving time for these crimes.

According to Mumola and Beck (p. 10): "As a percentage of all State prisoners, violent offenders fell from 54% in 1985 to 46% in 1995, property offenders fell from 31% to 24%, drug offenders rose from 9% to 23%, and public-order offenders rose from 5% to 7%." These researchers also state (p. 11): "Prisoners sentenced for drug offenses constituted the single largest

Table 7–3	Estimated Number of Sentenced Prisoners under State or Federal Jurisdiction, by Age and Education, 1992					
	Number of Sentenced Prisoners[a]			Number of Sentenced Prisoners per 100,000 Adult Residents[b]		
Age[c]	Less than High School	High School Graduate[d]	Some College or More	Less than High School	High School Graduate[d]	Some College or More
18–24	95,400	70,500	6,900	1,557	858	59
25–29	80,600	100,400	19,600	2,842	1,378	195
30–34	66,100	91,700	23,300	2,283	1,139	206
35 or older	91,200	130,500	65,200	343	308	126

Note: Estimates were calculated by multiplying the number of inmates by the estimated proportion in each age and educational category from the 1991 surveys of State and Federal inmates. All estimates were rounded to the nearest 100.

[a]Includes prisoners with a sentence of more than 1 year.

[b]Estimates of the adult resident population in each age and education category were obtained for the noninstitutional population from the U.S. Bureau of the Census, *Current Population Reports*, P20–476, "Educational Attainment in the United States: March 1993 and 1992." Estimates of the adult institutional population by age and educational level were derived from the 1991 surveys of State and Federal inmates.

[c]Excludes prisoners age 17 or younger.

[d]Includes general equivalency degree (GED).

Source: Tracy L. Snell. *Correctional Populations in the United States,* 1992. Bureau of Justice Statistics, January 1995, p. 51 (NCJ-146413).

group of Federal inmates (60%) in 1995, up from 34% in 1985. . . . The increase of more than 42,000 drug offenders accounted for more than 80% of the total growth in Federal inmates." Although the *number* of inmates serving time for drug offenses also increased in the state prisons, the greatest increase was seen in persons convicted of violent crimes. "As a percentage of the total growth in sentenced State inmates during the period [between 1985 and 1995], violent offenders accounted for 39% of the total growth, drug offenders 35%, property offenders 18%, and public-order offenders 8%" (p. 10).

Figure 7–3 illustrates how the number of state prisoners serving time for drug offenses has changed in relation to other types of crimes. Although the number of inmates serving time for violent offenses continues to be the greatest, no other category has experienced a greater *rate* increase than the drug offense category.

The greatest increase in incarceration rates over the past decade is in the drug offense category.

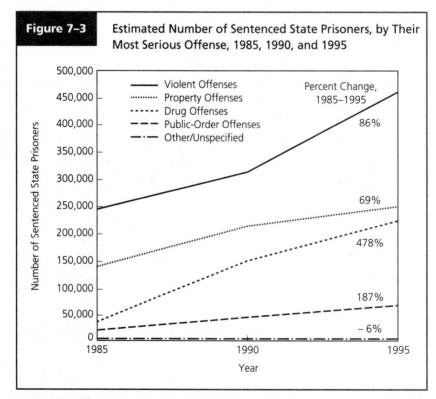

Figure 7–3 Estimated Number of Sentenced State Prisoners, by Their Most Serious Offense, 1985, 1990, and 1995

Source: Adapted from Christopher J. Mumola and Allen J. Beck. *Prisoners in 1996.* Bureau of Justice Statistics Bulletin, June 1997, p. 10 (NCJ-164619).

The Prison Facility

Today's prisons go by a variety of names, including correctional centers, correctional institutions, detention centers, reformatories, penitentiaries, prison camps and state and federal prisons. Although details of the prison facility may be very different among institutions, some commonalities exist among all prisons in the United States, including the process of prisoner classification and the designation of custody levels. Prisons also typically share basic similarities in construction and design, depending on the types of inmates housed in the facility and their correctional goals.

Prisoner Classification and Custody Level

Considering the diversity of the prison population and the variety of offenses inmates are convicted of, the need to classify prisoners is understandable.

➤ **Classification** is a process that divides a prison population into subgroups based on security and program needs. Such schemes are typically based on psychological and behavioral criteria. Separating prisoners into distinct custodial groups allows for better overall management of the prison population and for more effective use of available resources such as psychologists, psychiatrists, social workers and teachers. According to Austin (1994, p. 94): "Virtually every state prison system now relies on objective classification to guide inmate housing decisions. . . . Also, several national studies have documented the success of classification systems in improving safety and reducing costs." Austin concludes (p. 96):

> Classification plays a central role in managing a modern correctional facility and planning for its future needs. Without an objective classification system, it is impossible to determine which inmates should be separated from one another, how staff should be deployed, how best to control crowding, how to avoid unnecessary litigation and how to plan the next generation of correctional facilities. Without classification, a correctional facility can never be truly secure.

However, some scholars challenge this, suggesting that prisoners are classified primarily by public safety and custody or security needs.

Classification is not simply a one-time event for an inmate entering the prison system. Inmates are periodically reevaluated to make certain they
➤ are in the appropriate correctional setting. **Systemwide classification** involves decisions made by the correctional staff as to the degree of custody, level of supervision and institutional assignment of newly sentenced of-
➤ fenders. **Institutional classification** is assignment by the specific institution regarding tasks, housing and activities for the inmate within the
➤ confines established by the systemwide classification. **Reclassification** adjusts institutional classifications upon review and/or changes in the inmate's prison status.

Prisoner classification is an ongoing process that divides inmates into subgroups on the basis of security and program needs.

Classification systems, like other correctional components, must also adjust to changing times and shifts in prisoner demographics. Dallao (1997, p. 88) stresses the need for prisons to keep their classification systems current: "Although classification experts do not agree on the best way to classify inmates, they do agree on the importance of having an objective system which allows for discretionary staff input and which receives regular review. They also agree that a sound classification system—monitored and fine-tuned regularly—can be one of the most important security tools a facility can maintain."

Virtually every prison in the country classifies inmates and assigns them to appropriate housing units. Such units vary according to their security or custody level and are divided into the general categories of minimum-, medium- and maximum-security prisons. Several other alternatives also exist, such as open community facilities and high/close-security prisons. A number of sociological factors account for classification systems. For example, the development of new kinds of security reflects changes in technology, changes in administrative concerns (media interests, better record keeping, increased accountability), changes in inmate populations and changes in social sensibilities. Figure 7–4 illustrates the percentage of inmates

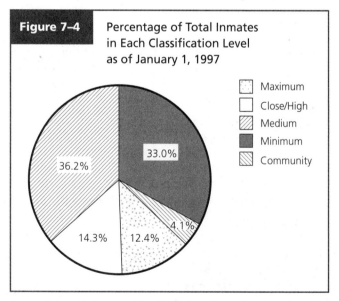

Figure 7–4 Percentage of Total Inmates in Each Classification Level as of January 1, 1997

Maximum
Close/High
Medium
Minimum
Community

33.0%
36.2%
14.3%
12.4%
4.1%

Source: George M. Camp and Camille Graham Camp. *The Corrections Yearbook, 1997.* South Salem, NY: The Criminal Justice Institute, 1997, p. 17. Reprinted by permission.

in each classification level at the beginning of 1997. Figure 7–5 shows the distribution of new prison beds being built or added as of January 1, 1997, by the various security levels. Note the emphasis on medium-security construction.

Minimum-Security Prisons. As the name implies, minimum-security prisons use very little perimeter security, if any, and are designed for low-risk offenders. Many inmates in these facilities are nonviolent first-time offenders, that is, they have no history of violence and did not commit a violent crime. One-third of state and federal prisoners are housed in minimum-security facilities (Camp and Camp, 1997, p. 17).

One focus of these facilities is reintegrating inmates into the community. Prisoners sentenced to minimum-security institutions may work offsite during the day with limited or no supervision. Therefore, assignment to such prisons depends on the inmate's perceived trustworthiness. Cost-efficiency is also a factor. Minimum-security prisons require less staff and less security.

> **Minimum-security prisons** impose little or no physical control over inmates and are designed for nonviolent offenders who are low risk for escaping. Their focus is to reintegrate inmates into the community.

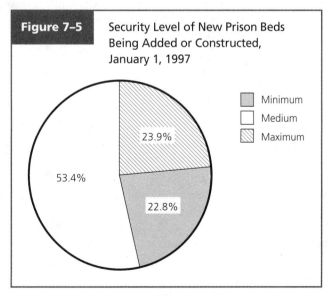

Figure 7–5 Security Level of New Prison Beds Being Added or Constructed, January 1, 1997

Minimum
Medium
Maximum

23.9%

53.4%

22.8%

Source: George M. Camp and Camille Graham Camp. *The Corrections Yearbook, 1997.* South Salem, NY: The Criminal Justice Institute, 1997, p. 67. Reprinted by permission.

Minimum-security prisons, by their nature, frequently serve as a transitional ground for those coming from higher-security institutions on their way to parole or total release. They are a logical compromise between medium-security prisons and community-based corrections.

Many believe the open environment of minimum-security prisons furthers the rehabilitation of inmates by bolstering their self-esteem and trusting them to act responsibly. Furthermore, the experience of many of these facilities has demonstrated that inmates are not likely to abuse the trust and freedom they are given.

Medium-Security Prisons. Unlike minimum-security facilities, medium-security prisons use perimeter controls generally including single or double fencing, sometimes topped with barbed wire or razor ribbon. These facilities do not permit the freedom of movement allowed in minimum-security prisons but are also not as restrictive as maximum-security prisons. These facilities focus on controlled access to programs.

> **Medium-security prisons** use perimeter controls such as fencing and allow inmates less freedom of movement than in minimum-security facilities but more than in maximum-security facilities. The focus is on controlled access to programs.

A shift in prison philosophy occurred during the post–World War II era from punishment to rehabilitation. A concurrent shift occurred away from maximum security toward medium security and, consequently, much of the construction in corrections over the past half-century was for medium-security institutions. The majority (36 percent) of state and federal prisoners are currently housed in medium-security facilities (Camp and Camp, p. 17).

Like minimum-security prisons, many medium-security prisons are constructed using an open interior physical design. However, prison staff can exercise a higher degree of control and lock down inmates in emergencies. Barring such emergencies, inmates are expected to be productively involved in industrial or educational activities. Privileges, such as receiving visitors and having access to various programs, are more restricted than in minimum-security prisons, yet many medium-security prisons provide opportunities for work release, furloughs and other types of programs.

High/Close-Security Prisons. These facilities are a step between the medium-security and maximum-security prisons in terms of degree of control over prisoners. Approximately 14 percent of all state and federal prisoners are held in these types of facilities.

Maximum-Security Prisons. Evidence shows that in the 1990s states are again paying more attention to maximum security as the offender population shifts to include more violent offenders. Because maximum-security prisons are designed to house high-risk, dangerous and violent repeat offenders, they have substantial perimeter controls including double fences, electrified fences or high solid walls. Armed guards posted in observation towers are common. Custody and security are the primary concerns, with little emphasis placed on prisoner rehabilitation.

Interior controls are just as strong as the perimeter controls. These facilities typically have very tight rules, and prisoners generally have substantial restrictions on their freedom of movement inside the prison and on their interaction with other inmates.

> **Maximum-security prisons** house violent offenders and those at high risk of escape and therefore use substantial perimeter controls such as double or electrified fences, high walls and armed guards posted in observation towers. Strict control of inmates on the interior is also a feature of these prisons, as the focus is on custody and security, not on treatment and rehabilitation.

Every state has at least one maximum-security prison. Approximately one-eighth of state prisoners are housed in maximum-security institutions. Although it may seem like this facility is as bad as it could get for a prisoner, there is still a more restrictive alternative.

Super-Maximum Prisons. Super-max or maxi-maxi prisons are the ultimate incarcerative experience for the worst of the worst. Alcatraz, one of the best

An armed guard stands watch in a high-tech control center of a security housing unit of California's Pelican Bay State Prison near Crescent City. This super-max facility uses video cameras and microphones to monitor the more than 1,000 high-risk prisoners housed there.

A New Home of Bars, Steel

America's Worst Inmates to Move to 'New Alcatraz' in Colorado

Editor's note: They call it Super Max, the latest in incarceration, a steel and concrete monument to maximum security. This new prison about to open in Colorado will house the worst federal prisoners, the kind who once were sent to Alcatraz. There will be no coddling of convicts there.

By Bob Unruh
Associated Press

Florence, Colo.
"An uncommon level of security." That's the understated way wardens describe the "new Alcatraz" that soon will welcome the nation's most violent, incorrigible federal prisoners.

The $60 million U.S. Penitentiary Administrative Maximum Facility will open in southern Colorado before the end of the year. It's the first federal prison ever built just for the most predatory inmates in the U.S. Bureau of Prisons. Nearly 500 of them will be sent there.

Alcatraz in San Francisco Bay was the home of their sort in years past. Then a federal penitentiary in Marion, Ill., was modified for the purpose. Now comes Super Max.

"There's no doubt this is a severe program," said John Vanyur, the prison's associate warden. "This is not a typical prison facility. It's one of a kind. And it's only used for this very small number of people."

There are motion detectors in underground crawl spaces, 1,400 remote-controlled sliding steel doors, cameras covering virtually every nook and cranny, and 12-foot chain-link fences topped with razor wire.

The 7-by-12 foot cells could be described as Spartan. They contain a polished steel mirror (glass is a weapon) riveted to the concrete wall. A steel toilet and shower are fixed to the walls. The bed is a slab of concrete covered with a mattress. The only other place to sit is an immovable concrete cylinder in front of a writing table, also concrete.

Cells are designed so inmates cannot make eye contact with other prisoners or see anything outside except the prison walls and the sky.

The worst inmates will be cell-bound 23 hours a day, five days a week. Those five days, they get an hour of solitary exercise in a concrete-walled room; the other two days, they don't get any exercise period.

In their cells, they will receive educational programming on a 12-inch black-and-white television and their meals on trays. The water in their showers is controlled from the outside. Inmates needing counseling from ministers or social workers will get it in their cells.

Inmates will be sent there from Marion and other federal prisons. Prison officials are not allowed to discuss who will call Super Max home, but they can generalize.

"They've demonstrated through highly assaultive behavior, predatory behavior and escape-related behavior that they cannot function in a less secure prison," said Louis Winn, an executive assistant at the prison. "They've proven themselves to be extremely dangerous and violent."

While many inmates sent to Colorado will be serving life sentences, Super Max will not be their home for life. Officials expect inmates to stay no longer than three years before returning to the relative freedoms of ordinary federal prisons.

During their time at Super Max, they will be kept on short leashes and monitored continually.

If inmates have to see doctors or dentists, they will walk only a couple of dozen paces and two correctional officers will accompany them, Winn said. One will walk in front with a baton, the only weapon allowed inside the prison, and one will walk behind, holding the chains connected to handcuffs the prisoner will be wearing behind his back.

Inmates are allowed up to three paperbacks, but no law books (only copies of applicable pages) so no contraband can be smuggled. Visitors remain beyond inch-thick plate glass designed to withstand hammer blows.

If an inmate participates in rehabilitation programs and stays out of trouble, his confinement can be modified so he can mingle with other inmates and visit the commissary.

"Buildings are only one part of the program," Vanyur said. "The key part is what the staff do and how they interact. They're the ones who have to preserve self-esteem and humanity issues—maintaining dignity but getting across the message.

"You go back to the Alcatraz example. . . . You all had the same haircut, walked in lockstep down the hallway and didn't speak during meals. Those elements of dehumanization, we don't have that here. Every individual has his own program. Caseworkers, psychologists and chaplains are going to come down and deal with him."

But the security measures go on and on and on.

Plumbing fixtures have automatic shut-offs so inmates cannot flood cells. Sprinklers and smoke-containment systems are built in. Matches and cigarette lighters are forbidden. Smokers must use a lighter built into each cell wall.

Handles on toothbrushes are cut off to prevent use as weapons. Only pencil stubs are allowed. Pictures of spouses (no nudity) are allowed, but frames are not.

Escape-minded inmates will have their hopes dashed. Between their cells and freedom lie seven layers of secured steel and concrete. Beneath the building is a crawl space with no outlet, monitored by the motion detectors.

Doors are remote-controlled by officers in fortified rooms within the prison. If they feel threatened, they can transfer control to another guard.

The prison is surrounded by cleared landscape, those 12-foot fences and razor wire and six towers occupied by armed guards. Guy wires will be strung over open areas to prevent helicopter escapes. In addition, there are other security systems federal officers would rather not have prisoners know about and will not discuss.

"There's obviously a message here, and the message is, we're not going to tolerate your violent behavior or predatory behavior, and, in fact, if you change that behavior, you eventually will get more privileges," Vanyur [states].

Source: Bob Unruh. "A New Home of Bars, Steel: America's Worst Inmates to Move to 'New Alcatraz' in Colorado." (Minneapolis/St. Paul) *Star Tribune*, December 11, 1994, pp. A10, A12. Reprinted by permission.

known super maximum-security facilities, was closed in 1963. The U.S. Penitentiary at Marion, Illinois, was built to replace Alcatraz. Federal facilities in Florence, Colorado, and Pelican Bay, California, are being heralded as the "new Alcatrazes." These two super-max prisons provide a level of custody and control unparalleled by any other prison in the country.

Differences Between Facilities for Men and Women

The first prison strictly for female inmates opened in 1873, but the construction of these facilities has not been as rapid as those for male prisoners. This is understandable given that the number of women sentenced to prison is but a fraction of the number of men similarly sentenced (6.3 percent of all sentenced prisoners in 1996 were women). However, the range of offenses committed by women is just as great as it is for men. Therefore, the need exists for a range of custody levels for women. Yet, because there are fewer facilities for females, many women's prisons contain a range of security levels within one institution. This differs from most prisons for men, where the facility is strictly of one custody level (for example, minimum-security or maximum-security only).

Nadel (1996, p. 2) notes: "Historically, each state has had only one women's facility that held all security classifications." Many states still lack a complete range of custody levels for female offenders and, consequently, women are often placed in the most readily available correctional facility instead of the most appropriate one. A few states also operate cocorrectional facilities, housing both male and female prisoners, the first of which was opened in 1971, but such facilities are being phased out. These coed facilities have some advantages, including better adjusted, more relaxed and well-behaved inmates resulting in fewer incidents of violence. Disadvantages of such facilities include the higher operational costs involved due to the need for more staff and the occurrence of sexual activity and possibility of pregnancies. Women's institutions attached to or affiliated with men's institutions typically are more security oriented. Furthermore, the staff-inmate ratio of women's prisons is normally higher than in men's prisons.

The physical design of women's prisons also differs from that of many men's prisons. Besides housing fewer inmates, many women's prisons appear less institutional and more homelike. Women's prisons tend more toward the campus, courtyard or free layout designs instead of the more orderly, traditional designs commonly used for men's prisons, particularly those of higher security levels.

Federal Bureau of Prisons

Since 1930, the Federal Bureau of Prisons (FBOP), an agency within the Department of Justice, has been responsible for running the country's federal facilities, which house those persons convicted of federal offenses. In 1979, the FBOP began using a new classification system to separate and assign prisoners to the appropriate facilities. The severity of the offense, the offender's prior record and the length of the sentence received are taken into consideration, and the

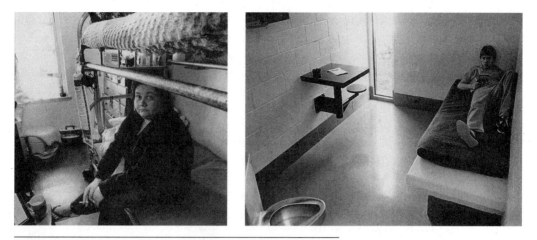

(Left) A female inmate sits on her bed at a Connecticut prison. Personal items such as the blanket, pillowcase and cloth calendar make the space feel more "homey," more like a dorm room than a prison cell. *(Right)* In contrast, a male offender lies on his bed, reading. This stark prison cell in Corvallis, Oregon, is typical of many facilities housing male inmates.

inmate is then assigned to one of six security levels. Security level 1 facilities are the least restrictive (minimum security); security level 6 facilities the most restrictive (super-maximum security). The prisons in Marion, Illinois, and Florence, Colorado, are examples of level 6 facilities. Federal security level designations are based on the same criteria as state security levels—presence of perimeter controls such as fences and walls, use of armed guards in observation towers, interior security measures, degree of separation of inmates and staffing levels.

FBOP classification personnel try to apply the "least restrictive" principle to keep the inmate population appropriately distributed and to avoid overcrowding in the higher security levels, where more intense correctional staff involvement and resources are needed. Efforts to place offenders in the least restrictive institution possible, closest to their homes, have resulted in less crowded higher-security-level institutions.

> The Federal Bureau of Prisons administers facilities that house persons convicted of federal offenses. Classification in the federal system is based on a six-level scale, with level 1 being the least restrictive and level 6 the most restrictive.

Architecture, Construction and Design

The architectural style, construction and design of a prison are directly affected by the custody level intended. Obviously, maximum-security prisons need more physical controls than minimum-security facilities. Whether inmates need to be kept physically isolated from each other and what services and programs will be made available to prisoners help determine what design is most suitable for the facility.

Early prison design focused on isolation and control. Consequently, many of today's maximum-security facilities resemble the earliest built prisons. As custody level decreases, the architecture of the facility tends to "relax." Figure 7–6 illustrates the various prison designs used in the United States.

The radial design or panopticon cell design was used by only one prison—that in Statesville. This design has rows of cells arranged like spokes on a wheel and places the control center at the hub of the wheel. A disadvantage of this design is that continuous surveillance of inmates is not possible due to the many blind spots inherent in the floorplan.

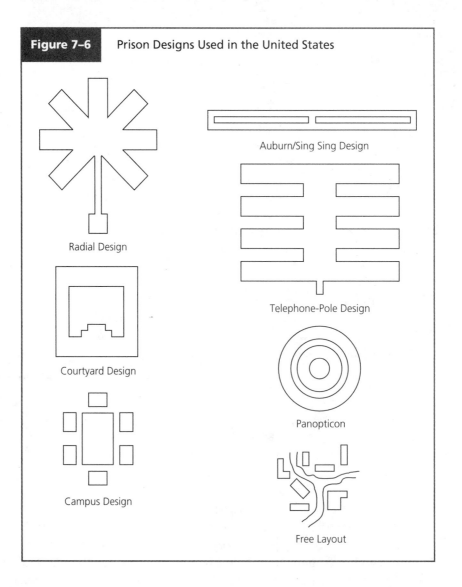

Figure 7–6   Prison Designs Used in the United States

Radial Design

Auburn/Sing Sing Design

Telephone-Pole Design

Courtyard Design

Panopticon

Campus Design

Free Layout

The telephone-pole design, as used in the federal U.S. Penitentiary at Leavenworth, Kansas, was the most commonly used plan for maximum-security prisons in this country. It allowed prisoners to be easily segregated in different wings according to classification levels, but it also posed a security risk by creating a corridor that may be blocked off by rioting inmates.

At the other end of the custody continuum, many minimum-security prisons have used the campus or free layout designs. These plans are characterized by lack of perimeter controls and other physical barriers. The architectural style is intended to reflect the correctional philosophy of these facilities—not to punish but to promote the rehabilitation and community reintegration of the inmates.

Between the rigidly confined telephone-pole design and the trustingly open campus and free layout designs is the courtyard design, more likely to be found in newer prisons. In this plan, a courtyard is centrally located, surrounded by the physical structure of the correctional facility. A corridor runs along the outer perimeter of the structure with individual cells and activity areas located along the interior perimeter, facing the courtyard.

> The telephone-pole design was most commonly used for maximum-security prisons; the campus and free layout designs are most frequently used for minimum-security prisons.

Although certain basic elements may work well in a variety of prison designs and for a variety of inmate populations, often the facility must be customized to achieve maximum effectiveness and efficiency. Coughlin (1992), in writing "How to Create a User Friendly Prison," says one of the most important considerations is to consult with those who will work in the facility. "Current line corrections officers, sergeants and lieutenants are your best sources of what works in today's prisons. Administrators, even though they were once line staff, are not working the blocks today, and they may not be as familiar with how equipment is actually used and what affects inmate behavior" (Coughlin, p. 92). The belief is that getting correctional staff involved in the design and construction of a prison will ultimately result in a better operating facility.

The construction of a facility also depends on the custody level intended. Differences are apparent between minimum- and maximum-security prisons regarding everything from cell layout and group/activity areas to door hinges and the type of toilet installed in each cell. Here, a distinction is made between detention hardware and builder's hardware. Builder's hardware includes materials used in "regular" structures such as offices whereas detention hardware includes specially designed materials for jails and prisons. Minimum-security facilities generally use a substantial amount of builder's hardware because the cost is lower, as is the need for fail-safe security devices. Maximum-security prisons, on the other hand, may use much more detention hardware to ensure the "safe keeping" of their more violence-prone inmate population (George, 1994, p. 86). This heavier grade hardware costs more and factors in to the heightened construction costs for maximum-security facilities.

Costs

Increasing costs of prison construction concern every taxpayer, and some correctional programs have found innovative ways to cut these costs while achieving other benefits. For example, Vestal (1994, p. 108) notes: "The California Department of Corrections (CDC) has learned that using inmate laborers in construction jobs not only teaches the inmates important job skills, but it also cuts costs and speeds up construction schedules."

As crime continues to make headlines, many citizens are clamoring for more prisons to be built. Few, however, realize how expensive it is to not just construct each prison but to operate and maintain such a facility. In fact, a prison built in California was too expensive to staff and run and is presently unused.

The cost of building a prison, or any other correctional facility, is typically presented in terms of cost per bed. According to Camp and Camp (p. 69), in 1996 the average construction costs per bed were:

- Minimum-security prison $31,184/bed
- Medium-security prison $50,376/bed
- Maximum-security prison $80,562/bed

Furthermore, these costs are expected to rise, with the following ranges forecast:

- Minimum-security beds $42,000–$45,000
- Medium-security beds $56,000–$71,000
- Maximum-security beds $84,000–$93,000

Considering an "average" prison in this nation is medium security and houses approximately 400 inmates, building such a facility, using the figures given by Camp and Camp, would cost over $20 million. And that is just to erect the structure. It would take another $15,000 per bed each year to operate the prison which, for the example just given, would total $6 million each year, or $180 million over 30 years, not adjusting for inflation. This high cost of construction and operation is one reason some are now considering the privatization of prisons, discussed at the end of the chapter.

A final consideration in the design and construction of prison facilities is the requirements set forth by the Americans with Disabilities Act (ADA), as discussed previously.

Administration, Management and Staffing

Prisons are administered by wardens or superintendents. In years past, many had no criminal justice or correctional background. Today, however, virtually all wardens have education and experience in criminal justice.

Responsibilities of prison administrators include interviewing and hiring corrections officers and other staff, terminating staff when necessary, developing policies to maintain facility security and staff and prisoner safety, implementing training programs for staff members and educational/vocational programs for inmates and overseeing general facility operations. Corrections management is discussed in Chapter 11.

Prison staff is a critical factor in the successful operation of the facility. A need exists nationwide to improve the quality of applicants for correctional positions. The federal prison system's, as well as some states', entry-level standards have been consistently higher than those for many state prisons, who typically require only that the applicant possess a high school diploma or GED (high school equivalency certificate) and a valid driver's license, be 21 or older and have never been convicted of a felony. Some states accept applicants who are only 18, rather young for a job with so much influence over inmates' rights and lives. Some states have raised their standards for all levels of correctional personnel. For example, many states now conduct extensive background checks on their applicants. Many proponents for higher standards are advocating the completion of college degrees, not just for entry-level personnel but for promotions to the positions of captain, warden and superintendent.

While few can argue against the benefits of higher education, other factors may be as or more important in preparing correctional staff for success in their field. Some experts believe that human relations skills may be more important to successful correctional officer employment than years of education. Correctional personnel are the topic of Chapter 12.

Operations

Prisons, like jails, must include in their operations a variety of services and programs for inmates. Prison operations differ from those of jails, however, in that jails are geared for the short-term stay of inmates and must deal with a relatively high turnover of prisoners, making the presentation and effectiveness of programs difficult.

Services and Programs

A variety of services are available to prison inmates, including food service, clothing provisions, health care (medical, dental, mental), visiting privileges, opportunities to exercise religious faiths, mail delivery, library access, commissary access and access to recreational facilities. The availability or lack of many of these services have been the focus of numerous prisoners' rights lawsuits, discussed in Chapter 14.

Food Service. Meals and dining procedures have changed greatly over the evolution of our prisons. While early prisoners had little if any choice over what they were served and were forbidden to talk while they ate, inmates today are given a greater variety in food choices and are allowed to converse during meals. Prison kitchens may consider the dietary restrictions of certain religious and ethnic groups, as well as the preferences of vegetarian inmates.

Health Care. Health care is one of the major services provided by a prison facility. With an aging prison population comes a corresponding range of age-related medical conditions. Tuberculosis (TB) has also been identified as an ailment that may spread rapidly in the prison environment. "Transmission of TB is of particular concern in correctional institutions, where the environment is often conducive to airborne transmission among inmates, health care workers, staff and visitors" (Mathews, 1994, p. 61). Furthermore, the increasing incidence of HIV-infected offenders has created many new concerns for both inmates and correctional staff, as discussed in Chapters 10 and 13.

Mental health services are also available to prisoners, as inmate suicide continues to be of great concern. "[T]he rate of suicide in prisons throughout the United States during the past 10 years was calculated to be 20.6 deaths per 100,000 inmates—a rate more than one and a half times greater than that of the general population, yet far below the rate of jail suicides." Furthermore, "states with small prison populations appear to have exceedingly high rates of suicide—often more than two and a half times greater than the national average" (Hayes, 1996, p. 92). The number of prison inmate suicides in 1995 was 160, and "47% of all inmate suicides were concentrated within the . . . five jurisdictions [of California, Texas, Pennsylvania, Georgia and the FBOP]" (Wees, 1996, p. 11).

While it is commonly acknowledged by corrections professionals that suicide among jail inmates is a critical problem—in fact it's the leading cause of death for persons in jail—many assume incorrectly that the "risk [of prisoner suicide] dissipates over time in prison as individuals become more comfortable with or tolerant of their predicaments and develop coping skills to effectively handle life behind bars" (Hayes, 1995, p. 433). According to Camp and Camp (p. 26) suicide is the third most common cause of death in prisons, behind natural causes and AIDS. Factors that may contribute to the high rate of suicide in prisons, and may lead to even higher levels in the future, are "recent mandatory sentencing laws, dramatic increases in death penalty and life sentences, overcrowded prison systems, increased cases of AIDS, and the 'graying' of inmate populations (inmates 55 years or older represent the fastest growing age group) [which] could instill despair and hopelessness in inmates" (Haycock, 1991).

Two national standards addressing prison suicide prevention policy are

1. Standard 3-4364 of the ACA's *Standards for Adult Correctional Institutions* (1990).
2. Standard P-58 of the National Commission on Correctional Health Care's *Standards for Health Services in Prison* (1992).

ACA Standard 3-4364 states, in part, there should be "a written suicide prevention and intervention program that is reviewed and approved by a qualified medical or mental health professional." NCCHC Standard P-58 states, in part: "The facility's plan for suicide prevention should include the following components: identification, training, assessment, monitoring, housing, referral, communication, intervention, notification, reporting and review." The National Center on Institutions and Alternatives (NCIA), in conducting a study for the National Institute of Corrections, combined the two standards and identified the six most critical components in a suicide prevention plan to assess how each state's department of corrections (DOC) and the FBOP was prepared to handle prison suicides.

From Table 7–4 it is seen that 41 DOCs (79 percent) had a complete suicide prevention policy, 8 DOCs (15 percent) did not have such a policy but did use some of the components identified and 3 DOCs (6 percent) did not address the issue of suicide prevention in any written policy (Hayes, 1996, p. 93). Furthermore, "only three departments of correction (California, Delaware and Louisiana) had suicide prevention policies that addressed all six critical components, and an additional five departments of correction (Connecticut, Hawaii, Nevada, Ohio and Pennsylvania) had policies that addressed all but one critical component. Thus, only 15 percent of all departments of correction had policies that contained either all or all but one critical suicide prevention component" (Hayes, 1996, pp. 93–94).

Hayes (1996, p. 94) concludes: "Recently, observers have noted that several developing trends suggest higher suicide rates in the future. Efforts to prevent future prison suicides will be predicated on several factors: further research, resources and progressive prison management."

Visiting Privileges. Prisoners as far back as those held in the Walnut Street Jail were allowed limited visitation. The quality of the visiting experience has improved greatly since then.

A range of visitation types and security levels exists, from the complete physical separation of closed visits, with floor-to-ceiling glazed glass between the inmate and the visitor in super-max prisons; to the limited- and informal-contact visits, where some level of physical contact is permitted; to the privacy afforded families, where the inmate and visitor(s) have minimal supervision.

Visitation poses a security risk for the facility, since visitors may attempt to smuggle weapons or drugs in to the inmate. Most prison administrators

Table 7–4	Suicide Prevention Protocols within Departments of Correction

DOC	Has Prevention Policy	Components Include					Admin. Review	Last Revision
		Training	Screening/ Assessment	Housing	Suicide Watch Levels (in minutes)	Intervention		
Alabama				x	15			May-93
Alaska		x	x		15, 30, 60			Feb-93
Arizona	x		x	x	10			Aug-89
Arkansas								
California	x	x	x	x	constant/unspecified	x	x	no date
Colorado	x	x		x	30, 60	.		Sep-93
Connecticut	x	x	x	x	constant, 15		x	Jul-92
Delaware	x	x	x	x	15	x	x	Jul-93
District of Columbia	x		x		15, 30, 60		x	Jun-93
Florida	x			x	constant, 15, 30			Oct-93
Georgia			x			x		Jan-91
Hawaii	x	x	x	x	constant, 15	x		Feb-93
Idaho	x		x			x	x	Nov-93
Illinois	x			x	10, 15			May-91
Indiana								
Iowa	x				15, 30			Mar-90
Kansas	x	x		x	10 to 15			Mar-93
Kentucky								
Louisiana	x	x	x	x	5 to 15	x	x	Sep-93
Maine		x	x		constant, 15			Draft/94
Maryland	x			x				Feb-92
Massachusetts			x	x				May-93
Michigan	x	x	x	x	10			Dec-91
Minnesota	x		x	x	15, 30			May-92
Mississippi	x			x	5			Nov-93
Missouri	x		x	x	15			Jun-92
Montana	x	x	x	x	15			May-93
Nebraska	x	x						Dec-93
Nevada	x	x	x	x	constant, 15		x	Aug-93
New Hampshire	x		x	x	15, 30, periodic	x		Aug-93
New Jersey	x			x	15	x		Jul-93
New Mexico	x			x	constant	x		Jan-92
New York		x		x	constant, 5, 15		x	Sep-92
North Carolina	x	x	x	x	constant, 15			Jul-93
North Dakota		x		x	15, 30			Sep-93
Ohio	x	x	x	x	5, 15		x	Dec-92
Oklahoma	x		x	x	15		x	May-92
Oregon	x	x	x	x	10 to 15			no date
Pennsylvania	x	x	x	x	constant, 15, 30		x	Apr-94
Rhode Island	x			x	15	x	x	Apr-88
South Carolina	x	x	x					Mar-86
South Dakota	x	x	x		15		x	Jun-91
Tennessee	x	x		x				Nov-92
Texas	x			x	15	x		Oct-93
Utah	x			x	15			Feb-94
Vermont	x		x	x	constant, 10 to 15			Apr-82
Virginia	x	x		x	constant, 15			Feb-92
Washington	x	x		x	constant, 15			Jun-84
West Virginia	x	x	x	x	15			May-87
Wisconsin				x	15			Apr-90
Wyoming	x	x	x	x	constant, 15	x		Oct-92
Federal Bureau of Prisons	x	x	x	x			x	Apr-90

Source: Lindsay M. Hayes. "Prison Suicide: Rates and Prevention Policies." *Corrections Today,* February 1996, p. 94. Reprinted by permission.

feel, however, that the benefits of visitation are worth the risks, since keeping contact with family members and friends seems to help the emotional well-being of inmates, translating into fewer disciplinary incidents within the facility. Furthermore, allowing an inmate to have contact with people on the outside helps prevent the total withdrawal of the prisoner from society and may help disrupt prisoner bonding by keeping inmates from turning to each other as their only source of company. Visitation can combat the inmate social system and prepare inmates for freedom in the outside world.

Recently, however, visitation privileges have become a sort of bargaining chip which some prison administrators have used to promote good behavior among the inmates. For example, some state Departments of Corrections reward good behavior with additional visitation rights and more contact visits (Wunder, 1995, pp. 6–9). Conversely, other state DOCs have reduced or eliminated certain visitation privileges for a variety of reasons, including cost containment and punishment. Wunder (p. 5) notes: "A maximum security prison in the District of Columbia has eliminated Annual Family Day, a time when inmates were allowed to participate in an outdoor event with their families." The elimination of family-oriented privileges reflects the harsher public view toward prisoners currently in vogue. The issue of visitation is discussed further in the chapter on prisoners' rights.

Programs. Besides numerous services, prisons may also provide a variety of programs for inmates. Programming may include treatment programs for drug and/or alcohol abuse, self-help programs, life-skills programs, vocational/technical skill development programs, adult education and literacy programs, cultural or ethnic programs and institutional or community service programs. Participation in such programs is voluntary by inmates, with prison officials able to revoke participation privileges for any number of reasons, including behavioral problems and cost containment.

One type of program that remains fairly controversial is the prison college program. McCollum (1994, p. 51) notes: "Prison college programs have a long history in the United States but their acceptability has ebbed and flowed over the years. Support of college programs in prison peaked in the 1960s and 70s, but became less popular in the 1980s and 90s." Opponents of such programs argue that law-abiding citizens have enough trouble acquiring the financial assistance to attend college, so why should federal tuition assistance be extended to convicted criminals? According to McCollum (p. 51): "A significant body of research has developed in recent years that demonstrates a positive correlation between higher education and postrelease success." She goes on to note: "Despite this, currently, at least in the United States, college programs continue to be the most vulnerable of all prison education programs." For example, Congress eliminated all Pell grants for inmates, thereby effectively eliminating most prison college programs.

Prison Industries

Prison industry (where inmates produce goods and services) has also been a controversial issue for corrections, as prison administrators, small businesses and labor unions have battled for the right to turn a profit and have debated the definition of fair competition. Nationally, a total of 6.6 percent of all confined prisoners were assigned to prison industries on January 1, 1997 (Camp and Camp, p. 81).

Prison labor has been around as long as the prisons themselves. According to Verdeyen (1995, p. 106): "The Auburn system of correctional philosophy that emerged in the 1800s set the stage for work programs and the use of inmate labor as we know it today. . . [by creating] the contract system . . . [under which] offenders were released to private manufacturers who supplied materials and machinery; prison management provided space and supervision." This arrangement, however, fell under heavy criticism from labor unions and the private business sector, who claimed such prison industries created unfair competition. As a result, the federal government drafted two pieces of legislation which effectively prevented the sale of prison-made goods to any private-sector markets. These two acts were the Hawes-Cooper Act of 1929 and the Sumners-Ashurst Act of 1935.

Prison industries continued to suffer throughout much of the middle part of this century but began making a comeback during the 1980s. One of the greatest proponents of the resurrection of prison industry was former Chief Justice Warren Burger. As Raspberry (1995, p. A27) put it: "It was his dream that America would one day see what had long been so obvious to him: that it made no sense (and did a great deal of harm) to warehouse prison inmates, virtually enforce their idleness and then release them—penniless, unskilled and bitter." In 1979, the Justice System Improvement Act was passed, authorizing the development of the Prison Industry Enhancement (PIE) certification program, which was later expanded by both the Justice Assistance Act of 1984 and the Crime Control Act of 1990. Verdeyen (p. 109) notes:

> A key provision of PIE for certified agencies is exemption from federal constraints placed on prison-made goods (Walsh-Healy Act and Sumners-Ashurst Act) by permitting the sale of such goods in interstate commerce and to the federal government. Also of importance to the PIE program is the mandatory requirement that comparable wages be paid at a rate that is not less than the federal minimum. With the earned wages, offenders can make a substantial contribution to society. Deductions from gross wages include room and board payments, federal and state taxes, family support and contributions to a state's crime victims program of at least 5 percent and not more than 20 percent of gross wages.

According to Verdeyen (p. 109): "PIE is a major development in state and county prison industries." Furthermore, "[s]ince the inception of the PIE concept in 1979, the programs have reached the level where there are 34 jurisdictions certified, gross earnings of offenders have exceeded $44 million and costs of incarceration have been reduced by over $8.2 million." The successes of PIE are heralded by inmates and employers alike. As Verdeyen (p. 110) notes: "One offender commented that the program allowed him to support his son and set money aside to have the necessities to be able to jump right into a job. Several employers have stated that the skill levels of the workers, in many instances, exceed the levels they encounter in the private sector."

> Prison industries suffered during the mid-1900s but began making a comeback during the 1980s. Today these industries are regarded as positive and beneficial enterprises by many inmates, correctional administrators and those in the private sector.

PIE is just one example of a successful prison industry program. The Free Venture model is another program, federally funded, which has attempted to create a realistic work environment for inmates by having them work full days, receiving wages based on their output and by providing them with useful job skills that will help them find employment once released (Connecticut Department of Corrections). Inmates in the federal prison system may be eligible for employment by UNICOR, the corporate trade name of Federal Prison Industries, Inc. This wholly owned government corporation sells products and services to other federal agencies. It supports the Federal Bureau of Prisons through employment of inmates in work programs.

By many standards, the efforts of these prison industries have been fairly successful, both in terms of giving inmates something meaningful to do and by providing financial support for the facility. Verdeyen (p. 108) states: "Cited by most correctional administrators as one of the most important programs in offender management today, correctional industry managers must address the complex and, oftentimes, divergent goals of maintaining institutional security while focusing on costs, production and customer satisfaction. . . losses are unacceptable . . . and usually have a major impact on operations." According to Camp and Camp (p. 85): "Forty-eight agencies reported gross sales of $1.4 billion for agency-operated prison industries during fiscal year 1996." Furthermore, "[p]rofit/losses ranged from a high of $12.1 million at the Federal Bureau of Prisons to a loss of $894,782 in Illinois."

The goods and services produced by prison industries have become quite diversified, as the labor unions and private business sectors have relaxed. Prison industry programs are now involved in telemarketing, data processing, computer-aided design, electronics, waste recycling, furniture manufacturing, textiles and metals and, most assuredly, the production of license plates. In fact, over 30 states still have inmates manufacturing license plates. Another example of a successful prison industry is the manufacture and sale of blue jeans under the name "Prisoner Blues." A listing of the prison industry products and services for 1996, by state, is given in Table 7–5.

Table 7–5   1996 Prison Industry Products and Services

	Agriculture/ Food	Garment/ Textiles	Vehicle/ Vehicle-Related	Wood Products/ Furniture	Paper Products/ Printing	Metal Products	Services	Business-Related/ Electronic Products	Janitorial Supplies	Misc.
Alabama		♦	♦	♦	♦	♦	♦		♦	♦
Alaska	♦	♦	♦	♦		♦	♦			
Arizona	♦	♦			♦	♦	♦			
Arkansas		♦	♦	♦	♦		♦	♦		♦
California	♦	♦		♦		♦	♦		♦	♦
Colorado	♦	♦		♦	♦	♦	♦	♦		♦
Connecticut		♦	♦		♦	♦	♦			♦
Delaware	♦	♦		♦	♦					
Dist. of Col.	♦	♦			♦	♦	♦			
Florida	♦	♦		♦	♦					♦
Georgia		♦		♦		♦			♦	♦
Hawaii	♦	♦	♦		♦		♦	♦		
Idaho	♦			♦	♦					
Illinois	♦	♦	♦	♦	♦		♦			♦
Indiana	♦			♦	♦	♦			♦	
Iowa		♦		♦	♦				♦	♦
Kansas		♦		♦	♦				♦	
Kentucky		♦		♦	♦	♦	♦		♦	
Louisiana		♦		♦	♦		♦		♦	
Maine		♦		♦						
Maryland	♦	♦		♦	♦					♦
Massachusetts		♦		♦	♦					♦
Michigan	♦	♦		♦		♦	♦			
Minnesota		♦	♦	♦	♦	♦	♦			♦
Mississippi		♦		♦	♦	♦				
Missouri		♦		♦	♦	♦				
Nebraska		♦	♦	♦	♦	♦	♦	♦	♦	
New Hampshire	♦			♦	♦	♦	♦			
New Jersey	♦	♦		♦	♦	♦	♦		♦	
New Mexico		♦		♦	♦	♦	♦		♦	
New York		♦		♦		♦	♦			♦
North Carolina	♦	♦	♦	♦	♦	♦	♦		♦	♦
North Dakota				♦	♦	♦				
Ohio			♦	♦	♦			♦		♦
Oklahoma	♦	♦		♦	♦		♦			
Oregon		♦		♦	♦	♦	♦			
Pennsylvania	♦	♦	♦	♦	♦	♦	♦		♦	♦
Rhode Island		♦	♦	♦	♦	♦	♦	♦		♦
South Carolina		♦		♦	♦	♦	♦			
South Dakota		♦		♦	♦	♦				
Tennessee		♦		♦	♦		♦			♦
Texas		♦		♦	♦	♦	♦		♦	♦
Utah	♦			♦	♦		♦			
Vermont				♦						
Virginia		♦		♦	♦	♦		♦	♦	♦
Washington	♦	♦			♦	♦	♦			♦
West Virginia		♦		♦	♦	♦				
Wisconsin	♦	♦		♦	♦	♦	♦	♦		♦
Wyoming		♦			♦	♦				
Federal		♦		♦	♦	♦	♦	♦	♦	
Total	21	43	12	45	44	32	31	9	16	21

♦ = prison industry produces/provides.

Source: George M. Camp and Camille Graham Camp. *The Corrections Yearbook, 1997.* South Salem, NY: The Criminal Justice Institute, 1997, p. 86. Reprinted by permission.

Some states have set up prison facilities to suit the economy of the region. For instance, agricultural prisons or prison farms have cropped up around the country, particularly in the South, where prisoners work to produce food for the other institutions in the state and for sale to the public. Lumber camps and road prisons have also been used by some states to meet their particular needs. Whether these are considered prison industries or not, such activities supplement the financial operations of correctional facilities. These programs may also instill work ethics and develop skills the inmates may find useful once released from prison.

Getting Out of Prison

All inmates spend time thinking about the day when they'll be released. While some prisoners find themselves serving life sentences with no chance of ever being freed, most inmates are eventually released from prison to return to society. This release may be the result of a variety of mechanisms, including

- Completion of the sentence (including reductions for good time).
- Executive clemency (pardon, amnesty, reprieve, commutation).
- Parole.
- Other forms of early release (sentence reduction, emergency release, early parole).

Of course, escape and death in prison are two other ways of getting out.

➤   Release from prison is either unconditional or conditional. As one might expect, **unconditional release** simply means the prisoner is freed from all government control, with no further restrictions or conditions to satisfy.

➤ **Conditional release,** however, means the offender is discharged from prison but must satisfy certain conditions while in the community to receive complete freedom and final release. Conditional release is further divided into

➤ two categories: discretionary or mandatory. **Discretionary release** is based on a decision by a parole board or other paroling authority and allows the re-

➤ lease of a prisoner prior to the expiration of the entire sentence. **Mandatory release** is defined by statute and is based on the offender serving the full sentence minus any good time credits. Mandatory release also takes into account any jail time served and credits received for program participation during incarceration. Since the mid-1970s, the distribution of parole cases between discretionary and mandatory release has changed. While about the same proportion of released prisoners are on parole today, a greater proportion are mandatory releases.

Conditional release is far more common, for both state and federal prisoners, than unconditional release, with over 80 percent of those released receiving supervision in the community. Furthermore, mandatory releases comprise slightly more than one-third of all conditional releases, with discretionary releases being most common.

> Release from prison may be either unconditional or conditional. Conditional release may be either discretionary or mandatory. The most prevalent form of release today is discretionary (conditional) release; the least prevalent is unconditional release.

Serving a Full Sentence

Since indeterminate sentencing leaves the period of incarceration open-ended, the ability of an inmate to serve a *full* sentence depends upon receiving a determinate sentence. Serving the length of the original sentence minus any good time credits constitutes serving a full sentence. Once the determined length of time has been served, the prisoner may receive either an unconditional prison release, in which complete freedom is restored and no further community supervision is required, or a supervisory (conditional) mandatory release, where some level of continued supervision is required of the offender. However, since prison overcrowding is a major concern, fewer and fewer inmates are being held to serve their entire original sentence.

Executive Clemency

➤ Prisoners may also be released via **executive clemency** procedures. This form of release derives its name from the person or governing body granting the release—an entity within the executive branch of government, either the governor of the state (the chief executive), the parole board or some other authorized board or commission. In the case of federal prisoners, the president, as chief executive, may extend executive clemency.

Executive clemency comes in a variety of forms:

➤ • **Pardon**—unconditional release absolving an individual from blame for a crime.

➤ • **Amnesty**—a pardon that applies to an entire class or group of individuals.

➤ • **Reprieve**—typically lessens the punishment received, the most common application involves the death penalty, with the reprieve acting as a temporary stay of execution.

➤ • **Commutation**—lessens the severity of punishment by shortening the sentence.

Executive clemency is a rare avenue by which to get out of prison. A far more common route is via parole.

Parole

The parole population comprises a substantial piece of the correctional picture. Approximately 700,000 adults were on parole at the end of 1995 (*Correctional Populations*, 1997, p. 2). According to Snell (p. iv): "The number of persons on parole grew 199% since 1980, more than that of any other correctional population." Parole has had many supporters and critics throughout the years. Proponents point out the importance parole plays in relieving some of the burdens of our overcrowded prisons, while opponents claim parole lets offenders off by shortening their stay behind bars and exposes the public to criminals who haven't yet paid their debt.

Cohen (1995, p. 2) states: "The term parole refers to both the process for releasing offenders from prison prior to the expiration of their sentences and to the period of conditional supervision in the community following imprisonment."

> **Parole** is the conditional release from prison before the expiration of the sentence and the period of supervision in the community following this release.

Violation of the conditions of parole typically sends the offender back to prison.

To better understand the philosophy and importance of parole, consider its history and use in the United States.

A Brief History of Parole. Parole practices in this country may be traced back to Europe. During the mid-1800s, Alexander Maconochie introduced "marks of commendation" as a way for prisoners to be rewarded for good behavior. The accumulation of so many marks earned inmates a chance for early release from prison, a practice that evolved into the use of good time credits. Sir Walter Crofton developed an indeterminate system of imprisonment whereby prisoners could earn early conditional release via "tickets of leave." Prisoners granted tickets of leave were expected to abide by the conditions of their early release and submit progress reports, with failure to do so resulting in their return to prison. Because parolees were unsupervised, the practice would not be recognizable as modern parole.

In the United States, good time laws were used for many decades before formal parole procedures were established. In 1817, New York became the first state to pass a good time law, allowing sentences to be reduced by as much as one-fourth the original length. It wasn't until 1876 that Zebulon Brockway established formal parole procedures at Elmira Reformatory. Brockway had all the elements of modern parole: indeterminacy, discretionary decisions and supervision (by volunteers). By 1916, every state had passed some form of good time law, but not until 1944 did all states have some mechanism for parole in place.

For several decades, parole was used regularly as a way to ease prisoners back into society and to relieve the pressures of prison overcrowding. However, in the 1970s, as the correctional philosophy swung away from the rehabilitative ideal and became more punitive, several states abolished parole and replaced indeterminate sentencing schemes with determinate ones. This movement was initiated in 1976 by Maine, followed by Arizona, California and Indiana the next year and Illinois and New Mexico in 1978. Many other states have since followed suit by reducing or completely eliminating parole. Although these states have done away with parole, they have implemented or retained other ways in which prisoners can obtain an early release, such as augmentation of the good time credit system.

In 1984, Congress passed the Comprehensive Crime Control Act, which set a course for parole to be abolished for federal prisoners starting November 1992. These state and federal cutbacks in parole have contributed to the overcrowded conditions in our nation's prisons, a problem discussed later in this chapter.

The Process of Parole. Parole as a release option is addressed quite early during the period of incarceration, although the actual release may still be a decade or more away. In many jurisdictions, a **release eligibility date** is determined during the first few months of the prisoner's incarceration. This is the first time that individual will be *considered* for release on parole. Many states use a formula or table to arrive at this date. An example of such a tool is shown in Table 7–6.

A variety of factors are taken into account to determine this date, such as the inmate's behavior while incarcerated, participation in programs, whether the inmate has a plan for life on the outside and if the inmate poses any public risk. Hoffman and Beck's Salient Factor Score Index is a tool that helps evaluate an offender's dangerousness. This index is weighted against those who have prior records and also considers the offender's age and drug dependency. Caution is needed in relying on such numerical scores as a basis for release because of false positives and negatives. A false positive happens when the score predicts individuals to be dangerous when, in fact, they are not. A false negative occurs when individuals are deemed not dangerous by the score when, in reality, they do present a public risk. The potential for either result should eliminate strict reliance on a number to determine if an individual should be released.

Those who fail to meet the various standards for release will continue to serve their sentence until another eligibility date can be set. For those who do receive parole, the length and conditions of the parole may vary substantially. For example, those serving time for murder usually draw longer parole lengths than those doing time for stolen property. Conditions of parole typically include regular meetings between the parolee and the parole officer at the parolee's home or place of employment, a requirement that the parolee receive permission to leave the county or state, a promise to act in a law-abiding manner, a requirement to acquire and hold a job, a prohibition on purchasing or using a firearm and submission to random or routine drug testing.

In many states the decision as to which prisoners receive parole is made by a parole board.

Table 7–6	Computing Parole Eligibility

Calculation of parole eligibility under parole regulations which use the twenty percent (20%) of time served criteria, for crimes committed after December 3, 1980, length of time to serve for parole eligibility [parole regulations 501 KAR 1:030 provides: 1 year up to but not including 2 years, 4 months to serve; 2 years up to and including 39 years, 20% of sentence received; more than 39 years, up to and including life, 8 years to serve]:

Since January 1975, KRS 532.120(3) allows for a deduction for time spent in custody prior to commencement of sentence.

Sentence Length Years	Original Parole Eligibility Years Minus Jail Time	Sentence Length Years	Original Parole Eligibility Years Minus Jail Time
1–23 months	4 months	19 years	3 years & 10 months
2 years	5 months	20 years	4 years
2 years & 6 months	6 months	21 years	4 years & 2 months
3 years	7 months	22 years	4 years & 5 months
3 years & 6 months	8 months	23 years	4 years & 7 months
4 years	10 months	24 years	4 years & 10 months
4 years & 6 months	11 months	25 years	5 years
5 years	1 year	26 years	5 years & 2 months
5 years & 6 months	1 year & 1 month	27 years	5 years & 5 months
6 years	1 year & 2 months	28 years	5 years & 7 months
7 years	1 year & 5 months	29 years	5 years & 10 months
8 years	1 year & 7 months	30 years	6 years
9 years	1 year & 10 months	31 years	6 years & 2 months
10 years	2 years	32 years	6 years & 5 months
11 years	2 years & 2 months	33 years	6 years & 7 months
12 years	2 years & 5 months	34 years	6 years & 10 months
13 years	2 years & 7 months	35 years	7 years
14 years	2 years & 10 months	36 years	7 years & 2 months
15 years	3 years	37 years	7 years & 5 months
16 years	3 years & 2 months	38 years	7 years & 7 months
17 years	3 years & 5 months	39 years	7 years & 10 months
18 years	3 years & 7 months		

More than 39 years, up to and including life . . . . 8 years

Persistent felony offender 1st degree . . . . 10 years

(Effective July 15, 1994—Persons found to be a Persistent Felony Offender in the First Degree based solely on Class D Felony charges would not be required to serve 10 years for parole review, but would fall under the twenty percent (20%) criteria set out above. Persistent Felony Offender in the First Degree based on Class A, Class B, or Class C Felonies would still be required to serve 10 years for parole review)

continued

Table 7–6	Computing Parole Eligibility—*Continued*

Calculation of Parole Eligibility under KRS 439.3401 (Parole for Violent Offenders) for Crimes Identified by the Department of Corrections, Office of General Counsel:

For crimes committed after July 15, 1986, time service for original eligibility—**MINUS JAIL TIME:**

Capital Offenses:

For the crimes of murder, or kidnapping *(which involves the death of the victim),*
or complicity to murder, or kidnapping *(which involves the death of the victim),*

    Sentences of a number of years . . . . . 50% of sentence imposed or 12 years—whichever is less

    Sentences of life . . . . 12 years

Class A & B Felonies:

For the crimes of manslaughter 1, rape 1, sodomy 1, assault 1, kidnapping *(where there is serious physical injury of the victim),* arson 1 *(where there is serious physical injury or death),* or complicity to manslaughter 1, rape 1, sodomy 1, assault 1, kidnapping *(where there is serious physical injury of the victim),* arson 1 *(where there is serious physical injury or death),*

    Sentences of a number of years . . . . . 50% of sentence imposed or 12 years—whichever is less

    Sentences of life . . . . 12 years

Exemptions from KRS 439.3401 for victims of domestic violence and abuse per KRS 439.3401(4), this section shall not apply to a person who has been determined by a court to have been a victim of domestic violence or abuse pursuant to KRS 533.060 with regard to the offenses involving the death of the victim or serious physical injury to the victim (exemption does not extend to rape 1st degree or sodomy 1st degree by the defendant). The findings of the court shall be noted in the final judgment.

Calculation of Parole Eligibility for Sentences of Death, or Life without Benefit of Parole for 25 years, Time Service for Original Eligibility—MINUS JAIL TIME:

    Death Sentence . . . . None

    Life without Benefit of Parole for 25 years . . . . 25 years

Source: Department of Corrections, Frankfort, KY, 1998.

> **The Parole Board.** The **parole board** is the authority charged with determining which prisoners should be released and under what conditions. In 1995, half of all entries to parole were based on parole board decisions (*Correctional Populations,* p. 2). The board also determines if parole should be revoked when violations occur and when an individual has satisfied the conditions of parole and is ready for final release.

Each state decides who and how many should make up the parole board. Some states have nearly 20 people on their parole board; others have only three. In most states, parole board members are appointed by the governor. Other states select board members from a civil service list.

Most states have a full-time parole board. Although great variation exists among the states regarding qualifications for parole board members, some state statutes list qualifications such as training or experience in law, criminal justice or related social science fields. The members of the parole board may be correc-

An inmate makes his case before a West Virginia parole board.
Behind him sits the sister of the man the inmate beat and robbed.
With her blessing, the inmate was paroled.

tions staff (institutional boards) or may be completely independent of the correctional system. Many states have chosen to include on their parole boards individuals from within the corrections profession *and* those outside the profession, to achieve a better balance. Such boards are known as *consolidated* parole boards, in contrast to the purely institutional or independent boards.

➤ In most states, the parole board conducts a **parole hearing** to determine if an inmate should be released on parole. During this hearing, all or part of the parole board interviews the inmate to evaluate various factors. Some states have an independent hearing examiner interview the inmate; other states rely solely on written reports from correctional staff to determine parole eligibility and never speak directly with the inmate being evaluated.

With an increasing number of individuals being placed on parole, parole boards and other paroling authorities are becoming busier and busier. Many parole board members have limited time to review the documentation for each case. Furthermore, as noted by Bartollas and Conrad (p. 257): "The capricious and arbitrary manner in which parole boards, especially in the past, decided when an inmate was ready for release has drawn strong criticism from inmates, prison reformers, and practitioners in the criminal justice system. The riot at Attica in New York in 1971 and the subsequent report that identified parole as a source of inmate discontent has also contributed to the unfavorable scrutiny of parole boards."

Some have strongly criticized the ability of parole boards to effectively determine which inmates may be safely released back to society. The pressure to clear bedspace and relieve overcrowding may be pushing parole authorities to release inmates who are poor candidates for parole, while the criminal justice system basically sanctions these questionable releases through mechanisms that protect paroling authorities from legal liability should they make a bad decision. As Fein ("Tonry, Fein Debate," 1993, p. 60) puts it:

> Most parole authorities receive legal immunity from making decisions that eventuate in the death or a lesser crime being committed against an innocent. Those parole officials recognize how intimidated they would be in making parole decisions if they asked themselves the question, "If I'm wrong, and a new crime occurs and I'm held liable. . . ."
>
> That in my judgment, is a good test of the level of confidence those who are on the firing line every day have in their ability to separate out those who are good candidates for intermediate parole, probation and other lesser punishments than prison in order to ensure public safety.

Clearly, the parole process is not perfect, and many states have chosen to abolish it. But many states still rely on parole to return inmates to society and to relieve the pressures on their overcrowded prisons. Once the inmate is released, it is the parole officer's task to supervise the parolee.

The Parole Officer. Many states have the same officers supervising both probationers and parolees. Indeed, the jobs are very much alike, seeking to make sure the offender abides by the conditions of the probation or parole. The parole officer is responsible for monitoring released individuals through regularly scheduled interviews, conducting routine or random drug tests, performing surveillance to ensure adherence to curfews and other restrictions, providing necessary counseling and referring the parolee to various community resources that may aid the parolee in finding work or receiving needed treatment or additional counseling.

The relationship between the parole officer and parolee can have a great impact on whether the parole is successful. Some inmates see the parole officer as an enemy, whose sole purpose is to catch them "screwing up" and return them to prison. Others view the parole officer as a friend, someone who wants to help them successfully complete their parole and achieve final release. Social skills and an ability to relate to a variety of personality types serve a parole officer well as the need to juggle an ever broadening range of offenders is becoming more common. The parole officer is discussed in detail in Chapter 12.

Types of Parole Releases. The type of parole release or reentry program granted depends on the inmate's individual needs and the variety of programs offered in a particular area. Common release programs include furloughs, work release, educational release, shock incarceration and halfway houses. Table 7–7 shows the number of inmates released to various programs during 1996.

➤ A **furlough** allows an inmate to go home unsupervised for a short period, typically 24 to 72 hours, although furloughs may extend to a week or longer.

Table 7–7	Inmates Released to Various Parole Programs in 1996

	Furloughs	Work Release	Study Release	Halfway Houses
Alabama		2,926		
Alaska[1]	839			839
Arizona		125		
Arkansas[2]	620	409		
Colorado[3]		2,216		
Connecticut	781			1,476
Delaware	101	297		
District of Columbia	48			1,212
Florida		4,200		
Georgia				1,313
Hawaii		337	7	4
Idaho[4]	4			
Illinois[5]		5,358		
Indiana	293	501	4	
Kansas[6]	10	411		
Kentucky	251			576
Louisiana[7]	4	1,046		
Maine	270	3,032	73	51
Massachusetts[8]	205			
Michigan				1,367
Minnesota	87	438		
Missouri[9]		1,282		550
Nebraska	477	664		
Nevada				349
New Jersey	1,127	225		1,838

[1]No furloughs resulted in felony. Misdem. not tracked but est. less than 10. [2]Incl. Dept. of Comm. Punishment which only has emerg. furloughs & est. 10 inm./furloughs. DOC furloughs incl. 286 meritorious, 607 emergency. [3]Work rel. is comm./ISP transitional programs. [4]Policy change resulted in large decrease over last year furloughs. [5]Inm. are admitted into work rel. before entering elec. det. [6]FY'96. Represents all entries to work rel. fac. (not work furloughs) during FY'96. [7]Inm. on furlough for medical reasons. Inm. on furlough who esc. were 0 but two died while on furlough. Work rel. and halfway houses are synonymous; this number represents work rel. halfway houses. [8]Furloughs are escorted. [9]Work rel. is monthly avg. [10]Work rel. is a combination work/study rel. [11]Halfway houses incl. parolees transferred from State Corr. Inst. to Comm. Corr. Centers. [12]Medical furloughs are granted only to terminally ill inm. with <1 yr. to live. [13]Work rel. est. [14]Work rel. figure is its ADP for 1/97. Halfway houses avg. 200/mo. [15]Numbers represent inm. placed during 1995. [16]Social furloughs only. Esc. was from social furlough only.

Source: George M. Camp and Camille Graham Camp. *The Corrections Yearbook, 1997.* South Salem, NY: The Criminal Justice Institute, 1997, p. 102, 104. Reprinted by permission.

continued

| Table 7–7 | Inmates Released to Various Parole Programs in 1996—*Continued* |

	Furloughs	Work Release	Study Release	Halfway Houses
New Mexico		200	50	
New York	17,274	7,370		
North Carolina		2,407	22	
North Dakota	7	73		
Ohio		913		836
Oklahoma	416	145	66	665
Oregon	11	139		
Pennsylvania[10,11]	108	295		1,738
Rhode Island		204		
South Carolina[12]	2	658		
South Dakota	60	242		93
Tennessee		1,572		
Utah				9
Vermont[13]	593	350		
Virginia[14]		151		2,400
Washington	33	2,669		
West Virginia	200	200	25	
Wisconsin[15]				546
Wyoming	6			560
Federal[16]	5,630			18,893
Total	**29,457**	**41,055**	**247**	**35,315**

Furloughs are generally reserved for offenders nearing the end of their sentence who have demonstrated their ability to behave and be trusted. Furloughs came under attack during the late 1980s when convicted murderer Willie Horton, sentenced to life *without parole,* was released on furlough, during which time he kidnapped and raped a woman and beat her fiancé. During 1996, 40 states permitted a total of 186,059 furloughs to 29,457 inmates (Camp and Camp, p. 104).

➤   **Work release** allows an inmate to leave the prison during the day, go to a job in the community and return to the prison after work. Work release goes by a number of names, including work furlough, day pass and day parole. Work release was one of the prison reforms suggested by Maconochie in the mid-1800s, and was first officially used in the United States in 1913 by Wisconsin's penal system. Typically the minimum-security facilities sponsor work release programs.

➤   **Educational release,** or study release, is like work release except that the inmate leaves the prison to attend classes. Many prisons offer such classes within the facility itself, but for those that don't, educational release is another way for inmates to be eased out of prison life and back into society.

➤   **Shock incarceration** is where an inmate is held in prison for a short time (the "shock"), typically 30, 60, 90 or 120 days, and then released on parole. This type of release is generally reserved for nonviolent first-time offenders. A form of shock incarceration known as "boot camp" is discussed later in the chapter.

➤   A **halfway house** is a place designed to ease the transition from life in prison to life in free society, where a parolee is provided with food, clothing, shelter and counseling. It may be a public or private facility, and the counseling and services provided to parolees vary greatly depending on the resources obtained by the facility. Such places impose "rules of the house" which parolees must abide by to maintain residency and are often in contact with a parolee's parole officer to confirm adherence to certain conditions of the parole.

When a parole officer learns that a parolee has violated any of the conditions of the parole, there is a good possibility that the court will begin parole revocation procedures.

Parole Revocation. Parole revocation occurs when a parolee either breaks the law or commits a technical violation of the conditions of parole, is taken into custody and is returned to prison, possibly to serve the remainder of the original sentence.

Several Supreme Court decisions have affected the granting and revocation of parole. The 1979 case of *Greenholtz v. Inmates of Nebraska Penal and Correctional Complex* determined "that prison inmates have no constitutional or inherent right to be conditionally released prior to the expiration of their sentence" ("Fourteenth Amendment," 1979, p. 468). However, once parole is granted, parolees do have certain due process rights which cannot be transgressed during the course of parole revocation proceedings.

The most notable case pertaining to parole revocation is *Morrissey v. Brewer* (1972). In 1967, Morrissey was convicted of check fraud and sentenced to seven years in the Iowa State Penitentiary. He received parole in June 1968 but was rearrested seven months later when his parole officer discovered Morrissey had purchased a car under a false name, obtained credit cards under a false name, given false information to an insurance company after his involvement in an auto accident and moved to a new residence without notifying his parole officer. Morrissey's parole was revoked and he was reincarcerated.

Morrissey took his case to court, claiming the revocation of his parole without a hearing violated his due process rights. The district court disagreed, ruling that the state's failure to conduct a hearing in conjunction with the parole revocation did not violate Morrissey's due process rights. Morrissey appealed, but the appellate court concurred with the district court's ruling. Morrissey finally had his case heard before the Supreme Court, which reversed the appellate court's ruling and set forth specific due process rights for persons entering parole revocation proceedings, including the right to written notice of the alleged violations, the disclosure of any evidence to support the allegations, the chance to be heard in person and to present witnesses and evidence, the opportunity to cross-examine adverse witnesses, the right to a judgment by a neutral body such as the parole board and receipt of a written statement of the reasons for the revocation of parole. As a result of *Morrissey v. Brewer,* two hearings now occur during parole revocation proceedings—a preliminary hearing by the parole agency to determine probable cause for revocation and a second hearing by a paroling agency to evaluate whether parole should, in fact, be revoked.

Two other cases, *Mempa v. Rhay* (1968) and *Gagnon v. Scarpelli* (1973), address parolees' right to have counsel present during revocation hearings. Basically, a parolee's right to counsel during such hearings is not a "given" but must be determined on a case-by-case basis.

Does Parole Work? Often, the frequency of parole revocations is used to evaluate whether parole is successful in reintegrating prisoners into society. Parole revocation is often the result of recidivism or the continuation of criminal activity, and recidivism rates are often looked at as ways of measuring the success or failure of a particular sanction. No standard has been established to determine what are high and low recidivism rates.

One report (Lillis, 1994, p. 7) indicates: "The number of adult parole revocations reached nearly 80,000 in 1993, approximately 22 percent of the total number of adults on parole in this country." The article also lists the primary reasons for parole revocation, many of which are technical violations such as failure to report, leaving the assigned area without permission or alcohol or drug use, not commission of new crimes (p. 9). Another report (*Correctional Populations,* p. 2) states: "Nearly half of all exits from parole [in 1995] were categorized as successful completions. Most of the remainders were returned to incarceration, but only 1 of every 9 parolees were returned to incarceration with a new sentence."

Other Forms of Early Release

In addition to parole as a way to ease prison overcrowding, other forms of early release have been used to reduce the number of inmates being held within a facility. These measures include *sentence reduction,* which shortens the sentences of selected groups of inmates such as nonviolent, first-time offenders; *emergency release,* where inmates nearing the end of their sentence are liberated to make room for an influx of new inmates; and *early parole,* where parole eligibility is moved up to make room for other incoming offenders. These measures are typically used when prisons are formally declared above capacity and ordered to reduce the number of inmates being held.

Critical Issues Facing Prisons Today

Many issues surround our nation's prisons today, from prison culture and the fear that these institutions add to the criminal tendencies of offenders, to concerns about prison overcrowding and the effectiveness of alternative programs like boot camps, to the privatization of prisons and the future of such institutions.

Prison Culture

Throughout this chapter, various ways have been discussed in which inmates may keep connected to the outside world. Visitation privileges and community release programs are but two examples of such efforts, the importance of which cannot be overemphasized, as most prisoners will one day return to society and will need to have the necessary social skills to maintain a healthy, crime-free existence. It has long been recognized, however, that the socialization that occurs in prison serves to draw the offender away from the values and norms of the community into an antisocial mindset. This socialization is
➤ part of a phenomenon identified by Donald Clemmer as **prisonization.** Clemmer, while employed as a correctional administrator, noticed that new inmates, "fish," were quickly educated by the more veteran inmates on the ways of life inside the prison. Notes Clemmer (1971, pp. 92–93):

> Every man who enters the penitentiary undergoes prisonization to some extent. The first and most obvious integrative step concerns his status. He becomes at once an anonymous figure in a subordinate group. A number replaces a name. He wears the clothes of the other members of the subordinate group. . . .
>
> After the new arrival recovers from the effects of the swallowing-up process, he assigns a new meaning to conditions he had previously taken for granted. The fact that food, shelter, clothing, and a work activity had been given him originally made no special impression. It is only after some weeks or months that there comes to him a new interpretation of these necessities of life. This new conception results from mingling with other men and it places emphasis on the fact that the environment *should* administer to him. . . .

According to Clemmer, not only does the prisoner come to expect to be taken care of but he also begins to identify with and learns to coexist with other criminals, gradually becoming criminalized and losing touch with any conventional values he may have had on the outside. As will be discussed in Chapter 12, correctional staff can be prisonized as well.

Another dangerous aspect of prison culture concerns the existence of prison gangs. It is common to find members of street gangs in prison. These gang members stick together as tightly on the inside as they did on the outside. For many new inmates, life behind bars may be very dangerous without the affiliation with and protection of a gang. This topic is discussed further in Chapter 8.

Overcrowding

It is no surprise that crime and prison construction are hot topics today. According to Irwin and Austin (p. 14): "Nationally, spending on corrections has become the fastest-growing item in state budgets. In 1995, state governments projected an 8 percent increase in correctional spending, while Medicaid was growing at 4.9 percent, higher education at 4.3 percent, and Aid to Families with Dependent Children at 2.1 percent." Yet despite the drive to create more bedspace for offenders, many prisons and jurisdictions still suffer from overcrowding. According to Camp and Camp (p. 54), at the beginning of 1997, 198 adult correctional agencies in 22 states were under court order to limit inmate populations.

Overcrowded prisons not only suffer because of stretched or insufficient resources but also place added stress on management and staff, who must maintain order within a facility holding more inmates than it was designed for. Debate exists whether such overcrowding contributes to higher levels of violence or increased spread of illness. Research suggests that prison crowding adversely affects both institutional management and employee satisfaction and stress. Overcrowding in prisons may be linked to violent deaths, suicides, psychiatric commitments and disciplinary infractions. Prison crowding has also led to numerous lawsuits filed by prisoners claiming inhumane conditions of confinement and other violations of their rights.

Various methods have been used to alleviate the pressures of overcrowding, including the release measures discussed earlier and the construction of more prisons. Another method to relieve prison crowding has been the use of alternatives to incarceration such as boot camps.

Boot Camps. Correctional boot camps, also referred to as shock incarceration, began in 1983 in response to the overcrowded status of our country's prisons. A **boot camp** is an alternative to prison where nonviolent, first-time (usually) offenders serve a relatively short sentence (typically 90 to 180 days) instead of their full prison sentence of several years or more.

Structured after the military boot camp, strict discipline and physical labor are elements of many shock incarceration programs. MacKenzie and Souryal (1994, p. 1) state: "Participation in military drill and ceremony, physical training, and hard labor is mandatory. Inmates begin their day before dawn and are involved in structured activities until 'lights out,' approximately 16 hours later." The authors also note: "The military-style regimen is generally supplemented with rehabilitative programming such as drug treatment/education or academic education . . ." and that "[a]s the boot camp program concept has developed over the years . . . rehabilitative programming has come to play a more prominent role in the day-to-day routine." The military discipline and physical elements are not part of all shock incarceration programs, however. "Though remaining highly structured, some programs have abandoned military-style

Young offenders stand at attention at this Florida boot camp.

training and have incorporated educational, wilderness, job corps, and industrial components" (U.S. Department of Justice, 1992, p. 79). After a judge has ruled shock incarceration the appropriate sentence, the offender may either agree to the placement or refuse and be placed in prison to serve a longer sentence.

> Boot camps generally house nonviolent, first-time offenders for short periods, and many emphasize discipline, physical training, hard labor and military drill. Education and behavior modification are also common elements of shock incarceration programs. Inmate consent is necessary for placement in shock incarceration.

Today, over half the states and the FBOP operate at least one boot camp. According to Camp and Camp (p. 97): "On January 1, 1997, 7,250 offenders were participating in boot camp programs in 32 agencies. Of those offenders, 587 were female (8.1%) and 6,663 were male (91.9%)." Figure 7–7 illustrates which states have shock incarceration programs. Table 7–8 shows when each state began using boot camps, how many are operating, the duration of their program, the daily cost per inmate and which states are planning to add shock incarceration programs.

Parent (1994, p. 8) notes: "Boot camps are in sync with calls for harsher punishment. They provide striking visual images that provoke visceral responses in members of the viewing public." Although these programs may satisfy the public's desire to see offenders sweat and toil to pay for their crimes, most criminal justice scholars give boot camps a failing grade, believing they are misused and have fallen short of their intended goals.

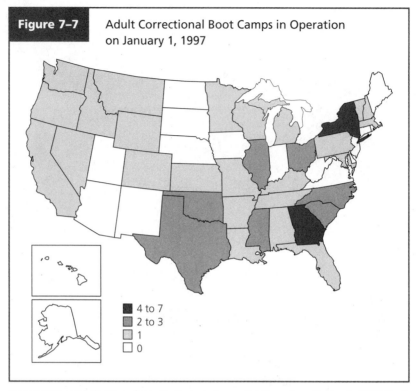

Figure 7–7   Adult Correctional Boot Camps in Operation on January 1, 1997

4 to 7
2 to 3
1
0

Source: George M. Camp, and Camille Graham Camp. *The Corrections Yearbook, 1997.* South Salem, NY: The Criminal Justice Institute, 1997, p. 99. Reprinted by permission.

Some critics claim judges are missentencing offenders to boot camps, placing non–prison-bound individuals in these programs, thereby widening the net. This net widening diminishes the effectiveness of the programming by denying a spot to a prison-bound offender for whom such alternatives were intended. According to MacKenzie (1994, p. 1): "Boot camps have two major goals—to change offenders and to reduce prison overcrowding. The principal findings are that most programs produce positive attitudinal changes in participants, have few if any effects on subsequent criminality, and are likely to reduce prison crowding only if program admissions are tightly controlled to assure that spaces are allotted to prison-bound offenders." Parent (p. 8) puts it more succinctly: "Most boot camps do not reduce recidivism, do not reduce prison populations, and do not reduce costs."

Regarding recidivism, Parent (p. 8) declares: "There is no evidence that existing boot camps significantly affect graduates' recidivism rates." A study of boot camp graduates in Georgia (National Criminal Justice Association, 1994, p. 5) revealed: "At the end of the five-year follow-up point, approximately half of all boot camp graduates had returned to prison." Furthermore, the same report states: "From all available accounts, boot camp graduates across the country are no more likely to succeed in community supervision programs than comparison groups of parolees." Based on this data, boot

Table 7–8	Boot Camps in Operation and Cost Per Inmate Per Day				

	Year First Opened	1/1/97 Boot Camps	Program Length (mos.)	'96 Daily Cost Per Inmate	Planned for 1997
Alabama[1]	1988	1	3	$ 21.44	0
Arkansas[1,2]	1990	1	15	$ 38.05	0
California	1993	1	6		0
Colorado	1991	1	3	$ 61.78	0
Florida[1]	1987	1	4	$ 50.13	1
Georgia[1]	1991	7	3	$ 26.00	0
Idaho[1]	1989	1	6	$ 38.10	0
Illinois	1990	3	4	$ 57.26	0
Kansas[3]	1991	1	6	$ 37.15	0
Kentucky[1]	1993	1	4.3	$ 31.56	0
Louisiana[1]	1987	1	6	$ 43.00	0
Maryland	1990	1	6	$ 39.64	0
Massachusetts[1,4]	1992	1	4	$ 56.01	0
Michigan[1]	1988	1	3	$ 68.46	0
Minnesota	1992	1	6	$149.12	0
Mississippi[1]	1985	3	5	$ 30.51	0
Missouri[1]	1994	1	3		0
Montana[1]	1993	1	3.5	$114.39	0
Nevada[1]	1991	1	6	$ 16.63	0
New Hampshire	1990	1	4	$ 50.96	0
New Jersey		0			1
New York[1]	1987	4	6	$ 64.27	0
North Carolina[1]	1989	2	3	$ 64.32	0
Ohio[1]	1991	2	3	$ 61.00	0
Oklahoma[1]	1984	2	4.5		0
Oregon[5]	1994	1	9	$ 65.00	0
Pennsylvania	1992	1	6	$121.39	0
South Carolina[6,7]	1987	2	3	$ 40.11	0
Tennessee[8]	1989	1	3.5	$ 64.06	0
Texas[9]	1989	2	3	$ 43.78	0
Vermont[1]	1993	1	4.5	$ 71.62	0
Washington[10]	1993	1	4	$ 75.85	0
Wisconsin	1991	1	6	$ 72.21	0
Wyoming[1]	1990	1	4	$ 39.00	0
Federal[1,11]	1991	3	6	$ 47.00	0
Average & Total	**1990**	**54**	**5**	**$ 56.77**	**2**

[1]Length of Program is based on number of days reported. [2]Cost is FY'96. [3]County boot camp oper. with state grant. [4]Prgm. cost incl. cost to house some med. security inmates at site. [5]Length of program is 6 mo. as inmate, plus 3 mo. transition leave under inst. juris. [6]Boot camp is a program created for inmates 17–25 yrs. old sentenced under Youth Offender Act with indeterminate sentences. Boot camps reported in previous yrs. refer to Shock incarceration program. [7]Shock incarceration prgm. is 3 months. [8]Length is 90–120 days. [9]Program length based on 75–90 days. [10]Work Ethic Camp. [11]Other programs opened in 1992, 1996.

Source: George M. Camp and Camille Graham Camp. *The Corrections Yearbook, 1997.* South Salem, NY: The Criminal Justice Institute, 1997, p. 98. Reprinted by permission.

camps have not succeeded in their goal to change offenders or make them any more law-abiding than those receiving standard parole.

While no significant difference has been documented regarding recidivism rates between boot camp graduates and regular parolees, a difference has been noted between the *attitudes* of those who've experienced shock incarceration and those exposed to traditional incarceration and parole. MacKenzie (p. 14) reports: "Boot camp graduates typically became more positive about their experiences and their future, and believed they had changed for the better. The results were surprisingly consistent. Graduates both from programs emphasizing physical training and work, and from programs incorporating major rehabilitation, treatment, and education components felt positive about their experiences." A report by the National Institute of Justice (NCJA, 1994, p. 5) states: "Offenders often cite the educational services and the drug counseling in particular as being helpful." MacKenzie et al. evaluated a shock incarceration program in Louisiana called IMPACT (Intensive Motivational Program of Alternative Correctional Treatment) and received positive comments from participating inmates (1993, p. 4).

Concerning the goal to reduce prison populations, Parent (p. 8) claims: "As typically designed and used, boot camps are more likely to increase prison populations, crowding, and total correctional costs than to decrease them." Parent offers some suggestions for administrators in using boot camps to reduce prison bedspace needs (p. 10):

1. "[B]oot camps should recruit offenders who have a very high probability of imprisonment."

2. "[B]oot camps should minimize failure rates . . . [by] refus[ing] to let inmates withdraw voluntarily during the first two or three weeks, when their muscles are most sore . . . [and should] intensively supervise boot camp graduates."

3. "[B]oot camps should select inmates who will receive a substantial reduction in time served for completing the boot camp."

4. "[A] large-scale boot camp operation is needed to make a substantial dent in a state's prison population."

Finally, Parent (p. 11) suggests: "Correctional agencies that operate prisons— not judges—should select participants." All these suggestions are intended to make boot camps more successful in keeping inmates out of prison.

The goals of reducing prison crowding and reducing costs are closely linked, as keeping offenders out of prison *should* ultimately lower the costs of such corrections. Doyle (1993, p. B2) explains: "Boot camps . . . cost more per day to run than conventional prisons because the programs have extensive drug-treatment programs and a high ratio of guards to prisoners. But the camps are supposed to save money in the long run by substituting six-month terms [or less] for a year or more in regular prisons, and by reducing the number of repeat offenders." According to a report by the U.S. General Accounting

Office (NCJA, 1993, p. 5): "[A]verage daily costs for prison boot camps tend to be higher due to the intense training and increased need for staff."

Despite the higher daily costs for boot camps, administrators hope the shorter time spent in this alternative will translate into savings. For example, a man convicted for possession of cocaine received the option of serving four years in prison or spending six months in a rigorous boot camp. He chose the boot camp which, using the average daily cost from Table 7–8, cost about $10,260 ($57/day for 180 days). Had he been sent to a minimum-security prison for even one year of the four-year sentence, the cost would have been over $18,500 ($50/day for 365 days). The full sentence would have cost nearly $75,000! Because the inmate successfully completed the boot camp and has found a job and stayed crime-free, his shock incarceration did contribute to a cost reduction.

However, not every inmate who enters a boot camp graduates, and not every graduate stays out of trouble and avoids a subsequent prison sentence. According to Doyle (p. B1), dropouts and escapes add to the higher costs associated with boot camps: "About 80 percent of the inmates who volunteered for the six-month Wisconsin program quit, escaped or otherwise failed to complete it, even though they faced the prospect of being sent to a conventional prison to serve longer sentences." These cases drive up the cost of corrections by combining the price of a regular prison term and the cost of the failed boot camp term. Therefore, as many critics believe, until the success rate of boot camps can be raised, the cost of corrections will continue to be exorbitant.

> Most boot camps have fallen short of their goals to reduce recidivism, reduce prison overcrowding and reduce costs. Many do, however, produce positive attitudinal changes, with boot camp participants feeling better about their shock incarceration experiences than regular prison inmates about their traditional incarceration.

Despite the marginal reviews of most boot camps, several programs have shown some success. Two successful programs quite different from each other in approach and philosophy are the Intensive Therapeutic Program in Georgia and the Work Ethic Camp in Washington.

The Valdosta (Georgia) Correctional Institution's Intensive Therapeutic Program (ITP) was begun in 1990 to handle the facility's "most troubled inmates, the ones . . . [who] would benefit most from the self-control and discipline ITP teaches" (Lewis, 1994, p. 132). Lewis (p. 130) states: *City and State* magazine named Valdosta 'most outstanding prison facility for 1993,' in part for the ITP, a 30-day boot-camp style program for hardened offenders that was begun . . . in an effort to reduce the high number of disciplinary infractions involving violence and to reduce the number of inmates who repeatedly served segregation time." According to Lewis (p. 132): "The purpose of [the] confrontational treatment is to break down the inmate's defenses to pave the way for rebuilding the person's ego in positive ways." This approach is similar to the philosophy used by the military in creating soldiers—break them down and then rebuild them. Lewis (p. 132) concludes: "The ITP is a model program for agencies looking for ways to cope with their segregation population. It provides inmates with constructive methods of responding to anger, frustration, fear and boredom. It also teaches coping mechanisms, builds pride and self-respect and teaches interpersonal communication skills—all of which are critical for reducing violence and improving morale in any facility."

Another successful program is the McNeil Island Work Ethic Camp in Washington State. This program is a nonmilitary model where "the relationship between inmates and their supervisors is closer to the link between employee and employer than between military grunt and drill instructor" (Sharp, 1995, p. 2). The program is newer, begun in 1993, and combines physical labor with abundant treatment and counseling sessions. Sharp reports:

> Some 125 closely supervised inmates—aged 18 to 28—spend eight-hour days pulling weeds, repairing fences, and cleaning and painting the ferries that travel from island to mainland. After the first month, inmates can then choose from dozens of prison jobs—from working in the recycling yard to cleaning up in the meat-packing center. . . .
>
> All that sweat is supplemented by substance: Adult education classes. Anger management. Planning for life after prison. Substance abuse counseling. And victim awareness. . . .
>
> For McNeil Island inmates who break the rules, push-ups aren't a punishment option. Some minor offenses earn extra physical work, but most penalties attempt to make a psychological change. An inmate who uses a racial slur, for example, has to write an essay on the cultural contributions of the ethnic group he demeaned.

In conclusion, Sharp (p. 5) cites two boot camp researchers' guidelines on how to create the most effective program: "In a 16-hour day, . . . no more than two or three hours should be given to military components, such as physical training and drill and ceremony. Drug treatment, counseling and therapy aimed at reducing and managing anger or aggression should consume four or five hours. The same amount of time should be given to services such as remedial education, job training or parenting classes."

Privatization

Another issue regarding prisons involves the concept of privately funded and/or ➤ operated facilities. **Privatization** is the provision of correctional services by organizations outside the governmental framework, either nonprofit or for profit. Camp and Camp (p. 79) state: "Fourteen jurisdictions had contracts with 47 privately operated prisons as of January 1, 1997. The agencies had their first privately operated prison open, on average, in 1992. Texas had 11, the largest number of contracts with privately operated prisons. Capacities . . . ranged from

1,500 at Bradshaw (Texas) to 20 at ECO in North Carolina. Costs per inmate per day ranged from \$92.31 at the New Mexico Women's Correctional Facility to \$24.54 at the Allen Correctional Center in Louisiana." Most of the private prison facilities operating in 1996 were on the lower end of the custody continuum: 17 were minimum security, 16 were medium security, 5 were minimum/medium security, 4 were minimum-restrictive security, 3 were multilevel security, 1 was low security and 1 was a community facility (Camp and Camp, p. 79).

Four forms of privatization are commonly used:

- Private-sector financing of correctional construction.
- Contract services (health care, food services, laundry).
- Operation only of prison industries.
- Total operation and management of correctional institution.

Private jails and prisons were common in the United States during the 19th century, but gradually fell into disfavor by the early 20th century. According to Shichor and Sechrest (1995, p. 458):

> The operation of prisons by the private sector became a vital option again during the 1980s and early 1990s for several reasons. First was the existence of a general sociopolitical climate favoring the reduction of taxes and the size of government. Second was the implementation of "get-tough" social control policies, particularly the "war on drugs," and increased mandatory prison sentences. . . . [which] resulted in an unprecedented increase in federal and state prison populations . . . [and] resulted in major problems of prison crowding. . . . The third reason is the general American "ethos" of laissez-faire economy, minimization of government control, and a firm belief in the abilities of the private sector to do a better job than the public sector.

Some believe the private sector is better equipped financially to deal with the economic strains facing today's governmental corrections facilities. Others argue that placing control over our country's criminals in the hands of independent, private enterprises will lead to more difficult regulation and monitoring of standards and potentially greater abuses of inmates' rights. These issues surrounding privatization are discussed in the final chapter of the text.

Summary

Like jails, the concept of prisons was brought to this country by the colonists. Unlike the Pennsylvania system of prisons, the Auburn system allowed inmates to eat and work together during the day. It also divided prisoners based on the nature of their offenses, setting the precedent for today's minimum-, medium- and maximum-security prisons.

The national incarceration rate has increased steadily over the past decade, with more than twice the number of sentenced inmates today than in

1985. The majority of prison inmates today are Black males, although it was not until 1991 that the number of Black males exceeded the number of White males in prison. The greatest increase in incarceration rates over the past decade is in the drug offense category.

Prisoner classification is an ongoing process which divides inmates into subgroups on the basis of security and program needs. Minimum-security prisons impose little or no physical control over inmates and are designed for nonviolent offenders who are low risk for escaping. Their focus is to reintegrate inmates into the community. Medium-security prisons use perimeter controls such as fencing and allow inmates less freedom of movement than in minimum-security facilities but more than in maximum-security facilities. The focus is on controlled access to programs. Maximum-security prisons house violent offenders and those at high risk of escape and therefore use substantial perimeter controls such as double or electrified fences, high walls and armed guards posted in observation towers. Strict control of inmates on the interior is also a feature of these prisons, as the focus is on custody and security, not on treatment and rehabilitation. The Federal Bureau of Prisons administers facilities that house persons convicted of federal offenses. Classification in the federal system is based on a six-level scale, with level 1 being the least restrictive and level 6 the most restrictive.

The custody level intended directly affects a prison's architectural style, construction and design. The telephone-pole design was most commonly used for maximum-security prisons; the campus and free layout designs are most frequently used for minimum-security prisons.

Prison labor has been around as long as the prisons themselves. Prison industries suffered during the mid-1900s but began making a comeback during the 1980s. Today these industries are regarded as positive and beneficial enterprises by many inmates, correctional administrators and those in the private sector.

Release from prison may be either unconditional or conditional. Conditional release may be either discretionary or mandatory. The most prevalent form of release today is discretionary (conditional) release; the least prevalent is unconditional release. Parole is the conditional release from prison before the expiration of the sentence and the period of supervision in the community following this release.

Boot camps generally house nonviolent, first-time offenders for short periods, and many emphasize discipline, physical training, hard labor and military drill. Education and behavior modification are also common elements of shock incarceration programs. Inmate consent is necessary for placement in shock incarceration. Most boot camps have fallen short of their goals to reduce recidivism, reduce prison overcrowding and reduce costs. Many do, however, produce positive attitudinal changes, with boot camp participants feeling better about their shock incarceration experiences than regular prison inmates about their traditional incarceration.

Discussion Questions

1. Discuss the fact that the United States imprisons a greater proportion of its citizens than any other nation in the world.

2. What factors might contribute to faster prison population growth in western states as compared to midwestern states? What might other regional differences be?

3. Do you think drug offenders should be put in prison when early release is being granted to violent offenders due to overcrowding?

4. How well does the classification process balance public safety/security needs with inmates' needs?

5. Might minimum-security prisons be easily replaced by some form of intermediate sanction and the space converted into medium- or maximum-security facilities?

6. Are the differences between men's and women's prison facilities appropriate? Fair?

7. Considering that research shows a positive correlation between higher education and postrelease success, should Pell grant funding for prison college programs be allowed again?

8. Should paroling authorities be legally immune when they make poor release decisions?

9. What are some innovative ways to ease prison crowding?

10. Is privatization of prisons a good or bad idea? Why? Is your answer different than it was regarding privatization of jails? If so, why?

References

American Correctional Association. *Standards for Adult Correctional Institutions*, 3rd ed. Laurel, MD, 1990.

Austin, James. "Objective Offender Classification Is Key to Proper Housing Decisions." *Corrections Today*, July 1994, pp. 94–96.

Bartollas, Clemens and Conrad, John P. *Introduction to Corrections*, 2nd ed. New York: Harper Collins Publishers, 1992.

Camp, George M. and Camp, Camille Graham. *The Corrections Yearbook, 1997*. South Salem, NY: The Criminal Justice Institute, 1997.

Clemmer, Donald. "The Process of Prisonization." In *The Criminal in Confinement*, edited by Leon Radzinowicz and Marvin Wolfgang. New York: Basic Books, 1971, pp. 92–93.

Cohen, Robyn L. *Probation and Parole Violators in State Prison, 1991*. Special Report: Bureau of Justice Statistics, August 1995 (NCJ-149076).

Connecticut Department of Corrections. *Free Venture Model in Corrections*. Hartford, CT: Department of Corrections, n.d.

Correctional Populations in the United States, 1995: Executive Summary. Bureau of Justice Statistics, June 1997 (NCJ-163917).

Coughlin, Thomas A., III. "How to Create a User Friendly Prison." *Corrections Today*, April 1992, pp. 88–94.

Dallao, Mary. "Keeping Classification Current." *Corrections Today*, July 1997, pp. 86–88.

Directory of Juvenile and Adult Correctional Departments. Lanham, MD: American Correctional Association, 1997.

Doyle, Pat. "Woes of Wisconsin Program Stir Doubts About the Concept." (Minneapolis/St. Paul) *Star Tribune*, November 1, 1993, pp. B1–B2.

"Fourteenth Amendment: Parole Release Determinations." *The Journal of Criminal Law and Criminology*, Vol.70, No.4, September/October 1979, p. 468.

George, Louis F. "Hardware for Prisons." *Security Technology and Design*, September 1994, pp. 86–88.

Haycock, J. "Crimes and Misdemeanors: A Review of Recent Research on Suicides in Prison." *Omega*, Vol. 23, No. 2, 1991, pp. 81–94.

Hayes, Lindsay M. "Prison Suicide: An Overview and a Guide to Prevention." *The Prison Journal*, Vol. 75, No. 4, December 1995, pp. 431–456.

Hayes, Lindsay M. "Prison Suicide: Rates and Prevention Policies." *Corrections Today*, February 1996, pp. 88–95.

Irwin, John and Austin, James. *It's About Time: America's Imprisonment Binge*, 2nd ed. Belmont, CA: Wadsworth Publishing Company, 1997.

Lewis, Richard. "Boot Camp Program Promotes Discipline, Improves Self-Esteem." *Corrections Today*, August 1994, pp. 130–132.

Lillis, Jamie. "Twenty-Two Percent of Adult Parole Cases Revoked in 1993." *Corrections Compendium*, August 1994, pp. 7–20.

MacKenzie, Doris Layton. "Boot Camps: A National Assessment." *Overcrowded Times*, August 1994, pp. 1, 14–18.

MacKenzie, Doris Layton; Shaw, James W.; and Gowdy, Voncile B. *An Evaluation of Shock Incarceration in Louisiana*. National Institute of Justice Research in Brief, Evaluation Bulletin, June 1993 (NCJ-140567).

MacKenzie, Doris Layton and Souryal, Claire. *Multisite Evaluation of Shock Incarceration*. U.S. Department of Justice, National Institute of Justice, November 1994 (NCJ-142462).

Mathews, Charles R. "Tuberculosis: Managing a Resurrected Plague." *The State of Corrections, Proceedings of the ACA Annual Conferences, 1993*. The American Correctional Association, 1994, pp. 61–64.

McCollum, Sylvia G. "Prison College Programs." *The Prison Journal*, Vol. 73, No. 1, March 1994, pp. 51–61.

Mumola, Christopher J. and Beck, Allen J. *Prisoners in 1996*. Bureau of Justice Statistics Bulletin, June 1997 (NCJ-164619).

Nadel, Barbara A. "Designing for Women: Doing Time Differently." *Corrections Compendium*, Vol. XXI, No. 11, November 1996, pp. 1–5.

National Commission on Correctional Health Care. *Standards for Health Services in Prisons*, 2nd ed. Chicago, IL, 1992.

National Criminal Justice Association. "Despite Studies, Boot Camps' Effects, Costs Remain Elusive, NIJ Report Says." *Juvenile Justice*, November 1994, pp. 1–2, 4–5.

National Criminal Justice Association. "GAO: Boot Camps Cheaper, but Recidivism Impact Still Uncertain." *Justice Research*, May/June 1993, pp. 3, 5–6.

Parent, Dale G. "Boot Camps Failing to Achieve Goals." *Overcrowded Times*, August 1994, pp. 8–11.

Raspberry, William. "Burger's Dream for Prison Justice." (Minneapolis/St. Paul) *Star Tribune*, June 30, 1995, p. A27.

Schoen, K.F. "Criminal Treatment." In *Criminal Justice 92/93*, edited by J.J. Sullivan and J.L. Victor. Guilford, CT: The Dushkin Publishing Group, Inc., 1992, p. 217.

Sharp, Deborah. "Boot Camps—Punishment and Treatment." Insert in *Corrections Today*, June 1995.

Shichor, David and Sechrest, Dale K. "Quick Fixes in Corrections: Reconsidering Private and Public For-Profit Facilities." *The Prison Journal*, Vol. 75, No. 4, December 1995, pp. 475–478.

Snell, Tracy L. *Correctional Populations in the United States, 1992.* Bureau of Justice Statistics, January 1995 (NCJ-146413).

"Tonry, Fein Debate Sentencing Policy." *Corrections Today,* October 1993, pp. 56–63.

U.S. Department of Justice, National Institute of Justice. *Searching for Answers—Annual Evaluation Report on Drugs and Crime: 1991.* July 1992.

Unruh, Bob. "A New Home of Bars, Steel: America's Worst Inmates to Move to 'New Alcatraz' in Colorado." (Minneapolis/St. Paul) *Star Tribune,* December 11, 1994, pp. A10, A12.

Verdeyen, Robert J. "Correctional Industries: Making Inmate Work Productive." *Corrections Today,* August 1995, pp. 106–110. Reprinted by permission.

Vestal, Kathy. "Inmate Labor Program Cuts Costs While Teaching Useful Job Skills." *Corrections Today,* April 1994, pp. 108–114.

Wees, Greg A. "Violence on the Rise in U.S. Prisons." *Corrections Compendium,* June 1996, pp. 9–12.

Wunder, Amanda. "The Extinction of Inmate Privileges." *Corrections Compendium,* June 1995, pp. 5–24.

Cases

Gagnon v. Scarpelli, 441 U.S. 778 (1973).

Greenholtz v. Inmates of Nebraska Penal and Correctional Complex, 99 S.Ct. 2100 (1979).

Mempa v. Rhay, 339 U.S. 128 Cir. 3023 (1968).

Morrissey v. Brewer, 408 U.S. 271 (1972).

SECTION III

The Human Factor—Behind the Bricks and Mortar

People are what corrections is really all about. Section III looks at the people who comprise corrections today—both the correctional "clients" and the professionals dedicated to their supervision and management. The section begins with an in-depth look at the broad categories of today's correctional clients—adult male and female offenders (Chapter 8) and juvenile offenders (Chapter 9). The general characteristics of each group are discussed, as are various aspects of the inmate culture and inmate needs.

Today's corrections system must deal not only with increased numbers of offenders but an increased variety of offenders as well. In addition to the general categories of male, female and juvenile offenders, corrections must handle a host of "special needs" offenders (Chapter 10), including elderly offenders, physically and mentally disabled offenders (mentally retarded or developmentally disabled offenders), mentally ill offenders (also called mentally disordered offenders and including the criminally insane), drug- and alcohol-dependent offenders, HIV-infected offenders, sex offenders and high-profile offenders.

As the number of offenders is increasing, so too is the number of correctional personnel required to supervise and tend to these offenders. Chapter 11 looks at the administration and management of corrections, including the overall staff structure of a correctional hierarchy; the network of entities involved in the corrections environment; how various positions are related to each other; definitions and levels of management; profiles of today's managers; correctional management's characteristics and functions; management styles, philosophies and techniques; and the accreditation process. Chapter 12 examines correctional personnel other than management, beginning with a look at custodial and surveillance personnel, such as correctional officers and probation and parole officers. The discussion then turns to treatment personnel (medical, psychological, educational, caseworkers/counselors, religious program, other programs) and support personnel. The chapter concludes with a discussion of the use of volunteers in corrections.

8

Correctional Clients: Adult Offenders

Do You Know

➤ Who the majority of correctional clients are and what the ratio of men to women is in prison? In jail? On parole? On probation?

➤ If inmate gangs and racial conflict are more prevalent in men's or women's facilities?

➤ What typically distinguishes prison gangs from street gangs and what prison gangs seek to achieve?

➤ When the first prison gang was recognized and what the extent of such gangs are in corrections today?

➤ What strategies are effective in dealing with the problem of prison gangs?

➤ What basic tenets are included in the inmate code?

➤ How the female prisoner growth rate compares to that of male prisoners?

➤ Whether women are more or less likely than men to be imprisoned for property and drug offenses? For violent offenses?

➤ What percentage of female prisoners are mothers?

➤ If, compared to male offenders, female offenders have shown greater or lesser endorsement of the inmate code and what factors may account for this?

➤ How an equal treatment policy for male and female inmates impacts each group?

I could kill everyone without blinking an eye. — *Charles Manson*

Can You Define

disruptive groups   prison gang   representing
inmate code   pseudofamilies   street gang

Introduction

T he focal point of corrections is necessarily the offender, the "correctional client." The nature and number of offenders determine how many facilities are needed, the security level of these facilities, the programming and services required and the number and type of staff needed.

Current data indicates no impending shortage of correctional clients, as the number of persons within the correctional scheme is at an unprecedented high. A U.S. Department of Justice report indicates an estimated 5.4 million American adults, about 2.8 percent of the total adult resident population, were under some form of correctional supervision in 1995 (*Correctional Populations*, 1997, p. iii).

This chapter takes an in-depth look at the broad categories of today's adult correctional clients—male and female. The general characteristics of each group are discussed, as are various aspects of the inmate culture and inmate needs.

Adult Offenders—An Overview

Data collected from 1985 to 1995 shows a consistent trend of increasing adult correctional populations. Table 8–1 presents the estimated number and percent of adult offenders under correctional supervision (jails, probation, prison and parole), categorized by sex and race. Notice the numbers for each category increase every year. It is interesting to note the number of Black offenders is disproportionately high, relative to their proportion of the general population (the African-American population is about 12 percent of the total U.S. population). This raises important, sensitive, controversial issues. Is the disproportionality due to discrimination or differences in conduct?

Figure 8–1 overviews where these adult offenders have been placed in the correctional system from 1980 to 1995. Notice that the prison, parole and jail

Table 8–1	Estimated Number and Percent of Adults under Correctional Supervision, by Sex and Race, 1985, 1990, 1995				

	Sex		Race		
Year	Male	Female	White	Black	Other
1985	2,606,000 (3.0%)	405,500 (0.4%)	1,941,600 (1.2%)	1,029,600 (5.2%)	40,300 (0.8%)
1990	3,746,300 (4.2%)	601,700 (0.6%)	2,665,500 (1.7%)	1,632,700 (7.9%)	49,800 (0.7%)
1995	4,546,400 (4.9%)	828,100 (0.8%)	3,210,200 (2.0%)	2,090,900 (9.3%)	73,300 (0.9%)

Source: Adapted from *Correctional Populations in the United States, 1995.* Bureau of Justice Statistics, May 1997, p. 6 (NCJ-163916).

populations have taken a fairly steady course upward while the probation population has continued to diverge away from the others, showing greater increases from one year to the next. As our prisons and jails face the pressure of overcrowding, it is understandable why the number of offenders placed on probation continues to grow more rapidly than the other categories.

Male Offenders

Most individuals under correctional supervision today are male. Historically, prison populations have been predominantly male. In fact, approximately 94 percent of all prison inmates on January 1, 1997, were men (Camp and Camp, 1997, p. 7). But prison is not the only place where men outnumber women. In 1995, 90 percent of jail inmates were men, 90 percent of parolees were men and about 79 percent of probationers were men (*Correctional Populations*, p. iii). Clearly, men comprise the majority of correctional clients.

> The majority of correctional clients are men. Men outnumber women in prison by nearly 19 to 1; in jail, 9 to 1; on parole, 9 to 1; and on probation, 4 to 1.

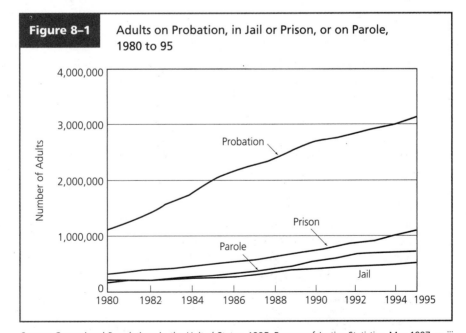

Figure 8–1 Adults on Probation, in Jail or Prison, or on Parole, 1980 to 95

Source: Correctional Populations in the United States, 1995. Bureau of Justice Statistics, May 1997, p. iii (NCJ-163916).

General Characteristics of Male Offenders

Much of the data concerning male offenders is limited to men in prison, but this information may reasonably apply to males at other stages of corrections. A typical male offender is poor, uneducated, unskilled, unemployed or employed in a low-paying occupation, addicted to alcohol and/or drugs and plagued by a variety of physical and mental health problems.

Many offenders, particularly male offenders, literally grew up in our country's criminal justice system, being in and out of numerous detention facilities as juveniles and progressing through the continuum of sanctions, eventually finding themselves in prison. For these offenders, correctional facilities feel like home. Prisoner Jack Henry Abbott (1981) explained this sense of belonging:

> Everyone in prison has committed crimes, could be called a criminal. But that does not mean everyone in prison *belongs* there. . . . Perhaps the great majority of prisoners belong there. They keep returning. I've seen at least one entire prison turn over in population. Almost every one of them (in fact, *everyone* I've seen) feels relieved to be back. They need shaves and showers; they are gaunt, starved-looking when they come in from outside. *Within a week* they are rosy-cheeked, starched-and-pressed, talking to everyone. Laughing a lot (hail-fellow-well-met). They fit in in prison. This is where they belong.

From this account it would seem that incarceration is a positive social experience for many prisoners. This is certainly not the case, however, for all inmates. The following discussion examines the inmate culture for those living in correctional facilities.

Inmate Culture in Men's Correctional Facilities

Drug and alcohol dependency are common among both male and female offenders. However, other factors, most having to do with the social climate of the facility, are quite distinct between male and female inmate populations. Because men's prisons are several times the size of women's prisons, the survival issue is a more significant problem. Therefore, some men may arm themselves for protection. Socially, men are less likely than women to seek out and build emotional relationships with persons of the same sex and, consequently, may feel more emotionally isolated while incarcerated. Furthermore, male prisoners must often deal with inmate gangs and racial conflicts. It appears that men face a more difficult incarceration than do most women. Exceptions, of course, do exist.

Inmate gangs and racial conflicts are more prevalent in men's facilities than in women's facilities.

Inmate Gangs

In many facilities for men, inmate gangs shape the social climate and organization of prisoners. Inmates without a gang affiliation are often at risk for victimization by those within a gang. Inmate leaders are commonly affiliated with a gang, and various gangs compete with each other for control over drugs and other contraband. In some states a gang member is given a stiffer sentence because of gang affiliation.

While street gangs have existed in this country for decades, prison gangs are a relatively recent phenomenon in our correctional system, presenting
➤ considerable challenges for corrections. A **street gang** is an association of individuals with an ongoing relationship who have identifiable leadership,
➤ claim control over a specific territory and engage in criminal activity. A **prison gang,** as defined by the National Institute of Corrections, is an "exclusive and surreptitious [group] of disruptive inmates who aim to control their environment by engaging in intimidating and threatening behaviors. They are also involved in criminal activity." Both types of gangs are also commonly referred to
➤ as **disruptive groups** by those in law enforcement and corrections. Drowns and Hess (1995, p. 418) state: "Prison gangs are better disciplined, more calculating and more sophisticated than street gangs." These authors also note that while street gangs thrive on notoriety, prison gangs rely on anonymity.

> Prison gangs are more sophisticated and covert than street gangs and are comprised of disruptive inmates seeking to control their environment through intimidation and threats.

Lately, the line of distinction that once clearly separated street gangs from prison gangs has become blurred. According to Welling (1994, p. 148): "Over the past several years, street and prison gangs have become more closely intertwined. As street gangs have grown and evolved, the more sophisticated prison gangs . . . have begun schooling and recruiting street gang members into their more established and structured organizations." Toller and Tsagaris (1996, p. 110) state: "Gangs in corrections are a manifestation of street gangs. . . . Knowing the dynamics of local street gangs is the first step toward understanding institutional gangs." Clarke (1992, p. 8) notes:

> Until recently, a differentiation was appropriately made between "street gangs" and "prison gangs." Although we can still tell which gangs originated in prison and which ones got their start on the streets, there are now street gangs active in prison systems and prison gangs operating in communities at large.
>
> Examples of prison gangs now seen on the streets are the Mexican Mafia, the Aryan Brotherhood, the Black Guerrilla Family, La Nuestra Familia and the Texas Syndicate. Street gangs now observed in corrections include the Bloods, the Crips, the Vice Lords, Hells Angels, the Skinheads and the Latin Kings.

Los Angeles police agencies are networking with prison personnel and vice versa to trace the swinging door of street-to-prison-to-street of gang members. This effort should serve as a model nationwide.

The Growth of Prison Gangs. The first recognized prison gang organized in 1950 at the Washington Penitentiary in Walla Walla and called themselves the Gypsy Jokers. From 1950 to 1970, only seven prison gangs were found in four states. In 1957, the Mexican Mafia began in the California prison system, and in 1969 the Disciples and Vice Lords appeared in Illinois' corrections (Fong et al., 1992, p. 60). In 1970, Utah saw the development of the Aryan Brotherhood, the Nuestra Familia and the Black Guerrilla Family, and by 1983, 17 other prison gangs had begun in 13 other states and the federal correctional system. Today, nearly every correctional system in the nation has had some experience with prison gangs, and estimates place the number of prison gang members around 3 percent of the total inmate population. Some states, such as Illinois and Pennsylvania, have disproportionately high percentages of gang members in their correctional facilities, with reports of 20 percent or more of the inmates holding gang affiliations. Furthermore, on the outside "[d]emographics are not encouraging," note Toller and Tsagaris (p. 110), "because the number of teenagers 15 to 19—a target population for gangs—is predicted to grow by 23 percent by the year 2005."

> The first recognized prison gang was the Gypsy Jokers in 1950. Today, nearly every correctional jurisdiction in the United States reports the presence of prison gangs, with approximately 3 percent of the national inmate population belonging to gangs.

Despite their slow start in the 1950s and 1960s, prison gangs seemed to flourish during the next several decades. Some believe the increasingly rapid development of prison gangs was fueled by court decisions in the 1960s and 1970s concerning prisoner rights, which effectively removed power from correctional administrators, thereby allowing gang activity to proliferate. Fong et al. (p. 60) note: "Correctional personnel, restricted by court-structured disciplinary procedures and threatened with the possibility of lawsuits, find it difficult, if not impossible, to maintain control over inmates. It is in this context of organizational crisis that prison gangs emerge for self-protection and power dominance." Buentello (1992, p. 58) explains how several court decisions served as catalysts for increasing gang activities in Texas:

> First, *Lamar v. Coffield* (1977) forced the agency to integrate inmates in the housing areas, intensifying existing racial tension. Because gangs form along racial lines, the decision made it easier for gang members to preach their ideology and gain more recruits.
>
> A second decision, *Guajardo v. Estelle* (1978), permitted inmates to correspond with other inmates throughout the agency. This decision allowed

gangs to use the mail system to recruit, extort and even order the deaths of inmates within the department as well as outside into the community.

Characteristics of Prison Gangs. A survey of literature by Fong et al. (p. 62) reveals that prison gangs, in general, share some common characteristics, including

- Organization along racial and ethnic lines.
- Members with similar preprison experiences.
- Adherence to a strict code of silence.
- Lifetime membership practice.
- A set of values including solidarity and loyalty.
- Hierarchical structure with defined lines of authority and responsibility.
- Clearly defined goals and objectives such as contract murder, extortion, drug trafficking, homosexual prostitution, gambling and protection.
- Achievement of goals and objectives through brutal and violent means.
- Antiauthority orientation.
- A hate and distrust of other gangs.
- Perception of themselves as political prisoners and victims of racial, economic and political inequality.
- A link to organized criminal activities on the streets.

Although prison gang members constitute only a small percentage of the total prisoner population, some studies report this group of inmates is responsible for more than half of the violence and other problems occurring in correctional facilities. Consequently, finding ways to manage prison gangs will help correctional administrators achieve better control over their entire facility.

Strategies to Deal with Gangs. "The increasing influence and presence in correctional facilities of street gangs has administrators scrambling for solutions. Because gangs—also known as Security Threat Groups (STGs)—have a record of disrupting operations and pose a continuous threat to the safety and security of inmates, staff, and the general public, administrators are deploying an array of weapons in a battle to diminish the gang presence" ("Anti-Gang Policies," 1996, p. 1). Gangs also pose problems in classification and housing decisions.

Several effective strategies have been developed to deal with the gang problem in corrections, beginning with identifying gang members. Training staff to be alert to gang identifiers is part of this challenge. At the Washington State Penitentiary in Walla Walla, as well as in most other prisons, all staff have adopted a mindset known as being "gang conscious." According to Riley (1992, p. 70): "This means always being aware that inmates may be gang members and considering the disruptions this may cause."

In Nebraska, a tracking program has been developed to identify gang members and follow their activity throughout the state. This program emphasizes the importance of communication between all criminal justice agencies as a strategy for dealing with gangs. Fletcher (1994, p. 1) states: "The program consists of several Nebraska law enforcement agencies, along with representatives from all institutions of the Nebraska Department of Corrections. In addition, the Omaha Police Department operates the Criminal Justice Network/Tracking Program, a similar system which works with probation, parole and other social agencies." The Nebraska program, like many others, uses common identifiers to recognize gang members, including (Fletcher, pp. 2–4):

➤
- Items worn only on the left or right side of the body, known as **representing.**
- Colors and emblems.
- Gym shoes: color of shoes and laces.
- Hair: style, accessories such as beads and barrettes.
- Pant legs rolled up on one side.
- Friendship beads.
- Fingernails.
- Meal trays: chosen to match gang colors.
- Hand signs.
- Graffiti.
- Tattoos.
- Gang slang.
- Symbols.

Fletcher (p. 2) cautions: "While a person may have one or more of these identifiers, it does not necessarily mean that he or she is a gang member. The best and safest thing to do is for unit staff to check for additional items and identifiers, along with interviewing the inmate and obtaining information from other inmates within the population." Interviewing incoming inmates is a common technique used in addressing the gang problem. Riley (p. 70) states:

> New inmates are screened by an intake committee. They are examined for tattoos and scars that might indicate an affiliation with a particular gang and are asked directly if they have gang affiliations. Some gang members will volunteer their affiliation, which helps in cell placements and work assignments. . . .
>
> For obvious reasons, we avoid placing rival gang members in the same cell. We keep contact between rival group members to a minimum by dividing the main facility into three sections, restricting movement and monitoring inmate traffic.

Separating rival gang members is seen as a critical move in preventing gang violence. Educating correctional staff about gang relations and identification techniques allows effective separation to take place. The Federal Bureau of Prisons uses such knowledge to better deal with the more violent groups. Trout (1992, p. 64) states: "The Mexican Mafia has long been at war with La Nuestra Familia and . . . has a long history of cooperation with the Aryan Brotherhood." Trout notes this information has proven very valuable in preventing violence between the Mexican Mafia and La Nuestra Familia as "incidents are virtually non-existent due to the BOP's policy of absolute separation between these two groups."

In Texas, a different approach is taken by placing any inmate positively identified as a gang member in administrative segregation. According to Buentello (p. 60):

> Removing these members from the general population reduced anxiety and fear among the general inmate population, and the number of inmates requesting protection status and unit transfers decreased.
>
> It became apparent gangs were having a difficult time recruiting and carrying out illegal activities from administrative segregation status. They became increasingly frustrated, which in turn lessened their effectiveness.

Such isolation techniques help explain why some prison gang members prefer anonymity for their actions. Avoiding notoriety helps avoid isolation and enables gang members to circulate among the general prisoner population in search of new recruits.

Toller and Tsagaris (p. 110) note: "Common elements of gang activity include unity, identity, loyalty and reward. The strategic challenge to corrections is to upset the gang's internal organization so that it cannot supply its members or potential recruits with these elements, and as a result, the gang's prestige and power decline. A more ambitious task is to offer corrections programs and activities that will replace gang activity."

> Strategies to manage prison gangs include identifying gang members, separating rival gang members, isolating confirmed gang members from the general prisoner population, training staff in how to recognize and separate gang members and maintaining internal and external communications to identify and track gang member activity. Disrupting the gang's internal organization and providing programs to replace gang activities are other strategies.

Racial Conflict

Racial conflict is another common part of the prison culture in men's facilities. Not only do gang members tend to organize along racial lines, but the general inmate population also tends to associate with those of common racial and ethnic backgrounds. However common or infrequent, it should be of no surprise that racial conflicts inevitably occur among correctional populations.

According to Hunt (1993, pp. 13–14): "Most new inmates (regardless of race or ethnicity) experience intense loss of personal identity . . . the inmate must struggle to define who he or she is in this new setting. . . . If the inmate tries to avoid this issue, other inmates will pressure him or her to identify with some group . . . avoidance will be judged as a weakness—and weak inmates do not survive in prison." Consequently, this racial or ethnic identification, because of its strong situational link to survival, heightens tension levels between those of different racial or ethnic groups.

Not only does racial conflict occur among inmates, but it also may exist between inmates and correctional staff.

Violence

Male prisoners, as a whole, commit more violent crimes and are, therefore, more dangerous than female offenders, although there are occasional exceptions. In the 1970s only 15 to 25 percent of the male population in prison were convicted of violent offenses. However, in most states, in the 1990s the number of violent offenders committing crimes against the person is almost 75 percent and growing. This is partially due to property offenders being placed in intermediate sanctions. Figure 8–2 shows how the number of violent offenders in prison outnumber those convicted of property, drug or public-order offenses.

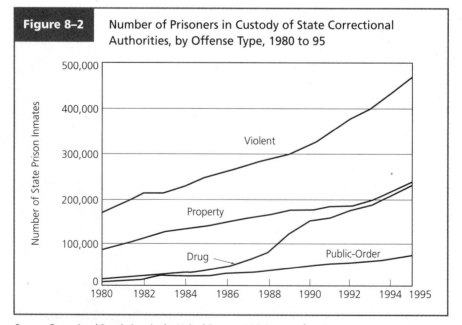

Figure 8–2 Number of Prisoners in Custody of State Correctional Authorities, by Offense Type, 1980 to 95

Source: Correctional Populations in the United States, 1995. Bureau of Justice Statistics, May 1997, p. 10 (NCJ-163916).

Violence in Prison: A Personal Perspective

by Jon Marc Taylor

For the past sixteen years, I have survived in the crucible of the maximum security keeps of various state prisons. During this tenure, I have been threatened innumerable times, punched with fists, slashed with a razor, bashed with a pipe, and poked with a shiv by other inmates, not to mention being inadvertently shot by a tower guard. Altogether, there are a half dozen scars on my body, with an uncountable number upon my psyche.

The violence I have suffered and inflicted has sadly been pretty much average fare for a convict. For the average inmate prison is a violent place, more violent than where he came from. For a small but growing number, though, prison is a safer, more regulated battleground than home ever was.

I am neither a player or punk, dealer, gambler nor gangbanger; just a student, 7 to 3 worker, and a general administrative pain in the ass. I mind my own business and get along pretty well with both staff and inmates, generally ignoring the instigators (of both groups) as much as possible. The incidents I have been involved in were unavoidable, because I had done everything (except run to protective custody) to avoid them. In one incident, I turned the wrong corner at the wrong time and was the wrong color. Later, after stitches in the noggin, I received an apology and, by way of peace offering, a C-note.

The purpose of this personal history is to preface my observations regarding violence in prison in general. I have seen three phases, or levels, of violence roll through the penitentiary. These waves have had different causes, eliciting different responses.

I fear the worst is yet to be seen.

When I first went down in 1980, the joint, a state reformatory (in name only), was still a gladiator school, with the average resident's age in the mid-twenties. Most of the inmates were doing time under the old indeterminate sentencing code—determinate sentencing with two-for-one good time credits having been enacted only a few years earlier—and still saw the parole board on a regular basis. One strategy of doing time then was to make a name for oneself during the first half of one's bit. Then "calm down" and "straighten up" on the flip side to show the board one had been reformed, or at least had grown up some.

This culture was the remnant of what I call the old school. The convict code (whatever that really is) was still talked about. There were old cons who still carried metal spoons in home made belt holsters, who spoke of the "old days" when convicts ran the joints, snitches died or wished they had, protective custody was rarely used, the place was wide open from breakfast to last count, and the cons and hacks stood toe to toe and threw down. Of course, these were mostly war stories by my rookie season, even then sounding mythical. But they were common enough to signify shared cultural norms.

These norms were one of a sharply divided culture of "us and them." Running to staff vying to be the first to snitch just for the sake of snitching was unheard of (as opposed to today's common practice). When discovered—or even suspected—the accused was seriously hurt or killed.

A clear hierarchy of crimes delineated the population. Murderers at the top, child molesters at the bottom, and drug dealers in a sort of limbo, circulating among all the strata.

continued

Violence in Prison: A Personal Perspective (*Continued*)

In fact, it was difficult for molesters even to exist in mainline population, while the killers usually held the best jobs and ran the joint as a sort of administrative syndicate, controlling housing and work assignments. Business was conducted, but there was a structure, a set of rules to the game. You incurred a debt, you paid it off or worked it off, usually on your knees. Everyone understood the rules and largely lived by them.

Preying on other cons was frowned upon, and if it became too flagrant the perpetrators were hurt for the good of the community. The basic concept was not to disturb the status quo. All in all there was a shared sense of unity and understandable mores. There was civilization, warped as it was, behind the walls.

Life in the joint then could be violent, but the violence had a purpose, a sort of logic to it. Fights occurred somewhere in the 32 acres nearly every day. Knives were ubiquitous. More than one gun or handful of shells were smuggled in. Serious injury and death was an all too possible occurrence. In the early to middle 80s, the administration tried to wrest greater control, resulting in intensified staff/inmate conflict. Fences went up, separating living areas from work areas. Unit feedings were staggered. Yard time was reduced and staggered.

Associations among inmates were limited to one's housing unit, recreational line (two to three units at a time), and work assignments. If a friend did not have a job and was in another unit, you never saw him. He might as well be in a different joint. Major shakedowns stripped comfortable customized cells, standardizing the accommodations to a spartan nature. Cell houses were usually locked down between line movements, ending the running of the ranges to blow off steam, visit friends or conduct business. The place was in constant turmoil as the structure of the society was forced to change. Nothing else was constant any longer. All changes were perceived as bad by the convict. The old ways, the old understandings eroded.

All officers, not just supervisors, were issued radios. Units received staff increases, though they remained dangerously undermanned. By the late mid-80s, inmate-on-inmate violence had reached a plateau and the focus shifted to inmate/staff conflict, with a series of riots and takeovers occurring.

After a series of clashes between housing units over the drug trade, control of punks, and general school yard pride, the takeover scared everyone. Prompted by a rogue unit of guards who routinely beat their charges with boots and clubs, a hit list of the participating officers was made after other efforts—inside and outside—failed to end the assaults. One morning, two inmates attacked several officers with shanks in front of the Captain's Office, trying to force their way into the Maximum Restraint Unit. Failing that, a running battle moved across the central yard, through the infirmary, and up into a housing unit. Eventually, four hostages were taken and a hundred or so inmates, who had not been involved in the original battle, ended up in control of a large cell house.

Largely unprepared, the DOC mobilized to deal with their worst nightmare in over twenty years. Through negotiation with state legislators, the ordeal ended peacefully a dozen hours later. The unplanned riot terrified everyone. The hostages' lives were in danger on more than one occasion. At one point, just hours before peace was negotiated, the DOC considered rushing the unit, an act that most assuredly would have resulted in lives lost on both sides.

Afterwards, everyone took a breath and slowly returned to the normal routine, with the shaken administration in clear control. Near the end of the decade, life remained relatively quiet. Movement was more controlled, but the general population still intermingled during worklines. Violence among inmates and between inmates and staff seemed reduced. Killings dropped off to rare events, with assaults on guards limited pretty much to dousings of urine and feces. Control units of varying degrees of isolation and deprivation began to be used. Trouble makers started to disappear from the mainline for six months to two years.

Also during this time, the quality of life improved in big and little ways. The major expansion of the college program, resulting from state grants matching the funding for federal Pell grants (brought about by an inmate lawsuit), allowed the university extension program to grow from 30 to 150 full-time students, employing 15 percent of the mainline population. The sense of purpose, of positive direction and involvement that the program provided cannot be understated, existing as it did amid the general milieu of prison apathy and negativity. The best minds and leaders in the population had a vested interest in keeping things calm so the semesters would not be interrupted. As the program grew, so did institutional stability.

At the same time, portable radios were sold, then crock pots, fans, and finally televisions. A daily movie was shown over the closed circuit system in addition to both public and private networks. The enhanced cell time stimulation also played a role in the period's calming effect. The new appliances also provided items a man could lose if he went to the hole, which remained as stark, barren and maddeningly monotonous as before. Overall, the staff, with a few notable exceptions, seemed to adopt the philosophy of live and let live.

The population began to age together. The average age was by now in the low 30s. There was, it seemed, only a relatively small turnover in the population. A period of stabilization, of peace, seemed to exist, allowing a consensus of coexistence to develop. One was not habitually looking over one's shoulder and arching blind corners. Fights were not altogether uncommon, but serious blood spilling was. Disturbances were random and isolated. In a sense, the population had matured. They sought stability and the maintenance of the standardized routine and what few luxuries they were allowed. They remembered the turmoil and horrors from earlier in the decade, and they saw no value in returning to those times.

By the turn of the decade, however, the environment had begun to change. Youngbloods, teenagers from harder times and meaner streets, began to arrive. The beginning of a new generation gap developed. The Youngbloods came from a different America than the older cons had. Life was meaner and tougher on the streets outside. The destructiveness of crack, worsened poverty and the futility of things never getting better had devastated a generation of young men. These offenders were even more poorly educated than the previous generation, their understanding of others less acute, and their desire to comprehend a situation beyond their own limited perspective nearly non-existent.

The youngsters were used to settling even minor disputes with guns and erratic violent

continued

Violence in Prison: A Personal Perspective (*Continued*)

eruptions. Face-to-face confrontations employing fists at the end of the block or calling someone out on the yard became less common, and explosive acts using more punishing weapons emerged as the norm.

The Youngbloods also seemed more antagonistic to the powers that be. Needless harassing of line staff took place, antagonizing everyone. Assaults on staff and among inmates increased. A few rotten apples in uniform geeked the hot heads, creating minor dramas for no other reason than their ability to do so. The stability of the now new-old ways were disrupted and an air of uncertainty settled over the prison.

More unsettling was the amount of time the new fish were bringing with them. These boys, and they largely were just boys, were routinely handed down 60, 90, 120, even 200 years. Essentially they had no future beyond these walls, with nothing to lose by lashing out in response to momentary anger, boredom, or frustration. Compounding the situation, programs were being scaled back from their already anemic levels, leaving fewer positive activities to engage in.

Games must and will be played, and if fewer organized options are available, those under control can and do create their own. These efforts mimic the life and death struggles for power and survival they dodged through on the streets. Only prison, without Uzis and Glocks, is actually a safer battleground on which to wage nihilistic wars of face and turf.

Ultimately it's all about the quest for respect, of others and of self. And if the system will not provide the socially accepted options of education, training and community involvement to achieve the earning of this respect, then those on the inside will do what they did on the streets that largely (at the very least perceptually) denied them the same options on the outside.

Civilization behind the walls has not collapsed, but it is ailing, just as it seems to be outside the walls.

Source: Jon Marc Taylor. "Violence in Prison: A Personal Perspective." *Corrections Compendium,* June 1996, pp. 1–3. Reprinted by permission of CEGA Publishing.

The violence which brought these offenders to corrections continues in their lives behind bars. As Johnson (1996, p. 77) states: "Most of today's prisons are formally known as correctional institutions, but this designation is more misleading than ever. As far as I and most other criminologists are concerned, the correctional institution as a type has largely passed from the prison scene. From the mid-1960s to the present, a new prison type has emerged. It is defined by the climate of violence and predation on the part of the prisoners that often marks its yards and other public areas. Known simply as the 'violent prison,' it has been aptly described as a 'human warehouse with a junglelike underground.' "

During 1996, the number of inmate-on-inmate assaults in prisons was 29,540, and the number of inmate-on-staff assaults in prisons was 13,724 (Camp and Camp, p. 36). Of these, 7,401 assaults on inmates required medical attention, and 938 were referred for prosecution; 2,192 of the assaults on staff required medical attention with 727 referred for prosecution.

Much of the violence in prison is perpetrated by younger inmates, victims themselves of a society where families are fractured and moral conscience is a foreign concept. Several inmates at the Oak Park Heights Correctional Facility in Minnesota had the following comments about the "new breed" of younger prisoner:

- "The problem here is the young punks who are coming in today. They don't care about anyone."
- "These punks don't give a damn about anything."

One inmate who had found a way to avoid conflict with such callous, youthful prisoners stated: "At least I feel safe in here. That's more than I can say about most of the prisons I've been in."

Homosexuality

Inmate homosexuality, both consensual and coerced, is a problem in any correctional institution. However, according to many researchers, a marked difference exists between the homosexual liaisons of male and female inmates. Homosexual acts in men's prisons are more frequently violent and coerced. In contrast, such homosexual encounters are less forced or one-sided with female inmates. The topic of sex in correctional facilities is covered further in Chapter 13.

Family Ties

Approximately half of all men in prison have children (Dallao, 1997, p. 96), and their family is an important part of their lives. Many of these prisoners consider the true punishment to be separation from loved ones:

- "This isn't too bad a prison as far as prisons go. The punishment is that I can't be with my family."
- "The people who are really being punished are my family. And I can't do anything about it." (Inmates at Oak Park Heights Correctional Facility in Minnesota)

When asked what they looked forward to, one inmate at a Florida correctional institution replied: "When my mom and family come to see me, which is once a month, plus when I get mail."

Humor

How often is it said, "At least you've kept your sense of humor"? Perhaps nowhere is such an attribute more valuable than for those behind bars. According to Terry (1997, p. 24):

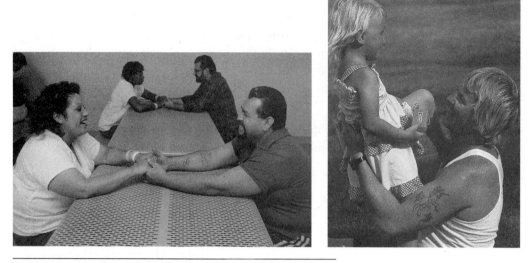

(Left) Visiting day at the Project PRIDE Boot Camp at the Santa Clara County Women's Jail. Inmates and adult visitors must remain on opposite sides of the table with their hands on top of it.
(Right) Maintaining the bonds with their children is very important to many prisoners. Here, an inmate father plays with his four-year-old daughter during a Fourth of July visit at the minimum-security state prison honor farm at Riverton, Wyoming.

Extensive research has been done in the hopes of better understanding the mechanisms underlying the socialization processes within the prison environment. Particular interest has been paid to the ways prison inmates adjust to, and cope with, confinement. . . .

Male prisoners exist in a world that suppresses the expression of one's true feelings. Any exhibition of emotion relative to pain of any sort is seen as weakness and is unacceptable. Yet human feelings (for most anyway) must be displayed somehow by inmates. This is accomplished through humor. . . .

Prison humor allows inmates to achieve control in two ways: It is the only social mechanism within the prison environment that allows feelings to be expressed and its expression cannot be controlled by authorities. Prison inmates use humor as a reply that undermines the strength of the many voices of the system that continuously attempt to manage and control them. It acts as proof of their power and their release from domination.

Keeping a sense of humor is one way to maneuver daily life behind bars. Other coping or survival mechanisms may be considered part of an inmate code.

Inmate Code

Another difference between male and female prisoners is the nature of their inmate code and the extent of its endorsement among offenders. An **inmate code** is an informal set of norms, a "code of conduct" to which offenders are expected to adhere. Researchers have noticed the inmate code is more extensive among male offenders than among female offenders. According to Sykes and Messinger (1960), six basic tenets comprise the inmate code:

1. Don't interfere with inmate interests (a.k.a. mind your own business).
2. Never rat on a con.
3. Do your own time.
4. Don't exploit fellow inmates.
5. Be tough; be a man; never back down from a fight.
6. Don't trust the hacks (guards) or the things they stand for.

> The inmate code consists of behavioral norms for offenders such as "mind your own business," "don't snitch on another inmate," "do your own time," "don't exploit fellow inmates," "stand up for yourself" and "don't trust the staff."

Although first described more than 40 years ago, today's inmates still abide by this unwritten code. It has been observed, however, that male inmates seem to have a much stronger commitment to this code than do female inmates.

The following quotes are excerpts from a survey conducted among inmates at a Florida correctional institution, providing a glimpse of the inmate code and prison culture in action:

- "Second time [incarcerated]—things are changing very quickly. A lot stricter rules and regulations. Rules are almost constantly changing, and they try to keep you locked down as long as possible. It really sucks, and I wish I could go back and start my life over, but now I can only learn from my mistakes."

- "Keep to yourself and don't get into NO one's business no matter what."

- "I don't fit into any group, nor do I feel like an outsider. I do my time and don't harass anyone unless it's brought to me."

- "As for the groups, there are several kinds. You got your 'child molesters' and 'baby rapers' and they stay to themselves. You've got members of several different organizations, which society calls gang members—Folk, Crip, Blood, Latin King, Aryan, Skin Head, Black Power, Black Panther—dope dealers and such. Then you've got the group that's sort of in between all that. I do my time and can get along with anyone who can get along with me."

- "Of course you're going to have your drugs, marijuana, cocaine, heroin, LSD, and others; even your homemade alcohol. But it's more than that. Just like you have rules to adhere by out there, we have those plus some unwritten ones, sort of a code of ethics."

- "My feelings for other inmates is nothin' 'cause they did what they did to get here just like I did, and they have their own problems."

- "I respect everyone until they go past the line and violate me and my space, but other than that it's all good."

- "You always have to stand up for yourself in here. If you don't, and you allow someone to take advantage of you, other people will be coming at you and you won't last very long. There are so many games and cons that people play on other people. You never allow someone (another inmate) to take anything from you. It's not like it is out there, where you can bring the law into it. It just doesn't work that way."

- ". . . just keep your mouth closed and stick to yourself and do your time 'cause this is a real serious spot and it ain't nothin' to play with."

- "Very very few [staff] are decent—you know, do their 8 hours and leave. Others want to be hard asses and do a lot of nitpicking."

- ". . . But to be real they [staff] treat all of us just like shit and if they have a bad day at home they take it out on us."

- "Nine out of every ten [staff members] will try to case you up and stab you in the back any chance they get."

- "Stay low profile. Don't communicate with officers unless [you] have to."

- "I wish that officers wouldn't use their uniforms to overpower inmates. Institutions would be a lot better if inmates and officers got along better. But that is impossible because officers bring home problems here and take it out on us."

- "Some staff are OK, but others are strictly by-the-book. Then others go out of their way to make it hard for us, like they've never made mistakes before."

The condition of the male offender has, for decades, been the yardstick by which correctional programs and services were evaluated. However, with their numbers constantly rising, much attention has recently been devoted to the female offender, and many are discovering that what has worked in the past for men does not necessarily work for women.

Female Offenders

Historically, women have comprised only a fraction of the total number of adults under correctional supervision, contributing in part to their being labeled the "forgotten offender." In 1995, women comprised about 6 percent of all prison inmates, 10 percent of jail inmates, 10 percent of parolees and about 21 percent of probationers (*Correctional Populations*, p. iii). And while their relative proportions are small, the numbers are significant considering the current growth rate of the female prison population is nearly double that of males.

Although their relative proportion is smaller, the female prisoner population is currently growing at about twice the rate of the male prisoner population.

It has been noted: "Between 1980 and 1994, the female prison population jumped roughly 480 percent (from 13,420 to 64,403), compared to an increase of 313 percent for the male prison population. . . . Although historically given little attention due to their comparatively small numbers, in the last decade both the number of female inmates and the average length of their sentences have increased dramatically" ("FBOP Focus," 1996, p. 5).

The higher incarceration rates for women may have been because discretion was curtailed or limited. Sentencing guidelines and mandatory-minimum sentences kept judges from using discretion, thereby driving up female incarceration rates. According to Ryan and McCabe (1997, p. 30), who compared profiles of adult female offenders in 1983 and 1993: "The sentencing pattern . . . changed. The number of sentences for 20 years or less was about the same; the number of sentences for more than 20 years doubled in 1993." However, as noted by McCarthy and McCarthy (1997, p. 305): "While this rapid growth in female crime has significant implications for corrections, which traditionally has allocated few resources for institutional *or* community-based programs for female offenders, there is little evidence that patterns of female criminality are truly changing."

General Characteristics of Female Offenders

Female offenders share many characteristics with male offenders and are very similar in terms of age, socioeconomic level and race/ethnic background. Snell and Morton (1994, p. 1) say of the female offender: "Most of the female State prison inmates were over age 30, at least high school graduates or holders of a GED, and members of a racial or ethnic minority. Large majorities were unmarried, mothers of children under 18, and daughters who had grown up in homes without both parents present. Before entering prison a large percentage of the women had experienced physical or sexual abuse." McCarthy and McCarthy (p. 305) state: "[F]emale criminal behavior appears to be a product of continuing social problems—the impact of physical and emotional abuse and extreme disadvantage, exacerbated by economic problems and drug and alcohol abuse." Owen and Bloom (1995, p. 174) compare characteristics of women prisoners based on their study of California prisoners and a study conducted by the Bureau of Justice Statistics (Table 8–2). Many female offenders struggle with depression, bitterness and guilt. As Rigert (1997b, p. A12) notes of women in federal prisons and prison camps:

| Table 8–2 | Characteristics of Women Prisoners: Comparison of the 1991 Bureau of Justice Statistics Data and the California Sample (*N* = 294) (Percentages) | |

Characteristic	Bureau of Justice Statistics 1991	California Sample
Race/ethnic Background		
White non-Hispanic	36.2	36.0
Black non-Hispanic	46.0	46.0
Hispanic	14.2	14.0
Other	3.6	4.0
Age (years)		
17 or younger	0.1	0.0
18–24	16.3	11.2
25–34	50.4	48.2
35–44	25.5	27.9
45–54	6.1	10.5
55 or older	11.7	2.2
Median age	31.0	33.0
Marital Status		
Married	17.3	16.0
Widowed	5.9	4.1
Divorced	19.1	23.1
Separated	12.5	12.2
Never married	45.1	42.9
Education		
8th grade or less	16.0	7.4
Some high school	45.8	28.2 (11.6% with GEDs)
High school graduate	22.7	14.6
Some college or more	15.5	25.7 (12.2% with technical school training)
Pre-arrest Employment		
Employed	46.7	46.3
Full-time	35.7	33.7
Part-time	11.0	12.6
Unemployed	53.3	53.7

Source: Barbara Owen and Barbara Bloom. "Profiling Women Prisoners: Findings from National Surveys and a California Sample." *The Prison Journal,* Vol. 75, No. 2, June 1995, p. 174. Copyright © 1995, *The Prison Journal.* Reprinted by permission of Sage Publications, Inc.

A heroin-addict shows the track marks on her arms. A correlation exists between such drug addiction and female criminal conduct.

Some of them adjust poorly: They eat too much or too little, sleep away their free time or hardly sleep at all, or use medication to drop out. Prison administrators say 8 to 10 percent of female inmates take antidepressants.

. . . But the women can't drop out during work hours. They are required to take jobs ranging from food service to factory work, for 12 cents to $1.15 an hour.

And many of them also keep busy after work and on weekends. Some focus on improving themselves and their prospects upon release. They plunge into hobbies, exercise and academic or vocational classes to fill their free time.

. . . Warden David Helman at the Pekin, Ill., correctional institution says prison helps some women: "I see them become stronger, more independent, developing some self-esteem. They have only themselves. They are not subservient."

The Unique Correctional Experience of Female Offenders

Many have noted the corrections experience is significantly different for women than for men, because men and women are treated differently by the courts and corrections systems. It has been suggested this differential treat-ment has to do with the nature of crimes committed by women and the role of many women as mothers.

Nature of the Offense

Compared to males, women are more likely to be arrested and imprisoned for property and drug offenses and less likely to be arrested and imprisoned for vi-olent offenses. According to McCarthy and McCarthy (p. 305): "Women's vio-lent crime is often the result of domestic abuse. . . . There is little indication that female criminals engage in significant amounts of predatory violence." Re-ferring to their study of female prisoners in California, Owen and Bloom (p. 165) state: "[T]he percentage of women in prison for violent offenses has decreased while the proportion of women in prison for drug-related offenses has increased substantially." Figure 8–3 presents the most recent available data illustrating the differences between male and female prisoner populations and the nature of their offenses. Keep in mind that although the actual numbers

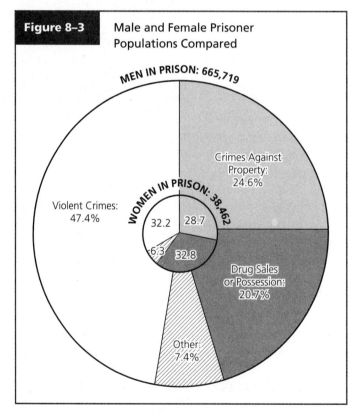

Figure 8–3   Male and Female Prisoner Populations Compared

MEN IN PRISON: 665,719

Crimes Against Property: 24.6%

Violent Crimes: 47.4%

WOMEN IN PRISON: 38,462

32.2   28.7

6.3   32.8

Drug Sales or Possession: 20.7%

Other: 7.4%

Source: Adapted from Tracy L. Snell and Danielle C. Morton. *Women in Prison: Survey of State Prison Inmates, 1991.* Special Report. U.S. Department of Justice, Bureau of Justice Statistics. March 1994, p. 3 (NCJ-145321).

today are greater than those given in the figure, the percentages (sizes of the pie slices) have changed little.

> Women are more likely than men to be arrested and imprisoned for property and drug offenses and less likely than men to be arrested and imprisoned for violent offenses.

Considering the nature of their offenses, women are generally viewed as less of a threat to society and, consequently, are more likely to receive probation or other intermediate sanction than be sentenced to time behind bars. When women are incarcerated, their sentences tend to be shorter than men's. According to Snell and Morton (p. 4): "Overall female prisoners had shorter maximum sentences than men. . . . Excluding sentences to life or death, women in prison had received sentences that, on average, were 48 months shorter than those of men (mean sentences of 105 and 153 months, respectively)." These authors note that part of this difference is the result of differences in crimes committed between women and men, with drug and property crimes carrying shorter sentences than violent crimes. However, data from the U.S. Department of Justice (*Compendium of,* 1997, p. 83) indicates that for each category of offense, including violent offenses, women received, on average, shorter sentences than men.

Table 8–3 shows how female offenders receive shorter sentences across the board.

The Incarcerated Mother

Many believe another factor in the decision to grant women lighter sentences is their role as caregiver. Approximately 80 percent of all incarcerated women have children (Dallao, p. 96). Furthermore, of the more than 1.5 million minors

| Table 8–3 | Average Sentence Lengths for Various Offenses, by Sex of Offender, 1994 (In Months) |

| | | | Felonies | | | | | |
| | | | **Property Offenses** | | | **Public-Order Offenses** | | |
Offender Characteristics	**All Offenses**	**Violent Offenses**	**Fraudulent**	**Other**	**Drug Offenses**	**Regulatory**	**Other**	**Mis-demeanors**
All offenders	61.4	95.9	15.8	20.8	81.1	16.1	45.0	8.7
Male	64.4	97.6	17.3	22.2	83.7	17.0	46.2	9.7
Female	36.3	58.5	10.6	11.0	58.3	9.7	26.5	0.7

Source: Compendium of Federal Justice Statistics, 1994. Washington, DC: U.S. Department of Justice, Bureau of Justice Statistics, 1997, p. 83 (NCJ-163063).

with a parent behind bars, 43 percent are under 7 years old. While many male prisoners also have children, in many cases, these men were not living with their children or playing an active role as caregiver. According to the most recent available data (Snell and Morton, p. 6), more female inmates than male inmates were living with their minor children before entering prison (Table 8–4).

| Table 8–4 | Children of State Prison Inmates, by Race and Sex of Inmates, 1991 |

| Characteristic | Percent of Female Inmates | | | | Percent of Male Inmates |
	All[a]	White	Black	Hispanic	All[a]
Have children					
No	21.9%	26.1%	20.4%	17.8%	36.1%
Yes	78.1	73.9	79.6	82.2	63.9
Under age 18	66.6%	61.6%	69.0%	71.6%	56.1%
Adult only	11.4	12.3	10.6	10.6	7.6
Number of inmates	38,658	13,983	17,754	5,521	669,732
Number of children under age 18[b]					
1	37.3%	40.7%	37.0%	31.2%	43.2%
2	29.9	30.8	28.4	33.3	28.9
3	18.1	17.5	18.2	19.8	15.2
4	8.5	6.5	9.0	10.0	6.8
5 or more	6.1	4.5	7.4	5.7	5.9
Lived with child(ren) under 18 before entering prison[b]					
No	28.3%	31.3%	24.5%	34.3%	47.1%
Yes	71.7	68.7	75.5	65.7	52.9
Where child(ren) under 18 live(s) now[b,c]					
Father/mother	25.4%	35.2%	18.7%	24.4%	89.7%
Grandparents	50.6	40.6	56.7	54.9	9.9
Other relatives	20.3	14.7	23.7	22.8	2.9
Friends	4.1	5.7	2.7	4.2	.4
Foster home	8.6	12.6	5.8	6.5	1.7
Agency or institution	2.1	2.1	1.8	2.1	.5
Alone	2.0	1.9	2.3	1.5	1.1

Note: Female prison inmates had an estimated total of 56,123 children under age 18, and male inmates had 770,841 minor children.
[a]Includes Asians, Pacific Islanders, American Indians, Alaska Natives, and other racial groups.
[b]Percents are based on those inmates with children under age 18.
[c]Percents add to more than 100% because inmates with more than one child may have provided multiple responses.
Source: Tracy L. Snell and Danielle C. Morton. *Women in Prison: Survey of State Prison Inmates, 1991.* Special Report, U.S. Department of Justice, Bureau of Justice Statistics, March 1994, p. 6 (NCJ-145321).

Nearly 80 percent of women prisoners have children, which may contribute to the shorter sentences they receive.

Furthermore, Snell and Morton (p. 6) found: "Among inmates with children under age 18, 25% of the women, but nearly 90% of the men, said that their children were living with the other parent." Dallao (p. 97) adds: "Fewer women than men in prison have spouses or significant others waiting for them on the outside." In other words, when men are imprisoned, most children still have their mothers to care for them, but when mothers are imprisoned, many fathers are nowhere to be found.

The maintenance of mother-child relationships through periods of incarceration has caused much concern and debate. Indeed, sentencing female offenders to probation or other intermediate sanctions allows them to remain home, able to care for their children while serving their sentences. But how can mother-child ties be maintained when the mother is behind bars? A 1990 survey conducted by the American Correctional Association (ACA) examined the impact on the relationship between mother and child caused by the mother's incarceration. Given that the average female offender has children and is the primary, if not sole, caregiver for those children, the potential for long-term damage is very great. According to Lord (1995, pp. 259–260):

> [I]f we are ever going to effectively intervene in the intergenerational connections of crime, abuse, drugs, and incarceration, we must recognize that these families are at risk. . . . These relationships cannot thrive on 2 hours a week or a month, and they cannot thrive on 1 week a year—they cannot thrive in prison. Everything that we are doing in prison to address family issues we can do better in free society and at considerably less cost. . . .
>
> Imprisonment should be the absolute last resort—for use when all else has failed and when there is concern for the safety of others.

Some facilities have arranged for children to stay with their mothers inside the facility for short periods, an arrangement unheard of in men's facilities. For example, Clark (1995, pp. 321–322), an inmate at Bedford Hills Correctional Facility, New York State's maximum-security prison for women, writes about

> . . . the extensive resources and activities of the Parenting Center and other programs in this prison (daily visiting, a Children's Center playroom for mothers and children, monthly bus transportation, weekend programs and weeklong summer programs for children to spend intimate quality time with their mothers, civilian advocates, peer counselors, groups and classes, and the Family Reunion Program's trailer visits) that enable many mothers to see their children regularly and comfortably; to communicate with caregivers and others such as

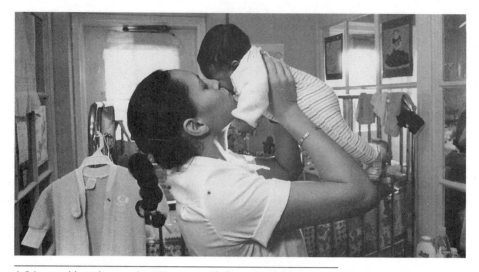

A 24-year-old mother, serving 15 years to life for a drug charge at the Bedford Hills Correctional Facility for Women in New York, snuggles her 9-month-old daughter. The mother had to give up her daughter later that year.

teachers, therapists, and social workers; and to improve their relationships with their children. There is also a nursery unit, which enables selected women who give birth while incarcerated to keep their babies for the first year.

Gray et al. (1995, p. 200) note: "[S]ome jails have experimented with allowing children to live with their incarcerated mothers. At the Neil J. Houston House in Boston, 15 inmate mothers live with their babies, usually for about 6 months. Similar programs exist at the federal level in Texas and California."

Most of the time, however, children of incarcerated women must try to cope without much contact with their mothers. According to Dallao (p. 97): "For these impressionable youngsters, the effects of their parents' crimes can alter and upset emotional development for years to come." Rigert (1997a, pp. A1, A10) notes:

Strict federal sentencing policies, enacted more than a decade ago, now require long prison terms for women as well as men, regardless of their responsibilities for children. Those policies were meant to eliminate discrimination and ensure equality in the sentencing of men and women, the rich and poor. But experts argue that the policies actually discriminate against women, because they don't allow judges to take into account family needs that remain when mothers go to prison.

One judge, James Rosenbaum in Minneapolis, declared: "Absolute gender equity in sentencing has turned out to be a war on children."

California law professor Myrna Raeder, an authority on women's issues in sentencing, added: "The lofty goal of gender neutrality has backfired, wreaking havoc in the lives of female offenders and their children." . . .

When judges do consider the role of mothers, they risk being slapped down by appeals courts.

Diaries from the Inside—Two Accounts

Following are excerpts from the journals of two women serving time in federal institutions for drug offenses. Note the common focus on children and the inmates' struggle to maintain their identities and roles as mothers, even from behind bars.

Lai Chiem Saelee

Lai Chiem Saelee is from Laos, where opium was legal and widely used. It isn't legal, however, in the United States, and that was her undoing. She arranged with another woman to import the drug for older Laotian men in Seattle.

Saelee, the mother of four, said she had planned to send most of her share of profits in the opium sales to her destitute family and to village people in Thailand and Laos.

Saelee has seen her children only twice during her five years in prison. Her husband's parents and brother are caring for them. The children are doing well in school. She calls them twice a week.

Saelee earns 12 cents an hour sweeping the prison yard. Like other noncitizen female drug offenders, she will be deported at the end of her sentence.

Meanwhile, she has been writing in her diary from federal prisons in Lexington, Ky., Danbury, Conn., and Dublin, Calif.:

1994

Lexington, (2,300 miles from her children in Seattle)

- **July 16:** I talk to my mother-in-law and baby Danny. He misses me so much and ask when I would get to transfer to Seattle . . . I cried when he ask me that. He also said mom don't worry I am a good boy and getting big.

- **Aug. 11:** I just so happy today I guess it's because my birthday. . . . Four people including my roommate. They are all celebrated and bought me gifts. It was so surprise me. . . . I then think about at home I never have someone do anything like this for me.

- **Sept. 29:** This is a day that my eyes filled with cloud and feeling hurt like a knife stick in my heart. I found out the bad news. . . . They are going to deport me. . . . I then ask to speak to my daughter Nancy. . . . They are deporting mommy back to Laos and never get to see you again.

Danbury (2,900 miles from her children)

- **Nov. 8:** Today this lady [roommate] was back. It's so stink she haven't wash her clothes for two week already. It made me sick.

- **Dec. 31:** My son said if nothing is important, don't call; it cost a lot of money for phone bill. I don't want to call, but I need to hear from my children's voice each week to help me through each day.

1995

- **Jan. 29:** I saw all my kids and I hug them so hard and play with them. It seemed so real. When I woke up, it was only dream.

- **Jan. 30:** [A manager tells her she is being transferred to Dublin, Calif., closer to her children.] I was shock. . . . I said, is this real? . . . After waiting two year God answer my pray.

Dublin (800 miles from her children)

- **March 7:** I feel depress. I didn't have enough money to spend to make phone call.

- **March 11:** [She breaks her leg roller-skating and is taken later to an outside

continued

clinic for surgery to install pins. She is in pain for weeks, can't work and relies on friends to bring her food.]

- **April 3:** I got four letters tonight. It made me happy. Also $100 from my son again. He wrote me a beautiful letter. Each one of them love me so much.

- **April 4:** When I get back to my room one of the roommate were smoking. It was smell terrible bad I could hardly breath. I said: "You smoke in here, please don't smoke, I am very allergic to smoking." . . . She said, "Yes, I smoke. . . ." I cannot live like this. . . . Also never help to clean the room. Very lazy person.

- **April 9:** Today my feel much happier cause my Thai friend would come and chat with in our native language. . . . We laughed so hard.

- **April 14:** This one [roommate] is really giving me headache. Lazy and strong mouth. Very messy, too. God please help me.

- **April 15:** I haven't see any family yet since 1993 in county jail.

- **April 17:** I have a bad news about my immigration. My appeal has been denied. I am so disappoint and upset, too. Why they are so cold heart never gave me a chance to stay here in the U.S. No matter what, they wanted me to send back to Laos. I cried and cried.

- **April 20:** I . . . got a letter from him [her husband] last night. It touch my heart knowing he loves me so much. He loves me more than I love him. I feel sorry, but I can't help him out. I wish I could go back to before so I can plea guilty for my crime.

- **May 21:** I have to borrow from my in-laws when I go home I'll work and pay back little by little. I love my children and I need to stay in U.S. [Another inmate told her she could get an attorney for $6,000

to keep her from being deported after her prison term is over. It was a scam. She lost the money.]

- **June 12:** This is the day I was arrested . . . in Seattle. It has been three years away from my children. At work I scream so loud, hey, you all, today is the day I got arrested. People laughed I laughed, too.

- **June 24:** My family I yell, hey I am here! . . . I was so excited and happy, nervous. . . . I saw my three youngest first and hug my tears came out and kids too. . . . We are all cried and happy. Pray Lord I got to see them. . . . We all walk together and share our joy. . . . We went back inside and chat not too long the time is over with it. Around 2:45 p.m. everyone started to cry. I put each one of my kids on my lap and hold them so tight telling them to study hard and be good.

- **July 6:** I can only imagine how life away from my children once I get deport to Laos. . . . I wonder is there a real God on the heaven or not?

1996

- **Feb. 26:** Today is sad day because my friend Sang is going home. I don't know if she will miss me as I miss her or not. But I know for sure that anyone goes home she will forget a friend who is still here in prison. It's okay prison is prison people come and go. . . . I realize one day will be my turn too just like that.

—*Saelee is due out in 2001. Her diary made available to the Star Tribune stopped in 1996.*

Gail Waggoner

After Gail Waggoner's then-husband led her into dealing marijuana, she became a cocaine addict and dealer, acting as a broker in

Naples, Fla., for distributors from Tennessee. One of the distributors, a longtime family friend, informed on Waggoner in exchange for a reduced sentence. Waggoner could have informed on 16 suppliers and dealers in exchange for a 16-month sentence. But she turned in none and received the mandatory minimum sentence of 10 years.

"I searched my conscience," she said. "If you give them more people, you are doing the same thing that got you here."

Still, Waggoner is bitter about the three men who received lighter sentences than hers because they helped the government.

Waggoner carries guilt to bed every night over what her crime did to her two children, Lisa and Fred. "I feel like I abandoned them, like I put them on a doorstep somewhere," she said. Her daughter dropped out of school and became an unwed mother. She said, "Mother, I just want something to love while you are gone; the way I loved you." Waggoner's son, a construction worker, is often depressed, even now. And Waggoner's mother cries for days after a visit. A new husband, Mark, also is in prison. In diary excerpts, she writes intermittently at the Marianna, Fla., prison of her life since 1992:

The First Few Days: 1992

- **Jan. 29:** Met some more of my cellmates. They range from terrorists to drug dealers to mothers who have killed to keep their children from going to prison.
- **Jan. 30:** The first female advance came today. Talked to my family and got accused of looking at someone's girlfriend.
- **Jan. 31:** Last night was really the worst one yet, cried in my sleep all night. . . . I really miss my family. I walked 3 miles and cried the whole way.
- **Feb. 1:** Everyone who has their loved ones with them, don't know how lucky they are. Please treasure every second.

- **Feb. 9:** Talked to the kids today. It seems as though I'm not needed at all anymore. Boy, that's tough.
- **Feb. 14:** I'm in the food warehouse cleaning . . . garbage cans. Boy, it sure stinks. I barfed the 1st hour.

Into the Second Year: 1993

- **July 29:** A lot has happened in this last 18 months. Became a granny, went through lots of emotional ups and downs. I can only thank God for helping me cope.
- **Dec. 4:** Ken brought Lisa and Taylor [Waggoner's grandchild] up as a B-day present. It was so wonderful. Taylor smiled the whole time. It was a wonderful gift. Thank you God.

On to the Third Year: 1994

- **Jan. 31:** Mark cut me off or out of his life tonight, whatever that means. I realize he is hurt and mad, but hurting someone else . . . is not the answer.
- **Feb. 9:** Lisa is pregnant again and doesn't trust me enough to tell me. This saddens me a great deal. Dear God I love my kids with all my heart and want them to come to me with anything.
- **May 4:** Oh, how happy I was 17 years ago. Today, yes, Lisa, the day you were born. You were such a beautiful baby, lots of black hair, dark eyes. Yes I had a wonderful gift from God. . . . I know, honey, I'm not there to be with you, but please know that in my heart and soul, I'm there.
- **Mothers Day, May 8:** I can't believe my kids. Surprised me and came to visit. . . . Baby Taylor, you're sure a beautiful child and just like your mother. I sure do wish I could go home and be the granma you need.
- **Sept. 28:** Dear God, I pray that you give us all the strength we need to get through this day. I lost a grand baby boy today. Lisa is going to need all the love and guidance that we can give her. I know that they say

---

Diaries from the Inside—Two Accounts (*Continued*)

there is an answer for everything. Help me see that. . . . I can deal with just about anything but my children hurting.

Fourth Year: 1995

- **Jan. 1:** I'm growing stagnant. I've run my rope. I feel as though I could draw all within myself very easily. Zombie material. I do not contemplate suicide, but next to it, whatever that may be. . . . I can do this and come out stronger and healthier. I went through the holidays with no one coming and survived.
- **Dec. 25:** Another Christmas. Only four more to go. How will I do that? Only by faith I'm sure.

Fifth Year: 1996

- **Jan. 13:** Another day down. Days have never meant so much. What a bad night for dreaming. I dreamt that Lisa was killed. I couldn't shake it, woke people up

making sad sounds. Tried to call, no one home. Great letter from Mark. We sure need some emotional contact.

- **Jan. 21:** Dear God, how I hate what I have done to my family.
- **Aug. 25;** Mom she tries so hard and never is rewarded. The kids are at an all-time low.
- **Dec. 22:** I'm feeling real sorry for all the lives I've touched and hurt by the crimes I've committed. I'm so sorry. Please forgive me. This was a hard visit on all of us. My sweet mother, God help her. She's so lonely and tired. I love her so. I pray God keeps her in his arms until I can get home. . . . Taylor she actually wanted to stay with me. She had to be pulled out of my arms. . . . She also asked me if I had been bad.
- **Dec. 25:** The kids and mom came up the 22nd and 23rd. They are truly the best. They still love me, even after what I've done to hurt us all.

—*Waggoner will be released in year 2000.*

Source: Lai Chiem Saelee and Gail Waggoner. "Diaries from the Inside." *Star Tribune,* Monday, December 15, 1997, p. A13. Reprinted by permission of the *Star Tribune,* Minneapolis-St. Paul.

Compounding the problem of trying to maintain contact with their children is the fact that correctional facilities for women aren't as numerous as facilities for men, meaning women are often transported many miles away from their families. In some cases, federal inmates are transported to institutions 2,000 miles or more away from where their children live. To many women inmates doing time far from their families, the phone becomes their lifeline to their children. Rigert (1997a, p. A11) states: "Known as 'phone queens' in prison, they call and call, negotiating discipline by phone, even help to settle arguments among contentious siblings."

Pregnant inmates are an additional concern for those handling female offenders. According to the ACA (1990), 4.2 percent of jail inmates and 6 percent of prison inmates were pregnant when they entered the facility. In addition to the medical needs of pregnant inmates, many other women arrive at prisons and jails in need of health care that, too often, is not readily available. Lord (p. 263) states: "Studies have shown that women come into prison with more medical needs than do men." Yet because many women's facilities are small, they lack the funding available to larger men's facilities for such services as comprehensive health care.

Offenders with a History of Abuse

The mental health needs of female offenders are of further concern. Carp and Schade (1992, p. 152) note: "A significant number of female offenders come from backgrounds of poverty, neglect and abuse." Such backgrounds should be considered when evaluating how a female inmate might respond to male corrections officers or other male authorities. In fact, regarding the placement of female offenders in some correctional alternatives like boot camps, Carol Shapiro, former assistant commissioner for New York City's corrections department, believes "the strictly military programs, especially, are no place for a woman who has a history of abuse by men. The last thing such an inmate needs is a male drill instructor screaming in her face . . ." (Sharp, 1995, p. 7).

Inmate Culture in Women's Correctional Facilities

The first moments upon arrival at prison can be terrifying, when the offender is uncertain where she fits in. Women quickly learn to adopt certain inmate identities and lifestyles as ways of adjusting to life behind bars. Carp and Schade (p. 154) state: "Women adapt to prison differently than men and are much less likely to engage in violence during incarceration. Instead, they seek to re-create or establish the kinds of relationships they are most familiar with: family bonds."

Kinships

➤ Women inmates frequently form **pseudofamilies** or substitute families with other incarcerated women. This kinship system plays a major role in many female inmates' lives. The most common relationship is that of mother-daughter, with some "mothers" having several "daughters" within the facility. Some female prisoners are very committed to such relationships and take their kinships very seriously. Others, however, regard it as more of a game.

The Inmate Code

This female kinship system interferes somewhat with several tenets of the inmate code. For example, the norm to "do your own time" is hampered by the apparent desire of female inmates to become involved in other inmates' problems. While male offenders are known to maintain emotional distance between each other, many females actively engage in relationships based on emotional involvement and concern. Consequently, female inmate subcultures often lack the taboo regarding involvement in other inmates' problems.

Another tenet, to avoid interacting with correctional staff, also appears to receive less endorsement from female inmates. Male inmates generally avoid interacting with officers for fear of being labeled a snitch. In contrast, female inmates often have more social interactions with staff.

> Generally, the inmate code receives less endorsement from female inmates than from male inmates, with such tenets as "do your own time" and "avoid interacting with the staff" being hampered by the kinship system of female inmates and their desire to engage in social interactions.

Homosexuality

Much has been written about the intimate relationships women cultivate behind bars. Women offenders are known to form close relationships during incarceration to alleviate feelings of loneliness and isolation and sometimes to ease sexual tensions. These liaisons differ from the sexual encounters of most male inmates in that they are almost always consensual, two-way agreements, not the coerced sexual relationships often found in men's facilities. As part of the pseudofamily organization, certain female offenders may assume more masculine, "fatherly" roles. One correctional officer explained sex in women's prisons this way:

> In the female facilities [sex is] not sold, it's not rape, it's just an agreement between two people that they're going to participate and there's a lot of participation.

Offenders in Community Corrections

For many offenders, male and female, there is no prison culture or inmate code because they serve their sentences in the community, in many cases free to pursue relationships with the same people (offenders and nonoffenders) they interacted with before being sentenced to corrections. However, offenders who serve time in halfway houses and other residential community corrections facilities do interact regularly with other offenders and are supervised closely by correctional staff and, consequently, may experience something similar to the prison inmate code described previously. According to McCarthy and McCarthy (p. 253):

> A 1978 study of an East Los Angeles halfway house revealed that the inmate code was alive and well in that community-based corrections facility. . . . The inmate code, which encourages loyalty to residents and distrust of staff, appeared to act as a significant barrier to reintegration. . . .
>
> Many inmates may settle in to the halfway house as they would adjust to prison—adopting a "do your own time" ethic that resists any outside intervention. Staff must work to demonstrate that the resident can try new behaviors without fear of failure, that there is real support for the resident's efforts to change, and that meaningful guidance and assistance are available.

When offenders are given probation or other nonresidential community corrections, however, and are allowed to serve their sentences in their own

Personal Account of a Former Probationer

Steve* was a 24-year-old college student when he was sentenced to 18 months of probation for conspiracy to sell marijuana.

I helped somebody that I thought was a friend get some marijuana for his girlfriend. I made a few phone calls for him and didn't think it was much of a big deal for someone who is your roommate, you know. Kinda' like when you know somebody who has something and somebody else who wants something . . . a free pass to the movie theater or whatever. I was trying to help get somebody some smoke. For reasons that will probably never be explained, he chose to turn me and my other roommate in to the police.

For the charge of conspiracy to sell marijuana, now I got 18 months of probation, which would be cut in half for good behavior. The terms of my probation were that I had to report once a month to the probation officer, pay a fee of $30, hold down a job, be subject to "random" monthly drug tests and random visits, any time of the day or night. (The drug tests happened at my monthly meeting with the probation officer—the only thing random about it was whether he decided to actually do the test.) I couldn't leave the county I lived in without written permission, and I had to go about my life knowing that if I got so much as a speeding ticket, it could bring up all the original charges and sentencing that I could have faced before we made the deal with the State Attorney's Office. So I really had to be careful and couldn't take a chance doing things you'd normally do, always looking back over your shoulder.

You had to know that if you went over to a friends house to watch a football game and somebody busted out a doobie, that you'd have to think twice about accepting it because there was a good chance it could show up on a drug test or something. And supposing you've been out having a drink with the guys and somebody does bust out that doobie, your judgment might not necessarily be 100%. It was really hard because of my social life, you know, college kids, the night life, drinking, partying . . . the whole attitude.

Also, when you live a couple miles from the county line, like I did, it's something to worry about. Every time you cross that line, you think, "Geez, I'm violating my probation 'cuz I don't have written permission." Getting pulled over for a taillight out could be bad news if you're in the wrong county. Furthermore, I was living and working in two different counties, and I didn't want to tell my probation officer where I'd moved to because my roommates still smoked. I didn't want the man to come down on them, you know, surprise visits and all. So I lied and said I was living at my mom's. Once I was even there when he showed up.

For some people it's a way of life, being on probation all the time, but I didn't feel I was one of those people, and I didn't want to be one of those people. For the people that get arrested 50 times a year, of course it's no big deal, but for me it was pretty serious. The night I spent in jail after my arrest, I was talking with one of the guys in the cell and we were discussing our situations. When the topic of probation came up, he said that he'd learned for him it was better to reduce the amount of probation by taking jail time. He said if he was faced with years of probation, he would actually ask the judge for jail time

*Not the subject's real name.   continued

Personal Account of a Former Probationer *(Continued)*

in lieu of the extra probation because he felt that chances are, if it was a lot of probation—if it was more than a year or so—that he'd probably end up screwing up and getting more jail time in the long run. If he violated his probation, whatever new trouble he got into would be multiplied by the old trouble, and he'd get in trouble three times as much for two times the mistakes. See, it's better to get into trouble when you're not on probation. So doing your time and then being set free means the next time you screw up, you only get nailed for what you just did. For me it wouldn't work because I knew I could behave. And I wasn't going to be in that kind of trouble again. I knew I could stay out of that kind of trouble.

My probation officer showed up at work a few times. It didn't really bug me that much because my bosses knew about it and didn't hold it against me. I really wasn't worried about what people would think, because I'm not that type of person. But the way it made me feel was just, like, an animal-in-a-cage kind of thing, I guess, when he showed up. The man's there to check up on you. It made you feel more like a scum bag. Like you weren't going to behave enough with the monthly requirements you were responsible for.

Everybody took it pretty well. Almost everyone, family and friends, they all knew I wasn't out there trying to make money selling this stuff and I was a decent person overall. It was just a nasty little situation that snuck up on me.

The probation seemed kinda' useless in some ways. The first probation officer I had was the only one who seemed like he gave a shit about his job. He seemed like he would do his job to the letter—he actually came out on a random visit on 4 or 5 occasions. None of the other probation officers I had to deal with did that. I expected the probation to be a little tougher. If they wanted to make it more effective, they should have been more random with the drug testing and done what the first guy did. Make the random visits. No one else appeared to care about that. And I'm guessing the guy probably had hundreds of people on probation he had to keep track of. That was the feeling that I got.

I think being suspended from school and the conditions the school placed on me were tougher than what the state gave me. I had to do 100 hours of community service and go to drug counseling every other week for a year to satisfy the school, plus pay the drug counselor fee of $45 each time I met with the guy. And all we really did was sit around and talk sports. It was a waste of time and money. I was no drug addict.

Probation itself was just punishment, nothing "correctional." The whole incident and everything else that happened is what taught me something. All the times that I went to the probation office, I never met anybody that was like me. The place was filled with negative people who seemingly had no goals or desire to do anything with their lives. It was a very depressing place. I really felt out of place.

Being on probation taught me a lot of things about people and taught me a little bit about myself. Who you can trust and who you can't trust. So even though it was a pain in the ass, it could've been a lot worse. It's just no fun knowing that you don't have any room to screw up.

homes, surrounded by their families and friends, how does this impact their lives? Do they, too, adopt a code involving loyalty to other probationers or a distrust of probation officers? Are such sentences considered punitive by offenders? Or are these sentences a mere inconvenience?

While variation is bound to exist among offenders and corrections practitioners regarding which type of correctional alternative is most appropriate for which offense(s) and whether such alternatives are punitive or "correctional," another debate surrounds offenders—whether men and women who commit crime should be treated equally by the criminal justice system, particularly corrections.

A Debate: Should Male and Female Offenders Receive Equal Treatment?

A first glance at facilities for men and women reveals the two sexes are not treated equally. Women's jails and prisons are smaller, have fewer controls and more freedom and privileges. Women generally are not violent and not escape prone, so less security is typically used for their facilities.

Regarding programming and services for female inmates, a debate has surfaced over whether the equal treatment of male and female inmates is beneficial or detrimental to the female inmates. The prevailing attitude among many, if not most, Americans is that men and women, whatever the situation or environment, should be treated equally. That philosophy extends to today's correctional dogma. However, several studies have shown that this equal treatment has had a negative impact on the female offender. A study by Jackson and Stearns (1995, p. 203) found "that equal treatment in the new generation jail led to negative outcomes for women." These authors conclude (p. 218):

> . . . the new generation jail is a success for men on many dimensions. Its ability to meet the needs of the women inmates in this study is more limited. The net result of the transfer of women and men into the new generation jail is that the women and men became more similar in their outcomes; they became this way as the result of a decline in the conditions of confinement for women and an improvement in those for men. In this manner, a policy of equal treatment for female and male inmates results in mostly negative effects on women.

> Some research indicates that a policy of equal treatment for male and female inmates tends to have negative effects for the women and positive effects for the men.

This same study also cites findings by Chesney-Lind and Pollock (1995), who "noted in the prison context, sentencing policy and detention programs that are applied to everyone equally—one of the guiding principles of contemporary policy—may have negative effects on women because the male experience is the measuring rod for fair treatment" (Jackson and Stearns, p. 205).

Some researchers have speculated how the results might change if the roles were reversed—if our jails and prisons were primarily geared toward handling female offenders and the same programs and techniques were then applied to the rising number of male inmates, how would the men fare?

Gray et al. looked at inmate needs and programming in jails that hold only women. They note (p. 186): "Most women in jail serve time in facilities that also house men. However, there are 18 jails nationally that house women only . . ." Some may assume that women-only facilities are better able to meet the needs of their inmates, such as providing education and training, maintaining bonds with children, overcoming drug and alcohol addictions and providing treatment and counseling for physical, sexual and emotional abuse. However, Gray et al. (p. 186) conclude: "[W]hen it comes to meeting most of these needs, the programming in women's facilities fails miserably." They state (p. 198): "Of the programming we examined here, exclusively women's jails best meet the needs of inmates in terms of alcohol and drug abuse treatment." Yet, "except for the availability of treatment programs that are often provided by community groups, such as Alcoholics Anonymous and Narcotics Anonymous, the programming in women's jails is woefully inadequate" (p. 199).

McCarthy and McCarthy (p. 326) state:

> A national survey of the use of intermediate sanctions for female offenders found that of the 110 programs studied, half were available to both males and females.
>
> Many of the programs were poorly designed for women. While the emphasis of most was on surveillance, the female offenders were in greater need of services—programs to promote economic self-sufficiency, including safe and reliable child care, skills training, and education. The vast majority of women had long-standing drug and alcohol problems, for which they were receiving little assistance.
>
> House arrest was considered a potential threat to women in situations of domestic violence, posing the potential to exacerbate drug and alcohol problems. Boot camps were described as especially inappropriate for women who have experienced the negative side of abusive control.

Robinson (1992, p. 258) adds: "The potentially positive aspects of the most common intermediate sanctions, those of keeping offenders in the community at less cost to the state and less disruption to the offender's life, may be contraindicated for women whose lives in the community are fraught with poverty, abuse, and mental illness."

While there appears to be some significant drawbacks for female offenders in "equal treatment" programs, Brown (1994, p. 2) points out that equal treatment does not necessarily mean *identical* treatment. Brown evaluated a shock incarceration program in South Carolina and reports that the program, which was not to discriminate based on the gender of the offender, *did* show gender biases early on. Separate men's and women's units were available, yet few judges would sentence female offenders to the program. Consequently, while the men's unit had a waiting list, the women's unit operated well below capacity, raising concerns about cost-effectiveness and the potential overcrowding of women's facilities by not using this available alternative. When faced with the option of closing the women's unit, corrections officials chose to keep it open. One reason for this decision was the issue of equal opportunity of treatment: "If men were given an opportunity to reduce their period of incarceration, then women certainly would be given parity in treatment" (p. 1). Brown (pp. 1–2) also states:

> Historically, women in prison have not been given equal treatment because they represented only a small segment of the inmate population. The number of women in prison is now increasing and the courts have ruled that the cost of providing programs, budget restrictions, and small numbers do not justify not providing programs comparable to those for men. Parity, however, does not require programs to be identical. In developing comparable programs for women in prison, there should be concern for the needs of the women and flexibility to provide better ways of meeting those needs.

According to Brown, the South Carolina program takes into consideration issues that concern female inmates more often than males, such as physical and psychological issues, including the offender's history of abuse, and family issues involving the care of children and balancing family with work.

The development of women's programs still appears to lag somewhat behind those for men, although many have realized that offering equal opportunities for treatment and programming for female inmates does not simply mean copying the program already in use for men. Effective programs for women may build from existing male programs but must also take into consideration the unique needs of female offenders.

Summary

The majority of correctional clients are men, with men outnumbering women in prison by nearly 19 to 1; in jail, 9 to 1; on parole, 9 to 1; and on probation, 4 to 1. Inmate gangs and racial conflicts are more prevalent in men's facilities than in women's facilities. Prison gangs are more sophisticated and covert than street gangs and are comprised of disruptive inmates seeking to control their environment through intimidation and threats. The first recognized prison gang was the Gypsy Jokers in 1950. Today, nearly every correctional jurisdiction in the United States reports the presence of prison gangs, with approximately 3 percent of the national inmate population belonging to gangs. Strategies to manage prison gangs include identifying gang members, keeping rival gang members separated, isolating confirmed gang members from the general prisoner population, training staff in how to recognize and separate gang members and maintaining internal and external communications to identify and track gang member activity.

Disrupting the gang's internal organization and providing programs to replace gang activities are other strategies.

Male inmates tend to adhere to the inmate code, which consists of behavioral norms for offenders such as "mind your own business," "don't snitch on another inmate," "do your own time," "don't exploit fellow inmates," "stand up for yourself" and "don't trust the staff."

Although their relative proportion is smaller, the female prisoner population is currently growing at about twice the rate of the male prisoner population. Women are more likely than men to be arrested and imprisoned for property and drug offenses and less likely than men to be arrested and imprisoned for violent offenses. Nearly 80 percent of women prisoners have children, which may contribute to the shorter sentences received by female offenders. Generally, the inmate code receives less endorsement from female inmates than from male inmates, with such tenets as "do your own time" and "avoid interacting with the staff" being hampered by the kinship system of female inmates and their desire to engage in social interactions.

Although many believe men and women should be treated equally, some research indicates that a policy of equal treatment for male and female inmates tends to have negative effects for the women and positive effects for the men.

Discussion Questions

1. Do you think the disproportionally high number of Blacks under correctional supervision is due to discrimination or real differences in conduct?

2. Do you think the higher number of males compared to females under correctional supervision is due to discrimination or real differences in conduct?

3. Which, if any, gangs exist in your local jails and prisons? What strategies have correctional administrators and staff devised to handle gangs in your area?

4. Do you agree with the Court's decision in *Lamar v. Coffield? Guajardo v. Estelle?*

5. Is it unreasonable to ever expect racial conflict to not be a problem among inmates? How might such tension be lessened?

6. If you were an inmate, would you support all six basic tenets of the inmate code? If so, why? If not, which would you not support and why?

7. Should women receive lighter sentences because they are more likely to be the sole caretaker of dependent children?

8. Should children be allowed to live with their incarcerated mothers? Incarcerated fathers?

9. Why are women more likely than men to form kinships with other inmates? Could this ever be possible among male inmates? Why or why not?

10. Do you support a policy of equal treatment for male and female inmates? Why or why not?

References

Abbott, Jack Henry. *In the Belly of the Beast.* Random House, 1981.

American Correctional Association. *The Female Offender: What Does the Future Hold?* Washington, DC: St. Mary, 1990.

"Anti-Gang Policies and Procedures Gain Prominence." *Corrections Alert,* Vol.3, No.18, December 16, 1996, pp. 1–2.

Brown, Sammie D. "South Carolina's Shock Incarceration for Women." *Corrections Compendium,* Vol.XIX, No.2, February 1994, pp. 1–3, 5.

Buentello, Salvadore. "Combating Gangs in Texas." *Corrections Today,* July 1992, pp. 58–60.

Camp, George M. and Camp, Camille Graham. *The Corrections Yearbook, 1997.* South Salem, NY: The Criminal Justice Institute, 1997.

Carp, Scarlett V. and Schade, Linda S. "Tailoring Facility Programming to Suit Female Offenders' Needs." *Corrections Today,* August 1992, pp. 152–159.

Chesney-Lind, M. and Pollock, J. "Women's Prisons: Equality with a Vengeance." In *Women, Law and Social Control,* edited by A. Merlo and J. Pollock. Boston: Allyn and Unwin, 1995, pp. 155–175.

Clark, Judith. "The Impact of the Prison Environment on Mothers." *The Prison Journal,* Vol. 75, No. 3, September 1995, pp. 306–329.

Clarke, Harold W. "Gang Problems: From the Streets to Our Prisons." *Corrections Today,* July 1992, pp. 8, 12.

Compendium of Federal Justice Statistics, 1994. Washington, DC: U.S. Department of Justice, Bureau of Justice Statistics, 1997 (NCJ-163063).

Correctional Populations in the United States, 1995. Bureau of Justice Statistics, May 1997 (NCJ-163916).

Dallao, Mary. "Coping with Incarceration—From the Other Side of the Bars." *Corrections Today,* October 1997, pp. 96–98.

Drowns, Robert W. and Hess, Kären M. *Juvenile Justice,* 2nd ed. St. Paul, MN: West Publishing Company, 1995. Reprinted by permission of the publisher.

"FBOP Focus on Female Offenders Raises Level of Concern." *Corrections Alert,* Vol. 3, No. 17, December 3, 1996, pp. 5–6.

Fletcher, Sharri. "Monitoring Gang Activity in Prison: Nebraska's Network Tracking Program." *Corrections Compendium,* Vol. XIX, No. 4, April 1994, pp. 1–4.

Fong, Robert S.; Vogel, Ronald E.; and Buentello, Salvador. "Prison Gang Dynamics: A Look Inside the Texas Department of Corrections." In *Corrections: Dilemmas and Directions,* edited by Peter J. Benekos and Alida V. Merlo. Cincinnati, OH: Anderson Publishing Co., 1992, pp. 57–77.

Gray, Tara; Mays, G. Larry; and Stohr, Mary K. "Inmate Needs and Programming in Exclusively Women's Jails." *The Prison Journal,* Vol. 75, No. 2, June 1995, pp. 186–202.

Hunt, Portia. "An Expression of African-American Culture in Correctional Settings." In *Understanding Cultural Diversity,* American Correctional Association. Fredericksburg, VA: BookCrafters, 1993.

Jackson, Patrick G. and Stearns, Cindy A. "Gender Issues in the New Generation Jail." *The Prison Journal,* Vol. 75, No. 2, June 1995, pp. 203–221.

Johnson, Robert. *Hard Time: Understanding and Reforming the Prison,* 2nd ed. Belmont, CA: Wadsworth Publishing Company, 1996.

Lord, Elaine. "A Prison Superintendent's Perspective on Women in Prison." *The Prison Journal,* Vol. 75, No. 2, June 1995, pp. 257–269.

McCarthy, Belinda Rodgers and McCarthy, Bernard J., Jr. *Community-Based Corrections*, 3rd ed. Belmont, CA: Wadsworth Publishing Company, 1997. Reprinted by permission of the publisher.

Owen, Barbara and Bloom, Barbara. "Profiling Women Prisoners: Findings from National Surveys and a California Sample." *The Prison Journal*, Vol. 75, No. 2, June 1995, pp. 165–185.

Rigert, Joe. "Justice Blind to Children." (Minneapolis/St. Paul) *Star Tribune*, December 15, 1997a, pp. A1, A10–A13.

Rigert, Joe. "Some Win Fight with Depression, Others Lose." (Minneapolis/St. Paul) *Star Tribune*, December 15, 1997b, p. A12.

Riley, William. "Taking a Two-Pronged Approach to Managing Washington's Gangs." *Corrections Today*, July 1992, pp. 68–71.

Robinson, Robin A. "Intermediate Sanctions and the Female Offender." In *Smart Sentencing*, edited by James M. Byrne, Arthur J. Lurigio and Joan Petersilia. Newbury Park, CA: Sage Publications, 1992, pp. 245–260.

Ryan, T.A. and McCabe, Kimberly A. "A Comparative Analysis of Adult Female Offenders." *Corrections Today*, July 1997, pp. 28–30.

Sharp, Deborah. "Boot Camps—Punishment and Treatment." Insert in *Corrections Today*, June 1995.

Snell, Tracy L. and Morton, Danielle C. *Women in Prison: Survey of State Prison Inmates, 1991*. Special Report, U.S. Department of Justice, Bureau of Justice Statistics, March 1994 (NCJ-145321).

Sykes, Gresham M. and Messinger, Sheldon L. "The Inmate Social System." In *Theoretical Studies in the Social Organization of the Prison*, edited by Richard A. Cloward et al. New York: Social Science Research Council, 1960, pp. 6–8.

Taylor, Jon Marc. "Violence in Prison: A Personal Perspective." *Corrections Compendium*, Vol.XXI, No. 6, June 1996, pp. 1–3.

Terry, Charles M. "The Function of Humor for Prison Inmates." *Journal of Contemporary Criminal Justice*, Vol. 13, No. 1, February 1997, pp. 23–40.

Toller, William and Tsagaris, Basil. "A Practical Approach Combining Security and Human Services." *Corrections Today*, October 1996, pp. 110–111, 115.

Trout, Craig H. "Taking a New Look at an Old Problem." *Corrections Today*, July 1992, pp. 62–66.

Welling, A. Dale. "Experts Unite to Combat Street and Prison Gang Activities." *Corrections Today*, August 1994, pp. 148–149.

Cases

Guajardo v. Estelle (1978).

Lamar v. Coffield (1977).

9

Correctional Clients: Juvenile Offenders

Do You Know

➤ How a status offender differs from a juvenile delinquent?

➤ What determines if and how a juvenile will enter corrections?

➤ What the most common disposition for juveniles adjudicated delinquent is?

➤ What the most common offenses of juveniles transferred to adult criminal court are?

➤ Which group is responsible for most of the violent offenses committed by juveniles and how early this criminal activity typically begins?

➤ What category of offense comprises the majority of delinquency cases? What category has shown the greatest percent increase in recent years?

➤ At what age the highest delinquency case rate occurs?

➤ Whether the majority of delinquency offenders are male or female?

➤ Whether White youth, Black youth or youth of other races have the highest delinquency case rate?

➤ What the primary goal of juvenile probation is?

➤ What community-based corrections for juveniles consist of?

➤ Whether most correctional facilities holding juvenile offenders are designated strictly for youths?

➤ If the inmate culture in juvenile facilities differs much from that in adult facilities?

➤ What some important programming and treatment needs of today's juvenile offenders are?

There was nothing to do.—Terrance Wade, age 15,
when asked why he and his friends allegedly raped, stomped,
stabbed and ultimately murdered a Boston woman

Can You Define

adjudication

aftercare

chronic juvenile
  offender

delinquent

delinquent act

detention centers

disposition

disproportionate
  minority
  confinement

foster group home

foster home

group home

juvenile

legal age

petition

serious juvenile
  offender

shelter

status offender

training school

upper age of original
  jurisdiction

violent juvenile
  offender

youth population at risk

Introduction

More than a century ago, Abraham Lincoln said: "A child is a person who is going to carry on what you have started. He is going to sit where you are sitting, and when you are gone, attend to those things you think are important. You may adopt all the policies you please, but how they are carried out depends on him. He will assume control of your cities, states and nations. He is going to move in and take over your churches, schools, universities and corporations. The fate of humanity is in his hands." Consider this statement, then think about the chapter opening quote. Something has gone terribly wrong with some of our nation's youth, and the problem lands directly at the door of corrections. Indeed, as Wilson (1994, p. 224) states: "[I]t is in the juvenile justice system that we will succeed or fail in reducing corrections populations. . . . If we do not address juvenile corrections fully, these children will end up as tomorrow's clients in the adult system."

Juvenile crime is a hot topic today, as the media continuously hands us stories of youthful car thieves, gun-toting teens and even children raping and murdering other children. As with adult offenders, juvenile corrections serves several important functions. These duties include protecting the public by removing juvenile offenders from the community, holding juvenile offenders accountable for their conduct and providing juvenile offenders with the educational, vocational, personal and social skills necessary to succeed in the community.

This chapter looks at juveniles in the correctional system beginning with some key definitions and how juveniles enter corrections, including waiver to adult criminal court. An overview of these youthful offenders, general characteristics of juvenile offenders, delinquency offenses and case rates are presented next, followed by age, gender and race differences. Next, correctional alternatives for juveniles are discussed. The chapter concludes with a discussion of programming and treatment needs of juvenile offenders.

Definitions

The age at which a youth becomes an adult, in the eyes of the law, is considered the **legal age.** An individual below the legal age is called a **juvenile.** Each state determines the legal age of its residents, with some as young as 16 and others as old as 19. Most states have set their legal age at 18. Offenders below the legal age are typically handled by the juvenile court, whereas those over the legal age are handled by the criminal (adult) court. However, the offenses of some juveniles are so severe as to warrant transfer to adult criminal court.

Juveniles who come in contact with the criminal justice system are classified as one of two types: status offenders and juvenile delinquents. **A status
offender** is a juvenile whose action would not be considered an offense had it
been committed by an adult. A status offense is an offense solely because of
the offender's age. Examples of status offenses include curfew violations, running away from home, drinking alcohol, smoking, habitual truancy and un-
governable behavior. Today, status offenders are usually not placed into
correctional facilities and are not considered *criminals*. However, the other
type of juvenile, the delinquent, is involved in criminal activity. A juvenile
delinquent is an individual below the legal age whose action would be a
crime if it were committed by an adult (for example, robbery, assault, murder). When a juvenile commits an act for which an adult could be prosecuted
in criminal court, it is called a **delinquent act,** not a crime.

A status offender is a juvenile who is *not* considered a criminal and whose action
would *not* be considered an offense had it been committed by an adult. In contrast,
a juvenile delinquent is an individual below the legal age who is involved in criminal
activity and whose action *would* be a crime if it were committed by an adult.

Underage drinking is a common
status offense.

Various levels of delinquency have been defined by the National Coalition of State Juvenile Justice Advisory Groups (1993, pp. 13–14):

➤ • **Serious juvenile offender**—A juvenile who has been convicted of a Part I offense as defined by the FBI *Uniform Crime Reports*, excluding auto theft or distribution of a controlled dangerous substance, and who was 14, 15, 16, or 17 years old at the time of the commission of the offense.

➤ • **Chronic juvenile offender**—A youth who has a record of five or more separate charges of delinquency, regardless of the gravity of the offenses.

➤ • **Violent juvenile offender**—A youth who has been convicted of a violent Part I offense, one against a person rather than property and who has a prior adjudication of such an offense, or a youth who has been convicted of murder.

Consider next how the courts process cases involving juveniles and how judicial decisions place juveniles into corrections.

How Do Juveniles Enter Corrections?

Clearly, differences exist between the handling of juveniles and adults by the criminal justice system. In fact the terminology used for juvenile offenders differs from that used for adult offenders. Juveniles who break the law are not "criminals," but rather "delinquents." They do not commit "crimes"; they commit "delinquent acts." And juveniles are not "arrested"; they are "taken into custody." Similarly, the steps taken to process a delinquency case, which may or may not result in a juvenile entering corrections, differ from those taken for adult criminal cases.

Butts (1996, p. 6) states: "Except in cases where a criminal-court transfer is granted, an adjudicatory hearing is generally held in all formally petitioned delinquency cases." A **petition** is a document alleging that a juvenile is a delinquent, status offender or dependent and asking the court to assume jurisdiction or requesting that an alleged delinquent be transferred to criminal court for prosecution as an adult. Butts continues: "During this [adjudicatory] hearing, the juvenile court determines whether the youth will be adjudicated a delinquent. The court then makes a dispositional decision that could include fines, restitution, probation, commitment to a residential facility, referral to another treatment program, or community service." Therefore, **adjudication,** similar to an adult (criminal) conviction of guilt, is a juvenile court judgment following a hearing, affirming that the juvenile is a delinquent, a status offender or a dependent, or that the allegations in the petition are not sustained.

➤ A **disposition** is like a sentencing decision made by the juvenile court, committing a juvenile to a confinement facility, placing the juvenile on probation or referring the juvenile to a particular course of treatment or care.

The disposition determines if and how a juvenile will enter corrections.

Figure 9–1 shows the number of delinquency cases processed by juvenile courts in 1993 and the percentage receiving various judicial dispositions. According to Butts (p. 6):

In 1993, 58% of all formally processed delinquency cases resulted in adjudication. In 28% of these cases, the youth was placed out of the home in a residential facility. More than half (56%) of all formally adjudicated delinquency

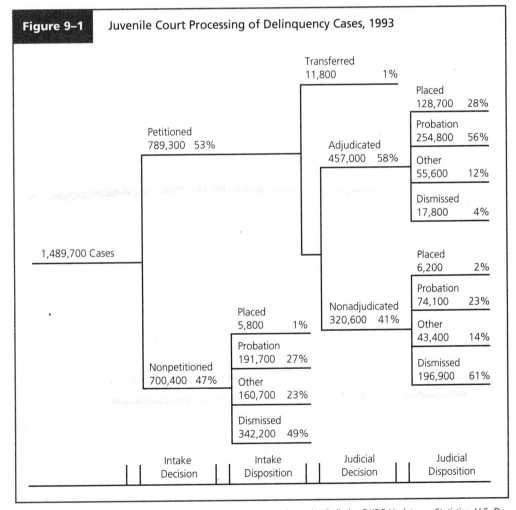

Figure 9–1 Juvenile Court Processing of Delinquency Cases, 1993

Source: Jeffrey A. Butts. *Offenders in Juvenile Court, 1993.* Juvenile Justice Bulletin: OJJDP Update on Statistics. U.S. Department of Justice, July 1996, p. 6 (NCJ-160945).

cases resulted in the juvenile being placed on probation. In 12% of formally adjudicated delinquency cases, the court ordered a juvenile to pay restitution or a fine, participate in some form of community service, or enter a treatment or counseling program—dispositions with minimal continuing supervision by probation staff.

From Figure 9–1 it is seen that, of all the delinquency cases brought before juvenile courts in 1993 which were *not* dismissed, most (520,600 or 35 percent) resulted in probation for the juvenile. About 17 percent of all cases resulted in a fine, restitution, community service or treatment/counseling program, and in approximately 9 percent of cases were juveniles actually committed to correctional facilities. The nature of the offense greatly affects the judicial disposition, as Butts et al. (1996) state: "Almost a third of those charged with violent offenses were committed." The various correctional alternatives available for youth are discussed in detail later in the chapter.

> Probation is the most common disposition for juveniles adjudicated delinquent.

Many argue that criminally minded youth are taking advantage of the less-punitive, more-rehabilitative philosophy of juvenile justice, hoping their age will spare them the harsh sentences that face adults convicted of similar crimes. The line separating juveniles from adults, however, is becoming less distinct as more and more violent youth are being tried in court as adults.

Waiver to Adult Criminal Court

With the number of violent juvenile offenses rising, many are seeking changes in the way juveniles are handled by the courts and the kinds of correctional sanctions they receive. Krisberg (1995, p. 122) states: "This past year, the states introduced more than 700 bills to move more troubled youngsters from specialized juvenile facilities to adult prisons. To some, juvenile corrections has come to symbolize soft-headed liberalism." Orenstein and Levinson (1996, p. 148) note: "It has become evident during the last several years that the political climate regarding the serious juvenile offender has moved toward retribution and away from an earlier, traditional nurturing attitude. Right or wrong, legitimate or not, this appears to be the reality at present and for the foreseeable future." Sickmund et al. (1997) state that from 1992 to 1995, 41 states enacted laws making it easier for juveniles to be tried as adults. Today, every state allows the transfer of juveniles to criminal court.

According to Butts (pp. 1–2): "The number of juvenile court cases transferred to criminal court grew 10% between 1992 and 1993. In contrast to previous years when property offenses were predominant among transferred cases, the largest group of transferred cases in 1993 involved person offenses. . . ."

This increased number of case transfers to criminal court is partly the result of an increase in the total number of juvenile cases being brought before the courts (23 percent more cases in 1993 than 1989) (Butts, p. 2). The *rate* of transfer to adult court has also increased. As the Department of Justice reports (*Privacy and Juvenile*, 1997, p. 9), the use of judicial waiver has increased substantially over the last few years. The most current available data (*Sourcebook*, 1997, p. 404) indicates 3.3 percent of all juveniles taken into police custody in 1995 were referred to criminal court, up from the 1.3 percent transferred to adult court in 1972, but down from 4.7 percent in 1994 and 5.5 percent in 1986.

Furthermore, the nature of the offenses being transferred changed from 1989 to 1993. Butts (p. 5) notes: "Between 1989 and 1993, the number of transferred person offense cases increased far more (115%) than did transfers of any other type of case (for example, 75% among public order cases and 12% among property offense cases)." According to Sickmund et al., the shift in types of transfers is partially due to new laws targeting violent juvenile offenders for automatic or presumptive waiver to criminal court. During 1995, of the estimated 7,888 juveniles held in local jails, more than three-quarters had been tried or were awaiting trial as adults (Gilliard and Beck, 1996, p. 1). Figure 9–2 shows how the offense profile of delinquency cases transferred to criminal court changed considerably between 1989 and 1993.

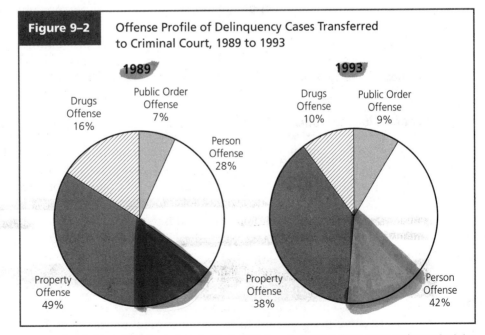

Figure 9–2 Offense Profile of Delinquency Cases Transferred to Criminal Court, 1989 to 1993

1989

Drugs Offense 16%

Public Order Offense 7%

Person Offense 28%

Property Offense 49%

1993

Drugs Offense 10%

Public Order Offense 9%

Person Offense 42%

Property Offense 38%

Source: Jeffrey A. Butts. *Offenders in Juvenile Court, 1993*. Juvenile Justice Bulletin: OJJDP Update on Statistics. U.S. Department of Justice, July 1996, p. 8 (NCJ-160945).
Note: Detail may not add to 100% because of rounding.

> Most juveniles who are transferred to criminal court have committed crimes against persons.

Sometimes juveniles are transferred to criminal court not by judicial waiver but because laws have been passed by a jurisdiction mandating such transfers. Butts et al. (1996) explain: "While 12,300 juveniles were judicially waived to adult status during 1994, others were statutorily excluded from juvenile court jurisdiction based on their age and offense or concurrent jurisdiction provisions. In 13 states the upper age of juvenile court jurisdiction is 15 or 16 years. Many states also exclude certain serious offenses—such as murder and other violent offenses—from juvenile court jurisdiction."

Who are these youth who find themselves face to face with corrections?

Juvenile Offenders—An Overview

Similar to adult offenders, the population of today's juvenile offenders is on the rise. A *Criminal Justice Newsletter* article ("Spending Not Keeping," 1996, p. 5) states: "Juvenile case filings reached 1.9 million in 1994, a 27-percent increase over 1990." All indications are that juvenile court caseloads will continue to grow. Indeed, a conservative count of arrests of persons under 18 in 1995 totaled 2,085,565, with some states not reporting (*Sourcebook*, pp. 372–375). As Fox (1996, p. 3) notes: "[T]he number of teenage offenders has grown in recent years, even as the population of teenagers has contracted. But now the teen population is on the upswing" (Figure 9–3).

General Characteristics of Juvenile Offenders

The youths who come in contact with the correctional system are very diverse. Drowns and Hess (1995, p. 412) note: "An investigation of the characteristics of inmates of public long-term juvenile institutions shows a pattern not unlike that of America's jails and prisons. The disadvantaged and the poor make up a large percentage of the [inmate] population." These authors also state (p. 217): "No one personality is associated with delinquency. However, some characteristics are common among delinquents. Those who become delinquent are more likely to be socially assertive, defiant, ambivalent about authority, resentful, hostile, suspicious, destructive, impulsive and lacking in self-control." Certainly, such youths pose quite a challenge for the corrections professionals to whom they are assigned.

Researchers in New York have demonstrated a strong link between mistreatment of youth and a range of subsequent problems when such youths reach adolescence ("Rochester Study," 1997, p. 5). These problems include increased risk of performing poorly in school, using drugs, committing acts of

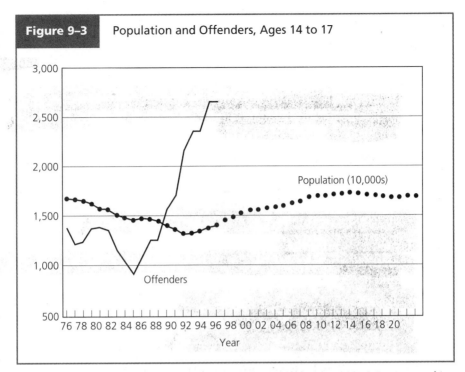

Figure 9–3   Population and Offenders, Ages 14 to 17

Source: Table from James Alan Fox. *Trends in Juvenile Violence*. Washington, DC: U.S. Department of Justice, Bureau of Justice Statistics, March 1996, p. 13. Data from FBI, Supplementary Homicide Reports, and Census Bureau, Current Population Survey and Population Projections of U.S.

serious and violent delinquency, displaying symptoms of mental illness and, for girls, becoming pregnant.

The Office of Juvenile Justice and Delinquency Prevention (OJJDP) (1993, p. 29) reports most chronic violent juvenile offenders possess the following characteristics:

- They are less attached to and monitored by their *family*.
- They have less commitment to *school* and attachment to teachers.
- More of their *peers* are likely to be delinquent, and they themselves are more likely to be gang members.
- They are more likely to reside in poor *neighborhoods* with high crime rates.

Furthermore, the OJJDP reports that while these chronic juvenile offenders make up a small proportion of the total number of delinquents (15 percent in one sample), they may be responsible for as much as 75 percent of the violent offenses committed by juveniles, and that "most chronic juvenile offenders start their criminal careers prior to age 12" (p. 29).

Chronic juvenile offenders, although a relatively small proportion of the delinquent population, are responsible for most of the violent offenses committed by juveniles, many beginning their criminal activity before reaching their teens.

A study group supported by the OJJDP drew the following conclusions about serious and violent juvenile (SVJ) offenders (Foote, 1997):

- SVJ offenders are a distinct group of offenders who tend to start early and continue late in their offending.
- From childhood to adolescence, SVJ offenders tend to develop behavior problems, including aggression, dishonesty, property offenses, and conflict with authority figures.

The National Coalition of State Juvenile Justice Advisory Groups (p. 14) lists the following characteristics as typical for serious or chronic juvenile offenders:

- A delinquency adjudication prior to the age of thirteen.
- Low family income.
- Between the ages of eight and ten being rated troublesome by teachers and peers.
- Poor school performance by age ten.
- Psychomotor clumsiness.
- Having a sibling convicted of a crime.

A study of felons between the ages of 12 and 18 in Ohio's juvenile prison system found that most youth who are chronic offenders are products of substandard social and economic environments (Thomas, 1996, p. A1). This study found

- More than 80 percent of juvenile felons in Ohio come from households with annual incomes below $10,000.
- More than 60 percent live with single mothers.
- 5 percent are homeless.
- Nearly 25 percent have children of their own.
- 75 percent of the girls and 50 percent of the boys have been sexually assaulted.
- 90 percent have substance abuse problems with alcohol, marijuana, crack or heroin.
- Approximately 30 percent have mental disorders.

According to one Ohio prison official: "These kids are the thowaways of society" (Thomas, p. A1).

Characteristics of Female Delinquents. As with adults, discussions of juveniles in the justice system have traditionally focused on the male offender. As Chesney-Lind and Shelden (1998, p. 2) state, "the academic study of delinquent behavior has, for all intents and purposes, been the study of male delinquency."

A female juvenile offender sits alone in her cell.

These authors have examined more closely the unique characteristics of girls in corrections and note some similarities (pp. 170–171):

- Most girls in correctional facilities are between the ages of 16 and 17.
- More than 18 percent were mothers at the time of their incarceration.
- Over 61 percent have experienced physical abuse.
- 54 percent had undergone sexual abuse.
- 80 percent had run away from home.
- Over half said they had attempted suicide.

The "offenses"[1] committed by these girls which place them into the justice system and, in many cases, the correctional system, are discussed shortly.

Delinquency Offenses and Case Rates

The types of crimes committed by juveniles are as diverse as those committed by adults. Table 9–1 shows the number of delinquency cases by offense from 1989 to 1993, with offenses ranging from criminal homicide to disorderly conduct.

---

[1]According to Chesney-Lind and Shelden (p. 166), parents may voluntarily commit their children to public and private juvenile facilities without official adjudication by the juvenile court. No formal "offense" need be committed or acknowledged by the juvenile justice system. Data from the Office of Juvenile Justice and Delinquency Prevention (*Juveniles Taken Into Custody*, 1992, p. 39) show that such "voluntary commitments" of female juveniles significantly outnumber those of male juveniles.

| Table 9–1 | Delinquency Cases by Offense, 1989 to 1993 |

Offense	Number of Cases		Percent Change	
	1989	1993	1989–93	1992–93
Total Delinquency	**1,211,900**	**1,489,700**	**23%**	**2%**
Person	**209,100**	**318,800**	**52**	**6**
Criminal Homicide	1,900	2,800	45	13
Forcible Rape	4,100	6,100	48	12
Robbery	22,800	35,600	56	5
Aggravated Assault	48,800	77,500	59	1
Simple Assault	110,400	166,400	51	10
Other Violent Sex Offenses	6,700	10,900	64	10
Other Person Offenses	14,300	19,400	35	−10
Property	**705,100**	**808,900**	**15**	**− 3**
Burglary	131,400	149,700	14	− 4
Larceny-Theft	318,500	353,700	11	− 2
Motor Vehicle Theft	67,900	61,100	−10	−14
Arson	6,700	8,200	21	0
Vandalism	82,900	117,100	41	0
Trespassing	49,700	60,500	22	5
Stolen Property Offenses	23,700	27,400	16	− 7
Other Property Offenses	24,200	31,300	29	−12
Drug Law Violations	**78,000**	**89,100**	**14**	**24**
Public Order	**219,700**	**272,800**	**24**	**8**
Obstruction of Justice	82,000	96,000	17	12
Disorderly Conduct	47,800	71,200	49	4
Weapons Offenses	25,200	47,200	87	16
Liquor Law Violations	15,800	13,200	−16	3
Nonviolent Sex Offenses	12,300	10,900	−11	−13
Other Public Order	36,700	34,400	− 6	8
Violent Crime Index*	**77,700**	**122,000**	**57**	**3**
Property Crime Index**	**524,600**	**572,600**	**9**	**− 4**

*Violent Crime Index includes criminal homicide, forcible rape, robbery, and aggravated assault.
**Property Crime Index includes burglary, larceny-theft, motor vehicle theft, and arson.
Note: Detail may not add to totals because of rounding. Percent change calculations are based on unrounded numbers.
Source: Jeffrey A. Butts. Offenders in Juvenile Court, 1993. Juvenile Justice Bulletin: OJJDP Update on Statistics. U.S. Department of Justice, July 1996, p. 2 (NCJ-160945).

From Table 9–1, it is seen that the number of delinquency cases rose for most of the offense categories (all but four) during a five-year span. Furthermore, this data represents a conservative account of delinquency cases. Butts (p. 2) elaborates: "Each case represents a youth processed by a juvenile court on a new referral, regardless of the number of individual offenses contained in that referral. The report categorizes cases involving multiple offenses according to the most serious offense. For example, a case involving both a charge of vandalism and a charge of robbery would be characterized as a robbery case."

According to Butts (p. 2): "A property offense was the most serious charge involved in 54% of these cases. The most serious charge was a person offense in 21% of the cases, a drug offense in 6%, and a public order offense in 18%. Larceny-theft, simple assault, burglary, and vandalism were the most common offenses in juvenile delinquency cases in 1993. Together, these four offenses made up more than half of the delinquency cases handled by juvenile courts during 1993."

But today's juveniles are not just shoplifting and vandalizing; they're killing people, and at a rate significantly higher than a decade ago. According to Fox (pp. 1–2): "[T]here are actually two crime trends going on in America—one for the young and one for the mature, which are moving in opposite directions. Since 1985, the rate of homicide committed by adults, ages 25 and older, has declined 25%. . . . At the same time, however, the homicide rate among 18–24 year-olds has increased 61% . . . [and] the rate of homicide committed by teenagers, ages 14–17, has more than doubled, increasing 172%." These trends are illustrated in Table 9–2 and Figure 9–4.

This rise in juvenile violence is reflected in the violent crime index, which increased 57 percent from 1989 to 1993 (Table 9–1). Butts (p. 2) states: "The largest relative percentage increases [between 1989 and 1993] occurred in cases involving weapons offenses (87%), violent sex offenses (excluding rape, 64%), aggravated assault (59%), and robbery (56%)." Table 9–3 shows the percent change in delinquency case rates from 1989 to 1993. Note the case rate is the number of
➤ cases disposed per 1,000 youth at risk. The **youth population at risk** is defined as the number of children from age 10 through the upper age of original jurisdiction. For example, if a state considers individuals to be adults on their 18th birth-
➤ day, the **upper age of original jurisdiction** is 17. Therefore, the delinquency and status offense youth population at risk in this state is the number of children ages 10 through 17 living within the geographic area served by the court.

> Most delinquency cases are for property offenses, although the greatest percent increase from 1989 to 1993 was in crimes against persons.

Age Differences

Different types of offenses appear to be committed more frequently by juveniles of a certain age. According to Butts (pp. 2–3): "Of all delinquency cases processed by the Nation's juvenile courts in 1993, 61% involved a juvenile under age 16. . . . Compared to caseloads of older juveniles, the caseloads of younger youth involved a smaller proportion of drug law violations (4% compared with 9%) and public order offenses (16% compared with 21%), but somewhat larger proportions of person offenses and property offenses."

Table 9–2	Trends in Homicide Offending Rates by Age (Rates per 100,000 Population)							
Year	Under 14	14–17	18–24	25+	Male	Female	White	Black
1976	.2	8.1	17.7	7.9	13.2	2.5	4.0	35.3
1977	.2	7.2	16.8	7.6	12.7	2.3	4.0	32.5
1978	.2	7.4	17.7	7.7	13.3	2.2	4.2	32.9
1979	.2	8.3	19.3	7.9	14.2	2.2	4.4	34.4
1980	.2	8.5	20.0	7.9	14.5	2.2	4.5	33.9
1981	.1	8.5	18.8	8.1	14.3	2.2	4.5	33.9
1982	.2	7.6	17.3	7.2	12.9	2.0	4.2	30.0
1983	.1	6.9	16.0	6.6	11.9	1.9	4.0	26.8
1984	.1	6.2	15.3	6.3	11.3	1.7	3.9	24.0
1985	.2	7.0	15.7	6.3	11.5	1.7	3.8	25.1
1986	.2	8.4	17.4	6.7	12.4	1.7	4.0	27.7
1987	.2	8.6	17.2	6.1	11.7	1.6	3.8	26.1
1988	.2	10.8	18.9	6.0	12.4	1.6	3.7	28.8
1989	.2	12.4	21.2	5.8	12.8	1.6	3.8	29.7
1990	.1	16.2	24.8	6.0	14.4	1.6	4.2	32.9
1991	.2	17.6	28.2	5.8	14.6	1.6	4.0	34.8
1992	.2	17.4	26.0	5.2	13.4	1.4	3.7	31.4
1993	.2	19.3	26.6	5.0	14.1	1.4	3.8	34.0
1994	.2	19.1	25.3	4.7	13.6	1.3	3.7	32.1

Source: Table from James Alan Fox. *Trends in Juvenile Violence.* Washington, DC: U.S. Department of Justice, Bureau of Justice Statistics, March 1996, p. 4. Data from FBI, Supplementary Homicide Reports, and Census Bureau, Current Population Survey. Includes known offenders only.

Table 9–4 profiles how the various categories of offenses are split among delinquents age 15 and younger and those age 16 and older. At first glance it may seem curious that the younger youth were involved in a greater proportion of offenses against persons and property. This might be explained, however, if one considers that older youth suspected of committing such serious offenses are more likely to be waived to adult court, thus not being counted in the juvenile court statistics.

Data also shows delinquency case rates generally increase with age, peaking at age 16 (Butts, p. 3). This trend is shown in Figure 9–5. According to this information, more than 10 percent of all 16- and 17-year-olds have committed an act that brought them in contact with the juvenile justice system.

The highest delinquency case rate occurs for juveniles age 16.

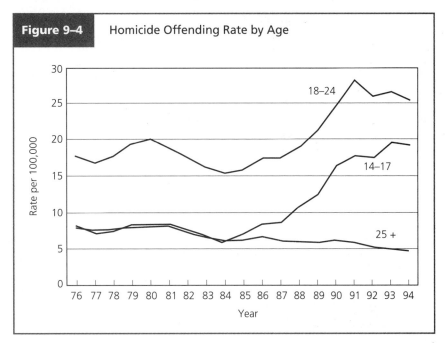

Figure 9–4   Homicide Offending Rate by Age

Source: Table from James Alan Fox. *Trends in Juvenile Violence.* Washington, DC: U.S. Department of Justice, Bureau of Justice Statistics, March 1996, p. 4. Data from FBI, Supplementary Homicide Reports and Census Bureau, Current Population Survey.

Table 9–3	Percent Change in Delinquency Case Rates, 1989 to 1993		

| | Case Rates | | Percent |
Offense	1989	1993	Change
Delinquency	47.8	54.6	14%
Person	8.2	11.7	42
Property	27.8	29.7	7
Drugs	3.1	3.3	6
Public Order	8.7	10.0	15

Case Rate = Cases per 1,000 youth at risk.
Note: Percent change calculations are based on unrounded numbers.
Source: Jeffrey A. Butts. *Offenders in Juvenile Court, 1993.* Juvenile Justice Bulletin: OJJDP Update on Statistics. U.S. Department of Justice, July 1996, p.3 (NCJ-160945).

Gender Differences

As with adult offenders, male juvenile offenders significantly outnumber female juvenile offenders. Also similar to adult offenders, male juveniles were involved more frequently than females in crimes against persons. According to the FBI's *Uniform Crime Reports* (*Crime in America*, 1995, p. 213), males under 18 are arrested three times more often than females under 18.

Table 9–4	Offense Profile of Delinquency Cases by Age at Referral, 1993	
Offense	**Age 15 or Younger**	**Age 16 or Older**
Person	22%	20%
Property	57	50
Drugs	4	9
Public Order	16	21
Total	100%	100%

Note: Detail may not total 100% because of rounding.
Source: Jeffrey A. Butts. *Offenders in Juvenile Court, 1993.* Juvenile Justice Bulletin: OJJDP Update on Statistics. U.S. Department of Justice, July 1996, p. 3 (NCJ-160945).

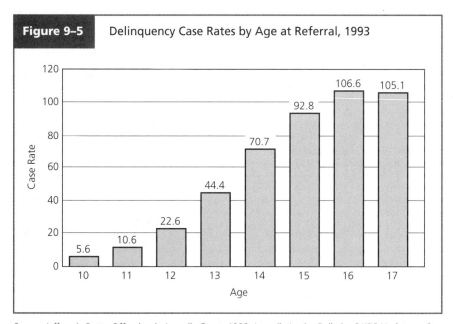

Figure 9–5   Delinquency Case Rates by Age at Referral, 1993

Source: Jeffrey A. Butts. *Offenders in Juvenile Court, 1993.* Juvenile Justice Bulletin: OJJDP Update on Statistics. U.S. Department of Justice, July 1996, p. 3 (NCJ-160945).

Some assert that females are narrowing this gap through increased levels of activity. Butts (p. 3) states: "Between 1989 and 1993, the delinquency case rate for males increased 13%. . . . Among female juveniles, the delinquency case rate grew 21%. . . . The person offense case rate for females was 56% higher in 1993 than in 1989, while the person offense case rate for males grew 38%. However, the 1993 person offense case rate for males was still more than three times greater than the corresponding rate for females." Chesney-Lind and Shelden (p. 10) counter: "[W]hile it could be argued that for some crimes girls are 'catching up,' the fact of the matter is that boys clearly outnumber girls for most major crimes, with the exception of larceny-theft." Table 9–5 shows the gender differences in juvenile arrests for various offenses in 1995.

> As with adult offenders, a vast majority of delinquent offenders are male.

Chesney-Lind and Shelden (p. 8) observe: "Status offenses play a more significant role in girls' arrests than boys' arrests. Status offenses accounted for 27.5 percent of all girls' arrests in 1995, but only about 10.5 percent of boys' arrests—figures that remained relatively stable during the past decade (and over previous decades as well)." These authors also note (p. 9): "Generally, official delinquency [the picture of delinquency derived from statistics maintained by law enforcement officers] is dominated by less serious offenses, and this is particularly true of female delinquency." These gender-based differences in offenses have significant implications for corrections professionals and how they handle juvenile offenders, as discussed later in the chapter.

Poe-Yamagata and Butts (1996, p. 1) note significant differences in how male and female delinquents are handled by the courts: "Delinquency cases involving females were less likely than those involving males to be processed formally, more likely to receive probation as the most restrictive disposition, and less likely to result in detention or out-of-home placement." These differences directly affect how many male and female juveniles enter the various components of corrections.

Race Differences

Delinquency is increasing among youths of all races. As with adult offenders, the greatest number of delinquency cases are reported for White individuals, followed by Blacks, with other races reporting the fewest cases (Table 9–6). According to Butts (p. 3): "In 1993 the number of delinquency cases involving white youth exceeded the number involving black youth by a margin of 2 to 1. Cases involving whites outnumbered those involving youth of other races by 18 to 1."

The data also reveals, however, that while the number of White delinquency cases increased 18 percent from 1989 to 1993, the number of cases involving Black juveniles increased 34 percent and cases involving youth of other races increased 32 percent. Nearly two decades' worth of data regarding juvenile-committed homicides shows an increase in offending rates primarily among Black males age 14 to 17 (Table 9–7). White males, age 14 to 17, have also shown an increase in homicide offending rates since 1976 but still remain far below those levels reported for Black males in the same age range. Homicide offending rates of females, both White and Black, have either stayed the same or decreased since 1976, yet the rates for Black females have consistently exceeded those for White females.

As was shown with adult offenders in Table 8–1, while Black juveniles comprise a smaller proportion of the general population than do White juveniles,

| Table 9–5 | Arrests of Persons under 18, by Sex, 1995 |

	Male		Female	
	Number	Percent	Number	Percent
Total	**1,399,547**	**100.0**	**482,039**	**100.0**
Index Crimes				
Homicide	2,245	*	138	*
Forcible Rape	3,769	*	84	*
Robbery	37,978	2.7	3,863	0.8
Aggravated Assault	46,695	3.4	11,418	2.4
Burglary	84,229	6.0	9,255	1.9
Larceny-Theft	238,889	17.1	114,778	23.8
Motor Vehicle Theft	48,719	3.5	8,490	1.8
Arson	6,283	0.4	874	0.2
Total Violent	90,687	6.5	15,503	3.2
Total Property	378,100	27.0	133,397	27.7
Total Index	468,787	33.5	148,900	30.9
Part II Offenses				
Other Assaults	106,028	7.6	40,515	8.4
Forgery/Counterfeiting	3,928	0.3	2,175	0.5
Fraud	13,242	0.9	4,676	1.0
Embezzlement	520	*	376	*
Stolen Property	25,799	1.8	3,559	0.7
Vandalism	84,206	6.0	10,007	2.0
Weapons	36,161	2.6	3,148	0.7
Prostitution	510	*	466	0.1
Other Sex Offenses	10,380	0.7	800	0.2
Drugs	116,627	8.3	16,696	3.5
Gambling	1,038	*	55	*
Offenses Against the Family	2,585	0.2	1,492	0.3
DUI	8,074	0.6	1,491	0.3
Liquor Laws	55,548	4.0	22,421	4.7
Drunkenness	12,009	0.9	2,243	0.5
Disorderly Conduct	82,793	5.9	26,512	5.5
Vagrancy	2,329	0.2	283	*
Curfew and Loitering	72,649	5.2	30,787	6.4
Runaway	74,713	5.3	101,657	21.1
All Other Offenses	221,621	15.8	63,780	13.2

*Less than 0.1 percent.
Source: Crime in America: Uniform Crime Reports, 1995. Washington, DC: U.S. Department of Justice, Federal Bureau of Investigation, 1995, p. 213. Table from Meda Chesney-Lind and Randall G. Shelden. *Girls, Delinquency, and Juvenile Justice,* 2nd ed. Belmont, CA: West/Wadsworth Publishing Company, 1998. Reprinted by permission.

Table 9-6	Percent Change in Delinquency Cases and Case Rates by Race, 1989 to 1993					
	Number of Cases			**Case Rates**		
Offense	**1989**	**1993**	**Pct. Chg.**	**1989**	**1993**	**Pct. Chg.**
White	816,300	962,100	18%	40.0	44.1	10%
Person	116,400	181,400	56	5.7	8.3	46
Property	501,600	555,900	11	24.6	25.5	4
Drugs	44,900	50,400	12	2.2	2.3	5
Public Order	153,400	174,400	14	7.5	8.0	6
Black	354,000	472,700	34%	92.8	115.4	24%
Person	86,100	127,700	48	22.6	31.2	38
Property	177,300	218,700	23	46.5	53.4	15
Drugs	31,500	36,600	16	8.3	8.9	8
Public Order	59,000	89,700	52	15.5	21.9	42
Other Races	41,600	54,800	32%	36.8	39.9	8%
Person	6,500	9,600	48	5.7	7.0	22
Property	26,200	34,300	31	23.1	25.0	8
Drugs	1,500	2,100	36	1.4	1.5	12
Public Order	7,400	8,800	18	6.6	6.4	-3

Case Rate = Cases per 1,000 youth at risk.
Note: Detail may not add to totals because of rounding. Percent change calculations are based on unrounded numbers.
Source: Jeffrey A. Butts. *Offenders in Juvenile Court, 1993.* Juvenile Justice Bulletin: OJJDP Update on Statistics. U.S. Department of Justice, July 1996, p. 4 (NCJ-160945).

cases involving Black delinquents occur at a disproportionately higher rate. Butts (p. 3) states: "The delinquency case rate for black youth . . . was more than twice the rate for white youth (115.4 compared with 44.1 per 1,000 youth). . . . In 1993 the person offense case rate for black youth was more than three times greater than the corresponding rate for white youth. The drug offense case rate for black youth was nearly four times the rate for whites. Similarly, the property and public order offense case rates for blacks were more than double the rates for whites." Church (1994, p. 72) notes: "In Iowa, where only 4.8 percent of youths are minorities, officials found a staggering 54 percent of youths in jail after waiver were African Americans." (Their cases were "waived" by the juvenile court, sending them to adult court, often to await trial in jail.)

Black youth have a higher delinquency case rate than do either White youth or youth of other races.

This overrepresentation of youths from racial and ethnic minorities in the juvenile justice system as compared with their numbers in the general youth

Table 9-7 Trends in Homicide Offending Rates by Age, Sex and Race Combinations (Rates per 100,000 Population)

	14–17				18–24				25+			
	Male		Female		Male		Female		Male		Female	
Year	White	Black	White	Black	White	Black	White	Black	White	Black	White	Black
1976	7.9	51.2	1.0	7.8	16.7	138.3	2.0	23.7	7.2	76.5	1.2	17.1
1977	7.6	44.8	.9	4.4	16.5	124.3	2.0	22.4	7.2	70.1	1.2	16.1
1978	7.7	44.4	.9	6.0	18.0	131.2	2.0	20.5	7.5	71.5	1.1	14.9
1979	9.2	47.1	.9	6.0	19.5	144.2	2.1	20.3	7.8	73.5	1.2	13.8
1980	8.9	48.9	.7	5.1	20.4	144.6	2.0	21.5	7.9	71.4	1.1	13.2
1981	8.4	55.0	1.0	6.3	19.8	135.5	1.9	17.8	8.2	72.4	1.1	13.5
1982	8.1	45.7	.9	4.4	17.5	120.8	2.0	18.6	7.6	62.3	1.1	11.6
1983	7.5	36.8	1.1	5.3	17.3	104.9	1.8	16.6	7.0	56.2	1.1	10.4
1984	6.9	33.4	.9	4.7	18.0	91.1	2.0	13.8	7.0	51.0	.9	9.2
1985	7.0	44.3	.7	4.9	17.2	101.3	1.8	13.3	7.0	50.2	.9	9.3
1986	9.0	51.0	.8	4.2	18.5	117.2	1.7	15.5	7.1	55.9	.9	9.8
1987	8.0	54.1	1.1	5.1	17.6	121.2	2.0	12.9	6.7	48.7	.9	8.4
1988	9.9	72.6	.8	5.2	16.9	146.9	2.0	15.2	6.4	50.5	.8	7.9
1989	11.5	84.6	.8	5.3	19.1	168.5	2.0	14.0	6.2	47.4	.8	8.3
1990	14.3	113.8	1.1	5.2	22.2	200.7	2.1	14.7	6.6	48.9	.8	7.7
1991	14.6	127.5	.9	7.7	23.2	241.2	1.9	15.7	6.3	46.4	.8	7.5
1992	14.4	122.5	1.0	7.5	21.7	219.0	1.7	12.8	5.5	42.6	.7	6.4
1993	14.4	151.6	1.0	6.7	20.9	215.8	1.6	14.3	5.5	39.7	.8	5.9
1994	15.6	139.6	1.1	6.7	20.9	201.0	1.6	13.1	5.3	35.5	.7	5.8

Source: Table from James Alan Fox. *Trends in Juvenile Violence.* Washington, DC: U.S. Department of Justice, Bureau of Justice Statistics, March 1996, p. 4. Data from FBI, Supplementary Homicide Reports, and Census Bureau, Current Population Survey. Includes known offenders only.

➤ population is known as **disproportionate minority confinement** (DMC). According to Shepard (1995, p. 114): "The juvenile corrections work force, including administrative and direct-service providers, is not diverse at all levels, and in spite of many years of civil rights struggles, there is still overt discrimination and racism." Others, however, disagree with this.

The Juvenile Justice and Delinquency Prevention Act of 1974 requires that "states develop a plan to reduce the proportion of juveniles detained or confined in secure detention facilities, secure correctional facilities, jails and lockups who are members of minority groups if such proportion exceeds the proportion such groups represent in the general population." As recent statistics demonstrate, however, disproportionate minority confinement still occurs more than two decades after passage of the act.

Time of Day

An interesting artifact of juvenile crime is the time of day many such offenses occur. According to a report by Fight Crime: Invest in Kids, a crime prevention group ("Juvenile Crime Rate," 1997, pp. 5–6), violent juvenile crime spikes between 3 and 4 P.M., right after schools let out, and about one-third of all violent juvenile crime occurs between 3 and 7 P.M. Figure 9–6 shows the time-of-day patterns for juvenile crime compared to adult crime.

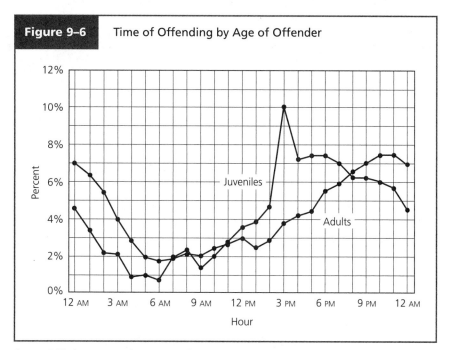

Figure 9–6 Time of Offending by Age of Offender

Source: Table from James Alan Fox. *Trends in Juvenile Violence.* Washington, DC: U.S. Department of Justice, Bureau of Justice Statistics, March 1996, p. 13. Data from FBI, National Incident-Based Reporting System (NIBRS) for South Carolina, 1991–92, and H. Snyder and M. Sickmund. *Juvenile Offenders and Victims: A National Report.*

Correctional Alternatives for Juveniles

As with adult offenders, juveniles may be placed along a correctional continuum, depending on the nature of their offense, their history and the availability of facilities or programs in their area. Since different states hold different philosophies regarding the way juvenile offenders should be handled, juveniles in one state may be more likely to receive correctional dispositions with a punitive thrust while those in another state are subject to a more rehabilitative correctional environment. Snyder and Sickmund (1995, p. 71) list which states' juvenile codes emphasize prevention and treatment goals, punishment goals or a balanced approach (Table 9–8).

As with adult offenders, the "least restrictive" alternative is to be used for juveniles when selecting correctional programs and services. For juveniles, this alternative is usually probation.

Probation

Probation is the most widely used disposition of the juvenile court. Recall from Figure 9–1 that more than half (56 percent) of all formally adjudicated

Table 9–8	States' Philosophical Goals Stated in Juvenile Code Purpose Clauses		
Prevention/Diversion/Treatment		**Punishment**	**Both**
Florida		Arkansas	Alabama
Idaho		Georgia	California
Kentucky		Hawaii	Colorado
New Hampshire		Illinois	Delaware
New Mexico		Iowa	Indiana
North Carolina		Kansas	Maryland
North Dakota		Louisiana	Massachusetts
Ohio		Minnesota	Nevada
Pennsylvania		Mississippi	Oklahoma
South Carolina		Missouri	Utah
Tennessee		New Jersey	Washington
Vermont		Oregon	
West Virginia		Rhode Island	
Wisconsin		Texas	

Note: Juvenile codes in states not listed did not contain a purpose clause.
Source: Howard N. Snyder and Melissa Sickmund. *Juvenile Offenders and Victims: A National Report.* Washington, DC: U.S. Department of Justice, Office of Juvenile Justice and Delinquency Prevention, 1995, p. 71.

delinquency cases in 1993 resulted in the juvenile being placed on probation and, of *all* the delinquency cases brought before juvenile courts in 1993 which were *not* dismissed, over a third (35 percent) resulted in probation for the juvenile. Torbet (1996, p. 1) states: "In 1993 nearly 1.5 million delinquency cases were handled by juvenile courts. Virtually every one of those cases had contact with a probation officer at some point. . . . Since 1929, when the first *Juvenile Court Statistics* report was published using 1927 data, probation has been the overwhelming dispositional choice of juvenile and family court judges."

According to Butts et al. (1995), a majority of cases (54 percent) in 1993 where juveniles received formal probation involved property offenses; 21 percent involved person offenses; 18 percent involved public-order offenses; and 7 percent involved drug law violations. As Table 9–9 shows, the greatest increase has been in the proportion of cases involving person offenses.

It is commonly assumed that the younger a person is, the greater the likelihood their behavior can be changed. Thus, the correctional philosophy traditionally taken with youth has been rehabilitative. According to Drowns and Hess (p. 379): "Probation is a guidance program to help juveniles overcome problems that may lead to delinquency and to keep an eye on juveniles who need supervision. It functions in the juvenile court as an alternative to a correctional facility and operates much like adult probation." These authors state the formal goal of probation is to improve the delinquent's behavior—in other words, rehabilitation. Other goals of juvenile probation are (1) to protect the community from delinquency, (2) to impose accountability on juvenile offenders and (3) to provide juvenile offenders with skills needed to live productively and responsibly in the community (Drowns and Hess, p. 387).

Table 9–9	Number and Percentage of Adjudicated Cases Placed on Formal Probation, 1989 and 1993		
Offense	**1989**	**1993**	**Percent Change**
Person	37,200 (17%)	53,900 (21%)	45%
Property	126,300 (58%)	136,600 (54%)	8%
Drugs	17,600 (8%)	17,500 (7%)	0%
Public Order	35,900 (17%)	46,800 (18%)	30%
Total Number of Cases Resulting in Formal Probation	216,900 (100%)	254,800 (100%)	17%

Note: Detail may not total 100 percent because of rounding.
Source: Adapted from Jeffrey A. Butts, et al. *Juvenile Court Statistics 1993*. Washington, DC: U.S. Department of Justice, Office of Juvenile Justice and Delinquency Prevention, 1995 (NCJ-159535).

When an offender, juvenile or adult, violates the conditions of probation, the probation officer often faces the unpleasant task of returning that offender to confinement. Here, a probation officer escorts a handcuffed violator back to juvenile hall.

The primary goal of juvenile probation is to improve the delinquent's behavior.

Probation for juveniles is not without its problems or critics. Unfortunately, probation is often the disposition of the juvenile court because no other options exist, as noted by Drowns and Hess (p. 384): "A problem commonly encountered at the dispositional stage is the paucity of available alternatives for helping or treating a youngster. . . . Often a youngster is placed on or continued on probation because of a lack of viable alternatives." They also state (pp. 379–380): "Often by the time a juvenile is placed on probation, the individual has a record of previous run-ins with the juvenile justice system, usually the police. The police regard probation as something juveniles 'get away with' or 'get off with.' Many juveniles who receive probation instead of being sentenced to a correctional facility view it the same way. Some youths have stated, 'I never see my P.O. [probation officer]. It's a joke! Don't ask me to tell you what he looks like, I can't remember.' "

As noted by McCarthy and McCarthy (1997, p. 351): "Although most juveniles on probation receive little counseling, some jurisdictions have developed special programs to meet the needs of serious delinquents or youths for whom assistance might make a difference." Programming and treatment needs of juvenile offenders are discussed at the end of the chapter.

When juveniles require more supervision or services than provided by probation, community-based corrections and intermediate sanctions are possible court dispositions.

Community-Based Corrections and Intermediate Sanctions

The philosophy behind community-corrections programs for juveniles is based on the need to integrate rather than isolate offenders. It is believed that isolating juvenile offenders from their normal social environment may actually encourage the development of a delinquent orientation, thus furthering delinquent behavior. Community-based corrections includes both nonresidential and residential alternatives.

A wide variety of nonresidential corrections programs exist, including community supervision, family crisis counseling, proctor programs and service-oriented programs such as recreational programs, counseling, alternative schools, employment training programs and homemaking and financial planning classes. Another alternative is the nonresidential day treatment program. According to Drowns and Hess (p. 393):

> Many state and local governments are turning to day treatment alternatives for delinquent juveniles because they appear to be effective and they are less costly than residential care. Alternatives might include evening and weekend reporting centers, school programs and specialized treatment facilities. Such programs can provide education, tutoring, counseling, community service, vocational training and social/recreational events.
>
> Such programs tend to be successful because they can focus on the family unit and the youth's behavior in the family and the community. They are also effective from a legal standpoint in those states that require that youths be treated in the least restrictive environment possible.

Community-based corrections also includes various types of nonsecure residential programs, such as shelters, group homes, foster homes, foster group homes and other nonsecure facilities such as correctional farms, ranches and camps for youth. The following brief descriptions of each program are taken from Drowns and Hess (pp. 394–396, Reprinted with permission.):

➤ • A **shelter** is a nonsecure residential facility where juveniles may be temporarily assigned, often in place of detention or returning home after being taken into custody or after adjudication while waiting for more permanent placement. Shelters usually house status offenders and are not intended for treatment or punishment.

➤ • The **group home** is a nonsecure facility with a professional corrections staff that provides counseling, education, job training and family-style living. The staff is small because the residence generally holds a maximum of 12 to 15 youths. The objective of the home is to facilitate

Several offenders take part in a lively debate during the "Changing Lives Through Literature" course at Middlesex Community College in Lowell, Massachusetts. The youth took the course in lieu of jail time as part of an alternative sentencing program.

reintegrating young offenders into society. Group homes are used extensively in almost all states.

➤ • A **foster home** is intended to be family-like, as much as possible a substitute for natural family settings. Small and nonsecure, they are used at any of several stages in the juvenile justice system. Foster care is not used as much for misbehaving children and those adjudicated youths in the area of community treatment as it is for children whose parents have neglected, abused or abandoned them.

➤ • The **foster group home** is a blend of group home and foster initiatives. They provide a "real family" concept and are run by single families, not professional staffs.

• Other nonsecure facilities—correctional farms, ranches and camps for youth are usually located in rural areas. These facilities are an alternative to confinement or regimented programs. The programs with an outdoor or rural setting encourage self-development, provide opportunities for reform and secure classification and placement of juveniles according to their capabilities. Close contact with staff and residents instills good work habits.

Community-based corrections for juveniles includes both nonresidential (community supervision, family crisis counseling, proctor programs, service-oriented programs and day treatment programs) and residential (shelters, group homes, foster homes, foster group homes and other nonsecure facilities such as correctional farms, ranches and camps) alternatives.

As with probation, however, community-based programs have been criticized for being too lenient for some juvenile offenders. Drowns and Hess (p. 396) comment:

> Court dispositions are often compromises among the pressures to secure deterrence, incapacitation, retribution and rehabilitation. Community-based programs do not permit the freedom of dismissal or of suspended judgments, but neither do they isolate offenders from the community as institutions do. Community programs are sometimes perceived as being easy on youngsters and, thus, as not providing sufficient punishment or supervision to ensure deterrence, incapacitation and retribution. Nonetheless, commitment to such programs represents a considerable degree of restriction and punishment when compared to dismissal, suspended judgment or informal processing out of the system at an early age.

When community-based corrections aren't "enough" but institutionalization is "too much," the court may impose a number of intermediate sanctions on youth, similar to those given to adults. These include intensive supervision, house arrest, electronic monitoring and boot camps. The elements of each alternative are the same for juveniles as for adults.

Juvenile Boot Camps

Although juvenile boot camps are fundamentally the same as those for adults, a brief discussion is appropriate here because of the recent attention focused on this alternative.

Boot camps for youthful offenders have received mixed reviews. According to Peters et al. (1997, p. 16): "The boot camp environment appears to create a setting that facilitates learning and academic education, even for such a troubled population. . . . A significant majority of youth improved at least one grade level in literacy and math skills in the equivalent of less than half an academic year, with many improving two grade levels or more." However, "boot camp participants probably participated in programs that were smaller and that afforded more personalized attention than they would have received otherwise. Offenders released immediately to probation received no such services and, therefore, were no better off academically than they had been before."

Similar to adult graduates of boot camps, juveniles completing boot camp still retain a high risk of recidivism, with estimates of rearrest rates ranging anywhere between 28 and 74 percent. Florida Senate Republican Leader Locke Burt (Kaczor, 1997, p. 6B) states: "If people were expecting a magic bullet, boot camps aren't it. But I think it does help some kids some of the time." Kaczor notes: "Teens at Bay County's camp in Panama City [Florida] don't need any studies to figure their odds for being arrested again. 'Sir, a 50-50 chance, sir,' said a thin 14-year-old boy. 'You just have to have enough will power to stay away from it, sir.' Does he have it? 'Sir, yes, sir.'"

For a small percentage of youthful offenders, none of the preceding alternatives are appropriate for the severity of their actions, and the court places them in correctional institutions.

Institutionalization

Of all the delinquency cases brought before juvenile courts in 1993 that were *not* dismissed, approximately 9 percent resulted in the juvenile being committed to a correctional facility. Juveniles are placed in numerous types of institutions, frequently with adult offenders. Estimates place the number of facilities holding juvenile offenders at over 11,000, of which only one-third are specifically designed for juveniles. The remainder are adult jails, police lockups and state correctional facilities.

> Juveniles may be held in a variety of correctional institutions, most often in facilities that also house adult offenders.

Commonly, juveniles are placed in **detention centers** which, unlike shelters or group homes, are secure, locked facilities that hold young offenders prior to and following adjudication. The National Juvenile Detention Association (NJDA) has clearly stated that juvenile detention is to be used for only those juveniles who are violent and/or who pose a serious threat to community safety. Even with these restrictions, our nation's detention centers are overflowing. According to Previte (1997, p. 76): "More than a half a million youths per year pour into secure, publicly-operated juvenile detention centers. More than half of the youths detained in the United States now are served in crowded facilities. In 1996, the Camden County (N.J.) Youth Center reached almost triple capacity. Newark reached 250 percent of capacity; Oklahoma City, 202 percent; Las Vegas, 183 percent; Chicago, 168 percent; Miami, 152 percent; and Dallas, which expanded into a new building only 20 months ago, 116 percent."

This serious shortage of detention space for violent juvenile offenders has created fervent debate about whether such juveniles should be housed in adult facilities. Some see housing violent juveniles in adult facilities as a common-sense approach. As Backstrom (1998, p. 14) asserts: "We cannot overlook the fact that today's juvenile offenders often are sophisticated, gang-connected juveniles committing violent crimes, and there are fewer reasons to be concerned about segregating these hard-core juvenile offenders from adults. . . . In many cases, 15- to 25-year-old offenders commit offenses together." Others, however, consider placing juveniles in adult prisons a very bad idea. Roush and Dunlap (1998, p. 15) state:

> There are significant differences between adults and children (person under
> 18 years old), and public safety is best served by correctional efforts that

restore youths to healthy, law-abiding lifestyles. The mission of adult corrections, as defined by politicians, the public and the courts, is at odds with these principles. . . . Research indicates that juveniles are five times more likely to be sexually assaulted and two times more likely to be beaten in prison than in a juvenile institution. Placing them in adult prisons constitutes deliberate indifference to their well-being and dehumanizes them. In addition to being costly in terms of time and resources, it prevents reconciliation and healing.

Nonetheless, when long-term institutionalization is the court's disposition, juveniles may be placed in jails or prisons, frequently next to adult offenders. The rising number of cases involving serious offenses committed by juveniles has more and more young offenders being transferred to adult status in the courts. Furthermore, the increased occurrence of juveniles being waived into adult institutions is posing new challenges for corrections. Orenstein and Levinson (p. 148) state: "As more and more juveniles are sentenced to adult correctional facilities, less is known about how adult authorities are dealing with this population." The results of an ACA survey conducted at the beginning of 1996, in which 29 state departments of corrections and 14 jails responded, show (Orenstein and Levinson, pp. 148–149):

- Regarding specialized needs and programs for juveniles waived to adult institutions, education was listed most frequently—47 percent indicated this was a special need, and 55 percent reported they were conducting special/innovative programs in education for their juveniles.

- In 1995, juveniles were committed into the adult system via:

Judicial waiver	59%
Legislative waiver	23%
Prosecutorial waiver	18%

- Types of offenses for which juveniles were committed to adult institutions:

Violent offenses	74%
Nonviolent offenses	26%

- How juveniles were classified in adult institutions:

The same as adults	41%
Classified by age	15%
Classified by offense	10%
Other	33%

- How juveniles were housed:

With other juveniles	50%
With general population	48%

- Special or innovative programming for juvenile population:

Special programming	50%
No special programming	40%

- Problems caused by the juvenile population:

Behavioral-related	70%
Dedicated spatial problems (sight, sound, separation)	19%
No problems	11%

- Future trends regarding the amount of juveniles in adult institutions:

Increase	79%
Reduction	0
No change	10%
Don't know	10%

Orenstein and Levinson (p. 149) conclude: "The adult correctional community does not appear to be prepared to manage and provide effective programming for these [juvenile] offenders. . . . The results indicate that more information and evaluation results are needed to assist the adult correctional community in developing effective strategies for the care and custody of its growing juvenile population."

Some juveniles are housed next to adult offenders even though the juveniles have been processed through the juvenile, not the criminal, justice system. For these correctional facilities, the OJJDP has identified specific criteria which must be met for compliance with the Juvenile Justice and Delinquency Prevention Act (JJDPA) ("OJJDP Issues," 1997, pp. 13–14):

- Sight and sound separation.
- Program activities (recreation, counseling, dining, sleeping) may not be shared by incarcerated juveniles and adults, although time-phasing of common nonresidential areas is permissible.
- Management, direct care and security staff must be separate between the two populations, although service staff (medical care, food service, laundry service) may serve both populations if acceptable under state law.
- Adherence to administrative standards defined by standing state laws, regulations or practice.

➤ Another secure alternative for young offenders is the **training school.** As Drowns and Hess (p. 410) explain: "Training schools exist in every state except Massachusetts, which abolished them in the 1970s. They vary greatly in size, staff, service programs, ages and types of residents. Some training schools resemble adult prisons, with the same distinguishing problems of gang-oriented activity, homosexual terrorism and victimization, which often leads to progressive difficulties or suicide."

Inmate Culture. The similarities between juvenile social structure and adult inmate cultures are great within correctional institutions. For example, the kinships commonly found among adult female inmates have also been observed among incarcerated female juveniles. A study conducted more than 20 years ago (Giallambardo, 1974) of girls in training schools found extensive networks of family roles. Some girls maintained "spousal" relationships including homosexual activities, while other girls were incorporated into families in such nonsexual roles as "sisters" or "cousins."

More recent research has shown these kinships persist among today's incarcerated girls (Chesney-Lind and Shelden, p. 185): "That many females in these facilities have come from extensively abusive families might be a strong reason for them to seek to create another family arrangement within which they can find love and acceptance." The inmate culture, in these instances, reinforces social contacts among youth and helps keep them "human."

For many incarcerated youths, however, the inmate culture fosters negativity and hardens their outlook on life. According to Drowns and Hess (p. 417): "The sociopolitical events produced in correctional institutions for youths are the same as those found in adult institutions." They also note (p. 419): "The world of institutionalization is not significantly different for females in a locked facility than for their male counterparts. Violence, role identity and establishing power are equally important for self-preservation."

> The inmate culture of juvenile facilities is very similar to that of adult facilities, with violence, role identity and the need to establish power important elements in survival.

A correctional worker at a Minnesota jail housing the worst juvenile offenders states:

> This is their environment, especially if they're here a long time. . . . They make a lot of contacts, they get a lot of reinforcement for their negative behavior, they tell their war stories. . . . They stop growing in a way. They don't have normal experiences. They have this siege mentality. . . . They're not working on their careers. They're already in their careers here. Their careers are being in the system. Detention for some of these kids is not so bad an option. They're safe. They get three meals a day. They get rest. They get attention. They say they don't like it, but they keep coming back (Brandt, 1993, p. B7).

When juveniles are released from correctional institutions, they may enter ➤ a stage known as aftercare. **Aftercare** is similar to adult parole in which youth are supervised for a limited time following release from a correctional facility but are still under control of the facility or the juvenile court.

The placement of juveniles in secure facilities such as detention centers, jails, prisons and training schools is the most restrictive disposition available to the court. The only more severe disposition is sentencing a juvenile to capital punishment.

Table 9–10	Executions of Juvenile Offenders, January 1, 1973, through December 31, 1997				
Name	**Date of Execution**	**Place of Execution**	**Race**	**Age at Crime**	**Age at Execution**
Charles Rumbaugh	9-11-1985	Texas	White	17	28
J. Terry Roach	1-10-1986	So. Car.	White	17	25
Jay Pinkerton	5-15-1986	Texas	White	17	24
Dalton Prejean	5-18-1990	Louisiana	Black	17	30
Johnny Garrett	2-11-1992	Texas	White	17	28
Curtis Harris	7-1-1993	Texas	Black	17	31
Frederick Lashley	7-28-1993	Missouri	Black	17	29
Ruben Cantu	8-24-1993	Texas	Latino	17	26
Chris Burger	12-7-1993	Georgia	White	17	33

Source: Victor L. Streib. *The Juvenile Death Penalty Today: Death Sentences and Executions for Juvenile Crimes over the Last Quarter Century, 1973–1997.* Ada, OH: Ohio Northern University, 1998. Reprinted by permission.

Juvenile Offenders on Death Row

When people think of the death penalty, they often do not consider its application to juvenile offenders. Yet, according to Snell (1996, p. 8) at year-end 1995, 51 of the 2,661 prisoners on death row (nearly 2 percent) had been 17 or younger at the time of their arrest.

Since the first execution of a condemned juvenile in 1642, 353 persons have been executed for juvenile crimes (Streib, 1998, p. 3). Since 1985, nine such executions have occurred. Table 9–10 lists details of some of these executions. The proportion of young offenders to whom the death penalty is given remains quite minuscule. For the vast majority of juvenile offenders, there remains the hope of rehabilitation and the chance to return to society a better person. For these youth, effective programming and treatment provided by correctional staff is critical.

Programming and Treatment Needs of Juvenile Offenders

Corrections must often provide programming and treatment to address the underlying causes of delinquent behavior. The variety of characteristics commonly found among juvenile offenders helps identify some of their major programming and treatment needs. Addiction, illiteracy and anger management are three such examples.

Drug abuse is common among juvenile offenders. According to a recent Justice Department report, 60 percent of juveniles in jail stated they use drugs regularly, and nearly 40 percent said they were under the influence of drugs when they committed crimes ("Tolerance of Juvenile," 1994, p. 6). The relationship between delinquency and drugs is well established. Not only do some drugs lower inhibitions so youth are apt to engage in behavior they would not do while not under such an influence, but also the need for money to buy drugs may lead to crimes such as thefts and burglaries. Drug treatment is one of the most obvious and necessary programs for delinquents to help them get out and stay out of the correctional loop. Drowns and Hess (p. 302) suggest: "During detention, a window of opportunity exists to identify youths on drugs and, therefore, at risk of becoming repeat offenders. Such youth can be put into drug-treatment programs, hopefully averting the drug-crime-drug cycle."

Educational and intellectual deficiencies are also common among juvenile offenders. Kearney and Thacker (1994, p. 86) state: "The typical 15-year-old male committed to the North Carolina Division of Youth Services scores four grade levels below his peers on a standardized achievement test." According to these authors, "[p]oor performance in school . . . is a predictor of future problem behavior." Curcio (1995, p. 28) notes: "In a recent survey of 157 prison wardens, 93 percent indicated that illiteracy was a problem for many youths in detention." Furthermore, as reported by Gemignani (1994, p. 2): "As many as 40 percent of youth in correctional facilities have some form of learning disability." Correctional facilities that handle juveniles need to address these learning and educational issues. Providing programs to help these young offenders improve their literacy and learning skills will contribute to keeping these youths from returning to corrections.

Violence, injury, depression and suicide are other issues facing juvenile corrections facilities. Many delinquent youth have problems with impulse control and anger management. In addition to anger, institutionalized youth may feel frightened, ashamed or despondent, conditions that may be made even worse in the overcrowded juvenile facilities. One report ("Tolerance of Juveniles," p. 6) notes: "Nearly half of confined juveniles are held in facilities with populations larger than they were originally designed to hold. Injury rates in crowded facilities are higher for both staff and inmates, at about 32,000 a year. Only one-quarter of detained youth live in institutions with anti-suicide programs, in a system where about 17,000 suicide attempts are made each year."

> Drug treatment, literacy and learning skills, anger management and suicide prevention are important programming and treatment needs of today's juvenile offenders.

It is especially important to realize that many juveniles in corrections are not so much offenders as they are victims—of abusive parents or boyfriends, gangs who won't let them go and so on. Also, breakdowns in family communications or clashes with parents' beliefs and expectations can drive juveniles from their homes, into the offense of running away, and then frequently into further offenses such as stealing to get food to eat, breaking into structures for shelter and so on. For these status offenders, probation, incarceration or many of the alternative sanctions in between are not the solution. For these juveniles, corrections becomes much more than a system for punishment or a process for rehabilitation. It becomes a lifeline, a doorway to a better future and, hopefully, an end to a cycle of violence their children will never need to know.

Summary

The terminology used to refer to juvenile offenders differs somewhat from that used to describe adult offenders. A status offender is a juvenile who is *not* considered a criminal and whose action would *not* be considered an offense had it been committed by an adult. In contrast, a juvenile delinquent is an individual below the legal age who is involved in criminal activity whose action *would* be a crime if it were committed by an adult.

The disposition determines if and how a juvenile will enter corrections. Probation is the most common disposition for juveniles adjudicated delinquent. The line separating juveniles from adults, however, is becoming less distinct as more and more violent youth are being tried in court as adults. Most juveniles who are transferred to criminal court have committed crimes against persons. Chronic juvenile offenders, although a relatively small proportion of the delinquent population, are responsible for most of the violent offenses committed by juveniles, many beginning their criminal activity before reaching their teens.

Most delinquency cases are for property offenses, although the greatest percent increase from 1989 to 1993 was in crimes against persons. The highest delinquency case rate occurs for juveniles age 16. As with adult offenders, a vast majority of delinquent offenders are male, and Black youth have a higher delinquency case rate than do either White youth or youth of other races.

As with adult offenders, juveniles may be placed along a correctional continuum, depending on the nature of their offense, their history and the availability of facilities or programs in their area. The least restrictive alternative for juveniles is usually probation, the primary goal of which is to improve the delinquent's behavior. Community-based corrections for juveniles includes both nonresidential (community supervision, family crisis counseling, proctor programs, service-oriented programs and day treatment programs) and residential (shelters, group homes, foster homes, foster group homes and other nonsecure facilities such as correctional farms, ranches and camps) alternatives. Juveniles may also be held in a variety of correctional institutions, most often in facilities that also house adult offenders. The inmate culture of juvenile facilities is very similar to that of adult facilities, with violence, role identity and the need establish power important elements in survival.

Corrections must often provide programming and treatment to address the underlying causes of delinquent behavior. Drug treatment, literacy and learning skills, anger management and suicide prevention are important programming and treatment needs of today's juvenile offenders.

Discussion Questions

1. Do you support a rehabilitative or punitive approach to treating juveniles? Why? Why might today's society be inclined to a "get tough on juveniles" attitude?

2. Should the legal age be uniform nationwide, like the legal drinking age? Why or why not? If so, what should it be set at?

3. Considering that most chronic juvenile offenders start their criminal careers prior to age 12, how "rehabilitative" do you think these youths are? Recall the definition of "chronic juvenile offender."

4. Do you believe most youth, at one time or another, commit an act for which they could be taken into custody? Did you ever take risks or commit delinquent acts as a youth?

5. Is juvenile probation effective or is closer supervision required of these youth?

6. Should parents, custodians or guardians of youth be actively involved in a youth's probation? Why or why not?

7. Do community-based corrections give judges more options in sentencing youth? Is this an advantage or disadvantage?

8. Should all violent juvenile offenders be committed to a secure facility? Why or why not?

9. Why do you think juvenile offenders are becoming more violent? Discuss contributing factors such as the breakdown of family values, the media, availability of weapons and so on.

10. What correctional alternatives are available for juvenile offenders in your area?

References

Backstrom, James C. "Housing Juveniles in Adult Facilities: A Common-Sense Approach." *Point/Counterpoint: Correctional Issues.* Lanham, MD: American Correctional Association, 1998, p. 14.

Brandt, Steve. "The In Crowd: Hennepin County's Jail for Juveniles Is Jammed." (Minneapolis/St. Paul) *Star Tribune,* April 11, 1993, pp. B1, B7.

Butts, Jeffrey A. et al. *Juvenile Court Statistics 1993.* Washington, DC: U.S. Department of Justice, Office of Juvenile Justice and Delinquency Prevention, 1995 (NCJ-159535).

Butts, Jeffrey A. *Offenders in Juvenile Court, 1993.* Juvenile Justice Bulletin: OJJDP Update on Statistics. U.S. Department of Justice, July 1996 (NCJ-160945).

Butts, Jeffrey A.; Snyder, Howard N.; Finnegan, Terrance A. et al. *Juvenile Court Statistics, 1994.* Office of Juvenile Justice and Delinquency Prevention, 1996.

Chesney-Lind, Meda and Shelden, Randall G. *Girls, Delinquency, and Juvenile Justice*, 2nd ed. Belmont, CA: West/Wadsworth Publishing Company, 1998.

Church, Vicky Turner. "Meeting Disproportionate Minority Confinement Mandates." *Corrections Today*, December 1994, pp. 70–72.

Crime in America: Uniform Crime Reports, 1995. Washington, DC: U.S. Department of Justice, Federal Bureau of Investigation, 1995.

Curcio, Sharon. "Finding Modern Ways to Teach Today's Youth." *Corrections Today*, April 1995, pp. 28–30.

Drowns, Robert W. and Hess, Kären M. *Juvenile Justice*, 2nd ed. St. Paul, MN: West Publishing Co., 1995. Reprinted by permission of the publisher.

Foote, Joseph. *Expert Panel Issues Report on Serious and Violent Juvenile Offenders*. Fact Sheet No. #68. Washington, DC: U.S. Department of Justice, Office of Juvenile Justice and Delinquency Prevention, October 1997.

Fox, James Alan. *Trends in Juvenile Violence*. Washington, DC: U.S. Department of Justice, Bureau of Justice Statistics, March 1996.

Gemignani, Robert J. "Juvenile Correctional Education: A Time for Change." *OJJDP Update on Research*. U.S. Department of Justice, Juvenile Justice Bulletin, October 1994 (NCJ-150309).

Giallambardo, R. *The Social World of Imprisoned Girls*. New York: Wiley, 1974.

Gilliard, Darrell K. and Beck, Allen J. *Prison and Jail Inmates, 1995*. Bureau of Justice Statistics Bulletin, July 1996 (NCJ-161132).

"Juvenile Crime Rate Spikes When School Lets Out, Study Indicates." *Criminal Justice Newsletter*, September 2, 1997, pp. 5–6.

Juveniles Taken into Custody: Fiscal Year 1992. Washington, DC: U.S. Department of Justice, Office of Juvenile Justice and Delinquency Prevention, 1992.

Kaczor, Bill. "Juvenile Boot Camps Show High Rearrest Rates." (Ft. Lauderdale) *Sun-Sentinel*, June 22, 1997, p. 6B.

Kearney, Gary and Thacker, Cindy. "Learning Model Facilitates Youths' Academic Success." *Corrections Today*, December 1994, pp. 86–90.

Krisberg, Barry. "The Legacy of Juvenile Corrections." *Corrections Today*, August 1995, pp. 122–124, 152–154.

McCarthy, Belinda Rodgers and McCarthy, Bernard J., Jr. *Community-Based Corrections*, 3rd ed. Belmont, CA: Wadsworth Publishing Company, 1997. Reprinted by permission of the publisher.

National Coalition of State Juvenile Justice Advisory Groups. *Myths and Realities: Meeting the Challenge of Serious, Violent, and Chronic Juvenile Offenders, 1992 Annual Report*. Washington, DC, 1993.

Office of Juvenile Justice and Delinquency Prevention. *Juvenile Justice*, Vol. 1, No. 1, Spring/Summer 1993, p. 29.

"OJJDP Issues Rules on Holding Youth Offenders." *NCJA Justice Bulletin*. January 1997, pp. 13–15.

Orenstein, Bruce W. and Levinson, Robert B. "Juveniles Waived Into Adult Institutions." *Corrections Today*, July 1996, pp. 148–149.

Peters, Michael; Thomas, David; and Zamberlan, Christopher. *Boot Camps for Juvenile Offenders*. Program Summary. Washington, DC: U.S. Department of Justice, Office of Juvenile Justice and Delinquency Prevention, September 1997 (NCJ-164258).

Poe-Yamagata, Eileen and Butts, Jeffrey A. "Female Offenders in the Juvenile Justice System." Statistics Summary: Office of Juvenile Justice and Delinquency Prevention, June 1996.

Previte, Mary Taylor. "Preventing Security Crises at Youth Centers." *Corrections Today*, February 1997, pp. 76–79.

Privacy and Juvenile Justice Records: A Mid-Decade Status Report. Washington, DC: Department of Justice, Bureau of Justice Statistics, May 1997 (NCJ-161255).

"Rochester Study Shows Links Between Abuse and Delinquency." *Criminal Justice Newsletter*, September 16, 1997, p. 5.

Roush, David W. and Dunlap, Earl L. "Juveniles in Adult Prisons: A Very Bad Idea." *Point/Counterpoint: Correctional Issues.* Lanham, MD: American Correctional Association, 1998.

Shepard, Karen B. "Understanding Disproportionate Minority Confinement." *Corrections Today,* June 1995, pp. 114–115.

Sickmund, Melissa; Snyder, Howard N.; and Poe-Yamagata, Eileen. *Juvenile Offenders and Victims: 1997 Update on Violence.* Washington, DC: Office of Juvenile Justice and Delinquency Prevention 1997 (NCJ-165703).

Sourcebook of Criminal Justice Statistics 1996. Washington, DC: U.S. Department of Justice, Bureau of Justice Statistics, 1997 (NCJ-165361).

Snell, Tracy L. *Capital Punishment 1995.* Bureau of Justice Statistics Bulletin, December 1996 (NCJ-162043).

Snyder, Howard N. and Sickmund, Melissa. *Juvenile Offenders and Victims: A National Report.* Washington, DC: U.S. Department of Justice, Office of Juvenile Justice and Delinquency Prevention, 1995.

"Spending Not Keeping Pace with Prison Populations, ABA Finds." *Criminal Justice Newsletter,* October 15, 1996, p. 5.

Streib, Victor L. *The Juvenile Death Penalty Today: Juvenile Death Sentences and Death Sentences and Executions for Juvenile Crimes over the Last Quarter Century, 1973–1997.* Ada, OH: Ohio Northern University, 1998.

Thomas. "Next Stop, Prison." *Washington Post,* March 18, 1996, p. A1.

"Tolerance of Juvenile Offenders Dwindles." *Law Enforcement News,* December 15, 1994, p. 6.

Torbet, Patricia McFall. *Juvenile Probation: The Workhorse of the Juvenile Justice System.* Juvenile Justice Bulletin. Washington, DC: U.S. Department of Justice, Office of Juvenile Justice and Delinquency Prevention, March 1996.

Wilson, John J. "Developing a Partnership with Juvenile Corrections." *Corrections Today,* April 1994, pp. 223–224.

10

Special Needs Offenders

Do You Know

➤ How often America's elderly inmate population is doubling in number?

➤ What difficulties mentally disabled offenders often encounter in correctional facilities?

➤ How mental retardation and mental illness differ?

➤ What percentage of the mentally ill in jail have committed no crime and why they are behind bars?

➤ What the most common offenses of mentally ill jail inmates are?

➤ If many male and female arrestees test positive for drugs and what drug is found most often in the urine of arrestees?

➤ What racial and gender differences exist among HIV-infected offenders?

➤ What age range and gender describe the majority of sex offenders? Whether most sex offenders are behind bars or serving time in the community?

Working together in multidisciplinary teams, corrections professionals will be better equipped to address the many challenges of accommodating inmates with special needs.
—Barbara A. Nadel

Introduction

Today's corrections system must deal not only with increased numbers of offenders but an increased variety of offenders as well. In addition to the general categories of male, female and juvenile offenders, corrections must handle a host of "special needs" offenders. Furthermore, longer sentences may add to the correctional challenge presented by these special needs prisoners.

George (1993, p. 191) states: "Special needs offenders can be defined as offenders who are best served by addressing the life circumstances that led to their involvement in the criminal justice system." Special needs offenders include elderly offenders, physically and mentally disabled offenders (including mentally retarded or developmentally disabled offenders), mentally ill offenders (also called mentally disordered offenders, including the criminally insane), drug- and alcohol-dependent offenders, HIV- and tuberculosis-infected offenders, sex offenders and high-profile offenders. It should be noted that these conditions may overlap—elderly offenders may also be physically disabled or mentally impaired, and HIV-infected offenders may also be drug-dependent. The special needs of such offenders and the special requirements of correctional facilities are the focus of this chapter.

Elderly Offenders

People in the United States are living longer. Due to factors including technological advances, improved medical care and better lifestyles and diets, the life span of people in this country has been steadily increasing. Some are even predicting the average life expectancy for Americans in the year 2000 could be in the low nineties.

This phenomenon, often called the "graying of America," is not only a major trend of the general population but is increasingly seen in our nation's correctional facilities. According to Cromwell (1994, p. 3):

> Since the mid-1970s, longer prison sentences and reductions in the use of parole have resulted in rapidly expanding numbers of elderly inmates in the correctional population. By 1992, nearly 14,000 prisoners in state and federal institutions were age 60 or older; 400 of them were over 85 years of age. Their ranks are doubling every four years. With the advent of "3 Strikes and You're Out" legislation in many states, the number of elderly inmates could increase dramatically in coming decades.

The population of America's elderly inmates is increasing rapidly, with their numbers doubling every four years.

The growing number of elderly inmates is placing extra financial strain on correctional systems.

As with the overall prison population, most elderly prisoners are male. Douglass et al. (1994, p. 152) state: "Black and Hispanic men are overrepresented in the elderly prison population, compared with the public at large. However, the extent of their overrepresentation is less significantly skewed than among younger inmates between 20 and 40 years of age."

Why the Elderly Inmate Population Is Increasing

Three forces contribute to the increase in elderly inmates:

- Older people may be committing more crimes.
- Longer sentences are being imposed on all offenders.
- Statutes such as the three-strikes law and mandatory-minimum sentences keep those with a history of criminal activity locked up longer.

Douglass et al. (p. 149) state: "Increasing crime committed by those older than age 50, the aging of the larger society that produces criminals, longer sentences for violent offenders and the accumulation of habitual offenders who are aging in prison are the main causes of [the] growth."

Defining Elderly

No specific age has been designated as the point at which someone becomes "elderly." Some studies use a minimum age of 55 to define the elderly population; others use age 50, 60 or 65. However, Silverman (1994, p. 145) claims: "If we only consider chronological age, we oversimplify the discussion—the diverse influences on this population indicate that we should consider the physiological age of the individual as well." We have all heard the phrase, "You're only as old as you feel." Therefore, **elderly** refers not only to an individual's chronological age but physiological age as well.

Needs of Elderly Inmates

An individual's physiological age is closely tied to the potential medical and health care needs of that individual. Some 80-year-old inmates require little or no medical care whereas some 50-year-old inmates require extensive medical attention. Pointing out the existence of "old" 40-year-olds and "young" 60-year-olds, Silverman (p. 145) advocates the "need to understand the factors that contribute to aging. Genetics, socioeconomic conditions, lifestyle, mental health and access to social and medical services all contribute to the acceleration or deceleration of aging and are key to assessing and defining 'old.' "

The health care administrator for Minnesota's prison system, Dana Baumgartner, in discussing the health care needs of elderly inmates, has stated (Halvorsen, 1995, p. B3): "The interesting thing about this population is that even though chronologically their age may be 55, biologically, because of their lifestyles, oftentimes they have organ systems that are much older. . . . For example, persons who have abused alcohol may have preexisting liver disease or pulmonary-related disease."

According to Cromwell (p. 3): "[T]he issue of long-term medical care for chronic disease presents the greatest challenge as the prison population becomes increasingly older. Inmates over age 60 have a much greater incidence of heart disease, cancer, kidney failure, and other chronic diseases." Such long-term care can be very costly, as evidenced by a study that compared the national average cost of incarceration for all inmates ($18,330/inmate) and the annual incarceration costs for inmates over 60 ($69,000/inmate) (Camp and Camp, 1994). Bradley (1990, p. 5) has projected the health care costs for elderly inmates will increase fourteenfold by the year 2005.

The mental state of many elderly offenders may also deteriorate, which can lead to emotional and behavioral problems with these inmates. According to George (p. 193): "Some older offenders develop Alzheimer's disease or become senile, which creates a significant problem for jails and prisons." These offenders may forget why they are behind bars, may feel paranoid about other inmates or correctional staff and may have difficulty remembering facility rules and regulations. One such inmate is described by Butterfield (1997, p. A12): "Stanley Wilson can no longer recall his age or why he was sent to prison. Alzheimer's has stolen his memory. His hazy mind wanders through space much more freely than his body these days, and he believes he will be released from his prison in western Pennsylvania 'this weekend.' Wilson is 59, though he looks at least 70."

In addition to medical and health care needs, elderly inmates have a host of other needs which present challenges to correctional administrators. Cromwell (p. 3) notes: "Older prisoners are often preyed on by younger inmates and they may require special housing facilities or other protective measures. More often than younger prisoners, they require special diets, medication, eye glasses, hearing aids, dentures, physical therapy, and even wheelchairs and Braille facilities."

Because vision capabilities and depth perception diminish with age, elderly inmates have more specific needs regarding visual elements of the facility. Silverman (p. 147) states: "Older inmates often have difficulty judging distance, requiring corrections administrators and designers to pay attention to stair riser heights or to consider eliminating stairs altogether. . . . To reduce confusion and avoid potential accidents, there should be a higher level of lighting, but glare should be eliminated."

Hearing loss is also common among older inmates. Silverman (p. 147) recommends: "To avoid disturbing and often confusing background noise, acoustical material should be used to reduce miscellaneous sound."

Physical movement is another challenge for many elderly inmates, a condition covered in the Americans with Disabilities Act (ADA) provisions for correctional facility design. According to Douglass et al. (p. 153): "[A]bout 20 percent of elderly inmates have some level of locomotion disability, limiting the number and configuration of settings that will be appropriate for their placement." Again, the use of stairs in facilities that house elderly prisoners must be carefully evaluated.

Other Concerns

Elderly inmates have other concerns that facility administrators should be aware of. Douglass et al. (p. 150) report the results of interviews conducted in 1991 with elderly Michigan inmates: "Sexual frustration, fear of having possessions stolen by younger inmates, concerns about dying in prison and anger at being confined were common themes of the unsolicited remarks made to interviewers."

Regarding the allocation of resources and division of programs and services, Silverman (p. 147) states: "[C]orrectional administrators need to consider how and where this special unit fits within the prison system and, assuming it is not a stand-alone unit, how it shares in the services and programs of other correctional units." Many have advocated the creation of separate, stand-alone units for elderly prisoners because of their special needs and their growing numbers. Neeley et al. (1997, p. 121) state: "[T]hese [elderly] inmates do better when they are away from the stress of interacting closely with younger offenders." Halvorsen (p. B3) notes: "The idea of geriatric prisons is being discussed nationwide as a crackdown on crime leads to longer sentences."

Competent staffing is another concern for administrators whose facilities house elderly inmates. Douglass et al. (p. 150) anticipate the growing need to build more nursing home–type facilities for inmates, recruit geriatricians to existing correctional hospitals and train custodial and nursing staff in gerontology to better meet the needs of this aging inmate population.

Security and Release of Elderly Inmates

Disagreement exists regarding the release of elderly offenders. Cromwell (p. 3) contends: "Humanitarian reasons aside, early release for long-term elderly prisoners has a solid economic justification. . . . The great majority of these older inmates would represent no further threat to society and could be safely released to the community." Cromwell adds that releasing these older offenders would free up bedspace for violent and predatory offenders. However, recent studies show that many of the elderly behind bars are such violent and predatory offenders.

The incarcerated elderly are more likely to have committed crimes such as homicide and sexual offenses than robbery and burglary. Butterfield (p. A12) notes: "While the stereotypical view of elderly inmates is that they are lifers who have committed their crimes in the distant past and therefore may be deserving of release, the reality is that most of them are new to the system." Recent BJS statistics reveal 25 percent of elderly inmates have been in prison for less than a year, 68 percent for less than five years and only 1 percent for thirty years or more. Furthermore, of all prisoners 55 and older, 67 percent are serving time for a violent crime, mainly murder, manslaughter and sexual assault (Butterfield, p. A12). A prison official in Minnesota believes security of elderly inmates is a critical issue since "90 percent of the older prisoners have committed murder or rape and other sex offenses" (Halvorsen, p. B3). Referring to elderly prisoners, this corrections professional states: "They are not good candidates for placement in the community unsupervised."

As with all other offenders, determining whether an elderly offender poses a threat to society is a crucial part of the release decision. Equally important is evaluating how ready or able that older offender is to handle a life of independence. Cromwell (p. 3) points out:

> . . . many have no place to go. They have lost or outlived their families and friends. Most have no job skills, and because of their age and criminal history, employment opportunities are minimal to nonexistent.
>
> In many cases, simply releasing aged prisoners without assuring alternative living arrangements, such as state-supervised nursing homes, would cause greater harm than requiring them to remain incarcerated.

More so than younger prisoners, older prisoners need programming to keep them current on how to survive outside the prison walls. Many technological advances and changes in the law may have occurred during their time behind bars, and simple things may have been forgotten over their lengthy incarceration. Silverman (p. 148) suggests: "Learning to fill out Social Security and rent applications and to write checks will make it less frustrating for older inmates when they re-enter the community."

The Elderly in Community Corrections

Little information is available regarding elderly offenders in community corrections programs, perhaps because many of the elderly who are committing crime today aren't doing the minor or nonviolent sorts of activities that would land them in community corrections. Most elderly offenders are new to the system, having committed sex offenses and other violent crimes that "earn" them a bed behind secure walls instead of in a more relaxed community facility. The few who have aged in prison and are of the nonviolent, property-offense typology are there usually because of an extensive criminal history.

A theory proposed by Craig (1998) to explain the lack of literature pertaining to elderly offenders in community corrections is quite simple: there just aren't very many elderly offenders sentenced to community corrections.

1. The number of elderly offenders in community corrections is so negligible as to not appear in any statistics or discussions of community corrections populations.

2. When the elderly do end up in community corrections, they do not present a significant management issue because they are not the wildly impulsive characters many 18- to 24-year-olds are. The elderly are a less reactive correctional clientele.

Nonetheless, some elderly offenders do serve their sentences in the community. These offenders, along with many of the elderly behind bars, frequently have disabilities.

Disabled Offenders

The Americans with Disabilities Act (ADA), signed into law in 1990 and put into effect in 1991, prohibits discrimination against persons with disabilities in many aspects of daily life in this country, including employment and transportation. Title II of the ADA applies to all public institutions, including correctional facilities, and covers all programs, services and activities provided by these facilities.

Defining Disabled

➤ The ADA defines **disability** as follows ("Agencies and Facilities," 1992, p. 143): "Anyone with a physical or mental impairment substantially limiting one or more major life activities, [who] has a record of such impairment, or is regarded as having such an impairment, is considered a person with a disability." The term *impaired* is frequently substituted for the word *disabled.*

The implications of the ADA are great for correctional institutions because of the rising number of offenders who fall within its scope. Appel (1995, p. 85) states: "The aging offender population (resulting from longer sentences and the aging of the general population), the debilitating effects of alcohol and drug abuse, and the injuries sustained through the violent behavior of inmates means that corrections will be responsible for an increasing number of disabled offenders."

Few statistics are available detailing the current size of the disabled inmate population in the United States. Table 10–1 shows the various categories of impairment recognized by the Florida Department of Corrections and illustrates how the number of inmates in each category has risen over a four-year period. This section focuses primarily on those offenders with physical impairments and mental deficiencies (for example, retardation). Offenders who are mentally *ill* are treated as a separate group of offenders, as are those whose impairments arise because they are elderly.

Accessibility to Programs and Services

Whatever programming and services a correctional facility offers inmates must be accessible to all individuals, including those with the disabilities covered by the ADA. Considering the various impairments and the individual ranges within each category (for example, partially blind to completely blind), this obviously presents a challenge for corrections. Instructors and program

Table 10–1	Impaired Inmate Survey			
Inmate Disabilities	**1990**	**1991**	**1992**	**1993**
Aged Inmates (60+)	557	582	606	696
Blind, Severe Vision & Eyes Impairment	21	21	35	31
Severe Hearing Impairment, Deafness	25	25	32	31
Lower Extremities, Wheelchair Required	67	78	169	163
Cardiovascular, Respiratory, Systemic Organic Disease, Physical Capacity	60	59	63	77
Upper Extremities, Spine, Shoulders, Hands	11	17	24	17
Severely Mentally Retarded	10	8	33	30
Total Inmate Population	44,362	44,905	48,176	51,029
Percent Impaired Inmates	1.69%	1.75%	1.99%	2.04%

Source: Table from Randall Atlas. "Advice on Surviving the Initial Steps Toward ADA Compliance." *Corrections Today,* December 1993, p. 130. Data from Florida Department of Corrections. Reprinted by permission.

leaders must be qualified and able to handle a broad spectrum of participants, and the curriculum must be presented in a format that these offenders can grasp (visual for the deaf, audible or in Braille for the blind, and so on).

Morton and Anderson (1996, p. 90) state: "Corrections personnel should not assume that because inmates have disabilities they cannot perform a particular job or participate in a specific program. Staff should explain the requirements of the job or program and ask inmates whether they can meet them."

Issues to address concerning disabled inmates and the construction and design of correctional facilities include doors and doorways; toilet facilities; beds; drinking fountains; fixed or built-in seating or tables; fixed benches; fixed or built-in storage; controls for lights, electrical receptacles, panic buttons and plumbing devices; visual alarms for those with hearing impairments; and telephones with variable volume control (Truitt, 1994). Such ADA design requirements frequently pose a greater financial burden for community corrections facilities than for larger, often better funded, institutions.

Mentally Retarded or Developmentally Disabled Offenders

There was a time when criminologists believed being mentally retarded effectively guaranteed leading a life of crime. Today it is recognized that such a correlation is absurd. However, mentally retarded individuals are not exempt from the ability to commit crime, nor are they exempt from being placed into the correctional system following conviction of such crime.

A blind inmate listens to stories on tape in one of the cubicles that serve as cells in the geriatric ward of this Huntsville, Texas, prison.

The American Association on Mental Retardation provides the following definition of **mental retardation:** ". . . significantly subaverage general intellectual functioning existing concurrently with deficits in adaptive behavior." An estimate made a decade ago concluded our nation's prisons alone were holding 25,000 mentally retarded offenders and that the number being held in jails was likely significant. Approximately 13 percent of juvenile offenders are estimated to be mentally retarded (Trupin et al., 1994, p. 30). Like all the other populations examined thus far (White, Black, male, female, adult, juvenile, elderly), it is presumed that the mentally retarded correctional population is increasing in number as well.

Problems and Needs of Mentally Disabled Offenders. Some problems frequently encountered by mentally disabled offenders include being the targets of practical jokes and sexual harassment by other inmates, high susceptibility to prison culture and inmate manipulation, abnormally high proneness to injury, difficulty adjusting to the rules and regulations of the facility, reluctance to partake in activities and programming due to a desire to hide their deficiencies and poor performance before review committees, resulting in more frequent parole denial (Santamour and West, 1985, p. 70). In fact, mentally retarded offenders have been found to serve an average of two to three years longer than other inmates for the same offense because of a higher incidence of parole denial.

> Mentally disabled offenders are often the targets of practical jokes and sexual harassment, are very susceptible to inmate manipulation, are abnormally prone to injury, have difficulty adjusting to the rules and regulations of the facility, are reluctant to partake in activities and programming due to a desire to hide their deficiencies and perform poorly before review committees, resulting in more frequent parole denial.

Corrections staff need to be especially aware of such mentally retarded offenders to ensure they are not being preyed upon by other inmates. Staff should also understand these offenders typically have more difficulty coping with the conditions of confinement and adjusting to the routine demanded of them behind bars. An example of one state's effort to afford appropriate treatment and care for these inmates is the Texas Department of Corrections' Mentally Retarded Offender Program, which identifies mentally deficient offenders, separates them from the general prisoner population and houses them in special units where they are able to receive suitable medical care and fair discipline. These inmates need to be protected.

Mentally Disabled Offenders and the Death Penalty. Much debate has been centered on mentally retarded offenders and the death penalty. Some claim such offenders lack the mental capacity to understand the nature of capital punishment and why they are being executed; others believe such offenders do possess the capacity to appreciate the seriousness of their crime(s) and should not receive preferential treatment based on their low IQ. It must be understood, however, that mental retardation is not the same as mental illness. Whereas mental retardation is a permanent condition of diminished mental capacity which no amount of counseling or treatment can cure, mental illness is often treatable and, in fact, mentally ill offenders may be highly intelligent. Furthermore, as discussed in Chapter 4, a diagnosis of mental illness often eliminates the death penalty as a sentencing option for the offender.

> Mental retardation is a permanent deficiency in mental capacity and is not treatable. Mental illness is a disease and is often treatable given the proper psychiatric care.

Mentally Ill Offenders

In the past, mentally ill offenders were hospitalized. Today, however, mentally ill offenders are frequently found in correctional populations and are becoming an increasingly serious problem for corrections. A movement begun over two decades ago with the passing of the Mental Health Act of 1974 deinstitutionalized thousands of mentally ill individuals. According to Gondles (1993, p. 6):

> It was during the '70s that the policy of diverting the mentally ill from hospitals to some of the more practical and cost-effective deliverable services was introduced. It was viewed as a good way to prepare these people for outpatient care in the community.
>
> Ironically, this movement became the catalyst for a problem that corrections inherited. . . .
>
> Many persons suffering from mental illness end up in our jails and prisons not only because they commit crimes of survival or endanger public safety, but also because they are simply unable to function independently or manage their lives without assistance.

Many believe the horrendous crimes that fill our newspapers and dominate our television news shows can only be committed by those who are "out of their minds." Indeed, how often has someone said, "He must've been crazy to do that!" Technically, however, crazy or insane offenders constitute only one of the four subgroups of mentally disordered offenders identified by Trupin et al. (p. 29), which are

- Those found not guilty by reason of insanity.
- Those incompetent to stand trial.
- Mentally disordered sex offenders.
- Mentally disordered prison inmates transferred to mental hospitals.

The final category recognizes that some offenders may enter the correctional system with no evidence of mental problems but, because of their inability to cope with the rigors of confinement, may deteriorate to a point where they become mentally ill. This disorder is sometimes referred to as **prison psychosis.** Factors that may lead to this disorder include:

- The prison routine.
- Fear of other inmates.
- Fear of assault or actual assault.
- Forced homosexual encounters.
- Breakdown in relationships with those outside the institution.
- Deterioration in the status of family outside the institution.
- Depression.

Trupin et al. (p. 29) note that an offender may actually succumb to more than one of these factors.

Mental illness among offenders is more common than many people realize. According to Trupin et al. (p. 28): "One national survey of 1,391 jails holding 62 percent of U.S. jail inmates found that more than one out of every 14 jail inmates have experienced mental illness. . . . Facility surveys indicate that between 6 and 8 percent of state prison populations have inmates with serious psychiatric illnesses." Furthermore: "Clinical studies suggest that 15 to 20 percent of all prison inmates need services associated with severe or chronic mental illness . . . [and] 29 to 56 percent of this population are estimated to need outpatient services during incarceration." An article reviewing the same national study states the problem is worsening, with nearly seven out of ten jails reporting they are seeing far more inmates with serious mental illness than they did a decade earlier ("Nation's Jails," 1992, p. A11).

Interestingly, this same national survey revealed that 29 percent of mentally ill individuals in jail have no charges against them but are behind bars because no psychiatric facilities are available ("Nation's Jails," p. A11). States vary considerably in their use of this practice. In Indiana, for example, a manic-depressive woman was held in jail for four months until a bed became available in a mental hospital, despite the fact she had committed no crime. According to one of the national survey's authors: "It is routine practice in Indiana, and many other states, to use local jails as (holding) facilities for mentally ill patients awaiting a hospital bed."

Nearly 30 percent of mentally ill individuals in jail have committed no crime but are being held behind bars until space becomes available in a mental hospital.

Many of the incarcerated mentally ill have, however, been convicted of a crime and are not simply waiting for a hospital bed to become available.

Common Crimes of the Mentally Ill

According to Trupin et al. (p. 29): "The four most common offenses cited by jails for arresting the mentally ill are assault and/or battery (cited by 41 percent of jails), theft (30 percent), disorderly conduct (29 percent), and drug- and alcohol-related offenses (29 percent). Many of these offenses are manifestations of a serious mental illness, which often goes untreated." Unfortunately, these offenders are unlikely to receive the help they need once they end up behind bars because "most [correctional] facilities in this country are not equipped to care adequately for the mentally ill offender" (Gondles, p. 6).

> The four most common offenses committed by the mentally ill in jail are assault and/or battery, theft, disorderly conduct and drug- and alcohol-related offenses.

Needs of Adult and Juvenile Mentally Ill Offenders

The needs of mentally ill offenders are varied, as they may suffer from a variety of "mood, thought or personality disorders; substance abuse problems; developmental disabilities; neuropsychological impairments; or a combination of these problems" (Trupin et al., p. 29). Meeting the needs of mentally ill juvenile offenders poses a further challenge to corrections. According to Trupin et al. (p. 30): "It is estimated that between 9.5 and 13.6 million youths out of an adolescent population of 86 million suffer from a diagnosable mental disorder. . . . Additionally, it is estimated that 3 to 26 percent of juvenile offenders have received psychiatric hospitalization and 38 to 66 percent have had outpatient counseling or treatment." Trupin et al. (p. 29) state that mentally ill juveniles differ from the chronic adult population in the following ways:

- The tendency to use illicit drugs.
- The tendency to drop out of treatment.
- The tendency to act more violently.
- The tendency to deny psychological problems.

These authors also note (p. 30): "While the needs of mentally ill youth who have no involvement in the juvenile justice system often go unmet, the additional stigma of criminal involvement lessens the possibility that juveniles will receive adequate assessment and treatment."

Correctional staff must be aware of the heightened level of suicide attempts among mentally disturbed offenders. Mentally ill offenders also tend to engage in disruptive behavior frequently and are often placed on medication to control their conduct. The need to administer and monitor these drugs regularly is another concern the correctional facility must address.

Corrections administrators must also consider the possibility they are being manipulated by offenders feigning mental illness. The condition of mental illness may preclude an offender from being executed, and while some inmates do slide into a depression or psychosis as a result of the impacts of prison life, others may only pretend in an attempt to have their death sentences commuted. A 1986 case, *Ford v. Wainright*, pertained to a death row inmate who became mentally ill while awaiting capital punishment and consequently could not be executed.

Many special needs offenders fall into more than one of the special needs categories. For example, a link has been identified between mental illness and addictive disorders. According to Gorski (1993, p. 78): "It has been estimated that 70 percent of offenders suffer from chemical dependence and, of those, the vast majority also have anti-social personality disorders." Gorski stresses the need to treat these disorders together, not separately, stating: "Because their behavior is driven by underlying personality and chemical use disorders, punishment alone will not stop offenders from using alcohol and drugs or from committing new crimes." Integrated treatment is often the most potent measure, combining elements that address the addiction but also improve the mental health of the offender. Gorski states: "The most effective institutional programs, such as those run by Interventions, Inc. in Dallas, Texas, and the Gateway Foundation in Illinois, teach four basic skills: self-motivation, initiating abstinence, maintaining abstinence and personal growth."

Addicted Offenders

Few can dispute the connection between drugs and crime. According to McBride and McCoy (1993, p. 257): "[T]here is strong empirical evidence of the statistical overlap between drug using and criminal behavior. Further, drug use is seen as increasing and sustaining criminal behavior." Offenders may be behind bars directly because of drug crimes (selling, manufacturing, using), or their need to support a drug habit may have led them to commit crimes such as robbery, burglary, prostitution or theft.

A Bureau of Justice Statistics (BJS) Executive Summary (1995, p. 2) reports: "The number of convicted drug offenders increased ninefold (from 19,000 to 172,300) from 1980 to 1992." But just because an offender has committed a drug crime does not necessarily mean that individual is an addict. Findings by Vito et al. (1993, pp. 348–349) indicate "although clients may have an admitted drug problem and a prior record of drug offenses, a current drug offense is not necessarily a good indicator of present abuse." Conversely, an addicted offender does not necessarily have to be behind bars as the result of a drug crime. The two issues, however—drug use and criminal behavior—are decidedly linked, and corrections professionals must be aware that many of the offenders they encounter will be suffering from a substance abuse problem.

According to a BJS national report (1992, p. 3), a 1990 drug use forecasting program showed a wide range in the rate of arrestees testing positive for drugs. The rate of male arrestees testing positive for drugs was 30 to 78 percent—anywhere from about one in three to nearly four out of five. For female arrestees, the rate of those testing positive for drugs ranged from 39 to 76 percent—two in five up to three out of four. Although these ranges are quite wide, the forecasting program calculated at least one-third of male and female arrestees tested positive for drugs. Furthermore, about 20 percent of both male and female arrestees tested positive for two or more drugs. The drug found most often in the urine of arrestees was cocaine. McBride and McCoy (p. 265) state: "a study of nonincarcerated delinquents in Miami, Florida . . . found that some three fourths of male and female delinquents used cocaine at least weekly."

> A substantial number of offenders use drugs regularly, and many are addicted. Over a third of all male and female arrestees tested positive for drugs, the most common being cocaine.

The problem of drug use doesn't end when offenders are placed behind bars. According to McBride and McCoy (p. 266): "There is also a body of research that indicates a high level of drug use among incarcerated individuals. In a study of Delaware prison inmates . . . 60% of the respondents reported the use of drugs, mostly marijuana, while in prison." Most prison systems now use regular urinalysis to detect such drug use.

Characteristics of Drug Offenders

A variety of factors may lead an individual to become an addict. According to Josi and Sechrest (1993, p. 356): "Substance abuse problems are lifestyle problems. They do not yield to counseling alone or just to employment, or job training, or other solutions to social problems." Although a number of elements may contribute to a person's drug problem, several commonalities have been found among different types of drug offenders. Vito et al. studied a drug testing program and drew some general conclusions about the offenders involved. Among their findings (p. 349): "Caucasians were more likely to test positive for marijuana (20.5%, 149/726), whereas Blacks had a higher positive rate for cocaine (24.9%, 232/931)." Vito et al. (pp. 349–350) also found:

Caucasians who tested positive for marijuana were more likely

- To be male.
- To be younger (mean age = 28.9).

- To have an admitted drug problem.
- To be supervised in some other manner than intensive supervision.

Blacks testing positive for marijuana were more likely

- To be male.
- To be younger (mean age = 30.05).
- To be property rather than drug offenders.
- To have an admitted drug problem.
- To be on probation (both felony and misdemeanant).

Vito et al. (p. 350) conclude: "Regardless of race, it appears that young males with admitted drug problems are likely to use marijuana." These authors also found that race was a factor in cocaine abuse (p. 350):

For Blacks, cocaine use was associated with

- A high number of prior alcohol and drug arrests.
- Females.
- Offenses other than drug, property, or violent crimes.
- An admitted drug problem.
- Probation.
- Levels of supervision other than intensive.

Whites who abused cocaine were likely

- To have a higher than average number of prior alcohol and drug arrests.
- To be cross-addicted (admitted problems with both drugs and alcohol).
- To be on probation and on some other level of supervision than intensive.

Wellisch et al. (1994, p. 2) noted the following characteristics of drug-abusing women offenders:

- Health problems, including physical or mental illness.
- History of unemployment and inadequate vocational skills.
- Psychosocial problems caused by abusive family conditions.
- Parenting issues (lack of family support, limited financial resources).
- Drug use with limited exposure to treatment.
- Involvement in the criminal justice system and child protective services.

Effects of Drug Use

Corrections professionals must be prepared for offenders who are drunk, high or otherwise under the immediate effects of drugs or who are suffering from the long-term debilitating effects of previous drug use. Besides addiction, drug use may lead to a variety of chronic physical problems. Alcoholic offenders may have serious liver damage or health problems brought on by years of poor nutrition. The BJS states (1992, p. 10): "Repeated use of opiates such as heroin impairs immune response. Compromised immune function may increase narcotic-dependent persons' susceptibility to the various infections that accompany use of unsterile, often shared injection equipment. Injecting drugs has been associated with viral hepatitis, infection and inflammation of the heart or valves, pneumonia, blood poisoning, meningitis, and in recent years with human inmunodeficiency virus (HIV) infection."

Drug users are also "at increased risk for extreme weight loss, dehydration, digestive disorders, skin problems, dental problems, gynecological and venereal infections, tuberculosis, hepatitis B, hypertension, seizures, respiratory arrest, and cardiac failure" (Daley and Przybycin, 1989). Furthermore, the diseases carried by drug-using offenders can place the rest of the inmate population at risk.

In addition to physical effects of drug use, addicted offenders may suffer from numerous psychological and emotional effects. Regarding juvenile drug users, the BJS (p. 11) notes: "These drug users are at higher risk than nonusers for a range of mental health problems including suicidal thoughts, attempted suicide, completed suicide, depression, poor conduct, and personality disorders." Adult drug users are equally susceptible to these drug-related mental health problems.

Needs of Addicted Offenders

Chemically addicted offenders need programming to help them overcome the physical and psychological harms of their drug use. Drug testing is one valuable tool in handling these offenders, and corrections professionals, particularly those in probation and parole functions, may have a significant impact on whether addicted offenders receive the necessary treatment. The findings of Vito et al. (p. 353) "strongly indicate that drug testing, together with treatment, enhances the effectiveness of community supervision and, consequently, public safety. . . . Probation and parole officers should make every effort to take advantage of drug testing as a treatment referral and client-monitoring tool. They should make every effort to identify clients in need of treatment, refer these clients to treatment, and keep these clients in treatment." Furthermore, successful completion of treatment lowers the likelihood of recidivism.

Addicted offenders also have other needs related to their immediate need to get off drugs. According to the BJS (1992, p. 199):

> Other treatment or services may include therapeutic communities, drug education, behavior modification, acupuncture, family therapy, relapse prevention training, and development of coping and interpersonal skills. Services intended to enhance offenders' ability to remain drug-free may also be provided. These might include

Substance abuse counseling provides a support network for addicted offenders and teaches them ways to live drug-free.

academic education, job training, job placement, employment interviewing and job-search skills training, life skills training (for example, cooking, health and hygiene, personal finance), field trips to cultural events, and parenting skills.

Providing access to 12-step programs such as Alcoholics Anonymous and Narcotics Anonymous is another route taken by many correctional facilities.

Regarding female offenders, Wellisch et al. (p. 1) note: "Although significant percentages of drug-abusing women offenders are in jail, prison, or under community supervision, little is known concerning their specific service needs." These authors further state (p. 5): "It is notable that services needed by women are more likely to be found in women-only programs than in programs that serve both men and women. This finding suggests that the specific needs of women are an afterthought in many programs."

One of the hazards associated with drug use is the increased risk of becoming infected with HIV. With the number of drug-using offenders on the rise, it follows that the number of HIV-infected offenders is also on the rise.

HIV-Infected Offenders

➤ **Human immunodeficiency virus (HIV)** destroys white blood cells in the body which are critical to fighting infection. HIV infection compromises the body's immune system, making a person more vulnerable to other illnesses.

HIV infection can also lead to **acquired immune deficiency syndrome (AIDS),** which encompasses a wide spectrum of reactions and symptoms and often leads to death. The Centers for Disease Control (CDC) requires that for a patient to be diagnosed with AIDS, the person must have one or more "opportunistic infections" or cancers in the absence of all other known underlying causes of immune deficiency. Symptoms associated with AIDS include fever, weight loss, diarrhea and persistently swollen lymph nodes.

The number of cases of HIV infection and AIDS is leveling off in the general American population due to education, yet the problem is still severe among today's correctional population. According to Maruschak (1997, p. 4): "At the end of 1995, the rate of confirmed AIDS in State and Federal prisons was more than 6 times higher than in the total U.S. population." She also reports 1,010 AIDS-related deaths among state inmates in 1995, accounting for over a third (34.2 percent) of all state prisoner deaths during the year, a rate of 109 deaths per 100,000 state inmates. Furthermore (p. 5): "The number of AIDS-related deaths in prison increased 94% from 1991 to 1995," making AIDS the fastest rising cause of state inmate deaths. Additionally (p. 8): "At midyear 1993, when the last national census of local jails was conducted, 1.8% of the inmates were known to be HIV positive."

Characteristics of HIV-Infected Offenders

While no segment of the population is immune to this disease, certain populations show a higher frequency of HIV infection. Lachance-McCullough et al. (1994, p. 200) note: "Minorities are disproportionately impacted by the AIDS epidemic. In fact, the sociodemographics of HIV/AIDS look strikingly similar to the sociodemographics of American prisons." Olivero (1992, p. 50) states: "Most of those infected in prison are disproportionately members of minority groups; they tend to be black and Hispanic."

Furthermore, female inmates have been shown to test positive for HIV at higher rates than male inmates. According to Maruschak (p. 6): "From 1991 to 1995 the number of male State inmates infected with HIV increased 28%, while the number of female inmates infected increased at a much faster rate—88%." Numerous other studies support this trend.

> HIV-infected offenders are more frequently minorities (Blacks and Hispanics) and women.

HIV-infected offenders are not distributed equally throughout the jails and prisons of the United States. Maruschak (p. 1) states: "New York held more than a third of all inmates (9,500) known to be HIV positive at yearend 1995."

Becoming HIV-Infected

HIV is not transmitted through casual contact such as holding hands, having a face-to-face conversation or the like. When body fluids are exchanged is where the risk of HIV infection lies. An individual may become infected with HIV several ways, including sexual intercourse with an infected person, sharing an intravenous needle with an infected person or receiving a blood transfusion from an infected person. Careful screening of donated blood has significantly lowered the risk of becoming HIV-infected during a transfusion. However, the other two well-known avenues of infection continue to pose great risk for those who travel them.

Many criminally active individuals often engage in other risk-taking behaviors, such as sharing needles or having unprotected sex with other intravenous drug users, thereby increasing their chances of contracting the virus. The CDC (1993) has concluded that the high rates of HIV infection and AIDS among women offenders are essentially the result of intravenous drug use and
➤ intercourse with male **injecting drug users (IDUs).**

Offenders who enter corrections already infected with the virus may transmit it to other inmates several ways. According to Olivero (p. 39): "No one knows the prevalence of illegal intravenous drug use inside jails and prisons. One possibility is that the scarcity of hypodermic needles within correctional facilities leads to greater sharing. Further, tattooing involving needles is also common in prisons." Homosexual activity among inmates is another way the virus is passed on.

Consequences of Being HIV-Positive Behind Bars

Although life is rarely easy for any inmate, it is often made even more difficult by being HIV-positive. Lachance-McCullough et al. (p. 213) note: "That dangers exist in being a known HIV positive prison inmate, ranging from social isolation to physical abuse, has been well documented in the literature." Olivero (p. 50) states: "It appears that inmates and some prison administrators share society's repulsion of AIDS victims. Prisoners found to be infected by AIDS are an 'outgroup' and are stigmatized within the prison community."

Many noninfected inmates are still uncertain how the virus is transmitted and, therefore, fear the presence of those who carry HIV. Consequently, AIDS education is becoming an increasingly important program for inmates in all prisons. Of course such education also serves to prevent further spread of the infection among inmates.

Correctional staff also have legitimate concerns about the transmission of HIV. The policy in prisons and jails is to assume all inmates are HIV-positive and to treat everyone the same, as they do in hospitals.

Many court cases have arisen over safety concerns of HIV/AIDS-infected inmates as well as the safety of other inmates and correctional staff. Olivero

(p. 43) notes: "The courts have held that the segregation of infected inmates for their safety is justified. The courts have also supported segregation policies despite the request of infected inmates to remain in the general population." However, Olivero (p. 45) also states: "The current trend is to 'mainstream' rather than routinely segregate those found to be AIDS infected. Such a policy permits all categories of infected inmates to remain in the general population."

Needs of HIV-Infected Offenders

Some persons infected with HIV may be asymptomatic, not even knowing they have the virus. Others may know they are HIV-positive but may be just as healthy as noninfected inmates. Still others, however, may have developed AIDS or other health problems as a result of the virus and may need substantial medical treatment. Inmates in the terminal stage of AIDS will need intensive medical care. Since HIV compromises the body's ability to fight infection and resist disease, those who are infected, whatever their stage of the disease, need to be kept away from inmates with contagious illnesses and other conditions that might overwhelm their suppressed immune system. When segregation is used to isolate HIV-infected inmates, these inmates need to be properly cared for and not denied services or programming available to the general prison population.

AIDS education may also serve the needs of the infected offender. By raising the level of knowledge among noninfected inmates and correctional staff, the stress caused by ignorance and fear should diminish, making life behind bars a little more tolerable for those who are HIV-positive. Such education also serves the general inmate population by providing them with knowledge on how to avoid becoming infected.

Martin et al. (1993) found that, of the 49 states that responded to their national survey, 48 had some type of HIV/AIDS education programming for inmates. Hogan (1994, p. 240) states:

> To encourage effective attitude and behavioral changes, educational programs must focus on the everyday meanings and interpretations to uncover the hidden risks that inmates are not aware of. The ingredients to good program content include the complete presentation of risky behaviors, sensitivity to racial, cultural and gender differences, effective selection of communication modes through the use of combining two learning paradigms, and ongoing evaluation of the program and its effectiveness.

Unfortunately, some predict a rather bleak outlook for HIV-infected offenders. Olivero (pp. 49–50) states: "The future for inmates infected with AIDS does not appear to be bright. Public attitudes have translated into government neglect for conditions inside prisons, especially in regard to prisoners with AIDS. . . . We can anticipate a future of overcrowded prison facilities, with little governmental attention or public outcry focused on the special needs of AIDS-infected inmates."

Prisoner Sean Paul Simon, 28, wearing a "spit shield," is escorted through the Butte County Superior Court lobby Thursday, July 17, 1997, in Oroville, California, by his lawyer and court security officers. Simon, who is HIV-positive, allegedly spit in a Butte County jailer's mouth two years earlier and was being arraigned for attempted murder. The State argued Simon's intent was to infect the jailer, who had not contracted the disease.

Those infected with HIV may also be coinfected with another type of infection, tuberculosis, a disease that poses great challenges for corrections officials and may spread rapidly among the closely confined population within correctional facilities.

Tuberculosis-Infected Offenders

Tuberculosis, or TB, is "an airborne disease, transmitted via droplet nuclei (e.g., the dried residue of droplets from sneezes or coughs) from patients who have pulmonary or laryngeal TB and who cough, laugh, spit, or otherwise emit sputum containing the TB bacteria (called *Mycobacterium tuberculosis*)" (Wilcock et al., 1996, p. 5). TB poses a much greater health risk among prison populations than does HIV because it spreads relatively easily through the air: "TB can be transmitted through repeated exposure in crowded, poorly ventilated environments; it does not require intimate contact" (Wilcock et al., p. 5). The bacteria destroys lung tissue, which is then replaced by fibrous connective tissue (scarring on the lungs). This thicker connective tissue is inelastic and interferes with breathing, hampering gas exchange and eventually causing suffocation.

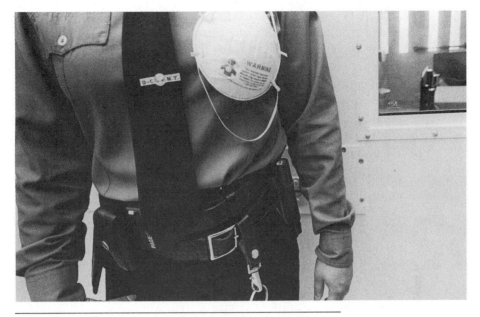

A correctional officer at the Rikers Island Contagious Disease Unit keeps a face mask handy. The CDU houses mainly inmates with TB.

Wilcock et al. identify the health concern presented by TB to corrections officials (p. 1): "Corrections facilities house men and women who often come from those segments of the community with high rates and risk of TB because of such factors as poverty, poor living conditions, substance abuse, and HIV/AIDS. Overcrowding in a correctional facility increases the potential for close and repeated contact with an active case of TB."

Similar to the situation with HIV and AIDS, an individual may be infected with TB but not show active symptoms of the disease. This is a dangerous scenario for corrections because individuals carrying TB can be infectious for a long time and therefore able to transmit the infection and disease to other inmates and staff. Consequently, TB-infected offenders are considered a special need population because of the medical need to identify, isolate and treat this group before the disease spreads.

A skin test called a purified protein derivative (PPD) is typically used to identify TB-positive individuals. Regarding TB infection among inmates during 1994, Wilcock et al. (p. 3) report: "(PPD) skin tests administered at intake produced positive reactions in more than 68,000 State/Federal and over 14,000 city/county inmates, according to survey responses." These numbers underestimate the true extent of the problem, as not every correctional facility in the country responded to the survey (p. 2). Nonetheless, the numbers indicate a significant number of TB-infected inmates among U.S. correctional populations.

Complicating the matter is the high incidence of false negative TB skin tests among those also infected with HIV. When an individual is coinfected with both HIV and TB, the PPD test for TB often comes out negative and the infected individual, logically, isn't treated. Furthermore, TB can become resistant to the leading medications, and the resistant strain may be spread among the other inmates and staff. Wilcock et al. (p. 1) note: "[R]ecent prison outbreaks of multidrug-resistant tuberculosis (MDR-TB) raise the threat of an often untreatable disease spreading in a closely confined population."

To combat the problem of TB, the Centers for Disease Control and Prevention (CDC) recommend all facility types screen incoming inmates and isolate those found to have symptoms. Wilcock et al. (p. 6) state:

> Symptom screening involves checking for signs and symptoms of TB through a systematic interview that inquires about persistent, productive cough; chest pain; coughing up blood; fever, chills, and night sweats; loss of appetite and weight loss; and tiring easily, especially during the preceding 6 weeks. Symptom screening should be performed as soon as possible. During the regular medical evaluation, inmates should be asked whether they have had TB disease, been treated, or received preventive therapy for TB.

An offender who is identified as TB-positive and infectious should be removed from the general inmate population (p. 7):

> A primary TB control measure is the isolation of infectious cases to prevent spreading the disease to other inmates. The most common and recommended isolation measure in prisons and jails is use of negative-pressure isolation rooms (i.e., isolation rooms with ventilation that does not flow into the general ventilation system) either in the infirmary or in a community hospital.

Just as corrections has a responsibility to protect society from those who have wronged it, so too does it have a responsibility to not release inmates who have acquired TB while incarcerated who may then spread the disease among the community. As Wilcock et al. (p. 12) conclude: "Following CDC guidelines, strong TB prevention, treatment, and control programs in correctional facilities can help contain the spread of TB within the greater community."

Sex Offenders

➤ Not surprisingly, as other segments of the correctional population are growing, so too are the number of sex offenders. A **sex offender** is one who commits a sexual act prohibited by law. In many states, sex offenders are the largest prison population. However, because of the nature of the offense, the extreme personal violation and the fact that many sex offenses are committed by offenders known to the victim (either a friend or family member), a high percentage are not reported to the police. Therefore, it is impossible to get an accurate picture of the total number of sex offenders in the United States.

According to Wees (1996, p. 10): "The nation's prisons held nearly 107,000 sex offenders in 1995, an increase of approximately 9% over the total reported in 1993." Greenfeld (1997, p. 2) notes: "On a given day about 234,000 offenders convicted of rape or sexual assault are under the care, custody, or control of corrections agencies. About 60% of these sex offenders are under conditional supervision in the community."

Most sex offenders prosecuted in the United States are men—a ratio of 200 to 300 men for every 1 woman. Most sex offenders in treatment programs are between 18 and 35 years old. Furthermore, research shows that many sex offenders began offending as juveniles and were victims of abuse themselves. As noted by Musk et al. (1997, p. 25): "Sixty to 80 percent of adult incarcerated pedophiles started acting on their pedophilia as juveniles. In fact, 30 to 50 percent of child sexual molestations are perpetrated by juveniles, which speaks to the problem faced in juvenile correctional facilities. Corollary to these facts, about half of inmate pedophiles were, themselves, sexually abused as children."

> Most sex offenders are between the ages of 18 and 35, the vast majority are men and many were sexually abused as children. Approximately two-thirds of sex offenders are serving their sentences in the community.

Types of Sex Offenders

Many sex offenders commit crimes where no physical contact takes place with another person (window peeping, indecent exposure and so on). One type of sex offender is the child sexual abuser, an adult who uses minors in a variety of sexual activities, including child pornography and sexual intercourse. A **pedophile,** or child molester, is sexually attracted to children. Musk et al. (p. 24) state: "Pedophilia is a sexual orientation, just like heterosexuality or homosexuality. . . . [P]edophiles do not ask to be sexually attracted to children." They frequently have little choice.

➤   Another type of sex offender is the **sexual predator,** an individual who commits violent sexual acts such as rape-mutilations and lust-murders. According to Greenfeld (p. 3): "After the latter half of the 1980's, the percentage of all murders with known circumstances in which investigators identified rape or another sex offense as the principal circumstance of the murder has declined from about 2% of murders to less than 1%." Furthermore: "Offenders in sexual assault murders are about 6 years younger on average than other murderers." These violent predators, about 1 percent of all sex offenders, are the ones typically locked up in maximum-security prisons, often on death row, and are generally deemed incapable of benefiting from any treatment program the facility might offer. The vast majority of sex offenders, however, are given less severe sanctions in an attempt to reform their deviant behavior.

Treatment of Sex Offenders

While many contend that certain types of sex offenders do not consciously choose to act the way they do, it is believed these offenders can benefit from behavior modification therapy and counseling, learning ways to control their urges or avoid situations that present the opportunity to commit a sex offense. As noted by Musk et al. (p. 28): "Approximately 1,500 programs nationally provide some form of treatment for sex offenders." Lotke (1996, p. 3) states: "Most research shows that sex offenders do indeed respond positively to treatment." Lotke continues: "The conclusion that treatment reduces recidivism can be refined further by distinguishing between different kinds of sex offenders. Treatment cuts the recidivism rate among exhibitionists and child molesters by more than a half, yet cuts recidivism among rapists by just a few percent. Juveniles respond very positively to treatment, indicating that treating sex offenders as soon as they are identified can prevent an escalation of their pathology."

Others, however, are more skeptical about the effectiveness of such therapy. Regarding pedophiles, Musk et al. (p. 24) note: "For most pedophiles, their condition is a curse which can destroy their lives, sometimes leading to decades of imprisonment." Yet: "Just as no therapy is likely to change the sexual orientation of a woman who prefers a man, it is improbable that therapy will change the desire of a pedophile for a child."

Nonetheless, most corrections professionals agree that many sex offenders need and can benefit from some form of treatment or counseling. Warehousing these individuals is *not* a solution. Since many categories of sex offenses are not pursued or prosecuted by the criminal justice system, many offenders are never placed in a position to receive treatment. And offenders of more violent sex offenses, such as rape-murders, sex-tortures and sex-mutilations, are deemed beyond the benefit or effectiveness of any form of treatment. Five types of sex offender account for the overwhelming majority of treatment program participants:

1. Rapists and would-be (attempted) rapists.
2. Child molesters (pedophiles).
3. Those who commit incest.
4. Exhibitionists and voyeurs.
5. Other offenders (those who break and enter, commit arson and so on, where the criminal action is sexually motivated).

Several exemplary sex offender treatment programs exist across the country. Oregon's Snake River Correctional Institution (SRCI) is a medium-security prison where 98 percent of the inmates are sex offenders. When the facility opened in 1991, only 18 to 20 percent of the inmate population consisted of sex offenders. But as SRCI developed and gained success with its sex offender treatment programs, non–sex offenders were gradually transferred out of the facility to make room for sex offenders, and within a year the proportion of sex offenders had grown to 98 percent.

Lester (1995, p. 168) notes: "Oregon's Department of Corrections and Mental Health and Developmental Disability Services Division, through an interagency agreement, have developed a comprehensive approach . . . not focused on curing the sex offender, but rather on providing sex offenders both internal (e.g., treatment) and external (e.g., lifetime registration, community notification, polygraphs) controls to manage their own behavior and to provide timely interventions when necessary." Interestingly, SRCI has experienced fewer behavioral/security issues than traditional prisons, and inmates report feeling safer there than at other correctional institutions (Lester, p. 170).

Some treatment programs exist in a "postcorrectional" environment, with offenders admitted after serving a criminal sentence. According to Harry and Shank (1996, p. 82): "Minnesota is among a handful of states taking new measures to address the problem of repeat sexual offenders. The trend is treatment with an emphasis on relapse prevention. The Minnesota difference is that sexual psychopaths can be committed civilly after completing criminal sentences if there is a mental or sexual disorder or dysfunction that is likely to lead to further offending." These authors state (p. 85): "The most promising new treatment focuses on helping sex offenders control the cycle of troubling emotions, distorted thinking and deviant fantasies that lead to their sex crimes."

A study sponsored by the National Institute of Justice (English et al., 1997, p. 3) details a five-part containment process for sex offenders in community corrections:

> The model process for managing adult offenders in the community is a containment approach that seeks to hold offenders accountable through the combined use of both offenders' internal controls and external control measures (such as the use of the polygraph and relapse prevention plans). A containment approach requires the integration of a collection of attitudes, expectations, laws, policies, procedures, and practices that have clearly been designed to work together. This approach is implemented through interagency and interdisciplinary teamwork.

According to this model, three basic elements work together to "contain" the sex offender (pp. 3–4):

1. *Therapists* trained to help sex offenders achieve personal control of their deviant sexual thoughts, feelings, impulses and behaviors.

2. *Probation and parole officers* who provide clear expectations and apply pressure through use or threatened use of sanctions to guarantee the offender complies with treatment and supervision conditions.

3. *Regular polygraph examinations* to monitor the offender's deviant fantasies and external behaviors, particularly access to victims.

As stated by English et al. (p. 4): "Maintaining close communication and acting as a team, the treatment provider, probation/parole officer, and polygraph examiner form a triangle of supervision, with the offender contained in the middle" (Figure 10–1). They conclude (p. 9):

> The five-part model process to contain adult sex offenders establishes a framework within which agencies and communities can develop specific practices to better promote public safety and victim protection and assistance. Just as the stringency of the supervision triangle should be tailored to the individual characteristics of each sex offender, so should the method of implementing the model process vary according to the needs of each community.
>
> Incremental improvement in the model process and in underlying case management practices will flow from new research findings and feedback from the field. But the bottom line of sex offender management in community settings should not change: public and victim safety first.

While some programs appear to have achieved success with the treatment of sex offenders, few correctional facilities have implemented such programs and

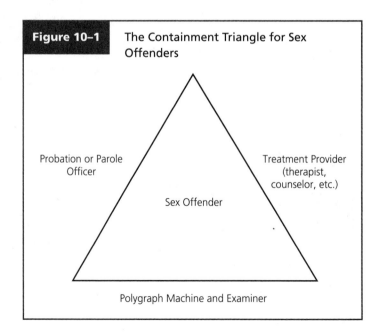

Figure 10–1   The Containment Triangle for Sex Offenders

Probation or Parole Officer

Treatment Provider (therapist, counselor, etc.)

Sex Offender

Polygraph Machine and Examiner

many correctional agencies lack a comprehensive community treatment alternative. Until such efforts are made successful, this serious problem will continue.

High-Profile Offenders

High-profile offenders, while relatively rare, are often the offenders the general public thinks of when they think of criminals, because of the unusual amount of media coverage involved. Because of their notoriety, these offenders have needs that lesser-known offenders do not have, including the need for protection from others who might themselves seek notoriety by causing harm to the high-profile offender.

These high-profile offenders are often placed in high-security facilities not only to keep them from getting out but to keep others from getting in to cause them harm. Within prisons, there are inmates who wish to bring harm to some high-profile offenders whose crimes were particularly gruesome. One report provides such an example ("Can Inmates Ever," 1995, p. 1):

> One of the nation's most infamous inmates was murdered in prison [in the fall of 1994]. Jeffrey Dahmer, who was serving 16 consecutive life terms for murdering, mutilating and cannibalizing 17 young men and boys, was one of two men bludgeoned to death at the Columbia Correctional Institution in Portage, Wis.
>
> . . . That fatal attack wasn't the first time Dahmer's life had been placed in jeopardy. [During the summer of 1994] he was the target of an attack with a homemade weapon fashioned from a toothbrush—but the weapon broke before it could cause any harm.

In a presentation to the American Jail Association addressing the topic of housing the high-profile inmate, Commander Daniel Burt (1996) related the experiences of the Los Angeles County Sheriff's Department. The Los Angeles County Jail system has housed numerous high-profile individuals over the years, including Errol Flynn, Bugsy Siegel, Sirhan Bishara Sirhan, Charles Manson, Bianchi/Bono, Richard Ramirez (the Night Stalker), Sean Penn, Christian Brando, Eric and Lyle Menendez and O.J. Simpson. Burt's presentation was meant to disseminate information regarding some lessons learned by L.A. County.

Although the geographic proximity of the entertainment industry heavily influences the number of high-profile persons housed at the L.A. County Jail, Commander Burt notes: "Today any jail manager can find himself/herself in a situation where a celebrity/notorious individual/superstar is in their custody" (for instance, the jail in the middle of Wyoming where convicted bomber Timothy McVeigh was initially held).

When a high-profile individual comes into a correctional facility, it can become "a very intense environment and busy place—literally overnight" (Burt). Correctional facilities face several critical areas of consideration when planning for the potential housing of a high-profile individual:

- Personnel selection.
- The physical plant.
- Security.
- Legal implications.
- The media.

Personnel selection is an important factor when handling high-profile offenders. Facilities should select the most mature individuals, those who are resistant to becoming "star struck" and are able to professionally distance themselves from the inmate. Thoroughly brief key personnel beforehand to ensure everyone understands the compromises that can occur when working with high-profile inmates. Integrity is also a factor—choose staff who won't be inclined to sell their story or otherwise exploit their involvement with the offender. The allure of the media and press offers can be very enticing and overwhelming. Rotate key personnel, and review policies concerning inappropriate staff/inmate relationships or fraternization. Constantly monitor for the beginning of inappropriate relationships and debrief the staff regularly about the situation. Discuss memorabilia issues with staff and the taking of items used by the inmate as momentos. Use video surveillance to cut down on staff "visits." Burt states: "Constant video monitoring on tape will prevent staff from *dropping by* to say hello to the *superstar.*"

Aspects of the physical plant also require consideration. There should be some degree of physical separation capabilities between the high-profile inmate and the general population. According to Burt: "[Y]ou will lose all order if the *superstar* frequently comes into contact with other inmates." Furthermore, "[m]eals, medical services, visitation, attorney conferences, to name a few, are best accomplished through separation from the rest of the facility population."

Security is an obvious concern. Burt notes: "The *eyes of the world* are on you and your facility—you don't want to lose him, you don't want him to be hurt, you don't want an embarrassing incident, that with anyone else would go unnoticed. Plan accordingly." Although escape is not likely, death threats can be, both from outside and within the correctional facility. As Burt states: "Be mindful of the *threat from within*—what better way for a fellow inmate to be recorded in history." Security at the courtroom is another issue, with many concerns about the media and spectators. The influx of mail can also create a security issue. Burt recommends: "Negotiate with the defense and use them as the first filter."

The legal aspects of housing a high-profile individual are another concern. Burt suggests: "Consider obtaining *dedicated counsel* to assist you with the endless legal issues and defense motions regarding how you house the high-profile inmate. *Remain as neutral as possible with respect to the prosecution vs. the defense. You will end up with everyone upset with you if you play any other role than the role of the 'jailer.'* Learn to 'whistle Dixie and the Battle Hymn of the Republic with equal enthusiasm!' "

Finally, correctional institutions need to consider the media when housing high-profile offenders. Burt has several recommendations regarding media relations: "Understand, and accept, that the media's first job is to get the story. . . . Know *your* media before you meet them for the first time in a crisis situation. . . [and] familiarize the media with appropriate aspects of your operations." It is advisable to designate a press information officer (PIO), one person who is trained to disseminate information to the media and who can build a rapport with these professionals. It is also recommended that correctional facilities have written policies regarding press relations and information leakage. This is another instance where a PIO can be valuable—train other staff members to direct all media questions to the PIO to ensure accuracy and protection of information the facility is not yet prepared to discuss.

Burt also advises: "The media *out of towners* will descend on you from all directions during a truly *big story* and you won't know who they are. Consider asking your local media to take charge and organize the others. Local *media associations* work wonders if you ask them to perform this service for you." A final word of advice: "Be impartial or else they'll kill you. Do not play favorites. Information that you release must be released to everyone at the same time."

Offenders connected to highly political or religious issues also pose special challenges to corrections. The antiabortionist serving time for murdering an abortion doctor or the militia member behind bars for bombing a federal building are examples of high-profile offenders who may require special attention to ensure their safety while incarcerated. Other possible high-profile offenders might include those in the criminal justice professions (judges, police officers, corrections officers and so on). The likelihood exists for these individuals to meet offenders they helped "put away." Therefore, this population may also require special handling.

Summary

Today's correctional system must deal not only with increased numbers of offenders but an increased variety of "special needs" offenders as well. The population of America's elderly inmates is increasing rapidly, with their numbers doubling every four years. Mentally disabled offenders are often the targets of practical jokes and sexual harassment, are very susceptible to inmate manipulation, are abnormally prone to injury, have difficulty adjusting to the rules and regulations of the facility, are reluctant to partake in activities and programming due to a desire to hide their deficiencies and perform poorly before review committees, resulting in more frequent parole denial.

Mental retardation is a permanent deficiency in mental capacity and is not treatable. Mental illness is a disease and is often treatable given the proper psychiatric care. Nearly 30 percent of mentally ill individuals in jail have committed no crime but are being held behind bars until space becomes available in a mental hospital. The four most common offenses committed by the mentally ill in jail are assault and/or battery, theft, disorderly conduct and drug- and alcohol-related offenses.

A substantial number of offenders use drugs regularly and many are addicted. Over a third of all male and female arrestees tested positive for drugs, the most common being cocaine. HIV-infected offenders are more frequently minorities (Blacks and Hispanics) and women. Most sex offenders are between the ages of 18 and 35, the vast majority are men and many were sexually abused as children. Approximately two-thirds of sex offenders are serving their sentences in the community, either on probation or parole.

Discussion Questions

1. Given that, on average, the annual cost of incarceration for elderly inmates is nearly $50,000 more, per individual, than for the general inmate population, can you think of ways to alleviate the financial burden of caring for these elderly offenders?

2. Which side do you tend to agree with: wider use of early release for elderly inmates or keeping elderly inmates incarcerated for as long as their sentences allow? Why?

3. Do you agree that mentally retarded offenders should *not* be immune from the death penalty? Why or why not?

4. For the nearly 30 percent of mentally ill individuals held in our nation's jails who've committed no crime but are awaiting space in a mental hospital, what might be some better alternatives?

5. Should people who receive capital punishment have their sentence commuted if they become mentally ill while incarcerated? Why or why not?

6. Considering the difficulties, if not impossibilities, in completely stopping all sexual or drug use activities in correctional facilities, should condoms or IV needles be made available to inmates to prevent the spread of HIV and other diseases?

7. Has your local correctional facility held any high-profile offenders recently? If so, what were some of the challenges it faced?

8. What programs for special needs offenders are available in your local correctional facilities? Have they met with success?

9. Discuss the plausibility, benefits and drawbacks of designating entire correctional facilities for specific groups of special needs offenders: geriatric, mentally ill, addicted and so on.

10. Which group of special needs offenders do you think poses the greatest challenge for corrections? Why?

References

"Agencies and Facilities Must Comply with New Federal Law on Disabled." *Corrections Today,* August 1992, p. 143.

Appel, Alan. "Requirements and Rewards of the Americans with Disabilities Act." *Corrections Today,* April 1995, pp. 84–86.

Bradley, Sarah. "Graying of Inmate Population Spurs Corrections Challenges." *On the Line,* Vol.13, March 1990, p. 5.

Bureau of Justice Statistics. *Drugs, Crime, and the Justice System: A National Report.* U.S. Government Printing Office, December 1992 (NCJ-133652).

Bureau of Justice Statistics Executive Summary. *Correctional Populations in the United States.* U.S. Department of Justice, April 1995 (NCJ-153849).

Burt, Daniel. "High-Profile Inmates: Housing the Superstar." Presentation to the American Jail Association, St. Louis, MO, May 22, 1996.

Butterfield, Fox. "Aging Prison Population Presents a New Burden for Jailers Across U.S." *New York Times,* quoted in (Minneapolis/St. Paul) *Star Tribune,* July 13, 1997, p. A12.

Camp, George M. and Camp, Camille G. *The Corrections Yearbook—1993.* South Salem, NY: Criminal Justice Institute, 1994.

"Can Inmates Ever Be Watched Closely Enough?" *On the Line,* Vol. 18, No. 2, March 1995, p. 1

Centers for Disease Control. *HIV/AIDS Surveillance Quarterly Report: Year-End Edition.* Atlanta, GA, February 1993.

Craig, Delores E. Assistant professor, Department of Administration of Justice, Wichita State University. Personal correspondence, January 9, 1998.

Cromwell, Paul. "The Graying of America's Prisons." *Overcrowded Times,* June 1994, p. 3.

Daley, B. and Przybycin, C. "Cocaine-Dependent Women Have Unique Treatment Needs." *Addiction Letter,* Vol. 5, No. 10, 1989.

Douglass, Richard L.; Lovett, William; and Lindemann, Mary. "Geriatric Inmates: What Can Be Done with This Growing Population?" *The State of Corrections: Proceedings from the ACA Annual Conferences, 1993.* The American Correctional Association. Springfield, VA: Goodway Graphics, 1994, pp. 149–153.

English, Kim; Pullen, Suzanne; and Jones, Linda. *Managing Adult Sex Offenders in the Community—A Containment Approach.* Research in Brief. Washington, DC: U.S. Department of Justice, National Institute of Justice, January 1997 (NCJ-163387).

George, Mildred M. "Treating Special Needs Offenders." *The State of Corrections: Proceedings from the ACA Annual Conferences, 1992.* The American Correctional Association. Arlington, VA: Kirby Lithographic, 1993, pp. 191–194.

Gondles, James A., Jr. "Planning for the Future of Mental Health Services." *Corrections Today,* December 1993, p. 6.

Gorski, Terence T. "A Prescription for Recovery from Addictive Behaviors." *Corrections Today,* December 1993, pp. 78–82.

Greenfeld, Lawrence A. *Sex Offenses and Offenders.* Executive Summary. Washington, DC: U.S. Department of Justice, Bureau of Justice Statistics, January 1997 (NCJ-163931).

Halvorsen, Donna. "Geriatric Inmates: Move Is Afoot to Start State's First Nursing Home for Elderly Prisoners." (Minneapolis/St. Paul) *Star Tribune,* June 5, 1995, p. B3.

Harry, Rick and Shank, Fred. "Treating Sex Offenders." *Corrections Today,* October 1996, pp. 82–85.

Hogan, Nancy Lynne. "HIV Education for Inmates: Uncovering Strategies for Program Selection." *The Prison Journal,* Vol. 73, No. 2, June 1994, pp. 220–243.

Josi, Don A. and Sechrest, Dale K. "An Evaluation of Substance Abuse Treatment Outcomes for Youthful Parolees." *The Prison Journal,* Vol. 73, Nos. 3 & 4, September/December 1993, pp. 355–378.

Lachance-McCullough, Malcolm L.; Tesoriero, James M.; Sorin, Martin D.; and Stern, Andrew. "HIV Infection Among New York State Female Inmates: Preliminary Results of a Voluntary Counseling and Testing Program." *The Prison Journal*, Vol. 73, No. 2, June 1994, pp. 198–219.

Lester, Thomas L. "Sex Offender Facility Committed to Change and Rehabilitation." *Corrections Today*, April 1995, pp. 168–171.

Lotke, Eric. "Sex Offenders: Does Treatment Work?" *Corrections Compendium*, Vol. XXI, No. 5, May 1996, pp. 1–3.

Martin, R.; Zimmerman, S.; and Long, B. "AIDS Education in U.S. Prisons." *The Prison Journal*, Vol. 73, No. 1, March 1993, pp. 103–129.

Maruschak, Laura. *HIV in Prisons and Jails, 1995*. Washington, DC: U.S. Department of Justice, Bureau of Justice Statistics Bulletin, August 1997 (NCJ-164260).

McBride, Duane C. and McCoy, Clyde B. "The Drugs-Crime Relationship: An Analytical Framework." *The Prison Journal*, Vol. 73, Nos. 3 & 4, September/December 1993, pp. 257–278.

Morton, Joann B. and Anderson, Judy C. "Implementing the Americans with Disabilities Act for Inmates." *Corrections Today*, October 1996, pp. 86–90, 140.

Musk, Henry; Swetz, Anthony; and Vernon, McCay. "Pedophilia in the Correctional System." *Corrections Today*, August 1997, pp. 24–29.

Nadel, Barbara A. "BOP Accommodates Special Needs Offenders." *Corrections Today*, October 1996, pp. 76–79, 136.

"Nation's Jails Holding More of Mentally Ill, Survey Shows." (Minneapolis/St. Paul) *Star Tribune*, September 10, 1992, p. A11.

Neeley, Connie L.; Addison, Laura; and Craig-Moreland, Delores. "Addressing the Needs of Elderly Offenders." *Corrections Today*, August 1997, pp. 120–123.

Olivero, J. Michael. "AIDS in Prisons: Judicial and Administrative Dilemmas and Strategies." In *Corrections: Dilemmas and Directions*, edited by Peter J. Benekos and Alida V. Merlo. Cincinnati, OH: Anderson Publishing Co., 1992, pp. 37–55.

Santamour, Miles and West, Bernadette. *Sourcebook on the Mentally Disordered Prisoner*. Washington, DC: U.S. Department of Justice, 1985.

Silverman, Charles. "Geriatric Inmates—Design and Health Care Considerations." *The State of Corrections: Proceedings from the ACA Annual Conferences, 1993*. The American Correctional Association. Springfield, VA: Goodway Graphics, 1994, pp. 145–148.

Truitt, Henry. "ADA Requirements for Cells in New Correctional Facilities." *The State of Corrections: Proceedings from the ACA Annual Conferences, 1993*. The American Correctional Association. Springfield, VA: Goodway Graphics, 1994, pp. 154–162.

Trupin, Eric; Rahman, Susan; and Jemelka, Ron P. "Mentally Ill Offenders: The Need for Incarceration Alternatives." *The State of Corrections: Proceedings from the ACA Annual Conferences, 1993*. The American Correctional Association. Springfield, VA: Goodway Graphics, 1994, pp. 28–35.

Vito, Gennaro F.; Wilson, Deborah G.; and Holmes, Stephen T. "Drug Testing in Community Corrections: Results from a Four-Year Program." *The Prison Journal*, Vol. 73, Nos. 3 & 4, September/December 1993, pp. 343–354.

Wees, Greg. "Sex Offenders in State and Federal Prisons Top 100,000 Mark." *Corrections Compendium*, May 1996, pp. 10–11.

Wellisch, Jean; Prendergast, Michael L.; and Anglin, M. Douglas. *Drug-Abusing Women Offenders: Results of a National Survey*. National Institute of Justice, Research in Brief. U.S. Government Printing Office, October 1994 (NCJ-149261).

Wilcock, Karen; Hammett, Theodore M.; Widom, Rebecca; and Epstein, Joel. *Tuberculosis in Correctional Facilities 1994–1995*. National Institute of Justice, Research in Brief. U.S. Department of Justice, July 1996 (NCJ-157809).

Case

Ford v. Wainright, 106 S.Ct. 2595 (1986).

11

Correctional Management

Do You Know

➤ What major characteristics describe a bureaucracy?

➤ Who the top correctional administrator is in each state and how they attain this position?

➤ Who the top manager is in a prison facility?

➤ What the basic functions of managers are?

➤ What correctional planning includes?

➤ How organizing relates to the other management functions?

➤ What steps are required in staffing a correctional department or facility?

➤ What the difference is between a manager and a leader?

➤ What the controlling function requires of managers?

➤ What four management styles are found in correctional facilities?

➤ What unit management is?

➤ What management by objectives requires?

➤ How total quality management might be applied in corrections?

➤ Which organization is the authority in setting professional correctional standards?

➤ Which organization is authorized to accredit correctional facilities?

➤ What a facility must do once it receives accreditation?

➤ What the benefits of accreditation are? Drawbacks?

Can You Define

accreditation

assessment centers

audit

authoritarian
  management

authority

autocratic management

budget

bureaucracy

Department of
  Corrections (DOC)

direct supervision
  management (DSM)

goal

Hawthorne effect

inmate control
  management

leader

management by
  objectives (MBO)

manager

objective

participatory
  management

performance-based
  standard

policy

power

shared-powers
  management

standards

total quality
  management (TQM)

unit management

warden

Introduction

The task of running a correctional institution, probation office or an entire system of such programs and facilities, is not as simple as it once was. There was a time when prisons and jails were so isolated from the outside world that little concern was given to what happened behind the walls. Top officials did virtually as they pleased, answering to no one except, perhaps, the governor, and even then there was little interference or regulation. This is no longer the case.

Not only must today's correctional managers know the field of corrections inside and out, but they must also be savvy in business practices, as the corrections profession continues to draw from techniques successfully used in corporate America. With increasing legal pressures and greater emphasis on accountability, correctional managers cannot afford to operate in the isolation enjoyed by their predecessors.

Several major trends have affected prison/corrections administration. These include public accessibility of information, greater media access to prisons and prisoners and legal changes growing out of the civil rights movement (including the "due process revolution"). These trends increase administrator visibility and accountability.

The administration and management of corrections is a topic of significant proportions. This chapter will outline the basic styles of management as well as general functions of administrators in a **Department of Corrections (DOC),** a maximum-security prison or any other specific correctional program. Consult any of the numerous volumes written on correctional administration for such details.

The chapter begins with a look at the overall staff structure of a correctional hierarchy, the network of entities involved in the corrections environment and how various activities are related to each other. Definitions and levels of management are presented next, followed by a profile of today's managers. Correctional management's characteristics and functions are discussed next, followed by management styles, philosophies and techniques. The chapter concludes with a discussion of what many have called one of the best management tools available—accreditation.

Overall Structure and Organization

Corrections does not exist as a distinct, centralized, solitary entity but rather as a complex, decentralized network of people, agencies, philosophies and efforts. Corrections is integrated into the larger society, reflects its sensibilities, responds to its current ideas about justice and addresses what it currently defines as the crime problem. Corrections is influenced by politics, sometimes heavily. Corrections operates within multiple environments. Stojkovic and Lovell (1992, pp. 180–192) define three levels of analysis useful in understanding the complex nature of corrections in the United States: the societal level, the DOC level and the service-delivery level. These three basic levels provide a bureaucratic foundation for the operation of today's corrections.

➤   The concept of **bureaucracy** was first described by Max Weber, a German sociologist and pioneer in the analytical method of sociology, including the study of formal organizations, as a way of describing an ideal organizational design leading to maximum effectiveness. Today's connotation, however, is less positive, often synonymous with delay, duplication and red tape. Following are some characteristics that describe organizations operating under a bureaucratic model:

1. A hierarchy of authority with a downward flow of power.
2. A division of labor with each position clearly defined and no overlap between positions.
3. A reliance on formal rules and procedures to guide the actions of employees (standard operating procedures, or SOPs).
4. An impersonal climate among and between superiors and subordinates and a separation between professional and personal affairs (to keep personal interests from interfering with job performance).
5. Employment and promotional decisions based on merit, with career tracks clearly defined.

> Major characteristics of a bureaucracy include a hierarchy of authority, a division of labor, formal rules and procedures, an impersonal climate and advancement based on merit.

Other characteristics may also be found in bureaucratic organizations, but these are some of the major elements—elements clearly recognizable among the three levels of correctional organization.

The Societal Level

The *societal level* refers to the political, economic and cultural conditions that affect corrections and help shape current policies and practices. This level is broad and nebulous, taking into consideration the abstract concept of social climate which sets the tone for current trends in corrections across the country. This is sometimes envisioned as a pendulum in which public policy swings back and forth between punitive and rehabilitative concerns, as illustrated in Chapter 1.

The Department of Corrections Level

The second level, the *DOC level*, refers to the general administrative entities found in each state that manage and coordinate the individual correctional efforts throughout that state. This level also applies to federal corrections. According to Stojkovic and Lovell (pp. 184–185), the "primary concern at this level is with the contexts for administration of corrections organizations, such as Departments or Divisions of Corrections, normally structured as major elements of state government, and the large organizations established to carry out corrections efforts for the federal government (e.g., the Federal Bureau of Prisons)." Figure 11–1 shows the internal and external environments of the DOC and the variety of entities that interact with and help create the network commonly referred to as corrections. The specific responsibilities of administrators at this level are discussed in the next section.

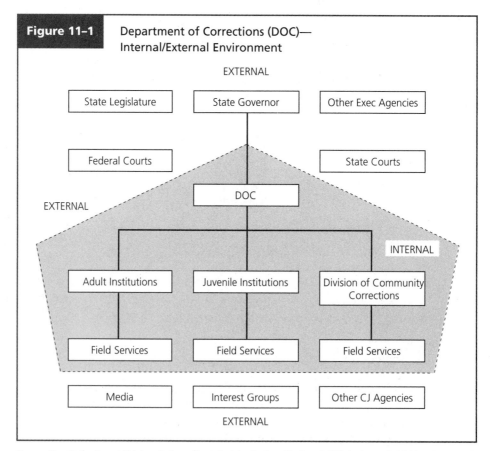

Figure 11–1   Department of Corrections (DOC)— Internal/External Environment

EXTERNAL

State Legislature   State Governor   Other Exec Agencies

Federal Courts   State Courts

EXTERNAL

DOC

INTERNAL

Adult Institutions   Juvenile Institutions   Division of Community Corrections

Field Services   Field Services   Field Services

Media   Interest Groups   Other CJ Agencies

EXTERNAL

Source: Stan Stojkovic and Rick Lovell. *Corrections: An Introduction.* Cincinnati, OH: Anderson Publishing Co., p. 186. Copyright © 1992 by Anderson Publishing Company. Reprinted by permission.

The Service-Delivery Level

Individual correctional facilities and programs are found on the third level of analysis: the *service-delivery level*. This level includes single organizations such as prisons, jails, probation field offices, halfway houses and other facilities that provide correctional services. Such organizations may be part of DOCs or the Federal Bureau of Prisons, or may be any of the many organizations established and controlled through local governments. Each facility operates as part of a larger system and also has an internal and external environment. The typical organization of an adult prison is shown in Figure 11–2. While a bureaucratic model prevails in many correctional settings, the human relations model has also been identified as having relevance for correctional programs and staff. Among the principal elements of the human relations model are

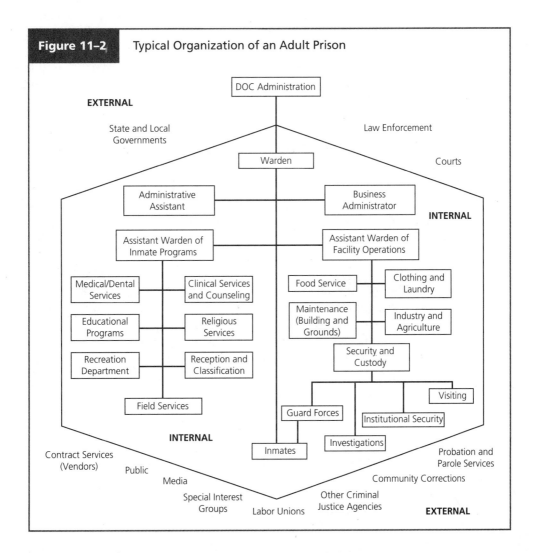

Figure 11–2 Typical Organization of an Adult Prison

1. Shared interests between employer and employee.

2. Recognition of individual differences and the primary importance of the individual.

3. An understanding of the importance of motivation and the need to work toward shared goals.

4. Human dignity, where employees are respected as people, not just as parts of the organization.

Support for the fourth element in the human relations model is provided by a classic experiment conducted during the 1920s and 1930s on employees at the Hawthorne plant of the Western Electric Company in Illinois. This study looked at factors influencing employee productivity. It was discovered that the personal attention directed by management toward their staff resulted in higher productivity even when other elements, such as work breaks, were taken away. This improved attitude and desire to work more productively as a result of improved human relations and working conditions, whether actually

➤ realized by the employees or not, was called the **Hawthorne effect.**

The bureaucratic and human relations models provide two different bases for the various administration and management styles prevalent in today's corrections.

Definitions and Levels of Management

The terms *management* and *administration* are often used interchangeably. In fact, many positions in corrections have more than one commonly used title.

➤ A **manager** controls and directs others, takes charge and coordinates human, material and financial resources to accomplish organizational goals. *To manage* is to get things done through others.

Managers are frequently separated into three levels: executive management, middle management or those commonly referred to as "managers" and first-line management or supervisors. Generally, executives oversee the managers, who oversee the supervisors, who oversee the rest of the staff—thus the hierarchy of authority. Other levels of management may exist depending on the extent of the bureaucracy. Managers must deal with both internal and external issues. Generally, the higher the level of management, the more "global" the issues. Top-level managers tend to focus on the big picture while first-line managers deal more with specifics, details and day-to-day operations.

Who Are Correctional Managers?

The top correctional administrator in the federal system is the director of the Federal Bureau of Prisons. Executive correctional administrators in each state are the

Three levels of correctional management discuss features of a new federal facility. Dr. Kathleen Hawk Sawyer, center, is director of the Federal Bureau of Prisons; Robert Matthews, left, is regional director of the southeast region; and Donald McKelvy, right, is warden of the new Federal Correctional Institute in Yazoo City, Mississippi.

director, commissioner or secretary of the DOC (titles vary by state), which is part of the executive branch of the state government. The top administrator is appointed by the governor and must perform a broad spectrum of functions, including supervising wardens of the state's correctional facilities, preparing and managing the budget, distributing resources among the state's organizations, developing correctional policies, coordinating media and public relations, interacting with the state's legislature and making long-range plans for the state's entire correctional system. In a number of states, the DOC has responsibility for community corrections, probation and parole as well.

> The top correctional administrator in each state is the director of the DOC, appointed by the governor and responsible for a broad spectrum of functions.

Interestingly, the management turnover rate in executive-level positions is very high according to McShane et al. (1991, p. 220): "State prison administrators have the highest rates of attrition of all prison employees." Camp and Camp (1997, p. 106) note: "As of July, 1997, the average length of time an agency director had been in office was 3.6 years. This ranged from a high of 19.1 years in New Jersey to 0.2 years in Maine." Directors may choose to leave because of job dissatisfaction or for a better job opportunity, but most commonly they leave

A female warden talks with prisoners at the Onondaga County
Correctional Facility in Jamesville, New York.

because of a change in state governor. The director's position in virtually all
states is viewed as a political job and is treated accordingly. The same holds true
in several states for appointed managers at other levels of the corrections hierarchy, such as wardens. Consequently, significant discontinuity is possible in correctional policies when administrators come and go.

➤   The administrator in a correctional institution is called a **warden** or superintendent. Because of the nature of the correctional hierarchy, a warden is the top-
level manager in the prison he or she is in charge of but is also considered middle
management when placed under the authority of the director of the DOC. This
discussion of management will refer primarily to the positions of warden and
deputy warden, with correctional officers being discussed in the next chapter.

> The top manager in a prison is the warden or superintendent.

Characteristics of Correctional Administrators

According to Camp and Camp (p. 107): "Wardens with the most years of service
as a warden, in 49 agencies reporting, averaged 14.1 years of service (as of July,
1997). This ranged from 37.7 years for a warden in Florida to 1.8 years for a
warden in Montana." A study of prison wardens' job satisfaction (Cullen et al.,
1993, p. 148) found the following characteristics among these administrators:

"The wardens are predominantly White, college educated, in their mid-40s, and have worked in corrections for nearly two decades, including 5 years at their current institution. Their career history shows that two thirds were in the military, one third were correctional officers, and a majority had held a treatment position in the field of corrections (e.g., counselor in prison, probation officer)."

Today's correctional managers are younger and better educated, although they do not necessarily possess a background in corrections. Women and minorities are still underrepresented in correctional management, although significant progress has been made in many states to lessen this disparity. Table 11–1 shows the distribution of wardens and superintendents by race, ethnicity, sex and facility type as of mid-year 1994.

Management Functions

The management focus changes at the different levels of administration. Executive managers are concerned about the "big picture," policy issues and the long-range goals of the correctional system, whereas middle and first-line managers are more concerned about the day-to-day application of policy and the details of correctional operations. Managers are responsible for some basic functions including planning, organizing, staffing, leading and controlling—a circular, interrelated set of processes.

> The basic functions of managers include planning, organizing, staffing, leading and controlling.

Planning

The planning function of management includes establishing goals and objectives. A **goal** is a broad, general, desired outcome; an **objective** is a specific, measurable way to reach a goal, usually to be accomplished under a specified time line.

Policy development is also part of the general planning function. A **policy** is a plan of action which, like an objective, leads to attaining the organization's goals. With well-defined policies in place, management and staff have a clear course of action to take under any variety of operating conditions. Failure to set policy leaves the institution open to crisis-centered management, an inefficient, potentially dangerous (both physically and legally) situation. Lawsuits and high staff burnout and turnover are possible consequences of crisis-centered management. Managers at the DOC level design broad, general policies for the state's corrections system and leave drafting of more specific policies to managers at each facility.

Table 11–1

Wardens and Superintendents by Race, Ethnicity, Sex and Type of Facility as of June 30, 1994

Jurisdiction	Total	White		Black		Hispanic/Other		Female Administrator/ Male Institution	Female Administrator/ Coed Institution	Male Administrator/ Female Institution	Male Administrator/ Coed Institution
		Male	Female	Male	Female	Male	Female				
State Juvenile Corrections	473	323	59	48	25	14	4	36	36	7	85
State Adult Corrections	1,239	859	115	168	46	45	6	90	8	32	50
Federal Bureau of Prisons	120	87	9	13	2	7	2	0	0	0	0
TOTAL	1,832	1,269	183	229	73	66	12	126	44	39	135

Source: Adapted from Sourcebook of Criminal Justice Statistics, 1995, pp. 92–93.

➤   A financial **budget** is a plan to manage expenditures within available resources during a certain period. Prison wardens usually maintain close contact with the deputy director for administrative services at the DOC to ensure
an acceptable budget is reached and adequate resources are provided.

> The planning function includes setting organizational goals and objectives, establish-
> ing policies and devising a budget.

Organizing

Management must bring order to the organization by subdividing the operation into workable departments and units, establishing programs and services, developing necessary positions to staff these departments and units,
defining methods of accountability for staff, establishing clear lines of communication and coordinating staff efforts to minimize overlap and redundancy and maximize effectiveness and efficiency. The other management
functions may be positively or negatively affected by organizational efforts
(for example, a well-organized system or facility will minimize problems with
staffing, simplify planning and enhance controlling).

> Organizing is an all-encompassing function that extends to and affects the other
> managerial functions.

Staffing

The staffing function is critical for managers; the successful operation of a corrections system or facility depends on having the right people doing the right
things. Institutional managers must be concerned not only with correctional
officers but with the other correctional personnel required to operate the facility, such as food service personnel, medical personnel, maintenance personnel
and programming staff (teachers, counselors). The level of direct involvement
by the director or warden varies among correctional departments and facilities, with some top-level managers very actively involved in staff selection and
others delegating such duties to mid-level human resource managers.

Determining how many and what type of staff are needed is the first step.
With budgets tight, management might be tempted to understaff a facility, but
such a decision may prove more costly in the end. Digges (1994, p. 4) states:
"Under-staffing a prison is asking for trouble. It can lead to disturbances, escapes, lawsuits, and worst of all severe injury or even death of staff."

Recruiting and selecting competent staff and placing them in appropriate
➤ positions are the next steps. Some states have found **assessment centers** particularly helpful in recruiting qualified staff. The assessment center originated

during World War II in the Office of Strategic Services (OSS). It provided rigorous identification and evaluation to thoroughly test selected attributes of prospective officers. As noted by Bennett and Hess (1996, p. 455), using assessment centers to select individuals eligible for promotion, especially at the upper levels, has become a trend.

Training staff, the next step, is a critical function of correctional managers. Sometimes overlooked but essential to the training program is orientation on the institution's mission, philosophy and goals. Training should cover the rules, regulations, policies and procedures of the facility. It should also provide training in human relations skills and strategies to avoid inmate manipulation, diffuse tense situations, maintain self-control during confrontations and make better decisions. Training should be ongoing as new techniques and technology are made available and as staff move into new positions. Unfortunately, many believe correctional personnel, correctional officers in particular, receive inadequate training because of lack of resources, which leads to poor job performance, low morale and an overall failure in the facility to operate efficiently and effectively.

Retaining staff is a final step for managers. Meeting this challenge can be enhanced by several factors. Corrections is an area of high stress, burnout and, consequently, turnover. Providing stress and anger management programs for staff is one way to improve retention levels. Evaluations, transfers and promotions are also part of the staffing function and help in retention by facilitating career development and improving job satisfaction. These processes also ensure that, as the organization's needs and conditions change, staff are repositioned accordingly.

A correctional officer receives training in self-defense.

Handling employee relations and grievances and conducting negotiations with union officials are other management functions.

> The staffing function involves determining how many and what type of staff are needed, recruiting and selecting competent staff, placing them in appropriate positions, training them (initial and ongoing) and retaining them.

When the manager is able to focus on the human element of the organization and influence the staff to work toward the organization's goals, that manager has also become a leader.

Leading

Leadership has many definitions, including

- Working with and through individuals and groups to accomplish organizational goals (Hersey and Blanchard).
- The activity of influencing people to strive willingly for group objectives (G.R. Terry).
- The exercise of influence (Luvern Cunningham).

➤ From these definitions, it follows that a **leader** is one who influences others by example, guides people and motivates them to achieve a common or organizational goal. Leading is a tricky function for many managers because managing sometimes serves to sabotage leading. While managing focuses on tasks and programs, leading focuses on people. Braiden (1994, p. 14) states:

> The most basic difference between leaders and managers is this: Managers think it is their job to run the organization well. That is why, more often than not, managers give themselves ulcers trying to know and control everything. Leaders know it is their job to make sure the organization is run well by others. Leaders concentrate on having the right people, in the right places, doing the right things.

The differences between management and leadership are shown in Table 11–2.

> A primary difference between managers and leaders is that managers focus on tasks while leaders focus on people.

Bennett and Hess (p. 76) note: "Managers may or may not be leaders, and leaders do not have to be managers. A true leader has the potential to influence from any position in the organization, formal or informal." Effective leadership skills are among a manager's most valuable assets.

Table 11–2	Management vs. Leadership

Management	Leadership
Does the thing right	Does the right thing
Tangible	Intangible
Referee	Cheerleader
Directs	Coaches
What you do	How you do it
Pronounces	Facilitates
Responsible	Responsive
Has a view on the mission	Has vision of mission
Views world from inside	Views world from outside
Chateau leadership	Front-line leadership
What you say	How you say it
No gut stake in enterprise	Gut stake in enterprise
Preserving life	Passion for life
Driven by constraints	Driven by goals
Looks for things done wrong	Looks for things done right
Runs a cost center	Runs an effort center
Quantitative	Qualitative
Initiates programs	Initiates an ongoing process
Develops programs	Develops people
Concerned with programs	Concerned with people
Concerned with efficiency	Concerned with efficacy
Sometimes plays the hero	Plays the hero no more

Source: Bill Westfall. "Leadership: Caring for the Organizational Spirit." *Knight Line USA,* May–June 1993, p. 9. Leaders Care for the Spirit reprinted with permission of Executive Excellence magazine, Provo, UT, Sept. 1992, p. 11.

Leading involves treating staff fairly and maintaining morale. Morale is bolstered when managers recognize and praise their subordinates' efforts. Rewarding staff for jobs well done is one of the best moves management can make because it shows personnel that management cares (recall the Hawthorne effect). Leading also involves providing opportunities for growth and fostering a sense of loyalty toward the correctional organization.

Controlling

The controlling function is perhaps what most people think of when they consider the role of managers. Controlling requires the manager to consider a variety of internal and external factors, how they interrelate and how they affect the correctional facility's operation. Furthermore, controlling requires the manager to influence, to the best of his or her ability, these internal and external factors so that their resulting actions benefit the correctional facility. In other words, managers have to *do* something to control outcomes, not just consider them.

> Controlling requires managers to set standards and expectations, know how internal and external factors affect the running of the facility and then *act* to influence these factors to benefit the facility.

Internal Control. Controlling internal factors involves monitoring the department or facility to determine if the goals are being met, supervising staff or those who supervise staff, monitoring inmates' status, evaluating individual and group performance against a set of standards and generally ensuring the correctional organization is on track. Open lines of communication with staff and offenders help managers control the facility's operations.

The controlling function for managers in correctional facilities is challenging because it involves managing people who do not want to be there. Although correctional officers directly supervise the inmates, managers are ultimately responsible for ensuring that the institution operates in a safe and secure manner. Managers need to evaluate the classification process used and make adjustments when appropriate. Managers need to know if programs are effective and if services can be improved or altered to better meet the inmates' needs. Obtaining feedback from inmates and staff helps managers better control the environment. Managers must also make decisions regarding use of good time credits and release options such as furloughs, community corrections and work release.

External Influences. Part of keeping control is maintaining rapport with external entities that affect the correctional system (DOC) or individual facility. For DOC directors, since politics influences corrections, good relations with the state legislature are essential to ensure support for the agency. Furthermore, the legislature passes laws which directly affect the state's correctional system. Similarly, the courts can make life difficult for corrections by issuing consent decrees requiring correctional facilities to meet certain conditions. The media is another external entity that plays a critical role in how the taxpaying public perceives corrections. Establishing and maintaining good communication with the media is pivotal to image management. A reporter who has to pull teeth to get a story may be less inclined to portray corrections favorably, whatever the nature of the story might be.

Controlling may also be thought of as implementing a management style. How a top-level manager chooses to "rule"—with an iron fist or a loose grip—

➤ is how he or she controls the organization. While managers always have the
authority to control, they do not always have the power to control. **Authority**
is the ability to command or enforce laws, rules and policy by virtue of rank or
➤ position—you listen to the boss because he or she is the boss. **Power,** however, is the ability to achieve action and results with or without legal right. Authority uses force. Power uses persuasion. It has been said: "Authority or force
is the use of 10,000 armed troops. Power is a wink." A manager has authority
while a leader has power. The various management styles and philosophies
rely, to some extent, on varying degrees of authority and power.

Management Styles and Philosophies

Correctional management styles have evolved over the decades in response to
a variety of factors, including inmate lawsuits and expanding prisoners'
rights, the increased professionalism of staff and some revolutions about the
general management process.

> Four management styles found in correctional facilities are autocratic or authoritarian
> management, participatory management, shared-powers management and inmate
> control management.

The management styles described are directly reflected by the age of the facility, the expectations of the public and the age/orientation of the administrator.

Autocratic Management

➤ **Autocratic** or **authoritarian management** was prevalent during the early
days of the American prison and was characterized by an almost tyrannical
rule by wardens, who had enormous power and very little accountability.
From the 1820s through the early 1940s, the warden was considered sovereign. These autocratic wardens took full control of their facilities, making
planning, staffing and operating decisions that, unless found unfavorable by
the governor, went unchallenged. Prisoners' rights were of no concern to the
warden. This style of management was rigid and formal, with decisions
made at the top and communication flowing mostly downward. The organizational climate was impersonal. Autocratic wardens did not seek input
from their employees, and, consequently, employees tended to regard management negatively.

In his classic study of prison management, *Governing Prisons* (1987), Di-
Iulio argued such a traditional, autocratic management style was the obvious

choice for those seeking a well-run correctional facility. He advocated a management structure where prison employees are given limited discretion, stating the best prisons "are organized along bureaucratic, even paramilitary, lines and operated strictly 'by the book' " (p. 237). While this style of management may still exist in some correctional facilities to a degree, it is not as common as it was in the past.

Participatory Management

➤ During the 1970s, **participatory management** grew in popularity among correctional managers due to innovations and results demonstrated in corporate management. It was shown that getting employees involved in decision making improved their commitment to organizational goals based on the principle that people are more likely to support that which they help create. Consequently, managers began fostering a participative climate, developing informal relationships with correctional staff and integrating the work group into an effective team. Under this management style, managers respect employees' views and opinions and solicit their input about the work environment.

Results of a study by Wright et al. (1997) of 73 federal prisons support the theory that a participatory management style is well-suited for corrections (p. 525): "Job autonomy and participation in decision making are associated with enhanced occupational outcomes including higher job satisfaction, stronger commitment to the institution, greater effectiveness in working with inmates, and less job-related stress." These authors also address the claim made by DiIulio, that a more traditional management style is optimal for prisons and how their research contradicts this assertion (p. 538): "DiIulio's judgement . . . runs counter to the large body of literature developed in other organizations. This divergence raises a question: Is management in prisons different from management in all other organizations? Research on prison workers' professionalization suggests that DiIulio may have been incorrect in his conclusions. A study of podular jails supports this position."

It is important to note that the participatory management style is not necessarily democratic—having a say is not the same as having a vote. While this management philosophy was, and still is, popular, fostering more positive feelings toward management among the staff, it certainly did not solve all the problems of correctional facilities.

Shared-Powers Management

The 1970s saw the development of another management philosophy inspired by a
➤ rehabilitative ideal known as **shared-powers management,** in which prison administrators sought to involve correctional staff *and* inmates in decision making.

Given this opportunity, many staff and inmates acted quickly to further their own group interests. Inmates pushed for development of grievance systems and formed associations, prisoner unions and other groups. In many cases, these prisoner groups acquired considerable power and authority, often at the expense of correctional staff and management. In response, correctional officers began to form their own unions in an attempt to retain some power and to address issues such as workplace safety.

In view of the demise of the rehabilitative ideal, the shared-powers management philosophy has lost most of its appeal among correctional administrators, who hope it will foster inmate compliance by allowing prisoners some input into decisions that affect their correctional existences. Care must also be taken to ensure that management's attention to inmate concerns and needs does not take away from administrative attention to staff needs. This is often a difficult act to balance and may lead to poor relations between management and staff. Top-level management must always use discretion to minimize potential abuse of inmate power.

Inmate Control Management

If inmate organizations and gangs become so powerful as to dominate facility management's decisions, the institution is operating under **inmate control management.** During the 1980s, facilities in California, Illinois and several other states came dangerously close to this type of management when inmate gangs wielded such power within the facilities that they sometimes successfully dictated prison policy. In some jurisdictions, inmate unions have successfully lobbied to abolish the indeterminate sentence and to establish certain worker rights for prisoners including minimum wages and collective bargaining.

Of course, variations of these basic management styles are numerous. No single approach is correct for all facilities and situations. In addition to differing management styles, several management techniques, some from corporate America, have been successfully implemented in correctional institutions.

Management Techniques

Management techniques differ from management styles in that they are more specific about a course of action to be taken. They define specific "points" for management to implement. This discussion of management techniques covers two methods developed within corrections (direct supervision and unit management) and two methods borrowed from the world of business and applied to corrections (management by objectives and total quality management).

Direct Supervision Management

The concept of direct supervision was first presented in Chapter 6. Recall that new (third) generation jails achieved successful inmate management by altering the facility's physical design, removing structural barriers and placing correctional officers in the same living area with the inmates. **Direct supervision management (DSM)** is not just an administrative approach but also an architectural approach to managing inmate populations. According to Pellicane (1991, p. 146): "The basic concept behind DSM is that through the design of cell clusters, or pods, and the management techniques of correctional officers, potentially violent situations can be diffused. DSM attempts to avoid the traditional method of reacting to crises and disturbances after they occur." The connection between correctional philosophy and architecture is as old as the modern prison era. Bentham worried about this connection.

Each pod is self-sufficient, with everything an inmate needs being located within the pod. Pellicane (p. 147) states: "By having this redundancy of services in each pod, movement of inmates through the facility is drastically reduced, thereby eliminating one of the primary causes of disturbances." Pellicane identifies five key principles on which DSM is based: "effective control and supervision, competent staff, staff and inmate safety, manageable and cost-effective operations, and accurate classification."

DSM also defines new roles for facility supervisors. According to Westbrook and Knowles (1994, pp. 171–172): "When a facility moves to direct supervision, first-line supervisors become managers. Rather than supervise inmate activities, they now manage their officers. . . . The new role of the first-line supervisor is to educate, coach, support, lead and motivate [the officers]."

Unit Management

A specific application of direct supervision is unit management, a concept originally developed in 1973 by Robert Levinson and Roy Gerard of the Federal Bureau of Prisons. Gerard (1991, pp. 32,34) writes: "Across the country, I am frequently introduced as the 'father of unit management.' If providing support during the early years of its development qualifies a person as a parent, then I accept responsibility. However, if I am the father, then Bob Levinson was the attending physician."

Levinson (1991a, p. 6) notes: "We don't build institutions the way we used to. Gone are the 'panopticons' and 'telephone poles' of yesteryear. They have been replaced by campus-like facilities. What brought this change about? The answer is functional unit management." Gerard (p. 32) states: "Unit management is a decentralized approach to institution management. . . . Unit management is not a program; it is a system to manage programs."

Unit management is a specific application of direct supervision and a system to manage programs.

According to Levinson (1991b, p. 44), the flexibility of unit management as a management tool has been demonstrated by its use in a variety of settings. It is built into the physical structure of newly constructed facilities and can also be modified to work in existing institutions. Its success has been undeniable. Levinson states: "To date, no system that has adopted unit management has subsequently abandoned it."

Accurate internal classification and programmatic separation are two vital elements of successful unit management. Because a central theme of unit management is having each unit function as a mini-institution, it is important that each unit consist of similarly classified inmates. Appropriate classification helps manage inmates by avoiding conflict and disturbances.

Classification also affects programmatic separation, another element important in unit management. As Levinson (1991b, p. 46) explains: "Programmatic separation is the practice of separating inmate predators from their prey in both living units and non-unit programs." Levinson cites a study of unit management in Missouri which found "that in institutions with unit management the likelihood of inmate-on-inmate victimization, if programmatic separations are *not* made, is highest in these areas: recreation/gymnasium, education classes, dining room, vocational shops and work assignments." Therefore, simply separating inmates based on classification for cell assignments does little to prevent victimization if all inmates are lumped together during programming or other activities.

Sherman R. Day, first director of the National Institute of Corrections, studied the 200-year history of American prisons and the characteristics of successful correctional programs. He concluded that unit management offered the best opportunity for such characteristics to exist within correctional institutions (Gerard, p. 34). Figure 11–3 itemizes Gerard's ten commandments of unit management to help correctional systems realize the full potential of this management approach.

Unit management has been successfully implemented in many individual facilities and throughout entire DOCs. For example, Missouri's entire correctional system has used unit management for nearly two decades. Pierson (1991, p. 30) identifies some benefits the Missouri DOC has received through this management technique:

- Closer interaction with inmates has improved security.
- The classic custody vs. treatment rivalry has been greatly toned down, if not eliminated. The experience of working in tandem . . . breaks down distrust between custody and nonsecurity staff.
- New career ladders were created, providing promotion opportunities for both security and noncustody personnel. In addition to improving staff morale, the new system encourages staff to view corrections as a career. This decreases staff turnover, increases interest in further training and cultivates in-house expertise.

Figure 11-3	Ten Commandments of Unit Management

1. The concept must be understood by and have the support of top-level administration.

2. There must be three sets of written guidelines:
   - a policy statement issued by the central office.
   - an institution procedures manual.
   - a unit plan for each unit.

3. There must be a table of organization that has unit managers at a "department head" level, giving them responsibility for staff and inmates assigned to their unit; this table has them and the head of security report to the same supervisor.

4. The unit's population size should be based on its mission:
   - General unit—150–250 inmates.
   - Special unit—75–125 inmates.

5. Inmates and unit staff should be permanently assigned to the unit; correctional officers should be stationed for a minimum of nine months.

6. Staffing should consist of:

	General Unit	Special Unit
Unit Manager	1	1
Case Manager	2	2
Corr. Counselor	2	2
Secretary	1	1
Mental Health	1/2	1

   - Part-time education, recreation and volunteer staff.
   - 24-hour coverage by correctional officers.

7. In addition to correctional officer coverage, unit staff should provide 12-hour supervision Monday through Friday and eight hours on each weekend day.

8. Staff offices should be located on the unit or as near to it as possible.

9. Unit personnel should receive initial and ongoing formal training concerning their roles and responsibilities.

10. Unit management audits conducted by knowledgeable central or regional office staff should occur on a regularly scheduled basis at least once a year.

Source: Roy E. Gerard. "The Ten Commandments of Unit Management." *Corrections Today,* April 1991, pp. 32–36. Reprinted by permission.

- Unit management has freed up time for top management to engage in long-range planning and other "big picture" activities such as improving the inmates' transportation system and evaluating alternative medical care providers.

Management by Objectives

A management technique from the business world which has had great appeal to correctional managers is management by objectives. First defined in the early

➤ 1950s by management theorist Peter Drucker, **management by objectives (MBO)** has managers and subordinates set goals and objectives together and then track performance to see that the objectives are accomplished. Timm (1992, p. 231) states:

> Management by objectives requires the participation and support of every member of the management team from the chief executive officer to the first-line supervisor. . . .
>
> When used as a total management approach, management by objectives produces excellent results. Indeed, it has been roughly estimated that MBO programs have been employed by over 80 percent of the industrial firms in the United States.
>
> The key to the MBO system is to get workers to participate in deciding and setting goals, both individually and in work groups. The performance achieved is then compared to these agreed-upon goals.

> Management by objectives (MBO) requires managers and subordinates to set goals and objectives together and to then track performance to ensure that the objectives are accomplished.

Total Quality Management

➤ Another management technique borrowed from the business world and applied to corrections is W. Edwards Deming's **total quality management (TQM).** A description of TQM is provided by Ash (1992, p. 82):

> TQM is the process by which traditional management practices are restructured to improve performance and product quality and customer satisfaction. The process involves strong quality leadership, customer-driven quality, employee participation, quality measurement and analysis, and continuous improvement.

Deming's famous "14 points" are not only applicable to corporate management but to criminal justice management as well, correctional management in particular:

1. Create constancy of purpose for improvement of product and service.
2. Adopt the new philosophy.
3. Cease dependence on mass inspection.
4. End the practice of awarding business on the basis of price tag alone.
5. Improve constantly and forever the system of production and service.
6. Institute modern methods of training on the job.
7. Institute modern methods of supervision.
8. Drive fear from the workplace.

 9. Break down barriers between staff areas.

10. Eliminate numerical goals for the work force.

11. Eliminate work standards and numerical quotas.

12. Remove barriers that rob people of pride of workmanship.

13. Institute a vigorous program of education and training.

14. Create a structure that will accomplish the transformation (Deming, 1982, p. 17).

Simonsen and Arnold (1994, pp. 164–166) state: "In corrections, we have seen various reports and studies in recent decades that have called for improved quality and productivity. . . . Rising crime rates in America put us as correctional managers in a tough situation. If we cannot improve quality and productivity, we lose support for our programs." These authors also note (p. 166):

> Local and state officials and taxpayers who are dissatisfied with crime control in America urge us to do something. They don't know what we should do, but they do know that what we are doing now seems too expensive and inefficient. Corrections must find a way to do more with what we currently have or we may soon find ourselves trying to do more with less.

According to Simonsen and Arnold (p. 166): "Some of the most likely applications for TQM in corrections include the following:

- identifying corrections' clients;
- developing methods to track performance; and
- ensuring that all team members seek continuous improvement in all operations."

Identifying clients is not always easy because corrections must answer to or consider so many people and agencies, including state and local elected officials, law enforcement agencies, the courts, inmates' attorneys and families, visitors, vendors, volunteers, the media and the taxpayers.

The second application, that of measuring performance, is also difficult. Simonsen and Arnold (p. 166) state: "Most correctional statistics are not qualitative but are based on quantitative measurements, making it difficult to define quality. Only by taking a new perspective—by looking at our clients' needs—can we attempt to evaluate performance in a more logical manner."

Finally, improving operations is another ongoing challenge for corrections. Improvement is best accomplished through small, continuous increments. Indeed, improving in incremental steps is the heart of TQM.

Some likely applications for total quality management in corrections include identifying correctional clients, tracking and measuring performance and ensuring that all team members continuously strive to improve operations.

Corrections usually can benefit from quality management. Creating and maintaining quality facilities are goals bolstered by another process—accreditation.

Accreditation—The Pursuit of Excellence

As correctional systems and facilities have aimed for greater professionalism and a higher degree of excellence, they have become increasingly involved in the complex process known as accreditation. But this pursuit of excellence had a simpler, more humble beginning and took nearly a century to evolve.

From Principles to Standards

When the American Correctional Association (ACA) was established in 1870, one of its first achievements was to publish a list of principles intended to improve working conditions for correctional staff and living conditions for prisoners (Phyfer, 1994, p. 184). For more than a century, these principles informally guided operations within corrections. But these informal principles, many believed, did not provide a solid foundation for the growing profession of corrections. Consequently, as Keve (1995, p. 92) states: "It was during the 1960s that the idea of accreditation began to be discussed seriously. But accreditation can exist only when it is based on detailed, unifying standards covering all aspects of program safety and quality." Recognizing the increasing need for formal national standards in corrections, the ACA responded by establishing a standards committee.

➤ Correctional **standards** "are the minimal qualification for sound correctional operation. They address physical conditions, policy and operations of correctional facilities and programs and are designed to safeguard the life, health and safety of staff and inmates" ("Answering Your Questions," 1994, p. 196). Standards are guidelines by which to measure or judge the adequacy of programs, facilities or activities. They allow self-regulation. According to Irving (1992, p. 62): "Standards are living and breathing; they can and must be changed, modified and deleted to reflect continuous improvement in the field." Indeed, the ACA's standards committee is constantly revising correctional standards to reflect changing practices and current case law.

The current trend is toward performance-based standards. According to Lehman and Myers (1995, p. 156): "Today, more and more corrections practitioners are endorsing the concept of performance-based standards. However, not everyone agrees about what exactly are performance-based standards."

To eliminate the confusion surrounding this new concept, the ACA's standards committee met in August 1994 to develop some definitions, including

➤ the following for a **performance-based standard:** "A statement that clearly defines a required condition or activity; communicates the intended result or value of that condition or activity; and quantitatively or qualitatively describes how performance can be measured" (Lehman and Myers, p. 156). These authors conclude (p. 160): "We believe performance-based standards are the next step in the history of standards. ACA's special initiative on performance-based standards will truly enhance the profession and help improve and advance the quality of correctional programs."

Correctional standards are divided into four categories and reflect, in decreasing order, the appropriate emphasis each should be given: mandatory, essential, important and desirable. As noted by Phyfer (1994, p. 184): "Professional ACA standards are prepared with several constituencies in mind. These include:

- the citizens who have been victimized by crime;
- the staff who work in correctional systems;
- the incarcerated inmates who serve sentences;
- the judges and court officers who impose sentences;
- the legislative and executive offices that are responsible for corrections; and
- the taxpayers who provide the fiscal support for corrections."

Roberts (1992, p. 56) states: "ACA standards represent sound management philosophy," and Huggins and Kehoe (1992, p. 40) note: "Standards manuals covering almost every correctional discipline have been published." Different standards apply to different correctional settings. For example, the ACA sets forth approximately 200 standards for probation departments (Dare, 1992, p. 48), while maximum security prisons have around 338 core standards ("Minnesota Facility," 1990, p. 5).

From Standards to Accreditation

Many professional organizations have a set of standards that dictate professional conduct and practice (for example, the American Bar Association, the American Medical Association). Such organizations often encourage members of the profession to comply with these standards by participating in a
➤ process called accreditation. **Accreditation** is a voluntary procedure that evaluates a facility's compliance with professional standards.

Accreditation is similar to credentialing. For example, as policing professionalizes, the credential (licensing) is rhetorically positioned to ensure that only "qualified" people are authorized to use deadly force. Accreditation has the same kind of rhetorical uses. The defensive elements, which are identified, are clear. Socially, accreditation does two things: (1) it allows administrators to position their institutions (to the public, the legislators and the courts) as meeting the minimum standards required of their kind of institution and (2) it creates a climate in which minimal enforceable expectations are raised (the results: safer, more humane facilities, protection from lawsuits and so on).

Bennett and Hess (p. 734) state: "Schools, colleges and hospitals frequently seek accreditation as recognition of their high quality. Those institutions lacking accreditation are often considered inferior." The same is becoming common in the field of corrections. In corrections, the ACA is the organization authorized to set professional standards, and the Commission on Accreditation for Corrections (CAC), begun in 1974, is the organization authorized to oversee evaluations for accreditation. The actual on-site evaluation of a correctional facility by the CAC is called an **audit.**

> In corrections, the ACA sets professional standards and the CAC determines, via audit, whether facilities applying for accreditation comply with the applicable standards.

Today, the "ACA and the [CAC] administer the only national accreditation program for all components of adult and juvenile corrections. Both ACA and the CAC promote improvement in the management of correctional agencies through the administration of a voluntary accreditation program and the ongoing development and revision of relevant, useful standards" ("Answering Your Questions," p. 196). Both the ACA's standards committee and the CAC are 20-member groups made up of corrections, criminal justice and other related professionals from across the country. Regarding the standards committee:

> The ACA president appoints 12 members of the committee for staggered six-year terms, while the Commission chairman appoints eight Commission members for two-year terms. Twice each year the committee holds public hearings on new standards proposals or standards revisions (Phyfer, 1992, p. 8).

Regarding the CAC, fifteen members of the commission are elected by ACA's membership and five are appointed from associations affiliated with corrections, including one each from the American Bar Association, the American Institute of Architects, the American Jail Association, the National Association of Counties and the National Sheriffs' Association ("Answering Your Questions," pp. 196–197).

The Accreditation Process

When a facility seeks accreditation, the first step is to contact the ACA for materials and documents. The ACA will develop an accreditation contract for the specific facility, and the accreditation process proceeds as follows ("Answering Your Questions," p. 197):

> After a facility or agency signs an accreditation contract, ACA sends the appropriate manual of standards and other materials. A regional administrator is appointed to advise the facility during the accreditation process. The facility's first step is to appoint an accreditation manager. After reviewing, revising and implementing

necessary changes in policy and operating procedure, the facility or agency undergoes an audit. Audits are conducted by a team of corrections professionals who are selected, trained and certified by the CAC. The audit team visits the facility, interviews staff and inmates, inspects facility records and observes operations. It then reports its findings to ACA and the CAC. If the facility complies with all mandatory standards and at least 90 percent of all nonmandatory standards, ACA will schedule an accreditation hearing before a panel of CAC members.

The accreditation process is a comprehensive evaluation of the correctional facility and involves examining all areas of operation, including security, medical services, environmental safety, waste management and storage of hazardous materials, facilities maintenance and operations, inmate case management, educational programming, record keeping, budget analysis and personnel administration.

Accreditation is *ongoing*. Once a facility is accredited, it must keep abreast of new and changing standards, submit annual reports to verify compliance with these standards and participate in reaccreditation every three years. Like the initial accreditation procedure, the reaccreditation involves a complete audit and another accreditation hearing.

> Accreditation is ongoing, with accredited facilities required to submit annual compliance reports and undergo reaccreditation, including a complete audit, every three years.

Who Gets Accredited?

Virtually any agency or facility involved in corrections can receive accreditation by the ACA/CAC provided they comply with the applicable standards. According to Keve (p. 93): "In 1978, the first accreditation awards went to four halfway houses; one year later, the Vienna Correctional Center in Illinois was the first prison to be accredited." Small jails and large prisons partake in the accreditation process; adult and juvenile facilities seek accreditation; probation and parole departments may be accredited. Correctional accreditation has even expanded to include organizations whose primary mission is to train corrections professionals. In 1993, the New Mexico Corrections Academy in Santa Fe became the first correctional training academy to receive accreditation. Keve states: "As of 1995, more than 1,400 correctional programs and institutions are involved in accreditation."

Benefits of Accreditation

The benefits of accreditation are numerous, which has helped propel ever higher the number of facilities seeking accreditation. Huggins and Kehoe

(p. 42) suggest: "Accreditation's major benefit to top administration comes from the knowledge that every aspect of operations and administration are now routinely and regularly reviewed." According to Stalder (1997, p. 20): "No other mechanism can be as effective in building partnerships, developing teamwork and fostering a sense of pride in a job well-done." An accreditation opinion survey (Ward, 1995, p. 80) of facilities having just been accredited revealed that "documentation, planning and coordination improved in all areas of the facility after being accredited." Furthermore, the surveyed facilities mentioned the following benefits of accreditation:

- Helps credibility in litigation cases.
- Makes staff aware of policy requirements.
- Promotes a sense of pride and ownership among staff.
- Offers a process through which program superiority can be demonstrated.
- Promotes teamwork, consistent effort and quality.
- Provides a structured, systematic approach to regularly monitor and review facility compliance with proper standards of operation.

Various areas examined during the accreditation process are listed in Table 11–3 with the survey respondents' opinions regarding whether accreditation improved each area. Concerning *prison* accreditation, Cross (1994, p. 115) concludes: "A certificate of accreditation can benefit a prison in many ways, including reducing costly and time-consuming litigation, increasing staff professionalism and morale, increasing community support, providing a credible assessment of the prison's strengths and weaknesses and offering a basis for increased funding."

According to Todd (1993, p. 164), during the mid-1980s, *small jails* in Ohio County were receiving constant criticism from the state's jail inspector regarding inmate life, health and safety standards: "Fire and safety procedures, sight and sound separation between men and women, key/security control, minimum staffing levels, medical needs, maintenance, juvenile detention, telephone and commissary use, recreation and psychiatric services—these were but a few of the areas in which the inspector found flaws." To satisfy the inspector, the county sheriff realized specific ACA standards would need to be met, a process tantamount to seeking accreditation. In becoming accredited, the jails realized a variety of benefits, including invaluable professional contacts, increased staffing, a lower potential for litigation and better morale (Todd, p. 165).

Dare (p. 48), in reviewing the benefits of accreditation to *probation services*, notes such advantages as "minimizing the potential for costly, time-consuming litigation; assessing our strengths and weaknesses; protecting the life, safety and health of staff and probationers; and improving our ability to provide quality investigations and supervision." Dare also states employee grievances diminished and the workload stabilized. "Additional benefits include more consistency in

Table 11–3	1994 Accreditation Opinion Survey Results		
	Much Improved	Improved	Not Affected
Facility staff understanding of facility policies	24	40	28
Inmate understanding of facility policies	8	46	16
Quality of facility	24	38	10
Overall fiscal management	14	20	38
Fiscal procedures	16	20	36
Personnel procedures	16	20	36
Staff training	30	24	18
Recordkeeping	32	38	2
Safety procedures	32	30	10
Security	20	32	18
Food service	12	38	22
Health care	12	42	18
Inmate rules	18	32	20
Work policies	10	30	32
Classification system	8	26	38
Academic and vocational programs	10	28	34
Library services	8	32	32
Inmate activities	12	36	22
Fire control	26	32	14
Sanitation	22	34	16
Inmate control	10	32	28
Inmate recreation program	8	36	26
Inmate release preparation	10	28	30
Religious services	8	22	42
Social services	8	28	36
Citizen volunteers	14	26	32

Source: Elizabeth Ward. "Accreditation: A Positive Step Toward Facility Improvement." *Corrections Today,* February 1995, p. 78. Reprinted by permission.

the quality and quantity of staff's work; enhanced training and orientation for new employees; access to additional resources, such as federal and state grants; and enhanced credibility among judges, the county commissioners, the corrections community and the media" (p. 50).

Regarding results at the Lansing Correctional Facility in Kansas, Roberts (p. 56) states:

> Accreditation has improved communication in the institution, which is essential to effective institutional management. Administrative staff are now more visible and available to listen to concerns presented by inmates and staff on the front lines where the "rubber meets the road." Healthy interaction between staff and inmates has created a more relaxed institutional environment.
>
> . . . The general feeling now is that if staff systematically attend to minor problems, they can prevent the onset of major problems.

Other improvements realized at the Lansing facility as a result of accreditation include a significant reduction in staff turnover rates; an increase in staff and inmate accountability; a decrease in inmate-on-inmate assaults, fires and disciplinary reports; and a general feeling by inmates, staff and the community that the institution is "a cleaner, safer and more secure facility" (Roberts, p. 56).

Huggins and Kehoe (p. 42) state: "[M]ost correctional administrators involved in the accreditation process see it as another form of insurance. The difference between traditional insurance and accreditation is that traditional insurance insures monies to pay judgments, while standards and accreditation are designed to avoid judgments." They note some insurance companies provide reduced premiums to accredited facilities.

> Benefits of accreditation are numerous and include minimizing the potential for litigation; increasing staff professionalism and morale; decreasing employee grievances and turnover rates; providing an assessment of the facility's strengths and weaknesses; enhancing credibility among judges, county commissioners, the corrections community and the media; increasing community support; offering a basis for increased funding and access to additional resources; protecting the life, safety and health of staff and offenders; and knowing all aspects of operations and administration are routinely and regularly reviewed.

Disadvantages of Accreditation

The accreditation process is not without its critics and drawbacks. DeLand (1998, p. 3) states: "Within the corrections community, it is often akin to heresy to criticize accreditation or standards; yet, there is strong disagreement among corrections professionals—even within the Association for State Corrections Administrators—over the value of ACA standards and accreditation." DeLand advocates internal audits as a superior way to evaluate correctional operations and practices.

An accreditation opinion survey revealed that disadvantages to accreditation included "the cost and time involved, the stress and extra work put on staff during the accreditation process, and the amount of paperwork required to prove compliance" (Ward, p. 80).

Drawbacks to accreditation include the cost and time involved, the stress and extra work put on staff and the amount of paperwork required to prove compliance.

Such disadvantages are not enough to keep facilities from seeking accreditation, however. According to Phyfer (1992, p. 8): "First-time contracts for accreditation continue to come in every week, even in the face of budget cuts, staff layoffs and an extremely poor economy. This shows that as corrections professionals we believe accreditation is truly the foundation of our profession."

Phyfer (p. 8) sums up the accreditation experience this way: "Speaking for myself, I can say that in my 25 years in corrections, standards and accreditation are the best management tool I have had available. I know the standards force me to address and document training, health, safety and numerous other issues. I have observed staff's pride in what their facility has accomplished by becoming accredited." Some have likened achieving accreditation to receiving a diploma or a medal—the true value lies in what you have to do to earn it. "In the case of ACA accreditation, it means your program or facility has been evaluated by experts and meets the standards set by the best in the field. It tells the world your program operates in a highly professional, humane, secure and consistent manner, that you and all your co-workers contribute to the effort, and that everyone—from the newest resident to the older veteran staffer—knows what is expected of him or her" ("Accreditation's Real Value," 1993, p. 210).

Summary

Major characteristics of a bureaucracy include a hierarchy of authority, a division of labor, formal rules and procedures, an impersonal climate and advancement based on merit. The top correctional administrator in each state is the director of the DOC, appointed by the governor and responsible for a broad spectrum of functions. The top manager in a prison is the warden or superintendent.

The basic functions of managers include planning, organizing, staffing, leading and controlling. The planning function includes setting organizational goals and objectives, establishing policies and devising a budget. Organizing is an all-encompassing function that extends to and affects the other managerial functions. The staffing function involves determining how many and what type of staff are needed, recruiting and selecting competent staff, placing them in appropriate positions, training them (initial and ongoing) and retaining them. Leading is guiding and motivating people to achieve an organizational goal. A primary difference between managers and leaders is that managers focus on tasks while leaders focus on people. Controlling requires managers to set standards and expectations, know how internal and external factors affect the running of the facility and then *act* to influence these factors to benefit the facility.

Four management styles found in correctional facilities are autocratic or authoritarian, participatory, shared-powers and inmate control. Unit management is a specific application of direct supervision and a system to manage programs. Management by objectives (MBO) requires managers and subordinates to set goals and objectives together and to then track performance to ensure that the objectives are accomplished. Some likely applications for total quality management in corrections include identifying correctional clients, tracking and measuring performance and ensuring that all team members continuously strive to improve operations.

In corrections, the ACA sets professional standards and the CAC determines, via audit, whether facilities applying for accreditation comply with the applicable standards. Accreditation is ongoing, with accredited facilities required to submit annual compliance reports and undergo reaccreditation, including a complete audit, every three years. Benefits of accreditation are numerous and include minimizing the potential for litigation; increasing staff professionalism and morale; decreasing employee grievances and turnover rates; providing an assessment of the facility's strengths and weaknesses; enhancing credibility among judges, county commissioners, the corrections community and the media; increasing community support; offering a basis for increased funding and access to additional resources; protecting the life, safety and health of staff and offenders; and knowing all aspects of operations and administration are routinely and regularly reviewed. Drawbacks to accreditation include the cost and time involved, the stress and extra work put on staff and the amount of paperwork required to prove compliance.

Discussion Questions

1. Have you personally experienced the Hawthorne effect in any of your previous employment situations? If so, share the experience with the class.

2. How would you rank the importance of the five basic management functions? Which is most important for a manager? Least important?

3. How important is it for a correctional manager to be a good leader?

4. Which is more useful to a correctional manager: authority or power? Why?

5. If you were a manager, which of the four management *styles* would you likely adopt? Why? Which do you think is most effective today?

6. Which management *style(s)* is/are used in your local correctional facilities?

7. Which management *technique(s)* is/are used in your local correctional facilities?

8. In the context of TQM, what are some ways to measure and evaluate the performance of a correctional facility? If your local correctional facility uses this technique, how do they measure and evaluate performance?

9. Are any of your local correctional facilities and programs accredited? If so, how long have they been accredited, how difficult was the process and what do they see as the pros and cons of accreditation? If not, why not?

10. Should accreditation of correctional programs and institutions be mandatory? Why or why not?

References

"Accreditation's Real Value Lies in What You Must Do to Earn It." *Corrections Today,* August 1993, pp. 210–211.

"Answering Your Questions About Standards and Accreditation." *Corrections Today,* April 1994, pp. 196–197.

Ash, Ronald W. "The ABCs of Developing TQM." *Security Management,* September 1992, pp. 82–84.

Bennett, Wayne W. and Hess, Kären M. *Management and Supervision in Law Enforcement,* 2nd ed. Minneapolis/St. Paul, MN: West Publishing Co., 1996.

Braiden, Chris. "Leadership: Not What (or Where) We Think." *Law Enforcement News,* April 15, 1994, pp. 14, 16.

Camp, George M. and Camp, Camille Graham. *The Corrections Yearbook, 1997.* South Salem, NY: The Criminal Justice Institute, 1997.

Cross, Carolyn A. "D.C. Prison Built in 1920 Meets Modern-Day Accreditation Standards." *Corrections Today,* June 1994, pp. 114–115.

Cullen, Francis T.; Latessa, Edward J.; Kopache, Renee; Lombardo, Lucien X.; and Burton, Velmer S., Jr. "Prison Wardens' Job Satisfaction." *The Prison Journal,* Vol. 73, No. 2, June 1993, pp. 141–161.

Dare, James E. "Accreditation in Probation Services: Looking Beyond the Basic Benefits." *Corrections Today,* May 1992, pp. 48–50.

DeLand, Gary W. "Rethinking the Value of Accreditation." *Point/Counterpoint: Correctional Issues.* Lanham, MD: American Correctional Association, 1998, p. 3.

Deming, W. Edwards. *Quality, Productivity, and Competitive Position.* Cambridge, MA: Institute of Technology, Center for Advanced Engineering Study, 1982.

Digges, Robert E., Jr. *Behind the Walls: A Correctional Officer's Story.* Ft. Oglethorpe, GA: R.E. Digges, Jr., 1994.

DiIulio, John J., Jr. *Governing Prisons: A Comparative Study of Correctional Management.* New York, Free Press, 1987.

Gerard, Roy E. "The Ten Commandments of Unit Management." *Corrections Today,* April 1991, pp. 32–36.

Huggins, M. Wayne and Kehoe, Charles J. "Accreditation Benefits Nation's Jails, Juvenile Detention Centers." *Corrections Today,* May 1992, pp. 40–42.

Irving, James R. "Supporting a Vital Process." *Corrections Today,* May 1992, p. 62.

Keve, Paul W. "From Principles to Standards to Accreditation." *Corrections Today,* August 1995, pp. 90–93.

Lehman, Joseph D. and Myers, Lawrence G. "Performance-Based Standards: What Are They, What Will They Do?" *Corrections Today,* July 1995, pp. 156–160.

Levinson, Robert B. "A Concept that Changed Corrections." *Corrections Today*, April 1991a, p. 6.

Levinson, Robert B. "The Future of Unit Management." *Corrections Today*, April 1991b, pp. 44–48.

McShane, Marilyn; Williams, Frank P., III; Shichor, David; and McClain, Kathy L. "Examining Employee Turnover." *Corrections Today*, August 1991, pp. 220–225.

"Minnesota Facility Earns Perfect Score." *On the Line*, Vol. 13, No. 4, September 1990, p. 5.

Pellicane, Anthony W. "New Jersey Saves Money Without Compromising Security." *Corrections Today*, July 1991, pp. 146–148.

Phyfer, George M. "Accreditation: Corrections' Foundation." *Corrections Today*, May 1992, p. 8.

Phyfer, George M. "123 Years of Evolution." *Corrections Today*, July 1994, p. 184.

Pierson, Timothy A. "One State's Success with Unit Management." *Corrections Today*, April 1991, pp. 24–30.

Roberts, Raymond N. "How Accreditation Helped Revitalize a Penitentiary Under Court Order." *Corrections Today*, May 1992, pp. 52–56.

Simonsen, Clifford E. and Arnold, Douglas G. "Is Corrections Ready for TQM?" *Corrections Today*, July 1994, pp. 164–169.

Stalder, Richard. "Accreditation: A Good Value for Corrections." *Corrections Today*, August 1997, p. 20.

Stojkovic, Stan and Lovell, Rick. *Corrections: An Introduction.* Cincinnati, OH: Anderson Publishing Co., 1992.

Timm, Paul R. *Supervision*, 2nd ed. St. Paul, MN: West Publishing Company, 1992.

Todd, James C. "Ohio County Finds Accreditation Offers Solutions for Small Jails." *Corrections Today*, July 1993, pp. 164–165.

Ward, Elizabeth. "Accreditation: A Positive Step Toward Facility Improvement." *Corrections Today*, February 1995, pp. 78–80.

Westbrook, Charles F., III and Knowles, Fred E., Jr. "Training First-Line Supervisors as Direct Supervision Managers." *Corrections Today*, July 1994, pp. 170–172.

Wright, Kevin N.; Saylor, William G.; Gilman, Evan; and Camp, Scott. "Job Control and Occupational Outcomes among Prison Workers." *Justice Quarterly*, Vol. 14, No. 3, September 1997, pp. 525–546.

12

Other Correctional Personnel

Do You Know

➤ What the primary responsibility of a correctional officer is?

➤ Who the majority of corrections personnel are?

➤ What a bona fide occupational qualification is?

➤ What the fundamental objective of a union is?

➤ What roles probation and parole officers commonly function in?

➤ Which correctional professionals are considered treatment personnel?

➤ What the range of support personnel includes?

➤ What individuals make up the correctional volunteer pool?

There is no field of endeavor more exciting and challenging than criminal justice and no component with more opportunities to "make a difference" than corrections. However, to paraphrase Woodrow Wilson: Corrections is as great, and only as great, as its employees. —*The Honorable Helen G. Corrothers*

Can You Define

bona fide occupational
   qualification (BFOQ)
collective bargaining
correctional officer

indigenous
   paraprofessional
parole officer
probation officer

psychiatrist
psychologist
union

Introduction

As the number of offenders are increasing, so too are the number of correctional personnel required to supervise and manage these offenders. Never have there been more opportunities for employment in corrections as there are today. As of January 1, 1997, the 52 adult correctional agencies (50 states, DC and the FBOP) employed 399,554 people (Camp and Camp, 1997, p. 109). Probation and parole agencies employed another 68,491 people (Camp and Camp, pp. 172–173). Additionally, employees working in the juvenile correctional systems total more than 40,000 (*Sourcebook*, 1995, p. 87). With construction of correctional facilities proceeding at a lively pace, efforts to staff these facilities are equally vigorous.

The focus of this chapter is on the variety of professionals working in corrections today, excluding management, and their vital roles in this field. Since an entire book could be devoted to each corrections professional (indeed, such books do exist), and since this text is designed to be an *introduction* to various topics within corrections, this chapter simply summarizes the primary corrections professionals and their basic duties and responsibilities.

The chapter begins with a look at custodial and security personnel, including the largest group of correctional employees—correctional officers—as well as probation and parole officers. The discussion then turns to treatment personnel (medical, psychological, educational, caseworkers/counselors, religious, other programs) and support personnel. The chapter concludes with a discussion of the use of volunteers in corrections. Administrative and management personnel, the topic of Chapter 11, are not discussed in this chapter. A listing of correctional job titles and descriptions is given in Appendix B.

Custodial and Security Personnel

Every individual employed in the field of corrections has, to some degree, a responsibility to control or supervise offenders. As Williamson (1990, p. 123) explains: "Corrections is a service industry and, as such, usually requires that all personnel (except those in highly specialized and professionalized roles) begin their careers at entry level positions—for example, custody and surveillance." Williamson also notes: "Those whose primary roles are custody and surveillance . . . are actually performing paraprofessional roles involving interpersonal and technical skills." These custodial and security personnel are the backbone of corrections, those who deal with offenders on the front line, day in and day out. Consequently, their ability to perform their duties is critical to the success of corrections.

A majority of correctional employees function within a security capacity. As of January 1, 1997, there were 237,041 individuals employed as uniformed staff in adult correctional systems, a number representing 59.3 percent of all correctional employees in adult facilities. *Uniformed staff* refers to "[a]ll correctional security staff including majors, captains, lieutenants, sergeants, and officers" (Camp and Camp, p. 111). Of these uniformed staff members, the vast majority hold the rank of correctional officer.

Correctional Officers

The ACA (1992, p. 3) states: "The purpose of corrections is no different from that of the other components of the criminal justice system; it is to protect the public."

> The primary responsibility of a **correctional officer** is to maintain order and control over those committed to custody and to prevent their escape.

Although in the past this function was summed up by the word *guard*, it is recognized today that those who perform this critical service do a lot more than just guard offenders. All correctional employees must also interact with offenders daily. Williamson (p. 126) states:

From a central control area, a correctional officer monitors two adjacent cell blocks in the Suffolk County Jail.

> It is very important that officers be able to judge human behavior appropriately and that they be able to interact with almost all types of personalities. . . . It is very important that officers recognize that maintaining order in prison institutions involves much more than merely opening and closing doors. It involves the supervision of human beings who, although they are in a secure environment, still have many options regarding the particular behaviors that they exhibit.

For these reasons, the ACA has approved a special resolution urging the discontinuance of the term *guard* and promoting use of the term *correctional officer* (see shaded box).

Correctional officers comprise the majority of corrections personnel today. As of January 1, 1997, there were 206,377 individuals employed as correctional officers in adult facilities (Camp and Camp, p. 112), accounting for 51.7 percent of all people working in adult correctional facilities. With the number of incarcerated individuals at an all-time high, it stands to reason that correctional officers are needed now more than ever.

> The majority of corrections personnel are correctional officers, who comprise nearly 52 percent of all corrections employees.

Harr and Hess (1996, p. 52) state: "Considering the new crime bill, the passage of '3 Strikes and You're Out' laws, the increased use of mandatory life without parole sentences and the efforts to achieve an 85% mandatory service of one's sentence, the need for correction officers will be even greater in the years to come." Wright (1993, p. xxix) notes that correctional officers are among the

ACA's Resolution on the Term *Correctional Officer*

WHEREAS, the duties of correctional personnel whose primary responsibility are custody and control require extensive interpersonal skills, special training and education; and

WHEREAS, correctional personnel are skilled professionals; and

WHEREAS, the term "guard" produces a false and negative image;

THEREFORE BE IT RESOLVED that the American Correctional Association adopt the term "correctional officer" as the official language in all Association publications, meetings, events and communications to describe custodial/security personnel; and

THEREFORE BE IT FURTHER RESOLVED that the Association actively promote the use of the term "correctional officer" and discourage the use of the word "guard" by the media, general public, educational institutions and publishers.

Source: "Resolution on the Term 'Correctional Officer.' " *Corrections Today,* April 1993, pp. 60, 146.

fastest growing occupations today, with projections calling for 61.4 percent more correctional officers being needed by the year 2005 than were employed in 1990. Table 12–1 shows the number of employees in adult correctional systems and how many of these individuals are correctional officers. Figure 12–1 shows how the total number of correctional officers has been increasing steadily since 1990, as well as the growth trends of minority and female correctional officers. The ratio of correctional officers to inmates varies from state to state and from institution to institution. At the beginning of 1997, the average U.S. officer-to-inmate ratio was 1 to 5.4 (Camp and Camp, p. 131).

Regarding recruitment and training of correctional officers, policies vary by jurisdiction. Nationwide, however, many enter the field of corrections as a stepping off point for future work in other areas of criminal justice. In most states the competition for police positions in law enforcement agencies is so great that many consider a position in corrections a viable option for entry into the criminal justice system, with plans to transfer to police work later. However, since corrections is the most rapidly growing segment of the criminal justice professions, more individuals are finding permanent employment here. In Illinois, local correctional officers are sheriff's office personnel and, like police officers in the state, must successfully complete basic corrections officer training, pass a state-level certification examination and participate in continuous in-service training. The educational and skill requirements for correctional officers are discussed shortly.

Lombardo (1989, pp. 51–57) divides correctional officer assignments into seven basic categories:

- Living unit officers—supervise housing units.
- Work detail supervisors—oversee work assignments.
- Industrial shop and school officers—maintain order and security in these locations.
- Yard officers—patrol, maintain order.
- Administration building assignments—building security, interact with public, little contact with inmates.
- Perimeter security—armed, little contact with inmates.
- Relief officers—provide relief for officers on days off.

Some correctional facilities routinely rotate correctional officers through these various assignments to prevent officers from getting "too close" to inmates and to break up the monotony. Assignment rotation also requires correctional officers to acquire competence in a variety of roles.

Roles of Correctional Officers. The roles of correctional officers are quite diversified. Stojkovic and Lovell (1992, p. 131) state "it is often said that the correctional officer is father, mother, babysitter, counselor, priest, and police officer to the prisoner." The correctional officer is also a disciplinarian, link between inmates and other staff, behavioral manager, environment setter, dispute

| Table 12–1 | Total Number of Employees and Number Employed as Correctional Officers in Adult Correctional Systems (by Sex, Race and Jurisdiction, as of January 1, 1997) |

Jurisdiction		Total	Sex		Race	
			Male	Female	White	Non-White
STATE DOCs*	All Employees	369,918	253,170	116,748	262,421	107,497
	Correctional Officers	195,241	154,030	41,211	132,897	62,344
FEDERAL BOP	All Employees	29,636	21,723	7,913	20,064	9,572
	Correctional Officers	11,136	9,833	1,303	7,027	4,109
TOTAL	All Employees	399,554	274,893	124,661	282,485	117,069
	Correctional Officers	206,377	163,863	42,514	139,924	66,453

*Includes Washington, DC
Source: Adapted from George M. Camp and Camille Graham Camp. *The Corrections Yearbook, 1997.* South Salem, NY: The Criminal Justice Institute, 1997, pp. 108, 112.

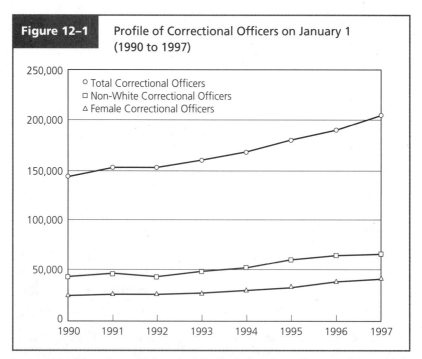

| Figure 12–1 | Profile of Correctional Officers on January 1 (1990 to 1997) |

Source: Adapted from George M. Camp and Camille Graham Camp. *The Corrections Yearbook, 1997.* South Salem, NY: The Criminal Justice Institute, 1997, p. 113.

A correctional officer, left, wipes tears from an inmate's face in the maximum-security women's prison at Bedford Hills, New York. In addition to serving as supervisor and disciplinarian, correctional officers may also provide emotional comfort and support to inmates.

settler, educator and consultant. The number of hats a correctional officer is expected to wear often depends on the facility in which he or she works. According to the *Occupational Outlook Handbook* (1993, pp. 295–296):

> Correction officers are charged with the safety and security of persons who have been arrested, are awaiting trial or other hearing, or who have been convicted of a crime and sentenced to serve time in a correctional institution. Many correction officers guard prisoners in small municipal jails or precinct station houses where their responsibilities are wide ranging, while others control inmates in large State and Federal prisons where job duties are more specialized. . . . Regardless of the setting, correction officers maintain order within the institution, enforce rules and regulations, and often supplement the counseling that inmates receive from psychologists, social workers, and other mental health professionals.

Role conflict or ambiguity is a well-documented phenomenon and can leave correctional officers wondering what their true function is. Stalder (1992, p. 45) expresses it this way:

> Your job as a correctional officer will often leave you scratching your head and wondering just how you fit into the system. As you enforce rules, resolve disputes, supervise housekeeping, distribute laundry, pass long nights in a guard tower, listen to complaints, announce counts, and spend long hours hoping nothing happens and wishing something would to break the monotony, you will have cause to reflect on how you fit in.

The Good, the Bad and the Ugly. Kelly (1996, p. 134) notes that employment in corrections can provide three things many look for in their work: opportunity, mobility and challenge. When asked if they would recommend their line of work to a close friend, several correctional officers responded:

- "Yes, to a friend that I felt was suited for it. Good opportunity for promotion, benefits, etc."
- "Yes. This job does have its rewards. It is a secure job and for me, I've gained lots of experience and maturity."
- "Yes . . . I have a very satisfying career, with good benefits to include promotional opportunity in line with my willingness to work!"

The correctional officer is a vital member of the corrections team, yet there are some negatives to this profession. In fact, the realities of being a correctional officer often come as a surprise to many who choose this career. When asked if the daily reality of their career was what they expected it to be before they began working, correctional officers' responses were mixed:

- "Yes. This is no easy job. Day to day interaction with inmates is hard."
- "I did not have a clue about what to expect. I just needed a job and expected to work hard, being confident I could do well."
- "[I didn't expect] the reality that things are not just black and white. There are people issues."

One corrections sergeant who'd spent many years as a line officer credits his success in corrections to his military background, adding: "The correctional officer training school is very different from the job. It's not as it appears on paper. I've seen many go through the school, get a job and quit fast because it's not what they expected."

The social environment surrounding correctional officers is, in several interesting ways, quite similar to that of the inmates they watch over. For example, Kauffman (1988, p. 85) notes the presence of an officer code: "Officers also possess a distinct subculture within prisons. Their own beliefs and code of conduct set them apart from administrators, social workers, and, of course, inmates." The nine norms comprising this "officer code" are (p. 86):

- Always go to the aid of an officer in distress.
- Don't "lug" drugs (bring them in for inmate use).
- Don't rat.
- Never make a fellow officer look bad in front of inmates.
- Always support an officer in a dispute with an inmate.
- Always support officer sanctions against inmates.
- Don't be a "white hat" or a "goody two-shoes."
- Maintain officer solidarity versus all outside groups.
- Show positive concern for fellow officers.

The following discussion is adapted from Officers at Risk: How to Identify and Cope with Stress, *and relates some of the emotions, feelings, fears, frustrations and disappointments of working in a correctional setting.*

Correctional officers often work in an antagonistic role with the population they serve. They may feel unsupported by the administration they work for, and they may see little success in reaching their assigned goal. They see the same inmates coming back time after time for the same offense, some spending the majority of their adult lives in prison—in small doses. While correctional officers do not deal with the victims as police officers do, they do deal with the victimization because every time they see an inmate return, they know that the system has failed again.

Many correctional officers indicate that their work has changed them and they have paid a large price as a result. Many correctional officers describe these changes as necessary to survive, but also as unanticipated. The changes frequently involve a loss of naiveté, a new awareness of the world, loss of the ability to trust, development of a cynical outlook and strained relationships with friends and family members.

The first change seems to be a loss of innocence. Many enter the corrections field unaware of the extent to which crimes and criminals pervade our society:

> I came in a little naive. Now that I think back, I came in here a happy-go-lucky, love everybody, you know, sunshine, rosy kind of guy. I was trusting. I was quite candid, and I got trampled on big time. I befriended people that I thought would be my friends forever, and that wasn't the case.

Another correctional officer described similar changes:

> I basically grew up in a white, middle-class community, and so I really didn't have that much to do with minorities or crime. I think once I got out of high school and got out of college and came here it was kind of disheartening to see how bad people could be.
>
> Some of my values, my beliefs about people changed. I think there's a tendency after you work here to say, "Don't give anyone the benefit of the doubt. They're just looking for something from you."

Many correctional officers become less trusting and more cynical because of their work:

> You're dealing with over a thousand people for eight hours a day that you just don't trust. That carries over outside of here in the way you deal with other people.

You may also learn that to display too much emotion is not acceptable. You learn not to appear vulnerable. One officer who had been taken hostage described how he and the others reduced the stress of the situation after being released: "I was tough. We didn't need any of this 'debriefing stuff.' We just went down to the saloon and got drunk." Alcohol seems to be used frequently as a stress reducer.

You may properly feel a fear and distrust of the population you deal with. Being called to handle an unknown situation raises concern: "Your adrenaline gets pumping. You don't know whether or not something's a setup to get you into an area."

Another officer verified the reality of that danger: "I've been taken hostage and I've been stabbed and assaulted many times." In response to danger from inmates, you learn to stick together. Your colleagues become extremely important to you:

> I guess I put my life in their hands every day. I feel good about the people I work with. After you've worked with them for awhile, it's almost like you can feel what their next move is going to be and you plan yours accordingly.

Many correctional officers find that as they become closer to their coworkers, their home relationships become strained. The job becomes very important and, as they learn who they are within the institution, it becomes more than just a job. It becomes a life: "You lived the job. In fact, we had rooms upstairs and a lot of guys stayed here. You just lived it." The increased importance of work frequently has a parallel decreased importance for the family.

Often inmates have a "working relationship" with correctional officers. Yet, since neither can afford to trust the other completely, correctional officers may work in an atmosphere of tension, distrust and the ever-present potential for danger. This danger, however, is offset with hours of dull routine. Obviously, the prison is not in a state of riot all the time. Correctional officers do not spend all their time responding to crises. Countless hours are spent simply waiting for something to happen. While they wait, however, they cannot really relax. They cannot totally prepare for the unexpected, even though they know that at some time it *is* going to happen.

Source: Dennis L. Conroy and Kären M. Hess. *Officers at Risk: How to Identify and Cope with Stress.* Incline Village, NV: Copperhouse Publishing Company, 1992. Reprinted by permission.

In addition to this subculture, some have noted that correctional staff may also succumb to prisonization much the same way inmates do, although to a lesser degree. While purportedly serving a survival function for officers within the facility, the effects of such prisonization may be quite devastating to these officers' relationships outside the facility. As noted by Kauffman (p. 235): "An officer highly rated by his superiors for his strong-arm tactics at work reported his home life in shambles. He found he had to 'concentrate' at home in order not to behave there as he did in the prison."

Digges (1994, preface) states: "Corrections is more than just a job. It is a lifestyle." And this lifestyle is certainly not for everyone. Harr and Hess (p. 51) state: "The working conditions in correctional institutions may be stressful or occasionally dangerous, as inmate riots have been known to claim the lives of corrections officers." As with police work, hospital work and many other professions, corrections operates around the clock. While most correctional officers work an eight-hour day, five days a week, these shifts may occur during the night, and the five days may include weekends and holidays.

According to Taylor (1995, p. 1): "For many reasons, such as low pay, long and odd hours, physical and social isolation, and unattractive and dangerous work environments, employment as a correctional officer shares many negative similarities with enlistment in the armed services, with few of

Table 12–2	Salaries of Correctional Officers, 1997			
	Entry Level	**After Training**	**After Probation**	**Maximum Salary***
Range among State DOCs	$14,736–$32,016	$14,988–$32,016	$15,432–$36,264	$19,376–$56,796
Federal BOP	$25,235	$25,235	$26,604	$38,360
National Average	$20,888	$21,357	$22,447	$33,229

*Kentucky does not have an upper salary limit.
Source: Adapted from George M. Camp and Camille Graham Camp. *The Corrections Yearbook, 1997.* South Salem, NY: The Criminal Justice Institute, 1997, p. 124.

the compensating benefits." Because of these factors, the turnover rate among correctional staff can be quite high. Taylor (p. 2) notes that "the national average annual turnover rate for correctional officers nears 15 percent, while at some institutions half of all new officers quit during their first year."

Salary ranges for correctional officers vary considerably by jurisdiction. Table 12–2 shows the range of salaries for correctional officers in 1997.

Regarding the professionalism of correctional officers, Blair and Kratcoski (1992, p. 117) state:

> The officer who is flexible, who adapts to the various situations, who can change from authority figure to counselor, depending on the type of interaction required, who has the good judgment to realize which rules and regulations need to be rigidly enforced and which ones can be bent, who really believes his/her work is important and contributes to the welfare of the community, approximates the image of a professional.

Educational Requirements and Skills. A quarter century ago, it was uncommon for correctional staff to have college degrees; in fact, many correctional positions did not even require applicants to hold a high school diploma. Today, however, the situation is quite different, as those seeking a career in corrections must consider numerous educational requirements and other qualifications ("Hiring of Correctional," 1994, p. 11):

> State requirements for correctional officers are similar nationwide. Most U.S. departments of corrections require that successful applicants meet a combination of the following criteria: over 21 years of age; high school diploma or GED equivalent; no felony convictions; in-state residency; U.S. citizenship; physical and mental fitness; previous work experience or advanced education; valid driver's license.

According to a recent survey of corrections agencies (Hill, 1997, pp. 3–6), 14 states and the Federal Bureau of Prisons require correctional officer recruits to have completed some college coursework, if not a two-year degree. Correctional officer training programs range from zero preservice hours in Wyoming to 640 hours in Michigan, with an average of 229 hours (Camp and Camp, p. 122). On-the-job training ranges from 8 hours in Wisconsin to 80 hours in Kansas, New Jersey, Wyoming and the District of Columbia.

Typical courses a correctional officer may need to complete during training include chemical agents, communicable diseases, crisis management, ethics, firearms, first aid, inmate classification, inmate gangs, inmate manipulation techniques, inmate mental health, inmate programs, life support/CPR, narcotics/dangerous drugs, professionalism, race relations, radio communications, report writing, security devices/procedures, self-defense, sexual harassment, special inmate populations, stress reduction and substance abuse awareness (Hill, pp. 10–11).

At the beginning of 1997, 34 agencies, including the Federal Bureau of Prisons, performed drug tests on all correctional officer applicants, and 14 agencies conducted drug tests on correctional officers holding probationary status (Camp and Camp, p. 130). The average probationary period for correctional officers increased from 8 months in 1990 to 9.4 months in 1997, with most agencies requiring either a 6-month or 12-month probationary period (p. 122).

Several efforts are currently being advocated as ways to enhance professionalism, improve job satisfaction and effectiveness among correctional officers and reduce the high level of employee turnover. One such effort is to raise the educational level of correctional officers. Many have argued that increasing the educational requirements of correctional officers will provide a personnel pool better equipped to handle the stresses of correctional work. Taylor (p. 2) states:

> [The] occupational complexity for the officer includes the ability to change offenders' behavior, an understanding of conflict dynamics and communication skills, a comprehension of the deprivations of imprisonment, and the awareness of cultural and ethnic diversity.
>
> With the requirements for correctional officers combining the tasks of a high-tech security guard with the abilities of a social worker, the need for college education becomes apparent in its teaching of complex analytical abilities, problem solving skills, and a heightened tolerance of ambiguity. Moreover, with the educational levels of offenders rising, evidenced by the expansiveness of prison college programs . . ., the educational levels of those staffing the institutions should meet or exceed those they supervise.

Supporters of this higher educational requirement believe education opens people's minds, expands their horizons and provides them with skills to handle challenges and conflict. The mere process of taking college courses and completing a degree forces one to think, make choices, prioritize, meet deadlines and follow through on commitments, regardless of the subjects studied. Such a process necessarily brings about a degree of maturity in the person going through it. Gone are the days when correctional officers were expected to be large, muscular men who maintained order strictly through fear, force and physical action. Correctional officers today must think and communicate to effectively control their wards.

Another effort to raise correctional officer effectiveness and take some of the guesswork out of the job is the development of codes of ethics or codes of conduct. Codes of ethics are presented in greater detail in Chapter 13.

The National Institute of Corrections has compiled a competency profile (Figure 12–2) to "aid staff, political leaders, media and the general public in understanding the importance and complexity of skills of corrections officers" (Hill, p. 2).

Women as Correctional Officers. Until the 1970s and 1980s, the only facilities in which women were allowed to work as correctional officers were those for female and juvenile offenders, and the only positions women were allowed to hold in male institutions were clerical. During the 1970s, with the passage of equal employment legislation, barriers to work in all correctional positions and institutions began to be dropped for women and minorities.

Although their numbers today remain substantially lower than those of White, male correctional officers, women (and minorities) are becoming more prevalent in the field. At the beginning of 1997, women comprised 31.2 percent of all employees in adult correctional facilities but only 20.6 percent of correctional officers in adult correctional systems (Camp and Camp, pp. 108, 112). Mississippi has the highest percentage of female officers by a wide margin—47.3 percent. Also high above the national average are Arkansas (37.0 percent), South Carolina (32.3 percent) and Texas (30.5 percent) (p. 112).

Prior to equal employment laws, many arguments were made for barring female correctional officers in male facilities, including: (1) women weren't strong enough, (2) their presence would be disruptive to prison operations (inmates would not follow their orders or would fight for their attention) and (3) the privacy of male inmates would be violated. Although some still try to use these objections, experience has shown they are unfounded. In fact, several studies have shown that female correctional officers have a normalizing effect, making the atmosphere of the facility seem more like the outside world.

Women in corrections have demonstrated their ability to meet or exceed the required levels of performance despite the fact most don't meet the old height and weight minimums originally set up for correctional officers—*male* correctional officers. These height and weight minimums were designated under the assumption that persons below such minimums would not be physically strong enough to perform the duties required of correctional officers. It was shown, however, that such limits were discriminatory to women as a class and that they were not directly related to the ability to perform the job.

Figure 12–2	Competency Profile of Correctional Officer

A CORRECTIONAL OFFICER ensures the public safety by providing for the care, custody, control and maintenance of inmates; and to carry out this mission, must:

I. Manage and communicate with inmates—
   A. Orient new arrivals on rules, procedures, and general information of facility/unit.
   B. Enforce rules and regulations.
   C. Conduct cell inspections (for contraband, obstructions, sanitation, jammed locks, etc.).
   D. Establish rapport (introduce self, use good body language, listen, etc.).
   E. Provide verbal and written counseling (i.e., disciplinary behavior, informational, confidential).
   F. Write disciplinary and incident reports.

II. Intervene in crises and manage conflicts—
   A. Employ the use of force continuum (minimum, less-than-lethal, lethal).
   B. Direct inmate movement.
   C. Observe, monitor and supervise movement of inmates/inmate property.
   D. Properly identify and escort inmates individually or in groups.
   E. Implement schedules for controlled movement of inmates at specified times.
   F. Restrict movement during scheduled physical counts of inmates.
   G. Receive/issue inmate passes/appointment slips.
   H. Implement emergency operating plans.
   I. Enforce custody/privilege/disciplinary restrictions.
   J. Receive/recommend inmate requests for bed, cell, or unit move.
   K. Maintain key, tool, and equipment control.
   L. Inspect keys, equipment, tools, and beepers.
   M. Report broken/missing keys, equipment, and tools.
   N. Inventory keys, equipment, and tools at beginning and end of shift.
   O. Maintain physical control of keys, equipment, and tools.
   P. Log keys, equipment, and tools in the work area.

III. Maintain Health, Safety, and Sanitation—
   A. Report changes in behavior.
   B. Search persons, personal property, and units.
   C. Report security violations.
   D. Submit health, safety, and sanitation recommendations to appropriate departments.
   E. Implement proper health procedures for inmates with infectious diseases.
   F. Implement health/safety memos and posters.
   G. Develop cleaning schedule.
   H. Supervise cleaning schedule.
   I. Ensure proper handling/labeling of hazardous materials.
   J. Supervise hygiene habits of inmates.

IV. Communicate with Staff—
   A. Establish positive rapport with other staff.
   B. Maintain constant communication with other staff and vigilance as to their work.
   C. Operate communication equipment per established guidelines.
   D. Document incidents, write reports, write recommendations going through chain-of-command.
   E. Brief oncoming staff for next shifts.
   F. Explain unusual procedures to staff.
   G. Participate in staff meetings.

V. Participate in Training—
  A. Participate in mandatory/elective training.
  B. Read daily log book and other information.
  C. Review new/updated post orders, administrative regulations, and memos.
  D. Participate in cross-training.
  E. Review and simulate emergency procedures (fire drills).
  F. Pursue continuing education opportunities.
  G. Seek additional training opportunities.

VI. Distribute Authorized Items to Inmates—
  A. Order/request authorized items.
  B. Take inventory of and distribute authorized items.
  C. Document the distribution of authorized items.

CORRECTIONAL OFFICER TRAITS & ATTITUDES

Professional	Perceptive
Dependable	Neat
Consistent	Compassionate
Fair	Analytical
Emotionally stable	Positive role
Empathetic	model

Ethical	Credible
Flexible	Leader
Punctual	Assertive
Self-motivated	Adaptable/
Cooperative	change-
Sincere	oriented
Sense of humor	
Optimistic	

KNOWLEDGE & SKILLS

Knowledge of:
Laws of jurisdiction
Policies & procedures
Force/necessary use of
Agency mission/purpose
Ethnic diversity
Equipment/tools
Available training
Stress management

Skills:
Written communication
Non-verbal communication
Stress management
All prison equipment/tools
Searching
CPR/First Aid
Leadership
Public relations
Management
Interpersonal communication

TOOLS & EQUIPMENT

Radios
Mechanical restraints (cuffs, waist chains, leg irons, flex-cuffs/soft restraints)
Badge
Whistle
Leather duty belts with accessories

Personal alarm devices/TAC alarms
Keys
Flashlight
Electronic control devices (Taser/stun gun)
Batons (straight/PR-24/riot baton)
Gloves (protective/leather/duty)
Uniforms/footwear
Helmets (riot/protective)
Polycaptor/riot shields
Stun shields
Body armor (vests, etc.)
Protective CPR/First Aid masks
Generators
Light stands
Computers
Telephone/paging systems
Airpacks/SCBA
Binoculars
Audio/visual aids
Equipment for opening/closing cell doors
Sallyports, entry gates, corridor grills
ID cards

Weapons:
Rifle/Shotgun
Handgun (37/38 mm)
Gas Gun
Dispersal of grenades
Rubber bullets
Chemical agents (CN/CS/mace)
Gas masks

Source: Gary Hill. "Correctional Officer Traits and Skills." *Corrections Compendium,* Vol. XXII, No. 8, August 1997, p. 2. Reprinted by permission of CEGA Publishing.

Standards directly related to the job to be performed are known as bona fide occupational qualifications, or BFOQs.

> A **bona fide occupational qualification (BFOQ)** is a requirement reasonably necessary to perform the job.

An example of a BFOQ for corrections work might be normal or correctable-to-normal vision and hearing since these senses are vital to adequate supervision of inmates.

To address privacy rights of male inmates supervised by female correctional officers, facilities have limited women correctional officers to general frisk and pat down searches and removed them from conducting strip searches or more invasive searches. Additionally, half-screens and doors have been installed in shower areas and on bathroom stalls to afford inmates a degree of privacy without sacrificing security.

Minority Correctional Officers. As facilities seek to hire more women, they are also realizing the need for more minority correctional officers. Johnson (1995, p. 96) states: "The large number of minority inmates, combined with an absence of minority correctional staff, often adds to the racial tension at a

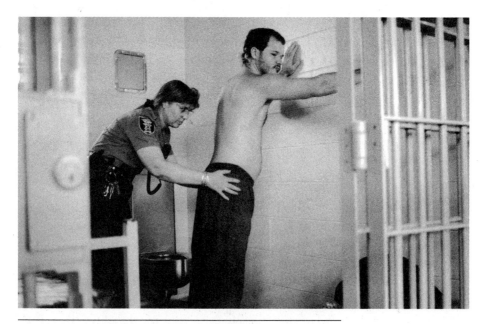

A female correctional officer pats down a male inmate during a cell search. Such practices have occasionally been called into question, as inmates claim privacy rights violations upon being searched by officers of the opposite sex.

correctional facility." As of January 1, 1997, non-Whites comprised 25.2 percent of all adult correctional system staff and 29.0 percent of correctional officers in these facilities (Camp and Camp, pp. 108,112).

Johnson (p. 96) notes: "There is a clear connection between institutional instability and a correctional staff that does not include people of color." Furthermore, he states (p. 97): "A diverse correctional staff can enhance communication between staff and inmates, add to the cultural awareness of staff, decrease racial tension, provide positive role models and enhance a department's public image." According to Hunt and Golden (1992, p. 61): "Transcultural correctional officers have a basic understanding of their own development as racial beings, and they can understand racial attitudes of other groups."

Sometimes, however, minority correctional officers feel they must walk a fine line between the interests of the inmates they share ethnicity with and the policies of the correctional administration, often predominantly White. Using an example of White vs. Black correctional officers, Hunt (1993, p. 15) notes:

> The African-American correctional officer will be evaluated differently by African-American inmates. The African-American officer is assumed to be familiar with the culture and will be tested by inmates. Correctional officers who are fair but firm will receive respect. Black correctional officers must prove that they have not "sold out" to the system. Selling out means acting white, being unfair to African-American inmates; taking sides with whites against blacks, especially when it's clear that whites are in the wrong; and not being assertive in situations where one's integrity is being questioned.

Conflict can easily arise for the minority correctional officer who must walk a tightrope between adhering to the officer code—"always support an officer in a dispute with an inmate" and "maintain officer solidarity versus all outside groups"—and not "selling out" to inmates of their own race, particularly when the nonminority officer(s) are wrong or out of line.

➤ **Unions.** A **union,** in a very general sense, is a group authorized to represent members of an agency or profession in negotiating such matters as wages, fringe benefits, working conditions and other elements of employment. Unionization of correctional officers evolved from a general trend in the unionization of public employees. Correctional officers were among the final groups of public workers to organize into unions, with a majority of states having correctional unions today. Most of these unions, however, are prohibited by law from striking.

The fundamental objective of a union is to improve employment conditions
➤ through a process known as collective bargaining. **Collective bargaining** is a process in which representatives of employees meet with representatives of management to establish a written contract outlining working conditions over a specific length of time, usually one to three years. The contract covers issues such as wages and benefits, hours of work and overtime, grievance procedures, disciplinary procedures, health and safety, employees' rights, seniority and contract duration.

> The fundamental objective of unions is to improve employment conditions through collective bargaining.

The unionization of correctional officers has not been a cure-all for the problems that plague this profession and has, in fact, created a number of problems for correctional employees. The biggest problem facing correctional officers is that most correctional unions cannot legally strike. They are, therefore, limited in their collective power against administration. However, unlawful strikes do occur. Such unlawful strikes often backfire on correctional unions by failing to evoke sympathy from the public and because forces such as the National Guard may be called in to substitute for the striking officers, thereby averting any real shutdown of the facility. Nonetheless, unions have frequently been effective in helping correctional officers get management's attention concerning employment issues.

Probation and Parole Officers

Like correctional officers, probation and parole officers are charged with supervising offenders. However, unlike correctional officers, probation and parole officers work outside the bars and high brick walls, in the community corrections environment. A **probation officer** supervises offenders diverted away from incarceration, whereas a **parole officer** supervises offenders recently released from incarceration yet not entirely free from the correctional system. Many jurisdictions use the same officer to supervise both probationers and parolees.

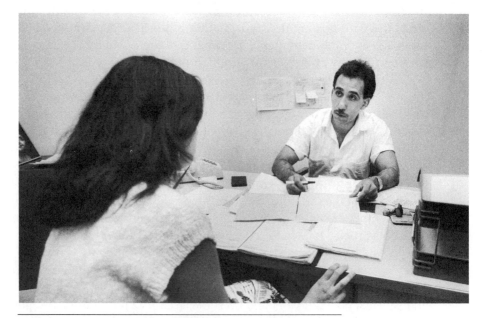

A parole officer meets with a woman recently paroled. In many agencies, parole officers also handle probation cases.

Who Works in Probation and Parole? As of January 1, 1997, there were 68,491 people employed in the areas of probation and parole: 32,036 (47 percent) strictly as probation officers, 10,401 (15 percent) strictly as parole officers and 26,054 (38 percent) as both probation and parole officers (Camp and Camp, p. 174). With the increased use of probation as a sentencing alternative, the number of officers needed to supervise offenders is expected to increase substantially over the next decade.

Similar to the correctional officer cohort, most probation and parole officers are White (69.7 percent). A significant difference, however, is that female probation and parole officers outnumber males—52.3 percent are women. The average salaries for probation, parole and probation/parole officers are fairly close to each other: probation officer, $32,369; parole officer, $33,750; and probation/parole officer, $31,466.

Torbet (1996, p. 1) offers a profile of the typical juvenile probation officer:

> Generally, juvenile probation officers are college-educated white males, 30–49 years old, with 5–10 years of experience in the field. Typically the officers earn $20,000–$39,000 per year and receive standard benefits packages, but not necessarily annual salary increases. The average caseload is 41 juveniles. Although probation officers have some arrest powers, they do not normally carry weapons.

Caseloads. Tremendous differences exist between the caseloads of probation and parole officers in different jurisdictions. According to Camp and Camp (p. 149): "Caseloads for probation officers ranged from 900 cases per officer in California to 60 cases per officer in Arizona. Among probation and parole officers, caseloads per officer ranged from 165 in Alabama to 53 in Ohio. Parole officers' caseloads varied from 176 cases per officer in the District of Columbia to 10 per officer in Vermont."

The number of cases probation or parole officers must handle necessarily affects their ability to carry out the myriad roles expected of them.

Roles of Probation and Parole Officers. Williamson (pp. 128–129) notes three basic roles of the probation/parole officer:

- Surveillance—supervising clients to ensure they are complying with the terms of their probation/parole. Degree of supervision may vary; some may be seen several times a week and others only once a month. Still others may be required only to check in by phone.

- Caseworker—conducting presentence and prerelease reports, helping offenders obtain the services of other private, community or governmental agencies.

- Counselor—assisting clients with personal problems or referring them to the appropriate individuals, programs or agencies.

> Probation and parole officers commonly function in a variety of roles, including surveillance, casework and counseling.

The job of the probation and parole officer is much more complex than these three basic roles would indicate. As Cosgrove (1994), himself a federal probation officer, states:

> What does a probation officer do? To this day, I suffer a violent, visceral pain whenever I hear some visiting academic discuss the "two hats" of the probation officer: cop or counselor. At last count we are at 33 hats and the number is growing.
>
> . . . Requirements for the job used to be listed as good writing skills and the ability to investigate, counsel and interview. If training speaks the employer's perceptions of what workers need to know, then consider the following programs which are offered to probation officers: Mental Preparation for Violent Confrontations, Dual Diagnoses, Child Abuse, Hate Groups, Sexual Deviance, Cultural Diversity, Negotiating Skills, Assertiveness Training, Fingerprinting, Ethics, Financial Investigation, Infectious Diseases, Chemical Abuse Seminars, Organized Crime Groups, Lexis/Nexis training. . . .

A significant part of a probation or parole officer's job involves understanding human nature, something that cannot be learned in a classroom. Carlton, retired after more than 25 years as a probation officer, states (1998): "The entire job is learning to deal with people and solving problems. However, the only way to gain that knowledge is to live and learn."

Part of understanding human nature is knowing when someone is being deceptive, and probation and parole officers usually develop a sixth sense about when a client is lying to them. Sometimes, however, such insight is not necessary. For example, the common practice of drug testing by probation and parole agencies often provides ample opportunity for probation and parole officers to hear how inventive some of their clients can be. As Carlton relates: "Our office did a lot of in-office drug testing. Many clients offer an excuse for having a 'positive' urine sample. Examples include:

1. I was in the room when others smoked marijuana, so it must be second-hand smoke.

2. Someone slipped something into my Mountain Dew.

3. I had sex with someone who used drugs."

It can truly be a challenge to counsel people who think such excuses are plausible because (1) they often don't see their actions as "wrong" and (2) in many cases they hold little, if any, respect for the correctional system and professionals dedicated to helping them get back on track. Many probation and parole officers tell with frustration of how their days are spent trying to keep track of people who repeatedly violate the terms of their probation or parole and are "constantly trying to get away with something." An innovative strategy used in Boston since 1992 has helped probation officers keep watch over juvenile offenders who violate their probation—allowing a probation officer to ride along with a police officer. As told by Butterfield (1997, p. 3):

> . . . on the first night Mr. Stewart [the probation officer] and Detective Fratalia drove together in 1992, they had not gone half a block before they heard on their radio that a boy had been shot nearby. The boy was one of Mr. Stewart's cases, and as he looked around the shooting scene, Mr. Stewart saw 35 other people he recognized as being on probation who should not have been out that late.
>
> "They were amazed to see me out there at night with the cops," Mr. Stewart recalled. "They tried to cover their faces. They were really afraid. They knew that, unlike the cops, I could recognize them."
>
> Many of these young people, he had come to learn, hate probation more than prison because they believe it interferes with their lives more.
>
> Detective Fratalia was also amazed. Where normally bystanders at a crime scene claim to have seen nothing, Mr. Stewart was able to elicit information about the shooting from the young people who faced having their probation revoked and going to jail, or—just as bad—spending more time on probation.

Maryland has also implemented a similar initiative as part of its "HotSpot Communities" program ("Maryland Puts Probation," 1997, p. 5):

> The component of the program that involves probation officers will assign officers to neighborhoods where their duties will be to work with community groups, police, and others to keep close track of individuals on probation or parole who live there.
>
> . . . the approach that the HotSpot Communities probation officers will take is very different from the traditional way probation officers function. Instead of spending much of their time in their offices, they will talk with community residents, share intelligence with police officers, and occasionally ride patrol with police officers.

Clearly, the roles of the probation and parole officer are ever-changing, evolving as the entire correctional system seeks to find better ways to handle its clients.

Treatment Personnel

Although it is common for correctional, probation and parole officers to counsel offenders, the corrections system also employs a wide variety of personnel whose primary responsibility is not the custody and surveillance of offenders but rather their treatment. Williamson (p. 132) states: "The traditional definition of the treatment function is limited to those programs directed at the change of long-term behavioral patterns, not merely the immediate control of overt behavior while incarcerated or under supervision. These programs typically include vocational and academic education, individual and group counseling, and similar activities."

Treatment professionals include medical staff, psychologists and mental health staff, caseworkers and counselors, correctional educators, chaplains and other religious personnel, recreational specialists and other program coordinators.

Medical Staff

A full range of medical professionals is required to service inmate populations, including physicians, surgeons, nurses, dentists, laboratory technicians and pharmacists. In general, those living the risky life of crime also tend to take risks with their health; consequently, many inmates come to corrections with more health problems than the average citizen. Additionally, as discussed in Chapter 10, the crowded prison environment holds great potential for the spread of contagious diseases such as TB.

Many smaller facilities are unable to afford a full-time, on-site medical staff and, as a result, frequently contract with area clinics and hospitals to provide such services. Larger institutions, however, usually provide full-time in-house medical staff. It is often difficult to attract health care workers to correctional

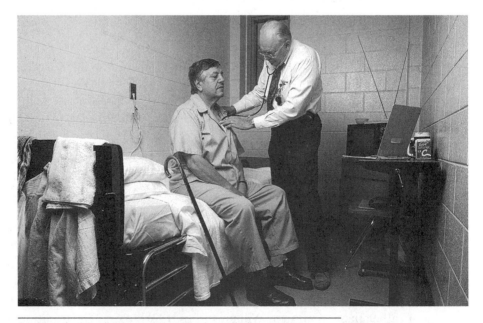

A prison physician listens to an inmate's heart during an exam.

facilities because of the low pay and unfavorable working conditions. When asked if the job was as expected and if there was anything they wished they'd known before taking the job, one chief health officer who had worked for 11 years as a corrections physician replied: "I had unrealistic expectations of inmates and the budget is more restrained than I expected. Furthermore, I wish I had known about the limited financial progression." Nonetheless, quality medical care is a court-mandated service for corrections, and a majority of health care workers are required to be licensed or certified by their respective licensing boards or agencies to practice in correctional settings.

Psychologists and Mental Health Staff

Recall from Chapter 10 the rising numbers of mentally retarded and mentally ill offenders being held in our nation's correctional facilities, how many jails now report seeing far more inmates with serious mental illness than they did a decade ago and how it has been estimated that one in five prison inmates require services associated with severe or chronic mental illness. For these reasons, corrections employs a variety of mental health professionals including psychiatrists, psychologists and counselors. These professionals comprise the mental health team, which may work either full-time or part-time within the facility.

An important distinction is made between psychiatrists and psychologists. A **psychiatrist** is a licensed medical doctor, or M.D., who specializes in the area of mental illness and is authorized to prescribe medication. A **psychologist** is not a medical doctor and, therefore, generally cannot prescribe drugs but can conduct psychological testing and treat mental disorders via therapy.

The educational requirements of mental health personnel vary, depending on their degree of involvement with offenders, whether there is a need for them to prescribe drugs and whether they work under the direction of another staff member. Psychiatrists, as mentioned, must possess an M.D. and be licensed. Psychologists are usually required to possess a Ph.D. and be licensed or certified. Requirements for counselors vary considerably.

In addition to treating offenders for mental illness, the mental health team administers and interprets numerous standardized tests for use by the correctional institution or parole authorities. Psychological profiles of offenders are frequently used for classification and parole decisions.

One senior psychologist tells of her experiences with the correctional population:

> A lot of what I do is crisis management. It is very difficult at times to sort out the real mental health problems from manipulation of the system. . . .
>
> I would probably not recommend this line of work to a close friend. The requirements, documentation for the job make it virtually impossible to provide good, quality, long-term therapy for those who need it. . . . Before I took this job, I wish I had known more about the politics involved, the rules, regulations and limitations. . . .

I have mixed feelings about the inmates I work with. There are some who are sincere in their need for help and willingness to change. There are others who will continually use the system. . . . Overall, I think the corrections system is ineffective. There is not enough rehabilitation done. Too often inmates' rights are violated. They are more often than not judged to be wrong in any grievance procedure. They need to be treated with more respect.

Caseworkers and Counselors

Mental health staff are not the only ones who use psychological concepts to treat offenders. Caseworkers and other counselors also rely on a variety of psychological techniques. According to Williamson (p. 137), social caseworkers may collect and analyze data pertaining to inmate classification, assist inmates in preparing preparole plans, help inmates achieve placement in various treatment and educational programs and counsel inmates during personal crises, such as the death of a family member. The various techniques used by caseworkers include alcohol and drug counseling programs, behavior modification, group counseling, milieu therapy, psychodrama, individual and group psychotherapy, reality therapy and transactional analysis.

Correctional counselors may use some of the preceding techniques, such as group counseling and alcohol and drug counseling, but generally do not use the stronger techniques that caseworkers and mental health personnel do. The primary responsibility of most correctional counselors is to collect and interpret data about inmates and to help inmates with programming decisions. Common counselor duties may include

- Keeping a file on each new resident.
- Determining treatment program objectives, methods, completion dates and long-range goals.
- Contacting program team members for meetings.
- Assisting parole boards and inmates with items needed for parole hearings.
- Interviewing inmates for work release programs, determining eligibility and writing recommendations to the department.

Correctional Educators

Educational programming in correctional facilities ranges from remedial reading and completion of the high school General Education Development (GED) test to vocational training and college degrees. Consequently, a wide array of correctional educators may be found in correctional settings throughout the country.

Many offenders are functionally illiterate or have a serious learning disability. A benchmark of a fifth grade reading level has been designated as the line between literate and functionally illiterate, with those reading below a fifth grade level falling into the latter category. Some estimates place the number of functionally illiterate inmates as high as 75 percent. The national cost of functional illiteracy has been estimated at more than $450 billion—over $230 billion in unrealized lifetime earnings and over $220 billion in social costs including welfare, unemployment and crime. As noted by Williamson (p. 135): "All prison systems are required by Public Law 94-142 to provide special education to those inmates under 21 who have learning deficiencies." Correctional educators work with these inmates to improve their reading and problem-solving skills so that they might attain a GED, often an acceptable substitute for a high school diploma. Many employers typically require one or the other when considering an individual for employment.

Educational efforts are also aimed at helping offenders prepare for specific areas of employment after release. Vocational training is often provided in areas such as auto repair, carpentry, data processing and food service. In many facilities, inmates are also allowed to pursue college degrees. These educators may work strictly for the corrections system or may be faculty at local colleges and universities. In the past, it was not uncommon for inmates to enter corrections with little or no education and, by the time of their release, have completed a college degree, in some cases a graduate degree. Recently, however, there have been significant cutbacks in college programs since Pell grants for inmates have been terminated.

Prison Chaplains and Other Religious Personnel

The freedom to practice religion is protected by the First Amendment of the Bill of Rights and extends to all Americans, free or incarcerated. Some people choose to make religion part of their daily life; others seek spiritual guidance only in times of crisis. Whatever the individual case, prison chaplains are correctional personnel employed to fill this niche. In early prisons, chaplains served as educators, social workers and counselors. As correctional facilities began hiring more treatment professionals, chaplains were able to focus solely on religious matters.

The prison chaplain runs the prison chapel, which is often interdenominational, given the wide variety of religious faiths that accompany a diverse correctional population. Facilities need not employ only one religious leader. They may have a Protestant chaplain, a Catholic priest, a Jewish rabbi and other religious leaders depending on the inmate population's denominational needs. Responsibilities of these religious personnel include leading regular worship services, performing funeral services, providing spiritual counseling to inmates, coordinating religious programming with other institutional programming and representing the correctional facility with various religious

A prison chaplain may organize a variety of religious programs involving both inmates and staff, such as this gospel choir at San Quentin's prison.

groups in the community. They also coordinate use of religious volunteers who come into the institution to meet with inmates.

One prison chaplain who has spent 13 years working in corrections speaks of the challenges of ministering to correctional clients: "The politics are worse than anyone can conceive. The one-on-one possibilities to teach and affect a productive lifestyle are greater. The inmate games and cons are troublesome at times. The ministry is great and enjoyable." He gives the following response when asked about the inmates he works with: "10% are con men that keep us alert and on guard at all times. 10% are truly not guilty of the crime they are here for but have great needs. 20% want to improve their lifestyle. 20% don't know any other way to live. 10% should be in mental institutions. 10% need to be in a medical facility. The rest can't wait to do it again."

Recreational Specialists

Inmates, like individuals in the community, benefit by having access to creative outlets. Recreational specialists organize programs such as sporting events, arts and crafts, movies and cultural events such as concerts and plays. Through these recreational activities inmates learn how to better use leisure time that they may have previously spent engaging in criminal activity. Recreational specialists' efforts help occupy inmates' time and diminish idleness, which often leads to inmate discontent and violence. Recreational activities also help improve inmates' emotional well-being, self-image and ability to socialize with others.

Self-Help Advisors

A preponderance of self-help groups are available to inmates, including Alcoholics Anonymous, Narcotics Anonymous, the Jaycees and Dale Carnegie courses. While inmates typically direct these programs, staff members may serve as a liaison or advisor to these groups.

Support Personnel

The list of support personnel in corrections can be long for large facilities and includes a wide variety of individuals. Personnel in support positions are needed to handle the abundance of resources required to operate a correctional facility. Williamson (p. 130) notes: "Facilities must be constructed, maintained and repaired. Raw materials must be acquired, stored and prepared for use or used to create products. Employees must be recruited, trained, supervised, evaluated and paid." Among the occupational support staff categories identified by Williamson (pp. 130–131) are the following:

Personnel Clerical and Assistant	Secretary
Computer Clerk and Assistant	Electronic Technician
Legal Clerk and Technician	General Facilities and Equipment
Laundry Plant Management	Inventory Management
Electronic Equipment Installation/Maintenance	Electrical Installation/Maintenance
Fabric and Leather Work	Wood Work
Machine Tool Work	Structural and Finishing Work
Metal Processing	Metal Working
Painting and Paperhanging	Plumbing and Pipefitting
Printing	Warehousing and Stock Handling
Quality Assurance and Control	Plant and Animal Work
Transportation/Mobile Equipment Maintenance	

Support personnel include a range of staff, from clerical workers and truck drivers to accountants and engineers.

Volunteers

With budgets stretched to their limits and the number and needs of inmates ever increasing, the role of volunteers in corrections has never been more vital. Volunteerism is not, however, a new concept to corrections. Parole and probation have their roots in volunteerism. John Augustus, the father of probation, was a volunteer, and Zebulon Brockway used volunteers to supervise released inmates.

Through the use of volunteers, many facilities are able to offer programs they could not otherwise afford. In fact, many of the positions previously discussed in this chapter are staffed by volunteers in many facilities throughout the country. The spread of volunteers has mandated the creation of a new position, the volunteer coordinator, in probation, and prisoner visitation and support (PVS) makes extensive use of volunteers.

Volunteers come from a variety of backgrounds. Costa and Seymour (1993, p. 110) note that corrections volunteers often come from local church groups, the business community and local colleges. "However, a growing number of volunteers are individuals who have personally felt the effects of crime in their lives—crime victims and former offenders."

> Correctional volunteers come from a variety of backgrounds and may be local church group members, part of the business community, students or professors at local colleges, crime victims and ex-offenders.

A former inmate returns to prison as a volunteer to educate male prisoners about HIV and AIDS. The volunteer is also HIV-positive.

Regarding crime victims as corrections volunteers, Costa and Seymour (pp. 110–112) state: "Crime victims serving as volunteers can offer a unique perspective to the people they serve. They can help both inmates and staff understand the traumatic effects crimes have on their victims, their families and society in general. In addition, volunteer service offers victims a chance to have input into the criminal justice system and therefore to affect the lives of other victims."

Many volunteers come from communities, cultures and socioeconomic levels vastly different from the offenders they serve. A volunteer who shares the same community, culture and socioeconomic status as offenders is identi-

➤ fied as an **indigenous paraprofessional** by McCarthy and McCarthy (1991, p. 389). As these authors point out (p. 390): "Not only have they shared the same culture and community as the offender, but they have also confronted some of the same problems, made some of the same choices, and experienced some of the same repercussions. They are thus in a special position to understand and communicate with offenders and to serve as a living illustration of the possibility of reform."

Corrections functions frequently staffed by volunteers include "chaplains, health education counselors, nurses, adult education teachers, family counselors, employment specialists, vocational counselors and trainers, and ex-offender support services specialists" (DC DOC, 1993, p. 124). Volunteers are also used in probation offices. According to Smith (1993, p. 80): "A volunteer probation officer program is an effective way to enhance a probation department and involve the community in the criminal justice system."

An innovative program in Maryland that depends on volunteers is a Girl Scout program for daughters of incarcerated mothers. The program, which is run by the Girl Scouts of Central Maryland (GSCM), relies heavily on volunteers for its success. Muriel Gates, special project coordinator for GSCM, states: "Without dedicated volunteers, we would not be able to serve these girls. These volunteers are the backbone of our organization. They do everything from coordinating transportation, making home visits to those without telephone service and escorting the children to the [correctional institution] meetings to organizing the community troop meetings and working with the mothers" (Moses, 1993, p. 134).

Other corrections groups that actively recruit volunteers include the International Association of Justice Volunteerism, the National Victim Center, Prison Fellowship, the Salvation Army, Volunteers of America, the Program for Female Offenders, Inc. and the Alston Wilkes Society ("Guide to Corrections," 1993, p. 138).

The ACA has published a handbook for correctional volunteers (*Helping Hands: A Handbook for Volunteers in Prisons and Jails,* by Daniel Bayse) and suggests that effective volunteers need to have certain qualities ("Volunteer Program Guide," 1993, pp. 68–70):

- Be ethical.
- Be a good listener.
- Be empathetic, but not gullible.
- Be respectful.
- Be genuine.
- Be patient.
- Be trustworthy.
- Be confrontive.
- Be objective—don't take sides.
- Expect hostility.
- Don't expect thanks.

It is uncertain exactly how many volunteers are serving corrections, but there is always room for more. According to Winter (1993, p. 20):

> Although it is estimated that the criminal justice system draws less than one half of 1 percent of the available volunteer pool in America, the 1990s seem to be a decade of increased justice volunteerism. Educated projections suggest justice volunteers are playing an important role in revitalizing America's criminal justice system. Establishing links between community volunteers and offenders is an ongoing challenge for correctional administrators.

Volunteers, whatever their number, are valuable members of the corrections team. Brenda Jones, volunteer executive director and founder of Parklands Community Center in Washington, DC, has said: "People who volunteer in prison are a special breed who really understand human suffering. They can serve as positive change agents to offenders" (DC DOC, p. 126).

Summary

As the number of offenders are increasing, so too are the number of correctional personnel required to supervise and tend to these offenders. With construction of correctional facilities proceeding at a lively pace, efforts to staff these facilities are equally vigorous.

Custodial and security personnel are generally called correctional officers. The primary responsibility of a correctional officer is to maintain order and control over those committed to custody and to prevent their escape. The majority of corrections personnel are correctional officers, who comprise nearly 52 percent of all corrections employees. Today, a greater percentage of correctional officers are women, as they have consistently demonstrated their ability to meet or exceed the required levels of performance for correctional officers. A bona fide occupational qualification (BFOQ) is a requirement reasonably necessary to perform the job.

Many correctional officers belong to unions. The fundamental objective of unions is to improve employment conditions through collective bargaining.

Probation and parole officers are also considered custodial/security personnel and commonly function in a variety of roles, including surveillance, casework and counseling.

Treatment professionals include medical staff, psychologists and mental health staff, caseworkers and counselors, correctional educators, chaplains and other religious personnel, recreational specialists and other program coordinators. Support personnel include a range of staff, from clerical workers and truck drivers to accountants and engineers.

The role of volunteers in corrections has never been more vital than today. Correctional volunteers come from a variety of backgrounds and may be local church group members, part of the business community, students or professors at local colleges, crime victims and ex-offenders.

Discussion Questions

1. Do you think a correctional facility with the average officer-to-inmate ratio of 1 to 5.4 is adequately staffed? When might such a ratio be too low? Too high?

2. Would you prefer to be a correctional officer in a small jail or a large prison? Why?

3. Regarding the realities of being a correctional officer, which ones came as a surprise to you? Which ones did you expect to be true?

4. Interview some correctional officers at your local correctional facilities and find out what surprised them most about the job. What's the most rewarding part? Most difficult part?

5. Since most correctional unions are prohibited by law from striking, what recourse do correctional employees really have in the event of a labor dispute? Are unions common among your local corrections?

6. Is it a good or bad idea to have the same individual serve as both a probation and a parole officer? Why?

7. Should inmates be offered free education? Why or why not? To what level?

8. Do your local correctional facilities and programs make much use of volunteers? If so, in what capacity? If not, why not?

9. Have you ever volunteered in a correctional setting? If so, share your experience.

10. Is there a shortage of qualified correctional employees in your local area? If so, what is your jurisdiction doing to remedy the situation?

References

American Correctional Association. *The Effective Correctional Officer.* Fredericksburg, VA: BookCrafters, 1992.

Blair, Robert and Kratcoski, Peter C. "Professionalism Among Correctional Officers: A Longitudinal Analysis of Individual and Structural Determinants." In *Corrections: Dilemmas and Directions,* edited by Peter J. Benekos and Alida V. Merlo. Cincinnati, OH: Anderson Publishing Co., 1992, pp. 97–120.

Butterfield, Fox. "In Boston, Nothing Is Something." *Subject to Debate* (A Newsletter of the Police Executive Research Forum), Vol. 11, Nos. 2&3, February/March 1997, pp. 1, 3–4.

Camp, George M. and Camp, Camille Graham. *The Corrections Yearbook, 1997.* South Salem, NY: The Criminal Justice Institute, 1997.

Carlton, Dale L. Retired from U.S. Probation Office. Responded to survey sent by author, 1998.

Conroy, Dennis L. and Hess, Kären M. *Officers at Risk: How to Identify and Cope with Stress.* Incline Village, NV: Copperhouse Publishing Company, 1992.

Cosgrove, Edward J. "ROBO-PO: The Life and Times of a Federal Probation Officer." *The Third Circuit Journal,* Vol. 12, No. 2, 1994.

Costa, Jeralita and Seymour, Anne. "Crime Victims, Former Offenders Contribute a Unique Perspective." *Corrections Today,* August 1993, pp. 110–113.

Digges, Robert E., Jr. *Behind the Walls: A Correctional Officer's Story.* Ft. Oglethorpe, GA: R.E. Digges, Jr., 1994.

District of Columbia Department of Corrections Office of Communications. "D.C. Honors Volunteers for Outstanding Service." *Corrections Today,* August 1993, pp. 124–126.

"Guide to Corrections Volunteer Groups." *Corrections Today,* August 1993, p. 138.

Harr, J. Scott and Hess, Kären M. *Seeking Employment in Criminal Justice and Related Fields,* 2nd ed. St. Paul, MN: West Publishing Company, 1996.

Hill, Gary. "Correctional Officer Traits and Skills." *Corrections Compendium,* Vol. XXII, No. 8, August 1997, pp. 1–12.

"Hiring of Correctional Officers Increasingly More Selective." *Corrections Compendium,* September 1994, pp. 8, 11.

Hunt, Portia. "Expression of African-American Culture in Correctional Settings." In *Understanding Cultural Diversity,* American Correctional Association. Fredericksburg, VA: BookCrafters, 1993.

Hunt, Portia and Golden, Liz. "Racial Differences and the Supervision of Inmates." In *The Effective Correctional Officer,* American Correctional Association. Fredericksburg, VA: BookCrafters, 1992.

Johnson, Tim. "Stressing the Value of Targeted Recruitment in Corrections." *Corrections Today,* June 1995, pp. 96–99.

Kauffman, Kelsey. *Prison Officers and Their World.* Cambridge, MA: Harvard University Press, 1988.

Kelly, Michael. "Is a Career in Corrections for You?" *Corrections Today,* July 1996, p. 134.

Lombardo, Lucien X. *Guards Imprisoned,* 2nd ed. Cincinnati, OH: Anderson Publishing Co., 1989.

"Maryland Puts Probation Officers on Patrol in Neighborhoods." *Corrections Journal* (Pace Publications), Vol. 2, No. 2, July 22, 1997, pp. 5–6.

McCarthy, Belinda Rodgers and McCarthy, Bernard J., Jr. *Community-Based Corrections,* 2nd ed. Pacific Grove, CA: Brooks/Cole Publishing Company, 1991. Reprinted with permission of the publisher.

Moses, Marilyn C. "New Program at Women's Prison Benefits Mothers and Children." *Corrections Today,* August 1993, pp. 132–135.

Occupational Outlook Handbook, 1992–1993 ed. U.S. Department of Labor, Bureau of Labor Statistics. Washington, DC: U.S. Government Printing Office, 1993.

"Resolution on the Term 'Correctional Officer.' " *Corrections Today,* April 1993, pp. 60, 146.

Smith, Brian M. "Probation Department in Michigan Finds Volunteers Make Fine Officers." *Corrections Today,* August 1993, pp. 80–82.

Sourcebook of Criminal Justice Statistics, 1995. U.S. Department of Justice, Office of Justice Program, Bureau of Justice Statistics. Washington, DC: U.S. Government Printing Office, 1995.

Stalder, Richard L. "Correctional Officer Role Ambiguity." In *The Effective Correctional Officer,* American Correctional Association. Fredericksburg, VA: BookCrafters, 1992.

Stojkovic, Stan and Lovell, Rick. *Corrections: An Introduction.* Cincinnati, OH: Anderson Publishing Co., 1992.

Taylor, Jon Marc. "A G.I. Bill for Correctional Officers." *Corrections Compendium,* December 1995, pp. 1–3.

Torbet, Patricia McFall. *Juvenile Probation: The Workhorse of the Juvenile Justice System.* Juvenile Justice Bulletin. Washington, DC: U.S. Department of Justice, Office of Juvenile Justice and Delinquency Prevention, March 1996.

"Volunteer Program Guide." *Corrections Today,* August 1993, pp. 66–70.

Williamson, Harold E. *The Corrections Profession.* Newbury Park, CA: Sage Publications, Inc., 1990.

Winter, Bill. "Does Corrections Need Volunteers?" *Corrections Today,* August 1993, pp. 20–22.

Wright, John W. *The American Almanac of Jobs and Salaries,* 1994–1995 ed. New York: Avon Books, 1993.

SECTION IV

Corrections at Work

Corrections is a dynamic field, with many changes and innovations occurring frequently. This section examines corrections at work, beginning with a look at special challenges facing corrections (Chapter 13), such as escape prevention, security, sex, contraband, gangs, riots, hostages, use of force, drugs and drug testing, recreation, work training, ethics, grievance procedures, ADA requirements and crowding.

The complicated issues of prisoners' rights are the topic of Chapter 14. General themes and topics are discussed and illustrated with the presentation of pertinent and landmark cases. The chapter looks at the distinction between rights and privileges, the evolution of prisoners' rights, categories of prisoner lawsuits and getting such lawsuits to and through the courts, sources of prisoners' rights and some of the collateral consequences of criminal conviction.

The future of corrections in the twenty-first century is the subject of the final chapter (Chapter 15). This chapter examines the progress that has occurred in corrections over the past 125 years, emphasizing the dynamic and ever-changing nature of the field of corrections. The discussion includes a look at how the pendulum is swinging back toward punitive corrections and the paradigm shift accompanying this movement, some of the major trends occurring in corrections and the impact of technology on corrections. The chapter concludes with a look at the many hats worn by those in corrections and asks, "Is corrections trying to do too much?"

13

Special Challenges for Corrections

Do You Know

➤ What type of prison suffers the highest incidence of inmate escape?

➤ What common methods are used to hinder escape attempts?

➤ What types of natural disasters corrections should be prepared for and what threat such disasters may pose to correctional facilities?

➤ How common sex in prison is and whether it is most often consensual or coerced?

➤ What may be considered contraband and how it gets into a facility?

➤ What two major elements are generally considered first-order causalities of riots? What are thought to be second-order causalities and the significance of these elements?

➤ What types of hostage situations may arise and what the most dangerous scenario is for a hostage?

➤ What is generally meant by "use of force"?

➤ What efforts are being made to handle the drug problem in correctional facilities?

➤ What a code of ethics embodies?

It is easy to propose impossible remedies.   —*Aesop, 550 B.C.*

consensual sex

contraband

deadly force

ethics

excessive force

first-order causalities

rape

second-order causalities

use of force

Introduction

C orrections has always been full of challenge: (1) the challenge to rehabilitate offenders while, at the same time, punishing them for their crimes and (2) the challenge to make offenders acknowledge their wrongful deeds while simultaneously helping them search for the good that lies within. The challenges presented in this chapter, including gangs, contraband and sex, illustrate the importance of the inmate social world. Prison gangs were discussed in detail in Chapter 8 but are mentioned again briefly here. The inmate social world is organized economically and politically, with gangs, contraband and other illicit activity a result of that structure. The economically active "players" can sometimes get (or manufacture) a number of things that they can trade for cash, goods or services.

The task of supervising our nation's correctional population is riddled with various special challenges. A discussion paper from the BJS Princeton Project (DiIulio, 1992, p. 13) suggests that we should not:

> [A]sk our correctional officials to somehow correct the incorrigible, rehabilitate the wicked, or deter the determined. But they do demand that, with the human and financial resources that society has provided, and with the requisite support of other social institutions, the officials must keep prisoners—keep them in, keep them safe, keep them in line, keep them healthy, and keep them busy—and to do so with fairness, without undue suffering, and as efficiently as possible.

This chapter examines some of these challenges, including escape prevention and natural disasters (keep them in); security, sex, contraband and gangs (keep them safe); riots, hostages and use of force (keep them in line); drugs and drug testing (keep them healthy); recreation and work training (keep them busy); ethics, grievance procedures, ADA requirements and legal rights (fairly); and crowding (without undue suffering). Each challenge is discussed separately, although overlap and interrelations exist among many of these correctional responsibilities. Many of these challenges exist for community corrections facilities, such as residential centers, as well as secure custody facilities like jails and prisons, although the issues have traditionally received more attention as they pertain to secure facilities. Some of the topics have already been presented in previous chapters; others are discussed at greater length later in the book. Where this is the case, the reader is referred to the appropriate chapter, although the topic is still mentioned here to call attention to its status as a special challenge for corrections.

Escape Prevention

For as long as captors have been holding others captive, the quest for an escape-proof design has been a challenge. With the opening of Alcatraz in 1934 came the hope that such a facility had, indeed, been established. When the prison closed in 1963, only a few men had ever attempted to escape from "the Rock." Whether these escaped convicts actually survived the rough, frigid, shark-infested waters and the two-mile trek to shore remains unknown, for no boat or bodies were ever located.

Escape is a problem administrators are constantly concerned about. Today, shows like *America's Most Wanted* and FBI flyers in post offices alert the general public to convicted felons who have escaped and are wanted by the authorities, while the search for escape-proof designs continues.

A *Corrections Compendium* survey reports (Lillis, 1994, p. 6) the number of prison escapes is decreasing overall, although some states are reporting increases. Of the 41 state correctional systems, the District of Columbia and the Federal Bureau of Prisons (FBOP) which responded, Lillis notes: "These systems reported 802 escapes out of a total average daily population of 652,982 in 1993. This is a drop of 4,991 from 1991's total of 5,793 escapes from 49 reporting systems." Mississippi, Pennsylvania, West Virginia, South Dakota and Oregon reported decreases in prisoner escapes, while Alaska, Delaware, the District of Columbia, Idaho, Kentucky, Maryland, Missouri, New Hampshire, Vermont and the FBOP reported increases in prisoner escapes and walkaways.

Since a primary purpose of corrections is to protect the public (ACA, 1992, p. 3), an important task is to prevent the escape of those serving time in correctional facilities. Naturally, the construction and design of correctional facilities centers around this fundamental correctional responsibility, but what specific measures are taken to ensure that inmates do not leave before their scheduled release date?

As discussed in the chapter on prisons, a facility's designated custody level has much to do with the escape-prevention measures taken. Minimum-security facilities house the least escape-prone inmates and generally have no fences, walls, locks, cameras or perimeter security and officers to ensure the offenders remain "in custody." It has been said that trust replaces walls in these facilities. However, six times as many escapes occur from low/minimum-security facilities than from high/medium-security facilities. According to Camp and Camp (1997, p. 19): "Of the total escapes/walkaways that occurred during 1996, most (89.9%) were walkaways from a work release or furlough program. Escapes from low/minimum security facilities accounted for 8.8% of all escapes, while escapes from high/medium security facilities only accounted for 1.4% of all escapes." Medium-security facilities, because they house more dangerous offenders, rely more on security measures, and maximum-security facilities rely heavily on such measures to keep inmates in.

Most prison escapes occur from work release or furlough programs. The majority of escapes from institutions occur at minimum-security facilities.

Several approaches have been used by states to lower their escape totals. Lillis (p. 6) states: "West Virginia has tightened furlough rules, work release eligibility, as well as security to limit its escapes. South Dakota attributes its decrease in escapes to physical plant improvements, better inmate and unit management, and more conservative policies. Oregon also has implemented strict policy on all escapes and has established a fugitive unit to search for its escapees."

The new super-max facility in Florence, Colorado, in considering the many ways inmates often escape, uses motion detectors in crawl spaces beneath the facility and is surrounded by 12-foot chain link fences topped with razor wire. Unruh (1994, p. A12) states:

> Escape-minded inmates will have their hopes dashed. Between their cells and freedom lie seven layers of secured steel and concrete. Beneath the building is a crawl space with no outlet, monitored by the motion detectors. . . .
>
> The prison is surrounded by cleared landscape, those 12-foot fences and razor wire and six towers occupied by armed guards. Guy wires will be strung over open areas to prevent helicopter escapes. In addition, there are other security systems federal officers would rather not have prisoners know about and will not discuss.

Clearly, perimeter controls are essential. Fences and walls topped with barbed wire or razor ribbon, floodlights, armed guards in towers and officers with dogs— all are used to keep inmates inside. While perimeter controls are crucial in escape prevention, many facilities are realizing that escapes can be short-circuited in other ways. Architectural designs, such as pods, and procedures that limit the movement of inmates between areas of the facility also reduce the opportunities for escape. Keeping inmates uninformed about the facility's design and what lies outside the prison walls are other methods used to hinder escape attempts. Regarding escape prevention at super-max, Vanyur (1995, pp. 92–93) states:

> The most critical . . . design feature that maximizes security and control is the degree to which each unit and cell is self-contained. Each unit has its own libraries, group and single recreation yards, barber shop, satellite feeding kitchen, unit team rooms, unit staff offices and physical examination room. Thus, inmates rarely need to leave their unit. . . . This greatly reduces inmate movement and escort around the facility, making it difficult for inmates to acquire a sense of the institution's layout. Inmates also have no view of the facility's exterior. Once inside, the only thing that can be observed in outdoor recreation yards is the sky. Inmates see neither the perimeter of the facility nor the surrounding countryside.

Perimeter controls, self-contained architectural designs that limit the movement of inmates between areas of the facility and keeping inmates uninformed about the facility's design and what lies outside the prison walls are common methods used to hinder escape attempts.

States experiencing increases in prisoner escapes attribute the rising number of breakouts to several causes, including rapid population turnover, overcrowding, increases in community-based programs, increased use of home detention (electronic monitoring), more inmates being placed in minimum-custody facilities, changes in how absconders are classified and an overall increase in the inmate population in general (Lillis, p. 6).

Natural Disasters

Natural disasters may also present a challenge for corrections, as staff try to react to the event while keeping inmates from taking advantage of the opportunity to perhaps escape. Depending on the geographic region of the facility, a variety of natural disasters may potentially affect correctional operations. Such events include tornadoes, hurricanes, floods and earthquakes. Facilities should have a natural disaster preparedness plan, including emergency evacuation procedures, and staff training should address what actions to take during a natural disaster.

> Natural disasters, such as tornadoes, hurricanes, floods and earthquakes, may strike regions in which correctional facilities are located, presenting inmates an opportunity to escape if emergency preparedness plans are not in place and executed properly.

In August 1992, Hurricane Andrew swept through South Florida, causing significant damage to two FBOP facilities. Regarding the storm's impact on the Metropolitan Correctional Center (MCC) in Miami, Samples (1992, p. 110) notes: "The wind flattened the prison's two perimeter fences, destroyed the perimeter detection system and seriously damaged the food and health service areas as well as the warehouse. Flying debris destroyed non-ballistics-resistant glazing, and other major security features were rendered inoperable. Water, electricity and phone service were cut off, leaving the institution totally dark and causing sewage to back up into the buildings." In the summer of 1993, heavy rains in the Midwest flooded the Missouri River affecting correctional facilities in Minnesota, Wisconsin, Iowa, Illinois and Missouri. According to Spertzel (1993, p. 159): "The flooding Missouri River severely damaged the Renz Correctional Center, a maximum security women's prison [in Missouri], destroying the prison's electronic security system and nearly three miles of perimeter fence."

Advance warning is possible with some natural events such as hurricanes, and weather services are often able to predict when flooding rivers will crest, thereby giving correctional facilities ample time to evacuate and relocate inmates. Other events, however, such as tornadoes and earthquakes, often strike with little or no warning and can literally place correctional facilities off guard when security systems and perimeter fencing are compromised.

Security

Moral, ethical and legal obligations demand that correctional practices administer to the safety and security of both inmates and the staff hired to supervise them. It is often challenging for staff to tend to inmates' safety and security needs when such activity places their own welfare in jeopardy. While the details of the issue of security differ between inmates and staff, the overall concerns are the same—to remain safe. The concept of security in corrections has several levels of meaning. As discussed in the previous section, the security of the facility greatly influences how often inmates are able to escape. This level of security may be thought of as external (perimeter) security or the security of the public outside the prison walls. This discussion will focus on internal security and the security of inmates and staff inside the prison walls.

Maintaining security is perhaps the foremost challenge on the minds of correctional staff. While this is not to suggest that they are any less concerned about prisoner escapes, their own lives are at risk when internal security breaks down. To achieve and maintain internal security, most facilities use such technology as electronically controlled doors and locking mechanisms, closed-circuit cameras to monitor corridors and exits, bullet-proof glass and upgraded detention hardware. Inmate identification has also been simplified through the use of technology such as electronic photo ID tags and bar coded wristbands. Architectural designs and supervisory approaches such as direct supervision also increase the security level inside a facility. Adequate classification processes further serve to improve a facility's security.

Security depends on more than just concrete and steel—it depends on appropriate staff training and response. Security is also impacted by the other issues under the broad umbrella of safety. Therefore, successfully addressing these other challenges improves the safety of both the inmate population and the correctional staff.

Sex

Sex behind bars, while prohibited except for conjugal visits in several states, does occur in prisons and jails. Saum et al. (1995, p. 427) state: "The sex restriction is thought to be necessary so that prison officials can satisfy the correctional goals of a safe and secure environment for those incarcerated. However, rules against these prohibited activities are violated and such behaviors do take place behind prison walls."

As with sex outside the confines of prison, sex in prison falls into two categories: consensual and coerced. **Consensual sex** is oral or anal sex that takes place between willing individuals who have agreed on the terms before the act occurs. Coerced sex, or **rape,** is oral or anal sex that is forced on someone.

While prison rape grabs attention because of its violent nature, many point out that a majority of the sexual encounters occurring in correctional institutions are not forced. Stojkovic and Lovell (1992, p. 364) acknowledge: "It is our impression that many people have been led to believe that prison rape is the predominant form of prison sex." This is not the case.

> Prison sex, although prohibited, does occur and is most often consensual.

Saum et al. (p. 413) interviewed Delaware prison inmates about the subject of sex behind bars and reported comments such as:

- "Sex still goes on in here. People I know don't use protection because it's not available. People are knowledgeable [about HIV] but still have sex."
- "Just like on the streets, you can get sex anytime if you have money."

Whether consensual or coerced, prison sex presents several challenges for corrections. Considering first consensual sex, although prohibited, many do not see this activity as a problem for corrections. Stojkovic and Lovell (p. 378) assert: "Concerning day-to-day sexual encounters among inmates, it is safe to conclude that sexual activity is going to occur and the only reasonable position of correctional staff is that it does not upset the order and stability of the prison." It has been argued that by allowing such sexual activity to take place, tension and, consequently, violence among the inmates is reduced and that such activity is, for lack of a better word, harmless.

While victimization is not the issue, spread of disease and, in the case of coed facilities, pregnancies are real concerns. The rate of HIV infection among inmates is of serious concern. The number of individuals suffering from AIDS is six times greater among state and federal inmates than it is among the general U.S. population (Maruschak, 1997, p. 4), and research shows a 94 percent increase in the number of AIDS-related deaths in prison since 1991 (p. 5). Since the medical needs of individuals suffering from AIDS can be quite extensive and expensive, the transfer of HIV among inmates through sexual contact is of great concern to prison administration.

For correctional officers, AIDS education and training is vital in maintaining an effective staff. Education on how the virus is transmitted allows staff to take precautions when necessary and can allay fears that might prevent staff from acting when needed. Correctional officers need to know what to do in situations where inmates are bleeding, biting or throwing urine or feces. Correctional officers must be knowledgeable so as not to endanger themselves, but they must also be prepared to respond without hesitation to emergency situations.

The spread of sexually transmitted diseases is also possible among inmates engaged in sexual relations. The medical staff needs to be aware of this activity and to make testing and treatment available. A debate is ongoing as to whether condoms should be made available to inmates, not to imply that prison management condones sexual activity among inmates but merely in response to the fact that such activity does occur and the negative consequences of unprotected sex warrant taking some precautions.

Sex for hire falls somewhere between consensual and coerced sex. Such economically motivated sexual activity may begin as a consensual act and progress to coerced acts when payment is not made. Conflicts over the amount and timeliness of payment or the quality of service rendered may lead to aggression.

Coerced sexual activity is another challenge altogether. Sexual victimization and rape, although not as common as consensual sexual activity, do occur among inmates and are not only damaging to the inmate being victimized but may also result in lawsuits against the facility. Stojkovic and Lovell (pp. 378–379) state "it is the responsibility of the staff to be continually aware of the possibility of victimization of weaker prisoners by the sexually aggressive inmates." This victimization may include one-on-one rape, gang rape, pimping weaker inmates and racially motivated sexual assaults.

The frequency of sex in prison depends greatly on the facility itself. According to Saum et al. (p. 428):

> There are a myriad of factors in a prison environment that work to either facilitate or discourage sexual activity. Each particular prison can differ with regard to its security level, type of population, number of inmates, single- versus multiple-occupancy cells, structured versus unstructured free time, and many other variables. All of these factors play a crucial role in the nature and frequency of sexual activity in a prison system. Thus sex in prison is likely to vary according to the conditions encompassing a specific prison.

Contraband

➤ Controlling contraband is an ongoing challenge for correctional staff. **Contraband** refers to a wide range of goods and services that are prohibited by institutional policy or not allowed without expressed permission from institutional management. Common forms of contraband include alcohol, illegal drugs and weapons. Paper money and gambling paraphernalia may also be considered contraband. Visitors are the most common route by which contraband enters the correctional facility, although correctional officers and delivery personnel have also occasionally been known to bring in contraband.

> Contraband may include alcohol, drugs and weapons. Visitors, correctional officers and delivery personnel are the usual routes by which contraband enters the correctional facility, although some is created inside the facility.

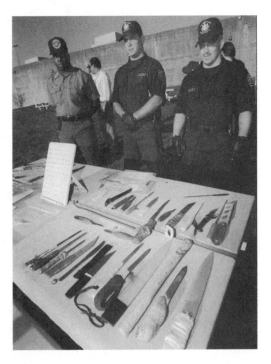

Corrections staff stand behind some of the homemade weapons confiscated during a three-day search inside and outside the Graterford State Prison.

While some forms of contraband can be fashioned inside the prison facility (such as knives or "shanks"), most is smuggled in from the outside. Contraband may also originate as legitimate pieces of prison property, such as kitchen knives taken by inmates for use as weapons. Visitors have been known to bring in books with the interior of the pages cut out to conceal weapons and drugs. Contraband may also come in through the mail. Drugs can be smuggled in inside balloons or condoms, which may be hidden in the visitor's mouth or other body cavities. Such containers, when swallowed, may successfully pass through the digestive system and be retrieved from the stool; they may also, however, rupture inside the body, killing the carrier.

Detection of contraband is not always easy. Metal detectors and pat down searches are used to locate weapons, and searches of bags and other materials are common. Efforts to eliminate contraband have included increased and more thorough checks of all persons entering the facility; routine "shakedowns" of inmates and their cells to uncover contraband; use of technology to help detect weapons, including metal detectors and drug-sniffing dogs; and architectural considerations that eliminate potential hiding spots for contraband. Certain areas of the facility, such as the kitchen and chemical/cleaning supplies closets, need special consideration to control the conversion of products and utensils into contraband. Stokes (1991, p. 154) notes:

> Inmates can be creative at finding hiding places for contraband and potential weapons. Consequently, many correctional kitchens use open shelves and pot racks instead of drawers and cabinets. Ceilings should be solid drywall, as prehung, laid-in acoustical tile ceilings provide unlimited hiding opportunities. . . .

Locked shadow boards for knives help control and track distribution of potential weapons. Some facilities use token systems or sign-out sheets to track sharp utensils. Other potential hazards are cleaning solutions and other chemicals. They, too, should be locked up.

According to a sergeant at a correctional facility in Florida, inmates can be quite inventive when trying to conceal their contraband, in this case home-made wine, called "buck":

After a few days of fermenting, buck usually gives off a very strong smell, a nasty smell, and so it's easy to find. But some inmates got a hold of a couple of five-gallon buckets, filled one up with buck and filled the other one up with soapy water. They attached the closed buck container to the open soapy container with a hose, so the buck fumes would pass through the detergent and escape "clean," smelling like nothing but soap.

Contraband poses an additional challenge to correctional staff and administration because in some institutions those inmates in "dealer" positions exercise a degree of control, sometimes substantial control, over inmates in "buyer" positions. Stojkovic and Lovell (p. 385) state:

The creation and perpetuation of a contraband market structure in prison . . . creates a situation in which dealers of illegal goods and services exercise a *legitimate* form of power over inmates, and that legitimacy is focused on the contraband market system. In effect, the distribution of contraband products through a marketplace provides the opportunity for key merchants or inmate leaders to develop a normative rule structure that supports the exchange of goods and services, yet in addition, enables stability to reign in the institutional environment.

Dealers seek to keep their marketplace—the prison—functioning in an orderly manner, a goal strikingly parallel to that of prison management. Consequently, in poorly run institutions, management often finds themselves caught between the duty to seize contraband, potentially disrupting the order within the facility, and allowing the contraband marketplace to exist to "keep the peace."

Another problem created by correctional contraband market systems is that they reinforce dealers' existing criminal behavioral patterns, which obviously impairs any attempt at rehabilitation. Further, because correctional officers are evaluated on how well they control their units, allowing contraband marketplaces to operate by "looking the other way" constitutes a sort of sanctioned corruption of authority (Stojkovic and Lovell, p. 387). These authors suggest: "One way to deal with the power of the contraband system is to create more legitimate jobs in the formal sector of the prison. In this way, prisoners would have greater sources of income through legitimate means and possibly reduce the power of the illegal sector of the prison economy."

Gangs

Prison gangs were discussed in detail in Chapter 8 as a critical part of the inmate culture. They are mentioned again here because of their connection to drugs, contraband and violence and to emphasize the significant challenge they pose for corrections. The power gangs wield behind bars may lead to a variety of disturbances or riots, either between groups of inmates or between inmates and correctional staff.

Riots

It can be a correctional officer's worst fear and prison management's worst nightmare—the inmates have taken control and a full-blown riot is underway. But management need not be at the mercy of the inmates. Boin and Van Duin (1995, p. 357) assert: "Most explanations of prison riots implicitly regard the causes of rebellious inmate behavior as the determinants of a riot's outcome. But little attention has been paid to the course of a riot. . . . We contend that the way in which prison administrations prepare for and handle this type of crisis can make the difference between a small-scale disturbance and a full-fledged riot. Crisis management should therefore be considered a critical variable in explaining a riot's outcome."

The nature of riots or disturbances include dorm fights, racial fights, gang fights, property damage, assaults on staff, inmate protests and work stoppages, refusal to lock down, refusal to give up food trays, hunger strikes, arson, refusal to leave the dining hall and refusal to return to dorms.

Two riots that received enormous publicity because of the extent of death and destruction involved were the Attica and New Mexico prison riots. The Attica Correctional Facility, opened in 1931, was thought to be riot-proof, yet in September 1971, inmates took control of a large section of the facility. They held a group of correctional officers hostage for four days before the prison was retaken by force. The final death toll was 43—32 inmates and 11 guards—39 of whom were killed by the state police during the final takeover by police and prison authorities. The New Mexico prison riot occurred in February 1980, when inmates took control of the entire prison and captured 12 correctional officers. Control of the prison was regained 36 hours later, but not before $100 million in damage was sustained and 33 inmates were killed. It is important to note that deaths can be the responsibility of either the authorities, as seen in Attica, or the inmates, as in New Mexico.

In October 1989, inmates at Pennsylvania's State Correctional Institution at Camp Hill were able to stage two back-to-back riots because the first one caught corrections off guard. According to Acorn (1991, p. 72): "Unfortunately, the Pennsylvania Department of Corrections was not well-prepared for the disturbance. Inmates were able to rise up not just once, but twice; the following day, they escaped

The aftermath of a prisoners' riot at Walpole State Prison in Massachusetts.

from their already damaged cells and took over the institution a second time. During the two days of rioting, 17 staff members were taken hostage, 123 employees and inmates were injured and 15 of the prison's 31 buildings were damaged or destroyed." The state Senate Judiciary Committee which investigated the incident identified "crowding as a major cause of the riot, but indicated poor staff training, lack of communication among top officials and institution staff, and indecisive action on legitimate inmate grievances were also to blame" (Acorn, p. 72).

On Easter Sunday, 1993, at the Southern Ohio Correctional Facility in Lucasville, inmates took control of the L-Block, holding 13 correctional officers hostage during an 11-day siege. The Lucasville riot has become perhaps the most investigated event in penal history, as Wilkinson (1994, p. 65) states: "Eleven internal and external committees studied various aspects of the disturbance, resulting in myriad recommendations." Security upgrades were completed, overcrowding and its negative impact on programming was addressed, the facility's problem of understaffing was corrected and disturbance preparedness training was enhanced.

Boin and Van Duin (p. 362) state: "Sloppy security procedures, the result of badly functioning prison administrations, may actually allow inmates to riot." Therefore, they contend the best way to deal with riots is to prevent them from ever happening. Figure 13–1 shows the types of riot proneness as a function of institutional security and living conditions.

Poor living conditions and a lack of institutional security are generally seen as two major contributors, or first-order causalities, to riot conditions.

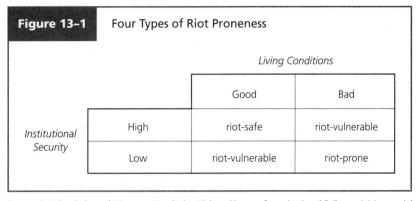

Figure 13–1   Four Types of Riot Proneness

		Living Conditions	
		Good	Bad
Institutional Security	High	riot-safe	riot-vulnerable
	Low	riot-vulnerable	riot-prone

Source: R. Arjen Boin and Menno J. Van Duin. "Prison Riots as Organizational Failures: A Managerial Perspective." *The Prison Journal,* Vol. 75, No. 3, September 1995, p. 363. Copyright © 1995, *The Prison Journal.* Reprinted by permission of Sage Publications, Inc.

Even when poor conditions and lax security exist, prisons need not fall victim to the devastation that occurred during the Attica and New Mexico riots. Boin and Van Duin note (p. 364): "[T]he Joliet (1975) and Michigan (1981) prison riots were characterized as a result of bad living conditions and failing security . . . , but these riots caused relatively modest damage in terms of injuries and financial costs." The differences in outcome may depend largely on what management does once a riot begins. Boin and Van Duin (p. 365) state: "As prison authorities find themselves confronted with a riot, . . . [they] will have to take some sort of action in order to cope with the threat and restore a state of normalcy. It is in this stage that the actions of prison authorities may make the difference between a food strike in an isolated cell block (a riot you will never hear about) and the over-taking of an entire institution (a riot you might never forget)."

Living conditions and security are designated by Boin and Van Duin as
➤ **first-order causalities** because they are what lead to a riot. **Second-order causalities** are what allow the disturbance to either be quelled or augmented— lack of preparedness, crisis response and management of the riot's aftermath (p. 366). These authors state (p. 369):

> It is our assumption that prison management can influence the level of prevention (with regard to the occurrence of first-order causalities) to a considerable degree, varying from adequate (decent living conditions/tight security) to inadequate (poor living conditions/low security). On the second dimension, the prison is analyzed in terms of the likeliness that second-order causalities will occur. Our hypothesis is that administrators are more likely to avoid second-order causalities when they are adequately prepared for crisis management.

Second-order causalities, those that allow a disturbance to either escalate or de-escalate, include lack of preparedness, crisis response and management of the riot's aftermath.

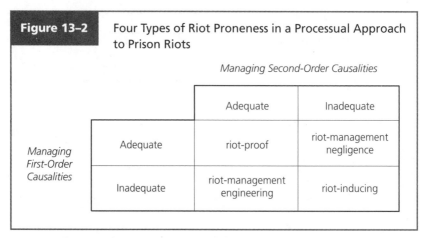

Source: R. Arjen Boin and Menno J. Van Duin. "Prison Riots as Organizational Failures: A Managerial Perspective." *The Prison Journal,* Vol. 75, No. 3, September 1995, p. 363. Copyright © 1995, *The Prison Journal.* Reprinted by permission of Sage Publications, Inc.

Figure 13–2 illustrates four comprehensive types of prison riot proneness.

Accessibility and familiarity with protective gear is critical to correctional staff who must respond rapidly to riot conditions. Protective gear such as helmets, face shields, shin and forearm guards, groin protectors and riot shields or pinning shields may be used not only during riots but also during disturbances of lesser degrees. Mosley (1991, p. 132) explains:

> In every correctional facility there is the potential for inmates to disturb daily operations. Officers must take quick control of such situations before they get out of hand. One technique used to handle disruptive inmates is the forced cell move. Used to remove inmates from their cells when they refuse to do so on their own, this technique requires organized teamwork and continuous training.
>
> Forced cell moves are often handled by a group of officers known as the special operations reaction team. The team, often called a SORT team, is similar to a law enforcement SWAT team, but is trained to handle potentially threatening situations inside the correctional environment.

Patrol dogs have also been used during inmate disturbances and riots. Dale (1994, p. 4) states: "Patrol dogs can . . . be adapted for use by Correctional Emergency Response Teams (CERT) during inmate disturbances. The dogs are taught to bite with the full mouth and hold upon the command of the handler in such a way that the dog uses the least degree of force. . . . U.S. courts categorize a Police Working Dog's use of force at the same level as the PR-24 baton—many degrees below 'deadly force.' " The use of force in corrections is another challenge, addressed shortly.

Community Riots

Disturbances in the community may also present a challenge for corrections as mass arrests fill correctional facilities beyond capacity in a short time. One

Members of a SORT unit at Rikers Island practice maneuvers wearing their riot gear.

such riot occurred in the wake of the Rodney King verdict in Los Angeles. According to Ruhren (1992, p. 178): "For five days—from April 29 to May 3—the horror of the Los Angeles riots gripped the nation. Newspapers reported 5,500 building fires, more than 50 deaths and about $700 million in damage." Ruhren also notes "the riots initially had a dramatic impact on the daily operations of the County's jails and corrections procedures. . . . During the week of the riots, approximately 9,000 inmates were processed at the inmate reception center of the sheriff's department; a normal book and release amount is only 600 to 800 per day."

Hostages

In many riot situations, hostages are taken. These hostages are most commonly correctional officers and other staff, although anyone inside the facility at the time of inmate takeover may conceivably become a hostage, including visitors and delivery personnel.

During the Lucasville riot, 13 correctional officers were taken hostage and one was killed before the disturbance was over. Larry Dotson, a correctional officer held hostage, recounts his ordeal (Unwin, 1994. Reprinted by permission):

> I had been working at Lucasville for about 26 months and had been involved in breaking up several fights. But as soon as I stepped out into that corridor I knew that this was not a routine disturbance. I saw an officer running out of the L-6 unit with two inmates running after him. They saw me and backed off, but when I went in to L-6, I saw John Kemper lying in a pool of blood. I realized there was nothing I could do for him, so I tried to defend myself and I was hit.

I was hit in the left side of the head with an object—a broom handle or a baton. I remember trying to defend myself and getting kicked, beaten and punched. I gave it everything I had until I lost consciousness. The next thing I remember, the inmates were bringing me into L-6 again where they locked me in the shower. . . .

The ultimate indignity was yet to come. They took my uniform away and gave me a set of inmate clothes. . . . they put a cotton ball over each eye and covered them with a head bandage. That bandage was never removed during the next 11 days. . . .

The only thing that they would tell me was that there was a lot of inmate activity throughout the institution. There was a lot of running and yelling, "Let us get at the hostages, let us have a crack at them." I asked my captors what was going to happen. I was told, "You're going to be okay. We'll give you the protection you need. The only thing we're concerned about is if outside forces come in. Then we're going to have to take care of business." . . .

I am proud of the fact that I try to live by the set of rules we stress at the academy: to be firm, fair and consistent. This reputation really works for you in a positive sense. There are always folks you are going to have conflicts with. But on the whole, I think that my work ethic was a strength for me. It was reflected in the attitude of the inmate who would come by and talk to me. He even walked me a few times, saying, "We gotta get you walking around a little bit." I didn't really want to because I felt that little cell was my one secure spot. Any time I was out of there, I thought, "This could be the last time." . . .

I realized that the less I said the better, because I didn't want to provoke them. I didn't want them to focus on my feelings at that point. The only time I would speak was when I was spoken to. Any time they would offer water or food, I would accept it whether I wanted it or not. I tried to be a model hostage.

I had learned these tactics during a training session about two months before the disturbance. I had completed my annual in-service training the first week of February, and I remember the instructor in hostage negotiations telling us what could happen and what to expect. . . .

Smith (1993, p. 174) states: "The more enlightened correctional systems have mandatory training on handling [hostage] situations; in some places this training includes instruction on what staff members should do if taken hostage. Most large institutions also have emergency response units that are specially trained to manage such disturbances."

According to Smith, two general types of hostage situations are planned and unplanned (p. 174): "Planned situations normally are intended to accomplish some preconceived goal, such as freeing a prisoner, forcing some type of political or social change, or publicizing a cause or a perceived wrong. . . . Unplanned situations usually arise out of panic. The hostage is simply a 'target of opportunity.' These situations almost always result in the hostage's survival." Smith also identifies four variations of hostage situations (pp. 174–175):

1. Single hostage/single hostage-taker—captor is least likely to harm hostage because hostage is the only bargaining tool.

2. Multiple hostages/single hostage-taker—slightly more dangerous for hostages.

3. Single hostage/multiple hostage-takers—similar to variation 1.

4. Multiple hostages/multiple hostage-takers—most dangerous scenario for hostages.

> Hostage situations may be planned or unplanned and may involve single or multiple hostages and hostage-takers. Generally, the more hostages involved, the more dangerous the situation for each hostage.

Smith offers some recommendations for individuals held hostage (p. 175), noting: "A number of behavioral dos and don'ts apply if an individual is taken as a hostage. For the most part, these principles apply to all the types and categories of hostage situations":

- Don't panic.
- Don't threaten or argue with your captor.
- Announce your behavior in advance.
- Buy time.
- Avoid "red-flag" subjects.
- Allow bonding to occur.
- Don't be a spokesperson.
- Find out what the hostage-taker wants.
- Carefully consider trying to escape.
- Try to communicate with the negotiators.
- Communicate the exit plan.

Smith (p. 181) also points out that probation and parole officers may become hostages: "While certainly not a frequent occurrence, probation and parole officers have in the past been taken hostage and held against their will for periods of time ranging from just minutes to several hours. The nature of their jobs—making unannounced home calls to convicted offenders who may be engaging in unlawful activities—places them in a very high-risk category."

Use of Force

The use of force has been a continuing challenge for those in criminal justice. In corrections, knowing when and how to use force is important not only in protecting the physical well-being of the inmate(s) and officer(s) involved and in restoring order to the facility but in protecting the officer(s) and the correctional facility from inmate lawsuits.

All American citizens, including incarcerated ones, have certain basic constitutional rights (prisoners' rights are the focus of Chapter 14), and correctional personnel must take care not to violate these rights through the use of unnecessary or excessive force. In *Hudson v. McMillan* (1992), the Supreme Court ruled that unnecessary force by a correctional officer against an inmate was a violation of the inmate's Eighth Amendment right against cruel and unusual punishment, even if the inmate did not sustain serious injury.

One reason this area is so challenging, and often confusing, is because of the various definitions concerning the degree of force, including general use of force, reasonable force, minimum force, nonlethal force, excessive force and deadly force. The definitions are not always clear-cut, leaving room for interpretation which may eventually lead to litigation. Henry et al. (1994, p. 108) state: "Use of force generally means reasonable force necessary to compel inmates to act or refrain from acting in a particular way, but there is no uniform definition or procedure for responding to such incidents. Florida's policy is one of the most inclusive, requiring that any physical touching of inmates by staff be reported as a use of force."

> **Use of force** generally means reasonable force necessary to compel an inmate to act or refrain from acting in a particular way.

The University of Illinois Police Training Institute's Use of Force Model, developed in 1991 by Dr. Franklin Graves and Professor Gregory J. Connor, may reasonably be applied to correctional settings and the officers employed therein. This model delineates five levels of offender behavior and corresponding levels of reasonable officer response (Figure 13–3).

Given the nature of correctional work—supervising the country's lawbreakers, some very violent—it is not surprising that use of force is unavoidable, even routine. It is recognized, however, that the potential exists for misuse of force and abuse of inmates by correctional staff. As Gondles (1994, p. 6) states: "Force, used under careful supervision for very legitimate causes, is sometimes a necessary part of our jobs. Excessive force is not. It has no place with those of us who value our work ethic and take pride in our jobs." **Excessive force** is force exceeding that necessary to control the situation. An extreme use of force, **deadly force,** is intended to cause death or serious injury.

Ross (1990, p. 66) states: "The first line of defense against potential litigation is clear, complete and well-written policies. . . . [T]o avoid liability, departmental policy and procedures should be current, comprehensive, consistent and constitutional." Yet, in a survey of state and federal adult correctional facilities,

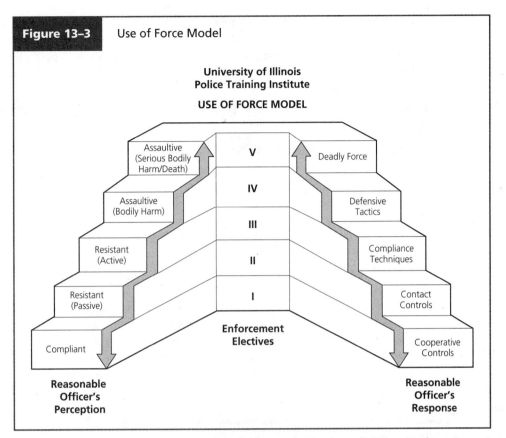

Figure 13–3   Use of Force Model

Source: Developed by Dr. Franklin Graves, Federal Law Enforcement Training Center (FLETC), and Professor Gregory J. Connor, University of Illinois Police Training Institute, 1991; modified in 1992. Reprinted from *The Police Chief,* p. 47, September 1996. Copyright held by the International Association of Chiefs of Police, Inc., 515 N. Washington St., Alexandria, VA 22314. Further reproduction without express permission from IACP is strictly prohibited.

Ross (p. 65) found "some confusion on the definitions for reasonable force, physical force and minimum force. Some respondents reported that their policy did not define maximum force nor did it define the meaning of physical force. Those agencies that did provide a definition failed to spell it out clearly."

Force may be physical, mechanical or chemical. Correctional officers may use self-defense tactics and other "hands only" maneuvers to restrain and control inmates. They may also use restraint devices such as handcuffs; weapons, including standard and electric batons, stun guns, Tasers and firearms; chemical spray devices such as oleoresin capsicum (OC), better known as pepper spray; and canines. Some facilities allow only certain officers to be trained in and to use specific applications of force such as stun guns and canines. Many other facilities train all officers in uses of force such as self-defense, chemical sprays and firearms, emphasizing that these applications are to be used as a last resort. For example, regarding the use of pepper spray (OC), Daley et al. (1995, p. 24) state: "It is critical that staff are trained how to use OC. Staff should be taught to negotiate with inmates first and to use OC only after talking fails and a threat exists. . . . [Staff] also need to be aware that inmates can take the OC canisters and turn them on staff. For this reason, [staff] need to avoid exposing their canisters by using a proper interview stance much like the technique used in protecting firearms."

These use of force applications remain controversial in many jurisdictions. Regarding the use of stun devices, Bryan (1994, p. 2) notes:

> The Federal Bureau of Prisons [and many other state correctional agencies] uses stun guns because they are non-lethal, but only CEO's have authorization to use them. . . .
>
> Florida reported that only selected staff are trained in the use of stun guns . . . [and] "that the display of a stun device . . . has very much been a deterrent to an inmate to continue uncooperative or combative behavior.". . .
>
> The District of Columbia, New York, Ohio, South Dakota, and Connecticut officials reported that stun gun use is not contained in their "Use of Force" policies. . . . New York reports it does not use stun guns in order to avoid "misuse and possible litigation." Ohio officials have decided that stun guns are "not appropriate for use of force policies."
>
> . . . Tennessee reported lawsuits which resulted from use of these devices. In each lawsuit "the Department's use of the stun gun was found to be appropriate."

Pepper spray as an acceptable use of force seems more widespread than stun devices among correctional facilities. Bryan (p. 23) states: "Most of the departments surveyed planned to continue using pepper spray. These departments claim that pepper spray provided a safer means of force and was less injurious to staff and inmates." However, "[o]pponents to the use of OC claim there is potential for abuse because it is biodegradable and after several minutes leaves no residue to show it has been used."

New use of force technology is being sought all the time. The National Institute of Justice (NIJ) Science and Technology office has been developing new "less than lethal" weapons for use by law enforcement and corrections officers, including a nontoxic sticky foam that, when sprayed on a subject, prevents that person from attacking, fleeing or even moving, and "an aqueous foam generator that can flood a common area with suds in a matter of seconds, making it impossible for those in the foam to see or hear" (Boyd, 1994, p. 164). These less than lethal uses of force have certain potential in corrections, particularly in riot control.

Proper staff training in using these kinds of force is necessary to prevent injury to inmates and staff and to avoid lawsuits. Borum and Stock (1992, p. 28) state:

> Once a facility has established a clear use of force policy, all corrections personnel should receive policy guidelines and training. The training should include a review of crucial definitions, the written policy, and relevant statutory and case law. . . .

A force continuum that provides a matrix by levels of subject resistance and officer force should be integrated into all use of force training. An officer should always be aware of these levels in any confrontation so he or she can know the appropriate range of responses available.

Borum and Stock also state that use of force training should include not only the basics such as firearms, defensive tactics and restraint techniques but also anger management, stress management and verbal skills. They note (p. 28): "Like performance skills to deal with stress, verbal skills are typically given very little attention in corrections training. Instruction in crisis intervention and de-escalation procedures should be given strong emphasis, since these skills are actually used more frequently than physical force."

Understanding inmates and their rejection of social control methods may also help correctional officers in their attempts to use force. Henry et al. (p. 110) state:

> . . . in situations where inmates have knowingly disobeyed an order, other inmates usually believe a minimal amount of physical force by staff is legitimate. However, if an inmate is defending his or her honor by fighting another inmate, other inmates see officers' force as illegitimate. . . . Inmates respond positively or negatively to force depending on the dynamics of the situation and the nature of the response. When correctional staff can anticipate inmates' response to different situations, they may be better prepared to resolve the incident quickly.

Drugs and Drug Testing

As discussed in Chapter 10, drug-addicted individuals are common in corrections systems across the country. For probationers and parolees, life in the community often presents numerous opportunities to purchase and use drugs. And as mentioned earlier, drug use is also a problem for correctional institutions. Drugs may be smuggled into the facility by visitors or correctional and delivery personnel hoping to "supplement" their income.

> Efforts to handle the drug problem in correctional facilities include searching visitors and their belongings, monitoring correctional and delivery personnel, conducting cell inspections and performing drug tests.

Some facilities use detector dogs to find narcotics, either as people are coming into the institution or during cell inspections. Dale (p. 4) notes: "Some states may use just one narcotic dog to serve all of the state's correctional facilities. Narcotic detector dogs are usually imprinted with (trained to find) the following odors: Marijuana/Hashish, Heroin/Opium, and Cocaine/Crack. They can also be imprinted with methamphetamine or other controlled substances."

Drug testing of inmates is commonly done when they arrive at the facility, to help with classification and programming decisions. Many facilities also test inmates while they are incarcerated to monitor drug use within the facility. Urine tests are one way corrections staff detect drug use. DuPont et al. (1990, p. 168) state: "Of the urine testing methods, the immunoassay tests are the most widely used because they can distinguish specific drugs, they are reliable and relatively inexpensive, and they detect drugs or drug by-products (metabolites) at levels low enough to indicate use within the past three to five days."

This time window for drug detection is adequate for many drugs, but others may go undetected while still others may linger long after the last use of the drug. Mieczkowski et al. (1993, p. 1) state: "Opiates and cocaine are water-soluble and quite rapidly excreted, generally within 48 to 72 hours. Only marijuana, which is fat-soluble, has a slow, relatively long-term urine excretion rate." According to DuPont et al. (p. 169): "Most drugs and their by-products cannot be detected after [three to five days]. Exceptions include marijuana and PCP, both of which can be detected up to 36 days after the last use in chronic, heavy users. Because these drugs are deposited in body fat and released over time, repeated urine tests can show continued drug use, although no drugs may have been used since the last urine test."

Hair testing is a newer technique also used to detect drug use. DuPont et al. (p. 169) explain: "Hair is nourished by small capillaries that carry the blood supply to hair roots. When drugs are used, the bloodstream carries the drug or its by-products to the hair shaft, where it is trapped. As hair grows, drug use is reflected in the hair." Drugs and their metabolites typically appear in the hair anywhere from three to seven days after drug use and remain there until that section of the hair strand is cut.

Although not perfect, the use of hair as the test medium has many advantages over urine. According to Mieczkowski et al. (p. 4): "Hair testing appears to have a number of advantages, including its less invasive method of collection, the extended time window of results, the stability of the medium, and the difficulty of tampering with the medium to evade positive test results. Some practical difficulties may occur from individuals with short or no head hair." It is possible, however, to use hair from anywhere on the body for this type of testing.

Hair testing has also been found to be more accurate than urine testing. Mieczkowski et al. report on a study of arrestees at the Pinellas County jail in Florida and a comparison of the results of hair testing, urinalysis and self-reports of drug use. They found (pp. 2–3) "a substantially greater proportion of positive hair assays than positive urine samples. . . . There were more than twice the number of positive hair test results for cocaine than positive urine tests (46.5 percent vs. 20.4 percent)." Table 13–1 compares the positive results for these arrestees and shows increasing percentages moving from self-reports

Table 13–1	Comparisons of Positive Outcomes: Self-Reports, Urinalysis and Hair Analysis (n = 303)			
	Self-reported Drug Use		**Assay Results**	
Have You Used	**In Prior 48 Hours**	**In Prior 30 Days**	**Urine (+)**	**Hair (+)**
Any cocaine?	25 (8.3%)	34 (11.2%)	62 (20.4%)	141 (46.5%)
Opiates?	0 (0.0%)	3 (1.0%)	5 (1.7%)	27 (8.9%)
Marijuana?	47 (15.5%)	94 (31.0%)	120 (39.6%)	n/a

Source: Tom Mieczkowski, Harvey J. Landress, Richard Newel and Shirley D. Coletti. *Testing Hair for Illicit Drug Use.* National Institute of Justice, Research in Brief. U.S. Department of Justice, January 1993, p. 3 (NCJ-138539).

to urinalysis to hair analysis, with hair analysis presenting the most accurate picture of drug use among inmates. Once drug use is detected, the next challenge for corrections is to treat and counsel these drug users, as discussed in Chapter 10.

Another challenge is substance abuse among corrections personnel. Stock and Skultety (1994, p. 66) note: "Overall, physical and psychological stress can lead corrections officers to perform their duties in a perpetual state of exhaustion. This can cause errors in judgment, lapses in coordination and even loss of response in basic muscle reflexes. To cope with such stressors, some officers turn to alcohol and other substances. Many correctional institutions have a 'hang out' bar nearby."

Correctional personnel who have a substance abuse problem generally do not admit to it, and correctional administrators have, in the past, been equally likely to look the other way when faced with such problems. But under the Americans with Disabilities Act, alcohol and drug abuse are now treated as impairments, for which employees have the right to treatment before termination (Stock and Skultety, p. 66). Interestingly, while only 978 jails performed drug testing on inmates as of June 30, 1993, 1,424 jails did drug testing of staff at the same date (Snell, 1995, p. 71). The most common instance for staff drug tests was for new hires and those staff on probation (1,067 jails).

Recreation

Recreation is an issue that has come under attack recently. Advantages to recreational activities in correctional facilities include keeping inmates busy and active, which has a positive impact on inmates' health (and reduces medical care costs for prisoners) while also providing an avenue to vent frustrations and avoid higher levels of violence. Recreational group activities also help inmates maintain the social and interpersonal skills they will need once released.

However, the abundance and extravagance of some institutions' recreational facilities has brought heavy criticism from the community. Criminal justice scholar John DiIulio explains how today's prisoners have come to receive such creature comforts:

> Prisons used to emphasize inmate discipline and forced labor, and wardens ruled the cellblocks with an iron fist. Beginning in the 1960s, federal courts stepped in. At first, judges ruled only that prisoners were entitled to nutritious meals, basic health services and protection against arbitrary discipline at the hands of guards. But a number of federal judges went well beyond such reasonable reforms and began ordering that prisoners be provided with expensive, untested treatment programs and a wide range of recreational opportunities regardless of the cost (Bidinotto, 1994, p. 68).

The precedents were set, and correctional facilities began constructing elaborate recreational facilities. One commissioner of corrections provides a typical prison administrator's justification for the abundance of recreational and physical-fitness amenities available to inmates: "We must attempt to modify criminal behavior and hopefully not return a more damaged human being to society than we received" (Bidinotto, p. 66). Other correctional administrators and politicians have rebuked these generous philosophies, calling for reforms that remove the resort-like atmosphere of many facilities. One Western Governor declares: "It's nonsense for them to say that convicts have a Constitutional right to taxpayer-provided services that many taxpayers can't afford on their own" (Bidinotto, p. 71).

Work Training and Educational Pursuits

Work training is an activity that is less criticized than recreation in corrections. Work training programs allow inmates to develop skills in anticipation of their release and eventual need to find employment. Common vocational training programs in prisons include auto repair, carpentry, electronics, data processing and food service.

In most facilities, inmates are also allowed to finish their high school educations by completing their GED, and many facilities permit prisoners to pursue college degrees. A recent survey ("Education Opportunities," 1997, p. 4) has shown that in 1996, more than 304,000 sentenced inmates (25.7 percent) were enrolled in some form of educational programming, ranging from adult basic education to postgraduate study. Inmates became ineligible to receive federal financial assistance via Pell grants during the 1994 to 1995 academic year, although some funds and private scholarships are still available to prisoners who wish to pursue a college degree.

Facilities that allow inmates to take college courses and complete their degrees have become increasingly criticized, when it is recognized many hard-working, law-abiding, middle-income families cannot afford to send

Inmates sit in their boot camp barrack, studying for GED class.

their own children to college. Convincing arguments have been made, however, regarding the potential payoff to society for educating such offenders. Consider the following points (Marks, 1997):

> "I frequently use the term, 'Pay me now, or pay me later,' " says J. Michael Quinlan, former director of the Federal Bureau of Prisons during the Reagan and Bush administrations. "Society should recognize that the cost of college is really very insignificant when you compare the cost of damage done by crime."
>
> Prisoners who receive at least two years of higher education have a 10 percent re-arrest rate, according to the Correctional Education Association (CEA). . . . That compares with a national re-arrest rate of about 60 percent. . . .
>
> The average cost of keeping an inmate in jail is $30,000 a year. The average Pell grant award to prisoners in 1994 was $1,500, according to the U.S. Education Department.

Ethics

Ethical behavior is expected of every professional, regardless of the field, but is especially critical for those involved in the criminal justice field, which includes corrections professionals. **Ethics** refers to a standard of conduct and moral judgment—doing what is considered right and just. Clear connections exist between ethics and the use of force, the dispensing of punishment and the treatment of prisoners. Ethics is a very important daily challenge touching practically every area within corrections.

With the expanding technology available to corrections, such as the stun guns and pepper spray discussed previously, comes an increasing complexity to professional performance. According to Falk (1995, p. 112):

> Proper training, supervision and discipline of officers using such devices are therefore crucial.
>
> In an effort to reduce [use of force lawsuits], federal, state and local governments and correctional authorities have undertaken more rigorous self-policing, typically by establishing a code of ethics or code of conduct. The Federal Bureau of Prisons (BOP) has established an excellent ethical code applicable to all its officers and employees.

A code of ethics is generally developed around a set of broad principles which incorporate ideals and standards applicable to members of the profession. Falk (p. 112) states: "In corrections, these principles include protecting inmates, protecting oneself and third persons, and preserving institutional integrity." Falk also notes that ethical obligations extend beyond mere "legal" requirements: "Ethical codes seek compliance with the 'lawful' needs of a particular community or profession—compliance with the spirit of the law, not just the letter of the law." The American Correctional Association's Code of Ethics is given in Appendix B.

> A code of ethics is developed around a set of broad principles which incorporate ideals and standards. In corrections, these include protecting inmates, protecting oneself and third persons and preserving institutional integrity. A code of ethics embodies the *spirit* of the law, not just the letter of the law.

Ethics touches every aspect of corrections, from probation practices to the medical treatment of terminally ill prisoners. Reams et al. (1997, p. 1) present the following hypothetical case:

> The county jail recently has initiated a screening program for suicide. In reviewing the results, the psychologist realizes that many more inmates than had previously been suspected are at suicide risk. He does not have the resources to adequately counsel all of them. Does he briefly interview all those at risk, knowing that his intervention will be insufficient? Does he select a few for more comprehensive treatment? How is the selection made?

Pollock-Byrne (1991, p. 257) discusses ethics as it relates to probation, parole and the mission of community supervision: "An ethical issue in . . . the mission of community supervision is the question of what society owes the offender." She discusses whether such community corrections should focus more on the victims of crime or on those who commit crime. As with many ethical issues, there are no simple answers.

Clearly, ethics is a challenging area for corrections, where unruly, hot-tempered, foul-mouthed inmates often test the patience of those holding the keys. But correctional personnel are in positions of considerable power over other individuals and must realize their actions hold potential for serious consequences. As Falk (p. 113) states: "Establishing a set of meaningful ethical standards demonstrates that members of the profession are willing to take responsibility for the conscientious exercise of their authority."

Grievance Procedures

When inmates are dissatisfied with their treatment and conditions of confinement, they have the right to petition to express grievances, as discussed in the next chapter. However, it is appropriate to mention this here as a challenge to corrections professionals who must know what is considered appropriate staff conduct when inmates express a desire to file grievances.

In *Stovall v. Bennett* (1979), a court ruling prohibited prison officials from intimidating, harassing or otherwise retaliating against inmates to discourage them from exercising their right to express grievances. However, in *Roberts v. Pepersack* (1966), the court ruled it permissible for correctional personnel to stop inmates from circulating protest petitions because of justifiable security concerns and the availability of other ways for inmates to communicate grievances (Krantz, 1988, p. 148). Correctional staff must be aware that inmates have the right to have their grievances heard by administration and that there are legitimate procedures by which inmates may file their grievances.

ADA Requirements

The Americans with Disabilities Act (ADA), discussed in Chapters 6 and 10, has had significant impacts on how correctional facilities are designed and what prison officials must keep in mind concerning not only disabled inmates, but disabled staff and members of the public as well. Van Sickle (1995, p. 106) states: "The ADA was written to ensure that people with disabilities have an equal opportunity to participate in or benefit from public programs, services and activities." Appel (1995, pp. 84–85) notes: "Of the five titles contained in the ADA, Titles I and II have a direct effect on corrections. These two titles deal with employment practices and access to public-sector services. In corrections, three distinct groups are protected under the ADA: staff, inmates and the public, both visitors and volunteers."

While some correctional administrators see ADA requirements as inconveniences which further burden their already stretched-thin budgets, compliance with the requirements will, ultimately, simplify and enhance the performance of correctional facilities and services. Bogard (1995, p. 8) states:

> Designers need to be aware of the full scope of rights the ADA offers to inmates, visitors and staff with disabilities, and not just simple regulations such as door widths, counter heights and accessible fixtures. By the same token, corrections professionals involved in the planning and design process must have a broader understanding about specific design regulations required by the ADA.

Some argue the cost of complying with these requirements will be too much to handle, given their already overstrained construction budgets. Appel (p. 85) notes that two new facilities recently completed in Philadelphia were able to meet ADA requirements with one costing just 3.6 percent of the total construction costs and the other costing a mere 0.83 percent of the total construction costs. With creative and proper planning, compliance need not be expensive.

Thompson and Ridlon (1995, p. 123) advise: "When a situation requires accommodating disabled staff members, the first step should be to consult with them directly. They will probably know better than anyone else what their needs are."

Bernsen and Gauger (1995, p. 100) point out that problems may be encountered with the unusual cell sizes needed to accommodate disabled inmates: "These potentially larger cells can interfere with the stacking of modular cells in multistory facilities."

Older, existing jail facilities are also subject to the requirements of the ADA and may present more of an economic challenge than new facilities. Significant renovations may be required to bring the facility into compliance. Title II focuses on equal access to services and calls for architectural modifications only as a last resort (Thompson and Ridlon, p. 122). Some facilities may avoid costly structural renovations by simply redesignating areas used by disabled inmates, visitors and staff (for example, moving visitation areas from the second floor to the first floor). Appel (p. 85) notes that with creative and proper planning, compliance need not be expensive.

Facilities concerned about the cost to renovate their physical structures to comply with the ADA must consider the cost of *not* completing such changes. Bernsen and Gauger (p. 97) note several instances at the St. Louis County jail where operational costs increased significantly due to a lack of facilities for disabled inmates:

> In one case, a quadriplegic offender spent six months at the county jail. This inmate required complete nursing care, including feeding, bathing and turning to prevent skin breakdown. Because there were no cells, toilet facilities or showers to accommodate disabled inmates, the nursing and custody staff were concerned whether they could provide adequate care to the inmate. After the offender

committed the crime and was apprehended, he was taken to St. Louis Regional Hospital, where he remained under guard until his condition stabilized. When the hospital was ready to release him, the county jail staff were not prepared to accept him, and he was detained at the hospital. While the staff contemplated their ability to care for the offender, hospital costs continued to accrue.

The ADA requirements are a challenge in their initial impacts—redesigning cells, relocating programs and services to be more accessible and so on—but corrections must be prepared to handle more and more disabled inmates, as mentioned in Chapter 10.

Legal Rights

Prisoners' rights are yet another challenge for correctional staff, especially since new cases are being tried all the time, with precedents being set and overturned almost constantly. Because this topic is so critical to corrections, it is the focus of an entire chapter (Chapter 14).

Crowding

Crowding has become a major concern of correctional facilities across the country. Newly constructed facilities are filling up fast, and some jails are being called upon to handle the "overspill" of state prisoners who have nowhere else to go. According to Snell (p. 19), of the jurisdictions with large jail populations (average daily inmate population of 100 or more) that were under court order for a specific condition of confinement, crowded living units were the number one subject of such court orders.

Crowding can precipitate inmate violence and riots. Consequently, keeping control over the degree of crowding can greatly affect tension levels within a facility. Following the Lucasville (Ohio) riot, a select committee on corrections was formed to investigate and identify the cause of the disturbance. This committee found that "[l]iving in extremely close proximity to a stranger frequently leads to stress, shortened tempers, impatience and what the committee has called a 'diminution of civility' " (Wilkinson, p. 65).

Crowding, besides putting people in closer proximity with one another, also takes up space that would otherwise be used for programming. The select committee's report notes (Wilkinson, p. 65): "Space which is intended for prison industries, recreation or vocational training has been converted to dormitory space to house inmates. . . . Education and work opportunities available to inmates are barely adequate to keep them productive when populations are at design capacity. When populations rise, it becomes impossible to keep a substantial proportion of inmates productive."

Summary

Corrections has always been full of challenge, and the task of supervising our nation's correctional population today is permeated with various special challenges.

Preventing prisoner escapes is a primary challenge. Not surprisingly, most prison escapes occur from work release or furlough programs. The majority of escapes from institutions occur at minimum-security facilities. Perimeter controls, self-contained architectural designs that limit the movement of inmates between areas of the facility and keeping inmates uninformed about the facility's design and what lies outside the prison walls are common methods used to hinder escape attempts. Natural disasters, such as tornadoes, hurricanes, floods and earthquakes, may strike regions in which correctional facilities are located, presenting inmates an opportunity to escape if emergency preparedness plans are not in place and executed properly.

Controlling sexual activity, contraband, gang activity and riots are ongoing challenges for correctional staff. Prison sex, although prohibited, does occur and is most often consensual. Contraband may include alcohol, drugs and weapons. Visitors, correctional officers and delivery personnel are the usual routes by which contraband enters the correctional facility, although some is created inside the facility. Prison gangs are a critical part of the inmate culture, and their connections to drugs, contraband and violence pose significant challenges for corrections. The power gangs wield behind bars may lead to a variety of disturbances or riots, either between groups of inmates or between inmates and correctional staff.

Poor living conditions and a lack of institutional security are generally seen as two major contributors, or first-order causalities, to riot conditions. Second-order causalities, those that allow a disturbance to either escalate or de-escalate, include lack of preparedness, crisis response and management of the riot's aftermath. In many riot situations, hostages are taken. Hostage situations may be planned or unplanned and may involve single or multiple hostages and hostage-takers. Generally, the more hostages involved, the more dangerous the situation for each hostage.

The use of force has been a continuing challenge for those in criminal justice. One reason this area is so challenging, and often confusing, is because of the various definitions concerning the degree of force, including general use of force, reasonable force, minimum force, nonlethal force, excessive force and deadly force. Use of force generally means reasonable force necessary to compel an inmate to act or refrain from acting in a particular way.

Drug-addicted individuals are common in corrections systems across the country and present numerous challenges, including the task of detecting such contraband as it enters correctional institutions. Efforts to handle the drug problem in correctional facilities include searching visitors and their belongings, monitoring correctional and delivery personnel, conducting cell inspections and performing drug tests.

Ethical behavior is especially critical for those involved in the criminal justice field, including corrections professionals, as clear connections exist between ethics and the use of force, the dispensing of punishment and the treatment of prisoners. Ethics is a very important daily challenge touching practically every area within corrections. A code of ethics is developed around a set of broad principles which incorporate ideals and standards. In corrections, these include protecting inmates, protecting oneself and third persons and preserving institutional integrity. A code of ethics embodies the *spirit* of the law, not just the letter of the law.

Discussion Questions

1. Given that most escapes from institutions occur from minimum-security facilities, what would you recommend be changed at these facilities to prevent such walkaways?

2. What natural disasters is your area susceptible to? How have local correctional facilities prepared for such events? Have any occurred recently?

3. Should corrections be concerned about stopping consensual sex among inmates? Why or why not?

4. What is your local correctional facility's policy for handling disturbances and riots? Have there been any recently? If so, what led up to the disturbance(s) and how effectively was (were) it (they) handled?

5. Do you find the definition of "use of force" fairly clear or rather confusing? Do you think Florida's policy regarding use of force is too restrictive?

6. Should routine drug tests be mandatory for all inmates, or is the common policy of testing upon "reasonable suspicion of use" effective? Fair?

7. Should inmates have access to recreational programs? If so, to what extent?

8. Do you believe most correctional professionals act ethically? If not, which areas need improving?

9. What elements are part of your personal code of ethics? How would these be beneficial in a correctional profession?

10. What do your local correctional facilities say their greatest challenges are?

References

American Correctional Association. *The Effective Correctional Officer.* Fredericksburg, VA: BookCrafters, 1992.

Appel, Alan. "Requirements and Rewards of the Americans with Disabilities Act." *Corrections Today,* April 1995, pp. 84–86.

Bernsen, Herbert L. and Gauger, Glenn E. "ADA's Impact: Requirements for Cell and Housing Design." *Corrections Today,* April 1995, pp. 96–102.

Bidinotto, Robert James. "Must Our Prisons Be Resorts?" *Reader's Digest*, November 1994, pp. 65–71.

Bogard, David M. "ADA's Impact on Architecture, Construction and Design." *Corrections Today*, April 1995, p. 8.

Boin, R. Arjen and Van Duin, Menno J. "Prison Riots as Organizational Failures: A Managerial Perspective." *The Prison Journal*, Vol. 75, No. 3, September 1995, pp. 357–379.

Borum, Randy and Stock, Harley. "Excessive Force Prevention Programs: An Essential Tool to Properly Train Staff and Protect Against Litigation." *Corrections Today*, June 1992, pp. 26–30.

Boyd, David G. "NIJ Enhances Weapons Technology." *Corrections Today*, April 1994, pp. 160–164.

Bryan, Darrell. "Dealing with Violent Inmates: Use of Non-Lethal Force." *Corrections Compendium*, Vol. XIX, No. 6, June 1994, pp. 1–2, 23.

Camp, George M. and Camp, Camille Graham. *The Corrections Yearbook, 1997*. South Salem, NY: The Criminal Justice Institute, 1997.

Dale, David. "K-9 Unit Operations in Corrections." *Corrections Compendium*, September 1994, pp. 4–6.

Daley, Dorothy E.; Hayes, Roger M.; Swint, Lloyd E.; and Henn, Frank W. "Oleoresin Capsicum: Don't Let the Fancy Name Fool You." *Corrections Today*, July 1995, p. 24.

DiIulio, John J., Jr. *Rethinking the Criminal Justice System: Toward a New Paradigm*. Washington, DC: Bureau of Justice Statistics, December 1992.

DuPont, Robert L.; Saylor, Keith E.; and Latimer, Sarah. "Drug Testing: Know Your Options." *Corrections Today*, August 1990, pp. 168–170.

"Education Opportunities in Correctional Setting." Survey Summary. *Corrections Compendium*, Vol. XXII, No. 9, September 1997, pp. 4–5.

Falk, James H., Sr. "Developing a Code of Ethics so COs Know How to Respond." *Corrections Today*, July 1995, pp. 110–113.

Gondles, James A., Jr. "Speaking About the Unspeakable." *Corrections Today*, May 1994, p. 6.

Henry, Patrick; Senese, Jeffrey D.; and Ingley, Gwyn Smith. "Use of Force in America's Prisons: An Overview of Current Research." *Corrections Today*, July 1994, pp. 108–114.

Krantz, Sheldon. *Corrections and Prisoners' Rights*. St. Paul, MN: West Publishing Co., 1988.

Lillis, Jamie. "Prison Escapes and Violence Remain Down." *Corrections Compendium*, June 1994, pp. 6–21.

Marks, Alexandra. "One Inmate's Push to Restore Education Funds for Prisoners." *The Christian Science Monitor*, March 20, 1997.

Maruschak, Laura. *HIV in Prisons and Jails, 1995*. Washington, DC: U.S. Department of Justice, Bureau of Justice Statistics Bulletin, August 1997 (NCJ-164260).

Mieczkowski, Tom; Landress, Harvey J.; Newel, Richard; and Coletti, Shirley D. *Testing Hair for Illicit Drug Use*. National Institute of Justice, Research in Brief. U.S. Department of Justice, January 1993 (NCJ-138539).

Mosley, Steven W. "Inmate Restraint Technique Requires Teamwork, Training." *Corrections Today*, July 1991, pp. 132–137.

Pollock-Byrne, Joycelyn M. "Moral Development and Corrections." In *Justice, Crime and Ethics*. Michael C. Braswell, Belinda R. McCarthy and Bernard J. McCarthy. Cincinnati, OH: Anderson Publishing Co., 1991, pp. 221–238.

Reams, Patricia N.; Smith, Martha Neff; Fletcher, John; and Spencer, Edward. "Making a Case for Bioethics in Corrections." *Corrections Compendium*, Vol. 24, No. 11, November 1997, pp. 1–3, 27–28.

Ross, Darrell L. "Study Examines Non-Deadly Physical Force Policies." *Corrections Today*, July 1990, pp. 64–66.

Ruhren, Karen Carlo. "How the L.A. Sheriff's Department Responded to the Influx of Inmates." *Corrections Today*, July 1992, p. 178.

Samples, F.P. Sam. "Weathering the Storm." *Corrections Today*, December 1992, pp. 108–113.

Saum, Christine A.; Surratt, Hilary L.; Inciardi, James A.; and Bennett, Rachael E. "Sex in Prison: The Myths and Realities." *The Prison Journal*, Vol. 75, No. 4, December 1995, pp. 413–430.

Smith, Albert G. "Developing an Action Plan to Resolve Hostage Situations." *Corrections Today*, August 1993, pp. 174–181.

Snell, Tracy L. *Correctional Populations in the United States, 1993.* U.S. Department of Justice, Bureau of Justice Statistics, October 1995 (NCJ-156241).

Spertzel, Jody K. "Coping with Disaster." *Corrections Today,* December 1993, pp. 158–160.

Stock, Harley V. and Skultety, Stephan. "Wrestling Demons in Our Own Ranks." *Corrections Today,* February 1994, pp. 66–68.

Stojkovic, Stan and Lovell, Rick. *Corrections: An Introduction.* Cincinnati, OH: Anderson Publishing Co., 1992.

Stokes, Judy Ford. "Food Service Design Helps Ensure Security." *Corrections Today,* July 1991, pp. 152–154.

Thompson, Arthur P. and Ridlon, Wesley. "How ADA Requirements Affect Small Jail Design." *Corrections Today,* April 1995, pp. 122–126.

Unruh, Bob. "A New Home of Bars, Steel: America's Worst Inmates to Move to 'New Alcatraz' in Colorado." (Minneapolis/St. Paul) *Star Tribune,* December 11, 1994, pp. A10, A12.

Unwin, Tessa. "Hostage Recounts 11 Days of Terror." *Corrections Today,* August 1994, pp. 66–72. Reprinted by permission.

Van Sickle, Darlene. "Avoiding Lawsuits: A Summary of ADA Provisions and Remedies." *Corrections Today,* April 1995, pp. 104–108.

Vanyur, John M. "Design Meets Mission at New Federal Max Facility." *Corrections Today,* July 1995, pp. 90–96.

Wilkinson, Reginald A. "Lucasville: The Aftermath." *Corrections Today,* August 1994, pp. 64–65, 74–76, 101, 143.

Cases

Hudson v. McMillan (1992).

Roberts v. Pepersack, 256 F.Supp. 415 (D.C.Md.), 1966.

Stovall v. Bennett, 471 F.Supp. 1286 (D.C.Ala.), 1979.

14

Prisoners' Rights and Other Legal Issues

Do You Know

➤ The difference between a right and a privilege?

➤ What collateral consequences of criminal conviction may occur?

➤ What impact *Ex parte Hull* and *Coffin v. Reichard* had on prisoners' rights?

➤ What the general categories of lawsuits are?

➤ What five common avenues for bringing cases to court are?

➤ What Section 1983 is and what significance it has in prisoners' rights cases?

➤ For prisoners, what cases based on First Amendment rights involve? Fourth Amendment rights? Fifth Amendment rights? Sixth Amendment rights? Eighth Amendment rights? Fourteenth Amendment rights?

Discussing the role of law in corrections is a relatively recent phenomenon. Most of the substantive rights and procedural safeguards accorded to the average citizen traditionally have not been provided to or even considered necessary for convicted offenders; and, lawyers and law schools have generally given little attention to the correctional process. This lack of concern by the legal profession is one of the reasons why corrections is a national disgrace.

—*Sheldon Krantz*

Can You Define

civil death

collateral consequences

deliberate indifference

Eighth Amendment

Fifth Amendment

First Amendment

Fourteenth Amendment

Fourth Amendment

"hands-off" doctrine

inmate litigation explosion

jailhouse lawyer

negligence

privilege

right

Section 1983

shakedowns

Sixth Amendment

stare decisis

substantive rights

writ of habeas corpus

Introduction

Although the opening quote is over a decade old, it still rings true regarding corrections, the law and the rights of offenders. Progress, while continuous, is moderate in this area of corrections. The wheels of justice often turn astonishingly slow. Indeed, it has been only during the past three decades that prisoners' rights have been given much consideration. It is an evolving field.

Given the complex environment in which corrections exists, it should come as no surprise that prisoners' rights can be extremely complicated. Krantz (p. 1) notes: "The correctional process consists of an incredibly complex and fragmented overlay of agencies and programs at federal, state and local levels. Included are pretrial diversion programs; probation and parole systems; jails and prisons; and community-based corrections such as half-way houses, work release, and community service programs. There are now even ways to be detained in one's own home under surveillance with electronic monitoring equipment."

This "complex and fragmented overlay" creates special problems concerning prisoners' rights, for courts at different levels and in different jurisdictions often rule oppositely on the same subject. For example, appeals courts frequently overturn decisions of lower courts. The location of an offender within the correctional system also has a great impact on how the court may rule on a particular issue.

One of the greatest difficulties surrounding prisoners' rights and the interpretation of the law is that court rulings rarely spell out an absolute decision about a particular topic that will apply, without question, to all other cases involving the same issue. Each case is evaluated individually, on its own merits, although precedents are frequently cited and previous rulings used to support a court's current decision. Injustices may occur against some inmates for essentially similar infractions, although the courts try, under stare decisis, to
➤ apply judicial precedents uniformly. **Stare decisis** is a policy of law requiring courts to abide by precedents when considering a similar set of facts. However, as you read through the cases concerning prisoners' rights, it will become evident that even rulings by the Supreme Court—the final word—do not necessarily hold from one case to the next.

This chapter discusses many topics already introduced, as inmate rights extend to all areas of corrections, including classification, disciplinary procedures, living conditions, medical care and access to libraries and reading materials. The immense number of cases relating to prisoners' rights makes it impossible to cover them all. However, general themes and topics are discussed and illustrated with pertinent and landmark cases. The chapter begins by distinguishing between rights and privileges. Next, the evolution of prisoners' rights is discussed, followed by categories of prisoner lawsuits and getting such lawsuits to and through the courts. Sources of prisoners' rights are covered next, including the First, Fourth, Fifth, Sixth, Eighth and Fourteenth Amendments to the Constitution. Relevant case law is also presented. The chapter concludes with a discussion of some collateral consequences of criminal conviction.

Rights and Privileges

People often talk of their "God-given right" or that someone "has no right" to do something. But from a legal standpoint, what is a right? Oran (1985, p. 271) provides the following definition: "One person's *legal* ability to control certain actions of another person or of all other persons. Every *right* has a corresponding *duty*. For example, if a person has a right to cross the street, most drivers have a duty to avoid hitting the person with their cars." Our founding fathers drafted the Constitution and the Bill of Rights to outline what the government saw as inalienable rights, those that could not be taken away. These documents are the basis of the legal rights prisoners have laid claim to.

➤   A distinction must be made between a right and a privilege. A **right** is a claim by one entity (an individual or individuals) that another entity has a
➤ legal obligation or duty to fulfill. A **privilege** is a favor or option that is not legally protected and may be denied one entity by another.

> A right is a legally protected claim, whereas a privilege is not legally protected.

Examples of inmate privileges include access to telephones, televisions and radios; smoking; exercise equipment and other recreation; commissary; and movies and other forms of entertainment. Although inmates may file lawsuits when these privileges are removed, the courts typically dismiss such cases recognizing the distinction between rights and privileges. Wunder (1995, p. 5) notes changes in privileges afforded to inmates today:

> Prison life is becoming less and less attractive with the elimination of sacred privileges like smoking. . . .
>
>   Some prison privileges are obvious candidates for elimination: free weights and popular movie rentals, for example. . . . A maximum security prison in the District of Columbia has eliminated Annual Family Day, a time when inmates were allowed to participate in an outdoor event with their families. Massachusetts inmates will no longer have annual banquets for veterans clubs, lifers organizations, and other inmate groups. In North Carolina, Christmas visits have been abolished. The elimination of family-oriented privileges reflects the extremely harsh public view toward prisoners that is currently in vogue. . . .
>
>   The reduction in privileges is also a byproduct of overcrowding and budget crunching.

Wunder (p. 5) also states that, of the U.S. DOCs that responded to a *Corrections Compendium* survey, approximately 42 percent of the survey respondents reported inmates have fewer privileges today than they did 10 years ago, 28 percent said inmates have more privileges and 30 percent said the number of privileges is about the same.

Inmate privileges are frequently seen by the public as luxuries and unnecessary expenses, and many prison administrators have begun eliminating such privileges to show a get-tough attitude to the voting taxpayers. Although privileges are not legally protected and may be stripped from prisoners at the discretion of prison management, some administrators are reluctant to remove these luxuries. According to Bryan (1995, p. 3):

> To ensure the security and order of prison facilities, administrators must consider inmates' reactions to the removal of some luxury items (weights, televisions, radios, etc.). Inmates often complain that one consequence of their incarceration is forced idleness and intolerable boredom. Inmate entertainment contributes to security since inmates who are able to passively occupy themselves are less likely to threaten the security and order of the facility.

Despite the potential negative repercussions of privilege removal, correctional administrators retain the ability to remove and restore inmate privileges as they see fit. As Bryan (1995, p. 3) states: "The courts have recognized that prison administrators have full authority and wide discretion in the use and control of privileges." The courts have taken a hands-off approach to inmate privileges, the same philosophy they used to have concerning prisoners' rights. Today, however, this is not always the case, as courts must respond to lawsuits brought by inmates who claim corrections has infringed on their rights.

Evolution of Prisoners' Rights

Throughout most of the history of corrections in the United States, prisoners have had comparatively few rights. The courts' reluctance to interfere with prison management stemmed from the belief that such intrusions would only make the administration of correctional facilities more difficult. Recall from Chapter 11 how early prison administrators were allowed to do essentially as they pleased, answering to no one except, perhaps, the governor, and even then there was little interference or regulation. This general unwillingness of the courts to become involved in how prisoners were treated was known as
➤ the **"hands-off" doctrine,** a principle that basically ignored prisoners' claims of mistreatment, cruel and unusual punishment or deplorable conditions of confinement. As a result, inmates sometimes suffered under conditions of squalor and inhumane treatment by correctional personnel and had nowhere to turn for help.

This hands-off attitude promoted the view that prisoners had *no* rights except those permitted by prison management, an attitude illustrated in the Virginia case of *Ruffin v. Commonwealth* (1871):

> During his term of service in the penitentiary, he is in a state of penal servitude to the State. He has, as a consequence of his crime, not only forfeited his liberty, but all his personal rights except those which the law in its humanity accords to him. He is for the time being the slave of the State. He is civiliter mortuus; and his estate, if he has any, is administered like that of a dead man.

➤ This **civil death** meant offenders, while incarcerated or on probation or parole, could not sign contracts, make decisions regarding their property, vote, hold public office, have a say in the custody of their children or marry. In fact, the wives of inmates sentenced to long terms or life were considered "widows" and were allowed to remarry as if their incarcerated husbands were dead.

Today, many state and federal statutes restrict some rights and privileges ordinarily available to citizens, including the rights to vote, to hold public office, to assist in parenting, to serve on a jury, to own firearms, to remain married and to have privacy. Such rights may be lost upon conviction, referred to
➤ as **collateral consequences** of criminal conviction, discussed in more detail later. Furthermore, once offenders have completed their sentences and are released back to the community, restoration of these civil rights is not always automatic. For example, many states consider a felony conviction grounds for divorce, bar felony offenders from serving on a jury and prohibit felony offenders from owning or possessing firearms.

> Collateral consequences of criminal conviction often include restrictions on or loss of the rights to vote, to hold public office, to assist in parenting, to serve on a jury, to own firearms, to remain married and to have privacy.

The hands-off doctrine and philosophy of the prisoner as a slave of the state began to change during the mid-twentieth century, as public attitudes concerning punishment vs. rehabilitation changed and the civil rights movement gained momentum. During the 1940s, some courts began to recognize prisoners' rights. The case generally considered to mark the beginning of prisoners' rights occurred in 1941 (*Ex parte Hull*).

At that time, it was common for correctional personnel to screen inmate mail, including prisoner petitions addressed to state and federal courts. Inmates wanting to express complaints and grievances to challenge the legality of
➤ their confinement were required to file a **writ of habeas corpus,** a document

that brought their case before a court. Consequently, these documents often wound up in the garbage, put there by correctional officers who claimed the petitions were improperly prepared and therefore unacceptable for submission to the court. In *Ex parte Hull*, the Supreme Court ruled that no state or its officers may abridge or impair a prisoner's right to apply to a federal court for a writ of habeas corpus, thereby eliminating the routine censoring and disposal of these prisoner petitions by correctional officers. The ruling declared that court officials, not correctional officials, held the authority to decide if such petitions were, in fact, prepared correctly. This was the first major decision on the right of access to the courts. Since this opinion, it is accepted that prisoners are guaranteed reasonable access to the courts.

> *Ex parte Hull* (1941) marks the beginning of prisoners' rights cases and was the first major decision asserting prisoners' right of access to the courts.

Three years later, in *Coffin v. Reichard* (1944), the Sixth Circuit Court extended federal habeas corpus to include the conditions of confinement, not just the fact of confinement, as was the subject of *Hull*. The significance of *Coffin v. Reichard*, therefore, is that it modified *Ruffin v. Commonwealth* and was the first case in which a federal appellate court ruled that prisoners do *not* lose all their civil rights as a condition of confinement.

> *Coffin v. Reichard* (1944) extended federal habeas corpus to include the conditions of confinement and was the first case in which a federal appellate court ruled that prisoners do not lose all their civil rights as a condition of confinement.

The Supreme Court has since ruled that, for state prisoners, federal habeas corpus petitions may generally be used only after these inmates have exhausted state remedies. Federal prisoners, of course, may file such writs directly with the federal court.

A third significant case establishing prisoners' right of access to the courts was *Cooper v. Pate* (1964). In this case, the court ruled that prisoners could sue the warden for depriving them of their constitutional rights under Title 42 of the United States Code, Section 1983, based on protections granted by the Civil Rights Act of 1871. This ruling allowed state prisoners to challenge the constitutionality of their imprisonment in federal courts.

Once the courts cracked open the door to prisoners' rights and allowed inmates access to the legal system, there was no holding these offenders back. Since then, cases have been filed challenging nearly every aspect of corrections. By the late 1960s and early 1970s, the courts (primarily federal district courts) began to seriously review prisoners' claims and regularly intervene on

their behalf, essentially reversing the hands-off doctrine that had prevailed earlier. Early efforts to bring prisoners' rights cases to court were slow and disorganized, yet the numbers continued to increase year after year, and inmates grew more and more adept at preparing their cases. The incredible upsurge in prisoners' rights cases over the past few decades has been called the
➤ **inmate litigation explosion.**

Although many cases have been filed since the *Hull* and *Coffin* decisions opened the door to prisoners' rights lawsuits in the early 1940s, there will doubtless be continued lawsuits filed concerning prisoners' rights. Since such rights have been won primarily through case law established by court decisions rather than statutory law enacted by legislation, each new case tried may set a precedent for further cases.

Categories of Lawsuits

Two general categories of lawsuits have been recognized: (1) rights of individ-
➤ ual prisoners, or **substantive rights,** and (2) rights concerning confinement conditions, which apply to all prisoners or a class of prisoners.

> Two general categories of lawsuits are rights of individual prisoners, or substantive rights, and rights concerning confinement conditions, which apply to all prisoners or a class of prisoners.

Others have categorized prisoner rights and the lawsuits filed concerning such rights another way: (1) access to court, (2) protection from cruel and unusual punishment, (3) civil rights and (4) protection of rights in decisions when adverse consequences are possible.

> Other categories of rights include access to court, no cruel and unusual punishment, civil rights and protection when adverse consequences are possible.

Getting Lawsuits to and through Court

Five common avenues to bring lawsuits to court are

1. State habeas corpus—an inmate-initiated hearing concerning confinement conditions.
2. Federal habeas corpus—available only after state remedies have been exhausted.

3. State tort suits—civil actions against a correctional employee for "negligence, gross or wanton negligence, or intentional wrong."

4. Section 1983 of the federal Civil Rights Act of 1871—may involve both injunctive relief and monetary damages.

5. The Civil Rights of Institutionalized Persons Act of 1980—allows the federal government to bring civil suits for equitable relief, but not damages, against state employees of any state institution.

> Five common avenues for bringing cases to court are (1) state habeas corpus, (2) federal habeas corpus, (3) state tort suits, (4) Section 1983 and (5) the Civil Rights of Institutionalized Persons Act of 1980.

Tort Suits

Torts are civil wrongs. State tort suits in corrections typically involve an inmate-plaintiff who claims the defendant (warden, correctional officer, facility) failed to perform a required duty owed to the plaintiff. Compensation for damages is the most common objective, and claims of negligence are frequently part of the allegations. **Negligence** is a failure to use a reasonable degree of care when that failure results in damage or harm to another individual.

Section 1983

Section 1983 of the Civil Rights Act of 1871 reads:

Every person who, under color of any statute, ordinance, regulation, custom, or usage, of any State or Territory, or the District of Columbia, subjects or causes to be subjected, any citizen of the United States or any person within the jurisdiction thereof to the deprivation of any rights, privileges, or immunities secured by the Constitution and laws, shall be liable to the party injured in an action at law, suit in equity, or other proper proceeding for redress. For the purposes of this Section, any Act of Congress applicable exclusively to the District of Columbia shall be considered to be a statute of the District of Columbia.

> For prisoners, cases based on Section 1983, the Civil Rights Act, challenge the conditions of confinement on the grounds that such conditions violate inmates' constitutional rights.

Section 1983 lawsuits may involve such issues as freedom of religion and the right to assembly (First Amendment), unreasonable body cavity searches (Fourth Amendment), excessive force by correctional officers or inmate-on-inmate assaults (Eighth Amendment) and access to law libraries (Fourteenth Amendment). According to Hanson and Daley (1995, pp. 1–2):

In the 1960s when the U.S. Supreme Court established that prisoners had constitutional rights, the number of cases filed was small. The Administrative Office of the U.S. Courts (AO) counted only 218 cases in 1966, the first year that state prisoners' rights cases were recorded as a specific category of litigation. The number climbed to 26,824 by 1992 . . . approximately one lawsuit for evpert [sic] thirty state prison inmates.

Figure 14–1 illustrates the national trends in the number of state prisoners and Section 1983 lawsuits.

Hanson and Daley (pp. 16–17) state:

. . . [of] the cases sampled, most [Section 1983] lawsuits are filed by inmates of state prisons (62%) with the rest from jail inmates (36%) and a few from individuals either paroled or released from a correctional institution (2%). Fewer than 1% are from offenders who are in mental health facilities.

. . . The largest number of Section 1983 lawsuits name correctional officers of prisons or jails as defendants (26%). The second largest group named is the heads of these institutions, such as wardens, deputy wardens, building directors, or jail administrators (22%). Medical staff . . . (9%), are the next largest group of defendants followed by elected officials . . . (7%).

. . . physical security, medical treatment, and due process are the most frequent issues in prisoners' complaints. The overwhelming majority of the issues are disposed of by court dismissals for failure to satisfy the basic requirements of a Section 1983 lawsuit. Virtually all prisoners act as their own attorney (i.e., *pro se*).

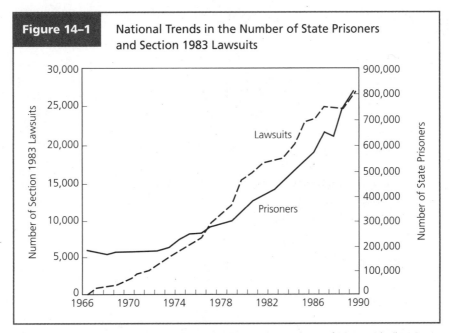

Figure 14–1 National Trends in the Number of State Prisoners and Section 1983 Lawsuits

Source: Roger A. Hanson and Henry W.K. Daley. *Challenging the Conditions of Prisons and Jails: A Report on Section 1983 Litigation.* U.S. Department of Justice, Bureau of Justice Statistics, January 1995, p. 3 (NCJ-151652).

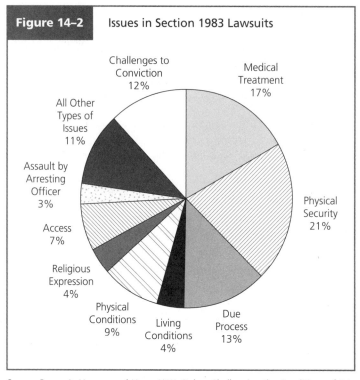

Figure 14–2 Issues in Section 1983 Lawsuits

Challenges to Conviction 12%

Medical Treatment 17%

All Other Types of Issues 11%

Physical Security 21%

Assault by Arresting Officer 3%

Access 7%

Religious Expression 4%

Physical Conditions 9%

Living Conditions 4%

Due Process 13%

Source: Roger A. Hanson and Henry W.K. Daley. *Challenging the Conditions of Prisons and Jails: A Report on Section 1983 Litigation.* Washington, DC: U.S. Department of Justice, Bureau of Justice Statistics, January 1995, p. 17 (NCJ-151652).

The court may, however, appoint counsel later to assist prisoners. Figure 14–2 shows the issues in Section 1983 lawsuits; Figure 14–3 shows the disposition of these cases. In Section 1983 litigation, 96 percent of all inmate-plaintiffs represent themselves (*pro se*) (Hanson and Daley, p. 21), and of the three possible outcomes of such cases—win nothing, win little and win big—94 percent of the prisoners win nothing (p. 36).

Many inmate lawsuits filed are dismissed by the courts, often through either (1) motions to dismiss, where the court, having read the prisoner's petition, rules that no basis exists for the suit; or (2) motions for summary judgment, where the court considers both the prisoner's petition and the correctional officials' side of the story and rules accordingly.

Sources of Prisoners' Rights

Prisoners' rights are rooted in a variety of sources, but are based primarily on the First, Fourth, Fifth, Sixth, Eighth and Fourteenth Amendments to the Constitution and on Section 1983 of the Civil Rights Act of 1871.

Consider next specific prisoners' rights and some major cases regarding each right, beginning with rights provided in the Constitution and the Bill of Rights.

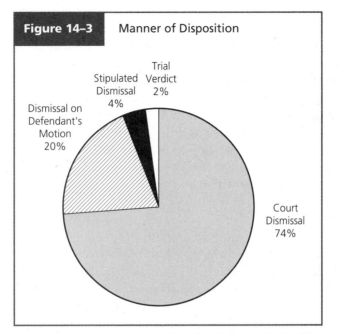

Figure 14–3 Manner of Disposition

Source: Roger A. Hanson and Henry W.K. Daley. *Challenging the Conditions of Prisons and Jails: A Report on Section 1983 Litigation.* Washington, DC: U.S. Department of Justice, Bureau of Justice Statistics, January 1995, p. 19 (NCJ-151652).

First Amendment Rights

➤ The **First Amendment** reads:

> Congress shall make no law respecting an establishment of religion, or prohibiting the free exercise thereof; or abridging the freedom of speech, or the press; or the right of the people peaceably to assemble, and to petition the Government for a redress of grievances.

For prisoners, cases based on First Amendment rights involve censorship of mail, expression within the institution, association within the institution, religion, appearance and visitation rights.

The First Amendment protects, among other things, individuals' freedoms of expression and association. The courts have recognized, however, that the security needs of correctional facilities often outweigh the individual needs for freedom petitioned by inmates in their lawsuits. While decisions have been made in favor of prisoners' First Amendment rights, many restrictions still exist, and for ample cause. For example, the censorship of mail, publications and prisoner manuscripts has been the topic of many prisoner lawsuits.

Prisoner Correspondence

Prisoner correspondence has been the focus of much litigation, perhaps because personal correspondence involves a nonincarcerated person who is also protected by the First Amendment.

Correctional administrators have provided several valid reasons why incoming and outgoing mail should be screened, including the need to detect incoming contraband such as drugs, weapons, tools of escape and pornographic materials. Justification for screening outgoing mail includes a need to protect the public from threatening or obscene letters, the need to stop correspondence that portrays the institution inaccurately or unfavorably and the need to identify escape or riot plans.

In *Prewitt v. State of Arizona ex rel. Eyman* (1969), the court ruled: "Mail censorship is a concomitant of incarceration, and so long as the censorship does not interfere with the inmate's access to the courts, it is a universally accepted practice." Recall that *Ex parte Hull* ended correctional interference in prisoner petitions reaching the court. In 1970, however, *Palmigiano v. Travisono* set an important precedent regarding censorship of prisoner mail. In this case, the court ruled that the First Amendment Freedom of Speech and Expression Clause (right to correspond) *did* apply to prisoners and set forth the following restrictions on correspondence censorship:

- The reading of outgoing inmate mail is unnecessary and violates the First Amendment rights of the parties involved unless pursuant to a valid search warrant.

- All incoming mail (except that from attorneys and other public officials) may be inspected for contraband.

- Incoming mail sent by someone not on an approved addressee list may be read and inspected to detect inflammatory writings and pornographic material; and mail from persons on an approved list may be inspected for contraband only but not read.

Palmigiano v. Travisono replaced total censorship with guidelines for limited censorship. Confusion still existed, however, on how to determine what to censor. Other cases at this time also upheld prisoners' First Amendment right to correspond without censorship, yet the courts disagreed on which test to apply in deciding these cases. Courts have used such tests as "compelling state interest," "clear and present danger," and "a regulation or practice which restricts the right of free expression that a prisoner would have enjoyed, if he had not been imprisoned, must be related both reasonably and necessarily to the advancement of some justifiable purpose" (Krantz, p. 137).

Wolff v. McDonnell (1974) looked at the issue of privileged communication between lawyers and their inmate-clients and censorship of such correspondence. The question was whether prison authorities could open such mail in the presence of inmates or whether the correspondence had to be delivered unopened if regular detection methods failed to indicate any contents as contraband. The Court ruled that correspondence from attorneys must be clearly identified with legal counsel's name and addresses in plain view on the envelope, and that prison authorities, in the presence of the inmate, may open and inspect such correspondence but may not read it, just look for contraband.

Another key case pertaining to prisoner correspondence was *Procunier v. Martinez* (1974), in which the Supreme Court considered whether correctional officials could censor specific prisoner writings, such as those in which inmates exaggerated complaints; expressed "inflammatory political, racial, religious, or other views or beliefs"; wrote about criminal activity; or used "lewd, obscene, or defamatory" language. Surprisingly, the Court sidestepped the issue of inmate rights, turning the focus of its ruling instead on the First Amendment rights of the nonincarcerated party with whom the inmate corresponds: "[C]ensorship of prison mail works a consequential restriction on the First and Fourteenth Amendment rights of those who are not prisoners." In determining whether a regulation on inmate correspondence violated any First Amendment rights, the Court set forth some criteria:

> First the regulation or practice in question must further an important or substantial governmental interest unrelated to the suppression of expression. Prison officials may not censor inmate correspondence simply to eliminate unflattering or unwelcome opinions or factually inaccurate statements. Rather, they must show that a regulation authorizing mail censorship furthers one or more of the substantial governmental interests of security, order, and rehabilitation. Second the limitation of First Amendment freedoms must be no greater than is necessary or essential to the protection of the particular governmental interest involved.

A fourth case related to censorship and the First Amendment is *Pell v. Procunier* (1974). The case, which dealt with face-to-face interviews between California inmates and members of the media, involved both the issues of freedom of expression and freedom of the press. The Supreme Court ruled that, although prisoners do have some First Amendment rights, they do not have a guaranteed right to conduct interviews with the press. Severe limitations may be put legitimately on prisoners' First Amendment rights to further the state's interest in security, order and rehabilitation. The Court further ruled that inmate access to the press was still possible through written correspondence and people on the outside.

Correspondence coming in for death row inmates poses a special challenge for corrections. Since prisoners on death row cannot be allowed to kill themselves before their execution, and because cases are known where inmates requested correspondence laced with poison (on the stationery, on the stamp or in the ink), these inmates commonly receive photocopies of correspondence sent to them by persons other than their lawyers.

Publications and Manuscripts

Much litigation has focused on how far prison officials can go to censor publications inmates wish to read and whether inmates should be allowed to publish books and other articles while incarcerated. In *Bell v. Wolfish* (1979), the Supreme Court approved a ban on incoming hardbound books, unless they had been mailed directly from publishers, book stores or book clubs, because such books may be used to smuggle contraband such as drugs, weapons or money. Today, corrections authorities commonly prohibit prisoners from receiving reading materials not sent directly from publishers and censor publications that are deemed inflammatory, obscene, racist or that may incite disruptive behavior (Krantz, p. 142).

Court rulings were very inconsistent, and a variety of tests were used to determine whether censoring was appropriate. Krantz (p. 143) notes: "After *Procunier v. Martinez,* most courts held that the standard of review formulated in that opinion for mail censorship cases applies equally to the censorship of publications."

Regarding prisoner manuscripts, many corrections agencies have restricted the ability of inmates to publish any works while behind bars. The courts, while recommending a broadening of such rights, have granted prison administrators wide discretion in cases involving prisoners' desire to publish books or other articles while incarcerated.

Freedom of Speech

Freedom of expression is another First Amendment right that prisoners have generally had limited. Most courts have severely restricted prisoners' freedom of expression. Litigated issues include the right to petition to express grievances, the right to engage in forms of protest such as work stoppages, and the right to solicit funds in support of political action. In *Roberts v. Pepersack* (1966), the court upheld disciplinary actions against an inmate who circulated materials calling for a collective protest against the prison administration for "mistreatment, inequities, and criminal neglect." The court ruled: "Attempts of prisoners to speak in a milieu where such speech may incite an insurrection against the authorities must be tempered. . . . In a prison environment, where the inmate tends to be more volatile than on the streets, strong restraints and heavy penalties are in order."

Courts do seem to side with prisoners in cases where regulations are overly broad or retaliation has occurred against prisoners for pursuing grievances. Recall that in *Stovall v. Bennett* (1979) the court ruled that prison officials were prohibited from intimidating, harassing or otherwise retaliating against inmates in an effort to discourage those inmates from exercising their right to express grievances.

It is sometimes difficult to balance *Roberts* and *Stovall*. While *Roberts* clearly supports the view that freedom of expression, as it pertains to prisoners, can be restricted, other court rulings and legal standards advocate greater leniency toward prisoners' freedom of expression. One rationale behind allowing freedom of expression is that prisoners can vent their frustrations. Such outlets for expression may defuse rather than exacerbate tensions.

Right to Assemble

For obvious security reasons, the courts have permitted prisons to restrict how prisoners are allowed to assemble. This has not meant, however, that all associations within the institution are prohibited. In *Goodwin v. Oswald* (1972), the court upheld prisoners' rights to form unions, stating that no state or federal law existed outlawing or prohibiting formation of prison unions. Prisoners sought unionization as a way to influence work conditions and wages, yet the Thirteenth Amendment permitted involuntary servitude for those convicted of crimes. Furthermore, because the state paid their wages, unionized prisoners were categorized as state employees and, therefore, prohibited from striking. Consequently, prisoners were unable to attain their associational goals using the Constitution as grounds for such rights.

In *Jones v. North Carolina Prisoner Union* (1977), the Supreme Court reversed a favorable decision, holding that state regulations that prohibited prisoners from soliciting others to join a union, barred all meetings of the union and refused delivery of union publications for distribution among the inmate population were not in violation of prisoners' First Amendment rights. The official ruling stated: "First Amendment associational rights . . . must give way to the reasonable considerations of penal management. . . . They may be curtailed whenever the institution's officials, in the exercise of their informed discretion, reasonably conclude that such associations . . . possess the likelihood of disruption to prison order or stability or otherwise interfere with the legitimate penological objectives of the prison environment."

Freedom of Religion

Religion has always played a vital role in corrections. It seems ironic that litigation in this area continues. Throughout history, Catholic priests, Protestant pastors and an occasional rabbi were available to inmates. Now there are so many

Native American inmates at the state prison in Las Cruces, New Mexico, construct a new sweat lodge with willow branches.

different religions, it is difficult to accommodate them all. In the Pennsylvania system, religion was used to coerce conformity and reform. Today, however, the ethnic and religious diversity of citizens is replicated behind prison walls so that one religion no longer adequately serves the religious needs of the present-day prisoner population. The courts and corrections find themselves challenged with identifying bona fide religious groups. The conflict between what constitutes an established religion and an individual's right to practice it has caused many problems in our country's correctional facilities.

The Supreme Court decision in *Cantwell v. Connecticut* (1940) held the constitutional guarantee of religious belief to be absolute, yet religious rights of prisoners were largely ignored until the 1960s. The Black Muslims brought the issue of religious rights for prisoners to the forefront. Although this group was first denied recognition as a bona fide religion, the courts eventually accepted it as genuine, stating Black Muslims were entitled to the same rights as those who practice more conventional faiths. Black Muslim ministers were permitted to conduct services in prisons (*Knuckles v. Prasse*, 1969), and Muslim inmates were allowed to use the Koran and other religious material. The court also gave prison officials much latitude to cancel privileges if activity turned to nonreligious concerns. In *Brown v. Johnson* (1985), the court ruled religious practices may be restricted for reasonable justification.

Another case, *O'Lone v. Estate of Shabazz* (1987), focused on a New Jersey prison's policy denying prisoners who worked outside the institution a chance to return to the facility earlier on Friday afternoons for the weekly Muslim service. The prison's reason for this restriction was based on security concerns and administrative burden. The Supreme Court upheld the prison's actions, ruling the restrictions were "reasonably related to legitimate penological interest."

Federal courts have consistently ruled that religious rights granted to one group must be granted to all such groups within a prison. One challenge, of course, is determining what qualifies as a religion. In some cases, this determination is fairly complex; in others, it's fairly simple. One so-called religion, the Church of the New Song, or CONS, founded by Harry Theriault, sought First Amendment protection and recognition available to the other religions practiced in prison. The religious beliefs of CONS included such dietary requirements as porterhouse steaks and sherry for its disciples. The Fifth Circuit Court of Appeals, however, denied any First Amendment rights to this group, stating "so called religious groups which tend to mock established institutions . . . are obviously shams and absurdities . . . whose members are patently void of religious sincerity" (*Theriault v. Carlson,* 1974). In another case, however, the right to practice Satanism has been upheld in court ("Practice of Satanism," 1995, p. 19):

> U.S. District Judge Edward W. Nottingham ordered a Federal prison near Denver to allow inmate Robert James Howard, Jr., to practice Satanism, a First Amendment right. . . . Judge Nottingham wrote that the prison forbade the performance of the plaintiff's Satanic rituals "based on the content of the plaintiff's beliefs—an unacceptable criteria according to the Supreme Court."
>
> The judge added that Howard is asking for "the same privileges granted to every other religious group" and did not ask to perform rituals involving bloodletting or violence. . . . [The judge] said his ruling "does not require prison officials to accommodate every form of Satanism, nor does it necessarily require them to allow each inmate to become a religion unto himself."

Legislation concerning freedom of religion made it easier for prisoners to win lawsuits. The Religious Freedom Restoration Act of 1993 (RFRA) states restrictions on the free exercise of religion must be justified by a "compelling state interest" and achieved by the "least restrictive means" possible. The NCJA reports (1995, p. 1):

> So far, inmates have claimed their civil rights have been violated because they were prohibited from: praying aloud in a foreign language; having access to religious facilities and services; having a special diet and meal schedule; ordering religious materials, including white supremacist literature that advocates a racial holy war; having long hair; and wearing certain clothing or jewelry, including a swastika medallion.

The NCJA also reports, however (p. 2): "By and large, when the states are able to demonstrate a direct link between the policy at issue and prison safety, the policies are upheld. For example, in two cases in which white supremacists demanded literature known to incite violence against minorities, the courts were quick to find a compelling state interest in safety that justified a prohibition of the possession of such material."

On June 25, 1997, in *City of Boerne, Texas v. Flores,* the U.S. Supreme Court declared RFRA unconstitutional "on the grounds that Congress impinged on the power of the judiciary and the states when it passed the law" ("Prison Officials Warn," 1997, p. 1). According to Sarah Vandenbraak, chief counsel for the Pennsylvania DOC, "RFRA encouraged people who did not have legitimate religious beliefs to file suit as a means to engage in behavior that ordinarily would not be allowed in a prison" (deGroot, 1997, p. 1). She adds (deGroot, p. 2): "For those inmates with legitimate religious beliefs, this isn't going to change anything. But it is going to take away the ability of the really litigious inmates to misuse religion as a cover for gang activity in the prison." RFRA cases filed by inmates have involved such claims as the right to engage in animal sacrifices, the right to burn Bibles, the right to group martial arts classes and the right to possess and distribute racist literature ("Prison Officials Warn," p. 6).

Some contend the loss of RFRA will make it more difficult for inmates to practice legitimate religions while incarcerated; others do not foresee much change. For example, Connecticut has a state RFRA still in place. Furthermore: "In a strictly legal sense, RFRA's repeal does not take away an inmate's right to practice his or her religion, as long as that practice does not compromise the safety of the facility" (deGroot, p. 1).

Krantz (p. 164) notes: "The majority rule . . . appears to be that prison officials can refuse to allow segregated prisoners to attend regular Sunday institutional religious services" (*Otey v. Best,* 1982). The courts have also upheld prison restrictions on certain acts and activities that do not fundamentally alter the ability of an inmate to practice a religion. Such acts include the wearing of hats and religious emblems, availability of special diets and meal times, the growing of long beards and other activities that might cause undue administrative burden and cost or compromise institutional safety and security. Restrictions on beards and personal appearance factors have been upheld for other prisoners separate from religious beliefs.

Appearance

Courts are generally reluctant to get involved in issues concerning prison restrictions on inmate appearance, such as hair length and facial hair. Most often, the courts have ruled that such restrictions do not violate inmates' constitutional rights and are valid restrictions based on institutional identification, hygiene and discipline needs. Furthermore, some contend that long hair, wherever it appears, may potentially allow for the concealment of contraband. However, some courts have allowed inmates to keep long hair when it is directly related to religious tenets (Krantz, p. 165).

Visitation

Visitation is considered by most courts to be a privilege and not a constitutionally guaranteed right. Some pertinent court decisions include

- *Walker v. Pate* (1966), allowing prison officials to deny visits by a prisoner's spouse if the spouse has a criminal record.
- *Rowland v. Wolff* (1971), denying visits by relatives based on an informant's statement that such persons had smuggled in contraband.
- *Polakoff v. Henderson* (1973), denying prisoners' rights to conjugal visits.
- *Block v. Rutherford* (1984), allowing restrictions on contact visits between pretrial detainees and visitors.

The final decision is significant because pretrial detainees retain a presumption of innocence and, as noted by Krantz (p. 156), "it has been argued that their rights to visitation do not have constitutional footing." In other words, they have not yet been convicted of a crime, so they should not be subjected to the same restrictions imposed on those who have been convicted. The Supreme Court ruled, however, against that argument, stating the correctional institution had sufficient security concerns to warrant restricting contact visits.

Fourth Amendment Rights

➤ The **Fourth Amendment** reads:

The right of the people to be secure in their persons, houses, papers, and effects, against unreasonable searches and seizures, shall not be violated, and no Warrants shall issue, but upon probable cause, supported by Oath or affirmation, and particularly describing the place to be searched, and the persons or things to be seized.

For prisoners, cases based on Fourth Amendment rights involve searches and seizures and the issue of privacy. These concerns also extend to offenders on probation and parole.

One of the first things inmates learn is that they do not enjoy the privacy that ordinary citizens do. Institutional security demands a limited degree of privacy. Krantz (1988, p. 166) notes: "Although the Fourth Amendment does not make any distinctions between classes of people, [*Stroud v. United States* (1919)] concluded that prisoners are not covered by any of its safeguards." Other early court rulings extended this opinion of denied Fourth Amendment rights to include probationers, parolees and those subject to border searches (p. 167).

During the 1970s, however, when the courts began ruling in favor of prisoners' rights, many courts deemed Fourth Amendment rights to not be automatically

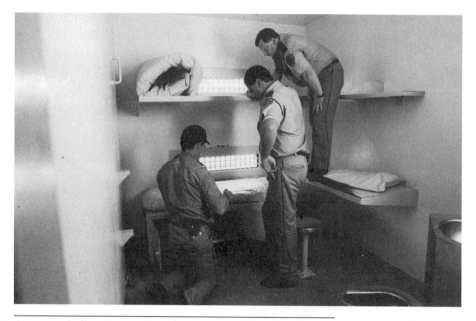

Correctional officers conduct a routine cell search for contraband.

forfeited upon incarceration. Recall the 1970 censorship case of *Palmigiano v. Travisono*. In this case, the court ruled "the right to be free from unreasonable searches and seizures is one of the rights retained by prisoners subject, of course, to such curtailment as may be made necessary by the purposes of confinement and requirements of security."

Security concerns have provided the grounds for many search and seizure cases. For instance, in *Moore v. People* (1970), the court ruled that searches conducted by correctional personnel "are not unreasonable as long as they are not for the purpose of harassing or humiliating the inmate in a cruel or unusual manner." In *Bell v. Wolfish* (1979), the Supreme Court ruled that unannounced cell searches, or **shakedowns,** did not require warrants, were not a violation of inmates' Fourth Amendment rights and were justified by the correctional facility's need to maintain security and order. If the *Bell* decision left any question as to how the Court felt about cell searches and the Fourth Amendment, those doubts were erased with the *Hudson v. Palmer* ruling in 1984, in which the Court declared: "the Fourth Amendment has no applicability to a prison cell."

The Supreme Court's decision in *Griffin v. Wisconsin* (1987) allowed the warrantless search of a probationer's home by a probation supervisor. In this case, a law enforcement officer had tipped off the probation supervisor that guns might be found in the probationer's home—an obvious violation of the conditions of probation. The Court ruled that the probation supervisor had reasonable grounds to believe such contraband was present in the probationer's home and that the warrantless search did not violate the probationer's

Fourth Amendment rights. The Court described probation as a sanction similar in form to incarceration and, as such, warrant requirements, probable cause and magistrate involvement were quite impractical given the need for quick decisions. Furthermore, the Court felt probation supervisors could act as impartial surrogate magistrates since they are, by regulation, responsible for the welfare of their probationers (Krantz, p. 363).

Body searches typically present a greater invasion of privacy than do cell searches. The courts, however, have been inclined to take a similar hands-off stance, allowing pat downs and strip searches as reasonable security and deterrence measures. *Bell* also addressed the issue of body cavity searches. Although the Supreme Court was aware of the potential for abuse in such invasive search procedures, it ruled nonetheless that body cavity searches were not unreasonable:

> The test of reasonableness under the Fourth Amendment is not capable of precise definition or mechanical application. In each case it requires a balancing of the need for the particular search against the invasion of personal rights that the search entails. Courts must consider the scope of the particular intrusion, the manner in which it is conducted, the justification for initiating it and the place in which it is conducted. A detention facility is a unique place fraught with serious security dangers. Smuggling of money, drugs, weapons and other contraband is all too common an occurrence (*Bell v. Wolfish,* 1979).

The Court's major concession to Fourth Amendment protection was that searches be conducted reasonably and nonabusively.

Certain privacy issue cases have met with limited success. For example, *Forts v. Ward* (1978) dealt with prisoners and correctional officers of the opposite sex. The court ruled that surveillance of female inmates by male correctional officers while the inmates showered, dressed, used the toilet facilities and slept was, in fact, a violation of the inmates' constitutional rights to privacy. However, later court decisions came to opposite opinions after balancing inmate privacy interests against sex discrimination in correctional staffing (Krantz, p. 177).

Bennett (1995, p. 91) notes: "Over the past decade and a half . . . [c]ourts have been more willing, within limits, to allow intrusion into inmate privacy." Two cases, *Turner v. Safley* (1987) and *Jordan v. Gardner* (1993), illustrate how court decisions "are at odds concerning inmates' constitutional right to privacy" (p. 108). In *Turner,* the Supreme Court sided with the administrator-defendant and the correctional policy allowing cross-gender searches, stating "when a prison regulation impinges on inmates' constitutional rights, the regulation is valid if it is reasonably related to legitimate penological interests." In *Jordan,* however, the court sided with the inmate-plaintiff, conceding that female inmates subjected to clothed body searches by male officers had, in fact, suffered a cruel and unusual punishment. Bennett (pp. 107–108) states: "In cases involving observation of nude inmates by opposite-sex officers, the courts generally have not found constitutional violations, upholding instead equal employment opportunities for officers. No hard-and-fast rules exist, however, for when cross-gender searches and observations become constitutional violations."

Searches have also been conducted on visitors, correctional officers and other corrections personnel, since it is known that these individuals may smuggle in contraband. While court rulings are split on these issues, the dominant view holds that the rights of visitors and corrections staff are lessened by the surrounding environment yet remain greater than those of prisoners (Krantz, pp. 174–175).

Urine testing has also led to litigation alleging violation of inmates', probationers' and parolees' Fourth Amendment rights (Collins, 1995, p. 160). Such cases have focused on "procedural deficiencies regarding proper chain of custody, Fourth Amendment search issues and the manner in which test results are admitted in judicial or administrative hearings." Other cases have challenged the reliability of drug testing and its results.

Fifth Amendment Rights

➤ The **Fifth Amendment** reads:

> No person shall be held to answer for a capital, or otherwise infamous crime, unless on a presentment or indictment of a Grand Jury, except in cases arising in the land or naval forces, or in the Militia, when in actual service in time of War or public danger; nor shall any person be subject for the same offense to be twice put in jeopardy of life or limb; nor shall be compelled in any criminal case to be a witness against himself, nor be deprived of life, liberty, or property, without due process of law, nor shall private property be taken for public use, without just compensation.

> For prisoners, cases based on Fifth Amendment rights involve interrogation and counsel, property rights and double jeopardy.

The Fifth Amendment does not come up often in prisoners' rights cases, but it may apply to inmates who are being questioned about offenses separate from those they are serving time for or those inmates involved in internal disciplinary proceedings. In *Baxter v. Palmigiano* (1976), the Supreme Court ruled:

> Prison disciplinary hearings are not criminal proceedings; but if inmates are compelled in those proceedings to furnish testimonial evidence that might incriminate them in later criminal proceedings, they must be offered "whatever immunity is required to supplement the privilege" and may not be required "to waive such immunity."

Compensation for prison labor has been another issue challenged under the Fifth Amendment, as inmates claim they are being deprived of property (competitive wages) without due process. Yet courts consistently reject just compensation arguments made on Fifth, Thirteenth and Fourteenth Amendment grounds.

Regarding the double jeopardy clause of the Fifth Amendment, inmates who commit disciplinary infractions, appear before a disciplinary board and are punished, frequently find themselves facing criminal prosecution for the same offense. According to the courts, this does *not* constitute double jeopardy.

Sixth Amendment Rights

▶ The **Sixth Amendment** reads:

> In all criminal prosecutions, the accused shall enjoy the right to a speedy and public trial, by an impartial jury of the State and district wherein the crime shall have been committed, which district shall have been previously ascertained by law, and to be informed of the nature and cause of the accusation; to be confronted with the witnesses in his favor, against him, to have compulsory process for obtaining witnesses and to have the Assistance of Counsel for his defense.

> For prisoners, cases based on Sixth Amendment rights involve the right to a speedy trial and the detainer problem.

Like the Fifth Amendment, the Sixth Amendment is not a frequently cited amendment in prisoners' rights lawsuits. This amendment applies to prisoners who have other criminal charges pending against them, for which they will stand trial. Often, detainers are filed against these inmates, ensuring their appearance before the prosecuting jurisdiction for the next trial once their current sentence is complete. Because it is argued that prisoners' abilities to defend themselves diminish with time, prisoners should be allowed to appear before court in a "speedy" fashion.

However, a 1969 case, *Smith v. Hooey*, involved an inmate at a federal institution who also had state criminal charges pending against him in Texas and who spent six years trying to get his trial. The detainer process apparently caused the delay. The court ruled that "upon petitioner's demand, Texas has a constitutional duty to make a diligent, good faith effort" to bring the prisoner to trial. As a result, many states took it to mean the right to a speedy trial was activated only *after* a prisoner demands it. However, because many prisoners are unaware of their right to a speedy trial or that detainers have been lodged against them, the rationale of *Smith v. Hooey* should not be limited to prisoners who make the demand.

Eighth Amendment Rights

➤ The **Eighth Amendment** reads:

> Excessive bail shall not be required, nor excessive fines imposed, nor cruel and unusual punishment inflicted.

For prisoners, cases based on Eighth Amendment rights involve cruel and unusual punishment, including overcrowding; solitary confinement; corporal punishment, physical abuse and the use of force; treatment and rehabilitation; the right not to be treated; and the death penalty.

The final protection of this amendment—that no cruel and unusual punishment be inflicted—has become the basis for numerous prisoner lawsuits. The Eighth Amendment is particularly popular among inmates filing lawsuits, for it protects against many conditions so often claimed to be found in penal institutions. However, like most of the other amendments discussed thus far, the Supreme Court did not consider the Eighth Amendment in relation to the conditions of correctional confinement until the 1970s.

A prisoner stands handcuffed to a metal bar under the sweltering Alabama sun. Some offenders are made to stay at the "hitching post" for entire days, prompting some, such as U.S. Magistrate Vanzetta Penn McPherson, to rally for the end of such barbaric punishment.

The general daily living conditions have been the subject of many inmate lawsuits and much court scrutiny. The first landmark case involving Eighth Amendment violations was *Holt v. Sarver* (1970), a class-action suit in which the court found deplorable, unconstitutional conditions in the Arkansas prison system:

> (1) the prison was largely run by inmate trusty guards who breeded hatred and mistrust; (2) the open barracks within the prison invited widespread physical and sexual assaults; (3) the isolation cells were overcrowded, filthy, and unsanitary; and (4) there was a total absence of any program of rehabilitation and training (Krantz, pp. 199–200).

A similar ruling was made in *McLaughlin v. Royster* (1972), in which the court ruled that poor living conditions were not enough to violate the Eighth Amendment: "what is required are inmates being exposed to conditions so dangerous and uninhabitable as to be shocking." The Eighth Amendment violations found in *Ruiz v. Estelle* (1980) resulted in massive changes within the Texas Department of Corrections, including changes in fire and safety regulations, health care, the number of inmates housed in each cell and the use of inmate guards.

Eighth Amendment violations are typically divided into two categories: (1) actions against individual prisoners, such as solitary confinement or corporal punishment and (2) conditions of the institution that all inmates are subject to and that constitute cruel and unusual punishment, such as overcrowding and lack of quality treatment services. *Holt, McLaughlin* and *Ruiz* used the Eighth Amendment to focus on the "totality of conditions" and how they combined to produce "cruel and unusual punishment," but the Eighth Amendment is frequently applied to separate, distinct aspects of corrections. Since *Holt* in 1970, prisoners have used almost every complaint imaginable about being incarcerated—everything from overcrowding and double-bunking to solitary confinement, the temperature of the cells, lack of privacy, quality of medical treatment, the death penalty and even such facts as the prison being located too far from family so as to preclude frequent visitation. Krantz (p. 190) notes: "It is clear from a reading of the cases which have attempted to interpret the Eighth Amendment that the term 'cruel and unusual punishment' has not been precisely defined. Instead, courts have applied a range of tests to determine its applicability to various factual patterns." Krantz summarizes the three tests as follows (pp. 190–191):

1. Whether under all the circumstances the punishment in question is ". . . of such character or consequences as to shock general conscience or be intolerable in fundamental fairness" (*Lee v. Tahash*, 1965).

2. If the punishment is greatly disproportionate to the offense for which it is imposed (*Weems v. United States*, 1910).

3. If the application of the punishment goes far beyond what is necessary to achieve its aim.

To summarize, the three tests applied to the phrase "cruel and unusual punishment" are: Is it shocking and undignified? Is it excessive? Could a lesser punishment achieve the same effect?

Overcrowding

Correctional overcrowding has already been discussed at several points, particularly as it contributes to inmate tension and violence. Overcrowding is also of concern to corrections because of its potential as a source for inmate grievances and lawsuits. As noted, many correctional facilities are currently operating under court orders to reduce crowding, a common situation.

Several key cases have been tried concerning overcrowding, including *Fischer v. Winter* (1983). In this case, the court ruled that California pretrial detainees at a women's detention facility had suffered cruel and unusual punishment due to the noise level, absence of privacy and shortage of space. In another case, *Battle v. Anderson* (1977), the court reached the same conclusion based on evidence that inmates in an Oklahoma prison were made to sleep in stairwells and garages and not given access to toilet or shower facilities.

In *Bell v. Wolfish* (1979), inmates challenged the conditions at New York's Metropolitan Correctional Center, claiming the double-bunking policy was a violation of their rights. Although this case produced favorable Eighth Amendment violation rulings for inmates in the lower courts, the Supreme Court failed to see any conditions that constituted cruel and unusual punishment, overturning the lower courts' decisions. It was demonstrated that the double-bunking occurred out of necessity due to lack of space and not intentionally to punish or deprive inmates in any way. Furthermore, as noted by the Court, the correctional facility was new, inmates spent only 7 to 8 hours in their cells each day, mostly sleeping during these periods, and inmates were normally released within 60 days (Krantz, p. 202).

Another case concerning an Ohio maximum-security prison, *Rhodes v. Chapman* (1981), involved prisoners serving longer terms who spent most of their time in their double-bunked cells. Yet the results of this case were surprisingly similar to *Bell*. The lower courts agreed with the prisoners' claims, then the Supreme Court overruled.

Legislation has been drafted to lessen the courts' involvement in cases alleging overcrowding. Call and Cole (1996, p. 92) state: "Section 20409 of the Violent Crime Control Act of 1994 contains several provisions that appear to be designed to diminish the role of federal courts in prison and jail overcrowding cases. . . . [but] they are not likely to bring about a substantial change." Although many strongly disagree, Call and Cole believe (p. 103): "Section 20409 may be void because it is an unconstitutional legislative restriction of judicial power that violates the constitutional requirement of separation of powers." They explain (p. 104):

Because it was added to the Act so late in the legislative process, no committee hearings considered Section 20409. Because the Act was so extensive, there was no significant floor debate on Section 20409. Consequently, Section 20409 is one of those pieces of proposed legislation that becomes law without the kind of careful consideration and debate that sheds light on the full ramifications of the legislation.

Solitary Confinement

At the other end of the spectrum from overcrowding is solitary confinement, which prisoners have also tried to have declared unconstitutional. Their lawsuits have claimed solitary confinement is psychological torture, constitutes excessive cruelty and inhumane treatment and is unnecessarily cruel when a less severe form of punishment would achieve the same purpose.

Following the decision in *McCray v. Burrell* (1975), the courts are nearly unanimous in their rulings that solitary confinement is not, per se, an unconstitutional form of punishment, although the overall conditions of solitary confinement and the length of time inmates remain in solitary confinement may constitute violations of the Eighth Amendment. *Hutto v. Finney* (1978), for example, limited the length of solitary confinement for Arkansas state prisoners to 30 days. *Fulwood v. Clemmer* (1962) determined the need to assess, case by case, the effects of solitary confinement on the prisoner's mental condition. In *Wright v. McMann* (1972), the court ruled it unconstitutional to deprive an inmate in solitary of clothing needed for warmth.

Courts have recognized solitary confinement as a valid correctional technique for disciplining troublesome offenders and for protecting the general inmate population and staff from such offenders.

Corporal Punishment, Physical Abuse and the Use of Force

Corporal punishment may have been a part of early American correctional methods, and is still practiced in many other countries (recall the caning of Michael Fay, an American youth in Singapore), but was declared unconstitutional in the United States over two and a half decades ago. Such punishment is now considered physical abuse and a violation of inmates' Eighth Amendment rights.

In *Talley v. Stephens* (1965), a federal district court ruled that whipping a prisoner with a leather strap was allowed if carefully controlled. Yet it was found that such whippings could not be controlled, and just three years later, a court in the same district ruled that such disciplinary measures did, in fact, constitute cruel and unusual punishment (*Jackson v. Bishop*, 1968). Three years later, in *Inmates of Attica Correctional Facility v. Rockefeller* (1971), the use of corporal punishment to enforce prison discipline was declared unconstitutional.

In many, if not most cases, corporal punishment fails the third test of cruel and unusual punishment: Does the application of the punishment go far

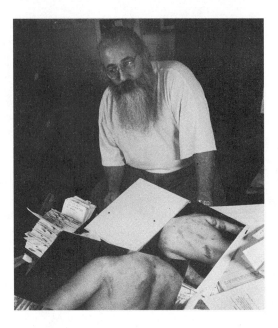

A staff photographer for Prison Legal Services in Plattesburg, New York, documents the brutal beatings of prisoners by correctional officers, violations of these inmates' Eighth Amendment rights.

beyond what is necessary to achieve its aim? Brutality by corrections officers against prisoners has usually been seen as a tort action rather than cruel and unusual punishment, although most courts, to date, have been reluctant to extend *Jackson v. Bishop* to include isolated assaults on prisoners by correctional officers as actionable under the Federal Civil Rights Act (Krantz, p. 195), or Section 1983, discussed shortly.

The use of force is required from time to time in correctional institutions (for example, an inmate refuses to go to segregation and institution staff must use force). Officers in our nation's jails and prisons are charged with the difficult task of supervising and controlling the lawbreakers of this country, people who have a hard time following rules. Such people frequently require a degree of prodding when it comes to following correctional staff's orders. Consequently, correctional officers and other personnel must exercise caution and restraint, no matter how provoking or infuriating an inmate may be, because the excessive use of force and use of deadly force have potentially serious legal consequences.

Landman v. Royster (1972) set, as the guideline for reasonable use of force, this test: Are property or lives in danger from this use of force? Recall from Chapter 13, in *Hudson v. McMillan* (1992), the Supreme Court ruled that unnecessary force by a correctional officer against a prisoner violated the prisoner's Eighth Amendment right against cruel and unusual punishment, even if the inmate did not sustain serious injury. Clearly, distinguishing between what is reasonable and what is unnecessary can be quite confusing.

Whitley v. Albers (1986) was brought by an inmate who had been shot by a correctional officer attempting to quell a disturbance. The Supreme Court ruled no Eighth Amendment violation had occurred, stating "only the 'unnecessary and wanton infliction of pain' constitutes cruel and unusual punishment" in a correctional setting, and that in efforts to maintain security, one must look at "whether force was applied in [a] good faith effort to restore discipline or maliciously and sadistically for the purpose of causing harm." Even this Supreme Court decision, however, is not absolute. Referring to *Spain v. Procunier* (1979), the use of force or chemicals, such as tear gas, to put down a disturbance *has* been held to constitute cruel and unusual punishment in some instances.

Improper inmate classification may lead to certain inmates being placed in more dangerous settings. Such classification errors may then lead to an increased likelihood of inmate-on-inmate assaults. Inmates have filed lawsuits after being assaulted by other inmates, claiming the correctional facility failed to adequately protect them from such attacks. In *Kish v. County of Milwaukee* (1971), the court hesitated to impose liability on prison officials for failing to protect inmates from assaults by other inmates. Although several cases have upheld inmates' constitutional right to some degree of protection from attacks by other inmates, the right is seldom applied in individual cases.

However, *Farmer v. Brennan* (1994) demonstrated that prisoners *can* win inmate-on-inmate assault lawsuits against prison administrations if they can prove "deliberate indifference." *Farmer* has become the defining case for such lawsuits, in which the Supreme Court's standard for inmate-on-inmate assaults was ruled as "deliberate indifference" by prison officials who "knew of a substantial risk of harm and recklessly disregarded that risk" (Vaughn and del Carmen, 1995, p. 70).

In this case, federal prisoner Dee Farmer was a preoperative transsexual, biologically male yet possessing feminine traits and dressing and acting effeminately. Although Farmer spent most of the early part of his sentence in administrative segregation, he was later moved to the general inmate population following a disciplinary infraction and transfer to another facility. After a week in the general population, Farmer was raped and physically assaulted in his cell when he ignored another prisoner's sexual advances. Farmer filed a lawsuit against the prison officials claiming their placement of him among the general inmate population demonstrated "deliberate indifference" and violated his Eighth Amendment right to protection from cruel and unusual punishment. Although the jury found Farmer had not been raped and he lost his case, Vaughn and del Carmen (pp. 82–83) note:

> *Farmer v. Brennan* is significant because it helps eliminate ambiguity as to when prison officials can be successfully sued for inmate-by-inmate assault. . . .
>
> The Supreme Court decision in Farmer offers both good news and bad news for prison administrators. The good news is that the Court's definition of "deliberate indifference" will make it difficult for prison plaintiffs to prevail in inmate-against-inmate assault litigation. The Court rejected the argument that officials are "deliberately indifferent" when they should have known of an "obvious risk" of potential harm to inmates. The bad news for prison administrators is that despite *Farmer*, inmates can, nonetheless, still win their

suits. The Court said that officials cannot be ostriches and ignore "unwelcome knowledge" . . . that "substantial risks" are present in their facilities. . . . The key to avoiding liability is for prison personnel to act reasonably in the face of known and substantial serious risk.

➤ **Deliberate indifference,** similar to but different from negligence, was first defined by the Court in *Estelle v. Gamble* (1976). The courts have, however, continued to struggle with this term. The Sixth Circuit Court of Appeals stated: "[P]art of the difficulty lies in the fact that there is a degree of inherent conflict between the two words chosen to express the standard. 'Deliberate' refers to action 'characterized by or resulting from slow, careful, thorough calculation and consideration of effects and consequences.' 'Indifference,' on the other hand, means to be 'marked by a total or nearly total lack of interest in or concern about something' " (*Marsh v. Arn*, 1991). Basically, "indifference" and "negligence" are the same, but the modifier "deliberate" adds the element of "recklessness" to the action (*Howell v. Evans*, 1991).

Treatment and Rehabilitation

Offenders may come into corrections with a variety of illnesses, diseases and disabilities. Others may exaggerate their problems to get better living conditions or more attention. Because incarceration prevents these individuals from personally seeking appropriate medical attention, it is argued that the correctional system owes a duty to these offenders to provide such services.

Medical and psychiatric treatment, and rehabilitation programs for such things as drug addiction and behavior modification, are not always available. Even when such services are provided, the quality is often questionable. Undoubtedly some correctional systems have adequate treatment facilities with competent staff. Others, however, are less than satisfactory and have frequently found themselves entangled in inmate lawsuits.

While the level of medical care required by law is subject to interpretation, some degree of medical treatment must be provided. In *Edwards v. Duncan* (1966), the court ruled that total and intentional denial of medical care is unconstitutional, and in *Newman v. State of Alabama* (1972), the court ruled that prisoners as a class do possess a constitutional right to medical care. The premier case concerning medical treatment in correctional facilities has been *Estelle v. Gamble* (1976). The plaintiff in this case was a Texas state prisoner, J.W. Gamble, who was injured in November 1973, when a 600-pound bale of cotton fell on him during routine prison labor. The prison physician treated Gamble for back strain by prescribing pain relievers and sent him to his cell for a month, after which time Gamble was declared fit for light work. Despite Gamble's 17 attempts to be treated for his condition, which had evolved into chest pains, migraines and blackouts, it was not until February 1974 that he was thoroughly examined. At that time it was determined Gamble needed hospitalization.

Gamble filed a Section 1983 lawsuit in which the court found he had not received adequate medical care and ruled in favor of the plaintiff. The Supreme Court, however, reversed this ruling, stating: "Deliberate indifference to the serious medical needs of prisoners constitutes unnecessary and wanton infliction of pain proscribed by the Eighth Amendment. This is true whether the indifference is manifested by prison doctors in their response to the prisoner's needs or by prison guards in intentionally interfering with the treatment once prescribed." Although this appeared to be an advance for the provision of medical care to prisoners, the Court went on to state that not all claims in inadequate medical care are protected by the Eighth Amendment. "An inadvertent failure to provide adequate medical care does not constitute an 'unnecessary and wanton infliction of pain.' Nor does an accident, simple negligence, or a disagreement as to treatment options" (Krantz, p. 215). Based on this standard, the Court ruled in favor of the defense, and in so doing, expressed reluctance to interfere with medical discretion as to the treatment chosen for a particular inmate-patient, another example of the hands-off approach to prisoners' rights.

A medical crisis facing more and more prisoners is AIDS. The rising number of HIV-infected inmates means prison doctors and medical staff will need to be knowledgeable on how to treat such patients. Constitutional issues surrounding AIDS in correctional facilities are just starting to be examined and include the right to treatment, the quality of care, the responsibility and failure to protect others from those infected with HIV and the right of HIV-positive inmates not to be isolated from the general population (Krantz, p. 217).

Regarding mental health treatment, the majority of cases have determined that failure to provide adequate treatment is a violation of Eighth Amendment rights. Regarding other treatment and rehabilitation programs, Krantz (p. 206) notes an absence of cases establishing a constitutional requirement that corrections provide such services to adult inmates. However (p. 207): "There has been far more active development on the issues of right to treatment or rehabilitative services in other types of institutional settings such as mental institutions and juvenile facilities."

Right to Treatment and to Refuse Treatment

Citizens in the community take for granted their right to seek or to refrain from seeking medical treatment and other services. Inmates, probationers and parolees, however, are often forced to submit to treatment or programming that corrections and medical personnel believe will further the correctional goals concerning these clients. In *Knecht v. Gillman* (1973), an appellate court ruled that prisoners who consent to a treatment procedure should later be allowed to rescind that consent.

Krantz (p. 221) notes the lack of consistency with which courts have handled cases involving informed consent:

Some courts, for example, have concluded that they will not intervene against forced medication as long as it has been determined that the decision was based upon competent professional judgment. . . .Others begin with a presumption that prisoners have a right to refuse such treatment unless there is a judicial determination that they are incompetent to do so and adequate procedural safeguards are provided to insure appropriate consideration is given to due process concerns. . . . Still others would simply neutrally balance the interests on a case-by-case basis.

Death Penalty

Capital punishment, as discussed in Chapter 4, is highly controversial, yet it wasn't until the late 1960s that its constitutionality was challenged in the courts. Although 38 states and the Federal Bureau of Prisons currently have the death penalty, there was a time when capital punishment was not practiced in this country.

The landmark case that suspended the death penalty across the nation was *Furman v. Georgia* (1972). This ruling effectively halted capital punishment throughout the United States and caused state courts to investigate their own application procedures and processes. In 1976, however, another Georgia case went before the Supreme Court and produced a controversial decision. In *Gregg v. Georgia,* the Court ruled that capital punishment for crimes of murder was not cruel and unusual punishment per se and, therefore, did not violate the Eighth Amendment. The two standards set forth by the Court regarding the death penalty and the Eighth Amendment were whether the punishment (1) involved unnecessary and wanton infliction of pain and (2) was grossly disproportionate to the severity of the crime. The Court noted that the death penalty had a long history of acceptance in the United States.

The death penalty has been and continues to be very controversial with the American public.

Other Eighth Amendment Issues

As shown, the Eighth Amendment has been applied to a variety of conditions that inmates claim constitute cruel and unusual punishment. One of the more recent claims concerns secondhand cigarette smoke, or ETS (environmental tobacco smoke). Bryan (1994, p. 2) notes:

Historically, tobacco and smoke have been viewed as a nuisance but not dangerous. However, it appears that society has begun to recognize the dangers of tobacco and the dangerous effects of second-hand smoke. . . . On June 18, 1993, the U.S. Supreme Court in *Helling v. McKinney* held that the Nevada Department of Prison "with deliberate indifference, exposed him

[McKinney] to levels of ETS [second-hand smoke] that pose an unreasonable
risk of serious damage to his future health."

As a result of this case, many correctional facilities have established smoke-
free environments and permit inmates and staff to smoke only in designated
areas or outside. Regarding smoking bans in correctional facilities, Tischler
(1998, p. 1) states:

> Smoking, it turns out, is part of the complex system of inmate privileges used to
> manage the inmate population, and is one of the few outlets that inmates have
> to release their pent-up frustrations. Many institutions have found that banning
> cigarettes altogether can be counterproductive, leading to volatile behavior,
> fights and an underground market for tobacco.

Tischler (p. 3) continues: "In Massachusetts, a number of inmates are arguing
that smoking bans constitute Eighth Amendment violations: 'needless and unnecessary pain and suffering.' Ironically, that is the same argument nonsmok-
ing inmates have successfully used to win smoking bans."

As with smoking, weight lifting in correctional facilities has been
touted as "a management tool that helps provide stress relief for inmates"
in addition to giving them something to do (Clayton, 1997, p. 1). However,
three states (Arizona, Georgia and North Carolina) have implemented full
bans on weight lifting in state prisons and jails, and ten states have partial
bans, primarily prohibiting use of free weights as they can be used as
weapons (Clayton, p. 3). States have run into legal trouble when they have
totally denied inmates access to exercise. In *Pearson v. Godinez* (1997), inmate Alex Pearson had accumulated so many restrictions for multiple disciplinary infractions that, under the facility's disciplinary policy, the
warden was authorized to deny Pearson access to the exercise yard for one
year. Pearson, however, filed suit, claiming cruel and unusual punishment
under the Eighth Amendment. The District Court of Illinois agreed, ruling
the restriction constituted an "extreme and prolonged" punishment and
was unconstitutional.

Another correctional management tool that has caused great debate is the
chain gang. Advocate Senator Charlie Crist (1998) states: "Chain gangs offer a
number of benefits. . . . [W]ork on the chain gangs is appropriate punishment. It puts criminals to work. It gives the opportunity to give back to the society they have taken from. Chain gangs and hard work ensure that prison is
not pleasant, which is what society and criminals need." Opponents, however,
claim chain gangs are a form of cruel and unusual punishment. According to
Brownstein (1998, p. 7): "[I]ntentionally degrading and humiliating inmates
not only makes for bad corrections policy, it violates the Eighth Amendment
to the Constitution. After all, as the U.S. Supreme Court has recognized: 'The
basic concept underlying the Eighth Amendment is nothing less than the dignity of man' (*Trop v. Dulles*, 356 U.S. 86, 100 [1958])."

Fourteenth Amendment Rights

➤ The **Fourteenth Amendment** reads:

> SECTION 1. All persons born or naturalized in the United States, and subject to the jurisdiction thereof, are citizens of the United States and of the State wherein they reside. No State shall make or enforce any law which shall abridge the privileges or immunities of citizens of the United States; nor shall any State deprive any person of life, liberty, or property, without due process of law; nor deny to any person within its jurisdiction the equal protection of the laws.

> For prisoners, cases based on Fourteenth Amendment rights involve equal protection based on race, gender and the availability of facilities and services.

Cases involving Fourteenth Amendment rights are concerned with equal protection and typically center around issues of race and gender. They may also involve the availability of facilities and services to various segments of the prisoner population.

Race Discrimination

In *Washington v. Lee* (1966), the court ruled that statutorily imposed racial segregation in corrections, without a compelling state interest, violates the Equal Protection Clause. In other words, prison officials must determine the need for security and discipline on a case-by-case basis. Segregating racial groups on the assumption that they will be in conflict violates the equal protection component of the Fourteenth Amendment.

Gender Discrimination

Gender-based cases include *Mary Beth G. v. City of Chicago* (1983), in which an equal protection violation was found regarding strip search practices. In this case, only female misdemeanants were required to submit to strip searches and body cavity exams; male misdemeanants were not subjected to these invasive procedures. In *Glover v. Johnson* (1979 and 1987), equal protection violations were found when female prisoners were offered fewer educational and vocational programs than were male prisoners and when programs available to women were of a lesser quality than those available to men.

Discrimination Against the Disabled

Special segments of the prisoner population may also file lawsuits claiming violations of their equal access rights under the Fourteenth Amendment. For example, correctional facilities are required by the Americans with Disabilities Act (ADA) to provide special accommodations, programming and services, such as sign language interpreters, to hearing impaired inmates. As Vernon (1995, p. 140) notes: "[T]he ADA gives inmates with disabilities tremendous legal leverage in obtaining such benefits. . . . Not providing interpreting services will likely lead to expensive and time-consuming class action lawsuits."

Disciplinary Hearings

The Fourteenth Amendment also covers due process rights in disciplinary hearings. Recall the case of *Wolff v. McDonnell* (1974) regarding censoring privileged communications between attorney and inmate-client. This case also involved the claim that Nebraska's disciplinary procedures, particularly those relating to loss of good time, were unconstitutional. As a result of this case, the Supreme Court determined that disciplinary proceedings were not the same as criminal prosecutions and that, therefore, a prisoner does not enjoy the full due process rights of a defendant on trial. The minimum requirements specified by the Court concerning such disciplinary proceedings included the following prisoners' rights:

- The right to receive advanced written notice of the alleged infraction.
- The right to have sufficient time to prepare a defense.
- The right to present documentary evidence and to call witnesses on his or her behalf.
- The right to seek counsel when the circumstances of the case are complex or if the prisoner is illiterate.
- The right to a written statement of the findings of the disciplinary committee and the maintenance of a written record of the proceedings.

Access to Court

Access to court is another issue frequently found in Fourteenth Amendment rights cases. Since the case of *Cooper v. Pate* (1964), a lengthy list of cases has been tried, each adding a new wrinkle to the "access to court" issue. The validity of access to court as a prisoner's right was solidified by the ruling in *Crug v. Hauck* (1971), in which the court stated "ready access to court is one of, perhaps *the* most fundamental constitutional right."

Considering the requirements set forth in *Wolff,* such as allowing an inmate sufficient time to prepare a defense, it was recognized that few resources were available to the inmate faced with such a task. It is a simple matter to allow prisoners to petition the court, but exceedingly difficult to equip them to submit such a petition in a form allowing the court to proceed. In *Younger v.*

Gilmore (1971), the court recognized the need for legal libraries inside correctional facilities to allow inmates to prepare sufficient petitions. In *Bounds v. Smith* (1977), the Supreme Court ruled that the state of North Carolina had a responsibility to furnish each correctional institution with an adequate law library. Many prison libraries include the standard legal references, the Supreme Court reports, state reports and federal and state statutes. Some states have gone even further in providing law libraries, some so extensive as to be envied by attorneys.

In *Johnson v. Avery* (1969), the Supreme Court ruled it was acceptable for inmates to assist each other with legal work and case preparation unless the correctional facility provided other reasonable legal assistance to inmates. This decision came before the major decisions requiring facilities to establish legal libraries. The later implementation of extensive law libraries permitted those inmates with sufficient interest to become extensively knowledgeable about the law, so much so they could provide legal advice to other inmates or to represent themselves before the court. Thus was born the **jailhouse lawyer.** Some facilities have dodged the extensive use of jailhouse lawyers by setting up legal assistance programs staffed by practicing lawyers or law students.

Establishing libraries and providing tools to help inmates become jailhouse lawyers inevitably led to abuses of the system. Some inmates file numerous frivolous lawsuits and nuisance suits, which only harm the credibility of those inmates filing legitimate suits. Consider *In re Green* (1981). Prisoner Green became a jailhouse lawyer who, during the 1970s, filed 600 to 700 lawsuits on behalf of himself and other prisoners, which the courts consistently found to be "frivolous, irresponsible, and unmeritorious."

Protection Against Adverse Consequences

The Fourteenth Amendment also offers certain protections when adverse consequences are possible, such as when the prisoner faces substantial loss of liberty. Three important Supreme Court cases involving such possible adverse consequences are *Mempa v. Rhay* (1968), *Gagnon v. Scarpelli* (1973) and *Morrisey v. Brewer* (1972), all discussed in Chapter 7. In *Mempa*, the Court ruled that the Sixth Amendment right to counsel may be extended to probationers during revocation hearings. In *Gagnon*, the Court ruled that the right to counsel in revocation hearings should be decided case by case and not automatically extended in all cases. *Morrisey* set forth specific due process rights for persons entering parole revocation proceedings, including the right to written notice of the alleged violations, the disclosure of any evidence to support the allegations, the chance to be heard in person and to present witnesses and evidence, the opportunity to cross-examine adverse witnesses, the right to a judgment by a neutral body such as the parole board and receipt of a written statement of the reasons for the revocation of parole.

At times it seems inmates are allowed to make a mockery of due process rights. Consider, for example, the three prisoners who plead not guilty to tunneling out of the Glades Correctional Institution in Florida. DiPaola and Friedberg (1995, p. 1B) report:

> It may seem absurd to hold trials for the convicted killers to determine if they fled the prison and were captured in Dade County, but legal experts say that is what will happen unless the escapees plead guilty.
>
> "It's called due process of law," said Mike Edmondson, spokesman for Palm Beach County State Attorney Barry Krischer. "Any criminal charge must stand on its own without consideration of past criminal history."
>
> . . . "Escape is a violation of a criminal law just like any other criminal violation," Circuit Court Judge Jack Cook said. "Even if you have a dozen eyewitnesses, you're still entitled to a trial and to have the state prove their case against you."

Selected Collateral Consequences

Certain rights may be lost or limited as the result of a criminal conviction. This loss of rights is known as collateral consequences and may include voting rights, judicial rights, domestic rights and property rights.

Voting Rights

The right to vote may be lost due to conviction of a crime. In most states, citizens convicted of felonies are disenfranchised in state and federal elections during and after incarceration. The Supreme Court ruling in *Richardson v. Ramirez* (1974) stated that the disenfranchisement of incarcerated offenders is unequivocally authorized by the Fourteenth Amendment, yet various court decisions indicate some ambivalence still prevails concerning voting.

In *Ray v. Commonwealth of Pennsylvania* (1967), the court ruled strongly against prisoners' constitutional right to vote: "Lawful incarceration brings about the necessary withdrawal or limitation of many privileges and rights, a withdrawal which is justified by the considerations underlying our penal system. . . . [I]t is only where fundamental, humane and necessary rights are breached that the constitutional protections become involved. These do not include the right to vote. . . ." Two years later, in *Kramer v. Union Free School District No. 15* (1969), another court declared voting was ruled a preferred right.

Several states still permit prisoners to vote. For example, the Massachusetts Constitution guarantees all state citizens the right to vote, regardless of any criminal convictions. Inmates in Maine and Vermont are also allowed to vote, as are those in Utah, except inmates convicted of treason or electoral law violations. John Reinstein of the American Civil Liberties Union believes voting should be considered a right, not a privilege, since "in that case, we could take it away from a lot of people. How about people who speed? How about people who don't pay their taxes?" ("Voting," 1995, p. 19).

Judicial and Property Rights

Judicial rights that may be restricted or lost following criminal conviction include the ability to sue or to enter into contracts. Again, courts in various districts have ruled differently on these topics. Much depends on whether the prisoner resides in a state that still practices civil death, although most states have discontinued its use. Convicted offenders may also find themselves with restricted pension and insurance rights.

Domestic Rights

Marriage, divorce, child bearing and sterilization may be seriously affected for someone serving time. In *Garner v. Garner* (1969) the court ruled that a sentenced prisoner held no right to file a counterclaim in a divorce suit. In fact, some jurisdictions still consider long-term or life imprisonment valid grounds for divorce. In many states, similarly restrictive rules against prisoners' right to marry have been upheld. In *Turner v. Safley* (1987), the Supreme

Doreen Lioy, center, walks with her head bowed as prison guards escort her out of the San Quentin Prison following her marriage to serial killer "Night Stalker" Richard Ramirez on October 3, 1996. Lioy told the media, "I just want to say I'm ecstatically happy today and very, very proud to have married Richard and be his wife."

Court ruled that the right to marry was, in fact, a fundamental right not lost simply due to incarceration, but also that marriage was subject to substantial restrictions as a result of incarceration. This Court ruling invalidated a Missouri regulation that required the prison superintendent to approve a prisoner marriage only if there were compelling reasons for such a marriage.

Cases involving parenthood and sterilization are controversial and not particularly common. In one paternity suit, inmate Steven Goodwin sought the right to father a baby. Mardon (1990, p. 172) notes: "Because courts have upheld the rights of prisons to deny conjugal visits, [Goodwin] has asked to be allowed to father a child by artificial insemination. . . . In 1988, a judge ruled that the right of reproduction was 'fundamentally inconsistent with imprisonment itself.' " Only once has the Supreme Court established restrictions in the area of prisoner sterilization, and the courts have upheld the constitutionality of several statutes that authorize the sterilization of criminals, despite offenders' claims the statutes allow for cruel and unusual punishment and are violations of equal protection and due process rights. Some courts, however, have ruled against the use of chemical or surgical castration as a condition of probation when no statutory direction exists (Krantz, pp. 111–112).

Summary

A right is a legally protected claim, whereas a privilege is not legally protected. Collateral consequences of criminal conviction often include restrictions on or loss of the rights to vote, to hold public office, to assist in parenting, to serve on a jury, to own firearms, to remain married and to have privacy.

Ex parte Hull (1941) marks the beginning of prisoners' rights cases and was the first major decision asserting prisoners' right of access to the courts. *Coffin v. Reichard* (1944) extended federal habeas corpus to include the conditions of confinement and was the first case in which a federal appellate court ruled that prisoners do not lose all their civil rights as a condition of confinement.

Two general categories of lawsuits are rights of individual prisoners, or substantive rights, and rights concerning confinement conditions, which apply to all prisoners or a class of prisoners. Other categories of rights include access to court, no cruel and unusual punishment, civil rights and protection when adverse consequences are possible. Five common avenues for bringing cases to court are (1) state habeas corpus, (2) federal habeas corpus, (3) state tort suits, (4) Section 1983 and (5) the Civil Rights of Institutionalized Persons Act of 1980.

For prisoners, cases based on Section 1983, the Civil Rights Act, challenge the conditions of confinement on the grounds that such conditions violate inmates' constitutional rights. Cases based on First Amendment rights involve censorship of mail, expression within the institution, association within the institution, religion, appearance and visitation rights. Cases based on Fourth Amendment rights involve searches and seizures and the issue of privacy. Cases based on Fifth Amendment rights involve interrogation and counsel, property rights and double jeopardy. Cases based on Sixth Amendment rights involve the right to a speedy trial and the detainer problem. Cases based on Eighth Amendment rights involve cruel and unusual punishment, including overcrowding; solitary confinement; corporal punishment, physical abuse and the use of force; treatment and rehabilitation; the right not to be treated; and the death penalty. Cases based on Fourteenth Amendment rights involve equal protection based on race, gender and the availability of facilities and services.

Discussion Questions

1. Do you think all the collateral consequences of criminal conviction are fair? Should those convicted of felonies ever be able to vote? Hold public office? Serve on a jury? Own or possess a firearm? Why or why not?

2. Should an activity such as smoking really be considered a right for inmates? What about other inmates' "right" to not be exposed to secondhand smoke?

3. Consider the phrasing of Section 1983 of the Civil Rights Act of 1871: "Every person who, under color of any statute, ordinance, regulation, custom, or usage, of any State or Territory, or the District of Columbia, subjects or causes to be subjected, any citizen of the United States or any person within the jurisdiction thereof to the deprivation of any rights, privileges, or immunities secured by the Constitution and laws, shall be liable to the party injured in an action at law, suit in equity, or other proper proceeding for redress." What does "under color of law" really mean? Are correctional officers and other staff liable for any action taken on the job? Only on direct orders from wardens? What about things they do after hours or off the clock?

4. How fair is it that correctional facilities be held liable for overcrowding when it's the courts who sentence so many individuals to incarceration and the taxpayers who control whether more bedspace is made available for these offenders? How can corrections better defend themselves in cases alleging violation of inmates' Eighth Amendment rights and overcrowding?

5. Is there something fundamentally wrong with our laws when inmates who escape from prison and are later captured in another jurisdiction are allowed to actually plead not guilty to the offense of escape? Do you think, in our efforts to create and maintain a system of justice that presumes everyone innocent until proven guilty, that it is too easy for criminals to abuse the justice system?

6. In your opinion, are any of the currently used forms of capital punishment "cruel and unusual"? Should the nation adopt only one method for the death penalty? If so, which one? If not, why not? What about when inmates are allowed to choose their own method of execution and then challenge that method as being cruel and unusual, as in the case of the obese inmate who chose hanging?

7. Have your local correctional facilities recently endured any instances of inmate litigation? If so, what did the cases involve and how were they decided?

8. How do you feel about inmates having access to legal libraries while incarcerated? Should they be allowed to prepare their own defense or should they be appointed legal counsel by the court? Why?

9. Should inmates be allowed to file as many petitions as they please, or should a limit be placed so they'd be more selective in bringing up their grievances? Is there potential for corruption in either scenario?

10. Overall, do you think inmates have too many rights? Why or why not?

References

Bennett, Katherine. "Constitutional Issues in Cross-Gender Searches and Visual Observation of Nude Inmates by Opposite-Sex Officers: A Battle Between and Within the Sexes." *The Prison Journal*, Vol. 75, No. 1, March 1995, pp. 90–112.

Brownstein, Rhonda. "Chain Gangs Are Cruel and Unusual Punishment." *Point/Counterpoint: Correctional Issues*. Lanham, MD: American Correctional Association, 1998, p. 7.

Bryan, Darrell. "Correctional Systems Wait for Nevada Decision: Does ETS Exposure Violate Inmates' 8th Amendment Rights?" *Corrections Compendium*, Vol. XIX, No. 5, May 1994, pp. 1–2.

Bryan, Darrell. "U.S. Courts Hand the Debate over Inmate Privileges to Corrections Officials." *Corrections Compendium*, Vol. XX, No. 6., June 1995, pp. 2–3.

Call, Jack E. and Cole, Richard. "Assessing the Possible Impact of the Violent Crime Control Act of 1994 on Prison and Jail Overcrowding Suits." *The Prison Journal*, Vol. 76, No. 1, March 1996, pp. 92–106.

Clayton, Susan L. "Weight Lifting in Corrections: Luxury or Necessity?" *On the Line*, Vol. 20, No. 5, November 1997, pp. 1, 3.

Collins, William C. "Urine Testing in Corrections: Legal Traps Remain for the Unwary." *Corrections Today*, April 1995, pp. 160–161.

Crist, Charlie. "Chain Gangs Are Right for Florida." *Point/Counterpoint: Correctional Issues*. Lanham, MD: American Correctional Association, 1998, p. 6.

deGroot, Gabrielle. "Supreme Court Invalidation of RFRA Could Reduce Frivolous Litigation by Inmates." *On the Line*, Vol. 20, No. 4, September 1997, pp. 1–2.

DiPaola, Jim and Friedberg, Ardy. "Three Plead Innocent to Glades Escape." (Ft. Lauderdale) *Sun-Sentinel*, February 11, 1995, pp. 1B, 5B.

Hanson, Roger A. and Daley, Henry W.K. *Challenging the Conditions of Prisons and Jails: A Report on Section 1983 Litigation*. Washington, DC: U.S. Department of Justice, Bureau of Justice Statistics, January 1995 (NCJ-151652).

Krantz, Sheldon. *Corrections and Prisoners' Rights*. St. Paul, MN: West Publishing Company, 1988.

Mardon, Steven. "Inmate Seeks Right to Father a Baby." *Corrections Today*, August 1990, p. 172.

National Criminal Justice Association. "Religious Freedom Law Raises Prison Safety Issues, State Says." *NCJA Justice Bulletin*, Vol. 15, No. 8, August 1995, pp. 1–2, 5–8.

Oran, Daniel. *Law Dictionary for Nonlawyers*, 2nd ed. St. Paul, MN: West Publishing Company, 1985.

"Practice of Satanism Among Inmates' First Amendment Rights." *Corrections Compendium*, January 1995, p. 19.

"Prison Officials Warn Against Restoring Religious Protections." *Corrections Journal*. Pace Publications, July 22, 1997, pp. 1, 6–7.

Tischler, Eric. "Smoking Bans Have Supporters, Detractors in Prison." *On the Line*, Vol. 21, No. 1, January 1998, pp. 1,3.

Vaughn, Michael S. and del Carmen, Rolando V. "Civil Liability Against Prison Officials for Inmate-on-Inmate Assault: Where Are We and Where Have We Been?" *The Prison Journal*, Vol. 75, No. 1, March 1995, pp. 69–89.

Vernon, McCay. "New Rights for Inmates with Hearing Loss." *Corrections Today*, April 1995, pp. 140–145.

"Voting: A Right or a Privilege for Prisoners?" *Corrections Compendium*, Vol. XX, No. 1, January 1995, p. 19.

Wunder, Amanda. "The Extinction of Inmate Privileges." *Corrections Compendium*, Vol. XX, No. 6, June 1995, pp. 5–24.

Cases

Battle v. Anderson (1977).

Baxter v. Palmigiano, 425 U.S. 308, 96 S.Ct. 1551, 47 L.Ed.2d 810 (1976).

Bell v. Wolfish, 441 U.S. 520, 99 S.Ct. 1861, 60 L.Ed.2d 447 (1979).

Block v. Rutherford, 468 U.S. 576, 104 S.Ct. 3227, 82 L.Ed.2d 438 (1984).

Bounds v. Smith, 430 U.S. 817, 97 S.Ct. 1491, 52 L.Ed.2d 72 (1977).

Brown v. Johnson, 743 F.2d 408 (6th Cir. 1985).

Cantwell v. Connecticut, 310 U.S. 296, 60 S.Ct. 900, 84 L.Ed. 1213 (1940).

City of Boerne, Texas v. Flores (1997).

Coffin v. Reichard, 143 F.2d 443 (6th Cir. 1944).

Cooper v. Pate, 378 U.S. 546 (1964).

Crug v. Hauck, 404 U.S. 59 (1971).

Edwards v. Duncan, 355 F.2d 993, 994 (4th Cir. 1966).

Estelle v. Gamble, 429 U.S. 97, 97 S.Ct. 285, 50 L.Ed.2d 251 (1976).

Ex parte Hull, 312 U.S. 546, 61 S.Ct. 640, 85 L.Ed. 1034 (1941).

Farmer v. Brennan, 114 S.Ct. 1970 (1994).

Fischer v. Winter (1983).

Forts v. Ward, 471 F.Supp. 1095 (D.C.N.Y. 1978).

Fulwood v. Clemmer, 206 F.Supp. 370 (D.C.D.C. 1962).

Furman v. Georgia, 408 U.S. 238, 92 S.Ct. 2726, 33 L.Ed.2d 346 (1972).

Gagnon v. Scarpelli, 411 U.S. 778 (1973).

Garner v. Garner, 59 Misc.2d 29, 297 N.Y.S.2d 463 (N.Y.Sup. 1969).

Glover v. Johnson, 478 F.Supp. 1075 (D.C.Mich., 1979); 659 F.Supp. 621 (E.D.Mich. 1987).

Goodwin v. Oswald, 462 F.2d. 1237 (2nd Cir. 1972).

Gregg v. Georgia, 428 U.S. 153, 96 S.Ct. 2909, 49 L.Ed.2d 859 (1976).

Griffin v. Wisconsin, ___ U.S. ___, 107 S.Ct. 3164, 97 L.Ed.2d 709 (1987).

Helling v. McKinney, 112 S.Ct. 3024 (1993).

Holt v. Sarver, 309 F.Supp. 362 (D.C.Ark. 1970).

Howell v. Evans, 922 F.2d 712 (11th Cir. 1991).

Hudson v. McMillan (1992).

Hudson v. Palmer, 468 U.S. 517, 104 S.Ct. 3194, 82 L.Ed.2d 393 (1984).

Hutto v. Finney, 437 U.S. 678, 98 S.Ct. 2565, 57 L.Ed.2d 522 (1978).

In re Green, 669 F.2d 779 (1981).

Inmates of Attica Correctional Facility v. Rockefeller, 453 F.2d 12, 23 (2d Cir. 1971).

Jackson v. Bishop, 404 F.2d 571 (8th Cir. 1968).

Johnson v. Avery, 393 U.S. 483, 485 (1969).

Jones v. North Carolina Prisoner Union, 433 U.S. 119, 97 S.Ct. 2532, 53 L.Ed.2d 629(1977).

Jordan v. Gardner, 986 F.2d 1521 (9th Cir. 1993).

Kish v. County of Milwaukee, 441 F.2d 901 (7th Cir. 1971).

Knecht v. Gillman, 488 F.2d 1136 (8th Cir. 1973).

Knuckles v. Prasse, 302 F.Supp. 1036 (D.C.Pa. 1969).

Kramer v. Union Free School District No. 15, 395 U.S. 621, 89 S.Ct. 1886, 23 L.Ed.2d 583 (1969).

Landman v. Royster, 346 F.Supp. 297, 312 (E.D.Va. 1972).

Lee v. Tahash, 352 F.2d 970 (8th Cir. 1965).

Marsh v. Arn, 937 F.2d 1056 (6th Cir. 1991).

Mary Beth G. v. City of Chicago (1983).

McCray v. Burrell, 516 F.2d 357, 367 (4th Cir. 1975).

McLaughlin v. Royster, 346 F.Supp. 297, 311 (E.D.Va. 1972).

Mempa v. Rhay, 339 U.S. 128 Cir. 3023 (1968).

Moore v. People, 171 Colorado 338, 467 P.2d (1970).

Morrissey v. Brewer, 408 U.S. 471 (1972).

Newman v. State of Alabama, 349 F.Supp. 278 (D.C.Ala. 1972).

O'Lone v. Estate of Shabazz, ____ U.S. ____, 107 S.Ct. 2400, 96 L.Ed.2d 282 (1987).

Otey v. Best, 680 F.2d 1231 (8th Cir. 1982).

Palmigiano v. Travisono, 317 F.Supp. 776 (D.C.R.I. 1970).

Pearson v. Godinez, U.S. District Court for the Northern District of Illinois, Eastern Division, No. 94 C 6591 (June 25, 1997).

Pell v. Procunier, 417 U.S. 817, 94 S.Ct. 2800, 41 L.Ed.2d 495, 71 O.O.2d 195 (1974).

Polakoff v. Henderson, 370 F.Supp. 690, 71 O.O.2d 106 (D.C.Ga. 1973).

Prewitt v. State of Arizona ex rel. Eyman, 315 F.Supp. 793 (D.C.Ariz. 1969).

Procunier v. Martinez, 416 U.S. 396, 94 S.Ct. 1800, 40 L.Ed.2d 224, 71 O.O.2d 139 (1974).

Ray v. Commonwealth of Pennsylvania, 263 F.Supp. 630 (D.C.Pa. 1967).

Rhodes v. Chapman, 452 U.S. 337, 101 S.Ct. 2392, 69 L.Ed.2d 59 (1981).

Richardson v. Ramirez, 418 U.S. 24, 94 S.Ct. 2655, 41 L.Ed.2d 551, 72 O.O.2d 232 (1974).

Roberts v. Pepersack, 256 F.Supp. 415 (D.C.Md. 1966).

Rowland v. Wolff, 336 F.Supp. 257 (D.C.Neb. 1971).

Ruffin v. Commonwealth, 62 Va. (21 Gratt.) 790 (1871).

Ruiz v. Estelle, 503 F.Supp. 1265 (S.D. Texas, 1980). Cert. denied, 103 S.Ct. 1438 (1980).

Smith v. Hooey, 393 U.S. 374, 89 S.Ct. 575, 21 L.Ed.2d 607 (1969).

Spain v. Procunier, 600 F.2d 189 (9th Cir. 1979).

Stovall v. Bennett, 471 F.Supp. 1286 (D.C.Ala. 1979).

Stroud v. United States, 251 U.S. 15, 40 S.Ct. 50, 64 L.Ed. 103 (1919).

Talley v. Stephens, 247 F.Supp. 683 (D.C.Ark. 1965).

Theriault v. Carlson, 495 F.2d 390 (5th Cir. 1974).

Trop v. Dulles, 356 U.S. 86, 100 (1958).

Turner v. Safley, 107 S.Ct. 2254 (1987).

Walker v. Pate, 356 F.2d 502 (7th Cir. 1966).

Washington v. Lee, 263 F.Supp. 27 (D.C.Ala. 1966).

Weems v. United States, 217 U.S. 349, 30 S.Ct. 544, 54 L.Ed. 793 (1910).

Whitley v. Albers, 475 U.S. 312, 106 S.Ct. 1078, 89 L.Ed.2d 251 (1986).

Wolff v. McDonnell, 418 U.S. 539, 94 S.Ct. 2963, 41 L.Ed.2d 935, 71 O.O.2d 336 (1974).

Wright v. McMann, 460 F.2d 126, 129 (2d Cir. 1972).

Younger v. Gilmore, 404 U.S. 15 (1971).

15

A Look Toward the Future: Corrections in the Twenty-First Century

➤ What paradigm shift has recently occurred in corrections?

➤ What the "get-tough" trend means?

➤ What trends are occurring in sentencing and the use of sentencing alternatives?

➤ What the trend is regarding victim involvement in offender matters?

➤ What the status of privatization of corrections is today?

➤ What are some arguments *for* privatization? *Against* privatization?

➤ What impacts technology is having on corrections?

Change is the law of life, and those who look only to the past or the present are sure to miss the future. —John F. Kennedy

Can You Define

paradigm shift   privatization

Introduction

Corrections has come a long way since 1870, when the first Congress of Correction, known then as the National Congress on Penitentiary and Reform Discipline, set forth 37 principles dealing with everything from sentencing practices, to the treatment of offenders, to the architecture of correctional facilities, to the training of staff and the administration of corrections. A recent historical overview ("Celebrating the Past," 1995, p. 32) states: "The corrections field has seen many advances since that first Congress, including the growth of the reformatory movement, the establishment of the juvenile court, the institution of supervised parole, acceptance of a system of classification of inmates as a method of treatment and the establishment of the Federal Bureau of Prisons, to name a few."

Through time, corrections has shifted between retribution and various pragmatic emphases. However, the technologies are different at each point, and society's attitudes have changed. Capitalism has been stronger at different points in history. With the ascendancy of capitalist ideas, individual responsibility, accountability and culpability have received greater emphasis. At other points, ideas of environmental impact on behavior have prevailed (not rigid determinism, only the worst forms of positivism adopted that view). When this occurred during the progressive era of the 1960s, social defense was emphasized and corrections focused on deterrence or rehabilitation or incapacitation. Public attitudes give the tilt to one or the other of the utilitarian emphases. When retributive thinking dominates, sensibilities shape what society is willing to accept as minimum, maximum and modal lengths of time and conditions of confinement. Retributive emphasis today is quite different in institutional practice, methods of implementation, public knowledge and concern from retributive emphasis in 1845.

Having reached the final chapter of this text, it should be evident that corrections is not static. It is constantly evolving, striving to keep up with the changing times and to meet the needs of an ever-changing population. A look at the history of corrections and its development clearly illustrates this point. Corrections is no longer where it was a century ago or even a decade ago, and will most likely be in a different place a decade from now, certainly a century from now. But where will that be?

Are there any trends to help predict which way corrections is moving? Yes, but trends are not guarantees, and predictions are not promises. Quinlan (1990, p. 6) states: "Overall changes in the U.S. criminal justice system have dramatically affected corrections in the past decade. Crime patterns and demographics have changed, and an increased enforcement emphasis reflects a shifting national mood against crime, particularly illegal drugs." Many note the pendulum is swinging back, away from corrections as a rehabilitative measure, toward corrections as a punitive measure. The development of boot camps and the elimination of parole in many states points to growing public demand that criminals be punished. People are fed up with crime, and the get-tough attitude appears to be gaining momentum. Hawk (1994, p. 72) notes the irony, however: "It is sad that a country founded on the principle of freedom should find itself so victimized."

This chapter examines where corrections seems to be heading as it nears the twenty-first century. The discussion begins with a look at how the pendulum is swinging back toward punitive corrections and the paradigm shift accompanying this movement. Next, some major trends in corrections are presented, including the get-tough attitude of the public, sentencing alternatives, victim involvement and privatization of corrections. The impact of technology is discussed next, with the chapter concluding with the question, "Is corrections trying to do too much?"

A Paradigm Shift—Which Way Is the Pendulum Swinging?

We are all aware of the cyclic nature of life and how things tend to swing from one extreme to the other—weather patterns and the years of drought or floods, how fashions tend to reappear after so many decades, how public attitude fluctuates between liberalism and conservatism.

➤   Many believe a **paradigm shift** is occurring in the field of corrections, from traditional methods of building more facilities to house rising numbers of offenders to looking for ways to handle circumstances that lead to criminality—illiteracy, lack of education, unemployment, poverty and drugs. As Crier (1993, p. 142) notes: "We all know building more buildings and locking people away without providing alternative solutions simply won't work. We cannot keep this up. So we must take responsibility. . . . We understand a new way of thinking is necessary." Others disagree that such a shift is occurring.

> A paradigm shift may be occurring in corrections, moving away from building more facilities as the solution to crime and toward the concept of dealing with circumstances that often lead to crime, such as illiteracy and lack of education, unemployment, poverty and drugs.

With incarceration rates at an all-time high and construction costs for new facilities beyond the means of many jurisdictions, today's criminal justice professionals are seeking new ways to better handle the crisis that looms before them. Rees (1990, p. 104) states:

Perhaps the time has come to scrap the old beliefs and approaches. Maybe jails and prisons are to be nothing more than places of incarceration—single-celled,

Some jurisdictions use offenders to help address the public about conditions that lead to crime. Here, a Texas prisoner stands before a gymnasium full of junior high students to talk about the importance of staying in school and staying off drugs.

secure environments, with all hope of rehabilitation placed upon the individual. Perhaps the new direction should be a war on criminal youth, with all the resources, money and personnel from the adult system re-channeled or concentrated on juvenile crime prevention, character building, behavior modification and education. Perhaps the preventive approach may prove more effective in the long run than the treatment approach.

Alban (1993, p. 14) has suggested stopping the pendulum between the extremes of punishment and rehabilitation: "On one hand we have boot camp programs that are too harsh, and on the other we have community corrections programs that are too lenient. Why can't we have boot camps with officers trained to listen and be sensitive to inmate problems and community correction centers that teach responsibility and use a little more discipline? You can't teach responsibility without using a certain amount of discipline, but you can teach discipline without brutalizing and demeaning people. I think it's time we try the middle ground."

Williams and Bissell (1990, p. 46) advocate a total systems approach for the crime problems of today: "Offenders entering the criminal justice system must be dealt with swiftly, justly and efficiently at every step. Such an approach can make the new century one of accomplishment and new hope in corrections. A 'band-aid' approach will not solve the problem. Construction, sentencing alternatives and treatment alone are not the answer, but together they can offer a comprehensive response."

As the pendulum swings, perhaps it will come to rest in a place we've never been, a place holding promise for solutions to correctional problems.

Trends in Corrections

In addition to the general change in philosophy slowly occurring in corrections, some more specific trends have also been identified, including

- The get-tough attitude.
- Changes in sentencing practices.
- Greater victim involvement.
- Privatization of certain aspects of corrections.

The Get-Tough Attitude

Public attitude has been discussed at several points. The trend of getting tough on crime has likely been fueled by a society tired of being victimized and their growing awareness that many crimes are committed by those who have already passed through the criminal justice. Research confirms that the public is correct. The "revolving door" image of corrections and the justice system has, unfortunately, shattered the public's faith in the ability of corrections to rehabilitate many offenders. Consequently, people are demanding tougher sanctions for repeat offenders and those convicted of particularly heinous crimes. Longer sentences and elimination of parole mean correctional facilities are overflowing, with little relief in sight.

> The get-tough trend has led to a call for mandatory sentences, 85 percent of time served and three-strikes laws, all designed to relay a no-nonsense attitude toward crime and repeat offenders.

A number of recent acts also reflect the growing national get-tough attitude by imposing more stringent sanctions on offenders. For example, the Comprehensive Crime Control Act of 1984 abolished parole in the federal correctional system, stiffened early release eligibility requirements and placed greater restrictions on how inmates may accumulate good time credits. The Bail Reform Act of 1984 allows judges to use pretrial detention for alleged offenders who either pose a danger to the community or are likely escape risks.

Considering the previous chapter's discussion on prisoners' rights and how pretrial detainees retain the presumption of innocence, the Supreme Court's consistent upholding of this act is testimony to how attitudes have shifted and how the protection and safety of the community is being placed above the rights of individuals.

Sentencing Alternatives

As discussed in Chapter 4, changes in sentencing philosophy have also been occurring throughout the nation's courts, directly affecting corrections. As indeterminate sentences are replaced by determinate sentences, and as mandatory sentences gain popularity, early release of offenders becomes less and less likely. This, too, has contributed to the overcrowding faced by many correctional facilities, although it is not within corrections' power to decide who receives a lengthy sentence or to draft laws calling for mandatory imprisonment for certain categories of crimes. Those are the respective responsibilities of the courts and the legislatures.

Another trend that, given the growing pressures of institutional overcrowding, shows signs of continuing is use of intermediate sanctions and alternatives to incarceration, including straight fines and day fines, forfeitures, restitution, community service, probation, intensive supervision, house arrest and electronic monitoring, day reporting centers and residential community corrections.

> Use of sentencing alternatives is another trend affecting corrections, as the terms of incarceration have gone from indeterminate to determinate and as intermediate sanctions have grown in use.

The future of community corrections is promising, as a more educated, tax-conscious public realizes building more prisons may not be the best solution to the burgeoning crime problem. Changes in the traditional roles of community corrections staff will continue, as described in Chapter 12 with probation officers. Similar to community policing trends, corrections will seek a more active partnership with the community in handling those who break the law.

Victim Involvement

Part of the paradigm shift presently occurring involves refocusing on the victims of crime. In criminal law, the alleged offender or defendant is accused of committing a wrong against the state, a legal relationship illustrated by the way the case is named (for example, *John Doe v. State of Alabama*). Although the crime may be robbery, assault or murder, the victim(s) of that crime are not formally recognized as part of the case and, until recently, have been granted very little voice in matters concerning those who caused them harm. Courts today, however, are allowing victims to play a more active role in criminal sentencing through testimony and victim impact statements.

An example of victim involvement is seen when Charles Manson appears before the parole board. The family members of his victims repeatedly organize and speak at these hearings to protest Manson's requests for early release.

Although in this particular case victim involvement has been occurring for many years, the increased voice given to victims is a growing trend today.

> Victims are being given greater recognition and input in decisions concerning offenders.

The Privatization of Corrections

➤ One of the most recent trends affecting corrections today is **privatization,** constructing and operating correctional facilities by for-profit (occasionally by nonprofit) organizations. Privatization is not new to corrections. According to Shichor and Sechrest (1995, p. 458): "The private operation of jails and prisons has a long and somewhat checkered history and tradition in Western countries, especially in England and America. This arrangement reached its peak during the industrial revolution in the 19th century and was discontinued completely in the early part of the 20th century." It wasn't until the 1980s that the private operation of prisons became an option again, and today, this trend may be accelerating.

> Correctional privatization, common in this country during the nineteenth century until discontinued in the early part of the twentieth century, began making a comeback during the 1980s and shows signs today of accelerated growth.

Correctional facilities have commonly contracted with private business for a variety of services, including medical and mental health care, drug treatment, counseling, food service, laundry service, remedial education, college courses, staff training, vocational training and construction. While such private sector contracts have existed for decades, the notion of having the entire facility operated entirely by nongovernmental, for-profit entities has caused debate.

The rapid growth of correctional privatization was brought about by numerous factors, including prison overcrowding, growing numbers of lawsuits concerning conditions of confinement, high staff turnover rates, explosive budgetary growth and a perceived lack of innovation and effectiveness in institutionalized corrections. Shichor and Sechrest (pp. 458–459) provide the following reasons for the resurgence of privatization:

> First [is] the existence of a general sociopolitical climate favoring the reduction of taxes and the size of government. Second [is] the implementation of "get-tough" social control policies, particularly the "war on drugs," and increasing mandatory prison sentences . . . [which result] in an unprecedented increase in federal and state prison populations . . . . The third reason is the general

A construction worker checks out the security system at a new privately operated prison in North Las Vegas, run by Corrections Corporation of America.

American "ethos" of laissez-faire economy, minimization of government control, and a firm belief in the abilities of the private sector to do a better job than the public sector.

Questions Concerning Privatization. Concerns exist on both sides of the debate. DiIulio (1988, p. 2) presents three sets of questions to consider concerning privatization of corrections:

1. Can private corrections firms outperform public corrections agencies? Can they produce and deliver more and better for less? What present and potential costs and benefits, if any, are associated with the private administration, construction, and financing of correctional institutions and programs?

2. Should the authority to administer criminal justice programs and facilities be delegated to contractually deputized private individuals and groups, or ought it to remain fully in the hands of duly constituted public authorities? What, if any, moral dilemmas are posed by private-sector involvement in these areas?

3. Does privatization present a single "either-or" bundle of policy alternatives or does it pose multiple choices?

Arguments exist both for those who support and those who oppose privatization.

The Pros of Privatization. Shichor and Sechrest (p. 459) state: "The major arguments for privatization are economic and administrative." Those who support privatization argue that private firms, motivated by profit margins, will operate more efficiently and economically, cutting out waste that so often accompanies government-run operations. Indeed, if corrections is considered a business, and today's correctional managers and administrators need a certain level of business savvy to succeed, private enterprise may do well in bringing their business sense to correctional facilities' operations. As DiIulio (1988, p. 2) notes: "[I]t is argued that private firms will be a source of technical and managerial innovations in a field in which most experts believe new methods are needed." Many other factors favor privatization.

> Arguments in support of privatization focus on economic and administrative issues.

The Cons of Privatization. Opponents to correctional privatization also present concerns, some of which take a pro argument and turn it into a con. For example, those who oppose privatization contend that profit margins, seen by proponents as motivators for positive outcomes, may become the primary focus, to the detriment of humane prisoner treatment. The bottom line may become more critical to private administrators than their wards. Opponents also fear that correctional personnel may become less qualified, not better qualified as proponents anticipate. DiIulio (p. 2) states: "Private firms, it is reasoned, have no incentive to reduce crowding (since they may be paid on a per-prisoner basis) or to foster less expensive (and to the private firm, less lucrative) alternatives to incarceration. . . . The firms' staffs, it is predicted, will be correctional versions of 'rent-a-cops'—ill-trained, under-educated, poorly paid, and unprofessional."

Other criticisms and objections concerning correctional privatization include the tendency to "showcase" certain facilities; legal issues; theoretical, moral and ethical issues; and the issue of symbolism. According to Shichor and Sechrest (p. 459): "[S]ome companies may 'showcase' some of their facilities by creating an artificial situation in which they perform above expectations for the purposes of gaining more business."

Legal issues surrounding privatization involve the nature of police power and who should have the right to deprive people of certain liberties. Shichor and Sechrest (p. 459) state: "It is maintained, especially by labor unions, that the state cannot contract out its police powers." For example, as noted by Thompson (1995, p. 29), the California correctional officers' union observed that state contracting agencies hold full liability for the actions of private contractors, and the union lobbied successfully to kill legislation authorizing such contracts for private correctional facilities. Several court cases, however, have upheld the constitutionality of private prisons.

The government does, however, have the legal authority to contract for private operation of correctional facilities, unless specifically prohibited by state law. In *Milonar v. Williams* (1982), the court ruled that operation of a private facility did not violate an offender's Eighth Amendment rights—the facility was considered an extension of the state. The court ruling in *Medina v. O'Neill* (1984) authorized states to delegate the power to imprison offenders to private prisons.

Opponents also pose theoretical questions and raise moral and ethical issues concerning privatization of corrections. Shichor and Sechrest (p. 460) state: "Imprisonment is a form of punishment. . . . The punishment of individuals who harm others is inherently a public function in modern society because it is imposed for the violation of the law, legislated by a body representing the state." They also note, however: "Privatization advocates, by and large, agree with this premise but argue that there is a difference between the decision to punish and to mete out punishment, on the one hand, and the administration of the punishment, on the other. There is general agreement that the punishment decision should be made by governmental authorities."

A final argument of privatization opponents is that prisoners may not respond well to private administration. Shichor and Sechrest (pp. 460–461) identify this issue as one of symbolism, stating: "Opponents of prison privatization claim that it makes a difference who is handling the inmates in a prison." To better illustrate the significance of symbolism, consider this rhetorical question (DiIulio, 1990): If a medal of honor was bestowed upon a citizen for a contribution to the country, and the ceremony was organized by a private company because it could execute it more cheaply, would it make a difference if the award presenter wore the pin of the private company rather than being a government representative? DiIulio believes it *would* make a difference and, extending this example to the issue of corrections, that the significance of symbolism is not lost on prisoners.

As further support of this point of view, Shichor and Sechrest (p. 461) cite a study of private security services that "found that citizens relate to private security personnel differently from the way they relate to sworn police officers." Based on this data, opponents of privatization believe prisoners may not respect the authority of private firms the way it is hoped they will respect government officials.

> Arguments against privatization focus on inmate welfare vs. profit margins; the potential decrease in officer qualifications; legal issues; theoretical, moral and ethical issues; and the issue of symbolism.

Privatization—Today and Tomorrow. Despite the concerns brought forth by opponents, support for and growth in privatization continues unabated. According to Thomas (1994, pp. 6,19):

> The number of firms that comprise the private corrections industry continues to expand. Competition between the firms that comprise the industry is intense. Facilities being operated by private firms house sentenced as well as

unsentenced prisoners, females as well as males, and prisoners of all possible security classifications. The number of jurisdictions that have made decisions to contract continues to grow. As is documented by government contract audits, contract renewal decisions, independent academic research, a striking paucity of successful prisoner litigation, and an impressive record of accreditation by the American Correctional Association, private firms continue to prove that correctional costs can be reduced significantly without a corresponding decrease in range and caliber of the service private vendors provide.

Although private facilities hold only a small percentage of the nation's prisoners, forecasts call for those numbers to increase rapidly. Thomas (p. 5) states: "[T]here are now 20 private management firms that have received contracts for the management of secure correctional facilities. An unknown but significant number of additional firms are actively pursuing their first contract awards." The status of private correctional facilities as of December 1996 is presented in Table 15–1. Table 15–2 shows the number and rated capacity of private adult correctional facilities in selected jurisdictions at the end of 1996.

Technology

Another consideration in the future of corrections concerns the role technology will play. In keeping with the computer revolution, many processes, such as booking, are becoming automated, and corrections personnel are now commonly required to be computer-literate. Stewart (1995, pp. 86–87) notes:

> In 1991, the U.S. Drug Enforcement Agency (DEA) developed an automated booking system to assist in coordinated criminal drug investigations. . . .
>
> Today, the DEA creates electronic files with high-quality images of fingerprints, mugshots, pictures of evidence and reports. These files can be remotely accessed from virtually anywhere.
>
> The DEA has found that using this automated system reduces offender processing time from one hour to 15 minutes. But more than just time is saved. Before automation, 30 to 40 percent of fingerprints and photographs taken were rejected. The automated system has virtually eliminated this problem.
>
> Other law enforcement agencies, such as the U.S. Marshals Service (USMS) and the Federal Bureau of Prisons (BOP), have faced similar problems. . . .
>
> The BOP has one of the best information systems in the justice system. The BOP's Sentry System, which was developed in-house, has been described as state of the art. However, as the BOP deals with an increasingly diverse prison population, it now requires far more complete information on its prisoners.

Information sharing remains a priority among criminal justice entities, including corrections, and computer technology enables more efficient, effective

Table 15-1   Private Adult Correctional Facility Census Summary for December 31, 1996

Management Firm	Rated Capacity of All Facilities Under Contract*	# Facilities Under Contract	Rated Capacity of Facilities Now in Operation	Prisoner Populations on 12/31/96	% Occupancy for Facilities in Operation	New Facilities to Open Within 12-18 Months	Expansion Anticipated Within 12-18 Months
Alternative Programs, Inc.	340	1	340	340	100.00%	0	0
Avalon Community Services, Inc.	144	1	144	144	100.00%	0	0
The Bobby Ross Group	2,164	3	1,872	1,800	96.15%	0	292
Capital Correctional Resources	1,908	3	1,616	1,601	99.07%	0	292
Cornell Corrections, Inc.	2,611	7	2,095	1,973	94.18%	1	516
Correctional Services Corporation	2,150	6	1,270	1,262	99.37%	2	880
Corrections Corporation of America	41,594	52	23,467	22,742	96.91%	16	18,127
Corrections Systems, Inc.	82	3	82	58	70.73%	0	0
Dove Development Corporation	295	1	295	68	23.05%	0	0
Fenton Security, Inc.	228	2	228	184	80.70%	0	0
Group 4 Prison Services, Ltd.	2,360	5	860	860	100.00%	2	1,500
The GRW Corporation	302	2	204	195	95.59%	0	98
Management & Training Corporation	2,978	4	2,978	2,761	92.71%	0	0
Maranatha Production Company, LLC	500	1	0	0	N/A	1	500
Securicor Custodial Services, Ltd.	800	1	0	0	N/A	1	800
U.S. Corrections Corporation	4,038	8	3,038	2,945	96.94%	2	1,000
Wackenhut Corrections Corporation	22,707	32	12,139	11,545	95.11%	14	10,568
Totals	**85,201**	**132**	**50,628**	**48,478**	**95.75%**	**39**	**34,573**
% Changes Since 12/31/95	**33.97%**	**26.92%**	**16.34%**	**29.77%**	**11.64%**	**85.71%**	**72.18%**

*Capacity figures include facilities under construction plus planned expansions of existing facilities.

Source: Charles W. Thomas, Dianne Bolinger and John L. Badalamenti. *Private Adult Correctional Facility Census*, 10th ed. Center for Studies in Criminology and Law. Gainesville, FL: University of Florida, 1997, p. 1. Reprinted by permission.

Table 15–2	Number and Rated Capacity of Private Adult Correctional Facilities, 1996

	Private Facilities of Geographical Location*		
	Number of	**Rated Capacities**	**Year-End Populations**
Arizona	5	4,742	3,389
Arkansas	2	1,200	NA
California	13	3,978	1,616
Colorado	5	1,980	781
District of Columbia	1	866	NA
Florida	10	6,215	3,492
Indiana	1	670	NA
Kansas	2	529	404
Kentucky	4	1,770	1,649
Louisiana	2	2,948	2,942
Minnesota	1	1,338	563
Mississippi	3	2,516	1,978
Nevada	1	500	NA
New Jersey	1	300	NA
New Mexico	6	4,033	842
New York	1	200	NA
North Carolina	2	1,000	NA
Ohio	1	2,016	NA
Oklahoma	4	3,648	1,749
Pennsylvania	1	1,200	855
Puerto Rico	3	3,000	973
Rhode Island	1	302	321
Tennessee	5	5,116	3,505
Texas	39	24,467	18,754
Utah	1	400	390
Virginia	2	2,500	NA
Washington	1	150	150

*The geographical location of facilities does not necessarily indicate contracting decisions made by agencies in those jurisdictions. Some states are contracting for the housing of their prisoners in other jurisdictions. Some states are providing sites only for federal facilities. Estimates include both facilities in operation and those under construction.
Source: Charles W. Thomas, Dianne Bolinger, and John L. Badalamenti. *Private Adult Correctional Facility Census,* 10th ed. Center for Studies in Criminology and Law. Gainesville, FL: University of Florida, 1997, pp. 35–37. Reprinted by permission.

Video cameras allow unarmed sheriff's deputies at the Santa Rita County Jail in Alameda County, California, to monitor inmates from glass control booths. Built in 1989 at a cost of $174 million, this ultramodern jail holds a daily average of 2,600 inmates, grouped into housing pods of about 30 prisoners, and uses video cameras to survey every corner of the facility. Dinner is served to inmates by a $6 million robot delivery system. Often, inmates don't even leave the facility to meet with their lawyers or public defenders—conferences and many court appearances are conducted via a video system linking the jail and Oakland, the county seat, over 30 miles away.

collaboration between agencies. To illustrate how this modernized information exchange can improve officer safety and cut correctional costs, Wilkinson and Ritchie-Matsumoto (1997, p. 64) present the following scenario:

> You are an inmate arriving at a prison reception center. Your fingerprints, along with your signature and voice track, are recorded electronically and then transferred to the local Bureau of Identification and Investigation at the touch of a button. You receive a "smart card," electronically coded with your demographic information, which provides your initial classification and identifies your treatment and programming needs. . . . There are no "bed counts" because you wear an electronic bracelet that monitors your location 24 hours a day. In fact, you may go the entire day without interacting with corrections personnel, although they'll be watching you closely.

As the military downsizes, private technology firms are shifting their focus toward other potential clients, including the corrections industry. According to deGroot (1997, pp. 60–62), some high-tech products and services now available to correctional facilities include

In prisons and other correctional facilities, telemedicine conferences allow prison physicians and other healthcare providers to consult with specialists around the world, thereby alleviating the need to maintain an extensive in-house medical staff.

- Ground penetrating radar (GPR) to detect inmate-made tunnels under prisons.
- Heartbeat monitoring devices to detect escape-minded inmates hiding in vehicles and containers about to leave the facility.
- Satellite monitoring for offenders on home detention.

Various facility areas, such as the canteen and library, use computerized "smart cards" similar to credit cards with information about the inmate to keep track of inmate purchases and checkouts. Inmates in some facilities now wear identification bracelets with bar codes for easier monitoring and processing. The South Carolina Department of Corrections has implemented an Offender-Based Correctional Information System (OBCIS) to handle such things as intake processing and assessment, inmate classification and needs assessment, release eligibility screening, inmate disciplinary and grievance tracking, institutional assignment and history, inmate transportation, education and program services tracking, medical reporting, inmate identification and inmate trust fund and canteen purchases (Ward et al., 1995).

Technology to better monitor offenders has also reached community corrections. For example, the Graphically Enhanced Network Information Enterprise (GENIE) system allows parole officers to minimize the time they spend with minimum-risk offenders, enabling them to focus on those offenders at higher

Technology has enhanced the task of monitoring probationers and parolees, as such offenders are now able to check in at a kiosk instead of reporting to a probation or parole office.

risk of repeat criminal activity. As Geiger and Shea (1997, p. 72) explain: "Under GENIE, offenders report to kiosks, at which they type in their names and answer a number of questions generated by the computer. Not only do the kiosks eliminate the need for each offender to meet face-to-face with a parole officer, but they have a built-in system for tracking offenders who don't report."

Computer on-line services are also affecting correctional training and communications. According to Vogel (1995, p. 162):

> It would serve agencies well to computerize many of the documents they use, such as agency rules and regulations, information bulletins, post orders, program descriptions, inmate manuals and personnel rules. . . . A bulletin board system (BBS) added to the PC [personal computer] will enable staff in every facility statewide to access up-to-date regulations. . . .
>
> A BBS also will allow facility managers to maintain a continuous dialogue with officers and staff facilitywide. Line staff will not have to depend on information trickling down from above. Role [sic] call announcements would be reinforced by the BBS message on the desktop PC.

Halasz (1997, p. 92) presents some reasons why on-line education is gaining popularity in the corrections environment: "Staff often are located too far from schools, colleges and training centers, or they have work schedules that don't allow them to attend classes. As for inmates, with Pell grants and with increasing restrictions on programs, most institutions are limited in the types of classes they can offer. But online education has the potential of closing the gap between the need for ongoing learning and skill-building, and the availability of such programs to correctional staff and inmates."

JUSTNET is an on-line information network available to corrections professionals seeking technology information. Some states have set up web sites for corrections personnel and, in some cases, the public, providing access to news and information about correctional facilities, contacts and jobs, data and reports, the organizational structure and histories of offenders confined in correctional facilities.

As discussed in Chapter 13, technology has also affected how correctional officers may control or restrain inmates. Development of oleoresin capsicum (pepper spray), stun devices, sticky spray foams and other less-than-lethal technologies has generated a variety of training and legal issues for corrections, and indications are that such technological advances will continue into the next millennium. Technology has also allowed for "chainless" chain gangs, as described in a *Law Enforcement News* article ("County Has a Shocking Message," 1997, p. 6): "The battery-powered stun belt is equipped with a receiver with electric prongs. If a prisoner tries to run or fight, an officer can press a button to trigger an eight-second burst of 50,000 volts from as far away as 300 feet. A prisoner wearing the belt would immediately fall to the ground, writhing in pain." Some, however, see this development as an Eighth Amendment rights violation waiting to happen.

> Technology is affecting various correctional processes, such as booking and inmate tracking, is simplifying and expediting communication throughout the correctional system and is providing new tools to help corrections personnel control inmates.

Technology has also affected accountability, as better record-keeping systems provide a "paper trail" which leads back to the individual(s) who made a decision. Zimring and Hawkins (1991, p. 174) contend:

> . . . the fact that information is cheaper, of better quality, and easier to retrieve will engender a feeling of accountability and will tend to produce a large number of "safe" decisions.
>
> In many systems, the safe decision is likely to involve the continuation of prosecution rather than its abandonment; a sentence of imprisonment rather than probation; a decision to hold in prison rather than to release.

Thus, this heightened sense of accountability generated by improved technology will undoubtedly have an impact on corrections.

Is Corrections Trying to Do Too Much?

Some have criticized the current state of corrections and the number of hats corrections has been forced to wear. It is but one element of the criminal justice system, whose primary function is to supervise criminal offenders, yet many expect corrections to manage and solve numerous social problems related to drug and alcohol abuse, child abuse, poor health care, mental illness, poverty, illiteracy, unemployment and lack of basic life skills. Although corrections is involved in handling persons with such problems, these issues are not the primary focus of corrections. They are the primary focus of other institutions, such as schools and health care facilities.

Our country must recognize that many of the incarcerated individuals have serious, chronic problems that extend far beyond their criminality. Because our correctional system was not designed to address the full spectrum of social problems, it is wholly unrealistic to expect corrections to provide lasting solutions for such problems, although many seem to expect exactly that. And from the previous chapters' discussions, it appears corrections is trying to keep up with those expectations and will continue to try to do so.

Clearly the future of corrections is filled with many challenges.

Summary

A paradigm shift may be occurring in corrections, moving away from building more facilities as the solution to crime and toward the concept of dealing with circumstances that often lead to crime, such as illiteracy and lack of education, unemployment, poverty and drugs.

The get-tough trend has led to a call for mandatory sentences, 85 percent of time served and three-strikes laws, all designed to relay a no-nonsense attitude toward crime and repeat offenders. Use of sentencing alternatives is another trend affecting corrections, as the terms of incarceration have gone from indeterminate to determinate and as intermediate sanctions have grown in use. Victims are being given greater recognition and input in decisions concerning offenders.

Correctional privatization, common in this country during the nineteenth century until discontinued in the early part of the twentieth century, began making a comeback during the 1980s and shows signs today of accelerated growth. Arguments in support of privatization focus on economic and administrative issues. Arguments against privatization focus on inmate welfare vs. profit margins; the potential decrease in officer qualifications; legal issues; theoretical, moral and ethical issues; and the issue of symbolism.

Technology is affecting various correctional processes, such as booking and inmate tracking, is simplifying and expediting communication throughout the correctional system and is providing new tools to help corrections personnel control inmates.

Discussion Questions

1. Should jails and prisons be nothing more than places of incarceration—single-celled, secure environments, with all hope of rehabilitation placed upon the individual?

2. Do you think the new direction for the next century should be a war on criminal youth, with all the resources, money and personnel from the adult system rechanneled or concentrated on juvenile crime prevention, character building, behavior modification and education?

3. Do you believe the preventive approach may prove more effective in the long run than the treatment approach?

4. On the correctional continuum from rehabilitation to punishment, where do you think today's national correctional philosophy falls? Where do you think society would like it to be? Where would you like it to be? Does it differ for adults and juveniles? Should it?

5. Is greater victim recognition and input in decisions concerning offenders a positive development in corrections? Why or why not?

6. Discuss the advantages and disadvantages of various aspects of corrections becoming computerized. Do you think it's wise for corrections to become too reliant on such technology, or is there no significant downside?

7. Do your local correctional facilities use computers for routine operations? Other kinds of technology?

8. Do you believe today's correctional systems try to do too much—that they "wear too many hats"?

9. Have your local correctional facilities privatized any of their functions? If so, which functions? If not, are they planning to in the future?

10. Discuss the following questions posed by DiIulio regarding privatization of correctional services:

    a. Can private corrections firms outperform public corrections agencies? Can they produce and deliver more and better for less? What present and potential costs and benefits, if any, are associated with the private administration, construction, and financing of correctional institutions and programs?

    b. Should the authority to administer criminal justice programs and facilities be delegated to contractually deputized private individuals and groups, or ought it to remain fully in the hands of duly constituted public authorities? What, if any, moral dilemmas are posed by private-sector involvement in these areas?

    c. Does privatization present a single "either-or" bundle of policy alternatives or does it pose multiple choices?

References

Alban, Lee. "It's Time to Find Some Middle Ground." *Corrections Today*, December 1993, p. 14.

"Celebrating the Past, Preparing for the Future." *Corrections Today*, June 1995, p. 32.

"County Has a Shocking Message for Criminals: The Chainless Chain Gang." *Law Enforcement News*, March 31, 1997, p. 6.

Crier, Catherine. "It's Time to Take Responsibility for Fixing Our Nation's Problems." *Corrections Today*, December 1993, pp. 142–143.

deGroot, Gabrielle. "Hot New Technologies." *Corrections Today*, July 1997, pp. 60–62.

DiIulio, John J., Jr. *Private Prisons*. U.S. Department of Justice, National Institute of Justice, 1988 (NCJ-104561).

DiIulio, John J., Jr. "The Duty to Govern: A Critical Perspective on the Private Management of Prisons and Jails." In *Private Prisons and the Public Interest*, edited by D.C. McDonald. New Brunswick, NJ: Rutgers University Press, 1990, pp. 155–178.

Geiger, Doreen and Shea, Mark. "The GENIE System." *Corrections Today*, July 1997, pp. 72–75.

Halasz, Ida M. "Cyber Ed?" *Corrections Today*, July 1997, pp. 92–95, 124.

Hawk, Kathleen M. "Corrections Must Take Action Using Courage, Creativity and Leadership." *Corrections Today*, April 1994, pp. 72–73, 222.

Quinlan, J. Michael. "Correctional Goals of the '90s: Building a Sound Foundation for the 21st Century." *Corrections Today*, February 1990, p. 6.

Rees, Chuck. "Will We Learn from Our Mistakes or Continue to Build on Them?" *Corrections Today*, February 1990, pp. 102–104.

Shichor, David and Sechrest, Dale K. "Quick Fixes in Corrections: Reconsidering Private and Public For-Profit Facilities." *The Prison Journal*, Vol. 75, No. 4, December 1995, pp. 457–478.

Stewart, James K. "Reinventing the Booking Process." *Corrections Today*, July 1995, pp. 86–87.

Thomas, Charles W. "Growth of Privatization Continues to Accelerate." *Corrections Compendium*, April 1994, pp. 5–9, 19.

Thompson, J. "The Privatization of Prisons Misses the Mark." *Peacekeeper*, April 1995, p. 29.

Vogel, Brenda. "Ready or Not, Computers Are Here." *Corrections Today*, July 1995, pp. 160–162.

Ward, John; Barrett, Tom; and Fowler, Lorraine. "South Carolina's Coordinated Response to Information Technology." *Corrections Today*, July 1995, pp. 78–84.

Wilkinson, Reginald A. and Ritchie-Matsumoto, Peggy. "Collaborations and Applications." *Corrections Today*, July 1997, pp. 64–67.

Williams, Sharon and Bissell, Cheryll. "A Total Systems Approach: Using the Past to Push Forward." *Corrections Today*, February 1990, pp. 44–46.

Zimring, Franklin E. and Hawkins, Gordon. *The Scale of Imprisonment*. Chicago, IL: The University of Chicago Press, 1991.

Cases

Medina v. O'Neill, 589 F.Supp. 1028 (1984).

Milonar v. Williams, 691 F.2d 931 (1982).

Jobs in Corrections

W hile correctional job titles and descriptions vary according to the structure and needs of each institution and agency, a few titles are commonly accepted. Occupations within corrections are as varied as those found outside the field. Some positions require a high degree of formal education and training; yet, there are opportunities for those with more modest education and experience. The education, training, and experience required for the following occupations differ from one place to another. Check with the Federal Bureau of Prisons, as well as your state or local correctional agency for specific job descriptions and requirements. Remember, advancement within the system is possible with continued education and training. The following is a sample of the types of opportunities available in the corrections field.

Managerial/Administrative Support

Warden/Jail Manager: Oversees all operations and programs within the superintendent facility.

Personnel/Human Resources Manager: Responsible for recruiting, advising, hiring, and firing staff; implements the institution's policies and procedures; provides leadership and supervision; advises and assists staff with benefits.

Employee Development Specialist: Plans, supervises, or leads programs designed to train and develop employees; consults with or guides management on employee training and development issues.

Budget Administrator: Plans and coordinates the use of resources for a facility.

Financial Manager: Maintains financial services such as auditing and credit analysis; coordinates financial policies and procedures.

Facility Manager: Manages and maintains buildings, grounds, and other facilities. Requires managerial skills and a broad technical knowledge of operating capabilities and maintenance requirements of various types of physical plants and equipment.

Safety Manager: Offers technical advice on or manages occupational safety programs, regulations, and standards. Requires knowledge of the techniques of safety and pertinent aspects of engineering, psychology, and other factors affecting safety.

Ombudsman: Acts as an unbiased liaison between inmates and facility administration; investigates inmate complaints, reports findings, and helps achieve equitable settlements of disputes between inmates and the correctional administration.

Librarian: Manages and cares for the facility's collection of books, recordings, films, and other materials.

Computer Specialist: Manages or designs use and maintenance of computer systems. This is an area of great need in the corrections field.

Researcher: Analyzes data for budgets and for projected needs and assists in the evaluation of programs.

Food Service Manager: Manages and supervises the operation of the institution's or department's food services, including the storeroom, kitchen, dining rooms, and procurement. Often requires certification as a registered dietitian and familiarity with federal, state, and local health codes and sanitary standards.

Correctional Officer: Supervises the treatment and custody of offenders in correctional institutions.

Probation/Parole Officer: Advises and counsels individuals who are on probation or parole; enforces and monitors compliance with the rules imposed on the offender by either the court or parole board.

Juvenile Services Officer: Advises and counsels juveniles in aftercare; evaluates and initiates treatment plans for juveniles in aftercare and makes referrals to appropriate support agencies.

Counseling/Training

Psychologist/Counselor: Works with inmates and corrections professionals. Provides counseling and testing. Generally requires professional training. Closely allied specialists may include art therapists and drama therapists. Certified drug and alcohol counselors are in great demand.

Chaplain: Offers religious guidance and spiritual counseling to inmates. Requires ordination by a recognized ecclesiastical body; chaplains may be called on to minister to inmates not of their faith.

Recreation Specialist: Plans, organizes, and administers programs that promote inmates' physical, creative, artistic, and social development.

Vocational Counselor: Provides educational programs or career training for inmates; determines learning needs, abilities, and other facts about inmates. May participate in discussions with other staff professionals to aid in inmate rehabilitation.

Vocational Instructor: Provides both classroom and hands-on training in a variety of trades.

Industrial Specialist: Assists or manages a prison industry, such as printing, carpentry, agriculture, and sign-making programs.

Juvenile Careworker: Supervises the treatment and custody of juvenile offenders in correctional or rehabilitation facilities. Often provides support and counseling to juvenile offenders and participates in the development and implementation of treatment plans.

Teacher: Leads classes on subjects for both juveniles and adult offenders. Requires a bachelor's degree plus certification by the state education authority in a specific subject area. Teachers certified in special education are in great demand.

Medical

Health System Administrator: Responsible for the administrative management of the health care delivery system and use of outside resources to provide patient care.

Medical Officer: Performs professional and scientific work in one or more fields of medicine. Requires, at a minimum, the degree of Doctor of Medicine and, in most states, a current license to practice medicine. Medical support staff may include physicians' assistants, nurses, nurses' assistants, and pharmacists.

For further discussion about the types of jobs in the field of corrections, consult the following books, which are available from the American Correctional Association.

Career Planning in Criminal Justice, by Robert C. DeLucia and Thomas J. Doyle, 1994, and *Inside Jobs,* edited by Stuart Henry, 1994.

Source: Michael Kelly. "Is a Career in Corrections for You?" *Corrections Today,* July 1996, pp. 135–136. Reprinted by permission.

American Correctional Association Code of Ethics

Preamble

The American Correctional Association expects of its members unfailing honesty, respect for the dignity and individuality of human beings and a commitment to professional and compassionate service. To this end, we subscribe to the following principles.

Members shall respect and protect the civil and legal rights of all individuals.

Members shall treat every professional situation with concern for the welfare of the individuals involved and with no intent to personal gain.

Members shall maintain relationships with colleagues to promote mutual respect within the profession and improve the quality of service.

Members shall make public criticism of their colleagues or their agencies only when warranted, verifiable, and constructive.

Members shall respect the importance of all disciplines within the criminal justice system and work to improve cooperation with each segment.

Members shall honor the public's right to information and share information with the public to the extent permitted by law subject to individuals' right to privacy.

Members shall respect and protect the right of the public to be safeguarded from criminal activity.

Members shall refrain from using their positions to secure personal privileges or advantages.

Members shall refrain from allowing personal interest to impair objectivity in the performance of duty while acting in an official capacity.

Members shall refrain from entering into any formal or informal activity or agreement which presents a conflict of interest or is inconsistent with the conscientious performance of duties.

Members shall refrain from accepting any gifts, service, or favor that is or appears to be improper or implies an obligation inconsistent with the free and objective exercise of professional duties.

Members shall clearly differentiate between personal views/statements and views/statements/positions made on behalf of the agency or Association.

Members shall report to appropriate authorities any corrupt or unethical behaviors in which there is sufficient evidence to justify review.

Members shall refrain from discriminating against any individual because of race, gender, creed, national origin, religious affiliation, age, disability, or any other type of prohibited discrimination.

Members shall preserve the integrity of private information; they shall refrain from seeking information on individuals beyond that which is necessary to implement responsibilities and perform their duties; members shall refrain from revealing nonpublic information unless expressly authorized to do so.

Members shall make all appointments, promotions, and dismissals in accordance with established civil service rules, applicable contract agreements, and individual merit, rather than furtherance of personal interests.

Members shall respect, promote, and contribute to a work place that is safe, healthy, and free of harassment in any form.

Adopted August 1975 at the 105th Congress of Correction

Revised August 1990 at the 120th Congress of Correction

Revised August 1994 at the 124th Congress of Correction

Source: American Correctional Association. Reprinted by permission.

Glossary

accreditation An ongoing, voluntary procedure that evaluates a facility's compliance with professional standards. [11]

acquired immune deficiency syndrome (AIDS) A condition encompassing a wide spectrum of reactions and symptoms, often leading to death. Brought about by HIV infection. The infected person must have one or more "opportunistic infections" or cancers in the absence of all other known underlying causes of immune deficiency. Symptoms associated with AIDS include fever, weight loss, diarrhea and persistently swollen lymph nodes. [10]

adjudication Similar to an adult (criminal) conviction of guilt, it is a juvenile court judgment following a hearing, affirming that the juvenile is a delinquent, a status offender or a dependent, or that the allegations in the petition are not sustained. [9]

aftercare Similar to adult parole in which youth are supervised for a limited time following release from a correctional facility but are still under control of the facility or the juvenile court. [9]

aggravating circumstances Serve to increase sentence length and include having a prior record of incarceration, causing severe bodily harm to the victim and preying on particularly vulnerable victims such as the elderly or the mentally or physically handicapped. [4]

alternatives to incarceration Include probation, straight fines and day fines, forfeitures, restitution, community service, intensive supervision, house arrest and electronic monitoring, day reporting centers and residential community corrections, boot camps and parole. [5]

amnesty A pardon that applies to an entire class or group of individuals. [7]

anomie Normlessness; the breakdown of societal norms as a result of society's failure to distinguish between right and wrong, often in response to rapid change. [1]

assessment centers Provide rigorous identification and evaluation to thoroughly test selected attributes of prospective officers; also used to select individuals eligible for promotion, especially at the upper levels. [11]

Auburn system Emphasized crime prevention through strict silence and fear of brutal punishment; sometimes referred to as the *congregate system*. [3]

audit An on-site evaluation of a correctional facility by the Commission on Accreditation for Corrections. [11]

authoritarian management Prevalent during the early days of the American prison and characterized by an almost tyrannical "rule" by wardens, who had enormous power and very little accountability; also called *autocratic management*. [11]

authority The power to command or enforce laws, rules and policy by virtue of rank or position; uses force. [11]

autocratic management Prevalent during the early days of the American prison and characterized by an almost tyrannical "rule" by wardens, who had enormous power and very little accountability; also called *authoritarian management*. [11]

bail The monetary "guarantee," deposited with the court, that a defendant will appear in court if released before trial. [6]

bona fide occupational qualification (BFOQ) A requirement reasonably necessary to perform the job. [12]

boot camp   An alternative to prison where nonviolent, first-time (usually) offenders serve a relatively short sentence (typically 90 to 180 days) instead of their full prison sentence of several years or more; also referred to as *shock incarceration*. [7]

Bridewell   Workhouse established in 1557 in London to house and employ the "dregs" of the city. [2]

budget   A plan to manage expenditures within available resources during a certain period. [11]

bureaucracy   Concept first proposed by Max Weber as a way to describe an ideal organizational design leading to maximum organizational effectiveness. Today's connotation, however, is less positive, often synonymous with delay, duplication and red tape. [11]

chronic juvenile offender   A youth who has a record of five or more separate charges of delinquency, regardless of the gravity of the offenses. [9]

civil death   Offenders, while incarcerated or on probation or parole, could not sign contracts, make decisions regarding their property, vote, hold public office, have a say in the custody of their children or marry. [14]

classical view   Humans have free will and are responsible for their own actions; focuses on crime. [1]

classification   Separates and organizes inmates once they enter the jail facility, to assess inmate risk and make housing decisions. [6,7]

collateral consequences   Rights that may be lost or limited as the result of a criminal conviction, including the rights to vote, to hold public office, to assist in parenting, to serve on a jury, to own firearms, to remain married and to have privacy. [14]

collective bargaining   A process in which representatives of employees meet with representatives of management to establish a written contract outlining working conditions over a specific length of time, usually one to three years. [12]

collective incapacitation   An alternative to selective incapacitation which seeks to impose lengthy terms of incarceration for all convicted offenders regardless of whether they are deemed a "poor risk" or a future danger to society. [4]

community service   Generally involves public service for nonprofit organizations. [5]

commutation   Lessens the severity of punishment by shortening the sentence. [7]

conditional release   (1) The defendant agrees to meet specific court-ordered conditions, such as participating in drug counseling, in exchange for pretrial freedom; (2) the offender is discharged from prison but must satisfy certain conditions while in the community to receive complete freedom and final release; divided into two categories: discretionary or mandatory. [6,7]

congregate system   Emphasized crime prevention through strict silence and fear of brutal punishment, with prisoners working and eating together as a group; also known as the *Auburn system*. [3]

consensual sex   Oral or anal sex that takes place between willing individuals who have agreed on the terms before the act occurs. [13]

contraband   A wide range of goods and services that are prohibited by institutional policy or not allowed without expressed permission from institutional management. [13]

corporal punishment   Inflicting bodily pain. [2]

correctional officer   Correctional staff member whose primary responsibility is to maintain order and control over those committed to custody and to prevent their escape. [12]

criminogenic   Contributing to the criminal attitude and outlook of those confined within their walls. [5]

day fines   Fines based on the offender's daily income, the amount of which is determined by the nature of the crime and the offender's ability to pay. [5]

day reporting centers (DRCs)   Nonresidential locations at which offenders must appear daily. [5]

deadly force   An extreme use of force intended to cause death or serious injury. [13]

deliberate indifference   Similar to but different from negligence, as the modifier "deliberate" adds the element of "recklessness" to the action. [14]

delinquent   An individual below the legal age whose action would be a crime if it were committed by an adult (e.g., robbery, assault, murder). [9]

delinquent act   An act for which an adult could be prosecuted in criminal court. [9]

Department of Corrections (DOC)   State agencies that oversee correctional functions and set policy. [11]

detention centers   Secure, locked facilities that hold young offenders prior to and following adjudication. [9]

determinate sentences   A type of limited discretionary sentence in which a degree of judicial discretion is removed but a range of sentence lengths is still allowed. [4]

determinism Views human behavior as the result of various environmental and cultural influences; crime is viewed as a consequence of many factors such as population density, economic status and legal definitions of crime. [2]

deterrence As a correctional objective, views punishment as a means to prevent future criminal actions. It is functional and proactive. [1]

direct supervision Achieved by removing structural barriers and placing correctional officers in the same living area with the inmates. [6]

direct supervision management (DSM) An administrative and architectural approach to managing inmate populations where the design of cell clusters, or pods, and the management techniques of correctional officers diffuse potentially violent situations. [11]

disability A physical or mental impairment substantially limiting one or more major life activities; the term *impairment* is frequently substituted for the word *disability*. [10]

discretion Freedom to make judgments. [1]

discretionary release Based on a decision by a parole board or other paroling authority and allows the release of a prisoner prior to the expiration of the entire sentence. [7]

discretionary sentences *See* **indeterminate sentences.** [4]

disposition Like a sentencing decision made by the juvenile court, committing a juvenile to a confinement facility, placing the juvenile on probation or referring the juvenile to a particular course of treatment or care. [9]

disproportionate minority confinement Overrepresentation of youths from racial and ethnic minorities in the juvenile justice system as compared with their numbers in the general youth population. [9]

disruptive groups Refers to street and prison gangs. [8]

distributive justice A form of injustice also known as social justice—the fairness of how property, money and prestige are divided within a society. [1]

educational release Like work release except that the inmate leaves the prison to attend classes; also called *study release*. [7]

Eighth Amendment Excessive bail shall not be required, nor excessive fines imposed, nor cruel and unusual punishment inflicted. [14]

elderly Refers not only to an individual's chronological age but his or her physiological age as well. [10]

electronic monitoring (EM) Uses telemetry devices to supervise an offender's whereabouts. [5]

ethics Refers to a standard of conduct and moral judgment—doing what is considered right and just. [13]

excessive force Force that exceeds what is necessary to control the situation. [13]

executive clemency Release from incarceration granted by an entity within the executive branch of government, either the governor of the state (the chief executive), the parole board or some other authorized board or commission; includes pardon, amnesty, reprieve and commutation. [7]

federalism A form of government where several states join together, yet retain certain powers at the state level. [1]

field citations A prebooking release used by arresting officers to release misdemeanants "on the spot" if they do not demand to appear before a judge. [6]

Fifth Amendment No person shall be held to answer for a capital, or otherwise infamous crime, unless on a presentment or indictment of a Grand Jury, except in cases arising in the land or naval forces, or in the Militia, when in actual service in time of War or public danger; nor shall any person be subject for the same offense to be twice put in jeopardy of life or limb; nor shall be compelled in any criminal case to be a witness against himself, nor be deprived of life, liberty, or property, without due process of law, nor shall private property be taken for public use, without just compensation. [14]

First Amendment Congress shall make no law respecting an establishment of religion, or prohibiting the free exercise thereof; or abridging the freedom of speech, or the press; or the right of the people peaceably to assemble, and to petition the Government for a redress of grievances. [14]

first generation jails Allowed only intermittent surveillance of inmates by correctional staff, minimized the interaction between inmates and staff and fostered a reactive management philosophy. [6]

first-order causalities What leads to a riot, such as living conditions and security. [13]

forfeiture A financial penalty involving the seizure of the offender's illegally used or acquired property or assets. [5]

foster group home   A blend of group home and foster initiatives; provide a "real family" concept run by single families, not professional staffs. [9]

foster home   Small, nonsecure homes used at any of several stages in the juvenile justice system; intended to be family-like, as much as possible a substitute for natural family settings. [9]

Fourteenth Amendment   SECTION 1. All persons born or naturalized in the United States, and subject to the jurisdiction thereof, are citizens of the United States and of the State wherein they reside. No State shall make or enforce any law which shall abridge the privileges or immunities of citizens of the United States; nor shall any State deprive any person of life, liberty, or property, without due process of law; nor deny to any person within its jurisdiction the equal protection of the laws. [14]

Fourth Amendment   The right of the people to be secure in their persons, houses, papers, and effects, against unreasonable searches and seizures, shall not be violated, and no Warrants shall issue, but upon probable cause, supported by Oath or affirmation, and particularly describing the place to be searched, and the persons or things to be seized. [14]

free will   People choose to act as they do and are responsible for those actions. This concept is at the heart of the classical approach to criminology and is also central to the contemporary return to retribution. [2]

fully secured bail   The defendant deposits the full bail amount with the court. [6]

funnel effect   The fact that the number of those committing crimes and the number being processed by the criminal justice system becomes fewer at each stage of the process. [1]

furlough   Allows an inmate to go home unsupervised for a short period, typically 24 to 72 hours, although may extend to a week or longer. [7]

gaols   Workhouses and jails in Europe. [2]

general deterrence   Deterrence intended to serve as an example to others. [1]

goal   A broad, general, desired outcome. [11]

good time   Credit earned by an inmate which reduces the duration of the incarceration. [4]

Greenwood scale   Devised by Peter Greenwood (1982) of the Rand Corporation, presumably provides a relatively accurate prediction of which offenders are most likely to commit future crimes. [4]

group home   A nonsecure facility with a professional corrections staff that provides counseling, education, job training and family-style living; the objective is to facilitate reintegrating young offenders into society. [9]

halfway house   A place designed to ease the transition from life in prison to life in free society, where a parolee is provided with food, clothing, shelter and counseling; may be a public or private facility. [7]

hands-off doctrine   General unwillingness of the courts to become involved in how prisoners were treated, basically ignoring prisoners' claims of mistreatment, cruel and unusual punishment or deplorable conditions of confinement. [14]

Hawthorne effect   An improved attitude and desire to work more productively as a result of improved human relations and working conditions, such as personal attention directed by management toward staff. [11]

house arrest   Requires the offender to remain within the confines of the home during specified times and to adhere to a strict curfew. [5]

hulks   Unseaworthy ships. [2]

human immunodeficiency virus (HIV)   A virus that destroys white blood cells in the body which are critical to fighting infection, compromising the body's immune system and making a person more vulnerable to other illnesses. HIV infection can also lead to AIDS. [10]

ideologies   Complex bodies of ideas, adopted because they provide answers to an entire range of questions, such as the causes of crime, moral significance of crime, the proper response to crime, etc. [1]

incapacitation   Making it impossible for the offender to commit further offenses. [1]

incarceration sentences   Include shock incarceration, placing offenders in confinement for a set period and then releasing them to serve probation, confinement in jail and confinement in prison. The four basic types: indeterminate (discretionary), determinate, presumptive, mandatory. [4]

indeterminate sentences   Judges and parole authorities have a great deal of latitude in determining the length of the sentence. The maximum sentence is determined by the legislature. Judges can't exceed this but can give a lesser sentence. Also called *discretionary sentences*. [2,4]

indigenous paraprofessional   A volunteer who shares the same community, culture and socioeconomic status as offenders. [12]

injecting drug users (IDUs)   Drug addicts who use hypodermic needles to put drugs into their bodies. [10]

inmate code   An informal set of norms, a sort of code of conduct, to which offenders are expected to adhere. [8]

inmate control management   When inmate organization and gangs become so powerful as to dominate facility management's decisions. [11]

inmate litigation explosion   The incredible upsurge in prisoners' rights cases over the past few decades. [14]

Inquisition   Begun in the thirteenth century, was one powerful means of holding people responsible for their actions. [2]

institutional classification   Assignment by the specific institution regarding tasks, housing and activities for the inmate within the confines established by the systemwide classification. [7]

intensive supervision programs (ISPs)   Emphasize offender control and surveillance by using frequent contacts between the probation officer and the offender, strict enforcement of conditions, random drug and alcohol testing, fulfillment of restitution and community service obligations, mandatory employment, house arrest and electronic monitoring, programs to help offenders "better" themselves (treatment programs, education classes) and regular checks of local and state arrest records. [5]

intermediate punishments   The continuum of increasingly restrictive correctional alternatives between standard probation and incarceration. [5]

intermediate sanctions   Same as *intermediate punishments*. [5]

jail   A place of confinement, typically administered by the county, with the sheriff in charge, and used to detain individuals prior to adjudication, sentenced offenders awaiting transfer to prison and those sentenced to a year or less of incarceration. [6]

jailhouse lawyer   An inmate with sufficient interest to become extensively knowledgeable about the law, so much so they could provide legal advice to other inmates or represent themselves before the court. [14]

just deserts   Individuals "get what's coming to them." They deserve what they get. [1]

justice model   One approach to sentencing; assumes offenders are self-directed, acting on free will and responsible for their crimes. [1,4]

juvenile   An individual below the legal age. [9]

leader   One who influences others by example, guides and motivates people to achieve a common or organizational goal. [11]

legal age   Age at which a youth becomes an adult, in the eyes of the law. [9]

lex talions   A concept based on the notion of "an eye for an eye." [1]

limited discretionary sentences   Determinate sentences and presumptive sentences. [4]

lockup   A temporary holding facility, commonly located in city halls or police stations and authorized to hold individuals for a maximum of 48 hours. [6]

management by objectives (MBO)   Defined by Drucker, has managers and subordinates set goals and objectives together and then track performance to see that the objectives are accomplished. [11]

manager   Controls and directs others; takes charge and coordinates human, material and financial resources to accomplish organizational goals; gets things done through others. [11]

mandatory release   Defined by statute and based on the offender serving the full sentence minus any good time credits; also takes into account any jail time served and credits received for program participation during incarceration. [7]

mandatory sentences   The sentence is fixed by law and must be given upon conviction, eliminating any judicial discretion to suspend the sentence or grant probation. Also known as *nondiscretionary sentences*. [4]

mark system   A system whereby prisoners could earn points (marks) for good behavior, thereby shortening their sentence, or lose marks for bad behavior, lengthening their sentence. [2]

maximum-security prisons   House violent offenders and those at high risk of escape; use substantial perimeter controls such as double or electrified fences, high walls and armed guards posted in observation towers; focus is on custody and security, not on treatment and rehabilitation. [7]

medical model   Assumes offenders are victims of society and their environment who need to be "cured." [1]

medium-security prisons   Use perimeter controls such as fencing and allow inmates less freedom of movement than in minimum-security facilities but more than in maximum-security facilities; focus is on controlled access to programs. [7]

mental retardation   Significantly subaverage general intellectual functioning existing concurrently with deficits in adaptive behavior. [10]

minimum-security prisons   Impose little or no physical control over inmates and are designed for nonviolent offenders who are low risk for escaping; focus is to reintegrate inmates into the community. [7]

mitigating circumstances   Weigh in favor of the defendant and serve to shorten the imposed sentence length. [4]

negligence   A failure to use a reasonable degree of care when that failure results in damage or harm to another individual. [14]

net widening   A negative consequence of diversion attempts, typically describing what happens when more diversion "to" other programs or agencies has occurred than true diversion "away" from the system. [5]

new generation jails   Used a podular configuration but removed physical barriers between staff and inmates to allow for direct supervision and foster a proactive management philosophy. Also called *third generation jails*. [6]

nondiscretionary sentences   *See* **mandatory sentences.** [4]

nonincarceration sentences   Include fines, restitution or victim compensation, probation, home confinement or house arrest, electronic monitoring and community service. [4]

objective   A specific, measurable way to reach a goal, usually to be accomplished under a specified time line. [11]

panopticism   Applying the technology of control through systematically observing and gathering information. [1]

paradigm   A model or a way of viewing an aspect of life such as education, politics, medicine or the criminal justice system. [1,15]

paradigm shift   A new way of thinking about a given subject. [1,15]

pardon   Unconditional release absolving an individual from blame for a crime. [7]

parole   The conditional release from prison before the expiration of the sentence and the period of supervision in the community following this release. [7]

parole board   The authority charged with determining which prisoners should be released and under what conditions. [7]

parole hearing   Conducted by the parole board to determine if an inmate should be released on parole, at which time the inmate is interviewed to evaluate various factors. [7]

parole officer   Supervises offenders recently released from incarceration yet not entirely free from the correctional system; roles include surveillance, casework and counseling. [12]

participatory management   Getting employees involved in decision making to improve their commitment to organizational goals. Under this management style, managers respect

employees' views and opinions and solicit their input about the work environment. [11]

pedophile   A sex offender who is sexually attracted to children; also called a *child molester.* [10]

Pennsylvania system   Emphasized religion and penitence; sometimes referred to as the *separate system.* [3]

penology   The study of the reformation and rehabilitation of criminals and of the management of prisons; based on the root word *penal,* which is derived from the Latin word *poenalis* meaning "punishment" and a similar Greek word *poine* meaning "penalty" or "fine." [1]

percentage bail   The defendant deposits part of the full bail amount, generally 10 percent, but again is responsible for the remainder following failure to appear in court. [6]

performance-based standard   A statement that clearly defines a required condition or activity; communicates the intended result or value of that condition or activity; and quantitatively or qualitatively describes how performance can be measured. [11]

petition   A document alleging that a juvenile is a delinquent, status offender or dependent and asking the court to assume jurisdiction or requesting that an alleged delinquent be transferred to criminal court for prosecution as an adult. [9]

plea bargaining   A preconviction agreement where a defendant pleads guilty in exchange for some concession from the prosecution. [4]

policy   A plan of action which leads to attaining the organization's goals. [11]

positivist view   Humans are shaped by their society and are the product of environmental and cultural influences; focuses on the criminal. [1]

power   The ability to achieve action and results with or *without* legal right; uses persuasion. [11]

presumptive sentences   A type of limited discretionary sentence removing a degree of judicial discretion but still allowing a range of sentence lengths. [4]

pretrial detention   The holding in jail until the trial of offenders determined by the judge to be a flight risk or a potential danger to self or society. [6]

pretrial release   An alternative to holding the offender in jail until trial. [6]

prison gang   An exclusive and surreptitious group of disruptive inmates who aim to control their environment by engaging in intimidating and threatening behaviors; they are also involved in criminal activity. [8]

prison psychosis A disorder where an offender enters the correctional system with no evidence of mental problems but, because of an inability to cope with the rigors of confinement, deteriorates to a point where he or she becomes mentally ill. [10]

prisonization Socialization that occurs in prison and serves to draw the offender away from the values and norms of the community into an antisocial mindset. [7]

privately secured bail A bondsman charges the defendant a fee (generally 10 percent of the bail amount) and agrees to cover the full bail amount should the defendant fail to appear in court. [6]

privatization The provision of correctional services by organizations outside the governmental framework, either nonprofit or for profit. [7,15]

privilege A favor or option that is not legally protected and may be denied one entity by another. [14]

probation *See* **standard probation**. [5]

probation officer Supervises offenders diverted away from incarceration; roles include surveillance, casework and counseling. [12]

pseudofamilies Substitute families formed by inmates while incarcerated. [8]

psychiatrist A licensed medical doctor, or M.D., who specializes in the area of mental illness and is authorized to prescribe medication. [12]

psychologist Not a medical doctor and, therefore, generally cannot prescribe drugs but can conduct psychological testing and treat mental disorders via therapy. [12]

rape Oral or anal sex that is forced on someone. [13]

recidivism Repeated offending. [1]

reclassification Adjusts institutional classifications upon review and/or changes in the inmate's prison status. [7]

rehabilitation Sees the purpose of corrections to be to correct deviant behavior. [1]

release eligibility date The first time an individual is considered for release on parole. [7]

release on own recognizance (ROR) The most commonly used pretrial release alternative, whereby a defendant basically exchanges his or her word, promising to appear in court, for pretrial freedom. [6]

representing Gang member wearing items only on the left or right side of the body. [8]

reprieve Typically lessens the punishment received; the most common application involves the death penalty, with the reprieve acting as a temporary stay of execution. [7]

residential community corrections Just short of actual incarceration and may take many forms, where residents may live either part-time or full-time at the center, depending on conditions set forth by the court. [5]

restitution Reimbursement of the victim by the offender, most often with money though occasionally with services. [5]

restorative justice Seeks to use a balanced approach involving offenders, victims, local communities and government in alleviating crime and violence and obtaining peaceful communities. [1]

retribution Punishment for the sake of punishment. [1]

retributivist model Rejected indeterminate sentencing schemes and the idea that rehabilitating criminals was the solution to the country's crime problems; took the focus away from rehabilitation of the offender and looked to other approaches for achieving justice. [4]

right A claim by one entity (an individual or individuals) which another entity has a legal obligation or duty to fulfill. [14]

second generation jails Used a podular configuration to remove blind spots and allow continuous visual supervision of inmates, but continued to keep inmates and staff physically separated and fostered a reactive management philosophy. [6]

second-order causalities What allows the disturbance to either be quelled or augmented, such as lack of preparedness, crisis response and management of the riot's aftermath. [13]

Section 1983 Part of the Civil Rights Act of 1871 which reads: Every person who, under color of any statute, ordinance, regulation, custom, or usage, of any State or Territory, or the District of Columbia, subjects or causes to be subjected, any citizen of the United States or any person within the jurisdiction thereof to the deprivation of any rights, privileges, or immunities secured by the Constitution and laws, shall be liable to the party injured in an action at law, suit in equity, or other proper proceeding for redress. [14]

selective incapacitation Seeks to keep those selected offenders predicted of future dangerousness locked behind bars while releasing nondangerous offenders on probation. [4]

selective release Seeks to set free selected offenders predicted to be of low risk for reoffending. [4]

sentencing commission   Not parole boards, but instead, consist of ex officio members and members appointed by the governor or mandated by the legislature. Their purpose is to develop and monitor presumptive sentences. [4]

Sentencing Reform Act   In 1984, created the United States Sentencing Commission and sought to achieve honesty, uniformity and proportionality in sentencing. [4]

serious juvenile offender   A juvenile who has been convicted of a Part I offense as defined by the FBI *Uniform Crime Reports*, excluding auto theft or distribution of a controlled dangerous substance, and who was 14, 15, 16 or 17 years old at the time of the commission of the offense. [9]

sex offender   Someone who commits a sexual act prohibited by law. [10]

sexual predator   An individual who commits violent sexual acts such as rape-mutilations and lust-murders. [10]

shakedowns   Unannounced cell searches. [14]

shared-powers management   Prison administration seeks to involve correctional staff *and* inmates in decision making. [11]

shelter   A nonsecure residential facility where juveniles may be temporarily assigned, often in place of detention or returning home after being taken into custody or after adjudication while waiting for more permanent placement; usually house status offenders and are not intended for treatment or punishment. [9]

shock incarceration   An inmate is held in prison for a short time (the "shock"), typically 30, 60, 90 or 120 days, and then released on parole; generally reserved for nonviolent first-time offenders. [7]

Sixth Amendment   In all criminal prosecutions, the accused shall enjoy the right to a speedy and public trial, by an impartial jury of the State and district wherein the crime shall have been committed, which district shall have been previously ascertained by law, and to be informed of the nature and cause of the accusation; to be confronted with the witnesses in his favor, against him, to have compulsory process for obtaining witnesses and to have the Assistance of Counsel for his defense. [14]

social contract   Montesquieu's philosophy whereby free, independent individuals agree to form a community and to give up a portion of their individual freedom to benefit the security of the group. [2]

sociological view of punishment   A broad view, perceiving punishment as a social institution. [1]

specific deterrence   Deterrence aimed at offenders which attempts to make the consequences of committing crime so severe that when the offenders are returned to society, they will not commit further crimes. [1]

standard probation   The least restrictive and most common of the correctional alternatives, allowing the offender to remain in the community under the limited supervision of a probation agency and subject to conditions set by the court. [5]

standards   The minimal qualifications for sound correctional operation which address physical conditions, policy and operations of correctional facilities and programs and are designed to safeguard the life, health and safety of staff and inmates; guidelines by which to measure or judge the adequacy of programs, facilities or activities; they allow self-regulation. [11]

stare decisis   A policy of law requiring courts to abide by precedents when considering a similar set of facts. [14]

station house citations   Prebooking releases which occur once the misdemeanant is taken to the police station for verification of information. If the arresting officer or desk sergeant is satisfied that the information checks out, the arrestee may be released, again to appear before the judge within five days for arraignment. [6]

status offender   A juvenile whose action would not be considered an offense had it been committed by an adult. [9]

street gang   An association of individuals with an ongoing relationship who have identifiable leadership, claim control over a specific territory and engage in criminal activity. [8]

substantive rights   Rights of individual prisoners, as opposed to rights that apply to all prisoners or a class of prisoners. [14]

summons   A request that an individual appear at a future court proceeding. A prebooking release, similar to an arrest warrant but does not require the defendant to be taken into custody. [6]

supervised release   The defendant is monitored by a pretrial officer via frequent phone calls and regular visits to the officer's office. This alternative may also incorporate house arrest, electronic monitoring and drug testing as conditions of the release and is used with defendants who pose more of a flight risk or threat to society. [6]

systemwide classification   Decisions made by the corrections department as to the degree of custody, level of supervision and institutional assignment of newly sentenced offenders. [7]

third generation jails   Used a podular configuration but removed physical barriers between staff and inmates to allow for direct supervision and foster a proactive management philosophy. Also called *new generation jails*. [6]

third-party release   An individual other than the defendant offers his or her word, guaranteeing the defendant's appearance in court, in exchange for the defendant's pretrial freedom. [6]

total institution   Concept developed by social scientist, Erving Goffman, to describe the environmental reality of prisons and their absolute dominance over prisoners' lives. [7]

total quality management (TQM)   The process by which traditional management practices are restructured to improve performance and product quality and customer satisfaction; involves strong quality leadership, customer-driven quality, employee participation, quality measurement and analysis, and continuous improvement. [11]

training school   A secure alternative for youthful offenders; some resemble adult prisons, with the same distinguishing problems of gang-oriented activity, homosexual terrorism and victimization, which often leads to progressive difficulties or suicide. [9]

unconditional release   The prisoner is freed from all government control, with no further restrictions or conditions to satisfy. [7]

union   A group authorized to represent members of an agency or profession in negotiating such matters as wages, fringe benefits, working conditions and other elements of employment. [12]

unit management   A specific application of direct supervision and a system to manage programs. [11]

unsecured bail   No money is actually deposited with the court but the defendant is responsible for the full amount in the event he or she fails to appear in court. [6]

upper age of original jurisdiction   The maximum age of an individual before the state considers him or her to be an adult. For example, if the state considers an individual to be an adult on his or her 18th birthday, the upper age of original jurisdiction is 17. [9]

use of force   Reasonable force necessary to compel an inmate to act or refrain from acting in a particular way. [13]

violent juvenile offender   A youth who has been convicted of a violent Part I offense, one against a person rather than property, and who has a prior adjudication of such an offense, or a youth who has been convicted of murder. [9]

warden   The administrator in a correctional institution; also called a *superintendent*. [11]

weekend jail   Programs similar to work release programs except that offenders need report to the jail only on weekends, working *and living* in the community during the week. [6]

work release   Allows inmates to maintain or obtain employment in the community while still serving their sentence, leaving only for work and returning to incarceration every evening; also called *work furlough, day pass* and *day parole*. [6,7]

writ of habeas corpus   A document that brings a case before a court. [14]

youth population at risk   The number of children from age 10 through the upper age of original jurisdiction. [9]

Author Index

Subject Index

Credits